GMAT®

GRADUATE MANAGEMENT ADMISSION TEST

17TH EDITION

EUGENE D. JAFFE, M.B.A., PH.D.
Professor of Business Administration
Head, MBA Programs
Ruppin Academic Center
School of Social Sciences and Management

STEPHEN HILBERT, PH.D.
Professor of Mathematics
Ithaca College

BARRON'S

Dedication

For Liora, Iris, and Nurit and for Susan

We would like to thank Mrs. Susan Hilbert and Ms. Dawn Murcer for keying the manuscript, Professor Shirley Hockett for helpful discussions, and Professor Justin Longenecker for his generous advice.

A very special thanks to Bobby Umar for his contribution to the Integrated Reasoning sections of this book. Bobby is a GMAT teacher in Toronto with 15 years' experience preparing students for the exam (*www.gmatbobby.com*). He holds an MBA and is President of Raeallan (*www.raeallan.com*), a motivational speaking and training company. He is also a TEDx speaker and an Executive Education instructor for the DeGroote School of Business.

All inquiries should be addressed to:
Barron's Educational Series, Inc.
250 Wireless Boulevard
Hauppauge, New York 11788
www.barronseduc.com

ISBN: 978-1-4380-0186-9 (Book)
ISBN: 978-1-4380-7306-4 (Book/CD Package)
ISSN: 1931–616X

GMAT®, Next Generation GMAT®, Computer-Adaptive GMAT®, GMAT CAT®, and Graduate Management AdmissionTest® are registered trademarks of the Graduate Management Admission Council™. The Graduate Management Admission Council™ does not endorse, and is not affiliated with, the owner or content of *Barron's GMAT*.

PRINTED IN THE UNITED STATES OF AMERICA
9 8 7 6 5 4 3 2 1

CONTENTS

REVIEW SECTION

SAMPLE TESTS

First Things First

This study guide goes further than most others on the market today. For starters, it gives you not just one, but three complete, up-to-date sample tests in addition to a diagnostic test. Each test question is similar in style to actual GMAT questions and comes with a complete answer explanation. By understanding why an answer is correct, you get insight into the GMAT's way of thinking—an invaluable asset when you're face to face with the actual exam.

"Why include a diagnostic?" you might ask. Well, because it can pinpoint areas that you haven't quite mastered. You can then devote more attention to studying what you don't know and less time reviewing those topics you do know.

Of course, tackling questions is only part of Barron's comprehensive approach to helping you prepare for the GMAT. Who couldn't use a refresher of critically important topics on the test? This is where Barron's shines. We delve into the subject matter that you need to master, bypass all irrelevant information that's not on the test (or is not likely to be on the test), and give you proven tactics, strategies, and advice for answering every question type.

By working your way through the book, you'll face test day with confidence and get the score you want. Isn't that what you expect from a book?

To all GMAT candidates, our heartfelt wishes for success on the test and reaching your goals in life.

What You Need to Know About the Next Generation

GMAT

The Basics

1

- → THE NEW TEST FORMAT
- → YOUR SCORES AND WHAT THEY MEAN
- → HOW THE CAT WORKS
- → PREPARING FOR THE GMAT
- → TEST-TAKING STRATEGIES
- → THE ART OF GUESSING
- → NAVIGATING THE COMPUTER SCREEN
- → OFFICIAL SCORES
- → THE SELF-SCORING TABLES
- → SUGGESTED STUDY PLAN

The purpose of the GMAT has always been to measure your ability to think systematically, using the knowledge and skills you have acquired throughout your years of schooling. Now, with the release of the Next Generation GMAT, the test seems more relevant to the real business world—requiring you to integrate your thinking and preparing you for the way business is done in the 21st century. That sounds daunting, doesn't it? But don't worry: the good news is that the test is not designed to measure your knowledge of specific business or academic subjects. No business experience is necessary. You are assumed to know basic algebra (but not calculus), geometry, and arithmetic. You should be able to write and apply formal written English and also compose an analytical essay. So far, that's not too bad.

In effect, the GMAT provides business school admission officers with an objective measure of your academic abilities. Remember, though, that the GMAT is just one criterion that schools consider. Business schools also look at your overall academic record, interviews, and references. Suppose you're an average student in a college that has high grading standards. Your overall grade average may be lower than that of a student from a college with lower grading standards. The GMAT allows you and the other student to be tested under similar conditions using the same grading standard. In this way, a more accurate picture of your all-around ability can be established.

Because the GMAT is (for the most part) a computer-adaptive test, it can be taken three weeks per month, six days a week, ten hours a day at 400 testing centers in the United States, Canada, and major cities throughout the world. That means you can take the test pretty much whenever you are ready. Just be sure to schedule it far enough in advance so that the schools of your choice will receive your results in time for the decision-making process. A few countries outside the United States, however, offer only the paper-and-pencil test, so be sure to check.

TIP

For exam fees, testing locations, and online registration, check the official website: *www.mba.com*.

THE NEW TEST FORMAT

The Next Generation GMAT consists of four parts: a Writing section that consists of one "analysis of an argument" essay, the new Integrated Reasoning section, a Quantitative test, and a Verbal test. You can take an optional five-minute break between each section.

See chart below.

Section	No. of Questions	Question Types	Time
Analytical Writing	1 essay	analysis of argument	30 minutes
Integrated Reasoning	12 questions	graphics interpretation table analysis two-part analysis multi-source reasoning	30 minutes
Quantitative	37 questions	problem solving data sufficiency	75 minutes
Verbal	41 questions	reading comprehension critical reading sentence correction	75 minutes

On the computer-adaptive test, the different types of verbal questions are mingled. The same is true for the quantitative questions. The total testing time is three and a half hours.

No-Nos

Aids such as handheld calculators, watch calculators, pens, watch alarms, dictionaries, translators, electronic devices, and beepers are not allowed in the testing room. You may not bring scratch paper, but laminated note boards will be handed out by the test administrator as needed. If you have some questions about procedures during the test, use the HELP function on the computer. However, remember that the time spent there will be at the expense of test time. Therefore, do yourself a favor and know what to expect from the CAT before taking the test.

YOUR SCORES AND WHAT THEY MEAN

One nice advantage to taking the computer-adaptive test is that unofficial scores on the Verbal and Quantitative sections are available upon completion. Official scores, including the Analytical Writing Assessment (AWA), are mailed out within ten days. As of press time, it was still unclear exactly how the scoring on the Integrated Reasoning section would be handled.

Scores are based on the number of questions answered correctly as well as their difficulty levels. A correct answer to a difficult question is worth more than a correct answer to an easy question. The total score ranges from 200 to 800. In general, no particular score can be called good or bad, and no passing or failing grade has been established. Scores above 750 or below 250 are unusual. In recent years, about two-thirds of all scores have fallen between 400 and 600, with the average being about 530.

What qualifies as an adequate GMAT score? There isn't one. Every university and college requiring the GMAT sets its own requirements. Average grades on the GMAT tend to differ by undergraduate major. Engineering students tend to score the highest, followed by science and social science majors, humanities majors, and business majors, in that order.

Most college catalogs do not state a minimum GMAT requirement. The annual reports of most MBA programs, though, tend to publish the average GMAT score of the last incoming student body. This is probably a good indication of what you need for admission. However, obtaining a score somewhat below that figure doesn't mean you're out of the running. First of all, it is an average figure. Second, the GMAT is *only one* criterion for admission. Your undergraduate record is equally important. You can also help yourself by writing an outstanding essay and wowing the admissions officer during a personal interview.

HOW THE CAT WORKS

In a CAT, each question is shown one at a time on a personal computer screen. Questions are of low, medium, or high levels of difficulty and every variation in between. The difficulty level of a particular question is a secret that only the test developer and computer know. For example, questions tend to be easy, medium-easy, medium, medium-hard, and difficult.

Not surprisingly, questions with a high difficulty level earn more points than easy ones. Again, how this is configured is a secret only the test developer and the computer know. So trying to figure out the difficulty of a particular question is pointless. Just do your best on each and every question.

Typically, the first question on the GMAT CAT is of medium difficulty. The difficulty level of the next question depends on your answer to the first question. If you answer the first question correctly, the next question will be of greater difficulty. If you answer the first question incorrectly, though, the next question will be less difficult, and so on. This procedure is repeated throughout the test. In this way, the computer constantly adjusts to your ability level.

Before you start the exam, you'll have time to become acquainted with the computer system. An interactive tutorial is available to help you. However, you can save a lot of time and gain confidence if you know how the CAT works in advance.

Sometimes the GMAT contains a few experimental questions. These questions may or may not be labeled as such. Just remember that they are not counted in your score. Nevertheless, you should do your best to answer them.

In the GMAT CAT, you must select an answer choice before you can proceed to the next question. You never have the option of skipping a question and coming back to it later. Once you enter and confirm your answer, you *cannot* change it. Furthermore, you can't go back and work on previous questions if you finish a section early. Some pros and cons of the CAT are highlighted in the table on the next page.

Suppose that you answer the first question correctly, then get a more difficult one that you also answer correctly, and then get an even harder one that you answer incorrectly. Will you get a lower score than, say, a candidate that answers the first question incorrectly and then gets an easier one that is answered correctly? No. Remember that difficult questions are worth more points than easier ones. There is little possibility that a candidate will receive a higher score from correctly answering only easy questions than another candidate who answers more difficult questions, even if the second candidate doesn't correctly answer as many questions.

What's the logic behind the policy of not skipping questions and not changing answers? Suppose that you gave a wrong answer to a question. The next question would be an easier one—one that, let's say, you answer correctly. If you were able to go back and change the previous question's wrong answer to the correct answer, the next question you received should have been an equally or more difficult question. You should not have received the easy

IMPORTANT

Only the Quantitative and Verbal sections are computer adaptive—the new Integrated Reasoning section is not.

TIP

Be sure to familiarize yourself in advance with how the GMAT CAT works.

CAREFUL

Answers that have been confirmed cannot be changed.

question that you answered correctly and that was scored accordingly. If you could change answers, the scoring system wouldn't work. Likewise, if skipping questions was allowed, the system would have no basis for determining the difficulty level of the next question.

These rules about skipping and returning to missed questions apply to both the Quantitative (problem-solving and data sufficiency) questions and the Verbal (reading comprehension, sentence correction, and critical reasoning) questions. **Neither the Integrated Reasoning section nor the essay are adaptive.** Your essay will be evaluated by faculty members from a number of academic disciplines, including management. It will also be rated by an automated essay-scoring system, developed by ETS, called an e-rater. After extensive testing, the e-rater system was found to agree 92 percent of the time with human readers, which is about the same rate at which two human readers agree.

Computer Skills Needed

Only basic computer skills are necessary for navigating the CAT. This means that if you know how to use a mouse and how to scroll, you'll be fine. You can download free test tutorials from *www.mba.com*. These will help you to review the basic skills of taking a computer-adaptive test, such as entering answers and accessing HELP. You should review these procedures *before* you arrive at the test center. Any time you spend on the HELP screen during the actual test is subtracted from the time you have to answer questions.

PROS AND CONS OF THE COMPUTER-ADAPTIVE TEST	
PROS	**CONS**
You can take the test at a time that is convenient for you throughout the year.	You cannot make notes on the computer screen and must rely only on note boards given at the exam.
You may register for the test by phone, fax, online, or mail and pay with a credit card.	You cannot skip a question.
More personal — only a few people will be taking the test at the same time in individualized testing alcoves.	You cannot return to a question once you have confirmed your answer.
You know your score (Verbal and Quantitative) immediately after the test. Official complete scores are available after ten days.	Those who have more experience using a computer should have an advantage in using the terminal.
You may cancel scores immediately after the test by indicating your decision on the computer screen.	You cannot see all of the Reading Comprehension test, but must scroll. The same is true for graphs and charts.
A timer is available on screen so that you can better pace yourself.	

PREPARING FOR THE GMAT

Perhaps the best way to prepare for the test is to acquaint yourself with the various types of questions on the exam. The analyses of typical GMAT questions found in the next chapter are designed for this purpose. Pay particular attention to the test-taking tactics for answering the different types of questions.

Next, make sure you know how the CAT works. Pacing yourself is very important. Every minute you spend in the HELP function equals valuable time lost.

When you feel you understand this material completely, take the Diagnostic Test and evaluate your results. A low score in any area indicates what you need to concentrate on during your preparation. Study the appropriate review section until you feel you have mastered it. Then take one of the sample GMAT tests. Continue this pattern until you are completely satisfied with your performance. For best results, try to simulate exam conditions as closely as possible when taking sample tests. Do not take any unscheduled breaks, do not allow any interruptions, strictly adhere to time limits, and do not use any outside aids other than scratch paper. Make sure you answer each question in order. While taking the diagnostic and sample tests, do not change any previous answers.

REMEMBER

You can't skip any questions.

TEST-TAKING STRATEGIES

1. **THE FIRST FIVE OR SO QUESTIONS COUNT MORE THAN LATER QUESTIONS.** Budget a little more time for these questions. You have about $1\frac{3}{4}$ minutes for each verbal question and 2 minutes for each quantitative question. So be prepared to spend more time with the initial questions, which set the difficulty level for the rest of the test.

2. **BE SURE TO FINISH EACH SECTION.** You can receive a substantial penalty for not finishing a section, so keep abreast of how much time you have remaining. If you are running out of time, guess on the final questions.

REMEMBER

Familiarity with the test saves valuable time.

3. **IF YOU ARE NOT SURE OF AN ANSWER, GUESS.** You will not be penalized for choosing a wrong answer. So if you are running out of time, guess. Also, since you have to select an answer in order to proceed to the next question, guessing is a must.

4. **PACE YOURSELF.** Keep track of your time and the number of questions remaining to be answered. A time icon and a clock appear on the screen.

5. **CONFIRM YOUR ANSWER ONLY WHEN YOU ARE CONFIDENT THAT IT IS CORRECT.** Remember, you cannot return to a previous question. Additionally, you must confirm your answer in order to move to the next question.

6. **BE CAREFUL ABOUT SECTION EXIT AND TEST QUIT COMMANDS.** Once you confirm a section exit, you cannot go back. Don't touch the test quit command unless you want to end the session. Once you have pressed the test quit command, you have no chance of continuing the test. Be careful.

7. **DON'T DAWDLE.** Since you have to answer the current question before proceeding to the next one, don't spend too much time on any one question. If you don't know the answer, do your best to eliminate one or two choices, make a selection, and move on. If you're approaching the end of a test and time is running out, guess on the remaining questions because you will incur a serious penalty if you do not complete the section. That's a far better strategy than leaving questions unanswered. Besides, you just might guess correctly, boosting your score.

THE ART OF GUESSING

Your chances of selecting the correct answer by randomly guessing is 1out of 5, or 0.20, which is rather low. However, suppose you're able to eliminate two answers but are still unsure of the correct answer. You now have a 0.33 probability of randomly guessing the correct answer. Obviously, if you are able to eliminate three choices, you then have a 50-50 chance of selecting the correct answer.

There's a decided difference between randomly guessing and making educated guesses. You make an educated guess when you can eliminate three choices, increasing the odds of selecting the correct answer. Believe it or not, you can often eliminate three choices for most questions. The next section describes how.

EXAMPLE: CRITICAL REASONING QUESTION

The college tenure system provides long-term job security for established professors, but at the same time prevents younger instructors from entering the system. But instructors are familiar with current teaching material and therefore may provide students with a better education. Thus, it is a shame that many students are unable to be taught by instructors who cannot find employment because of the tenure system.

Which of the following is an assumption made in the argument above?

(A) Most tenured professors do not make an effort to provide quality education.
(B) Most instructors are against the tenure system.
(C) University students generally prefer to be taught by instructors.
(D) Instructors have received their graduate degrees more recently than professors.
(E) Tenured professors are not as familiar with current teaching material.

In this type of question, the assumption is usually one of the answer choices rather than part of the text. In any case, let us see how you can readily eliminate several choices. Alternative (B) cannot be assumed; simply no evidence points in this direction. Likewise, no evidence is given for choice (C). Choice (D) is true by definition. However, it is not even remotely part of the text and therefore is not an assumption. By the process of elimination, choices (A) and (E) remain.

Choice (A), if true, would certainly buttress the claim that it is a shame that students cannot be taught by new instructors rather than by tenured professors. However this assumes that instructors are better teachers than professors. Instructors would be better either if professors did not make an effort to provide quality education (A) or if professors were unfamiliar with up-to-date teaching materials (E). So both alternatives are plausible. If we have to guess, we have a 50-50 chance of answering correctly. However, choice (E) claims that instructors are "familiar" with teaching materials but that professors are not as familiar with them.

So (E) is the assumption. The argument runs like this:

1. New instructors are familiar with teaching materials and can thus provide students with a better education than professors.
2. The college tenure system prevents instructors from entering the system.

3. Professors are not as familiar with current teaching materials.

4. It is a shame for students that they cannot be taught by instructors.

The conclusion "it is a shame that many students are unable to be taught by instructors" is buttressed by the addition of the premise (choice E) that professors are not familiar with current teaching materials.

Here's another example of how two or three alternatives may be quickly eliminated.

EXAMPLE: READING COMPREHENSION QUESTION

Some economists believe that the United States can be utilized as a "land bridge" for the shipment of containerized cargo between Europe and the Far East. Under the land-bridge concept, containerized freight traveling between
Line the Europe Line and the Far East would be line shipped by ocean carrier to the
(5) United States East Coast, unloaded and placed on special railway flatcars, and shipped via railroad to a West Coast port. At this port, the containers would then be loaded on ships bound to a Far East port of entry. This procedure would be reversed for material traveling in the opposite direction. Thus, a land transportation system would be substituted for marine transportation during
(10) part of the movement of goods between Europe and the Far East.

If a land-bridge system of shipment were deemed feasible and competitive with alternative methods, it would open a completely new market for both United States steamship lines and railroads. At present, foreign lines carry all Far East–Europe freight. American carriers get none of this trade, and the all-
(15) water route excludes the railroads. The system established by a land bridge could also serve to handle goods now being shipped between the United States West Coast and Europe, or goods shipped between the Far East and the United States Gulf and East Coasts. Currently, there are 20 foreign lines carrying West Coast freight to Europe via the Panama Canal, but not one United
(20) States line. Thus, in addition to the land bridge getting this new business for the railroads, it also gives the United States East Coast ships an opportunity to compete for this trade.

While this method of shipment will probably not add to the labor requirements at East and West Coast piers, it does have the potential of absorbing
(25) some of the jobs that the containerization of current cargo has eliminated or could eliminate. Thus, the possibility of creating new jobs for longshoremen is not an expected benefit of such a system, but it will most certainly create other labor requirements. The land-bridge concept has the potential of offering new job openings for United States railway workers and seamen. In addition, there
(30) would be expansion of labor requirements for people in the shipbuilding and container manufacturing business.

By making United States rail transportation an export service, the landbridge system would have a favorable effect on our balance of payments. Such a system also has the potential of relieving the United States gov-
(35) ernment of part of the burden it now bears in the form of subsidies to the shipping industry. The federal government subsidizes the construction and operation of scheduled vessels. Some 52 percent of the income from their

---

operation comes from the government in that these ships are used for all our military and other government-related export shipments. The land-bridge (40) requirement for scheduled sailings could effect a shift from the use of these scheduled lines for shipment of government goods to commercial cargo of the land bridge. This would then open some of the lucrative government business to the unscheduled, unsubsidized lines.

According to the passage, the major alternative to a U.S. land bridge is the

(A) Panama Canal

(B) Suez Canal

(C) air-freight system

(D) all-land route

(E) military transport system

Choice (C) may be quickly eliminated because it is not mentioned. Alternative (E), military transport system, can also be eliminated because it is a user and not a choice. An all-land route (D) is analogous to the U.S. land bridge and so cannot be correct. So three answers have been quickly eliminated. The choice is between (A) or (B). If we read the passage carefully, we note that the Suez Canal (B) is not mentioned. However, the Panama Canal (A) is noted as the existing alternative to a land bridge.

NAVIGATING THE COMPUTER SCREEN

While you will have the opportunity to try out the so-called testing tools of the CAT before taking the test, you will have an advantage if you are already familiar with them beforehand. These testing tools consist of a number of icons or commands by which you navigate the test.

Quit Program

If you click this, you end the test. Do this only if you have completed the entire test.

Section Exit

Clicking this button ends a test section and enables you to go on to the next test section. If you have used up all your time, the program exits the section automatically. So use this button only if you have completed the section in less than the allotted time. If you still have some time remaining and you click this button, you will be able to reverse your decision by pressing the command that appears on the bottom of the screen.

Time

Clicking this icon shows you how much time (shown in hours, minutes, and seconds) remains on the test. In any case, the time will appear in a flashing mode when your allotted time is nearly up.

? Help

Clicking this button activates the HELP function. This function contains directions for the question you are working on, directions for the section you are working on, general directions, how to scroll, and information about the testing tools. When you want to exit the help function, click the *Return to Where I Was* tool.

Next and Answer Confirm

Both of these buttons work in sequence. When you are sure of your answer, click the *Next* button to move on to the next question. The *Answer Confirm* button will then become dark. Clicking it will save your answer and bring the next question to the screen. You should also practice the word-processing tools needed for the AWA. They are similar to those used on typical word-processing programs such as Word for Windows or WordPerfect. The typing keys available are as follows:

Page up—moves the cursor up one page.

Page down—moves the cursor down one page.

Backspace—removes the text to the left of the cursor.

Delete—removes text to the right of the cursor.

Home—moves the cursor to the beginning of a line.

End—moves the cursor to the end of a line.

Arrows—moves the cursor up, down, left, and right.

Enter—moves the cursor to the beginning of the next line.

There are also *Cut*, *Paste*, and *Undo* functions.

OFFICIAL SCORES

You can see your unofficial score on the Verbal and Quantitative parts of the exam immediately after the test. Official scores, including those for the AWA, will arrive by mail within approximately ten days.

You may repeat the test once per calendar month. However, if you repeat the test, your scores from that and the two previous tests will be sent to all institutions you designate as score recipients. Many schools average your scores if you take the test more than once.

You can cancel your scores if you act before leaving the test center. You have to indicate this on the computer screen after completing the test. However, if you cancel your scores, the fact that you took the test will be reported to all the places you designated.

Therefore, canceling your scores is generally not advantageous unless you have some reason to believe that you have done substantially worse on the test than you should have. For example, if you became ill while taking the exam, you might choose to cancel your scores. Once a score is canceled from your record, it cannot be put back or reported at a later date.

THE SELF-SCORING TABLES

You can use the Self-Scoring Table for each sample test in this book to evaluate your weaknesses in particular subject areas. These tables should help you plan a highly effective study program. After completing a sample test, turn to the Answers section that immediately follows each test. Count the number of *correct* answers you had for each section. This is your correct score for that section. Now turn to the section Evaluating Your Score, which follows

TIP
Remember that you cannot see your scores before canceling them.

REMEMBER
Unless you have a reason to expect a substantial improvement in your score, retaking the exam is *not* usually worthwhile.

the Answers Explained section of each test. Record your scores in the appropriate score boxes.

In the Self-Scoring Table as shown below, add your Quantitative score to your Verbal score to get your total score. The following procedure outlines how to convert your total score into an approximate scaled score to determine your performance on this test.

1. Find the total number of correct answers you achieved in the Quantitative section.
2. Find the total number of correct answers you achieved in the Verbal section.
3. Add the numbers from steps 1. and 2. to obtain the total number of correct answers you achieved in the Verbal and Quantitative sections. We will call this number **T** (your total score).
4. Find the score that corresponds to your value of **T** in the scoring table.

T should be a number less than or equal to 78. Find your equivalent scaled score in the table below.

SELF-SCORING TABLE

T	Score	T	Score	T	Score	T	Score
78	800	59	660	40	510	21	370
77	790	58	650	39	500	20	360
76	790	57	640	38	490	19	350
75	780	56	630	37	490	18	340
74	770	55	620	36	480	17	340
73	760	54	620	35	470	16	330
72	760	53	610	34	460	15	320
71	750	52	600	33	460	14	310
70	740	51	590	32	450	13	300
69	730	50	580	31	440	12	290
68	720	49	580	30	430	11	280
67	720	48	570	29	430	10	270
66	710	47	560	28	420	9	260
65	700	46	550	27	410	8	250
64	690	45	550	26	400	7	240
63	690	44	540	25	400	6	230
62	680	43	530	24	390	5	220
61	670	42	520	23	380	4	210
60	660	41	520	22	370	<4	200

IMPORTANT

This chart refers only to Quantitative and Verbal sections scoring. For details on Integrated Reasoning scoring, see page 17 or go to *mba.com*.

In the example below, your approximate score would be calculated as follows.

1. Suppose your Quantitative score is 13.
2. Suppose your Verbal score is 27.
3. Your Total is 27 + 13 = 40. So **T** = 40
4. The score that corresponds to **T** = 40 is 510.

SUGGESTED STUDY PLAN

Let's face it. You probably already have an idea of how to prepare for the GMAT. If so, great. Do whatever works for you. In case you don't have the foggiest clue about how to prepare, here's a suggested study plan that takes full advantage of this guide.

1. Familiarize yourself with the purpose and format of the GMAT CAT (Chapter 1).
2. Study the analysis of each type of question on the exam (Chapter 2).
3. Take the Diagnostic Test (Chapter 3), and use the Self-Scoring Table to approximate the score you might earn on the actual exam.
4. Study the review sections (Chapters 4, 5, 6, 7, 8, 9, and 10). Spend more time on areas you're unsure of, and skim over those you have down pat.
5. Take the three sample GMAT model tests (Chapters 11, 12, and 13), and evaluate your results.
6. If necessary, review any remaining troublesome topics.
7. Congratulate yourself on a job well done and look forward to showing what you know on test day.

Now let's get down to business!

Test Specifics

2

→ **ANALYTICAL WRITING ASSESSMENT**
→ **ANALYSIS OF AN ARGUMENT**
→ **THE NEW INTEGRATED REASONING SECTION**
→ **READING COMPREHENSION**
→ **SENTENCE CORRECTION**
→ **CRITICAL REASONING**
→ **PROBLEM SOLVING**
→ **DATA SUFFICIENCY QUESTIONS**
→ **LONG-TERM STRATEGY FOR DATA SUFFICIENCY QUESTIONS**

A logical first step in preparing for the GMAT is to familiarize yourself with all types of questions that usually appear on this exam. The following analysis explains the purpose behind each type and the best method for answering it. Tactics for handling each of the different types of questions are also given. These tactics provide practical tools and advice to help you prepare for the exam and take it more efficiently. Samples of the questions with a discussion of their answers are also included.

ANALYTICAL WRITING ASSESSMENT

The AWA section is designed to assess your ability to think critically and to communicate complex ideas. The writing task now consists of only one essay prompt that requires you to take a position on a particular issue and present a critique of the conclusion derived from a specific way of thinking. The issues are typically taken from topics of general interest related to business or other subjects.

TIP

There is no spell-check or grammar check on the computer for the writing section.

ANALYSIS OF AN ARGUMENT

EXAMPLE

The computerized water irrigation system to be installed by farmers will prevent crops from drying out. The soil moisture is measured by sensors in the ground that send signals back to the irrigation control system. On the basis of this information, the system automatically regulates the amount and time of irrigation.

Discuss how logically persuasive you find this argument. Are there inferred assumptions? In presenting your point of view, analyze the sort of reasoning used and its supporting evidence. In addition, state what further evidence, if any, would make the argument more sound and convincing or would make you better able to evaluate its conclusion. What might weaken or strengthen the argument?

Test-Taking Tactics

1. **UNDERSTAND WHAT YOU'RE BEING EXPECTED TO ANALYZE.** An argument question asks you to discuss the persuasiveness of a claim and express a point of view on a subject, while supporting that point of view with evidence. You may be asked to defend or refute an argument.

2. **IDENTIFY THE PARTS OF THE ARGUMENT.** Make sure to read the prompt very carefully and address all the aspects of the argument in your response.

3. **STATE HOW CONVINCING (OR UNCONVINCING) YOU FIND THE ARGUMENT.** The persuasiveness of an argument depends on its logic, which is whether the conclusion follows from the evidence presented. You are also asked to discuss what would make the argument more persuasive or would help to evaluate its conclusion. In this instance, you need to provide more evidence that will buttress the conclusion.

In the example above, the conclusion is found in the first sentence: the irrigation system will prevent crops from drying out. What evidence is given that the irrigation system will indeed perform this task? Overall, the argument is sound and convincing, assuming that proper irrigation is all that is needed to keep crops from drying out. What could strengthen the conclusion? You might include evidence that similar systems are already in place and working.

This last point is important because the passage provides no evidence about the reliability of the system. Moreover, there may be a question of cost effectiveness. Will farmers be willing to adopt such a system? If you could provide evidence of these factors, the conclusion would be strengthened.

TIP

Always be sure to identify the conclusion of the argument.

INTEGRATED REASONING

In June 2012, a brand new Integrated Reasoning section was added to the GMAT. This section basically tests your ability to extract and decipher information and data from multiple sources and formats. This Barron's guide breaks down everything you need to know about the new IR section and includes strategies and methodologies you will need in order to succeed on test day. *Please refer to the Integrated Reasoning section on page 167 for details.*

Why the New Section?

Over the past few years, the Graduate Management Admission Council (GMAC), the organization that owns and operates the GMAT exam, surveyed 740 management faculty around the world to determine how to improve the GMAT as a measure of student success in an MBA program. According to the GMAC:

> "Today's businesses and organizations demand managers who can make sound decisions, discern patterns, and combine verbal and quantitative reasoning to solve problems. The Integrated Reasoning section will measure these skills."
> (Source: *http://www.mba.com/the-gmat/nex-gen/find-out-whats-changing.aspx*)

Section Details

The new Integrated Reasoning section contains 12 questions, many of which have multiple parts, and has a 30 minute time limit. A special online calculator is available for use on only this part of the GMAT. The Integrated Reasoning section will be scored separately from your GMAT score (from 200–800) and from your AWA score (from 0–6). This section will be scored on a scale from 1–8, in intervals of 1. There are no partial points given, which means that if a question has three Yes/No statements, you need to get all three correct in order to get full credit. For more details on scoring in the Integrated Reasoning section, go to *mba.com*.

The Integrated Reasoning section is designed to measure your ability to review data in multiple formats using various methods, to identify key issues and trends, to apply high-level reasoning, and to organize information in order to make an informed decision. For this, you will need to be comfortable with synthesizing information from charts, tables, graphs, spreadsheets, e-mails, and letters in paragraph form. As with the rest of the GMAT, you will not need prior business knowledge to answer Integrated Reasoning questions. The new Integrated Reasoning section can be best summarized as a blend of the GMAT Quantitative and Critical Reasoning sections along with some argumentative logic, thus the use of the term *integrated.*

Note that the Integrated Reasoning section is not computer adaptive like the quantitative and verbal sections, which become easier or more difficult in response to your performance. This means the questions are preselected, just like in a simple paper and pencil test. Therefore, you should expect a diverse mix of question types and difficulty levels. *Again, for further information and strategies on Integrated Reasoning questions, see page 167.*

READING COMPREHENSION

Reading comprehension questions test your ability to analyze written information and include passages from the social sciences, the physical and biological sciences, and sometimes the humanities.

The typical Reading Comprehension section consists of three passages with approximately 15 questions in total. Each passage is approximately 350 words long. You will be allowed to scroll through the passages when answering the questions. However, many of the questions are based on what is implied in the passages rather than on what is explicitly stated. Your ability to draw inferences from the material is critical to completing this section successfully. Inference questions will be identified. Main idea and specific questions are also generally identified as such. You are to select the best answer from five alternatives.

Types of Questions

Reading comprehension questions usually fall into several general categories. In most questions, you will be asked about one of the following.

MAIN IDEA

In main idea questions, you may be asked about the main idea or theme of the passage, about a possible title, or about the author's primary objective. Usually the main idea refers to the passage as a whole, not to some segment or part of the passage. The main idea can sometimes be found in the first paragraph. It will be a statement that gives the overall theme of the passage. In many cases, it will be in the form of an argument, including a premise and conclusion.

A frequent question on Reading Comprehension tests asks you to select the title or theme that best summarizes the passage.

EXAMPLE 1

Government policy in Frieland has traditionally favored foreign investment. Leaders of all political parties have been virtually unanimous in their belief that foreign investment in Frieland would contribute to speeding that coun-
Line try's economic development, a major priority of both the ruling coalition and
(5) opposition parties. Of special interest to the government were those industries that exported a significant share of their total output.

Since Frieland had a relatively small population, there was a limit to the amount of goods that could be produced for the local market. Also, the government did not want to encourage foreign investors to compete with local
(10) industry, even though new industries might alleviate the already high unemployment rate.

Which of the following is the best possible title of the passage?

(A) Government Policy in Frieland
(B) How to Provide Employment
(C) Attracting Foreign Investment
(D) The Economics of Developing Countries
(E) Foreign Investment and Economic Development

All of the above alternatives can be found in the passage with the exception of (D). We don't know if Frieland is a developing country. However, note that the words "foreign investment" are mentioned three times in the passage. In lines 3–4, these words are linked with economic development.

Clearly, the main idea or subject is foreign investment.

Additional questions may ask you to identify the author's purpose in writing the passage.

REMEMBER

The main idea is often found in the first paragraph.

EXAMPLE 2

It can be concluded that the aim of the author is to

(A) increase foreign investment.

(B) protect local industry from foreign competition.

(C) increase unemployment benefits for workers.

(D) develop a theory of foreign investment.

(E) increase the indigenous population of Frieland.

(A) is the correct answer. The author explains under what conditions foreign investment would be beneficial to Frieland.

SUPPORTING IDEAS

In supporting idea questions, you may be asked about the idea expressed in one part of the passage rather than about the passage as a whole. This type of question tests your ability to distinguish between the main idea and those themes that support it, some of which may be explicitly stated or implied.

EXAMPLE

Some economists believe that the United States can be utilized as a "land bridge" for the shipment of containerized cargo between Europe and the Far East. Under the land-bridge concept, containerized freight traveling between
Line the Europe Line and the Far East would be shipped by ocean carrier to the
(5) United States East Coast, unloaded and placed on special railway flatcars, and shipped via railroad to a West Coast port. At this port, the containers would then be loaded on ships bound to a Far East port of entry. This procedure would be reversed for material traveling in the opposite direction. Thus, a land transportation system would be substituted for marine transportation during
(10) part of the movement of goods between Europe and the Far East.

If a land-bridge system of shipment were deemed feasible and competitive with alternative methods, it would open a completely new market for both United States steamship lines and railroads. At present, foreign lines carry all Far East–Europe freight. American carriers get none of this trade,
(15) and the all-water route excludes the railroads. The system established by a land bridge could also serve to handle goods now being shipped between the United States West Coast and Europe, or goods shipped between the Far East and the United States Gulf and East Coasts. Currently, there are 20 foreign lines carrying West Coast freight to Europe via the Panama Canal, but

(20) not one United States line. Thus, in addition to the land bridge getting this new business for the railroads, it also gives the United States East Coast ships an opportunity to compete for this trade.

While this method of shipment will probably not add to the labor requirements at East and West Coast piers, it does have the potential of absorbing (25) some of the jobs that the containerization of current cargo has eliminated or could eliminate. Thus, the possibility of creating new jobs for longshoremen is not an expected benefit of such a system, but it will most certainly create other labor requirements. The land-bridge concept has the potential of offering new job openings for United States railway workers and seamen. In (30) addition, there would be expansion of labor requirements for people in the shipbuilding and container manufacturing business.

By making United States rail transportation an export service, the land-bridge system would have a favorable effect on our balance of payments. Such a system also has the potential of relieving the United States gov(35) ernment of part of the burden it now bears in the form of subsidies to the shipping industry. The federal government subsidizes the construction and operation of scheduled vessels. Some 52 percent of the income from their operation comes from the government in that these ships are used for all our military and other government-related export shipments. The land-bridge (40) requirement for scheduled sailings could effect a shift from the use of these scheduled lines for shipment of government goods to commercial cargo of the land bridge. This would then open some of the lucrative government business to the unscheduled, unsubsidized lines.

The main idea in this passage is that the United States may be utilized as a land bridge for the shipment of containerized cargo between Europe and the Far East. This is evidenced by the first sentence in the passage. Supporting ideas would include any facts or arguments that buttress the main idea. A number of these may be found in the passage:

1. The opening of a new market (paragraph 2).
2. Creating new jobs (paragraph 3).
3. Expanding labor requirements (paragraph 3).

1. According to the passage, if a land-bridge system were feasible, it would

    (A) create employment in the bridge-building industry.

    (B) decrease the amount of air freight.

    (C) create a new market for steamship lines and railroads.

    (D) make American railroads more efficient.

    (E) increase foreign trade.

2. The author implies that which of the following would be provided employment by the development of a land bridge?

    I. Dockworkers

    II. U.S. railway workers

    III. U.S. sailors

    (A) I only

    (B) III only

    (C) I and II only

    (D) II and III only

    (E) I, II, and III

The answer to question 1 is choice (C), which refers to supporting idea (1) listed on page 20 and summarized in paragraph 2 of the passage. A land bridge would create a new market for U.S. steamship lines and railroads.

Question 2 is developed from an idea implied in the passage. Answer choice (D) is correct. Paragraph 3 argues that new jobs will be created for U.S. railway workers and sailors but not for dockworkers.

DRAWING INFERENCES

Drawing inference questions ask about ideas that are not explicitly stated in a passage. These questions refer to meanings implied by the author based on information given in the passage. Typical questions include:

1. The author feels (believes) that . . .

2. In reference to (event), it may be inferred that . . .

Refer to the land-bridge passage on page 19. Which of the following does the passage suggest might least benefit from a land bridge?

(A) U.S. railway workers

(B) U.S. sailors

(C) U.S. scheduled shipping lines

(D) U.S. unscheduled shipping lines

(E) U.S. government

Choice (C) is correct. The author gives specific reasons why each of the answer choices might benefit from a land bridge except scheduled shipping lines. The final paragraph states that the land bridge "would then open some of the lucrative government business to the unscheduled, unsubsidized lines." This implies that the scheduled lines would not benefit.

SPECIFIC DETAILS

In specific detail questions, you may be asked about specific facts or details the author has stated explicitly in the passage. This sort of question may take the following forms:

1. Which of the following statements is mentioned by the author?

2. All of the following are given as reasons for (topic) EXCEPT:

3. The author argues that . . .

EXAMPLES

Refer to the land-bridge passage on page 19.

1. According to the passage, the major alternative to a U.S. land bridge is the
   (A) Panama Canal.
   (B) Suez Canal.
   (C) air-freight system.
   (D) all-land route.
   (E) military transport system.

2. The passage states that a land bridge would improve United States
   (A) foreign trade.
   (B) balance of payments.
   (C) railroad industry.
   (D) international relations.
   (E) gold reserves.

3. A land bridge would not
   (A) aid U.S. steamship lines.
   (B) handle goods shipped between Europe and the Far East.
   (C) create new jobs for dockworkers.
   (D) supply new business for U.S. railroads.
   (E) create business for unscheduled shipping lines.

The answer to specific detail questions must always be found in the passage. These questions do not deal with implications or inferences. The answer to question 1 above is (A). Paragraph 2 discusses using the Panama Canal as a route for freight lines. The answer to question 2 is (B), which is given in paragraph 4. The answer to question 3 is (C). Paragraph 3 specifically states that dockworkers would not benefit from a land bridge.

APPLYING INFORMATION FROM THE PASSAGE TO OTHER SITUATIONS

This type of question asks you to make an analogy between a situation described in the passage and a similar situation or event listed in the question. Unlike other types of questions, these do not describe situations given in the passage. Rather, they describe situations analogous to those in the passage. In order to answer this kind of question, you must be able to draw a parallel between the situation in the question and its counterpart in the passage.

EXAMPLE

The Danes are widely renowned for their business orientation, which is reflected in their export promotion policies. Without any raw materials of their own, except for agricultural produce, the Danes obtain a third of their
Line GNP from their export trade. This magnitude has been achieved only through
(5) a thorough exploitation of export potential and the implementation of a wide range of promotional activities. The latter emphasize the practical rather than the theoretical, and actual business encounters rather than such indirect, and previously popular, means as cultural events and Danish weeks.

Which of the following countries should succeed in exporting?
(A) Countries without domestic raw materials.
(B) Countries with a growing GNP.
(C) Countries with a practical approach to business.
(D) Countries with a thoroughly produced and diverse promotional campaign.
(E) Countries with some export potential based on a wide range of products.

This question asks you to project the Danish experience to similar events in other countries. The analogy, of course, is "what helped the Danes to export will help other countries as well." What helped the Danes in this case was the "implementation of a wide range of promotional activities." The correct answer is (D). Note that you were not asked to comment on the validity of the analogy but only to identify the parallel case.

TONE OR ATTITUDE OF THE PASSAGE

Questions about tone or attitude may appear on the test and involve the author's style, attitude, or mood. In order to determine attitude, look for key words, such as adjectives that reveal if the author is pessimistic, critical, supportive, or objective about an event, idea, or situation in the passage.

Typical questions include:

1. For what audience is the passage intended?

2. The passage indicates that the author expresses a feeling of
   (A) hope.
   (B) confidence.
   (C) enthusiasm.
   (D) instability.
   (E) pleasure.

3. It can be concluded that the author of the passage is
   (A) sympathetic to John Doe's ideas.
   (B) uncritical of John Doe's interpretation of history.
   (C) politically conservative.
   (D) a believer in mysticism.
   (E) a political dilettante.

Authors' Techniques

A reader can detect certain techniques used by authors, depending on the subject matter of the material.

SOCIAL STUDIES

If the subject matter of the passage is about social studies, authors tend to:

- Make comparisons ("The ABC company uses a production process that can be likened to . . .").
- Describe cause and effect relationships ("The development of the harbor can be attributed to . . .").
- Describe their opinion or reasoning ("The author belongs to which of the following schools of thought?").

SCIENCE

If the subject matter is from the sciences, writers deal with:

- Problem solving ("Serious unemployment leads labor groups to demand . . .").
- Cause and effect ("Government investment in industry should result in . . .").
- Classification of things and events ("According to the passage, the waves occur most frequently in the area of . . .").
- Experimentation ("Given present wave-tracking systems, scientists can forecast all of the following EXCEPT:").

LITERATURE

If the subject matter is literature, authors tend to:

- Create moods ("Which of the following best describes the author's tone in the passage?").
- Narrate events ("The author's treatment of the topic can be best described as . . .").
- Describe settings and characters ("The main character is a person attempting to . . .").

THE LOGICAL STRUCTURE OF THE PASSAGE

These types of questions test your understanding of the overall meaning, logic, or organization of a passage. You may be asked how several ideas in a passage are interrelated or how a passage is constructed, classifies information, compares situations, or describes events. You may be asked about the strengths or weaknesses of the argument the author is making, to identify assumptions, or to evaluate counterarguments.

The following are some typical questions.

1. John Doe's judgment that he failed was based on an assumption. Which of the following could have served as that assumption?
2. Which of the following, if true, weakens the above argument?
3. If the statement in the passage is true, which of the following must also be true?
4. Which of the following conclusions can be drawn from the passage?

DETERMINING THE MEANING OF WORDS FROM THE CONTEXT

When a question asks for the meaning of a word, you can usually deduce the definition from the context of the passage.

TIP

You are not required to know the meaning of technical or foreign words.

EXAMPLE

During the 1980 campaign to clean the streets of undesirables and criminal elements, a force of 10,000 special police was used to maintain order. Nevertheless, many of the hunted crime figures fought back with live weapons Line and the streets looked like a battlefield. Almost as many police officers were (5) injured as were criminals. This year's action will have to be better planned.

The planned action can be described as a

(A) police offensive.
(B) political campaign.
(C) battle.
(D) law and order.
(E) none of the above.

The passage tells us that this year's action will have to be planned better. From this, we know that it is being compared to something that happened before, which occurred during 1980. That was the campaign to clean the streets. Therefore, the best answer choice is (A). We know that the meaning of action is the police offensive described in the passage.

Test-Taking Tactics

1. **READ THE QUESTION FIRST AND THEN THE PASSAGE.** Why? Doing so enables you to identify the question type. However, do not read the answer choices at this time. If you are familiar with the question type, such as identifying a main idea or drawing inferences, you will know what to look for when you read the passage. After you know the question type, carefully read the passage.

   Read as quickly as you can but not in haste. Each Reading Comprehension passage contains about 350 words. Even if you read at a medium rate of 300 words a minute, you will read the passages in approximately 1 minute, leaving approximately 1.5 minutes per question.

   If the question asks you to identify the main idea, remember that it will often be found in the opening sentences or in the summary part of the passage. In order to identify the main idea, first determine the object, person, or thing that is the subject of the passage. Ask yourself, "What is the main point the author is making?"

2. READ ALL THE ANSWER ALTERNATIVES. Read all the answer choices. Never assume you have found the correct answer until you have considered all the alternatives. Choose the best possible answer on the basis of what is written in the passage and not on your own knowledge from other sources.

3. IDENTIFY THE MAJOR QUESTION TYPE. Before taking a Reading Comprehension test, make sure that you are thoroughly familiar with the major question types. This will save you time on the test and increase your effectiveness in choosing the correct answer. You will save time because you will know in advance what to look for and how to read the passage. You will be more effective because you will immediately know what reading tactic to apply.

Sample Passage and Questions

To familiarize yourself with the GMAT, read the passage through and then answer the questions, making sure to leave yourself enough time to complete them all.

TIME: 10 minutes

Political theories have, in fact, very little more to do with musical creation than electronics theories have. Both merely determine methods of distribution. The exploitation of these methods is subject to political regulation and is quite rigidly
Line regulated in many countries. The revolutionary parties, both in Russia and else-
(5) where, have tried to turn composers on to supposedly revolutionary subject matter. The net result for either art or revolution has not been very important. Neither has official fascist music accomplished much either for music or for Italy or Germany.

Political party influence on music is just censorship anyway. Performances can be forbidden and composers disciplined for what they write, but the creative stimulus
(10) comes from elsewhere. Nothing really "inspires" an author but money or food or love.

That persons or parties subventioning musical uses should wish to retain veto power over the works used is not at all surprising. That our political masters (or our representatives) should exercise a certain negative authority, a censorship, over the
(15) exploitation of works whose content they consider dangerous to public welfare is also in no way novel or surprising. But that such political executives should think to turn the musical profession into a college of political theorists or a bunch of hired propagandists is naïve of them. Our musical civilization is older than any political party. We can deal on terms of intellectual equality with acoustical engineers,
(20) with architects, with poets, painters, and historians, even with the Roman clergy if necessary. We cannot be expected to take very seriously the inspirational dictates of persons or of groups who think they can pay us to get emotional about ideas. They can pay us to get emotional all right. Anybody can. Nothing is so emotion-producing as money. But emotions are factual; they are not generated by ideas. On the con-
(25) trary, ideas are generated by emotions; and emotions, in turn, are visceral states produced directly by facts like money and food and sexual intercourse. To have any inspirational quality there must be present facts or immediate anticipations, not pie-in-the-sky.

1. The author is making a statement defending

    I. intellectual freedom.
    II. the apolitical stance of most musicians.
    III. emotional honesty.

    (A) I only
    (B) II only
    (C) I and II only
    (D) I and III only
    (E) I, II, and III

2. The tone of the author in the passage is
    (A) exacting.
    (B) pessimistic.
    (C) critical.
    (D) optimistic.
    (E) fatalistic.

3. The author's reaction to political influence on music is one of
    (A) surprise.
    (B) disbelief.
    (C) resignation.
    (D) deference.
    (E) rancor.

4. According to the author, political attempts to control the subject matter of music
    (A) will be resisted by artists wherever they are made.
    (B) may succeed in censoring but not in inspiring musical works.
    (C) will succeed only if the eventual goal is the common good.
    (D) are less effective than the indirect use of social and economic pressure.
    (E) have profoundly influenced the course of modern musical history.

Answers

1. **(D)**   2. **(C)**   3. **(C)**   4. **(B)**

Analysis

1. **(D)** The author is arguing that musicians will not conform to any control over their creativity. Thus, they want to be intellectually free and emotionally honest. It does not mean that they could not be active in politics (apolitical).
2. **(C)** The author is critical of attempts to censor the arts, especially music.
3. **(C)** The author does not find censorship surprising (lines 12–13), nor does he take it seriously (lines 21–24). He is resigned to attempts at censorship, although he does not believe it can inspire creativity.
4. **(B)** See paragraph 2.

Now that you have reviewed the answers, look at the same passage marked with cues to the major question types.

Political theories have, in fact, very little more to do with musical creation than electronics theories have. Both merely determine methods of distribution. The exploitation of these methods is subject to political regulation and is quite rigidly
Line regulated in many countries. The revolutionary parties, both in Russia and else-
(5) where, have tried to turn composers on to supposedly revolutionary subject-matter. The (net result) for either art or revolution has not been very important. Neither has official fascist music accomplished much either for music or for Italy or Germany.

<u>Political</u> party-influence on music is just censorship anyway. Performances can be forbidden and composers disciplined for what they write, but the creative stimu-
(10) lus comes from elsewhere. Nothing really "inspires" an author but money or food or love.

(That) persons or parties subventioning musical uses should wish to retain veto power over the works used is not at all surprising. (That) our <u>political masters</u> (or our representatives) should exercise a certain negative authority, a censorship, over the exploita-
(15) tion of works whose content they consider dangerous to public welfare is also in no way novel or surprising. (But that) such <u>political executives</u> should think to turn the musical profession into a college of <u>political theorists</u> or a bunch of hired propagandists is naïve of them. Our musical civilization is older than any <u>political party</u>. We can deal on terms of intellectual equality with acoustical engineers, with architects,
(20) with poets, painters, and historians, even with the Roman clergy if necessary. We cannot be expected to take very seriously the inspirational dictates of persons or of groups who think they can pay us to get <u>emotional about</u> ideas. They can pay us to get <u>emotional</u> all right. Anybody can. Nothing is so <u>emotion-producing</u> as money. (But) <u>emotions</u> are factual; they are not generated by ideas. (On the contrary), ideas are
(25) generated <u>by emotions</u>; and <u>emotions, in turn</u>, are visceral states produced directly by facts like money and food and sexual intercourse. To have any inspirational qual-
ity there must be present facts or immediate anticipations, not pie-in-the-sky.

Note the marked passage above. Cue words have been circled. For example, in the first paragraph, the cue words "net result" have been circled. These words refer to the sentences above and to the main idea found in the first sentence: that politics and the arts are foreign to each other and that political regulation of music and the arts does nothing for them.

The second paragraph contains a supporting idea and a specific detail. The word *that,* which appears three times at the beginning of the third paragraph, signals that a statement is to be made. The first two introduce a supporting idea to the effect that it is not surprising to find censorship of artistic works considered to be dangerous to a (totalitarian) state. The *but* before the third *that* signals a different thought. Although censorship may be applied, it will not politicize the musical profession. A second *but* and the phrase *on the contrary* signal that the following ideas or details present a contrasting argument to what was previously presented.

Since the main idea is concerned with the politicizing of the arts, the word *political* was underlined every time it appeared. Since musical or artistic creation is also a subject of the passage, the word *emotional* was underlined. As can be seen from the marked passage, underlining was done very sparingly.

By now looking at the passage as a whole, we can see that the first paragraph contains the main idea.

The second paragraph contains supporting ideas and details either buttressing or negating the main idea. The last paragraph sums up and gives a conclusion. This is a typical structure of a Reading Comprehension passage. You will find that questions will usually follow this order.

REMEMBER

The main idea is *usually* found in the first paragraph and the conclusion in the last paragraph.

SENTENCE CORRECTION

The Sentence Correction part of the Verbal section tests your understanding of the basic rules of English grammar and usage. To succeed on these questions, you need a command of sentence structure, including tense and mood, subject and verb agreement, proper case, parallel structure, and other basics. No attempt is made to test for spelling or capitalization. However, the Verbal section does test punctuation, including commas and semicolons.

In the Sentence Correction part of the test, you will be given sentences in which all or part of the sentence is underlined. You will then be asked to choose the best phrasing of the underlined part from five alternatives. Choice (A) will always be the original phrasing.

Test-Taking Tactics

1. **REMEMBER THAT ANY ERROR IN THE SENTENCE MUST BE IN THE UNDERLINED PART.** Do not look for errors in the rest of the sentence.

2. **IF YOU DETERMINE THAT THERE IS AN ERROR IN THE UNDERLINED PART OF THE SENTENCE, IMMEDIATELY ELIMINATE ANSWER CHOICE (A)**, which always repeats the wording of the original sentence. Also eliminate any other answer alternatives that repeat the specific error. Then concentrate on the remaining answer alternatives to choose your answer.

3. **DO NOT CHOOSE AS AN ANSWER ANY ALTERNATIVE THAT CHANGES THE MEANING OF THE ORIGINAL SENTENCE.**

4. **DETERMINE IF THE PARTS OF THE SENTENCE ARE LINKED LOGICALLY.** Are the clauses of a sentence equal? (Do they contain *and*, *or*, and so on?) Instead, is one clause subordinate to another? (Are they linked with *because*, *since*, *who*, and so on?)

5. **LOOK AT THE CHANGES MADE IN THE ANSWER ALTERNATIVES.** This will tell you what specific error or usage problem is being tested. This can be particularly helpful if you know that the original sentence contains an error—your ear tells you the sentence is wrong—but you cannot pinpoint the error. Reading the possible choices will help you identify the error and then select the answer you think is correct.

6. **BE AWARE OF THE COMMON GRAMMAR AND USAGE ERRORS TESTED ON THE GMAT.** Among the most common errors are errors in verb tense and formation and errors in the use of infinitives and gerunds in verb complements; errors in pronoun case and

agreement with subject and object; errors in the use of adjectives and adverbs, especially after verbs of sense; and errors in comparatives, connectors, parallel construction, and unnecessary modifiers.

The GMAT also commonly tests easily confused words, such as affect and effect, afflict and inflict, and prescribe and proscribe. Be sure you know the meaning and spelling of these words and check that they are used correctly in the sentence.

Chapter 6—"Sentence Correction"—reviews those errors in grammar and usage commonly found on the GMAT. Examples of incorrect and correct sentences are given. A list of frequently misused words and prepositional idioms is provided.

Sample Question

Since the advent of cable television, at the beginning of <u>this decade, the video industry took</u> a giant stride forward in this country.

(A) this decade, the video industry took

(B) this decade, the video industry had taken

(C) this decade, the video industry has taken

(D) this decade saw the video industry taking

(E) the decade that let the video industry take

Answer

(C)

Analysis

The phrase "Since the advent . . ." demands a verb in the present perfect form. Thus, *has taken*, not *took*, is correct. Choice (E) changes the meaning of the original sentence.

CRITICAL REASONING

The Critical Reasoning part of the Verbal section is designed to test your ability to evaluate an assumption, inference, or argument and to find missing premises or conclusions. Each critical reasoning passage consists of a short statement containing several sentences. Occasionally, there are longer passages, and these tend to be more difficult. Each question or assumption has five answer choices. Your task is to evaluate each of the five possible choices and to select the best one.

Types of Critical Reasoning Questions

Inference or Assumption

Flaws

Statements of Fact

Missing Premises

Missing Conclusions

Weakening an Argument

Supporting an Argument

INFERENCE OR ASSUMPTION

These questions test your ability to evaluate an assumption, inference, or argument. You will be given a statement, position, argument, or fact and will be asked to identify a conclusion or claim and the premise on which it is based.

EXAMPLE

Four years ago, the government introduced the Youth Training Program to guarantee teenagers leaving school an alternative to the dole. Today, over 150,000 16 and 17 year olds are still signing on for unemployment benefits. However, the numbers have dropped below those of previous years.

Each of the following, if true, could account for the above EXCEPT:
(A) The program provides uninteresting work.
(B) It is difficult to find work for all the program's graduates.
(C) The number of 16- and 17-year-old youths has increased over the past four years.
(D) Unemployment benefits are known while future salaries are not.
(E) Youths are unaware of the program's benefits.

The correct answer is (C). The fact that the number of 16- and 17-year-old youths has increased does not explain why unemployed high school graduates do not opt for the training program. All other answer alternatives do give possible reasons.

FLAWS

In this type of question, you are asked to choose the best alternative answer that either represents a flaw in the statement position or, if true, would weaken the argument or conclusion.

EXAMPLE

Many people are murdered by killers whose homicidal tendencies are triggered by an official execution. Since 1977, for each execution there were about four homicides. . . . If each of the 1,788 death row prisoners were to be executed, up to 7,152 additional murders would be one of the results.

Which of the following, if true, would weaken the above argument?
(A) The rate of murders to executions is 1 to 1.66.
(B) There is no relationship between executions and murders.
(C) Executions result from the higher incidence of violent crime.
(D) The death penalty will be abolished.
(E) Not all death row prisoners will be executed.

The correct answer is (B). The author's assumption is that there is a relationship between executions and homicides. As executions increase, so will homicides—at a given rate. Of course, if (D) occurred, presumably the homicide rate, according to the author's argument, will decline. However, (B) is the strongest argument—if true—against the author's premise.

STATEMENTS OF FACT

With this type of question, you will be asked to find the answer that best agrees with, summarizes, or completes the statement.

EXAMPLE

When Herodotus wrote his history of the ancient world, he mixed the lives of the famous with those of the everyday. He wanted not only to record the events that shaped his world but also to give his readers a taste of life in past times and faraway places.

Which of the following best summarizes the above?
(A) Herodotus performed the tasks of both historian and journalist.
(B) Historians alone cannot reconstruct times and social circles.
(C) Herodotus relied on gossip and hearsay to compile his essays.
(D) Herodotus's history was based on scanty evidence.
(E) Herodotus preferred writing about the elite, rather than the lower classes.

The correct answer is (A). Herodotus wrote about all classes of people, recording not only momentous events but also the mundane. Therefore, he could be classified as a historian and as a journalist.

MISSING PREMISES

EXAMPLE

This academic year, enrollment has declined by 10 percent at Duramia College, a four-year, on-campus business administration studies institution. Last year, corporate employment rates declined by about the same percent while unemployment rose. These statistics conclusively show that worsening employment is primarily responsible for the decline in enrollment at Duramia College.

Which of the following is an assumption upon which the argument relies?
(A) Duramia College has a large number of liberal arts students.
(B) Liberal arts studies have declined in popularity throughout the country.
(C) New dormitories are under construction at the college.
(D) Tuition has risen by 5 percent at Duramia.
(E) Employment and student enrollment rates have moved in the same direction over the last several years.

The conclusion in this passage follows two premises. The first premise is that enrollment at the college has decreased this year. The second premise states that corporate employment decreased while unemployment rose last year. The conclusion reasons that employment conditions affect student enrollment. However, additional evidence is needed to support the linkage between employment and enrollment. Answer choice (E) does this by showing that employment and enrollment rates have trended together.

MISSING CONCLUSIONS

EXAMPLE

A record number of start-ups were established last year in Innovatia, an emerging economy. These start-ups were responsible for the majority of new jobs created. This new job creation was in addition to increased employment at existing high-tech companies at the same time. This year, new start-ups will not provide more jobs per company than did start-ups last year.

Which of the following assertions can be drawn from the above information?
(A) Existing companies provide more employment than new start-ups.
(B) Existing companies will not add as many new jobs as they did last year.
(C) Unless there will be a large number of start-ups this year, Innovatia will not break last year's record for new jobs created.
(D) More new jobs were created in Innovatia last year than jobs lost.
(E) Established companies lost fewer jobs than did start-up companies.

This passage does not contain a conclusion. So it must be found as one of the answer choices. Since new start-ups provided the majority of new jobs and it is estimated that each start-up will provide fewer jobs this year, more start-ups will have to be formed if last-year's record will be broken, answer choice (C). No evidence supports the other answer choices.

WEAKENING AN ARGUMENT

EXAMPLE

During the past year, attendance at baseball games in the United States has declined by 15 percent. Over the same time period, attendance at basketball games in the United States has declined by 10 percent. The decrease in attendance at these games conclusively shows that the popularity of sports has declined.

Which of the following, if true, best weakens the argument?
(A) The price of an entrance ticket to a baseball game increased by 5 percent, while a ticket to a basketball game increased by 10 percent.
(B) Attendance at both sports increased slightly over the previous three years.
(C) Sales of seasonal tickets (for all games) at both sports have not declined.
(D) The salaries of athletes in both sports increased last year by 20 percent.
(E) Attendance at football, soccer, hockey, and tennis competitions have remained steady over the past three years.

TIP

Whenever there is an "if true" clause, assume that each answer choice is true.

This question requires a careful reading of the conclusion, "The popularity of sports has declined." The evidence presented in the passage takes into consideration the attendance at only two sporting events, baseball and basketball. However, the conclusion refers to sports in general. So if it can be shown that attendance at other sports has not declined, such as answer choice (E), the conclusion is weakened. Answer choices (A), (B), and (C) refer to the two sports mentioned, not sports in general. Answer choice (D) has no relevance to spectator attendance.

SUPPORTING AN ARGUMENT

EXAMPLE

Over the last several years, visits to medical clinics by people over the age of 65 with minor illnesses has declined. Some professionals in the medical field attribute this decline to the increased use of the Internet by this age group. They would rather get free medical advice for minor illnesses on the Internet than have to pay for a visit to a clinic.

Which of the following could support the conclusion to this passage?
(A) Most people over the age of 65 have had the value of their income reduced by inflation.
(B) People over the age of 65 consume more vitamins than any other age group.
(C) People over the age of 65 are frequent users of fitness clubs.
(D) Doctors do not like to treat patients for minor illnesses.
(E) People of all ages are concerned about their health.

The conclusion in this passage reasons that people over the age of 65 would rather obtain free medical advice for minor illnesses. This age group has increased their use of the Internet and therefore can obtain medical advice via this medium. A reason for this preference is that their incomes have been eroded by inflation (A). This population thus has less money to spend on going to a medical clinic. Answer choices (B) and (C), even though they may be true, cannot lead to the conclusion. Answer choice (D) might seem to be the right answer, but it does not mean that doctors will not treat patients. Answer choice (E) does not explain how people deal with minor illnesses.

Test-Taking Tactics

1. **FIRST, READ THE QUESTION AND THEN READ THE PASSAGE.** If you can identify the question type, you will know what to look for in the passage.

2. **LEARN TO SPOT CRITICAL REASONING QUESTION TYPES.** If you are able to recognize what a question is asking, you will know what reasoning tactic to apply. For example, if you recognize a question is asking about flaws in reasoning, you realize that you must identify the argument and conclusion in the passage. If the question is "Which of the following, if true, would weaken the above argument?" you must find the author's argument by identifying the premise(s) and conclusion. In the factual type of question, such as "Which of the following best summarizes the statement above?" or "If the information in the statement is true, which of the following must also be true?" you look for the main facts and what is claimed from the facts. The next step is to determine to what extent the conclusion is substantiated by the facts. When deciding whether or not the conclusion is substantiated, rely on only the facts presented in the passage and not on any outside information. Moreover, assume that the facts are true, without making any value judgment.

3. **LOOK FOR THE CONCLUSION FIRST.** Critical reasoning questions are preceded by an argument or statement that has a conclusion or claim. While it may seem logical

that a conclusion appears at the end of a passage, the conclusion might be given at the beginning or in the middle. Clues to help you find the conclusion are given in Chapter 8—"Critical Reasoning."

4. **FIND THE PREMISES.** Premises are facts or evidence. Determine whether or not the conclusion logically follows from the premises or whether it is merely alleged. A conclusion may not follow even though the premises may be true. You must determine the legitimacy of assumptions and conclusions. A number of methods for doing this are given in the Critical Reasoning section, pages 233–250. A typical question might ask you to attack or find a fact that weakens an argument. You must find the premise (one of the answer alternatives) that defeats the author's assumption.

EXAMPLE

The United States gives billions of dollars in foreign aid to Balonia. Leaders of Balonia resent foreign aid. The United States should discontinue direct foreign aid to developing countries.

Which of the following statements, if true, would weaken the above argument?
(A) Balonia doesn't need foreign aid.
(B) Balonia isn't a developing country.
(C) Balonia is ruled by a dictator.
(D) Balonia's balance of payments is in surplus.
(E) Balonia's economy is growing.

In the above argument, only one example (that of Balonia) was used as a premise for reaching the conclusion that foreign aid should be discontinued. If it could be shown that Balonia is not a developing country, choice (B), then the premise would be false and the conclusion would be invalid.

5. **DO NOT BE OPINIONATED.** The statement in a question may contain a specific point of view. Do not form an opinion about the statement or its claim. Concentrate on the structure of the argument and whether or not the structure and logic are valid. Accept each statement, argument, or trend as fact. Then proceed accordingly.

6. **DO NOT BE OVERWHELMED BY UNFAMILIAR SUBJECTS.** You are not expected to be familiar with subject matter in a particular field, such as economics or political history. Most scientific and technical words will be explained.

PROBLEM SOLVING

The Problem-Solving part of the Quantitative section is designed to test your ability to work with numbers. A variety of questions deal with the basic principles of arithmetic, algebra, and geometry. These questions may take the form of word problems or require straight calculations. In addition, questions involving the interpretation of tables and graphs may be included.

Based upon past tests, between 50 and 55 percent of the questions in a Quantitative section will be problem-solving questions.

Test-Taking Tactics

1. **ANSWER THE QUESTION THAT IS ASKED.** Read the question carefully. If your answer matches one of the choices given, your answer is not necessarily correct. Some of the choices given correspond to answers you would obtain by making simple errors, such as adding instead of subtracting or confusing area and perimeter.

EXAMPLE 1

If $x + y = 2$ and $x = 4$, then $x + 2y$ is

(A) –4

(B) –2

(C) 0

(D) 2

(E) 8

Since $x = 4$, then $x + y = 2$ means that y must be –2. Choice (B) is –2. However, choice (B) is not the answer to the question. The question asks for the value of $x + 2y$, not for the value of y. The correct answer is (C) since $x + 2y$ is $4 + 2(–2) = 0$. If you forgot the minus sign and used $y = 2$ in evaluating $x + 2y$, your answer would be 8, which is choice (E).

To give you practice in avoiding these types of mistakes, some of the choices given on the sample tests in this book will be answers you would obtain if you made simple errors. After you have worked through the tests, you will know how to avoid errors of this kind.

TIP

Budget your time well so you can get to every question.

EXAMPLE 2

How much will it cost to fence in a field that is 12 feet long and 42 feet wide with fence that costs $10 a yard?

(A) $180

(B) $360

(C) $504

(D) $540

(E) $1,080

If you multiply 12×42, you get 504. However, 504 is the area of the field in square feet. You actually need to determine the perimeter of the field. The perimeter of the field is $12 + 12 + 42 + 42 = 108$ feet. If you multiply 108 by $10, you get $1,080, which is choice (E). However, this answer is incorrect. The price is $10 per yard. You must change the perimeter from feet to yards before calculating the price, 108 feet $\div$ 3 = 36 yards since there are 3 feet in 1 yard. Then multiply 36 yards $\times$ $10 per yard = $360, which is answer choice (B).

2. **DON'T PERFORM UNNECESSARY CALCULATIONS.** If you can, answer the question by estimating or doing a rough calculation rather than by figuring it out exactly. The time you save can be used to check your answers.

EXAMPLE

Find the value of $2x + 2y$ if $x + 2y = 6$ and $x + y = 10$.
(A) –4
(B) 6
(C) 10
(D) 14
(E) 20

You could solve for x and y and then evaluate $2x + 2y$. It is much faster to use the fact that $2(x + y)$ is $2x + 2y$, so the correct answer is $2(10)$ or 20, which is choice (E).

3. **LOOK AT THE ANSWER CHOICES BEFORE YOU START TO WORK ON THE PROBLEM.** For some questions, checking the answers may be easier and quicker than solving the problem.

EXAMPLE

Which of the following numbers is the closest to the square root of 0.0017?
(A) 0.005
(B) 0.05
(C) 0.13
(D) 0.4
(E) 0.04

To answer this question, do not try to find the exact square root of 0.0017 and then see which of the choices is closest to your answer. Instead, simply square each answer choice and then determine which is closest to 0.0017. Choice (E) is the correct answer because $0.04 \times 0.04 = 0.0016$, which is closer to 0.0017 than the square of any of the other choices.

4. **USE INTELLIGENT GUESSING TO IMPROVE YOUR SCORE.** You have to answer each question in order to see the next question. If you have no idea of the correct answer, you must make a random guess. In most cases, though, you should be able to eliminate at least one answer choice. After eliminating all the incorrect choices that you can, you should guess one of the remaining choices.

In problem solving, you may be able to eliminate one or two choices by performing a quick estimate. Look at each choice offered. Some choices may obviously be incorrect. This tactic can be very useful for inference questions.

If *xy* is positive, then which of the following conclusions is valid? (*x* and *y* are integers.)

  I. *x* must be positive.

  II. *x* is not zero.

  III. *x* must be negative.

(A) Only I

(B) Only II

(C) I and II only

(D) II and III only

(E) I, II, and III

Since 0 times any number is 0 it is easy to see that II is valid. Even if you can't go any further on this problem, you know that the correct answer must be a choice that has II as part of the answer.

So you know that choice (A) is incorrect. Guess one of the remaining choices.

What is the product of 21.84 × 32.78?

(A) 615.9152

(B) 715.8152

(C) 715.902

(D) 715.9152

(E) 725.9152

Since the product asked for will be greater than 21 × 32, which is 672, you can eliminate choice (A).

Each factor has two decimal places, so the answer must have four decimal places. Since 8 × 4 = 32, the correct answer must have 2 in the fourth decimal place. Therefore, you can eliminate choice (C). If you can't do the calculation, then guess (B), (D), or (E). The correct answer is (D).

5. **USE YOUR LAMINATED NOTE BOARD TO COPY AND MARK UP THE DIAGRAMS.** Make copies of diagrams and make whatever marks will help you to answer questions. If you are given the dimension of part of a diagram, write it on the diagram. If you are told parts are equal, mark them as equal. Cross out answers you have eliminated as you work on a problem. If a diagram is not supplied, draw a picture wherever possible.

6. **HOLD THE EDGE OF THE NOTE BOARD UP TO THE SCREEN AS A RULER.**

7. **CHECK YOUR WORK IF YOU CAN.** If you can check your work quickly, do so. This will help you avoid silly mistakes. For example, if you are asked to solve an equation, check that your answer actually does satisfy the equation. In many questions, you can catch an obvious error by simply asking if your answer makes sense or by looking at an easy case of the problem.

What is the solution set to the inequality $2x > 5x - 18$?

(A) $x > 6$

(B) $x < 6$

(C) $x > -6$

(D) $x < -6$

(E) $x > \dfrac{18}{7}$

The correct answer is (B). However, making an algebra mistake could give one of the other choices. For instance if you thought the answer was (C), try $x = -5$ and see if it works and then try $x = -7$ and see if it doesn't work. Since $x = -7$ satisfies $2x > 5x - 18$, answer (C) must not be correct. If you thought (A) was the answer, then check that $x = 7$ works and $x = 5$ doesn't work. Remember, choosing an incorrect answer at the beginning of the test can have a larger effect on your score than choosing an incorrect answer did on the old paper-and-pencil GMAT.

8. **IF A PROBLEM INVOLVES UNITS, KEEP TRACK OF THE UNITS.** *Make sure your answer has the correct units.* If a problem asks for the area of a figure, then your answer should be in square inches or some square measurement. Volumes should be in cubic measurements. Speed is measured in miles per hour or feet per second.

Avoid making careless mistakes by *quickly* checking your work.

EXAMPLE

How much fence will be needed to enclose a rectangular field that is 20 feet long and 100 feet wide?

(A) 120 feet

(B) 140 feet

(C) 200 feet

(D) 240 feet

(E) 2,000 feet

The correct answer is 240 feet, which is the perimeter of the field. If you made a mistake and multiplied length × width (i.e., you found the area of the field), then your answer would be 20 feet × 100 feet = 2,000 square feet, which is not the same as choice (E). If you looked at only the number 2,000 and not the units, you might have made the wrong choice.

9. **USE NUMERICAL VALUES TO FIND OR CHECK ANSWERS THAT INVOLVE FORMULAS.** Some questions will have answers that use given quantities whose numerical value is not given. For example, a question may ask for the cost of making y objects and the answer choices will all involve y. In such problems, assigning a value to y that is easy to use when making calculations can simplify the problem and enable you to check your answer.

EXAMPLE 1

The first 100 copies of a poster cost x cents each. After the first 100 copies have been made, extra copies cost $\frac{1}{4}x$ cents each. How many cents will 300 copies of the poster cost?

(A) 100x

(B) 150x

(C) 200x

(D) 300x

(E) 400x

The correct answer is $100x$ plus $200 \times \frac{1}{4}x$ or $150x$, which is choice (B). Set x equal to some whole number. Since the problem includes the fraction $\frac{1}{4}$, choose a number divisible by 4. So let $x = 8$. The first 100 copies will cost 800 cents. Extra copies will cost $\frac{1}{4} \times 8 = 2$ cents each. So 200 extra copies will cost $200 \times 2 = 400$ cents. The total cost will be $800 + 400$, or 1,200. By letting $x = 8$, the answer choices are (A) 800, (B) 1,200, (C) 1,600, (D) 2,400, and (E) 3,200. So choice (B) is correct.

When assigning variables, avoid using the number 0 or 1 since 0 times any number is 0 and 1 times a number does not change the number. If the answer contains more than one unknown quantity, assign different numbers to each quantity.

This technique can sometimes help you eliminate answers to a problem so that you can make an intelligent guess.

In many cases, you can eliminate all the incorrect choices by this technique. Start with the easiest formula to compute and work toward the hardest. If the formulas are complicated, this approach may take too much time. So be sure to check the time left and the number of questions left in the section before you use this approach with complicated formulas.

EXAMPLE 2

Box seats for a ball game cost $\$b$ each, and general admission seats cost $\$g$ each. If 10,000 seats are sold and x of the seats are box seats, which expression gives the fraction of money made on seat sales that came from box seats?

(A) $\dfrac{bx}{xb + (10,000 - x)g}$

(B) $1 + (10,000 - x)g$

(C) $\dfrac{bx}{10,000}$

(D) $\dfrac{b}{(b + g)}$

(E) $\dfrac{x}{10,000}$

Since 10,000 – x general admission tickets are sold, the total income from seat sales is $bx + (10,000 – x)g$. Thus, the fraction made on box seats sales is $\dfrac{bx}{bx+(10,000-x)g}$, which is choice (A). If you couldn't solve this problem, assign values to each quantity. For instance, let $b = 20$, $g = 10$, and $x = 2,000$. (Note that $x = 5,000$ is not a good choice since the number of box seats and general admission seats will be identical.) Then 2,000 box seats were sold and 8,000 general admission seats were sold. The total from box seats is $2,000 \times 20 = 40,000$, and the total from general admission seats is $8,000 \times 10 = 80,000$. So the total from ticket sales is 120,000. Since 40,000 came from box seats, the fraction that came from box seats is $\dfrac{40,000}{120,000} = \dfrac{1}{3}$. The value of answer (C) is $\dfrac{40,000}{10,000} = 4$, so (C) is wrong; the value of (D) is $= \dfrac{20}{(20+10)} = \dfrac{2}{3}$, which is wrong; and the value of (E) is $\dfrac{2,000}{10,000} = \dfrac{2}{10}$, which is wrong. The value of (B) is $1 + (8,000)(10) = 80,001$, which is incorrect. So the only possible answer is (A). When you substitute the values into choice (A), the result is $\dfrac{40,000}{[40,000+(8,000)10]} = \dfrac{40,000}{120,000} = \dfrac{1}{3}$, which agrees with the correct answer. So the correct answer is (A).

10. **ALWAYS REMEMBER THAT X OR Y COULD BE NEGATIVE, ESPECIALLY IF YOU NEED TO KNOW WHETHER IT IS "LARGER THAN" OR "SMALLER THAN" SOME OTHER NUMBER.** For example, if $x = 3y$, this does not imply that x is greater than y. If $y = –1$, then x is –3, which is less than –1.

11. **ALWAYS REMEMBER THAT $X^2 = a$ HAS BOTH A POSITIVE AND A NEGATIVE ROOT.** For example, $x^2 = 4$ does not mean that $x = 2$. This equation has two solutions, $x = 2$ or $x = –2$.

12. **TRANSLATE THE INFORMATION YOU ARE GIVEN INTO NUMERICAL OR ALGEBRAIC EQUATIONS TO START WORKING A PROBLEM.** If the problem contains more than one variable, keep track of what each variable represents. Using variables that suggest what each variable represents is helpful. For example, if you have the equation Profit = Revenue – Cost, use the variables P = Profit, R = Revenue, and C = Cost. The equation becomes $P = R – C$, which is much more informative than $x = y – z$.

Long-Term Strategy for Problem Solving

1. **PRACTICE ARITHMETIC.** Most Problem-Solving sections contain one or two basic computational questions, such as multiplying two decimals or finding the largest number in a collection of fractions. If you are used to using a calculator to do all your arithmetic, these easy questions may be difficult for you unless you practice your math skills. You already know how to do basic computation; you just need to improve your speed and accuracy. See Chapter 8—"Math"—for computational details and practice.

2. **TRY TO THINK QUANTITATIVELY.** If you want to be a good reader, you should read a lot. In the same way, if you want to improve your quantitative skills, you should exercise them frequently. When you go grocery shopping, try to figure out whether the giant size is cheaper per ounce than the economy size. When you look at the news, try to make

comparisons when figures are given. If you·get used to thinking quantitatively, the Problem-Solving sections will be much easier for you and you will feel more confident about the entire exam.

SAMPLE PROBLEM-SOLVING QUESTIONS

DIRECTIONS: Solve the following sample questions, allowing yourself 12 minutes to complete all of them. As you work, try to use the tactics just described. Any figure that appears with a problem is drawn as accurately as possible. All numbers used are real numbers.

TIME: 12 minutes

1. A train travels from Albany to Syracuse, a distance of 120 miles, at the average rate of 50 miles per hour. The train then travels back to Albany from Syracuse. The total traveling time of the train is 5 hours and 24 minutes. What is the average rate of speed of the train on the return trip to Albany?

   (A) 60 mph
   (B) 50 mph
   (C) 48 mph
   (D) 40 mph
   (E) 35 mph

2. A parking lot charges a flat rate of x dollars for any amount of time up to two hours, and $\frac{1}{6}x$ for each hour or fraction of an hour after the first two hours. How much does it cost to park for 5 hours and 15 minutes?

   (A) $3x$
   (B) $2x$

   (C) $1\frac{2}{3}x$

   (D) $1\frac{1}{2}x$

   (E) $1\frac{1}{6}x$

3. How many two-digit numbers are divisible by both 5 and 6?

   (A) none
   (B) one
   (C) two
   (D) three
   (E) more than three

4. What is 1 percent of .023?

   (A) .00023
   (B) .0023
   (C) .23
   (D) 2.3
   (E) 23

5. A window has the shape of a semicircle placed
   on top of a square. If the length of a side of
   the square is 20 inches, how many square
   inches is the area of the window?

   20

   (A) 400
   (B) 200π
   (C) $50(8 + \pi)$
   (D) $200(2 + \pi)$
   (E) $400(1 + \pi)$

6. Which of the following sets of values for
   w, x, y, and z, respectively, are possible if
   ABCD is a parallelogram?

   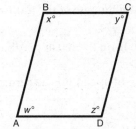

   I.   50, 130, 50, 130
   II. 60, 110, 70, 120
   III. 60, 150, 50, 150

   (A) I only
   (B) II only
   (C) I and II only
   (D) I and III only
   (E) I, II, and III

7. John weighs twice as much as Marcia. Marcia's weight is 60% of Bob's weight.
   Dave weighs 50% of Lee's weight. Lee weighs 190% of John's weight. Which of
   these 5 persons weighs the least?

   (A) Bob
   (B) Dave
   (C) John
   (D) Lee
   (E) Marcia

8. There were *P* people in a room when a meeting started. *Q* people left the room during the first hour, while *R* people entered the room during the same time. What expression gives the number of people in the room after the first hour as a percentage of the number of people in the room who have been there since the meeting started?

(A) $\dfrac{(P-Q)}{(P-Q+R)}$

(B) $100 \times \dfrac{(P-Q+R)}{(P-Q)}$

(C) $\dfrac{(P+R)}{(P-Q)}$

(D) $100 \times \dfrac{(P-Q)}{(P-Q+R)}$

(E) $100 \times \dfrac{(P+R)}{(P-Q)}$

Answers

1. **(D)**   2. **(C)**   3. **(D)**   4. **(A)**   5. **(C)**   6. **(A)**   7. **(E)**   8. **(B)**

Analysis

1. **(D)** The train took $\dfrac{120}{50} = 2\,\dfrac{2}{5}$ hours to travel from Albany to Syracuse. Since the total traveling time of the train was $5\,\dfrac{2}{5}$ hours, it must have taken the train 3 hours for the trip from Syracuse to Albany. Since the distance traveled is 120 miles, the average rate of speed on the return trip to Albany was $\left(\dfrac{1}{3}\right)(120)$ mph = 40 mph.

2. **(C)** It costs x for the first 2 hours. If you park 5 hours and 15 minutes there are 3 hours and 15 minutes left after the first 2 hours. Since this time is charged at the rate of $\dfrac{x}{6}$ for each hour or fraction thereof, it costs $4\left(\dfrac{x}{6}\right)$ for the last 3 hours and 15 minutes. Thus the total $x + \dfrac{4}{6}x = 1\,\dfrac{2}{3}x.$

3. **(D)** Since 5 and 6 have no common factors any number divisible by both 5 and 6 must be divisible by the product of 5 times 6 or 30. The only two digit numbers divisible by 30 are 30, 60, and 90. So, the correct answer is (D).

4. **(A)** Remember that the decimal equivalent of 1 percent is .01. To find 1 percent of .023 you simply multiply .023 by .01. The answer must have five decimal places since .023 has three decimal places and .01 has two decimal places. Therefore, the correct

answer is .00023 or choice (A). This is an example of the type of simple calculation that many versions of the GMAT will have in one question in the Quantitative section.

5. (C) Copy the diagram onto the note board and mark up the diagram by dividing the given figure into a square and a semicircle as shown below. Label all the lengths that you are given.

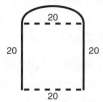

The area of the window is the area of the square plus the area of the semicircle. The area of the square is 20^2 or 400 square inches. The area of the semicircle is $\frac{1}{2}$ of πr^2 where r is the radius of the semicircle. Since the side of the square is a diameter of the semicircle, the radius is $\frac{1}{2}$ of 20, or 10 inches. The area of the semicircle is $\frac{1}{2} \times \pi \times 100 = 50\pi$ square inches. Therefore, the area of the window is $400 + 50\pi = 50(8 + \pi)$. Note that you must be able to change your answer into the correct form to answer this question.

6. (A) The sum of the angles of a parallelogram (which is 4-sided) must be $(4 - 2)180° = 360°$. Since the sum of the values in III is 410°, III cannot be correct. The sum of the numbers in II is 360°, but in a parallelogram opposite angles must be equal so x must equal z and y must equal w. Since 60° is unequal to 70°, II cannot be correct. The sum of the values in I is 360° and opposite angles will be equal, so I is correct.

7. (E) John weighs twice as much as Marcia, so John cannot weigh the least. Marcia's weight is less than Bob's weight, so Bob's weight is not the least. Dave's weight is $\frac{1}{2}$ of Lee's weight, so Lee can't weigh the least. The only possible answers are Marcia or Dave. So only (B) and (E) are possible; if you can't get any further, you should choose one of the two as your answer, since you have eliminated three choices. Let J, M, B, D, and L stand for the weights of John, Marcia, Bob, Dave, and Lee respectively. Then $D = .5L = .5(1.9)J$. So $D = .95J$. Since $J = 2M$, we know $M = .5J$. Therefore Marcia weighs the least. It may help to write the 5 names (or initials) on your note board and cross out each incorrect choice as you work through the problem.

8. (B) Although this problem looks difficult, it is fairly simple if you approach it in a step-by-step manner. First, express the number of people in the room after the first hour. There were P to begin with and Q left while R entered, so after the first hour there were $P - Q + R$ in the room. Second, express the number of people who have been in the room since the meeting started. R people entered while the meeting was in progress, so $P - Q$ people were in the room the entire hour. Therefore $\frac{(P-Q+R)}{(P-Q)}$ is the desired expression. But the question asks for a percentage. To change a number

(fraction) into a percentage, simply multiply the number by 100. The correct answer is (B). If you can't work this out, you can let $P = 100$, $Q = 40$ and $R = 20$. For these values, 80 people are in the room after the first hour and there are 60 people left in the room at the end of the hour who were there at the start. So $80/60 = 1.33$ and $1/3\%$ is the correct answer. Now eliminate the answers that give an incorrect result. (A) gives $60/80$, (C) gives $120/60 = 2$, (D) gives $100 \times (60/80) = 75$, and (E) gives $100 \times (120/60) = 200$, so (B) must be the correct answer.

DATA SUFFICIENCY QUESTIONS

Data Sufficiency questions, which also appear in the Quantitative section, are designed to test your reasoning ability. Like the Problem-Solving questions, they require you have a basic knowledge of the principles of arithmetic, algebra, and geometry. Each Data Sufficiency question consists of a mathematical problem and two statements containing information relating to it. You must decide whether the problem can be solved by using information from: (A) the first statement alone, but not the second statement alone; (B) the second statement alone, but not the first statement alone; (C) both statements together, but neither alone; or (D) either of the statements alone. Choose (E) if the problem cannot be solved, even by using both statements together. Usually 18 of the 37 questions on the Quantitative section of the GMAT are Data Sufficiency problems. Approaching these problems properly will help you achieve a high score. As in the Problem-Solving section, time is of the utmost importance. Approaching Data Sufficiency problems properly will help you use this time wisely.

Test-Taking Tactics

1. **MAKE SURE YOU UNDERSTAND THE DIRECTIONS.** Reread the paragraph above. Make sure you know what is being asked. If you have never seen this type of question before, make sure you do the practice problems that follow. At first, these questions may seem difficult. Once you have worked through several examples, you will start to feel comfortable with them.

2. **DON'T WASTE TIME FIGURING OUT THE EXACT ANSWER.** Always keep in mind that you are never asked to supply an answer for the problem. You are only asked to determine if sufficient data are available to find the answer. Once you know whether or not it is possible to find the answer from the given information, you are done. If you waste time figuring out the exact answer, you may not be able to finish the entire section.

EXAMPLE

The profits of a company are the revenues the company receives minus the costs that the company pays. How much were the profits of the XYZ Company in 2009?
(1) The XYZ Company had revenues of $112,234,567 in 2009.
(2) The costs of the XYZ Company were $102,479,345 in 2009.

The information given states that to find the profit, you need to know both the revenues and the costs. So it is easy to see that both (1) and (2) are needed and that the profit could be determined using (1) and (2). So the answer is (C). Do not compute the profit. If you perform the subtraction needed to compute the profit, you are just wasting time that could be spent on other problems.

3. **DRAW A PICTURE WHENEVER POSSIBLE.**   Make a copy of any diagrams on your note board, and mark them up. If a diagram is not supplied, draw one. Pictures can be especially helpful in any question that involves geometry.

4. **DON'T MAKE EXTRA ASSUMPTIONS.**   You are allowed to use only the information given and facts that are always true (such as the number of hours in a day) to answer these questions. Do not make assumptions about things such as prices rising every year. If you are given a diagram, don't assume two lines that appear to be perpendicular are perpendicular unless you are given specific information that says the lines are perpendicular. If an angle looks like a 45° angle, don't assume it is 45° unless you are given that fact.

5. **USE A SYSTEM TO WORK THROUGH THE QUESTIONS.**   Try to adopt a consistent approach to these types of problems. The system explained in detail that follows will help you answer the questions and also let you make intelligent guesses.

REMEMBER

You're not expected to solve Data Sufficiency problems. So don't waste time trying to do so.

System for Data Sufficiency Questions

A systematic analysis can improve your score on Data Sufficiency sections. By answering three questions, you will always arrive at the correct choice. In addition, if you can answer any one of the three questions, you can eliminate at least one of the possible choices so that you can make an intelligent guess.

The three questions you need to ask are:

I.   Is the first statement alone sufficient to solve the problem?
II.   Is the second statement alone sufficient to solve the problem?
III.   Are both statements together sufficient to solve the problem?

A good way to see this is to use a decision tree.

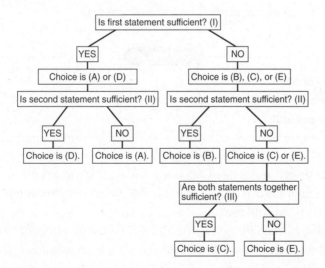

First, answer question I. It asks whether the information in statement (1) is sufficient to solve the problem without any additional information. The answer is either YES or NO.

- If the answer to question I is YES, the possible choices are limited to (A) and (D). Only responses (A) and (D) require that statement (1) provide enough information on its own to solve the problem.

Next answer question II. It asks whether the information in statement (2) is sufficient to solve the problem without any additional information. The answer is either YES or NO.

- If the answer to question II is YES, then statement (2) alone is sufficient to solve the problem. Since the responses to both questions I and II are YES, the answer is (D). Either statement (1) or statement (2) alone is sufficient to determine the solution. If the answer to question II is NO, the answer is (A). Only statement (1), but not statement (2), can be used to solve the problem.
- What if the answer to question I is NO? What if statement (1) alone is *not* sufficient to solve the problem? Then choices (A) and (D) are no longer possibilities. The responses are limited to (B), (C), and (E). Choice (B) means that statement (2) alone provides enough information to solve the problem. Choice (C) requires that information in statements (1) and (2) be combined to find the solution. Choice (E) says that even when combined, statements (1) and (2) do not provide enough information to answer the problem.

Next answer question II. If the answer is YES, statement (2) provides enough information on its own to solve the problem. Since question I is NO and question II is YES, the answer is choice (B).

- If the answer to question II is NO, answer question III. It asks whether combining statements (1) and (2) would provide enough information to solve the problem. If the answer is YES, then choice (C) is correct. The information in statements (1) and (2) can be combined to find the solution. If the answer to question III is NO, then choice (E) is correct. The answer cannot be determined by combining statements (1) and (2).

Practicing this system will improve your ability to solve Data Sufficiency problems!

6. **IN MANY CASES, YOU CAN USE SIMPLE VALUES TO CHECK QUICKLY WHETHER A STATEMENT FOLLOWS FROM A GIVEN STATEMENT.** This can be especially useful in deciding that a statement does *not* follow from a given statement.

EXAMPLE

Is k a multiple of 6?
(1) k is a multiple of 3.
(2) k is a multiple of 12.

Write out some simple multiples of 3 ($3 \times 1 = 3$, $3 \times 2 = 6$, and so on). Since 3 is not a multiple of 6 but 6 is a multiple of 6, "k is a multiple of 6" does not follow from "k is a multiple of 3." So statement (1) is not sufficient.

The only possible choices are (B), (C), or (E). Write some multiples of 12 (for example, 12, 24, 36, 48, . . .). All these are multiples of 6 since 12 is 2×6. So statement (2) is sufficient. The correct answer is (B).

7. REMEMBER THAT IF SUFFICIENT INFORMATION IS GIVEN TO SHOW THAT THE ANSWER TO THE QUESTION IS NO, THAT MEANS SUFFICIENT INFORMATION IS PROVIDED TO ANSWER THE QUESTION.

EXAMPLE

Is n an even integer?
(1) $n = 3k$ for some integer k.
(2) $n = 2j + 1$ for some integer j.

The first statement is not sufficient since $3 \times 2 = 6$, which is even, but $3 \times 3 = 9$, which is odd. The second statement is sufficient since it means that n is odd. This means that the answer to the main question is "no," and therefore (B) is the correct choice.

LONG-TERM STRATEGY FOR DATA SUFFICIENCY QUESTIONS

Practice Working Data Sufficiency Questions. Most people have not had much experience with these types of questions. The more examples you work out, the better you will perform on this section of the test. By the time you have finished the sample exams, you should feel confident about your ability to answer Data Sufficiency questions.

SAMPLE QUESTIONS

Read the following directions carefully and then try the sample Data Sufficiency questions below. Allow yourself 8 minutes total time. All numbers used are real numbers. A figure given for a problem is intended to provide information consistent with that in the question but not necessarily consistent with the additional information contained in the statements.

DIRECTIONS: Each of the following problems has a question and two statements that are labeled (1) and (2). Use the data given in (1) and (2) together with other available information (such as the number of hours in a day, the definition of *clockwise*, mathematical facts, etc.) to decide whether the statements are *sufficient* to answer the question. Then choose

(A) if you can get the answer from **(1) ALONE** but not from **(2)** alone
(B) if you can get the answer from **(2) ALONE** but not from **(1)** alone
(C) if you can get the answer from **BOTH (1) and (2) TOGETHER**, but not from (1) alone or (2) alone
(D) if **EITHER** statement **(1) ALONE OR** statement **(2) ALONE** suffices
(E) if you **CANNOT** get the answer from statements **(1) and (2) TOGETHER**, but need even more data

All numbers used are real numbers. A figure given for a problem is intended to provide information consistent with that in the question but is not necessarily consistent with the additional information contained in the statements.

TIME: 8 minutes

1. A rectangular field is 40 yards long. Find the area of the field.

   (1) A fence around the entire boundary of the field is 140 yards long.
   (2) The field is more than 20 yards wide.

2. Is X a number greater than zero?

   (1) $X^2 - 1 = 0$
   (2) $X^3 + 1 = 0$

3. An industrial plant produces bottles. In 2001 the number of bottles produced by the plant was twice the number produced in 2000. How many bottles were produced altogether in the years 2000, 2001, and 2002?

   (1) In 2002, the number of bottles produced was 3 times the number produced in 2000.
   (2) In 2003, the number of bottles produced was one-half the total produced in the years 2000, 2001, and 2002.

4. A man 6 feet tall is standing near a pole. On the top of the pole is a light. What is the length of the shadow cast by the man?

   (1) The pole is 18 feet high.
   (2) The man is 12 feet from the pole.

5. Find the length of RS if z is 90° and $PS = 6$.

   (1) $PR = 6$
   (2) $x = 45°$

6. Working at a constant rate and by himself, it takes worker U three hours to fill up a ditch with sand. How long would it take for worker V to fill up the same ditch working by herself?

   (1) Working together but at the same time U and V can fill in the ditch in 1 hour $52\frac{1}{2}$ minutes.
   (2) In any length of time worker V fills in only 60% as much as worker U does in the same time.

7. Did John go to the beach yesterday?

   (1) If John goes to the beach, he will be sunburned the next day.
   (2) John is sunburned today.

Answers

1. **(A)**	3. **(E)**	5. **(D)**	7. **(E)**
2. **(B)**	4. **(C)**	6. **(D)**	

Analysis

1. **(A)** The area of a rectangle is the length multiplied by the width. Since you know the length is 40 yards, you must find out the width in order to solve the problem. Since statement (2) simply says the width is greater than 20 yards, you cannot find out the exact width using (2). So (2) alone is not sufficient. Statement (1) says the length of a fence around the entire boundary of the field is 140 yards. The length of this fence is the perimeter of the rectangle, the sum of twice the length and twice the width. If we replace the length by 40 in $P = 2L + 2W$, we have $140 = 2(40) + 2W$, which can be solved for W. On the test don't waste time calculating W or the area. At this point you know that (1) alone is sufficient. So the correct choice is (A).

2. **(B)** Statement (1) means $X^2 = 1$. However, this equation has two possible solutions, $X = 1$ and $X = -1$. Thus using (1) alone, you cannot deduce whether X is positive or negative. Statement (2) means $X^3 = -1$. However, this equation has only one possible (real) solution, $X = -1$. Thus X is not greater than zero, which answers the question. Statement (2) alone is sufficient, which means the correct choice is (B).

3. **(E)** T, the total produced in the three years, is the sum of $P_0 + P_1 + P_2$, where P_0 is the number produced in 2000, P_1 the number produced in 2001, and P_2 the number produced in 2002. You are given that $P_1 = 2P_0$. Thus $T = P_0 + P_1 + P_2 = P_0 + 2P_0 + P_2 = 3P_0 + P_2$. So we must find out P_0 and P_2 to answer the question. Statement (1) says $P_2 = 3P_0$; thus, by using (1) if we can find the value of P_0 we can find T. But statement (1) gives no further information about P_0. Statement (2) says $\frac{1}{2}T$ equals the number produced in 2003, but it does not say what this number is. Since the relationship between production in 2003 and production in the individual years 2000, 2001, or 2002 is not given, you cannot use (2) to determine P_0. Thus, (1) and (2) together are not sufficient. The correct answer is (E).

4. **(C)** Sometimes it may help to draw a picture. By using proportions or similar triangles the height of the pole, h, is to 6 feet as the length of shadow, s, plus the distance to the pole, x, is to s.

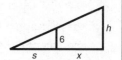

So $\frac{h}{6} = \frac{s+x}{s}$. Thus, $hs = 6s + 6x$ by cross-multiplication.

Solving for s gives $hs - 6s = 6x$, so $s(h - 6) = 6x$, so $s = \frac{6x}{h-6}$.

Statement (1) says $h = 18$; thus $s = \frac{6x}{12}$. So using (1) alone, we cannot deduce the value

of x. Thus (1) alone is not sufficient. Statement (2) says x equals 12. By using (1) and (2)

together, we deduce $s = 6$. However, by using (2) alone, all we can deduce is that $s = \frac{72}{h-6}$,

which cannot be solved for s unless we know h. Thus using (1) and (2) together gives the answer but using either statement (1) alone or (2) alone is not sufficient. The correct choice is (C).

5. **(D)** Since z is a right angle, $(RS)^2 = (PS)^2 + (PR)^2$, so $(RS)^2 = (6)^2 + (PR)^2$, and RS will be the positive square root of $36 + (PR)^2$. Thus, if you can find the length of PR, you can solve the problem. Statement (1) says $PR = 6$, thus $(RS)^2 = 36 + 36$, so $RS = 6\sqrt{2}$.

Thus, (1) alone is sufficient. Statement (2) says $x = 45°$. Since the sum of the angles in a triangle is $180°$ and z is $90°$ then $y = 45°$. So, x and y are equal angles. That means the sides opposite x and opposite y must be equal or $PS = PR$. Thus, $PR = 6$ and $RS = 6\sqrt{2}$. So (2) alone is also sufficient. The correct answer choice is (D).

6. **(D)** Statement (1) says U and V can work together to fill in the ditch in $1\frac{7}{8}$ hours. Since U can fill in the ditch in 3 hours, in 1 hour Worker U can fill in one-third of the ditch. Hence, in $1\frac{7}{8}$ hours, U would fill in $\left(\frac{1}{3}\right)\left(\frac{15}{8}\right) = \frac{5}{8}$ of the ditch. So V fills in $\frac{3}{8}$ of the ditch in $1\frac{7}{8}$ hours. Thus, V would take $\left(\frac{8}{3}\right)\left(\frac{15}{8}\right) = 5$ hours to fill in the ditch working by herself. Therefore, statement (1) alone is sufficient. According to statement (2), since U fills the ditch in 3 hours, V will fill $\frac{3}{5}$ of the ditch in 3 hours. Thus, V will take 5 hours to fill in the ditch working alone. The correct answer is choice (D).

7. **(E)** Obviously, neither statement alone is sufficient. John *could* have gotten sunburned at the beach, but he might have gotten sunburned somewhere else. Therefore, statements (1) and (2) together are not sufficient. This problem tests your grasp of an elementary rule of logic rather than your mathematical knowledge.

SUMMARY

The purpose of this chapter was to introduce you to the various types of Qualitative and Quantitative questions that appear on the GMAT. For each type of question, test-taking strategies and tactics were suggested. The diagnostic test is followed by individual chapters that focus on each type of question. The chapters look more closely at these kinds of questions and contain more details, explanations, strategies, and examples. You should review each of these chapters before you attempt to take the three full sample tests.

Test

PREVIEW

Diagnostic Test with Answers and Analysis

3

→ **TEST**

→ **ANSWERS**

→ **ANALYSIS**

→ **EVALUATING YOUR SCORE**

Now that you have become familiar with the various types of questions appearing on the GMAT and have had a chance to sample each type, you probably have an idea of what to expect from an actual exam. The next step, then, is to take a sample test to see how you do.

The Diagnostic Test that follows has been designed to help you with the types of questions that will appear on the new GMAT. When taking it, try to simulate actual test conditions as closely as possible. For example:

- Time yourself as you work on each section so that you don't go over the allotted time limit for that section.
- Answer each question in order.
- Do not allow yourself to change any previous answers once you have started on the next question.
- Do not use outside aids (except for scratch paper).

After you have completed the test, check your answers and use the self-scoring chart to evaluate the results. Use these results to determine which review sections you should spend the most time studying before you attempt the 3 sample GMATs at the end of the book. To assist you in your review, all answers to quantitative section questions are keyed so that you can easily refer to the section in Chapter 9—"Math"—that discusses the material tested by a particular question.

In the CAT, the quantitative test will contain two types of questions: Problem Solving and Data Sufficiency. The verbal test will be made up of three types of questions: Reading Comprehension, Critical Reasoning, and Sentence Correction. There will also be an Analytical Writing section and an Integrated Reasoning section. After you have finished using this book, you will be so familiar with the structure of each type of question that you will be able to identify it according to the passage or the structure of the question, and to solve it using the techniques that you learned by taking the tests in this book.

DIFFICULTY RATINGS

Each question in the Quantitative and Verbal sections of the Diagnostic test and the 3 sample tests in the book has been assigned an approximate level of difficulty. See the key on page 103.

ANSWER SHEET
Diagnostic Test

INTEGRATED REASONING SECTION

1. i. Ⓐ Ⓑ Ⓒ Ⓓ
   ii. Ⓐ Ⓑ Ⓒ Ⓓ

2.

Alpha Company	Beta Company	Rate of Increase
○	○	100
○	○	300
○	○	550
○	○	700
○	○	800
○	○	950

3.

Yes	No
○	○
○	○
○	○

4.

Yes	No
○	○
○	○
○	○

5. Ⓐ Ⓑ Ⓒ Ⓓ Ⓔ

6.

Total Distance Traveled to/from Work	Average Rate to/from Work	Mathematical Expression
○	○	$\dfrac{RT}{(T+10)}$
○	○	$\dfrac{2RT}{(T+20)}$
○	○	$2RT^2$
○	○	$(R-5)(T+20)$
○	○	$2RT$

7. i. Ⓐ Ⓑ Ⓒ Ⓓ
   ii. Ⓐ Ⓑ Ⓒ Ⓓ

8. Ⓐ Ⓑ Ⓒ Ⓓ

9.

True	False
○	○
○	○
○	○

10. i. Ⓐ Ⓑ Ⓒ Ⓓ
    ii. Ⓐ Ⓑ Ⓒ Ⓓ

11.

Would Help Explain	Would Not Help Explain
○	○
○	○
○	○

12. Ⓐ Ⓑ Ⓒ Ⓓ Ⓔ

ANSWER SHEET
Diagnostic Test

QUANTITATIVE SECTION

1. Ⓐ Ⓑ Ⓒ Ⓓ Ⓔ	11. Ⓐ Ⓑ Ⓒ Ⓓ Ⓔ	21. Ⓐ Ⓑ Ⓒ Ⓓ Ⓔ	31. Ⓐ Ⓑ Ⓒ Ⓓ Ⓔ
2. Ⓐ Ⓑ Ⓒ Ⓓ Ⓔ	12. Ⓐ Ⓑ Ⓒ Ⓓ Ⓔ	22. Ⓐ Ⓑ Ⓒ Ⓓ Ⓔ	32. Ⓐ Ⓑ Ⓒ Ⓓ Ⓔ
3. Ⓐ Ⓑ Ⓒ Ⓓ Ⓔ	13. Ⓐ Ⓑ Ⓒ Ⓓ Ⓔ	23. Ⓐ Ⓑ Ⓒ Ⓓ Ⓔ	33. Ⓐ Ⓑ Ⓒ Ⓓ Ⓔ
4. Ⓐ Ⓑ Ⓒ Ⓓ Ⓔ	14. Ⓐ Ⓑ Ⓒ Ⓓ Ⓔ	24. Ⓐ Ⓑ Ⓒ Ⓓ Ⓔ	34. Ⓐ Ⓑ Ⓒ Ⓓ Ⓔ
5. Ⓐ Ⓑ Ⓒ Ⓓ Ⓔ	15. Ⓐ Ⓑ Ⓒ Ⓓ Ⓔ	25. Ⓐ Ⓑ Ⓒ Ⓓ Ⓔ	35. Ⓐ Ⓑ Ⓒ Ⓓ Ⓔ
6. Ⓐ Ⓑ Ⓒ Ⓓ Ⓔ	16. Ⓐ Ⓑ Ⓒ Ⓓ Ⓔ	26. Ⓐ Ⓑ Ⓒ Ⓓ Ⓔ	36. Ⓐ Ⓑ Ⓒ Ⓓ Ⓔ
7. Ⓐ Ⓑ Ⓒ Ⓓ Ⓔ	17. Ⓐ Ⓑ Ⓒ Ⓓ Ⓔ	27. Ⓐ Ⓑ Ⓒ Ⓓ Ⓔ	37. Ⓐ Ⓑ Ⓒ Ⓓ Ⓔ
8. Ⓐ Ⓑ Ⓒ Ⓓ Ⓔ	18. Ⓐ Ⓑ Ⓒ Ⓓ Ⓔ	28. Ⓐ Ⓑ Ⓒ Ⓓ Ⓔ	
9. Ⓐ Ⓑ Ⓒ Ⓓ Ⓔ	19. Ⓐ Ⓑ Ⓒ Ⓓ Ⓔ	29. Ⓐ Ⓑ Ⓒ Ⓓ Ⓔ	
10. Ⓐ Ⓑ Ⓒ Ⓓ Ⓔ	20. Ⓐ Ⓑ Ⓒ Ⓓ Ⓔ	30. Ⓐ Ⓑ Ⓒ Ⓓ Ⓔ	

VERBAL SECTION

1. Ⓐ Ⓑ Ⓒ Ⓓ Ⓔ	12. Ⓐ Ⓑ Ⓒ Ⓓ Ⓔ	23. Ⓐ Ⓑ Ⓒ Ⓓ Ⓔ	34. Ⓐ Ⓑ Ⓒ Ⓓ Ⓔ
2. Ⓐ Ⓑ Ⓒ Ⓓ Ⓔ	13. Ⓐ Ⓑ Ⓒ Ⓓ Ⓔ	24. Ⓐ Ⓑ Ⓒ Ⓓ Ⓔ	35. Ⓐ Ⓑ Ⓒ Ⓓ Ⓔ
3. Ⓐ Ⓑ Ⓒ Ⓓ Ⓔ	14. Ⓐ Ⓑ Ⓒ Ⓓ Ⓔ	25. Ⓐ Ⓑ Ⓒ Ⓓ Ⓔ	36. Ⓐ Ⓑ Ⓒ Ⓓ Ⓔ
4. Ⓐ Ⓑ Ⓒ Ⓓ Ⓔ	15. Ⓐ Ⓑ Ⓒ Ⓓ Ⓔ	26. Ⓐ Ⓑ Ⓒ Ⓓ Ⓔ	37. Ⓐ Ⓑ Ⓒ Ⓓ Ⓔ
5. Ⓐ Ⓑ Ⓒ Ⓓ Ⓔ	16. Ⓐ Ⓑ Ⓒ Ⓓ Ⓔ	27. Ⓐ Ⓑ Ⓒ Ⓓ Ⓔ	38. Ⓐ Ⓑ Ⓒ Ⓓ Ⓔ
6. Ⓐ Ⓑ Ⓒ Ⓓ Ⓔ	17. Ⓐ Ⓑ Ⓒ Ⓓ Ⓔ	28. Ⓐ Ⓑ Ⓒ Ⓓ Ⓔ	39. Ⓐ Ⓑ Ⓒ Ⓓ Ⓔ
7. Ⓐ Ⓑ Ⓒ Ⓓ Ⓔ	18. Ⓐ Ⓑ Ⓒ Ⓓ Ⓔ	29. Ⓐ Ⓑ Ⓒ Ⓓ Ⓔ	40. Ⓐ Ⓑ Ⓒ Ⓓ Ⓔ
8. Ⓐ Ⓑ Ⓒ Ⓓ Ⓔ	19. Ⓐ Ⓑ Ⓒ Ⓓ Ⓔ	30. Ⓐ Ⓑ Ⓒ Ⓓ Ⓔ	41. Ⓐ Ⓑ Ⓒ Ⓓ Ⓔ
9. Ⓐ Ⓑ Ⓒ Ⓓ Ⓔ	20. Ⓐ Ⓑ Ⓒ Ⓓ Ⓔ	31. Ⓐ Ⓑ Ⓒ Ⓓ Ⓔ	
10. Ⓐ Ⓑ Ⓒ Ⓓ Ⓔ	21. Ⓐ Ⓑ Ⓒ Ⓓ Ⓔ	32. Ⓐ Ⓑ Ⓒ Ⓓ Ⓔ	
11. Ⓐ Ⓑ Ⓒ Ⓓ Ⓔ	22. Ⓐ Ⓑ Ⓒ Ⓓ Ⓔ	33. Ⓐ Ⓑ Ⓒ Ⓓ Ⓔ	

WRITING ASSESSMENT

Time: 30 minutes

> DIRECTIONS: Write a clear, logical, and well-organized response to the following argument. Your response should be in the form of a short essay, following the conventions of standard written English. On the CAT, your answer should be the equivalent of an essay that would fill three pages of lined $8^{1}/_{2}'' \times 11''$ paper. If you are taking a paper test, write legibly. Essays that are illegible or that are written on a topic other than the one outlined in the question will not be scored.

The Japanese always have to consult a companion or call a conference to solve even the most trivial things. In India, there are definite rules for family members (and this is also true for other social groups), so that when one wants to do something, one knows whether it is all right by following those rules. Because of the rule system, things get done more quickly in India.

Discuss how logically persuasive you find the argument. In presenting your point of view, analyze the sort of reasoning used and its supporting evidence. In addition, state what further evidence, if any, would make the argument more sound and convincing or would make you better able to evaluate its conclusion.

STOP

ON THE ACTUAL GMAT,
AFTER YOU HAVE CONFIRMED YOUR ANSWER,
YOU CANNOT RETURN TO IT.

INTEGRATED REASONING SECTION

Time: 30 minutes

12 questions

This section consists of four types of questions: Graphics Interpretation, Table Analysis, Two-part Analysis, and Multi-Source Reasoning.

> **DIRECTIONS:** The new Integrated Reasoning section consists of four question types. Some require the use of both quantitative and verbal skills. Others involve the use of graphics, tables, or text material. The questions also use various response formats.
>
> For each question, review the text, graphic, or text material provided and respond to the task that is presented. *Note: An onscreen calculator is available in this section on the actual test.*

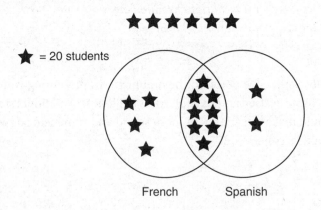

★ = 20 students

French   Spanish

1. Refer to the Venn diagram above. Each ★ represents 20 students at Westbury College. Complete each statement according to the information presented in the diagram.

   i. If one student is selected at random from the entire student body, what is the probability that the student will be taking French, Spanish, or both?

   (A) 3 out of 8
   (B) 2 out of 5
   (C) 1 out of 2
   (D) 7 out of 10

   ii. If a student is taking at least one of the two language courses offered at Westbury College, what is the probability that the student will also be taking the second language course?

   (A) 5 out of 6
   (B) 4 out of 7
   (C) 7 out of 8
   (D) 9 out of 10

2. Alpha Company has a total of 12,000 employees. The number of employees is growing at a constant rate. Beta Company has a total of 15,000 employees. The number of employees is growing at a constant rate. Business analysts have projected that if each organization continues to grow at the same rate, they will both have the same number of employees 6 years from now. After 8 years, Alpha Company will have more employees than Beta Company.

In the table below, identify the rates of increase, in number of employees per year, for each company based on the projections above. Choose only one option in each column.

Alpha Company	Beta Company	Rate of Increase (employees per year)
○	○	100
○	○	300
○	○	550
○	○	700
○	○	800
○	○	950

3. The table below displays population and GDP data from 2010.

Country	GDP (in trillion $)	Rank in GDP	Population (in millions)	Rank in Population
United States	$ 14.59	1	310.2	3
Japan	$ 5.46	2	126.8	10
China	$ 5.93	3	1,330.1	1
Germany	$ 3.28	4	82.3	15
France	$ 2.56	5	64.1	21
United Kingdom	$ 2.25	6	61.3	22
Brazil	$ 2.09	7	201.1	5
Italy	$ 2.05	8	58.1	23
India	$ 1.73	9	1,173.1	2
Canada	$ 1.58	10	33.8	36
Russia	$ 1.48	11	139.4	9
Spain	$ 1.41	12	40.6	32
World	$63.12		6,830.6	

For each of the following statements, select *Yes* if the statement can be shown to be true based on the information in the table. Otherwise, select *No*. (Note: This table is not sortable.)

Yes No

○ ○ Of the countries that produced at least 4% of the world's GDP in 2010, no country made up less than 1% of the world's population.

○ ○ Only 3 countries made up both 3% of the world's population and 3% of the world's GDP in 2010.

○ ○ Both the 2010 median population and median GDP of the countries in the chart are less than their respective averages.

E-mail 1: E-mail from **marketing manager** to supply coordinator.

July 10, 9:42 A.M
Yesterday I spoke with the manager of Store #2351, and he says his sale of orange juice boxes is exceeding expectations. He wants to run the sale another two weeks to drive in-store traffic and wants to make sure that we have enough inventories to deliver for the display. How is our inventory tracking? Do we need to make special arrangements with our warehouse in order to ship enough supplies?

E-mail 2: E-mail from **supply coordinator** in response to marketing manager's July 10, 9:42 A.M. message.

July 10, 10:24 A.M
We originally sent them 12 lots of product last week, and they have gone through 8 this week. If he wants to extend the sale another 2 weeks, we need to consider that there should be some decrease in the amount sold when we plan our order. I would estimate somewhere around a 50% drop-off in sales for weeks 2 and 3. The warehouse maintains an inventory of 600 lots minimum weekly, sends out product in lots of 6 at a time, and requires special requests be made only if we want lots other than multiples of 6. Do you want to make a special request from the warehouse?

E-mail 3: E-mail from **marketing manager** in response to the supply coordinator's message.

July 10, 10:53 A.M
I want to make a special request only if it means we would not have to destroy product. I like to keep my special requests to a minimum. The store manager swears that the drop-off in sales for weeks 2 and 3 should be only 25%. However, I'm leaning toward your call, even though it would be nice to sell more product to the store. Heck, it's better to have product sold out than to have lots left over. Plus the shelf life should help.

4. Consider each of the following statements. Does the information in the three sources support the inference as stated?

Yes No

◯ ◯ The marketing manager and supply coordinator are in conflict over this situation.

◯ ◯ The supply coordinator will likely make two special requests from the warehouse and order 4 lots in week 2 and 4 lots in week 3.

◯ ◯ The supply coordinator and the marketing manager will both support making a special request with the warehouse.

---

5. Given that a lot contains 500 units and each sells for $4 with a 25% margin, how much profit will the company expect to make from the special request lot sent for week 3?

(A) $1,000
(B) $2,000
(C) $3,000
(D) $4,000
(E) $8,000

---

6. Alice likes to run to work in the morning. However, she prefers to walk home after the long workday. She runs at a rate of R mph in T minutes. On the way home however, her speed is 5 mph slower and her time is 20 minutes longer.

In terms of variables R and T, select the expression that represents the total distance Alice travels to work and back. Also select the expression that represents Alice's average rate to and from work.

Total Distance Traveled to/from Work	Average Rate to/from Work	Mathematical Expression
◯	◯	$\dfrac{RT}{(T+10)}$
◯	◯	$\dfrac{2RT}{(T+20)}$
◯	◯	$2RT^2$
◯	◯	$(R-5)(T+20)$
◯	◯	$2RT$

7. The following graph shows economic data from 1999.

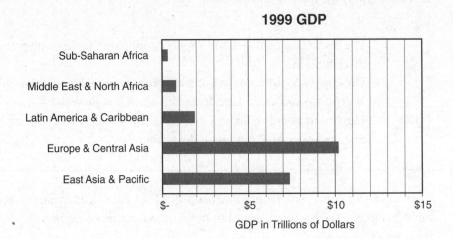

1999 GDP

Complete each statement according to the information presented in the diagram.

i. The ratio of the Europe and Central Asia 1999 GDP to the East Asia and Pacific 1999 GDP is closest to which of the following?

(A) 2 to 1
(B) 3 to 2
(C) 4 to 3
(D) 8 to 7

ii. Middle East and North Africa's 1999 GDP is approximately what percent of Latin America and Caribbean 1999 GDP?

(A) 27%
(B) 37%
(C) 47%
(D) 57%

Questions 8 and 9 refer to the following information and tables.

UltraCopy, one of the top 5 photocopier stores in the region, offers several deep discounts for large purchases at its store. In order to receive the discount, the store requires volume purchases as per the chart below.

UltraCopy Discounts on Volume Sales

	Black and White Copies	Color Copies	Bound Projects
1,000–5,000 units	20%	10%	10%
5,001–10,000 units	30%	20%	15%
10,001+ units	40%	25%	15%

The second chart outlines the price for copies and bound projects.

UltraCopy Pricing for Copies and Binding

	Black and White Copies	Color Copies	Bound Projects
Single sided	$0.10 per page	$0.30 per page	
Double sided	$0.15 per page	$0.50 per page	
Plastic binding			$0.30 per booklet
Coil binding			$1.00 per booklet

Jennifer is planning a very large scale 3-day conference in May. She is exploring options for designing and printing her 20-page programs for all the attendees. She estimates that there will be anywhere from 7,000–10,000 attendees. However, many participants lose their programs and require another one on the second day. Jennifer also wants to ensure the highest quality of program without going over budget.

8. Which of the following options would result in the lowest cost?

   (A) 7,000 color copies, double sided with coil binding
   (B) 15,000 black and white, single sided, plastic binding
   (C) 5,000 color copies, single sided, coil binding
   (D) 10,001 color copies, double sided, plastic binding

9. Answer the following True or False statements.

   True False
   ○ ○ If Jennifer's budget is $45,000, she can opt for the highest quality program and 15,000 units.
   ○ ○ It is cheaper to have 15,000 black-and-white, single-sided units than the same number of color, and double-sided units, regardless of binding.
   ○ ○ Given Jennifer's needs, the printing option that generally has the least effect on overall cost is the binding.

10. The scatter plot below charts the daily sales of Julie's Ice Cream Store during the month of May, 2011.

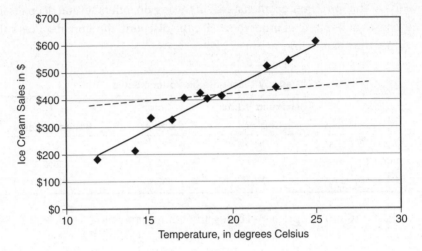

Complete each statement according to the information given by the graph.

i. What is the relationship between the outdoor temperature and Julie's Ice Cream Store sales?

(A) nonlinear
(B) positive
(C) negative
(D) quartic

ii. How does the slope of the regression line compare with the slope of the dashed line?

(A) The slope of the regression line is less than the slope of the dashed line.
(B) The slope of the regression line is equal to the slope of the dashed line.
(C) The slope of the regression line is greater than the slope of the dashed line.
(D) The slope of the regression line is undefined and cannot be compared with the slope of the dashed line.

The table below displays the Best Picture Oscar winners from 1996–2010.

Movie	Box Office Gross (in million $)*	Box Office Rank	Metacritic Score	Metacritic RANK
The English Patient	$64	12	87	5
Titanic	$496	1	74	12
Shakespeare in Love	$73	10	87	5
American Beauty	$108	8	86	7
Gladiator	$187	3	64	15
A Beautiful Mind	$155	4	72	13
Chicago	$134	5	82	11
The Lord of The Rings: The Return of The King	$364	2	94	1
Million Dollar Baby	$65	11	86	7
Crash	$53	14	69	14
The Departed	$132	6	86	7
No Country for Old Men	$64	12	91	3
Slumdog Millionaire	$98	9	86	7
The Hurt Locker	$15	15	94	1
The King's Speech	$114	7	88	4

*The box office gross is up to the time of the Oscar telecast.

11. For each of the following statements, select *Would help explain* if it would, if true, help explain some of the information in the table. Otherwise select *Would not help explain.*

Would Help Explain	Would Not Help Explain	
◯	◯	Most Best Picture winners are usually raved by critics (85+ rating) more often than are box office hits ($100+ million gross).
◯	◯	*Lord of the Rings* was considered a sure bet for winning Best Picture with odds of 1:10, the lowest odds in Oscar history because it was both a critic's darling and the highest-grossing picture in its year.
◯	◯	After a movie had won Best Picture, it would get an Oscar bump and make considerable box office gains afterward.

12. Based on the table above, which one movie was neither a critic's darling nor a big box office contender yet still won the Best Picture Oscar?

(A) *American Beauty*
(B) *Chicago*
(C) *Crash*
(D) *Shakespeare in Love*
(E) *Slumdog Millionaire*

STOP

ON THE ACTUAL GMAT,
AFTER YOU HAVE CONFIRMED YOUR ANSWER,
YOU CANNOT RETURN TO IT.

QUANTITATIVE SECTION

Time: 75 minutes

37 questions

This section consists of two types of questions: Problem Solving and Data Sufficiency.

Problem Solving

DIRECTIONS: Solve each of the following problems; then indicate the correct answer.

NOTE: A figure that appears with a problem is drawn as accurately as possible so as to provide information that may help in answering the question.

Numbers in this test are real numbers.

Data Sufficiency

DIRECTIONS: Each of the following problems has a question and two statements that are labeled (1) and (2). Use the data given in (1) and (2) together with other available information (such as the number of hours in a day, the definition of *clockwise*, mathematical facts, etc.) to decide whether the statements are *sufficient* to answer the question. Then fill in space

(A) If you can get the answer from **(1) ALONE** but not from (2) alone

(B) If you can get the answer from **(2) ALONE** but not from (1) alone

(C) If you can get the answer from **BOTH (1)** and **(2) TOGETHER** but not from (1) alone or (2) alone

(D) If **EITHER** statement **(1) ALONE OR** statement **(2) ALONE** suffices

(E) If you **CANNOT** get the answer from statements (1) and (2) **TOGETHER** but need even more data

All numbers used in this section are real numbers.

A figure given for a problem is intended to provide information consistent with that in the question, but not necessarily with the additional information contained in the statements.

All figures lie in the plane unless you are told otherwise.

Figures are drawn as accurately as possible; straight lines may not appear straight on the screen.

1. If the length of a rectangle is increased by 20 percent and the width is decreased by 20 percent, then the area

   (A) decreases by 20%
   (B) decreases by 4%
   (C) stays the same
   (D) increases by 10%
   (E) increases by 20%

2. It costs x dollars each to make the first 1,000 copies of a compact disc and y dollars to make each subsequent copy. If z is greater than 1,000, how many dollars will it cost to make z copies of the compact disc?

   (A) $1{,}000x + yz$
   (B) $zx - zy$
   (C) $1{,}000\,(z - x) + xy$
   (D) $1{,}000\,(z - y) + xz$
   (E) $1{,}000\,(x - y) + yz$

3. How many two-digit integers satisfy the following property? The last digit (units digit) of the square of the two-digit number is 8.

   (A) none
   (B) 1
   (C) 2
   (D) 3
   (E) more than 3

4. Ms. Taylor purchased stock for $1,500 and sold $\frac{2}{3}$ of it after its value doubled.

   She sold the remaining stock at 5 times its purchase price. What was her total profit on the stock?

   (A) $1,500
   (B) $2,000
   (C) $2,500
   (D) $3,000
   (E) $4,500

5. City B is 8 miles east of city A. City C is 6 miles north of city B. City D is 16 miles east of city C, and city E is 12 miles north of city D. What is the distance from city A to city E?

(A)   10 miles
(B)   20 miles
(C)   24 miles
(D)   30 miles
(E)   42 miles

6. If x is a number satisfying $2 < x < 3$ and y is a number satisfying $7 < y < 8$, which of the following expressions will have the largest value?

(A) x^2y

(B) xy^2

(C) $5xy$

(D) $\dfrac{4x^2y}{3}$

(E) $\dfrac{x^2}{y}$

7. The median salary of the employees in the sales department in 1999 was $\$x$. The average raise for the next year was $\$800$ per employee. What was the median salary of the employees in the sales department in 2000?

(1) $x = 48{,}000$

(2)   The range of the salaries in the sales department in 2000 was $\$12{,}000$.

8. If 50 apprentices can finish a job in 4 hours and 30 skilled workers can finish the same job in $4\frac{1}{2}$ hours, how much of the job should be completed by 10 apprentices and 15 skilled workers in 1 hour?

(A) $\dfrac{1}{9}$

(B) $\dfrac{29}{180}$

(C) $\dfrac{26}{143}$

(D) $\dfrac{1}{5}$

(E) $\dfrac{39}{121}$

9. If the shaded area is $\frac{1}{2}$ the area of triangle ABC and angle ABC is a right angle, then the length of line segment AD is

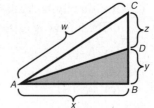

(A) $\left(\frac{1}{2}\right)w$

(B) $\left(\frac{1}{2}\right)(w + x)$

(C) $\sqrt{2x^2 + z^2}$

(D) $\sqrt{w^2 - 3y^2}$

(E) $\sqrt{y^2 + z^2}$

10. There are 4 quarts in a gallon. A gallon of motor oil sells for $12 and a quart of the same oil sells for $5. The owner of a rental agency has 6 machines and each machine needs 5 quarts of oil. What is the minimum amount of money she must spend to purchase enough oil?

(A) $84
(B) $94
(C) $96
(D) $102
(E) $150

11. A store has a parking lot which contains 70 parking spaces. Each row in the parking lot contains the same number of parking spaces. The store has bought additional property in order to build an addition to the store. When the addition is built, 2 parking spaces will be lost from each row; however, 4 more rows will be added to the parking lot. After the addition is built, the parking lot will still have 70 parking spaces, and each row will contain the same number of parking spaces as every other row. How many rows were in the parking lot before the addition was built?

(A) 5
(B) 6
(C) 7
(D) 10
(E) 14

12. A piece of wood 5 feet long is cut into three smaller pieces. How long is the longest of the three pieces?

(1) One piece is 2 feet 7 inches long.

(2) One piece is 7 inches longer than another piece and the remaining piece is 5 inches long.

13. *AC* is a diameter of the circle and *B* is a point on the circle. *ACD* is a straight line. What is the value of *x*?

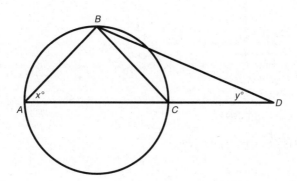

(1) $AB = BC$

(2) $x = 2y$

14. What is the value of *y*?

(1) $x + 2y = 6$

(2) $y^2 - 2y + 1 = 0$

15. Two pipes, *A* and *B*, empty into a reservoir. Pipe *A* can fill the reservoir in 30 minutes by itself. How long will it take for pipe *A* and pipe *B* together to fill up the reservoir?

(1) By itself, pipe *B* can fill the reservoir in 20 minutes.

(2) Pipe *B* has a larger cross-sectional area than pipe *A*.

16. *AB* is perpendicular to *CD*. Is *A* or *B* closer to *C*?

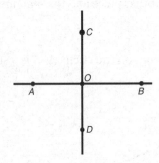

(1) *OA* is less than *OB*.

(2) *ACBD* is not a parallelogram.

17. Is *xy* greater than 1? *x* and *y* are both positive.

(1) *x* is less than 1.

(2) *y* is greater than 1.

18. Does $x = y$?

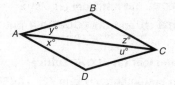

(1) $z = u$

(2) $ABCD$ is a parallelogram.

19. Train T leaves town A for town B and travels at a constant rate of speed. At the same time, train S leaves town B for town A and also travels at a constant rate of speed. Town C is between A and B. Which train is traveling faster? Towns A, C, and B lie on a straight line.

(1) Train S arrives at town C before train T.

(2) C is closer to A than to B.

20. Does $x = y$?

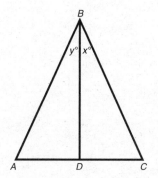

(1) BD is perpendicular to AC.

(2) AB is equal to BC.

21. What is the value of $x + y$?

(1) $x - y = 4$

(2) $3x + 3y = 4$

22. Did the XYZ Corporation have higher sales in 1988 or in 1989? Assume sales are positive.

    (1) In 1988, the sales were twice the average (arithmetic mean) of the sales in 1988, 1989, and 1990.

    (2) In 1990, the sales were 3 times those in 1989.

23. Is *ABDC* a square?

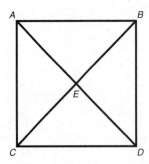

    (1) *BC* is perpendicular to *AD*.

    (2) *BE = EC*.

24. *k* is an integer. Is *k* divisible by 12?

    (1) *k* is divisible by 4.

    (2) *k* is divisible by 3.

25. If *n* is a positive integer less than 100, what is the value of *n*?

    (1) *n* is an even integer.

    (2) n^3 is less than 200.

26. What was the price of a dozen eggs during the 15th week of the year 2004?

    (1) During the first week of 2004 the price of a dozen eggs was 75¢.

    (2) The price of a dozen eggs rose 1¢ a week every week during the first four months of 2004.

27. Is *DE* parallel to *BC*? *DB = AD*.

    (1) *AE = EC*

    (2) *DB = EC*

28. If the area of a rectangle is equal to the area of a square, then the perimeter of the rectangle must be

    (A) one half of the perimeter of the square
    (B) equal to the perimeter of the square
    (C) equal to twice the perimeter of the square
    (D) equal to the square root of the perimeter of the square
    (E) none of the above

29. Which of the following are possible values for the angles of a parallelogram?

      I. 90°, 90°, 90°, 90°
     II. 40°, 70°, 50°, 140°
    III. 50°, 130°, 50°, 130°

    (A) I only
    (B) II only
    (C) I and III only
    (D) II and III only
    (E) I, II, and III

30. For every novel in the school library there are 2 science books; for each science book there are 7 economics books. Express the ratio of economics books to science books to novels in the school library as a triple ratio.

    (A) 7 : 2 : 1
    (B) 7 : 1 : 2
    (C) 14 : 7 : 2
    (D) 14 : 2 : 1
    (E) 14 : 2 : 7

(A) If you can get the answer from **(1) ALONE** but not from **(2)** alone

(B) If you can get the answer from **(2) ALONE** but not from **(1)** alone

(C) If you can get the answer from **BOTH (1)** and **(2) TOGETHER** but not from (1) alone or (2) alone

(D) If **EITHER** statement **(1) ALONE OR** statement **(2) ALONE** suffices

(E) If you **CANNOT** get the answer from statements (1) and (2) **TOGETHER** but need even more data

31. There are 50 employees in the office of ABC Company. Of these, 22 have taken an accounting course, 15 have taken a course in finance, and 14 have taken a marketing course. Nine of the employees have taken exactly two of the courses, and one employee has taken all three of the courses. How many of the 50 employees have taken none of the courses?

    (A) 0
    (B) 9
    (C) 10
    (D) 11
    (E) 26

32. If $x + y = 4$ and $x - y = 3$, then $x + 2y$ is

    (A) $\dfrac{1}{2}$

    (B) 3.5
    (C) 4

    (D) $4\dfrac{1}{2}$

    (E) $7\dfrac{1}{2}$

33. How much interest will $2,000 earn at an annual rate of 8 percent in 1 year if the interest is compounded every 6 months?

    (A) $160.00
    (B) $163.20
    (C) $249.73
    (D) $332.80
    (E) $2,163.20

34. If *BC* is parallel to *AD* and *CE* is perpendicular to *AD*, then the area of *ABCD* is

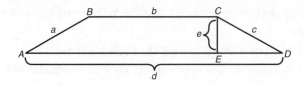

(A) *bd*

(B) *bd* + *ac*

(C) *ed*

(D) *e*(*b* + *d*)

(E) .5*eb* + .5*ed*

35. If the price of steak is currently $1.00 a pound, and the price triples every 6 months, how long will it be until the price of steak is $81.00 a pound?

(A) 1 year

(B) 2 years

(C) $2\frac{1}{2}$ years

(D) 13 years

(E) $13\frac{1}{2}$ years

36. If $\dfrac{x}{y} = \dfrac{2}{3}$, then $\dfrac{y^2}{x^2}$ is

(A) $\dfrac{4}{9}$

(B) $\dfrac{2}{3}$

(C) $\dfrac{3}{2}$

(D) $\dfrac{9}{4}$

(E) $\dfrac{5}{2}$

(A) If you can get the answer from **(1) ALONE** but not from (2) alone

(B) If you can get the answer from **(2) ALONE** but not from (1) alone

(C) If you can get the answer from **BOTH (1)** and **(2) TOGETHER** but not from (1) alone or (2) alone

(D) If **EITHER** statement **(1) ALONE OR** statement **(2) ALONE** suffices

(E) If you **CANNOT** get the answer from statements (1) and (2) **TOGETHER** but need even more data

37. What is the maximum number of points of intersection of two circles that have unequal radii?

(A) none
(B) 1
(C) 2
(D) 3
(E) infinite

STOP

ON THE ACTUAL GMAT,
AFTER YOU HAVE CONFIRMED YOUR ANSWER,
YOU CANNOT RETURN TO IT.

VERBAL SECTION

Time: 75 minutes
41 questions

Reading Comprehension

DIRECTIONS: This section contains three reading passages. You are to read each one carefully. When answering the questions, you will be allowed to refer back to the passages. The questions are based on what is stated or implied in each passage.

Critical Reasoning

DIRECTIONS: For each question in this section, choose the best answer among the listed alternatives.

Sentence Correction

DIRECTIONS: This part of the section consists of a number of sentences in each of which some part or the whole is underlined. Each sentence is followed by five alternative versions of the underlined portion. Select the alternative you consider both most correct and most effective according to the requirements of standard written English. Answer (A) is the same as the original version; if you think the original version is best, select answer (A).

In considering the answer choices, be attentive to matters of grammar, diction, and syntax, as well as clarity, precision, and fluency. Do not select an answer that alters the meaning of the original sentence.

1. Typically, the entrepreneur is seen as an individual who owns and operates a small business. But, simply to own and operate a small business—or even a big business—does not make someone an entrepreneur. If this person is a true entrepreneur, then new products are being created and new ways of providing services are being implemented.

   Which of the following conclusions can best be drawn from the above passage?
   (A) An owner of a large business may be an entrepreneur.
   (B) Someone who develops an enterprise may be considered an entrepreneur.
   (C) Entrepreneurs do not own and operate small businesses.
   (D) Entrepreneurs are the main actors in economic growth.
   (E) Entrepreneurs are investors.

2. The principal reason for our failure was quite apparent <u>to those whom we had brought</u> into the venture.
   (A) to those whom we had brought
   (B) to them whom we had brought
   (C) to the ones whom we had brought
   (D) to those who we had brought
   (E) to those who we had brung

Questions 3–8 are based on the following passage.

There are three basic styles of political leadership: traditional, modern technical bureaucratic, and charismatic. Traditional leaders base their claim to leadership on the assertion that they are the clear and logical successors to a line of leaders that
Line stretches back in time and that is legitimized by practice. They are leaders because
(5) of historical forces, and they claim the right and obligation to continue. They often imply that their leadership is necessary to main social order on the right course. Traditional political orders, while conservative, are not rigid or unyielding to change, but they may be slow to implement a schedule of changes or react to changing conditions. They expect change to occur over relatively extended periods of time.
(10) As defined by Max Weber, a charismatic leader possesses particular characteristics that set him apart from normal leaders. A charismatic leader is, in a word, unique. He possesses personal characteristics that are suited to a particularly intense leadership style; and he is capable of creating or participating in an intense, reciprocal psychological exchange with his followers. His actions and proposals are legitimized
(15) by reference to some awe-inspiring source, religious, historical, natural, or mystical. The charismatic leader will promulgate substantial and convincing images of a new order, perhaps ordained in heaven, that will raise the community to new levels of activity and accomplishment, or in another variant, restore the community to its rightful place in the world. Another characteristic of charismatic leaders is their reso-
(20) nant rhetorical gift—resonant in the sense that they can raise sympathetic responses from their followers.

Modern bureaucratic leadership is predicated on the premise of adequate short-term performance in government. Modern bureaucratic leaders promise to transform society through the application of management skills. These leaders believe

(25) that contemporary problems can be solved, that people can positively change their physical and social environment if only given the chance and the right organization, and that these changes can lead to several possible social, economic, and political outcomes.

(Adapted from: Roy R. Andersen, Robert F. Seibert, and Jon G. Wagner (1998), "Political Leadership in the Contemporary Middle East," *Politics and Change in the Middle East*, New Jersey: Prentice-Hall, pp. 202–203, 207–208, and 211.)

3. Which of the following is NOT mentioned in the passage as a distinguishing characteristic of a charismatic leader?
    (A) inspirational
    (B) popular
    (C) convincing
    (D) forceful
    (E) exceptional

4. The primary purpose of the passage is to
    (A) show how leadership styles affect domestic politics
    (B) illustrate which leadership style is the most effective
    (C) identify the advantages and disadvantages of several leadership styles
    (D) present some characteristics of several leadership styles
    (E) argue that leadership styles are influenced by a nation's culture

5. The passage suggests which of the following propositions?
    (A) Both bureaucratic and charismatic leaders promise to transform society through effective management skills.
    (B) Traditional leaders resist any modernization, while modern bureaucratic leaders support it.
    (C) Charismatic leaders ensure their power base owing to their oratorical skills.
    (D) Traditional leadership is based on long-term performance expectations, while modern bureaucratic leadership is short term.
    (E) Charismatic leaders offer themselves as a substitute for traditional and bureaucratic leadership.

6. It can be inferred that the author believes that
    (A) tradition is a legitimizing symbol of leadership
    (B) many charismatic leaders have mystical powers
    (C) only bureaucratic leaders possess management skills
    (D) traditional leadership is determined by historical right but bureaucratic leadership is elected
    (E) a traditional leader may also be charismatic

7. It can be inferred from the passage that
   (A) bureaucratic leaders' survival in power depends on the consequences of their policy choices, not their charismatic or traditional appeal
   (B) charismatic leaders will often focus strongly on making the group that they appeal to feel distinct and unique
   (C) bureaucratic leaders emphasize rules and regulations
   (D) traditional leaders are viewed as having control and power because those holding the position before them had control and power
   (E) people follow others that they personally admire

8. Which of the following statements best applies to a charismatic leader according to information in the passage?
   (A) Charm and grace are all that is needed to create followers.
   (B) Self-belief is a fundamental need of leaders.
   (C) Be very persuasive, and make very effective use of body language as well as verbal language.
   (D) Be willing to tell other people what to do, but have the respect of other people as well.
   (E) Change what others think and feel.

9. During the incumbent president's term of office he succeeded in limiting annual increases in the defense budget by an average of 5 percent. His predecessor experienced annual increases of 8 percent. Therefore, the incumbent president should be given credit for the downturn in defense outlays.

   Which of the following statements, if true, would most seriously weaken the above conclusion?
   (A) Some generals have claimed that the country's defenses have weakened in the past year.
   (B) More soldiers were drafted during the former president's term of office.
   (C) The incumbent president advocates peaceful resolution of international disputes.
   (D) The average annual inflation rate during the incumbent president's term was 4%, while during his predecessor's term it was 10%.
   (E) A disarmament treaty with a major adversary was signed by the incumbent president.

10. Nobody denies that economic development is essential for poorer nations. But in advanced economies there is mounting evidence that an increase in consumption adds little to human happiness and may even impede it. Unless we can radically lower the environmental impact of economic activity we will have to devise a path to prosperity that does not rely on continued growth.

Which of the following is an assumption on which the author's argument depends?
(A) Economic development is the only way to achieve happiness.
(B) More people in developed countries than in developing countries claim that they are satisfied with their quality of life.
(C) There is little correlation between consumption and happiness.
(D) Economic development is not essential for developed countries.
(E) Concerns about the environment in developed economies are a factor determining economic policy.

11. Although he was the most friendly of all present and different from the others, he hadn't hardly any friends except me.
(A) different from the others, he hadn't hardly any friends except me
(B) different than the others, he had hardly any friends except me
(C) different from the others, he had hardly any friends except me
(D) different than the others, he hadn't hardly any friends except I
(E) different from the others, he hardly had any friends except I

12. It was us who had left before he arrived.
(A) us who had left before he arrived
(B) we who had left before he arrived
(C) we who had went before he arrived
(D) us who had went before he arrived
(E) we who had left before the time he had arrived

13. Buy Plenty, a supermarket chain, had successfully implemented an in-store promotional campaign based on video messages flashed on a large screen. The purpose of the campaign was to motivate customers to purchase products they had not planned to buy before they entered the store. The sales manager of Build-It Inc., a chain of do-it-yourself hardware stores, saw the campaign and plans to introduce it at Build-It locations.

The sales manager's plan assumes that
(A) supermarket and hardware products are the same
(B) products cannot be sold successfully without a video sales campaign
(C) supermarket chains do not sell hardware products
(D) consumer decision-making to buy products does not differ substantially when it comes to both supermarket and hardware products
(E) in-store campaigns are more effective than out-of-store advertising and sales promotion

In the 1970s, Charles Kowal at Mount Palomar Observatory discovered Chiron, an asteroid whose orbit was in the vicinity of Saturn and Uranus, far from other known asteroids.

Line
(5)
In the 1990s, robotic telescopes began to comb the Kuiper Belt, the region of the solar system beyond the orbit of Neptune. More than 400 objects were discovered there, with the biggest object about half the size of Pluto.

Last year, the farthest asteroid to date was found: Sedna, named after an Inuit goddess who dwells in a cave at the bottom of the Arctic Ocean. Sedna has a very eccentric orbit that takes it nearly 1,000 times farther from the Sun than Pluto and
(10)
outside the Kuiper Belt.

In early January 2005, the same team that discovered Sedna found a larger body. From its light and absence of infrared radiation, the team of Brown, Trujillo, and Rabinovitz are certain that the object's size is between that of Pluto (1,485 miles across) and our moon (2,160 miles across).

(15)
Its temporary name is 2003 UB313. Presently, the object is 9 billion miles from the sun, about three times as far as Pluto. At this distance from the Sun, 2003 UB313 has a surface temperature of 415° below zero.

This Kuiper Belt object takes 560 Earth years to orbit the Sun. 2003 UB313's orbit has a tilt of 44 degrees to the plane of the solar system, more than twice the tilt of
(20)
Pluto (the previous planet record holder). Its minimum solar distance is 3.3 billion years, close to the edge of Neptune's orbit.

2003 UB313's orbit is well known due to its being captured on wide angle photographs taken in 2003 by the 4-foot-wide Schmidt telescope on Mount Palomar.

Will UB313 be called the tenth planet? The decision is up to the International
(25)
Astronomical Union.

Asteroids are mini-planets, most of which are located in the asteroid belt, between the orbits of Mars and Jupiter. The largest of the belt asteroids is Ceres, about 700 miles across (i.e., roughly the size of Texas). Most asteroids are much smaller, typically less than a mile across.

(30)
While most asteroids keep their distance from Earth, there are probably 1,000 asteroids that are located in the inner solar system and may cross Earth's orbit.

Last summer, a robotic telescope discovered a 1,000-foot-wide asteroid that crosses Earth's orbit. The object is 99942 Apophis. Once Apophis' orbit was determined, its future positions decades ahead were generated by computer.

(35)
There was a shock when an early study showed Apophis to be on a collision course with Earth in 2029. More early observations were utilized to refine Apophis' orbit; new calculations showed that on April 13, 2029, Apophis would instead pass 22,000 miles from Earth, which is a little less than three Earth diameters. Apophis will then be visible to the naked eye from Europe and western Africa.

14. The author provides information that would answer which of the following questions?
    (A) What are some of the causes of asteroids?
    (B) Who is Charles Kowal?
    (C) What are asteroids?
    (D) When will Neptune collide with Earth?
    (E) How far are asteroids from the sun?

15. It may be inferred from the passage that
    (A) the Kuiper Belt includes 1,000 asteroids
    (B) Apophis was calculated to be in the inner solar system
    (C) most asteroids are dangerously close to Earth
    (D) there is no inherent danger from falling asteroids
    (E) asteroid research is not very advanced scientifically

16. According to the passage,
    (A) new asteroids are named by those who discover them
    (B) Sedna is the farthest asteroid from Earth
    (C) the largest asteroid is Pluto
    (D) Apophis is about the size of Pluto
    (E) UB313 will be named after Brown, Trujillo, and Rabinovitz

17. Which of the following titles best describes the contents of the passage?
    (A) "The Impact of Asteroids on the Solar System"
    (B) "What Is the Tenth Planet?"
    (C) "How Asteroids Are Discovered"
    (D) "The Search for Asteroids"
    (E) "The Discoveries of Charles Kowal"

18. She is the sort of person who I feel would be capable of making these kind of statements.
    (A) sort of person who I feel would be capable of making these kind of
    (B) sort of a person who I feel would be capable of making these kind of
    (C) sort of person who I feel would be capable of making these kinds of
    (D) sort of person whom I feel would be capable of making these kinds of
    (E) sort of person whom I feel would be capable of making this kind of

19. The movement to ownership by unions is the latest step in the progression from management ownership to employee ownership. Employee ownership can save depressed and losing companies.

    All of the following statements, if true, provide support for the claim above EXCEPT
    (A) Employee-owned companies generally have higher productivity.
    (B) Employee participation in management raises morale.
    (C) Employee union ownership drives up salaries and wages.
    (D) Employee union ownership enables workers to share in the profits.
    (E) Employee union ownership makes it easier to lay off redundant workers.

20. The burning of coal, oil, and other combustible energy sources produces carbon dioxide, a natural constituent of the atmosphere. Elevated levels of carbon dioxide are thought to be responsible for half of the greenhouse effect. Enough carbon dioxide has been sent into the atmosphere already to cause a significant temperature increase. Growth in industrial production must be slowed, or production processes must be changed.

Which of the following, if true, would tend to weaken the strength of the above conclusion?
(A) Many areas of the world are cold anyway, so a small rise in temperature would be welcome.
(B) Carbon dioxide is bad for the health.
(C) Most carbon dioxide is emitted by automobiles.
(D) Industry is switching over to synthetic liquid fuel extracted from coal.
(E) A shift to other energy sources would be too costly.

Questions 21–25 are based on the following passage.

The institutions engaged in artistic or scientific activity are centrally concerned with the maintenance and extension of cultural systems. The growth of government patronage of these areas suggests that facilitation and production of culture has
Line become a major state activity in the United States. The objectives underlying this
(5) state intervention are not well understood. The central purpose of this paper is to evaluate the relative strengths of several alternative explanations for the government's involvement in the production of culture. A second purpose is to suggest the likely impact of government patronage on the physical sciences, social sciences, and arts in America.
(10) Four distinct models for explaining the state's growing interest in the production of culture can be identified. One model emphasizes the value of patronage for the maintenance of the cultural institutions in question. A second model stresses the utility of the investment for capital accumulation. A third model points toward the value of supporting science and art for the administration of government programs.
(15) The fourth model identifies the ideological potential of science and art as a primary reason for government patronage.
Science and art for their own sake. The first model of government patronage is predicated on the structural-functionalist assumption that the government is a relatively neutral instrument for the articulation and pursuit of collective goals in a
(20) society with relatively autonomous subsystems. Pure science and art are vital societal subsystems, and the government moves to protect and develop these areas to ensure the continued production of culture for the benefit of all members of society. Thus, the government intervenes directly as the final patron of public goods that would otherwise be unavailable.

(25)   Two important corollaries follow from this formulation, which makes it empirically testable. First, the timing of government intervention should primarily be related to economic crises faced by the arts and sciences themselves, not to crises in the political system, economy, or elsewhere. Second, government intervention should generally take the form of protecting the paradigm of the arts and sciences. Specifically,

(30)   federal funding should be allocated to the most creative artists and organizations, as defined by the relevant artistic community. Similarly, funding should be preferentially bestowed on scientists whose research is making the greatest contribution to the advance of the scientific discipline, regardless of its relevance for outside problems or crises.*

*Reprinted from Michael Useem, "Government Patronage of Science and Art in America," pp. 123–142 in Richard A. Peterson, ed., *The Production of Culture*, © Sage Publications, Inc.

21.   Which of the following best summarizes the four culture production models mentioned in the passage?
  (A)   They are based on economic criteria.
  (B)   They explain why government should support cultural activities.
  (C)   They argue against government intervention.
  (D)   They are not well understood.
  (E)   They argue for a separation of government and the arts.

22.   The major objective of the passage is to
  (A)   increase appreciation for the arts
  (B)   provide an ideological basis for artistic funding
  (C)   explain why government supports cultural activities
  (D)   evaluate government involvement in the production of culture
  (E)   demonstrate cultural activities in the United States

23.   The passage suggests that a corollary of government support of artistic and scientific activity is
  (A)   funding should be provided by government only as a last resort
  (B)   funding will be geared to projects of value to the government
  (C)   funding is to be provided only to nongovernmental employees
  (D)   funding by the government is self-defeating
  (E)   funding by the government is inflationary

24.   A conclusion reached by the author of the passage is that
  (A)   the arts and sciences have been funded by the government for different reasons.
  (B)   government is a neutral observer of the arts and sciences.
  (C)   government intervention in the arts and sciences is declining.
  (D)   the arts and sciences are not dependent on government funding.
  (E)   politics and science go together.

25. The idea that government should support the arts and sciences only when the market does not provide enough funds belongs to which school?
    (A) "their own sake"
    (B) "business application"
    (C) "government programs"
    (D) "ideological control"
    (E) all of the above

Questions 26–27 are based on the following passage.

Contrary to charges made by opponents of the new trade bill, the bill's provisions for taking action against foreign countries that place barriers against American exports is justified. Opponents should take note that restrictive trade legislation in the 1930s succeeded in improving the U.S. trade balance even though economists were against it.

26. The author's method of rebutting opponents of the new trade bill is to
    (A) attack the patriotism of its opponents
    (B) attack the opponents' characters rather than their claims
    (C) imply an analogy between the new trade bill and previous trade legislation
    (D) suggest that economists were against both pieces of legislation
    (E) imply that previous legislation also permitted retaliatory action against foreign countries

27. Opponents of the new legislation could defend themselves against the author's strategy by arguing that
    (A) the fact that past trade legislation improved the trade balance does not mean that the present bill will do the same
    (B) economists are not always right
    (C) the United States had a trade deficit both in the 1930s and at the time of the new bill
    (D) the new law is not as strong as the 1930s bill
    (E) America's new trading partners have also passed similar legislation

28. Beside me, there were many persons who were altogether aggravated by his manners.
    (A) Beside me, there were many persons who were altogether aggravated
    (B) Beside me, there were many persons who were all together aggravated
    (C) Besides me, there were many persons who were altogether aggravated
    (D) Besides me, there were many persons who were altogether irritated
    (E) Beside me, there were many persons who were all together irritated

29. The owner, who was a kind man, spoke to the boy and he was very rude.
    (A) , who was a kind man, spoke to the boy and he
    (B) was a kind man and he spoke to the boy and he
    (C) spoke to the boy kindly and the boy
    (D) , a kind man, spoke to the boy who
    (E) who was a kind man spoke to the boy and he

30. Because we cooperated together, we divided up the work on the report that had been assigned.
    (A) together, we divided up the work on the report that had been assigned
    (B) together, we divided the work on the report that had been assigned
    (C) , we divided up the work on the report that was assigned
    (D) , we divided the work on the assigned report
    (E) we divided up the work on the assigned report

31. During 1999, advertising expenditures on canned food products increased by 20 percent, while canned food consumption rose by 25 percent.

    Each of the following, if true, could help to explain the increase in food consumption EXCEPT
    (A) Advertising effectiveness increased
    (B) Canned food prices decreased relative to substitutes
    (C) Canned food products were available in more stores
    (D) Can opener production doubled
    (E) Per-capita consumption of frozen foods declined

32. Inflation rose by 5.1 percent over the second quarter, up from 4.1 percent during the first quarter of the year, and higher than the 3.3 percent recorded during the same time last year. However, the higher price index did not seem to alarm Wall Street, as stock prices remained steady.

    Which of the following, if true, could explain this reaction of Wall Street?
    (A) Stock prices were steady because of a fear that inflation would continue.
    (B) The president announced that he was concerned about rising inflation.
    (C) Economists warned that inflation would persist.
    (D) Much of the quarterly increase in the price level was due to a summer drought's effect on food prices.
    (E) Other unfavorable economic news had overshadowed the fact of inflation.

33. "Ever since I arrived at the college last week, I've been shocked by the poor behavior of students and the unfriendly attitude of the townspeople, but the professors are very erudite and genuinely helpful. Still, I wonder if I should have come here in the first place."

    Which of the following, if true, would weaken the student's conclusion that the college may not have been the best choice?
    (A) Professors are not always helpful to students.
    (B) The college has more than 50,000 students.
    (C) The college is far from the student's home.
    (D) Not all professors have doctorates.
    (E) The narrator was unsure of staying at the college.

34. The senator rose up to say that, in her opinion, she thought the bill should be referred back to committee.
    (A) rose up to say that, in her opinion, she thought the bill should be referred back
    (B) rose up to say that she thought the bill should be referred back
    (C) rose up to say that she thought the bill should be referred
    (D) rose up to say that, in her opinion, the bill should be referred
    (E) rose to say that she thought the bill should be referred

35. I don't know as I concur with your decision to try and run for office.
    (A) since I concur with your decision to try to
    (B) that I concur in your decision to try to
    (C) as I concur in your decision to try to
    (D) that I concur in your decision to try and
    (E) that I concur on your decision to try to

36. Jones, the president of the union and who is also a member of the community group, will be in charge of the negotiations.
    (A) who is also a member of the community group
    (B) since he is a member of the community group
    (C) a member of the community group
    (D) also being a member of the community group
    (E) in addition, who is a member of the community group

37. A local garbage disposal company increased its profitability even though it reduced its prices in order to attract new customers. This was made possible through the use of automated trucks, thereby reducing the number of workers needed per truck. The company also switched from a concentration on household hauling to a concentration on commercial hauling. As a result of its experience, company management planned to replace all its old trucks and increase the overall size of the truck fleet, doubling hauling capacity.

The company's plan, as outlined above, takes into consideration each of the following EXCEPT

(A) Commercial clients have more potential than household customers.
(B) The demand for garbage removal services is sensitive to price.
(C) Demand for garbage removal services would increase in the future.
(D) Doubling of capacity would not necessitate a substantial increase in the workforce.
(E) Doubling of capacity would not cause bottlenecks, leading to a decrease in productivity.

38. Every town with a pool hall has its share of unsavory characters. This is because the pool hall attracts gamblers and all gamblers are unsavory.

Which of the following, if true, cannot be inferred from the above?

(A) All gamblers are unsavory.
(B) All pool halls attract gamblers.
(C) Every town has unsavory characters.
(D) All gamblers are attracted by pool halls.
(E) An explanation of what attracts gamblers.

39. In an August 2000 poll, 36 percent of voters called themselves Republican or said they were independents leaning toward being Republicans. In November 2004, the Republican figure rose to 47 percent. But in a later survey, the Republicans were down to 38 percent. Therefore, the Democrats are likely to win the next election.

Which of the following, if true, would most seriously weaken the above conclusion?

(A) Republicans were a minority in 2004, but a Republican president was elected.
(B) People tend to switch their votes at the last minute.
(C) People vote for the best candidate, not for a political party.
(D) No one can predict how people will vote.
(E) It has been shown that 85% of Republicans vote in an election, compared to 50% of the Democrats.

40. Average family income is right where it was 20 years ago, even though in most families these days, both husbands and wives are working.

The above statement implies all of the following EXCEPT
(A) Even though nominal family income may have increased, prices have risen at an equal rate.
(B) More husbands and wives are working today than 20 years ago.
(C) It was more prevalent for only one spouse to work 20 years ago than it is today.
(D) Wives earn more than husbands today.
(E) Prices were lower 20 years ago.

41. The instructor told the student to hold the club lightly, keeping his eye on the ball, and drawing the club back quickly, but that too much force should not be used on the downward stroke.
(A) to hold the club lightly, keeping his eye on the ball, and drawing the club back quickly, but that too much force should not be used
(B) to hold the club lightly, keep his eye on the ball, and drawing the club back quickly, and that too much force should not be used
(C) to hold the club lightly, keep his eye on the ball, draw the club quickly back, and not use too much force
(D) to hold the club lightly, keep his eye on the ball, draw the club back quickly and that too much force should not be used
(E) he should hold the club lightly, keeping his eye on the ball, drawing the club back quickly, and not using too much force

STOP

ON THE ACTUAL GMAT,
AFTER YOU HAVE CONFIRMED YOUR ANSWER,
YOU CANNOT RETURN TO IT.

INTEGRATED REASONING

1. **i.** D

ii. B

2.

Alpha Company	Beta Company	Rate of Increase
◯	◯	100
◯	⬤	300
◯	◯	550
◯	◯	700
⬤	◯	800
◯	◯	950

3.

Yes	No
◯	⬤
◯	⬤
⬤	◯

4.

Yes	No
◯	⬤
◯	⬤
⬤	◯

5. A

6.

Total Distance Traveled to/from Work	Average Rate to/from Work	Mathematical Expression
◯	⬤	$\dfrac{RT}{(T+10)}$
◯	◯	$\dfrac{2RT}{(T+20)}$
◯	◯	$2RT^2$
◯	◯	$(R-5)(T+20)$
⬤	◯	$2RT$

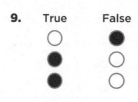

7. **i.** C

ii. C

8. B

9.

True	False
◯	⬤
⬤	◯
⬤	◯

10. **i.** B

ii. C

11.

Would Help Explain	Would Not Help Explain
⬤	◯
⬤	◯
◯	⬤

12. C

ANSWER KEY
Diagnostic Test

QUANTITATIVE SECTION

1. B	11. D	21. B	31. C
2. E	12. D	22. A	32. D
3. A	13. A	23. E	33. B
4. D	14. B	24. C	34. E
5. D	15. A	25. E	35. B
6. B	16. A	26. C	36. D
7. E	17. E	27. A	37. C
8. B	18. C	28. E	
9. D	19. C	29. C	
10. B	20. C	30. D	

VERBAL SECTION

1. B	12. B	23. B	34. E
2. A	13. D	24. A	35. B
3. B	14. C	25. A	36. C
4. D	15. B	26. C	37. E
5. D	16. B	27. A	38. C
6. A	17. D	28. D	39. E
7. D	18. C	29. D	40. D
8. E	19. C	30. D	41. C
9. D	20. C	31. D	
10. E	21. B	32. D	
11. C	22. D	33. B	

SELF-SCORING GUIDE
Analytical Writing

Evaluate your essay (or have a friend or teacher evaluate it for you) on the following basis. Read your essay completely, paying special attention to its logical organization and use of examples and facts to buttress its claims or position. Assign a holistic score between 0 and 6, using the scale below.

6 OUTSTANDING

Cogent, well-articulated analysis of the issue or critique of the argument. Develops a position with insightful reasons and persuasive examples. Well organized. Superior command of language and variety of syntax. Only minor flaws in grammar, usage, and mechanics.

5 STRONG

Well-developed analysis or critique. Develops a position with well-chosen examples or reasons. Generally well organized. Clear control of language and variety of syntax. Minor flaws in grammar, usage, and mechanics.

4 ADEQUATE

Competent analysis or critique. Develops a position with relevant reasons or examples. Adequately organized. Adequate control of language, but may lack syntactic variety. May have some flaws in grammar, usage, and mechanics.

3 LIMITED

Competent but clearly flawed analysis or critique. Vague or limited in developing a position. Poorly organized. Weak in using relevant examples or reasons. Language used imprecisely or lacking in sentence variety. Contains major errors or frequent minor errors in grammar, usage, and mechanics.

2 SERIOUSLY FLAWED

Serious weaknesses in analysis and organization. Unclear or seriously limited in presenting or developing a position. Disorganized. Few relevant examples or reasons. Frequent serious problems in language and sentence structure. Numerous errors in grammar, usage, or mechanics that interfere with meaning.

1 FUNDAMENTALLY DEFICIENT

Little evidence of ability to organize and develop a coherent response to issue or argument. Severe and persistent errors in language and sentence structure. Pervasive pattern of errors in grammar, usage, and mechanics that severely interfere with meaning.

0 UNSCORABLE

Illegible or not written on the assigned topic.

ANSWERS EXPLAINED

Integrated Reasoning Section

1. i. (D) The first thing you need to determine is how many students attend Westbury College. Counting the number of symbols reveals 20 stars, which means the student body is 400 students. The number of stars within the circles in the Venn diagram total 14. Therefore the ratio is 14:20 and the answer is **D**.

ii. (B) This probability is based on a smaller subgroup of students taking a language course. The number of stars in the center region (representing those students taking both courses) is 8. The ratio is 8:14, and therefore the answer is **B**.

2. (300 for Beta Company, 800 for Alpha Company) The correct answer is 800 employees per year for Alpha Company and 300 employees per year for Beta Company. The best way to solve this question is to pick two values from the chart and systematically get to the combination that works. However, doing this may be time consuming. An easier method is to use algebra to simplify your work.

According to the paragraph, 6 years from now, both companies will have the same number of employees. Therefore, you get the following equation, where A and B represent the number of new employees for Alpha and Beta, respectively:

$$12,000 + 6A = 15,000 + 6B$$

When you simplify the equation, you get:

$$A = 500 + B$$

This tells us that Alpha Company is gaining 500 extra employees per year. The only combination in the chart that works is 300 and 800.

3. (No, No, Yes)

i. If you calculate 4% of the world's GDP, you would get $63.12 \times 0.04 = 2.52$. This means that the top 5 countries each have a GDP above 4%. France has the lowest-ranking population of these 5 countries. So you should compare its population with the world population. Minimize your calculator use as much as possible. You can see that 64.1 is less than 1% of 6,830.6. Therefore, there is a country that produced at least 4 percent of the world's GDP in 2010 that makes up less than 1% of the world's population. Thus the answer is **No**.

ii. Calculate 3% of the world's GDP and 3% of the world's population:

$$\text{GDP: } 63.12 \times 0.03 = 1.89$$

$$\text{Population: } 6,830.6 \times 0.03 = 204.9$$

The only countries with populations higher than 204 million are the United States, China, and India. India clearly has the lowest GDP, which is under the 1.89 that you just calculated. Therefore only 2 countries meet the requirement. The answer to the question is **No**.

iii. If you sort the table based on either GDP rank or population rank, the median would be those countries ranked 6th and 7th. However, you should also notice that the populations of China and India create a weighted average that is far above the median. The same can be said of the GDP of the United States, which is far above that of the rest of the countries shown in the list. You do not need to use the calculator to determine the actual averages of either the GDP or the population since they are both clearly above their respective medians. Thus the answer is **Yes**.

4. (No, No, Yes)

i. The tone of the e-mails is positive and informal. The marketing manager says he is leaning toward the supply coordinator's call. Both of them are just trying to determine the number of lots required based on the math and their sales forecast. The answer is **No**.

ii. The normal lot size sent by the warehouse is 6 at a time. The marketing manager says that a special request may be necessary in order to avoid destroying products. He also says that he would like to keep the special requests down to a minimum. The supply coordinator will therefore want to order 6 lots in week 2 and then make just one special request of 2 lots for week 2. They will anticipate selling 4 lots each in weeks 2 and 3. Although we don't know the exact shelf life, it is a reasonable assumption that the 2 lots not sold in week 2 can be carried over to week 3. The answer is **No**.

iii. The marketing manager is open to making special requests, and he supports the sales call of the supply coordinator. Given that both are aligned with the 50% decrease sales call, the store will be expected to sell 4 lots each in weeks 2 and 3. This will require a shipment of 6 lots in week 1 and then a special request of 2 lots in week 3. The answer is **Yes**.

5. (A) This is tricky. The question specifically asks for the profit from the product sent in the week 3 lot. Since week 2 will have 6 lots, week 3 will then require just 2 lots. Even though the company expects to sell 4 lots in week 3, only 2 lots are from the week 3 shipments. The margin means that each unit will deliver $1 in profit. The following equation shows the profit:

$$\text{2 lots} \times \text{500 units/lot} \times (0.25)4 = \$1,000 \text{ profit}$$

6. ($2RT$ and $\dfrac{RT}{(T+10)}$) The best way to answer this question is to use a chart and plug in the values given in the question. (These are shown in bold.) From those values, you can infer the other calculations and fill in the chart.

	Going to Work	Coming from Work	Total
Distance	RT	$(R-5)(T+20)$	$RT+(R-5)(T+20)$
Rate	R	$R-5$	
Time	T	$T+20$	$2T+20$

i. Although we have a complicated equation for the total distance, we can solve this conceptually. The distance to and from work is exactly the same. Since the distance going to work is RT, the total distance is twice as much. Therefore the answer is $2RT$.

ii. To calculate Alice's average rate, you need to find (total distance)/(total time). Use your knowledge from part (i):

$$\text{Average rate: } \frac{2RT}{(2T+20)}$$

This reduces to the correct answer, which is $\frac{RT}{(T+10)}$.

7. i. (C) If you look at the first graph, Europe and Central Asia's GDP is slightly more than $10 trillion while East Asia and Pacific's GDP is approximately $7.5 trillion. A 10:7.5 ratio is the same as the ratio 20:15, which can be reduced to 4:3. The answer choice is **C**.

ii. (C) If you look at the first graph, Middle East and North Africa's 1999 GDP is a bit less than $1 trillion while Latin America and Caribbean's 1999 GDP is a bit less than $2 trillion. Therefore, Middle East and North Africa's 1999 GDP is approximately half, or 50%, of Latin America and Caribbean's 1999 GDP. The only answer choice close enough is **C**.

8. (B) By using the information from the two different charts, you can calculate each answer choice and determine which one is the cheapest. However, doing that might take a long time. Instead, start by calculating the cost of answer choice C, which has the lowest number of copies. The calculation is broken down into the copying cost plus the binding cost.

Copying cost:
5,000 copies × 20 pages per program × $0.30 per page × 0.9 discount = $27,000

Binding cost:
5,000 copies × $1 per binding × 0.9 discount = $4,500

Total cost:
$31,500

As you can see, the printing costs are far greater than the binding costs, even when you choose the more expensive binding. This means you should look for the cheapest printing costs first. So just calculate the copying costs.

A: 7,000 copies × 20 pages per program × $0.50/2 per page × 0.8 discount = $28,000

B: 15,000 copies × 20 pages per program × $0.10 per page × 0.6 discount = $18,000

D: 10,001 copies × 20 pages per program × $0.50/2 per page × 0.75 discount = $37,503.75

Choice B clearly has a much lower printing cost. The binding costs for choice B can be calculated:

$$15{,}000 \text{ copies} \times \$0.30 \text{ per program} \times 0.85 \text{ discount} = \$3{,}825$$

The total printing and binding costs for option B are $21,825, which is far below the costs of any of the other options. Thus the answer is **B**.

9. (False, True, True)

i. If Jennifer opted for the highest-quality program, the program would be in color, single sided, and with coil binding. Calculate the cost for 12,000:

Copying cost:

$$12{,}000 \text{ copies} \times 20 \text{ pages per program} \times \$0.50/2 \text{ per page} \times 0.75 \text{ discount} = \$45{,}000$$

This cost is already at the $45,00 budget, without even considering the binding costs. Adding the binding costs would make this option over budget. Therefore the answer is **False**.

ii. Use the calculations you did for question 10 to compare the two options. Copying costs for 15,000 units in black and white and also single sided are $18,000. You know that color copies, even when double sided, are 2.5 times the cost of black and white copies. Therefore, there is no need to calculate. You can estimate that color copies will cost approximately $18,000 × 2.5 = $45,000 just for copies alone. Clearly, the answer is **True**.

iii. As shown in question 10, the binding cost is much less than the printing cost. Whether the copies are in black and white or in color or whether they are single sided or double sided affects the printing costs more than does binding. In other words, binding tends to have the least effect on the overall cost. Therefore the answer is **True**.

10. i. (B) If you look at the graph and the trend line, you can clearly see a positive relationship between the outdoor temperature and the daily sales. The relationship is closer to linear than not. Therefore the answer is **B**.

ii. (C) If you look at the graph, the slopes of both the regression line and the dashed line are positive. However, the regression line has a higher slope than the dashed line. Therefore the answer is **C**.

11. (Would help explain, Would help explain, Would not help explain)

i. The first thing you should do is look at the table and get a sense of what the information is showing you. The movies are ranked by their gross box office and by their Metacritic rating. If you sort by either, you can get a sense of (and hopefully remember) when the movies came out and how popular or critically acclaimed they were. The question defines what it means to be "raved by critics" and a "box office hit." By using these definitions, you can sort the Metacritic rating and see that 10 movies have a rating higher than 85 and 8 movies have a box office gross higher than $100 million. Therefore the table **would help explain** the statement.

ii. You are given a definition of a "sure bet"—a movie with strong critical reviews and high box office grosses. In fact, by sorting, you will see that *Lord of the Rings* is tied for the highest Metacritic score of 94 and is the second highest grossing movie with $364 million. Therefore, the table **would help explain** the statement.

iii. The table does give a sense of each movie's box office gross at the time of the Oscar telecast. However, there is no way to measure the defined "Oscar bump" mentioned. Therefore, the chart **would not help explain** the statement.

12. (C) By sorting through the Metacritic rating, you can see only five movies that have ratings under 85. From those, simply look over to the box office grosses. Only one movie, *Crash*, made under $100 million. Therefore the answer is **C**.

Quantitative Section

(Roman numerals at the end of each answer refer to the section of Chapter 9 in which the appropriate math principle is discussed.)

1. If the length of a rectangle is increased by 20 percent and the width is decreased by 20 percent, then the area

   (A) decreases by 20%
   (B) decreases by 4%
   (C) stays the same
   (D) increases by 10%
   (E) increases by 20%

   (B) Let L be the original length and W the original width. The new length is 120 percent of L, which is $1.2L$; the new width is 80 percent of W, which is $.8W$. The area of a rectangle is length times width, so the original area is LW and the new area is $(1.2L)(.8W)$ or $.96LW$. Since the new area is 96 percent of the original area, the area has decreased by 4 percent. (I-4)   ★★☆

2. It costs x dollars each to make the first 1,000 copies of a compact disc and y dollars to make each subsequent copy. If z is greater than 1,000, how many dollars will it cost to make z copies of the compact disc?

   (A) $1,000x + yz$
   (B) $zx - zy$
   (C) $1,000(z - x) + xy$
   (D) $1,000(z - y) + xz$
   (E) $1,000(x - y) + yz$

   (E) The first 1,000 copies cost x dollars each, so altogether they will cost $1,000x$ dollars. Since z is greater than 1,000, there are $z - 1,000$ copies left, which each cost y dollars. Their cost is $(z - 1,000)y$. Thus the total cost is $1,000x + (z - 1,000)y$. However, this is not one of the answer choices. But $(z - 1,000)y = zy - 1,000y$, so the total cost is $1,000x - 1,000y + yz$ or $1,000(x - y) + yz$, which is choice (E). If you want to check your work, let $x = 5$, $y = 2$, and $z = 3,000$. (II-3)   ★★☆

3. How many two-digit integers satisfy the following property? The last digit (units digit) of the square of the two-digit number is 8.

   (A) none
   (B) 1
   (C) 2
   (D) 3
   (E) more than 3

   (A) When two integers are multiplied, the units digit of the product is the last digit of the product of the last digit of each of the integers. For example, the product of 22×18 is 396. The last digit of 396 is 6. And 6 is also the last digit of 16, which is the product of 2 (the last digit of 22) times 8 (the last digit of 18). When an integer is squared, the last digit of the square is the last digit of the square of the last digit. Squaring an odd number gives an odd number, and odd numbers cannot end in 8. Squaring a number that ends in 0 gives a number that ends in 0. Squaring a number that ends in 2 or 8 gives a   ★★★

number that ends in 4. Squaring a number that ends in 4 or 6 results in a number that ends in 6. So no integer squared ends in 8. Therefore, the correct choice is (A). (I-1)

★★★ **4.** Ms. Taylor purchased stock for $1,500 and sold $\frac{2}{3}$ of it after its value doubled. She sold the remaining stock at 5 times its purchase price. What was her total profit on the stock?

(A) $1,500
(B) $2,000
(C) $2,500
(D) $3,000
(E) $4,500

(D) Two-thirds of the stock cost $\frac{2}{3}$ of $1,500, or $1,000. So, when its value doubled, it was worth $2,000. The profit on this part of the stock is $2,000 – $1,000 = $1,000. The remaining stock cost $1,500 – $1,000 = $500. Five times the purchase price for this part of the stock is 5 × $500 = $2,500. The profit on this part is $2,500 – $500 = $2,000. So the total profit is $1,000 + $2,000 = $3,000, which is choice (D). (II-3)

★★★ **5.** City B is 8 miles east of city A. City C is 6 miles north of city B. City D is 16 miles east of city C, and city E is 12 miles north of city D. What is the distance from city A to city E?

(A) 10 miles
(B) 20 miles
(C) 24 miles
(D) 30 miles
(E) 42 miles

(D) Drawing a picture makes this problem easy. One way to solve the problem is to use coordinate geometry. Let A have coordinates (0,0); then the coordinates for B, C, D, and E are (8,0), (8,6), (24,6), and (24,18), respectively. So the distance from A to E is the square root of $24^2 + 18^2 = \sqrt{576+324} = \sqrt{900}$, which is 30. (III-9)

★★★ **6.** If x is a number satisfying $2 < x < 3$ and y is a number satisfying $7 < y < 8$, which of the following expressions will have the largest value?

(A) x^2y
(B) xy^2
(C) $5xy$
(D) $\dfrac{4x^2y}{3}$
(E) $\dfrac{x^2}{y}$

(B) From the information given you know that x and y are both positive and that $x < y$. So, we know that xy is positive. Since $xy = xy$ and $x < y$, we have that $x(xy) < y(xy)$, so (A) < (B). Since $5 < 7 < y$, we know that $5(xy) < y(xy)$, so (C) < (B). Since $x < 3$, we know $\left(\frac{4}{3}\right)x < 4$ so $\left(\frac{4}{3}\right)x(xy) < 4xy$ so (D) < (B). Since $y > 7$ and $x < 3$, (E) is obviously less than (B). Therefore, (B) has the greatest value and is the correct choice. (II-7)

7. The median salary of the employees in the sales department in 1999 was $\$x$. The average raise for the next year was $\$800$ per employee. What was the median salary of the employees in the sales department in 2000?

(1) $x = 48,000$

(2) The range of the salaries in the sales department in 2000 was $\$12,000$.

(E) STATEMENT (1) alone is not sufficient. If every employee received a raise of $\$800$, then the median in 2000 would be $x + 800$, but raises could be distributed in several different ways and still have the average raise equal to $\$800$. For example, if the top 10 percent received all the increases and everyone else received no increase, the median would not change from 1999. Information about only the range gives us the difference between the largest and smallest salaries; this does not let us find the middle salary, which is what we need for the median. So STATEMENT (2) along with STATEMENT (1) is not sufficient. (I-7) ★★☆

---

8. If 50 apprentices can finish a job in 4 hours and 30 skilled workers can finish the same job in $4\frac{1}{2}$ hours, how much of the job should be completed by 10 apprentices and 15 skilled workers in 1 hour?

(A) $\dfrac{1}{9}$

(B) $\dfrac{29}{180}$

(C) $\dfrac{26}{143}$

(D) $\dfrac{1}{5}$

(E) $\dfrac{39}{121}$

(B) Since 10 is $\dfrac{1}{5}$ of 50, the 10 apprentices should do $\dfrac{1}{5}$ as much work as 50 apprentices. Since 50 apprentices did the job in 4 hours, in 1 hour 50 apprentices will do $\dfrac{1}{4}$ of the job. Therefore, 10 apprentices should do $\dfrac{1}{5}$ of $\dfrac{1}{4} = \dfrac{1}{20}$ of the job in an hour. ★★★

Since 15 is $\dfrac{1}{2}$ of 30, 15 skilled workers will do half as much work as 30 skilled workers. The 30 skilled workers finished the job in $4\frac{1}{2}$ hours, which is $\dfrac{9}{2}$ hours, so in 1 hour they will do $\dfrac{2}{9}$ of the job. Therefore, 15 skilled workers will do $\dfrac{1}{2}$ of $\dfrac{2}{9} = \dfrac{1}{9}$ of the job in 1 hour. So both groups will do $\dfrac{1}{20} + \dfrac{1}{9} = \dfrac{9}{180} + \dfrac{20}{180} = \dfrac{29}{180}$ of the job in 1 hour. (II-3)

9. If the shaded area is $\frac{1}{2}$ the area of triangle ABC and angle ABC is a right angle, then the length of line segment AD is

(A) $\left(\frac{1}{2}\right)w$

(B) $\left(\frac{1}{2}\right)(w + x)$

(C) $\sqrt{2x^2 + z^2}$

(D) $\sqrt{w^2 - 3y^2}$

(E) $\sqrt{y^2 + z^2}$

(D) Since angle ABC is a right triangle, we know that the length of AD squared is equal to the sum of y^2 and x^2. However, none of of the answers given is $\sqrt{x^2 + y^2}$.

The area of triangle ABC is $\left(\frac{1}{2}\right)x(y + z)$, and the area of triangle ABD, which is $\left(\frac{1}{2}\right)xy$, must be one half of $\left(\frac{1}{2}\right)x(y + z)$.

So $\left(\frac{1}{4}\right)xy + \left(\frac{1}{4}\right)xz = \left(\frac{1}{2}\right)xy$, which can be solved to give $y = z$. Since angle ABC is a right triangle, $w^2 = (y + z)^2 + x^2 = (2y)^2 + x^2$. So $w^2 = 4y^2 + x^2$. Since we want $x^2 + y^2$, we subtract $3y^2$ from each side to get $w^2 - 3y^2 = y^2 + x^2$. Therefore, the length of AD squared is $w^2 - 3y^2$. (III-4, III-7)

---

10. There are 4 quarts in a gallon. A gallon of motor oil sells for $12 and a quart of the same oil sells for $5. The owner of a rental agency has 6 machines and each machine needs 5 quarts of oil. What is the minimum amount of money she must spend to purchase enough oil?

(A) $84
(B) $94
(C) $96
(D) $102
(E) $150

(B) The total amount of oil needed is $6 \times 5 = 30$ quarts, or 7 gallons and 2 quarts. Since the cost of oil per quart is cheaper when you purchase by the gallon, the owner should buy at least 7 gallons of oil. However, in order to get the remaining 2 gallons, it is cheaper to buy 2 quarts individually rather than another gallon. So the minimum amount is $7 \times \$12 + 2 \times \$5 = \$84 + \$10 = \$94$. The correct answer is (B). (II-3)

11. A store has a parking lot which contains 70 parking spaces. Each row in the parking lot contains the same number of parking spaces. The store has bought additional property in order to build an addition to the store. When the addition is built, 2 parking spaces will be lost from each row; however, 4 more rows will be added to the parking lot. After the addition is built, the parking lot will still have 70 parking spaces, and each row will contain the same number of parking spaces as every other row. How many rows were in the parking lot before the addition was built?

(A) 5
(B) 6
(C) 7
(D) 10
(E) 14

(D) Call s the number of spaces in each row and r the number of rows in the parking lot before the addition is built. The parking lot had 70 parking spaces, so $sr = 70$. Since after the addition is built there will be 4 more rows, 2 fewer spaces in each row, and a total of 70 spaces, we know that $(s-2)(r+4) = 70$. You could solve these two equations by algebra, but it would be rather lengthy and there is a faster method. Since the number of rows and the number of spaces must be positive integers, you are looking for a way to write 70 as the product of two factors s and r with the additional property that $s-2$ and $r+4$ also have 70 as their product. Writing 70 as a product of primes, we get $70 = 2 \times 35 = 2 \times 5 \times 7$. Therefore, the only possibilities for s and r are listed here:

s	r	s	r
1	70	10	7
2	35	14	5
5	14	35	2
7	10	70	1

Now just check whether any pair of solutions (s, r) has the property that $s-2$ and $r+4$ is a solution. For example, if $s = 5$ and $r = 14$, then $s-2 = 3$ and $r+4 = 18$, which are not solutions. But if $s = 7$ and $r = 10$, then $s-2 = 5$ and $r+4 = 14$, which is also a solution. It is easy to see this is the only solution that works. So before the addition was built, there were 10 rows, each with 7 spaces. (I-1)

★★☆ **12.** A piece of wood 5 feet long is cut into three smaller pieces. How long is the longest of the three pieces?

(1) One piece is 2 feet 7 inches long.

(2) One piece is 7 inches longer than another piece and the remaining piece is 5 inches long.

(D) STATEMENT (1) alone is sufficient. Since 2 feet 7 inches is more than half of 5 feet, the piece that is 2 feet 7 inches long must be longer than the other two pieces put together.

STATEMENT (2) alone is sufficient. Since one piece is 5 inches long, the sum of the lengths of the remaining two pieces is 4 feet 7 inches. Since one piece is 7 inches longer than the other, $L + (L + 7$ inches$) = 4$ feet 7 inches, where L is the length of the smaller of the two remaining pieces. Solving the equations yields $L + 7$ inches as the length of the longest piece. (II-2)

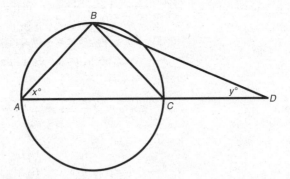

★★★ **13.** *AC* is a diameter of the circle and *B* is a point on the circle. *ACD* is a straight line. What is the value of *x*?

(1) $AB = BC$

(2) $x = 2y$

(A) Since *AC* is a diameter, angle *ABC* is inscribed in a semicircle and is therefore a right angle.

STATEMENT (1) alone is sufficient since it implies that the two other angles in the triangle must be equal. Since the sum of the angles of a triangle is 180°, we can deduce that $x = 45$.

STATEMENT (2) alone is not sufficient. There is no information about the angle *ABD*; so STATEMENT (2) cannot be used to find the angles of triangle *ABD*. (III-6)

★★★ **14.** What is the value of *y*?

(1) $x + 2y = 6$

(2) $y^2 - 2y + 1 = 0$

(B) STATEMENT (2) alone is sufficient, $y^2 - 2y + 1 = (y - 1)^2$, and the only solution of $(y - 1)^2 = 0$ is $y = 1$.

STATEMENT (1) alone is not sufficient.

$x + 2y = 6$ implies $y = 3 - \dfrac{x}{2}$, but there are no data given about the value of *x*. (II-2)

15. Two pipes, *A* and *B*, empty into a reservoir. Pipe *A* can fill the reservoir in 30 minutes by itself. How long will it take for pipe *A* and pipe *B* together to fill up the reservoir?

(1) By itself, pipe *B* can fill the reservoir in 20 minutes.

(2) Pipe *B* has a larger cross-sectional area than pipe *A*.

(A) STATEMENT (1) alone is sufficient. Pipe *A* fills up $\frac{1}{30}$ of the reservoir per minute.

STATEMENT (1) says pipe *B* fills up $\frac{1}{20}$ of the reservoir per minute, so *A* and *B* together fill up $\frac{1}{20} + \frac{1}{30}$ or $\frac{5}{60}$ or $\frac{1}{12}$ of the reservoir per minute.

You should not waste any time actually solving the problem. Remember, you only have to decide if there is enough information to let you answer the question.

STATEMENT (2) alone is not sufficient. There is no information about how long it takes pipe *B* to fill the reservoir. (II-3)

★★☆

---

16. *AB* is perpendicular to *CD*. Is *A* or *B* closer to *C*?

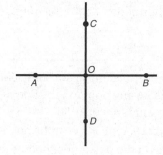

(1) *OA* is less than *OB*.

(2) *ACBD* is not a parallelogram.

(A) STATEMENT (1) alone is sufficient. Draw the lines *AC* and *BC*; then *AOC* and *BOC* are right triangles since *AB* is perpendicular to *CO*. By the Pythagorean theorem, $(AC)^2 = (AO)^2 + (CO)^2$ and $(BC)^2 = (OB)^2 + (CO)^2$; so if *AO* is less than *OB*, then *AC* is less than *BC*.

STATEMENT (2) alone is not sufficient. There is no restriction on where the point *D* is. (III-5, III-4)

★★☆

---

17. Is *xy* greater than 1? *x* and *y* are both positive.

(1) *x* is less than 1.

(2) *y* is greater than 1.

(E) STATEMENTS (1) and (2) together are not sufficient. If $x = \frac{1}{2}$ and $y = 3$, then *xy* is greater than 1, but if $x = \frac{1}{2}$ and $y = \frac{3}{2}$, then *xy* is less than 1. This is a good example of the use of specific values for *x* and *y* to decide whether the given statements are sufficient to deduce the desired conclusion. (II-7)

★★☆

★★☆ **18.** Does $x = y$?

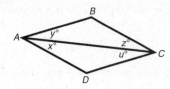

(1) $z = u$

(2) *ABCD* is a parallelogram.

(C) STATEMENT (1) alone is not sufficient. By moving the point *B* along the original side *BC*, we can have either $x = y$ or $x \neq y$ and still have $z = u$.

STATEMENT (2) alone is not sufficient. It implies that $x = z$ and $y = u$, but gives no information to compare x and y.

STATEMENTS (1) and (2) together, however, yield $x = y$. (III-5)

★★☆ **19.** Train *T* leaves town *A* for town *B* and travels at a constant rate of speed. At the same time, train *S* leaves town *B* for town *A* and also travels at a constant rate of speed. Town *C* is between *A* and *B*. Which train is traveling faster? Towns *A*, *C*, and *B* lie on a straight line.

(1) Train *S* arrives at town *C* before train *T*.

(2) *C* is closer to *A* than to *B*.

(C) STATEMENT (1) alone is not sufficient. If town *C* were closer to *B*, even if *S* were going slower than *T*, it could arrive at *C* first. But if you also use STATEMENT (2), then train *S* must be traveling faster than train *T* since it is further from *B* to *C* than it is from *A* to *C*.

So STATEMENTS (1) and (2) together are sufficient.

STATEMENT (2) alone is insufficient since it gives no information about the trains. (II-3)

★★☆ **20.** Does $x = y$?

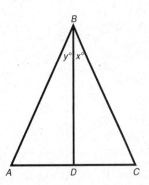

(1) *BD* is perpendicular to *AC*.

(2) *AB* is equal to *BC*.

(C) STATEMENT (2) alone is not sufficient since *D* can be any point on the line *AC* if we assume only STATEMENT (2).

STATEMENT (1) alone is not sufficient. Depending on the position of point *C*, x and y can be equal or unequal. For example, in both of the following triangles *BD* is perpendicular to *AC*.

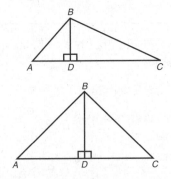

If STATEMENTS (1) and (2) are both true, then $x = y$. The triangles *ABD* and *BDC* are both right triangles with two pairs of corresponding sides equal; the triangles are therefore congruent and $x = y$. (III-4)

21. What is the value of $x + y$?

(1) $x - y = 4$

(2) $3x + 3y = 4$

(B) STATEMENT (2) alone is sufficient since $3x + 3y$ is $3(x + y)$. (Therefore, if $3x + 3y = 4$, then $x + y = \dfrac{4}{3}$.)

STATEMENT (1) alone is not sufficient, since you need another equation besides $x - y = 4$ to find the values of x and y. (II-2)

---

22. Did the XYZ Corporation have higher sales in 1988 or in 1989? Assume sales are positive.

(1) In 1988, the sales were twice the average (arithmetic mean) of the sales in 1988, 1989, and 1990.

(2) In 1990, the sales were 3 times those in 1989.

(A) STATEMENT (1) alone is sufficient. We know that the total of sales for 1988, 1989, and 1990 is three times the average and that sales in 1988 were twice the average. Then the total of sales in 1989 and 1990 was equal to the average. Therefore, sales were less in 1989 than in 1988.

STATEMENT (2) alone is insufficient since it does not relate sales in 1989 to sales in 1988. (I-7)

---

23. Is *ABDC* a square?

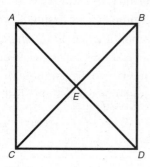

(1) *BC* is perpendicular to *AD*.

(2) *BE = EC*.

(E) STATEMENTS (1) and (2) together are not sufficient since points *A* and *D* can be moved and STATEMENTS (1) and (2) will still be satisfied. (III-5)

---

24. *k* is an integer. Is *k* divisible by 12?

(1) *k* is divisible by 4.

(2) *k* is divisible by 3.

(C) List the first few numbers that are divisible by 4, such as 4, 8, 12, 16, 20, 24, . . ., and list the first few numbers that are divisible by 3, such as 3, 6, 9, 12, 15, 18, 21, 24, ... Notice that the integers that appear in both lists are divisible by 12. STATEMENT (1) alone is not sufficient, since 24 and 16 are both divisible by 4 but only 24 is divisible by 12.

STATEMENT (2) alone is not sufficient since 24 and 15 are divisible by 3 but 15 is not divisible by 12.

STATEMENT (1) implies that $k = 4m$ for some integer m. If you assume STATEMENT (2), then since k is divisible by 3, either 4 or m is divisible by 3. Since 4 is not divisible by 3, m must be. Therefore, $m = 3j$, where j is some integer and $k = 4 \times 3j$ or $12j$. So k is divisible by 12. Therefore, STATEMENTS (1) and (2) together are sufficient. (I-1)

★☆☆ **25.** If n is a positive integer less than 100, what is the value of n?

(1) n is an even integer.

(2) n^3 is less than 200.

(E) Statement (1) alone is not sufficient since there are many even positive integers less than 100, such as 2, 4, and 6. Statement (2) alone is not sufficient since $2^3 = 8$ and $4^3 = 64$, which are both less than 200, and 2 and 4 are positive integers that are less than 100. Statements (1) and (2) together are not sufficient since 2 and 4 are both even integers that are less than 100 and both of their cubes are less than 200.

★☆☆ **26.** What was the price of a dozen eggs during the 15th week of the year 2004?

(1) During the first week of 2004 the price of a dozen eggs was 75¢.

(2) The price of a dozen eggs rose 1¢ a week every week during the first four months of 2004.

(C) You need (1) to know what the price was at the beginning of 2004. Using (2) you could then compute the price during the 15th week. Either statement alone is insufficient. You should not actually compute the price since it would only waste time. (II-6)

★★★ **27.** Is DE parallel to BC? $DB = AD$.

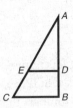

(1) $AE = EC$

(2) $DB = EC$

(A) (1) alone is sufficient since the line connecting the midpoints of two sides of a triangle is parallel to the third side. (2) alone is insufficient. In an isosceles triangle statement (2) would imply that ED is parallel to BC, but in a nonisosceles triangle, (2) would imply that ED and BC are not parallel. (III-4)

28. If the area of a rectangle is equal to the area of a square, then the perimeter of the rectangle must be

(A) one half of the perimeter of the square
(B) equal to the perimeter of the square
(C) equal to twice the perimeter of the square
(D) equal to the square root of the perimeter of the square
(E) none of the above

(E) Let L be the length and W be the width of the rectangle, and let S be the length of a side of the square. It is given that $LW = S^2$. A relation must be found between $2L + 2W$ and $4S$. It is possible to construct squares and rectangles so that each of (A), (B), (C), and (D) is false, so (E) is correct. For example, if the rectangle is a square, then the two figures are identical and (A), (C), and (D) are false. If the rectangle is not equal to a square, then the perimeter of the rectangle is larger than the perimeter of the square, so (B) is also false. (III-7)

---

29. Which of the following are possible values for the angles of a parallelogram?

 I. 90°, 90°, 90°, 90°
 II. 40°, 70°, 50°, 140°
 III. 50°, 130°, 50°, 130°

(A) I only
(B) II only
(C) I and III only
(D) II and III only
(E) I, II, and III

(C) Since a parallelogram is a four-sided polygon, the sum of the angles of a parallelogram must be $(4 - 2)180° = 360°$. (A diagonal divides a parallelogram into two triangles, and the sum of each triangle's angles is 180°.) Since the sum of the angles in II is not 360°, II is not possible. But I and III both consist of angles whose sum is 360°. Also, since in both I and III opposite angles are equal, (C) is the correct choice. Note that a rectangle is also a parallelogram, so I does give possible values for the angles of a parallelogram. (III-3, III-5)

---

30. For every novel in the school library there are 2 science books; for each science book there are 7 economics books. Express the ratio of economics books to science books to novels in the school library as a triple ratio.

(A) 7 : 2 : 1
(B) 7 : 1 : 2
(C) 14 : 7 : 2
(D) 14 : 2 : 1
(E) 14 : 2 : 7

(D) If you know two ratios, $A : B$ and $B : C$, you can combine them into a triple ratio if B is the same number and represents the same quantity in both ratios. We know that the ratio of economics books to science books is 7 : 1 and that the ratio of novels to science books is 1 : 2. However, we can't combine this into the triple ratio 7 : 1 : 2 since 1 in the first ratio represents science books and 1 in the second ratio represents novels. We need science books as the middle term in the triple ratio, so we express the second ratio as: The ratio of science books to novels is 2 : 1. Now, the ratio of economics books to science books is 7 : 1 and the ratio of science books to novels is 2 : 1. Since a ratio is unchanged if both sides are multiplied by the same positive number, we can also express the ratio of economics books to science books as 14 : 2. Finally, we can combine these into the triple ratio 14 : 2 : 1 of economics books to science books to novels. (II-5)

★★★ **31.** There are 50 employees in the office of ABC Company. Of these, 22 have taken an accounting course, 15 have taken a course in finance, and 14 have taken a marketing course. Nine of the employees have taken exactly two of the courses, and one employee has taken all three of the courses. How many of the 50 employees have taken none of the courses?

(A) 0
(B) 9
(C) 10
(D) 11
(E) 26

(C) A diagram helps.

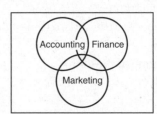

We want to know how many people are not in any of the sets. The easy way to do this is to find the number in at least one of the sets and subtract this number from 50. To find the number of employees in at least one set, *do not count the same employee more than once.* If you add 22, 15, and 14, an employee who took exactly two of the courses will be counted twice, and employees who took all three courses will be counted three times. So the number who took at least one course is the number in accounting plus the number in finance plus the number in marketing minus the number who took exactly two courses minus 2 times the number who took all three courses = $22 + 15 + 14 - 9 - (2 \times 1) = 51 - 9 - 2 = 40$. Since 40 of the employees took at least one course, $50 - 40 = 10$ took none of the courses. (II-4)

★★☆ **32.** If $x + y = 4$ and $x - y = 3$, then $x + 2y$ is

(A) $\dfrac{1}{2}$

(B) 3.5

(C) 4

(D) $4\dfrac{1}{2}$

(E) $7\dfrac{1}{2}$

(D) Add $x + y = 4$ to $x - y = 3$ to obtain $2x = 7$. Therefore, $x = 3\dfrac{1}{2}$. Since $x + y = 4$, y must be $4 - 3\dfrac{1}{2} = \dfrac{1}{2}$. So $x + 2y = 3\dfrac{1}{2} + 2\left(\dfrac{1}{2}\right) = 4\dfrac{1}{2}$. (II-2)

33. How much interest will $2,000 earn at an annual rate of 8 percent in 1 year if the interest is compounded every 6 months?

(A) $160.00
(B) $163.20
(C) $249.73
(D) $332.80
(E) $2,163.20

(B) The interest is compounded every 6 months. At the end of the first 6 months, the interest earned is $2,000(.08)$\left(\frac{1}{2}\right)$ = $80. (Don't forget to change 6 months into $\frac{1}{2}$ year since 8 percent is the annual—yearly—rate.) Since the interest is compounded, $2,080 is the amount earning interest for the final 6 months of the year. So the interest earned during the final 6 months of the year is $2,080(.08)$\left(\frac{1}{2}\right)$ = $83.20. Therefore, the total interest earned is $80 + $83.20 = $163.20. (I-4)

★★☆

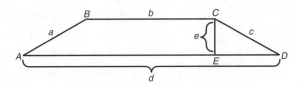

34. If BC is parallel to AD and CE is perpendicular to AD, then the area of $ABCD$ is

(A) bd
(B) $bd + ac$
(C) ed
(D) $e(b + d)$
(E) $.5eb + .5ed$

(E) Since BC is parallel to AD, the figure $ABCD$ is a trapezoid. The area of a trapezoid is the average of the parallel sides times an altitude. Since CE is perpendicular to AD, e is an altitude. So the area is $e\left(\frac{1}{2}\right)(b + d) = \left(\frac{1}{2}\right)eb + \left(\frac{1}{2}\right)ed$. Since $\frac{1}{2} = .5$, (E) is the correct answer. (III-7)

★★★

35. If the price of steak is currently $1.00 a pound, and the price triples every 6 months, how long will it be until the price of steak is $81.00 a pound?

(A) 1 year
(B) 2 years
(C) $2\frac{1}{2}$ years
(D) 13 years
(E) $13\frac{1}{2}$ years

(B) The price will be $3.00 a pound 6 months from now and $9.00 a pound 1 year from now. The price is a geometric progression of the form 3^j, where j is the number of 6-month periods that have passed. Since $3^4 = 81$, after 4 six-month periods the price will be $81.00 a pound. Therefore, the answer is 2 years since 24 months is 2 years. (II-6, I-8)

★★☆

★★☆ **36.** If $\frac{x}{y} = \frac{2}{3}$, then $\frac{y^2}{x^2}$ is

    (A) $\frac{4}{9}$

    (B) $\frac{2}{3}$

    (C) $\frac{3}{2}$

    (D) $\frac{9}{4}$

    (E) $\frac{5}{2}$

(D) Since $\frac{x}{y} = \frac{2}{3}$, $\frac{y}{x}$, which is the reciprocal of $\frac{x}{y}$, must be equal to $\frac{3}{2}$. Also, $\frac{y^2}{x^2}$ is equal to $\left(\frac{y}{x}\right)^2$, so $\frac{y^2}{x^2}$ is equal to $\left(\frac{3}{2}\right)^2 = \frac{9}{4}$. (I-2, I-8)

★★★ **37.** What is the maximum number of points of intersection of two circles that have unequal radii?

    (A) none

    (B) 1

    (C) 2

    (D) 3

    (E) infinite

(C) Since the radii are unequal, the circles cannot be identical, thus (E) is incorrect. If two circles intersect in three points, they must be identical, so (D) is also incorrect. Two different circles can intersect at 2 points without being identical, so (C) is the correct answer. (III-6)

Verbal Section

1. Typically, the entrepreneur is seen as an individual who owns and operates a small business. But, simply to own and operate a small business—or even a big business—does not make someone an entrepreneur. If this person is a true entrepreneur, then new products are being created and new ways of providing services are being implemented.

Which of the following conclusions can best be drawn from the above passage?
(A) An owner of a large business may be an entrepreneur.
(B) Someone who develops an enterprise may be considered an entrepreneur.
(C) Entrepreneurs do not own and operate small businesses.
(D) Entrepreneurs are the main actors in economic growth.
(E) Entrepreneurs are investors.

(B) Answer (B) is the best choice. Note the cue word "then" before "new products" and "new ways." An entrepreneur is one who creates or implements change, not necessarily an investor, as in answer (E). Answer (A) is true (the owner of a large business may be an entrepreneur), but it is not the best conclusion that can be drawn from the passage. It is a necessary but insufficient condition. Note that the text states that to own a small or large business does not make someone an entrepreneur. Answer (C) is not supported by the passage and not enough information is given to conclude answer (D).

2. The principal reason for our failure was quite apparent <u>to those whom we had brought</u> into the venture.

(A) to those whom we had brought
(B) to them whom we had brought
(C) to the ones whom we had brought
(D) to those who we had brought
(E) to those who we had brung

(A) No error. Choice (B) uses the incorrect personal pronoun "them," choice (C) does not contain a pronoun, choice (D) uses the incorrect pronoun who ("who" replaces a subject, not an object), and choice (E) uses the incorrect pronoun "who," and the incorrect past participle "brung."

The passage for questions 3–8 appears on page 82.

3. Which of the following is NOT mentioned in the passage as a distinguishing characteristic of a charismatic leader?
(A) inspirational
(B) popular
(C) convincing
(D) forceful
(E) exceptional

(B) A charismatic leader may be popular, but this is not mentioned in the passage.

★☆☆ **4.** The primary purpose of the passage is to

(A) show how leadership styles affect domestic politics

(B) illustrate which leadership style is the most effective

(C) identify the advantages and disadvantages of several leadership styles

(D) present some characteristics of several leadership styles

(E) argue that leadership styles are influenced by a nation's culture

(D) The author describes some characteristics of each leadership style.

★★☆ **5.** The passage suggests which of the following propositions?

(A) Both bureaucratic and charismatic leaders promise to transform society through effective management skills.

(B) Traditional leaders resist any modernization, while modern bureaucratic leaders support it.

(C) Charismatic leaders ensure their power base owing to their oratorical skills.

(D) Traditional leadership is based on long-term performance expectations, while modern bureaucratic leadership is short term.

(E) Charismatic leaders offer themselves as a substitute for traditional and bureaucratic leadership.

(D) The first paragraph states that traditional leaders *expect change to occur over relatively extended periods of time,* which means over the long term. The first sentence of the third paragraph states that modern leaders seek short-term performance outcomes.

★☆☆ **6.** It can be inferred that the author believes that

(A) tradition is a legitimizing symbol of leadership

(B) many charismatic leaders have mystical powers

(C) only bureaucratic leaders possess management skills

(D) traditional leadership is determined by historical right but bureaucratic leadership is elected

(E) a traditional leader may also be charismatic

(A) The first paragraph states that traditional leaders stake their claim to leadership through a long line of predecessors that is *legitimized by practice.*

★★★ **7.** It can be inferred from the passage that

(A) bureaucratic leaders' survival in power depends on the consequences of their policy choices, not their charismatic or traditional appeal

(B) charismatic leaders will often focus strongly on making the group that they appeal to feel distinct and unique

(C) bureaucratic leaders emphasize rules and regulations

(D) traditional leaders are viewed as having control and power because those holding the position before them had control and power

(E) people follow others that they personally admire

(D) The second sentence of the excerpt states that *traditional leaders base their claim to leadership on the assertion that they are the clear and logical successors to a line of leaders that stretches back in time and that is legitimized by practice.* Therefore, it may be inferred that the power of a present-day traditional leader stems from the power inherent in his predecessor(s).

---

8. Which of the following statements best applies to a charismatic leader according to information in the passage?
   (A) Charm and grace are all that is needed to create followers.
   (B) Self-belief is a fundamental need of leaders.
   (C) Be very persuasive, and make very effective use of body language as well as verbal language.
   (D) Be willing to tell other people what to do, but have the respect of other people as well.
   (E) Change what others think and feel.

   (E) This is a very short statement that tells much about charismatic leaders. This information is embodied in paragraph 2, which states that they *will promulgate substantial and convincing images of a new order, perhaps ordained in heaven, that will raise the community to new levels of activity and accomplishment.*

---

9. During the incumbent president's term of office he succeeded in limiting annual increases in the defense budget by an average of 5 percent. His predecessor experienced annual increases of 8 percent. Therefore, the incumbent president should be given credit for the downturn in defense outlays.

   Which of the following statements, if true, would most seriously weaken the above conclusion?
   (A) Some generals have claimed that the country's defenses have weakened in the past year.
   (B) More soldiers were drafted during the former president's term of office.
   (C) The incumbent president advocates peaceful resolution of international disputes.
   (D) The average annual inflation rate during the incumbent president's term was 4%, while during his predecessor's term it was 10%.
   (E) A disarmament treaty with a major adversary was signed by the incumbent president.

   (D) If inflation averaged 4 percent and spending increased 5 percent, the *real* value of defense outlays actually increased 25 percent. During the former president's term, outlays actually declined faster than inflation, indicating a real decrease of 25 percent. The passage and the conclusions concern defense outlays only; the strength of the defenses (A), number of draftees (B), presidential views (C), or international treaties (E) are not mentioned in the passage and no direct inferences can be made; therefore all other alternatives are not relevant. The argument may be summarized as follows:

   (1) Annual increases of incumbent were 5 percent.
   (2) Annual increases of predecessor were 8 percent.

These two premises lead to a conclusion: 5% < 8%. However, converting the nominal to real increases, as we showed previously, weakens the conclusion.

★★★ **10.** Nobody denies that economic development is essential for poorer nations. But in advanced economies there is mounting evidence that an increase in consumption adds little to human happiness and may even impede it. Unless we can radically lower the environmental impact of economic activity we will have to devise a path to prosperity that does not rely on continued growth.

Which of the following is an assumption on which the author's argument depends?
(A) Economic development is the only way to achieve happiness.
(B) More people in developed countries than in developing countries claim that they are satisfied with their quality of life.
(C) There is little correlation between consumption and happiness.
(D) Economic development is not essential for developed countries.
(E) Concerns about the environment in developed economies are a factor determining economic policy.

(E) Concerns about the environment in developed economies are a factor determining economic policy. This assumption is derived from the last section in the statement that if the environmental impact on economic activity (presumably pollution, excessive water use, etc.) is not lowered, a different path to prosperity will have to be devised. In other words, a different economic policy will have to be chosen. Choices (A) and (D) are not supported by the statement. Choice (B) is incorrect because while the author mentions the important of economic development for "poorer nations" and the relations between consumption and happiness in "advanced economies," there is not comparison between the two and the quality of life. Choice (C) is wrong because on the contrary, the author argues that there is a relation between consumption and happiness.

★★☆ **11.** Although he was the most friendly of all present and <u>different from the others, he hadn't hardly any friends except me</u>.
(A) different from the others, he hadn't hardly any friends except me
(B) different than the others, he had hardly any friends except me
(C) different from the others, he had hardly any friends except me
(D) different than the others, he hadn't hardly any friends except I
(E) different from the others, he hardly had any friends except I

(C) This corrects the double negative (*hadn't hardly*). *Different from* is the correct idiom. *Me* is the correct form of the pronoun after the preposition *except*.

★★☆ **12.** It was <u>us who had left before he arrived</u>.
(A) us who had left before he arrived
(B) we who had left before he arrived
(C) we who had went before he arrived
(D) us who had went before he arrived
(E) we who had left before the time he had arrived

(B) *We* is correct; a predicate pronoun is in the nominative case. *Had went* is an incorrect verb form (either *went* or *had gone*). (E) is not only wordy, but the tense sequence also is wrong (the *leaving* occurred before the *arriving*).

13. Buy Plenty, a supermarket chain, had successfully implemented an in-store promotional campaign based on video messages flashed on a large screen. The purpose of the campaign was to motivate customers to purchase products they had not planned to buy before they entered the store. The sales manager of Build-It Inc., a chain of do-it-yourself hardware stores, saw the campaign and plans to introduce it at Build-It locations.

   The sales manager's plan assumes that
   (A) supermarket and hardware products are the same
   (B) products cannot be sold successfully without a video sales campaign
   (C) supermarket chains do not sell hardware products
   (D) consumer decision-making to buy products does not differ substantially when it comes to both supermarket and hardware products
   (E) in-store campaigns are more effective than out-of-store advertising and sales promotion

   (D) Build-It's sales manager assumes via analogy that consumers behave the same way when it comes to buying do-it-yourself hardware products as they behave in a supermarket even though no evidence for this is given in the passage. Choice (A) cannot be inferred, and there is no evidence to support choice (B), (C), or (E).

The passage for questions 14–17 appears on page 86.

14. The author provides information that would answer which of the following questions?
   (A) What are some of the causes of asteroids?
   (B) Who is Charles Kowal?
   (C) What are asteroids?
   (D) When will Neptune collide with Earth?
   (E) How far are asteroids from the sun?

   (C) Asteroids are defined as mini-planets, most of which are located in the asteroid belt (paragraphs 9 and 10).

15. It may be inferred from the passage that
   (A) the Kuiper Belt includes 1,000 asteroids
   (B) Apophis was calculated to be in the inner solar system
   (C) most asteroids are dangerously close to Earth
   (D) there is no inherent danger from falling asteroids
   (E) asteroid research is not very advanced scientifically

ANSWERS EXPLAINED

(B) Beginning on line 30, there is a discussion about asteroids that may cross the Earth's orbit. These asteroids are in the inner solar system. The next paragraphs mention the possibility that Apophis "crosses Earth's orbit." Therefore, it is in the inner solar system.

★★☆ **16.** According to the passage,
(A) new asteroids are named by those who discover them
(B) Sedna is the farthest asteroid from Earth
(C) the largest asteroid is Pluto
(D) Apophis is about the size of Pluto
(E) UB313 will be named after Brown, Trujillo, and Rabinovitz

(B) Sedna is the farthest asteroid (paragraph 3).

★★☆ **17.** Which of the following titles best describes the contents of the passage?
(A) "The Impact of Asteroids on the Solar System"
(B) "What Is the Tenth Planet?"
(C) "How Asteroids Are Discovered"
(D) "The Search for Asteroids"
(E) "The Discoveries of Charles Kowal"

(D) The focus of the passage is the search for asteroids. Almost every paragraph discusses the search.

★★★ **18.** She is the sort of person who I feel would be capable of making these kind of statements.
(A) sort of person who I feel would be capable of making these kind of
(B) sort of a person who I feel would be capable of making these kind of
(C) sort of person who I feel would be capable of making these kinds of
(D) sort of person whom I feel would be capable of making these kinds of
(E) sort of person whom I feel would be capable of making this kind of

(C) An adjective should agree in number with the noun it modifies (*these kinds*). Although in choice (E) *this kind* is also correct, *whom* is not because *who* is needed as the subject of *would be*. In choice (B) *sort of a* is not a correct idiom.

★★★ **19.** The movement to ownership by unions is the latest step in the progression from management ownership to employee ownership. Employee ownership can save depressed and losing companies.

All of the following statements, if true, provide support for the claim above EXCEPT
(A) Employee-owned companies generally have higher productivity.
(B) Employee participation in management raises morale.
(C) Employee union ownership drives up salaries and wages.
(D) Employee union ownership enables workers to share in the profits.
(E) Employee union ownership makes it easier to lay off redundant workers.

(C) Statement (C) is the best choice because increased salaries and wages will make the company less profitable and thus not help save a losing company. All other statements, if true, would lend credence to the claim.

---

20. The burning of coal, oil, and other combustible energy sources produces carbon dioxide, a natural constituent of the atmosphere. Elevated levels of carbon dioxide are thought to be responsible for half of the greenhouse effect. Enough carbon dioxide has been sent into the atmosphere already to cause a significant temperature increase. Growth in industrial production must be slowed, or production processes must be changed.

★★★

Which of the following, if true, would tend to weaken the strength of the above conclusion?
(A) Many areas of the world are cold anyway, so a small rise in temperature would be welcome.
(B) Carbon dioxide is bad for the health.
(C) Most carbon dioxide is emitted by automobiles.
(D) Industry is switching over to synthetic liquid fuel extracted from coal.
(E) A shift to other energy sources would be too costly.

(C) Choice (C) would weaken the conclusion the most. If most carbon dioxide is emitted by automobiles, then cutting industrial production or changing production processes would solve a small part of the problem. Alternative (A) weakens the conclusion, but not as much. It does not attack the basic premise of the passage—namely, that industrial production is responsible for elevated carbon dioxide levels. It also disregards the effect of a temperature increase even in cold areas. Alternative (B) adds to the conclusion. Alternative (D) would not change the conclusion because liquid fuel may also produce carbon dioxide (in actuality, it produces quite a bit). Alternative (E) does not weaken the conclusion because even if a shift to other energy sources were too costly, this does not mean that slowing of or changes in production would be too costly.

The passage for questions 21–25 appears on page 88.

---

21. Which of the following best summarizes the four culture production models mentioned in the passage?
(A) They are based on economic criteria.
(B) They explain why government should support cultural activities.
(C) They argue against government intervention.
(D) They are not well understood.
(E) They argue for a separation of government and the arts.

★★★

(B) The author states on lines 5–7 the central purpose of the passage, which is to evaluate several alternative explanations (models) of the government's involvement in the production of culture. The question asks you to select which answer choice best summarizes the four models. Paragraphs 2–4 give arguments why the government should support cultural activities.

★★☆ **22.** The major objective of the passage is to
   (A) increase appreciation for the arts
   (B) provide an ideological basis for artistic funding
   (C) explain why government supports cultural activities
   (D) evaluate government involvement in the production of culture
   (E) demonstrate cultural activities in the United States

   (D) According to lines 5–7 in the passage, "The central purpose of this paper is to evaluate the relative strengths of several alternative explanations for the government's involvement in the production of culture."

★★★ **23.** The passage suggests that a corollary of government support of artistic and scientific activity is
   (A) funding should be provided by government only as a last resort
   (B) funding will be geared to projects of value to the government
   (C) funding is to be provided only to nongovernmental employees
   (D) funding by the government is self-defeating
   (E) funding by the government is inflationary

   (B) Choice (B) belongs to the third model, which emphasizes value of patronage to the government (lines 13–14). The other answer choices are not mentioned in the passage.

★★☆ **24.** A conclusion reached by the author of the passage is that
   (A) the arts and sciences have been funded by the government for different reasons.
   (B) government is a neutral observer of the arts and sciences.
   (C) government intervention in the arts and sciences is declining.
   (D) evaluate government involvement in the production of culture
   (E) politics and science go together.

   (A) Answer choice (A) reflects the four models about the government's funding objectives: the utility of the investment, maintaining cultural institutions, the value of supporting science and art, and ideological reasons. Thus, the author is trying to show empirically how the government funds the arts and sciences but for different reasons, i.e., as a consumer, as an influencer, and as a subsidizer.

★☆☆ **25.** The idea that government should support the arts and sciences only when the market does not provide enough funds belongs to which school?
   (A) "their own sake"
   (B) "business application"
   (C) "government programs"
   (D) "ideological control"
   (E) all of the above

(A) The idea expressed in the question is suggested by the science and art for "their own sake" model. This idea is supported by lines 23–24, which state that *the government intervenes directly as the final patron of public goods that would otherwise be unavailable*, i.e., not purchased or supported by nongovernmental or market forces.

---

26. The author's method of rebutting opponents of the new trade bill is to
    (A) attack the patriotism of its opponents
    (B) attack the opponents' characters rather than their claims
    (C) imply an analogy between the new trade bill and previous trade legislation
    (D) suggest that economists were against both pieces of legislation
    (E) imply that previous legislation also permitted retaliatory action against foreign countries

(C) The author refers to 1930s trade legislation to justify the new bill. Therefore, choice (C) is the best answer. There is no information to conclude (A) or (B); the author does not attack the character of the opposition, nor their patriotism. In choice (D), it is assumed that the opposition infers that economists were against both pieces of legislation, but there is no evidence of this in the passage. Choice (E) is wrong because the passage does not stipulate what sort of action was permitted by the earlier legislation.

---

27. Opponents of the new legislation could defend themselves against the author's strategy by arguing that
    (A) the fact that past trade legislation improved the trade balance does not mean that the present bill will do the same
    (B) economists are not always right
    (C) the United States had a trade deficit both in the 1930s and at the time of the new bill
    (D) the new law is not as strong as the 1930s bill
    (E) America's new trading partners have also passed similar legislation

(A) The opponents could argue that two similar pieces of legislation passed and implemented at different times may not have the same effect because they face a different set of circumstances. Even though both bills may have similar provisions, they may be applied under different sets of economic and political conditions. Therefore, (A) is the best answer. Alternatives (C) and (E) strengthen the author's argument rather than the opponent's rebuttal. Alternative (B) may be so, but it does not necessarily apply in this case. There is not enough information to conclude (D).

★★☆ **28.** Beside me, there were many persons who were altogether aggravated by his manners.

(A) Beside me, there were many persons who were altogether aggravated

(B) Beside me, there were many persons who were all together aggravated

(C) Besides me, there were many persons who were altogether aggravated

(D) Besides me, there were many persons who were altogether irritated

(E) Beside me, there were many persons who were all together irritated

(D) *Besides* means "*in addition to.*" *Irritated* is correct. A person is irritated; a situation or condition is aggravated.

★★☆ **29.** The owner, who was a kind man, spoke to the boy and he was very rude.

(A) , who was a kind man, spoke to the boy and he

(B) was a kind man and he spoke to the boy and he

(C) spoke to the boy kindly and the boy

(D) , a kind man, spoke to the boy who

(E) who was a kind man spoke to the boy and he

(D) The appositive, *a kind man*, can easily replace the clause *who was a kind man*. The words *and he*, where the antecedent of *he* is vague, should be replaced by *who*, which refers specifically to the boy.

★★☆ **30.** Because we cooperated together, we divided up the work on the report that had been assigned.

(A) together, we divided up the work on the report that had been assigned

(B) together, we divided the work on the report that had been assigned

(C) , we divided up the work on the report that was assigned

(D) , we divided the work on the assigned report

(E) we divided up the work on the assigned report

(D) *Together* and *up* are included in the meaning of other words in the sentence. The adjective *assigned* is preferable stylistically to the adjective clause *which was assigned*.

★★☆ **31.** During 1999, advertising expenditures on canned food products increased by 20 percent, while canned food consumption rose by 25 percent.

Each of the following, if true, could help to explain the increase in food consumption EXCEPT

(A) Advertising effectiveness increased

(B) Canned food prices decreased relative to substitutes

(C) Canned food products were available in more stores

(D) Can opener production doubled

(E) Per-capita consumption of frozen foods declined

(D) The problem in this example is finding cause and effect. However, some plausible relationships exist. Assuming a positive relationship between advertising outlay and consumption, if advertising is more effective, a smaller increase in expenditure should lead to an increase in consumption, the conclusion in (A), even though we do not have information about the absolute, base amounts of either advertising or consumption expenditures. If people buy more of a substitute product when its price is lower, then alternative (B) will occur. If canned food is made more available, consumption should increase (C). If consumption of substitute products decreases (E), canned products should increase. However, an increase in can opener production may be a result of increased canned food consumption (D), and not the other way around.

---

32. Inflation rose by 5.1 percent over the second quarter, up from 4.1 percent during the first quarter of the year, and higher than the 3.3 percent recorded during the same time last year. However, the higher price index did not seem to alarm Wall Street, as stock prices remained steady.

Which of the following, if true, could explain this reaction of Wall Street?
(A) Stock prices were steady because of a fear that inflation would continue.
(B) The president announced that he was concerned about rising inflation.
(C) Economists warned that inflation would persist.
(D) Much of the quarterly increase in the price level was due to a summer drought's effect on food prices.
(E) Other unfavorable economic news had overshadowed the fact of inflation.

(D) Answer (D) is most appropriate. If most of the quarterly inflation was due to a rise in food prices caused by a drought, then other prices rose less or no more than in the last quarter. Because the drought is probably a temporary phenomenon, it may be expected that the price level will decline next quarter. A fear that inflation would continue (A), an announcement by the president that he was concerned about inflation (B), economists' warnings about inflation (C), and other unfavorable economic news (E) would all tend to cause stock prices to decline and cause alarm on Wall Street.

---

33. "Ever since I arrived at the college last week, I've been shocked by the poor behavior of students and the unfriendly attitude of the townspeople, but the professors are very erudite and genuinely helpful. Still, I wonder if I should have come here in the first place."

Which of the following, if true, would weaken the student's conclusion that the college may not have been the best choice?
(A) Professors are not always helpful to students.
(B) The college has more than 50,000 students.
(C) The college is far from the student's home.
(D) Not all professors have doctorates.
(E) The narrator was unsure of staying at the college.

(B) If, as the passage states, the narrator spent only a week at a college that has more than 50,000 students, how could he or she possibly draw a conclusion about the entire group. This is an example of an overgeneralization, so choice (B) is correct. Choice (A) would support the conclusion. Choices (C), (D), and (E) are irrelevant to the issue.

★★★ **34.** The senator <u>rose up to say that, in her opinion, she thought the bill should be referred</u> <u>back</u> to committee.

    (A) rose up to say that, in her opinion, she thought the bill should be referred back

    (B) rose up to say that she thought the bill should be referred back

    (C) rose up to say that she thought the bill should be referred

    (D) rose up to say that, in her opinion, the bill should be referred

    (E) rose to say that she thought the bill should be referred

(E) Choices (A), (B), (C), and (D) all say *rose up*, which is redundant. (A) and (B) use another redundant phrase, *referred back*. The phrase *in her opinion* is also unnecessary.

★★★ **35.** I don't know <u>as I concur with your decision to try and</u> run for office.

    (A) since I concur with your decision to try to

    (B) that I concur in your decision to try to

    (C) as I concur in your decision to try to

    (D) that I concur in your decision to try and

    (E) that I concur on your decision to try to

(B) Choice (A) includes the phrase *concur with*, which is incorrect. Choice (C) is wrong because *as* should not appear after the verb *to know*. In addition, the infinitive *try* should be followed by *to*, and one concurs *in* a decision (not *on*), so Choices (D) and (E) are incorrect.

★★☆ **36.** Jones, the president of the union and <u>who is also a member of the community</u> <u>group</u>, will be in charge of the negotiations.

    (A) who is also a member of the community group

    (B) since he is a member of the community group

    (C) a member of the community group

    (D) also being a member of the community group

    (E) in addition, who is a member of the community group

(C) Nouns in apposition must be parallel to one another: "Jones, the *president* . . . and a *member* . . ."

37. A local garbage disposal company increased its profitability even though it reduced its prices in order to attract new customers. This was made possible through the use of automated trucks, thereby reducing the number of workers needed per truck. The company also switched from a concentration on household hauling to a concentration on commercial hauling. As a result of its experience, company management planned to replace all its old trucks and increase the overall size of the truck fleet, doubling hauling capacity.

The company's plan, as outlined above, takes into consideration each of the following EXCEPT
(A) Commercial clients have more potential than household customers.
(B) The demand for garbage removal services is sensitive to price.
(C) Demand for garbage removal services would increase in the future.
(D) Doubling of capacity would not necessitate a substantial increase in the workforce.
(E) Doubling of capacity would not cause bottlenecks, leading to a decrease in productivity.

(E) There is no evidence that the doubling of capacity is linked to productivity. All other answer choices can be inferred. Choice (A) is inferred from the fact that the company switched from household to commercial customers. Choice (B) is inferred from the company's decision to lower charges, which will result in greater demand for its services. Choices (C) and (D) are inferred from the decision to switch to labor-saving trucks.

---

38. Every town with a pool hall has its share of unsavory characters. This is because the pool hall attracts gamblers and all gamblers are unsavory.

Which of the following, if true, cannot be inferred from the above?
(A) All gamblers are unsavory.
(B) All pool halls attract gamblers.
(C) Every town has unsavory characters.
(D) All gamblers are attracted by pool halls.
(E) An explanation of what attracts gamblers.

(C) The statement's conclusion is that all towns have unsavory characters. This conclusion is false. According to the passage, only towns with pool halls have unsavory characters; and since we cannot infer that all towns have pool halls, conclusion (C) is wrong. Alternatives (A) and (B) are stated in the passage, while alternatives (D) and (E) can be deduced. A diagram will help:

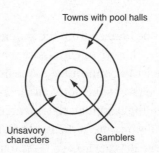

The argument may be summarized as follows:

1. Pool halls attract gamblers.
2. Gamblers are unsavory.
3. *Therefore*, towns with pool halls have unsavory characters.

Check this argument and the diagram with alternative statements in this question.

★★☆ **39.** In an August 2000 poll, 36 percent of voters called themselves Republican or said they were independents leaning toward being Republicans. In November 2004, the Republican figure rose to 47 percent. But in a later survey, the Republicans were down to 38 percent. Therefore, the Democrats are likely to win the next election.

Which of the following, if true, would most seriously weaken the above conclusion?
(A) Republicans were a minority in 2004, but a Republican president was elected.
(B) People tend to switch their votes at the last minute.
(C) People vote for the best candidate, not for a political party.
(D) No one can predict how people will vote.
(E) It has been shown that 85% of Republicans vote in an election, compared to 50% of the Democrats.

(E) 85 percent of 38 percent is 32 percent, while 50 percent of 62 percent is 31 percent; therefore, it can be expected that more Republicans will vote. Alternative (A) shows that even though 47 percent of the voters called themselves Republicans, the Republican Party won the election. In the latest poll, the proportion of Republicans declined to 38 percent. (A) weakens the conclusion but not as strongly as (E). Alternatives (B) and (C) hold equally for both Republicans and Democrats. Alternative (D) weakens the conclusion but not as much as (E); the fact that no one can predict how people will vote does not imply that results cannot be forecast with a high probability.

★★★ **40.** Average family income is right where it was 20 years ago, even though in most families these days, both husbands and wives are working.

The above statement implies all of the following EXCEPT
(A) Even though nominal family income may have increased, prices have risen at an equal rate.
(B) More husbands and wives are working today than 20 years ago.
(C) It was more prevalent for only one spouse to work 20 years ago than it is today.
(D) Wives earn more than husbands today.
(E) Prices were lower 20 years ago.

(D) Alternative (D) cannot be implied from the statement. There is no information in the statement that implies that wives earn more than husbands. Alternative (A) may be implied because as wives contributed to the household nominal income, if prices increased at the same rate as the nominal income, real income stayed the same. Alternatives (B) and (C) are implicit in the statement. If the added income contribution of wives leaves average family income at the level of 20 years ago, then the reason must be that the prices were lower 20 years ago, so (E) is implied.

41. The instructor told the student <u>to hold the club lightly, keeping his eye on the ball,</u> ★ ★ ★
<u>and drawing the club back quickly, but that too much force should not be used</u> on the
downward stroke.

(A) to hold the club lightly, keeping his eye on the ball, and drawing the club back
quickly, but that too much force should not be used

(B) to hold the club lightly, keep his eye on the ball, and drawing the club back quickly,
and that too much force should not be used

(C) to hold the club lightly, keep his eye on the ball, draw the club quickly back, and
not use too much force

(D) to hold the club lightly, keep his eye on the ball, draw the club back quickly and
that too much force should not be used

(E) he should hold the club lightly, keeping his eye on the ball, drawing the club back
quickly, and not using too much force

(C) Four infinitives are in parallel form and much clearer than the mixture of an infinitive (*to hold*), two verbals (*keeping* and *drawing*), and a clause (*too much force should
not be used*).

EVALUATING YOUR SCORE

Tabulate your score for each section of the Diagnostic Test according to the directions on page 11 and record the results in the Self-Scoring Table below. Then find your rating for each score on the Self-Scoring Scale and record it in the appropriate blank.

SELF-SCORING TABLE		
Section	**Score**	**Rating**
Quantitative		
Verbal		

SELF-SCORING SCALE—RATING				
Section	**Poor**	**Fair**	**Good**	**Excellent**
Quantitative	0–15	15–25	26–30	31–37
Verbal	0–15	15–25	26–30	31–41

Find your approximate GMAT score by using the scoring table that follows.

*Important note: Up-to-date scoring guidelines for the Integrated Reasoning section can be found at *mba.com*.

SCORING TABLE

Add the number of correct answers on the Quantitative test and the number of correct answers on the Verbal test to find **T**, your total number of correct answers.

T should be a number less than or equal to 78. Find your equivalent scaled score in the table below.

Again, this table refers to Quantitative and Verbal scores only. For specifics on Integrated Reasoning scoring, go to *mba.com*.

T	Score	T	Score	T	Score	T	Score
78	800	59	660	40	510	21	370
77	790	58	650	39	500	20	360
76	790	57	640	38	490	19	350
75	780	56	630	37	490	18	340
74	770	55	620	36	480	17	340
73	760	54	620	35	470	16	330
72	760	53	610	34	460	15	320
71	750	52	600	33	460	14	310
70	740	51	590	32	450	13	300
69	730	50	580	31	440	12	290
68	720	49	580	30	430	11	280
67	720	48	570	29	430	10	270
66	710	47	560	28	420	9	260
65	700	46	550	27	410	8	250
64	690	45	550	26	400	7	240
63	690	44	540	25	400	6	230
62	680	43	530	24	390	5	220
61	670	42	520	23	380	4	210
60	660	41	520	22	370	<4	200

The following Review sections cover material for each type of question on the GMAT. Spend more time studying those sections for which you had a rating of FAIR or POOR on the Diagnostic Test.

Review

SECTION

Essay Writing

4

→ **THE GMAT ANALYTICAL WRITING ASSESSMENT**

→ **HOW TO WRITE AN ESSAY IN 30 MINUTES**

→ **ANALYSIS OF AN ARGUMENT**

→ **SAMPLE ESSAYS**

THE GMAT ANALYTICAL WRITING ASSESSMENT

The Analytical Writing Assessment (AWA) consists of one essay question, which you will have 30 minutes to complete.

In general, the questions (and the reduction of the number of multiple-choice questions) will probably favor persons accustomed to expressing their thoughts in concise and well-organized written English. The Analytical Writing Assessment will be the first portion of the test administered, so be prepared to start when you are fresh.

Your essay will be scored by two graders, who are college and university instructors from various schools and departments experienced in teaching and evaluating writing, or the essay will be scored by computer. Essays are scored "holistically," which means that it will be assigned one score (between 0 and 6, with 0 being the lowest and 6 the highest) by each reader, based on its overall quality. The two scores for your essay are averaged to produce the writing score, which is reported on a scale of 0 to 6, rounded off to the nearest half point.

Writing an Essay

Many students dread the thought of writing an essay on an assigned topic, but it need not be that difficult. Writing an essay that will receive a holistic score of 4, 5, or even 6 requires no more than some common sense, a little on-the-spot planning, familiarity with the standards of written English, and a healthy amount of practice. Indeed, the best way to improve your writing ability is through practice. The more you write, the more comfortable and confident you become with the process.

This chapter cannot substitute for a writing course or for a lifetime of practice, but it will outline some helpful points and strategies for improving your writing and scoring higher on the GMAT Analytical Writing Assessment.

The Essay Topic

The essay question on the GMAT requires you to analyze an argument. You will be expected to explore some complexities of the topic, to take a position, and to demonstrate critical reasoning abilities. The questions will not require you to have any pre-existing knowledge of the subject or any specific business training or experience. Some topics may relate to business, but others will be about areas of general interest or current events and issues.

General Strategy

The most important thing your essay must do is take a position. Even if you are not entirely sure that you would always agree with that position, *take a position*. You are not deciding on an irrevocable course in life—you are writing an essay to be assessed on the basis of how well it is written. Support your position with examples organized in a logical order; restate your position in a conclusion. Remember that there are no right or wrong answers to these questions, just well-written or poorly written ones. Don't try to guess what the graders' feelings about the issue might be so you can agree. Take a position upon which you can develop examples and supportive arguments. Make it a specific position; don't try to be too broad: it is much easier to put together ideas about banning automatic assault rifles than it is to discuss the use or misuse of firearms in general.

The second most important thing your essay needs is good organization. Stop and plan before you begin writing. Place your arguments or examples in the most logical order and provide reasonable transitions between them. Usually, three examples are enough.

Finally, you need to concentrate on writing a good beginning and a good conclusion. Your opening sets the stage and draws the reader in; your conclusion clinches your point and leaves your argument fresh in the graders' minds when they assign a score.

> ### OVERALL STRATEGY
>
> 1. Narrow the topic.
> 2. Take a position.
> 3. Use three examples or points and connect them logically.
> 4. Write a good, interesting opening and a strong, memorable conclusion.

HOW TO WRITE AN ESSAY IN 30 MINUTES

Don't be misled by the title of this section. It promises more than it can deliver. For one thing, writing an essay in 30 minutes may be a contradiction in terms. An essay is essentially the product of a writer's thinking about a topic. It expresses a point of view arrived at after reflection, analysis, or interpretation of a subject or issue. When you are given an assignment only 30 minutes before the essay is due, you can't expect to pore over the topic for long. If you think too deeply, before you know it you'll have thought the allotted time away.

A second reason to distrust the title is that no one learns to write well by reading a "how-to" book on the subject. You learn essay writing by taking a pen in hand, by messing around with ideas and words, and by experimenting, practicing, and doing. Many of the in-class essays you've had to produce for social science or humanities courses have probably been good training for the kind of instant essay required by the GMAT Analytical Writing Assessment. In your classes, though, success was often determined by how closely your essay resembled what the teacher had in mind. That's not true on the GMAT, which won't give you a topic with a predetermined answer. You can't study for this essay writing test the way you can study calculus or Spanish. What you need to know is already lodged inside you. The task you face on test day is to organize your ideas and put them into readable form on a piece of paper, which takes practice, practice, practice. Just as athletic skills improve with repetition, so do essay writing skills. All you need each time you schedule a writing session is 30 minutes.

The next several pages will take you inside essay writing. By entering the territory, you won't become a world-class author of essays, but you'll see what most good writers do as they write essays. You'll be shown what works and what to watch out for.

Principles of Good Writing

Success in essay writing depends in large measure on how completely you can master the following guidelines:

1. Study the topic closely.
2. Narrow the topic unmercifully.
3. Decide what point(s) to make about the topic.
4. Collect ideas and arrange them in order.
5. Start with an appealing and informative introduction.
6. Develop your ideas fully with specific examples and details.
7. Guide readers with transitions.
8. Use words that are plain, precise, lively, and fresh.
9. Omit needless words.
10. Vary your sentences.
11. End your essay unforgettably.
12. Follow the conventions of standard English.

Refer to these guidelines often. If your writing usually demonstrates mastery of these principles, you're undoubtedly a terrific writer. To be a still better one, though, you must know that occasionally one or more of the principles ought to be set aside. When a principle leads you to say something barbaric, ignore it for the time being. Let your intuition and good judgment guide you instead. The principles, after all, merely describe what most good writers do; they are not commandments.

Through experience, accomplished essayists have absorbed good writing habits into their craft. Professionals needn't be reminded, for example, to cut needless words from their writing or to prefer the plain word to the pompous one.

The Process of Writing an Essay

To start, plan what to do during each stage of the process. The first stage, *prewriting*, consists of all you do before you actually begin writing the text of your essay. During the second stage, *composing*, you are choosing the words and forming the sentences that contain your thoughts. And finally, during the *revising and proofreading* stage, polish and refine the text of your essay word by word, making it true, clear, and graceful. Actually, the lines between the stages are not at all distinct. Sometimes it helps to put words on paper during the prewriting stage. Writers compose, revise, and proofread simultaneously. New ideas may sprout at any time. No stage really ends until the final period of the last sentence is securely in place—or until time is up.

In spite of the blurry boundaries between the stages of the writing process, it pays to keep the functions of each stage in mind as you study in detail how the dozen principles of good writing contribute to the growth of a successful essay.

1. STUDY THE TOPIC CLOSELY

Obviously, your work on the GMAT essay question should start with a meticulous reading of the topic. Read it more than once, underscoring key ideas and words until you know it intimately. If in doubt, read it again.

Here is a typical essay topic for your scrutiny.

EXAMPLE

Concerned about the survival of democracy, the president of the University of Chicago, Robert Maynard Hutchings, once wrote, "The death of democracy is not likely to be an assassination from ambush. It will be a slow extinction from apathy, indifference, and undernourishment." However, the history of the United States also contains examples of commitment, defiance, and passion that led to change.

While democracy may still be alive and well, situations often arise that do not coincide with the democratic principles on which America was founded. Using examples based on your studies, reading, or on personal experience, write an essay that illustrates your view on the current health of democracy.

Before reading the explanation, briefly write your understanding of what the topic asks you to do:

_____

_____

_____

_____

_____

Explanation: The basic task is clearly spelled out in the last clause: *write an essay that illustrates your view on the current health of democracy.* The prompt and everything else merely creates a context for the task and provides some general clues to the meaning of "health of democracy." Other essential information is that the essay must use examples drawn from your studies—that is, course work or independent study; your reading, which includes fiction and nonfiction read for school or on your own; or relevant personal experiences.

All told, the topic gives students considerable leeway for interpretation. In fact, lengthy and complicated topics like this one often encourage students to blaze their own trails. Shorter topics, on the other hand, often tighten the reins on creativity.

Although writing about one's experience has a lot of merit, not every GMAT question allows students to write a personal response. But when possible, it's an option that may be too good to refuse, especially when the topic leaves you cold. Students are leading authorities on their own lives and times. With a little finesse, almost any topic on the GMAT can be shaped into an interesting and readable personal essay.

2. NARROW THE TOPIC UNMERCIFULLY

Because a GMAT topic must suit a multiethnic, multicultural, and multitalented student audience, it is bound to be very broad. Your first job is to reduce it to a size snug enough to fit the time and space allotted. In fact, the quality of the essay you write could depend on how narrowly you define the topic. Think small. A cosmic approach won't work, and you are not likely to err by narrowing the topic too much. If you were to run out of things to say about a narrowed topic, the simple solution would be to expand the main idea in midstream, a far easier task than hacking away at an overweight topic after you've already filled most of a page.

It would be beyond the hope and talent of most students to compose a substantive 300 or 400 word essay on such topics as *democracy*, *psychology*, or *jazz*—subjects so vast you could probably fill a barn with books about them. The same holds true for any general subject, from *alcoholism* to *zoology*. Therefore, to keep your essay from being stuck in a mess of generalities, narrow the topic ruthlessly.

Try building a ladder of abstraction. Start at the top with the most general word. As you descend the ladder, make each rung increasingly specific. When you reach the bottom, you may have a topic sufficient for a short essay. Here are some examples:

SUBJECT: *Democracy*

Democracy	*Highest level of abstraction*
Democracy in conflict with totalitarianism	*Too broad for a short essay*
People's rights vs. government control	*Still too broad*
Freedom of press vs. government restrictions	*Still too broad*
The right to print opinions vs. censorship	*Still broad, but getting there*
The right to print a scandalous story in a school newspaper	*Possible topic for a short essay*
What happened to Pete when *The Globe* published a story about incompetent teachers	*Distinct possibility for an essay*

SUBJECT: *Alcoholism*

Alcoholism	*Highest level of abstraction*
The effects of alcoholism on society	*Extremely broad for a short essay*
Family problems resulting from alcoholism	*Still too broad*
Alcoholism as a cause of broken families	*Very broad, but getting closer*
The effects of alcoholism on children from broken homes	*Good only for a lengthy research paper*
The experience of Betsy G., the daughter of an alcoholic	*A definite topic for a short essay*

Each subject has been pared down to a scale appropriate for a GMAT essay. Topics on the bottom rungs offer students a chance to write a thorough essay. Focusing on a single idea may deny them the chance to demonstrate the scope of their knowledge. The GMAT, however, is not a place to show off breadth, but rather to display depth. Business school applications show breadth. For the present, it's depth that counts.

PRACTICE IN NARROWING TOPICS

Reduce several of the following subjects to a level of specificity concise enough to be used for a GMAT essay. Try constructing a ladder of abstraction for each one. Put the broadest topic on the top. Don't stop descending until you have a topic suitable for a short essay.

Youth and Age	Calamities
Procrastination	Probability
Jealousy	Truth
Taking Risks	Style
Change vs. Permanence	Wonder

SUBJECT: *Zoology*

Zoology	*Highest level of abstraction*
The study of mammals	*Too broad*
The study of primates	*Still very broad*
Researching the behavior of chimpanzees	*Still too broad*
Teaching of chimps	*Still rather broad*
Training chimps to distinguish colors	*A reasonable topic*
My job in the primate lab working on the color recognition project	*A fine topic for a short paper*

3. DECIDE WHAT POINT(S) TO MAKE ABOUT THE TOPIC

An essay needs a point. Nothing will disappoint a reader more than arriving at the end only to discover that the essay lacks a point. Essays may be written with beautiful words, contain profound thoughts, and make readers laugh or weep. But without a point, sometimes called a *main idea* or a *thesis*, an essay remains just words in search of a meaning. After they've finished, readers may scratch their heads, say "Huh?" and resent having wasted their time. Don't confuse the topic of an essay with its point, for even a pointless essay is likely to be about something. But a topic isn't enough. An essay must also say something about its topic. It can be basically factual, but it should express a point of view about an issue.

Finding a Point for Your GMAT Essay

TOPIC: The topic will be given to you in the instructions for writing the essay.

Purpose: The purpose of the essay will be explained by the wording of the topic. Look for such words as *describe, compare, contrast, persuade, explain, report, analyze,* and *interpret.* Each requires a slightly different response. Or the purpose of the essay may be left up to you.

Point: The point is the essay's main idea or thesis, or what the essay demonstrates, proves, or argues.

Even if you have no particular opinion on a certain topic, the hard fact is that you must still try to create the illusion that you care deeply about the issue. Doing so may rub your conscience the wrong way, but rather than raise a stink, which won't get you anywhere, make the best of it. This time go along to get along. Don't regard it as a cop-out. Rather, consider it a survival tactic, a challenge to your resilience and creativity, qualities that schools and businesses seek and admire.

Faced with the prospect of writing an essay about a topic that leaves you cold, you have some choices to make: Fake it, fight it, drop it, or psych yourself to do the best you can.

TIP

Above all, your essay must take a stand on an argument.

1. **Fake it.**   Writing to say something even when you have nothing to say inevitably leads to words on a page that sound forced, like a conversation you might have with an aging aunt at Thanksgiving. Not a good choice.

2. **Fight it.**   Some resentful students turn on the test or the test makers by attacking the admissions testing system in America. They write statements declaring their refusal to participate in a dehumanizing charade that fails to take into account each student as a unique individual. After the test, such students may feel relieved for having spoken their minds, but their position also will have irreparably damaged their chances of being admitted to the school of their choice. While admissions officials generally approve of individual initiative and an independent spirit, they won't bother with students who respond defiantly to a GMAT essay question. Not a good choice.

3. **Drop it.**   Although this is the only foolproof way to keep yourself from writing a pointless essay, it's not a viable option when you're striving for good grades and high test scores. Not a good choice.

4. **Psych yourself.**   This is the most promising solution. Begin by asking yourself ten or a dozen questions about the topic. Start with easy questions and work toward the harder ones.

Here, for example, are questions on the general topic

Dangerous Pursuits:
   What are some dangerous pursuits?
   Why do some people go bungee jumping?
   Why don't I go bungee jumping?
   Why does my cousin Henry go?

After a while, the questions and answers become more provocative:

   When is it okay to gamble with your life?
   Does the state have the right to forbid you from
      risking your life?
   At what point in lawmaking does the government
      overstep its bounds?

Obviously, at the beginning of a 30-minute essay test, you won't have time to ask and answer dozens of questions, but the more thoughts you can generate, the richer your writing will be.

If self-psyching fails to work, try this alternative: As rapidly as possible write a list of anything, literally anything, that might qualify as a response to the topic. Like pulling a stopper, making a list often starts the flow of ideas. Your mind makes connections as one idea calls up memories of another, and then another. Don't be particular. After a short time, review the list and choose the idea that holds promise for your essay. Even if the list doesn't thrill you, pick the least objectionable item and begin to write on it. Who knows, you may have accidentally stumbled upon a rich lode of ideas. Writers often discover what they really want to say only after they've written for a while, even as long as 10 minutes. After that, time and space won't permit a complete rewrite, but a few crucial sentences could change the emphasis of what they've written, and they can quickly relocate ideas and restructure their essays with neatly drawn arrows.

Sometimes a better thesis suddenly swims into view halfway through the test. Should you change course or stick with what you have? It takes courage to return to "Go" and to start over. Because of time and space restraints on the GMAT, a switch could be fatal. In general, the new idea ought to be out of this world to justify trashing what you've written.

If you find yourself in such a predicament, don't switch unless you'll never again be able to look yourself in the eye. Grit your teeth and finish what you began. Resist the temptation to shift from your original idea even if you don't believe in it anymore. You won't be penalized for hypocrisy, but you will surely damage your essay with a confusing or ambivalent presentation.

Normally, the wording of a GMAT essay question forces you to take a position on the issue or topic. It might say to you directly, "State your opinion," or ask "Do you agree or disagree?" Your view then becomes the point, or thesis, of your essay. In the essay itself the thesis is usually stated outright in a simple declarative sentence, as in these examples:

TOPIC: Democracy   Thesis: Democracy is a far more cumbersome form of government than dictatorship.
TOPIC: Psychology   Thesis: In the discipline of children, instilling a fear of punishment is more effective than promising a reward.
TOPIC: War   Thesis: War is hell.

On the other hand, the thesis of an essay may be so strongly implied by the cumulative weight of evidence that stating the thesis is unnecessary. Whichever way you decide to inform the reader of your essay's thesis—by announcing it directly or by weaving it subtly into the fabric of the text—be sure to lock onto it as you write. Let it guide you from the opening lines to your conclusion. Omit material that causes the essay to wander from its point. Readers will appreciate an essay that rarely deviates from a well-defined path.

4. COLLECT IDEAS AND ARRANGE THEM IN ORDER

Unless you are blessed with a lightning-quick mind that instantly analyzes issues and draws conclusions in a logical sequence, you'll have to gather and organize ideas for your essay the way ordinary mortals do. You'll search your knowledge and experience for ideas and examples to support your thesis. You'll keep them in mind as you write, note them on paper as you think of them, or prepare a sketchy outline. Jotting down a brief list of ideas that occur to you, or possibly preparing a sketchy outline, is all it takes.

While you reflect on your jottings, a better thesis may come to mind, or you may run into new ideas that bolster your first one. Before you write a word on your answer sheet, though, you probably should devote at least a few minutes to collecting your thoughts. Obviously, on the GMAT, you'll have to think rapidly, but better in haste than not at all.

The Formula

Most essays are variations and adaptations of the formula. Using the formula will not make your prose immortal, but it could help turn a muddle of words into a model of clear thinking. The formula is simply an all-purpose plan for putting ideas into a clear, easy-to-follow order. It uses a beginning, a middle, and an end. It's not sensational, but it works for virtually any essay. Its greatest virtue is simplicity. Each part has its place and purpose within the essay:

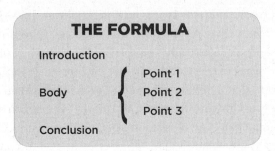

THE FORMULA

Introduction

Body { Point 1 / Point 2 / Point 3

Conclusion

The formula prescribes a three-stage structure for an essay. It also requires a body consisting of three points. Why three? Mainly because three is a number that works. If you can make three different statements about a topic, you probably know what you're talking about. One is too simple, two is better but is still shallow. Three, however, is thoughtful. It suggests depth. Although every short essay needn't include three points to support its thesis, three carries a voice of authority. If you can't think of three, stick with two, and don't make up a third that is simply a rehash of one of the first two disguised as something new. Psychologically, three also creates a sense of wholeness for the reader, like the beginning, middle, and end of a story. It's no accident that the number three recurs in all literature, from *The Three Little Pigs* to *The Bible*.

The order of ideas is important too. What comes first? Second? Third? The best order is the clearest order, the arrangement that readers can follow with the least effort. No plan is superior to another provided you have a valid reason for using it. The plan least likely to succeed is the aimless one, the one in which you state and develop ideas in the random order they happened to come to mind. It's better to rank your ideas in the order of importance. Decide which provides the strongest support of your thesis. Although your best argument may be listed first in your notes, save it for last on the essay. Giving it away at the start is self-defeating, because everything that follows will be anticlimactic. In other words, work toward your best point, not away from it. An excellent way to plot three good ideas is to lead with your second best, save your best for the end, and sandwich your least powerful idea between the others. This structure recognizes that the end and the beginning of an essay are its critical parts. A good opening draws the reader in and creates an all-important first impression, but a memorable ending, coming last, is what readers have fresh in their minds when they assign you a grade.

TIP

Be sure to write a powerful ending.

5. START WITH AN APPEALING AND INFORMATIVE INTRODUCTION

The opening lines of an essay tell readers what to expect. If the opening is dull or confusing, readers will brace themselves for a less than thrilling reading experience. Some essays become clear and engaging by the second paragraph, but an essay with an unimaginative start begins with a handicap, and the writer will have to work that much harder to overcome the reader's first impressions.

It pays, therefore, to write an opening that stops readers in their tracks. Begin with something to lure the reader into the piece. Use a hook—a phrase, sentence, or idea to grab your readers so firmly that they'll desperately want to read on. Hooks must be very crisp, very clean. They must surprise, inform, or tickle the reader in an instant, and say "Read on; you'll be glad you did." A dull hook just won't do. In a short essay, a hook can't take up more than a couple of lines. Anything longer will erode the heart of the essay.

A concise one-sentence opening is probably harder to write than a longer one. In other words, you can't fool around when space is tight. It's not unheard of for students, smitten with an inventive idea, to write half a page before they start to deal directly with the topic. Some students need that much space to put their thoughts in order. Either way, on the GMAT, beware of an introduction that drags on.

Beware also of openings that are too cute or too precious, as in

Little did George Washington know as he sat sipping a brew on the veranda at Mount Vernon with his little woman Martha beside him, that . . .

Be thoughtful and clever, yes, but not obnoxious. Above all, steer clear of an all-inclusive opening that grandiloquently reviews the history of humankind in fifteen words or less, as in

Throughout recorded time, humanity has struggled to keep the flame of freedom alive, . . .

Be intelligent and perceptive, yes, but not pompous.

Techniques for pulling readers into the body of an essay are unlimited. Yet many successful openings are merely unique variations of one of these popular formats:

1. Begin with a brief incident or anecdote that relates to the point of your essay.

   When Joan S. entered Springdale College early last September, she didn't know that she had left her constitutional rights at the campus gate.

2. State a provocative idea in an ordinary way or an ordinary idea in a provocative way. Either will arrest the reader's interest.

   That a person is supposed to be innocent until proven guilty is an alien concept in my university.

3. Use a quote from the test question, Bruce Springsteen, or any other source—maybe even your grandmother. But be sure the quote relates to the topic of your essay and says it better than you can.

   "All animals are equal, but some animals are more equal than others." George Orwell said that.

4. Knock down a commonly held assumption or define a word in a new and startling way.

   When Ulov, a Russian immigrant, arrived in Shaftsbury, Vermont, he learned that freedom does not mean cutting down a neighbor's maple tree.

5. Ask an interesting question or two, which you will answer in your essay.

   Is true democracy possible? Or is it just an ideal to work for?

6. Make an unexpected connection between your topic and a bit of culture. By offering readers a second layer of meaning, your writing is enriched.

    We'll get by with a little help from our friends. That, at least, was the hope of Hurricane Andrew's victims after the winds died down.

7. Create suspense by waiting until the end of your opening passage to reveal your topic.

    Matt Damon takes his everywhere, while Julia Roberts takes hers to bed. Rob Lowe keeps one in each Porsche, and Jennifer Jason-Leigh has one made of gold. Happiness, for all these stars, depends on having a cell phone at their fingertips.

If none of these techniques works for you, or if you don't have time on the GMAT to devise a good hook, rely on the direct approach. Just declare your thesis right up front. But don't phrase it like an announcement, as in "In this essay, I am going to prove that democracy is not dead." State your point, as in "Democracy is far from dead," and take it from there.

If at first you can't find a suitable opening, don't put off writing the rest of your essay. Just skip a few lines and begin with the body of your essay. As you write, a pleasing opening idea might strike you. Add it later. Whatever you do, though, be sure that your opening fits your writing style and personality. Work hard to get it right, but not so hard that it will seem forced or too cute or too long. Ideally, it should introduce your topic so naturally and unobtrusively that readers will not even realize that they are being enticed into reading past the first sentence.

6. DEVELOP YOUR IDEAS FULLY WITH SPECIFIC EXAMPLES AND DETAILS

Precise, well-documented information is far more convincing than general and unsubstantiated opinion. In an essay, the information used to give credence to the writer's main point is commonly called *development*. Because development indicates how deeply a student can think—a matter of great concern to business schools—it counts heavily in grading GMAT essays. Development does not mean number of words. An essay of a thousand words can still be underdeveloped. Some students, unaware of the difference between development and throwing the bull, fill their essays with verbal waste. They write even when they have nothing to say. Perhaps you've done it yourself on occasion. Be assured that essays short on development but long on refuse will be found wanting by GMAT readers, who know bull when they see it.

Nor is development simply the range of evidence summoned to uphold a thesis. Not every good essay needs, say, three or five or a dozen supporting ideas. The fact is that superior development skills can be demonstrated on the GMAT with a single vivid example. It's depth that counts.

Each paragraph in your essay should contribute to the development of the main idea. It should contain facts, data, arguments, examples—testimony of all kinds to corroborate the thesis. If you are unsure how a particular paragraph lends support to the thesis, cross it out or revise it. If you're perplexed, just imagine how your readers will feel. Be merciless with your writing. Even though you may admire a paragraph, give it the boot if it doesn't help to make your case.

A paragraph indentation ordinarily signals readers to get ready for a change in thought or idea. Yet not every new paragraph signals a drastic change in direction. It may simply move the essay ahead one small step at a time. Paragraphs also permit readers to skim your writing. Readers in a hurry focus on opening and closing sentences and skip what lies between, but you can force readers to slow down by varying the location of the most important idea in each paragraph, usually called the *topic sentence*.

While topic sentences come in assorted guises, they share a common trait. They are helpful in keeping both writers and readers on the track. When you write, assume that readers have a poor sense of direction. Given half a chance, they'll lose their way. Therefore, remind them often of where they are. Lead them with topic sentences, but be sure that whatever you say in the rest of the paragraph supports what the topic sentence says.

7. GUIDE READERS WITH TRANSITIONS

Readers need to be guided through an essay. Consider them visitors in a strange place. As the writer you must show them around by setting up verbal guideposts. Tell them where they are going, show them their progress, and remind them often of the destination. If you've done your job, they should be ready for what they find at the end. By repeatedly alluding to the main idea, you'll not only compel readers to focus on your point, but you'll keep readers at your side from start to finish.

Help readers along, too, by choosing words that establish relationships between one thought and the next. This can be done with words such as *this*, which happens to tie the sentence you are reading to the one before. (The word *too* in the first sentence of this paragraph serves the same function; it serves as a link between this and the earlier paragraph.) The English language is rich with words and phrases that serve to tie sentences and ideas together. Here is a brief thesaurus of common transitions grouped according to their customary use. With a bit of thought, you probably can think of others.

When you **ADD** ideas	*in addition, furthermore, moreover, further, besides, too, also, and then, then too, again, next, secondly, equally important*
When you **COMPARE or CONTRAST**	*similarly, likewise, in comparison, in like manner, however, in contrast, conversely, on the other hand, but, nevertheless, and yet, even so, still*
When you cite an **EXAMPLE**	*for example, for instance*
When you **REINFORCE** an idea	*indeed, in fact, as a matter of fact, to be sure, of course, in any event, by all means*
When you show **RESULTS**	*as a result, as a consequence, consequently, therefore, thus, hence, accordingly*
When you express a **SEQUENCE** or the passing of **TIME**	*soon after, then, previously, meanwhile, in the meantime, later, at length, after a while, immediately, next*
When you show **PROXIMITY**	*here, nearby, at this spot, near at hand, in this vicinity, on the opposite side, across from, adjacent to, not far from*
When you **CONCLUDE**	*finally, in short, in other words, in a word, to sum up, in conclusion, in the end*

Not every sentence needs to be tied to the previous one with a particular transitional word or phrase. The ideas themselves sometimes create a natural link.

Whenever you use a transition to tie one sentence to another, you do your readers a favor. You guarantee them a smooth trip through your essay. Otherwise, each sentence stands like a disconnected link in a chain, and readers bump along, often losing the point you are trying to make. Although many sentences won't contain transitions, three or four sentences in succession without a link of some sort may leave readers doubting that this trip is worth taking.

8. USE WORDS THAT ARE PLAIN, PRECISE, LIVELY, AND FRESH

Use Plain Words

That's a principle easy to say but hard to live by when you're hoping to impress readers with your intellect and sophistication. Yet nothing, truly nothing, conveys your erudition better than plain words. However big your vocabulary, never use a complex word on the GMAT essay to show off. You'll get no extra credit for an essay crammed with ornate, multisyllabic words used for no other purpose than to sound ornate and multisyllabic. There's always a risk, in fact, that words that sound profound to you may seem pompous to your readers. Or worse, they could make you appear foolish.

The student who wrote, "I am of the opinion that a prerequisite for parenthood includes disbursement of penal adjudication among siblings with an even, dispassionate hand," needs a basic lesson in plain writing. How much clearer to have written, "I think that good parents should know how to be fair in disciplining their children" or "I think that being equally strict with all their children is a prerequisite of being good parents." Words should be like gifts, carefully chosen to give pleasure to someone you like. High gloss is not a measure of value. You won't gain much by dressing ordinary ideas in fancy robes or from trying to appear more impressive than you already are.

This admonition to use plain words, however, shouldn't be regarded as a license to use current, everyday slang or street talk in your essays. Spoken language, which contains many colorful words and expressions like *chill*, *pig out*, *dissed*, and *freak out*, has its place, but its place is not in a GMAT essay unless you definitely need current lingo to create an effect that you can't get any other way. If you must write slang terms, don't highlight them with quotation marks. Why call attention to the fact that you can't think of standard or more original words?

Use plain words even for profound thoughts—correction, *especially* for profound thoughts. By writing "I think. Therefore, I am," the seventeenth-century philosopher René Descartes reshaped the way humans think about existence. He could have used more exotic words, of course, words more in keeping with the florid writing style of his time, but his statement probably derives its power from its simplicity. A sign of true intelligence is the ability to convey deep meanings with simple words.

Simple doesn't necessarily mean short. It's true that the plain words tend to be the short ones, but not always. The word *fid* is short, but it's not plain, unless you are a sailor, in which case you'd know that a fid supports the mast on your boat or is used to pry open a tight knot in your lines. On the other hand, *spontaneously* is five syllables long. Yet it is a plain and simple word because of its frequent use. It springs, well, spontaneously from the mouth.

For any GMAT essay, a plain, conversational style is appropriate. The language should sound like you. In formal writing, custom requires you to remove yourself from stage center and focus on the subject matter. At some point in your schooling, you may have been warned never to use "I" in an essay. That caveat may apply to some forms of exposition, but not to GMAT essays. In fact, GMAT topics often encourage first-person responses by asking you to state your opinion or preference. How do you do that without using "I"? It can be done,

TIP

Be yourself when you write. Your writing will come across as genuine.

of course, by using pronouns like *one*, as in "When *one* is getting ready for graduate school, *one* sometimes writes funny," or *you*, as in "Sometimes *you* feel like a dope," or by avoiding pronouns altogether. But an essay that expresses the writer's personal opinion will sound a lot more natural when cast in the first-person singular.

GMAT essay readers are old hands at rooting pretense out of student writing. Unless students are exceptionally astute, they usually give themselves away by using elaborate words that fall a mite short of precise diction. Writers who leave no clue that they are posing as bright, witty, clever, articulate people, on the other hand, are probably bright, witty, clever, and articulate enough to write essays in their natural voice, so why pretend?

The point is, don't be phony! Just let your genuine voice ring out, although the way you speak is not necessarily the way you should write. Most speaking is vague, clumsy, confused, and wordy. Consider writing as the casual speech of someone who speaks exceedingly well. It's grammatically correct and is free of pop expressions and clichés. Think of it as the kind of speech expected of you in an interview. Or maybe even the way this paragraph sounds. You could do a lot worse!

Use Precise Words

Hazy, vague, and abstract words fade as quickly from a reader's memory as last night's dream. They indicate a lack of clear and precise thinking. How much easier it is to say that a book is *good*, *interesting*, or *exciting* than to search for words that will precisely describe the book's appeal. Similarly, it's more convenient to resort to words like *nice, fine, stupid, boring*, and *pretty* than to explain in detail what you mean by each word. But to write something that will stick in a reader's mind, use well-defined, hard-edged words. Exact words help you express exact thoughts. To write precisely is to write with pictures, sounds, and actions that are as vivid in words as in reality. Exact words leave a distinct mark; general ones, only a blurry impression.

Good writers often experience the world more intensely than other people. Like artists, they think visually. They listen hard to the sounds and voices around them and are extra-sensitive to smells, to tastes, and to the feel of things. They keep their senses at full throttle in order, as the writer James Baldwin once said, "to describe things which other people are too busy to describe." They understand that good writing must sometimes appeal to their readers' senses.

To evoke a strong response from your readers, make use of the principle that a picture is worth a thousand words. Actually, whether it's more or less than a thousand is debatable, but the point is clear: words should help readers *see*. Therefore, *show* more than you *tell*! Instead of describing your uncle as "absent-minded," show him stepping into his morning shower with his pajamas on. Rather than saying that your room is a "mess," show the pile of wrinkled clothes in the corner and the books and Snickers wrappers scattered on the floor next to your unmade bed. The same principle applies to smells: "Her breath was foul with a stale whiskey stench"; to sounds: "the hum and throb of big machines in the distance"; to touch: "the feel of cool, linen bedsheets"; and to tastes: "a cold, sweet drink of clear water on a hot day." In short, by writing vividly, you prevent readers from misinterpreting what you have to say.

Essays bogged down in detail no doubt grow tedious both to read and to write. Authors need to choose what readers need to see and know. Excessive analysis is boring, but so is too little. A balance is best. No one can tell you precisely how to achieve the balance. The feel of what seems right takes time and practice. In the end, the content and purpose of an essay will have to determine how detailed it needs to be. Every time you mention a meal, it's not necessary to recite the menu unless there's a good reason for doing so. When you use an abstract word, ask what is more important, to give details to readers or to push on to other matters? The context, as well as your judgment and experience as a writer, will determine what you can expect readers to understand. To get the knack a little more quickly, reread any interesting passage from a book or other publication. Pick out the details and the broad statements. What did the passage show, and what did it tell? Since the passage held your interest, perhaps you will have found a model worth emulating in your own writing.

By no means does this plea for verbal precision suggest that abstract words be eliminated from the language. After all, we need them to talk to each other about *beauty, love, fairness, satisfaction, power, enlightenment,* and thousands of other notions that exist in our hearts and minds. The ability to think abstractly, to invent theories, to express feelings, and to articulate ideals and lofty principles is a gift that separates human beings from all other creatures, and we should delight in it, but remember that most readers are an impatient lot. They will reject essays that don't, at some point, come down to earth.

Use Lively Language

Active and Passive Verbs: Unlike the machine-scored multiple-choice questions, your GMAT essay will be read by people—real people with feelings, moods, likes and dislikes, and the capacity to laugh, grow angry, and be moved. They are usually teachers who know that student writing can be lively, interesting, and clear. Like any readers, they will be put off by writing that is dull.

The most efficient way to inject life into your writing is to pay close attention to your choice of verbs. Verbs, as you've no doubt been taught, show action or state of being. To a writer, the fact that verbs show action is extremely important. Active verbs stimulate interest by waking up the language. They create movement, perform, stir things up, and move around. They excel all other words in their power to restore life to lifeless prose. They add energy and vitality to sentences, and, as a bonus, they help you to write more economically.

While *active* verbs are full of life, *being* verbs are not. They stagnate. They don't do anything but connect one thought to another, especially forms of the verb *to be: is, are, was, were, am, has been, had been, will be.* When used in sentences, each of these being verbs joins a subject to a predicate, and that's all. In fact, the verb *to be* in all its forms acts much like a verbal equal sign, as in "Seven plus three *is* ten" (7 + 3 = 10) or "Sam *is* a genius" (Sam = genius), or "Your GMAT score *is* going up" (That = good news!). Because *being* verbs (and equal signs) show little life, use active verbs whenever possible.

Here are some ways to pump life into sluggish sentences:

1. Try to substitute an active verb drawn from another word in the sentence.

> BEING VERB: Monica and Phil *were* the highest scorers on the GMAT practice test.
> ACTIVE VERB: Monica and Phil *scored* highest on the GMAT practice test.
> The verb *scored* has been drawn from the noun *scorers.*
> Active verbs may also be extracted from adjectives:

> BEING VERB: Achievement *is* the determining factor in GMAT grades.
> ACTIVE VERB: Achievement *determines* GMAT grades.

The verb *determines* has been drawn from the adjective *determining.*

2. Sometimes it's preferable to find an altogether new verb:

> BEING VERB: It *is* logical that admission to business school is the result of a student's effort and achievement.
>
> ACTIVE VERB: Logic *dictates* that a student's effort and achievement lead to business school admission.

Being verbs are perfectly acceptable in speech and writing. We can hardly get along without them. But use them sparingly in your essays. As a rule of thumb, if more than one in four of your sentences relies on a form of the verb *to be* as its main verb, you may be depending excessively on passive verbs.

When you start to weed *being* verbs out of your writing, you're likely to find that some sentences resist easy change. Some need to be thoroughly recast. Subjects become verbs, verbs turn into nouns, unnecessary phrases are eliminated entirely—alterations that result in sentences that bear little resemblance to the original. At the same time, though, your writing may get an unexpected lift. Verb-swapping tends to eliminate needless words, thereby improving your writing.

Once you get into the habit of clearing dead verbs out of your prose, you may notice that certain nouns limit your options for using active verbs. That is, certain nouns, when used as the subject of a sentence, determine your chances for finding a lively verb. Some abstract nouns, in fact, cut the choices drastically. Take, for example, sentences starting with "The reason," as in "The reason for taking the GMAT is . . ." Verb choices are also severely reduced by subject nouns like *thought, idea, issue, way, notion, concept,* or any other essentially abstract nouns. The same holds true for sentences that begin with "There," as in "There are 2,400 colleges in America," and often for sentences that begin with "It," as in "It is difficult to choose just one." On the other hand, nouns that name people, places, concrete objects, or events almost cry out for active verbs. When the subject can perform an action, like a person, for instance, you'll never run out of verb choices.

As these examples illustrate, whenever you insert a concrete, easy-to-define noun in place of an abstraction, you are apt to write a tighter, more energetic, and more readable sentence.

> ABSTRACT: The *cause* of the strike was the students' demand for freedom.
> DEFINITE: The *students* struck for freedom.

> ABSTRACT: The *way* to the dean's office is down the next corridor.
> DEFINITE: The next *corridor* goes to the dean's office.

> ABSTRACT: *There* are students who are good in chemistry but not in physics.
> DEFINITE: Some *students* excel in chemistry but not in physics.

Being verbs are not the only verbs that sap the life out of sentences. They share that distinction with several other verbs, such as any form of *to have, to come, to go, to make, to move,* and *to get.* They are convenient and versatile, but because of constant use, such verbs pale next to more animated verbs. But, like *being* verbs, they are indispensable. When they show up in your writing, stick with them only if you can swear that no other words will do. Unless they fit perfectly, however, trade them in for better, livelier ones.

> DULL: The line to the lunch counter *moved* very slowly.
> LIVELY: The line *crept* (crawled, poked, inched) to the lunch counter.

Note that by using a more animated verb, you eliminate the need for "very slowly," which would be redundant.

> DULL: The dean *gave* permission to the students to eat in the staff room.
>
> LIVELY: The dean *permitted* the students to eat in the staff room.

Active and Passive Sentences

To write lively prose, also keep in mind the distinction between *active* and *passive* sentences. A passive sentence is one in which the performer of the action is not mentioned until late in the sentence or is left out altogether. Any time you restructure passive sentences, you pep up the prose.

> PASSIVE: This book was recommended by my teacher.
>
> ACTIVE: My teacher recommended this book.

> PASSIVE: It was bought for me by my mother.
>
> ACTIVE: My mother bought it for me.

Although active sentences usually sound more natural and interesting, sometimes a passive sentence will work better. When it's immaterial who performed an action, for example, or when the actor can't be identified, passive voice makes perfect stylistic sense.

> ACTIVE: The exam proctor gave the starting signal at 8:30.
>
> PASSIVE: The starting signal was given at exactly 8:30.

In the passive version the important fact is the starting time. Who gave the signal is secondary.

Use Fresh Language

Here's your chance to do yourself and your readers a favor. Instead of relying on safe, customary language, take a chance now and then and give your readers a verbal surprise. GMAT essay readers, especially after reading hundreds of predictable essays on the same topic, will do cartwheels for something fresh, something new—a word, a phrase, a sentence still wet behind the ears. A pleasant verbal surprise or two will give your readers, as well as your essay, a boost.

A verbal surprise is simply a unique and interesting choice of words. You don't have to turn exotic phrases in order to dazzle your reader. Common words, deftly used, will do the job just as well—better, probably, for they will sound more natural than something forced onto the page just to sound unusual.

> ORDINARY: He wrote a magnificent essay on baseball.
>
> SURPRISING: He pitched a magnificent essay on baseball.

Since essays are not normally *pitched*, the unexpected shift from *wrote* to *pitched* is modestly surprising. The verb *pitched* works well only because the topic is baseball. It might be silly in an essay on another topic.

> ORDINARY: The shark bit the swimmers.
>
> SURPRISING: The shark dined on the swimmers.

Changing *bit* to *dined* suggests good manners and gentility, qualities that sharks rarely enjoy.

ORDINARY:	The gunshot frightened the pigeons, which flew away.
SURPRISING:	The gunshot filled the sky with frightened pigeons.

The ordinary sentence states literally what happened: the sound of the gunshot scared the pigeons silly. In the second version, though, the shot becomes a vital force with the power to fill the sky. Both the pigeons and the sentence have sprung to life.

Surprise with Comparisons

Does this sound familiar? You can't find the words to express a feeling that you have inside you. You know what you want to say, but the words won't come. Although our language is filled with wonderful words to describe virtually anything, sometimes emotions and experiences seem almost inexpressible. How, for instance, do you show the look you got from the bus driver when you didn't have the exact fare? How do you describe street sounds at 5 o'clock on a summer morning or the feel of clean bedsheets?

Comparisons are economical. They condense a lot of thought and feeling into a few words. Ernie Pyle, a famous newspaper correspondent in World War II, reported his stories as though they were being told by the average GI lying in a foxhole. He said, "I write from a worm's eye point of view." What a terrific comparison! Who ever thought that worms have eyes, much less a point of view? The idea gives a fresh slant to the old expression "bird's eye view" and cleverly emphasizes Pyle's position on the battlefield.

Similes ("Norma babbles like a brook") and *metaphors* ("Norma is a babbling brook") compare something known (a babbling brook) to something unknown (Norma). Little kids use such figures of speech instinctively. Because their vocabularies are limited, they compare what they know with what they can't yet express. "When my foot is asleep, it feels like seltzer," says a boy to his daddy, or "Today is chocolate sunshine." As people grow up, they lose the knack of making colorful comparisons and have to relearn it. When you actively look for comparisons, they sprout, like weeds in the garden, all around.

Cut Out Clichés

Every familiar combination of words, such as "I couldn't care less," or "you've got to be kidding," or "what a bummer," was once new, cool, or poetic. But constant repetition turned them into clichés, and clichés, by definition, have lost their zing and their power to surprise. Still, clichés crowd our conversations, swamp our airwaves, and deluge the media. Like the air we breathe (a cliché), we hardly notice them. In an essay, however, especially one that is supposed to demonstrate your unique cast of mind, you must avoid clichés like the plague. "Like the plague," in fact, is one you should avoid, along with other secondhand phrases and expressions like *the bottom line, how does that sit with you, to touch base with, off the top of my head, I'm outta here, a point well taken, two sides of the same coin, getting psyched, go off the deep end, life in the fast lane, for openers, flipped out, get off my back, get a life!, super, so amazing, at the cutting edge of*, and would you believe, *would you believe?* Using such trite phrases and expressions declares that you'd rather borrow what someone else has said than think of something on your own. Spewing one cliché after another is also the sign of a poverty-stricken mind.

Expunge clichés that sneak into your prose *when your back is turned, when your defenses are down*, and *when you least expect them*. Be vigilant, and purge them from your prose. Don't use an expression that you've ever heard or seen before. If you've written a phrase with a familiar ring, drop it, not *like a hot potato*, but just as quickly.

Your GMAT essay won't be penalized for an absence of inventive and scintillating expressions, but it is sure to suffer if infested with clichés. Get into the habit of expelling all trite phrases from your writing vocabulary. *Half the battle*, as they say, is knowing a cliché when you see one. The other half—removing them—is still to be fought and won.

9. OMIT NEEDLESS WORDS

In *Hamlet*, the old windbag Polonius knew what he was talking about when he said "Brevity is the soul of wit." What he meant, in brief, is that Brief is Better. Never use two words when one will do. Readers want to be told quickly and directly what you have to say. They value economy and resent reading more words than necessary.

Here's a word to the wise:

Work through all the sentences you write by examining each one and crossing out all the words you don't definitely need.

Actually, that's 21 words to the wise—probably more than are needed.

Go through every sentence you write and cross out unnecessary words.

That's better—11 words of free advice, but still too many. The sentence could be trimmed still further:

Cut extra words out of every sentence.

Aha! This streamlined version contains just 7 words, one third of the original. If you can regularly trim that proportion of words from your writing without changing meaning or intent, you will have gone about as far as you can to make your writing interesting, although a ruthless, sharp-eyed editor might cut even more:

Omit unnecessary words.

The ultimate goal in economical writing is to make every word count, so that omitting a single word will alter or distort the meaning.

Sentences are trimmed by squeezing them through various wringers.

Wringer #1. Look for repetition. Then combine sentences.

> FAT: In his last and final year in college, Bill was elected to be the head of the statewide SADD organization. As head of the statewide organization, he learned about the details of laws dealing with DWI convictions and had many experiences talking in public to large groups of people. (49 words)
>
> TRIMMED: Elected head of the statewide SADD organization in his senior year, Bill learned about DWI laws and spoke often to large groups. (21 words)

Wringer #2. Look for telltale words like *which, who, that, thing, all*. They sometimes indicate the presence of fat.

> FAT: Football is a sport that millions of fans enjoy. (9 words)
>
> TRIMMED: Millions of fans enjoy football. (5 words)

Wringer #3. Look for phrases that add words but little meaning.

FAT: *By that point in time*, people will be ready for a change. (12 words)

TRIMMED: By then, people will be ready for a change. (9 words)

FAT: Hamlet returned home *as a result of* his father's death. (10 words)

TRIMMED: Hamlet returned home because his father died. (7 words)

FAT PHRASES

what I mean is	I mean
on account of	
due to the fact that	because
in the final analysis	
the bottom line is	finally
few and far between	
insignificant in number	few
each and every one	each
this is a subject that	this subject
ten in number	ten
at the age of six years old	at age six
most unique	unique
true fact	fact
biography of his life	biography
in regard to	
with regard to	
in relation to	about
with reference to	

Wringer #4. Search for redundancies. Countless words are wasted on reiteration of what has already been said, on restating the obvious, on repeating the same ideas, on saying the same darn thing again and again.

FAT: While carefully scrutinizing her patient's medical history, the doctor seemed fully absorbed by what she was reading. (17 words)

Because scrutinize means "to study carefully," the word "carefully" is unnecessary. Also, absorbed by what she was reading repeats what has already been stated.

TRIMMED: While scrutinizing her patient's medical history, the doctor seemed absorbed. (10 words)

After you've pared your sentences to the bone, study the remains. Cut away still more by tracking down little words like *the, a, an, up, down, its,* and *and.* Don't remove whatever gives writing its energy and character, but neither should you spare yourself the pain of removing what you worked hard to put in. Throwing away your precious words may feel sometimes as though you are chopping off your hand, but count on it, your writing will gain life and strength without unnecessary words.

10. VARY YOUR SENTENCES

In writing, it's easy to fall into a rut by repeatedly using the same sentence pattern. To avoid boring your readers to death, serve them a variety of sentences. Your prose will be invigorated and your readers will be happy. Because English is such a pliant language, sentences can be endlessly revised until you've got a mix that works.

You probably know that most simple declarative sentences start with the subject, followed by the verb:

The peaches (subject) *are* (verb) not yet ripe or ready to eat.
They (subject) *left* (verb) for the airport at dusk.
This policy (subject) *is* (verb) not easy to enforce.

Several sentences in a row with this subject-verb pattern will make writing sound like a chapter from a grade-school primer. Take steps to more mature prose by checking an essay you've recently written. If several of your sentences lead off with the subject, try starting some of them with a preprositional phrase, with an adverb or adjective, or with some other grammatical unit. By varying sentence openings, you make your writing bolder and more readable.

The following pairs of sentences illustrate ways in which a subject can be shifted from its customary position:

BEFORE THE SHIFT: Poison ivy thrives in the woods.
AFTER THE SHIFT: In the woods, poison ivy thrives.

After a prepositional phrase the subject of the sentence appears.

BEFORE: Poison ivy is apparently one of the most poisonous plants.
AFTER: Apparently, poison ivy is one of the most poisonous plants.

Obviously, the revised sentence begins with an adverb.

BEFORE: Many people still don't know what it looks like.
AFTER: Still, many people don't know what it looks like.

Well, here the sentence subject is snuck in after an opening connective.

BEFORE: People should keep their eyes peeled for an innocent-looking three-leaved plant on a single stem whenever they go out to the country.
AFTER: Whenever people are out in the country, they should keep their eyes peeled for an innocent-looking three-leaved plant on a single stem.

After introducing this sentence with a dependent clause, the writer named the subject and then added the rest of the sentence.

BEFORE: A prudent person should take a shower with plenty of soap and water as soon as possible after brushing up against the plant to guard against infection.
AFTER: To guard against infection after brushing up against the plant, a prudent person should take a shower with plenty of soap and water as soon as possible.

To revise this sentence the writer began with a *verbal*, in this case "to guard," the infinitive form of the verb. Verbals look and feel a lot like verbs (hence, their name), but are not. (The infinitive form of any verb, for example, cannot serve as the main verb of a sentence.) Verbals, though, come from verbs, which explains the resemblance.

BEFORE: Some people walk through patches of poison ivy without worrying, thinking that they are immune.

AFTER: Thinking that they are immune from poison ivy, some people walk through patches of the stuff without worrying.

Hoping to add diversity to sentence openings, the writer began this sentence with another kind of verbal, known as a *participle*. Most of the time the *-ing* ending is a clue that the word is a participle.

BEFORE: Such people, who were unconcerned about becoming infected, may be shocked to discover that their immunity has suddenly disappeared.

AFTER: Unconcerned about becoming infected, such people may be shocked to discover that their immunity has suddenly disappeared.

Determined to try something different, the writer picked an adjective that happens to sound like a verb because of its *-ed* ending.

Another variation to try occasionally is the sentence with a paired construction. Two equal and matched ideas are set against each other, often differing by only one or two words:

It wasn't that David caught poison ivy, it was poison ivy that caught him.
"Ask not what your country can do for you, ask what you can do for your country."
—John F. Kennedy, January 20, 1961

The strength of such a sentence lies in the balance of parallel parts. Each part could stand alone, but together the thought is expressed more vigorously.

No rule of thumb governs the proportion of sentences in an essay that should depart from the usual subject-verb word order. Much depends on the intent and content of the essay.

Don't deliberately scramble up sentence types just to make a sentence potpourri, for you may end up with a mess on your hands. Be guided always by what seems clearest and by what seems varied enough to hold reader interest.

Use of Repetition

Contrary to what this book has stated previously, repetition deserves a place in an essay writing repertoire. Some kinds of repetition are boring, true, but adept use of repetition lets a writer stress important ideas in an unusual way. People naturally repeat words for emphasis, anyway, as in "I love you. I love you very much," and "Knock it off. I said knock it off!"

While effective repetition leaves its mark, accidental repetition can be annoying. Watch out for avoidable repetitions:

At the end of the hall stood a clock. The clock said five o'clock.
Columbus made three voyages. The voyages took him across the Atlantic.

Usually, combining such sentences will keep you from ending one sentence and starting the next one with the same words:

The clock at the end of the hall said five.
Columbus made three voyages across the Atlantic.

Occasionally sentences are plagued by a word or sound that won't let go. One student wrote:

Maybe some people don't have as much freedom as others, but the freedom they do have is given to them for free. Therefore, freedom is proof enough that the best things in life are free.

Another student wrote:

The members of the assembly remembered that November was just around the corner.

These authors weren't listening to the sound of their own words. Had they read their sentences aloud, their ears would probably have noticed that the record seemed to be stuck. In fact, reading your work aloud allows you to step back (Hold it! Those two words—aloud and allows—should not be allowed to stand. They sound sour, don't you agree?) Anyway, when you say your written words out loud, you gain perspective and notice repetitive bumps that need repair. Or better still, let your essay cool for a spell, then recruit a friend to read it to you. That's how to achieve real objectivity.

Short and Long Sentences

Sentences can be written in any length, from one word to thousands. A long sentence demands more from readers because, while stepping from one part of the sentence to the next, they must keep track of more words, modifiers, phrases (not to speak of parenthetical asides), and clauses without losing the writer's main thought, which may be buried amid any number of secondary, or less important, thoughts. Short sentences are easier to grasp. A brief sentence makes its point quickly and often with considerable force, as in this passage about a family trip:

For three days, my parents and I sat in our Toyota and drove from college to college, looking for the perfect place for me to spend the next four years. For 72 hours we lived as one person, sharing thoughts and dreams, stating opinions about each college we visited, taking guided tours, interviewing students and college officials, asking directions a hundred times, eating together in town after town, and even sleeping in the same motel rooms. But mostly, we fought.

The blunt closing sentence, particularly after a windy 46-word sentence, produces a mild jolt. To be sure, it's meant to shock, but placing a tight, terse sentence against a long one intensifies the effect. Like all stylistic techniques, this one mustn't be used too often. Overuse dilutes its impact, but when it works well, it's indelible.

Short and long sentences create the rhythm of writing. Because readers usually pause, subconsciously at least, at every period, short sentences slow the tempo. Long sentences may speed it up, but the pace depends a lot on the placement of clauses, the amount of parenthetical matter, and word choices.

In any case, a string of short, simple sentences can be as tiresome to read as series of long, complex ones strung end to end. A balance is best. A sequence of four or five equally short (or long) sentences should be given the fission-or-fusion treatment. That is, split the big ones and combine the others.

Passages consisting of short sentences can also be made more readable by fusing ideas.

When sentences are combined, words are excised and the writing often becomes livelier. Not only that, but when some ideas are subordinated to others, not every thought receives equal emphasis.

STRATEGIES TO VARY YOUR SENTENCES

Start sentences with:

1. A prepositional phrase: *In the beginning, From the start, In the first place*
2. Adverbs and adverbial phrases: *Originally, At first, Initially*
3. Dependent clauses: *If you follow my lead, When you start with this*
4. Conjunctions: *And, But, Not only, Either, So, Yet*
5. Verbal infinitives: *To launch, To take the first step, To get going*
6. Adjectives and adjective phrases: *Fresh from, Introduced with, Headed by*
7. Participles: *Leading off, Starting up, Commencing with*
8. Inversions: *Unique is the writer who embarks . . .*

Use a variety of sentence types.

Balance long and short sentences.

Combine series of very short sentences.

Dismember very long sentences.

11. END YOUR ESSAY UNFORGETTABLY

When you reach the end of your GMAT or any other essay, you can lift your fingers from the keyboard and be done with it, or you can leave your readers a little gift to remember you by. What you leave can be a little piece of insight, wisdom, or humor to make readers glad that they stayed with you to the end. It may be something to tease their brains, tickle their funny bones, or make them feel smart.

Whatever you give, choose it carefully, and let it spring naturally from the text of your essay. A good essay can easily be spoiled by an ill-fitting ending. Also, don't be tempted to use an ending that is too coy, corny, or cute, such as *that's all, folks*; *it was a dream come true*; *a good time was had by all*; *tune in next week—same time, same station*; or *a nice place to visit, but I wouldn't want to live there*. These are outrageously trite endings that leave behind an impression that the writer was either too cheap to leave a better gift or too dull to think of something classier. Readers will appreciate almost any gift you give them, provided you've put some thought into its selection. Don't spoil a fresh essay with a stale conclusion.

Nor must you tack on an ending just for the sake of good form. The best endings grow organically out of the essay's content. Endings are so crucial in works of creative art that specific words have been designated to name them. A piece of music has a *coda*, a story or play, a *denouement*, a musical show, a *grand finale*. When an ending approaches, you sense it at hand and expect soon to be bathed with a feeling of satisfaction. Good endings please both heart and mind.

Choose the gift judiciously. Leave behind a memento of your thinking, your sense of humor, or your vision. Even an ordinary thought, uniquely presented, will shed an agreeable afterglow.

1. Have some fun with your ending. A reader may remember your sense of humor long after forgetting the essay that struck his funny bone.

    SUBJECT: Stricter gun control laws
    GIFT: On this issue, the legislature has taken a cheap shot at many law-abiding citizens.

2. End with an apt quotation taken from the essay, from the assigned topic, or from some other source.

> SUBJECT: The nobility of the teaching profession
>
> GIFT: As a wise person once said, "Catch a fish and you feed a man his dinner, but teach a man to fish, and you feed him for life."

> SUBJECT: The costs of racial disharmony
>
> GIFT: Now, more than ever, Rodney King's question, "Can we all get along?" has a new meaning.

3. Finish by reviewing the paper's main point, but with new words. Add a short tag line, perhaps.

> SUBJECT: The low quality of art supplies used in school, arguing that money should be devoted to support the art program.
>
> GIFT: Colors fade rapidly when exposed to sunlight, a true indication of the paint's poor quality. How frustrating!

> SUBJECT: The purported death of democracy
>
> GIFT: Our victory over the forces of the communist menace must mean that democracy has the power to endure and must mean that it is healthy.

4. Project your readers into the future. What will happen in the months or years ahead?

> SUBJECT: Being adventurous
>
> GIFT: By late spring I had my fill of studying the river; it was time to get a raft and try the rapids myself.

> SUBJECT: The misuse of our environment
>
> GIFT: We must all do our part to save the planet, or there won't be a planet left to save.

TIP

Always finish your essay with some kind of ending—but not a summary.

A catchy conclusion isn't always needed, but some sort of ending is necessary to make readers feel they've arrived somewhere. They won't be satisfied with an essay that just evaporates. A short one is better than none at all. Stay away from summary endings, particularly when the essay is short, as on the GMAT. It's insulting, in fact, to review for the readers what is evident on the page in front of them. Readers are intelligent people. Trust them to remember what the essay says.

12. FOLLOW THE CONVENTIONS OF STANDARD ENGLISH

This book is too lean to house a complete handbook of standard English usage. For a full treatment of English usage, however, see "Sentence Correction"—Chapter 7 or go to the library and check out one of the hefty books on the subject. Look, for instance, at H. W. Fowler's *Modern English Usage*, the definitive reference work, in which you can find a page-long discussion of such arcane usage questions as the difference between *farther* and *further*, or when to use *that*, as in "Is it my Mazda Miata *that* is parked illegally?" and when to use *which*, as in "Yes, your Mazda Miata, *which* is now being ticketed, is parked illegally." Numerous other books, such as *The New York Times Manual of Style and Usage* and *The Careful Writer* by Theodore M. Bernstein are packed with solutions to literally thousands of usage problems.

Unhappily, there is no particular logic to standard English usage. Like the famous definition of pornography, it's hard to define but easy to spot when you see it. Standard English is merely a badge of an educated person, the level of writing and speech expected of people who are literate and who, to some degree, must depend on their language skills to help them make their way in the world.

ESSAY TOPICS FOR FURTHER PRACTICE

DIRECTIONS: Write a clear, logical, and well-organized response to the following argument. Your response should be in the form of a short essay, following the conventions of standard written English. Your answer should fit on three pages of lined $8\frac{1}{2}"\times11"$ paper; on your computer, the equivalent would be a word count of approximately 1,000.

Eight topics are suggested for practice, but if you write on the same topic again and again, the number of topics is two, three, or even ten times as many. Since it's virtually impossible to write the same essay twice, you could try the same topic over and over without repeating yourself. Each time you write on the same topic, choose another point of view to defend. They say that one sign of erudition is the ability to argue both sides of an issue equally well. Then compare the results.

ANALYSIS OF AN ARGUMENT

1. **If a person achieves greatness in fields such as the arts, science, politics, or business, that person's achievements are more important than any of his or her personal faults.**

   Discuss how well reasoned the above argument is. You will have to consider the assumptions that underlie the writer's thinking. Describe alternative explanations or counterexamples that might weaken his or her conclusion. You must come up with evidence that would strengthen or refute the argument or identify what changes would make the argument more logically sound.

2. **The following is an excerpt from a meeting of the Board of Directors of a security products manufacturing firm:**

   "The Director of Safety and Security Services reported that according to the company's research over the past five years, wearing photo badges by employees prevented theft. His conclusion was based on the results of research conducted on a sample of fifteen client companies. He decided to recommend that future customers should adopt photo badges at work as an effective theft prevention practice."

   Discuss how well reasoned the above argument is. You will have to consider the assumptions that underlie the writer's thinking. Describe alternative explanations or counterexamples that might weaken his or her conclusion. You must come up with evidence that would strengthen or refute the argument or identify what changes would make the argument more logically sound.

3. The following was published in a marketing magazine:

"Our correspondent learned that Eurocoffee, a privately owned coffee manufacturer, plans to introduce a new line of European gourmet coffee products. Because there are many competing brands on the market, the brand manager believes that the best way to gain customers for the brand is to concentrate on print and TV ads for the introduction of its new line of coffees. It conducted a temporary sales promotion campaign that offered free samples, price reductions, and discount coupons for the new brand."

Discuss how well reasoned the above argument is. You will have to consider the assumptions that underlie the writer's thinking. Describe alternative explanations or counterexamples that might weaken his or her conclusion. You must come up with evidence that would strengthen or refute the argument or identify what changes would make the argument more logically sound.

4. The following appeared on *The New York Times* website:

"With the health care system at the center of the political debate, a lot of scary claims are being thrown around. The dangerous ones are not those that are false; watchdogs in the news media are quick to debunk them. Rather, the dangerous ones are those that are true but don't mean what people think they mean."

Discuss how well reasoned the above argument is. You will have to consider the assumptions that underlie the writer's thinking. Describe alternative explanations or counterexamples that might weaken his or her conclusion. You must come up with evidence that would strengthen or refute the argument or identify what changes would make the argument more logically sound.

5. The following appeared in the health section of a local newspaper:

"Ten women participated in a consumer panel studying the effectiveness of a new hair coloring agent called 'Washaway'. Once a month, the participants applied 'Washaway' on their hair. At the end of two months most participants reported a marked improvement in the way their hair looked and felt. Thus it appears that 'Washaway' is truly effective in improving hair color."

Discuss how well reasoned the above argument is. You will have to consider the assumptions that underlie the writer's thinking. Describe alternative explanations or counterexamples that might weaken his or her conclusion. You must come up with evidence that would strengthen or refute the argument or identify what changes would make the argument more logically sound.

6. The following announcement appeared in a fashion magazine:

"The ShoeBest shoe manufacturing company has developed a leather substitute for men's shoes lasting three times as long as conventional leather shoes. However, the composition of the substitute was not as supple as leather. In order to test consumer acceptance of the innovation, management decided to distribute the shoes among company employees and have them wear them for a six month period. After that, the marketing department would ask their opinions of the shoes, and if favorable, the shoes would be marketed to the public at large."

Discuss how well reasoned the above argument is. You will have to consider the assumptions that underlie the writer's thinking. Describe alternative explanations or counterexamples that might weaken his or her conclusion. You must come up with evidence that would strengthen or refute the argument or identify what changes would make the argument more logically sound.

7. By law, tobacco products may not be advertised on television. Some people think that foods that are unhealthy for children, such as candy and heavily sugared cereals, should also be banned from television advertisements. Opponents view such a ban as an infringement of basic freedoms.

Discuss how well reasoned the above argument is. You will have to consider the assumptions that underlie the writer's thinking. Describe alternative explanations or counterexamples that might weaken his or her conclusion. You must come up with evidence that would strengthen or refute the argument or identify what changes would make the argument more logically sound.

8. The following announcement appeared in a medical journal:

"College researchers say that if you were born after the year 2000, you will very likely live to be 100. If you knew you were to live until the age of 100, you would probably organize your life very differently."

Discuss how well reasoned the above argument is. You will have to consider the assumptions that underlie the writer's thinking. Describe alternative explanations or counterexamples that might weaken his or her conclusion. You must come up with evidence that would strengthen or refute the argument or identify what changes would make the argument more logically sound.

SAMPLE ESSAY

Below is a sample essay.

Analysis of an Argument

The following was published by a non-governmental organization (NGO).

Globalization shapes and distorts cultural patterns in developing countries. The Westernization, particularly the Americanization, of culture presents a formidable threat to the cultural integrity of the non-Western World.

Discuss how logically persuasive you find the above argument. In presenting your point of view, analyze the sort of reasoning used and supporting evidence. Are there inferred assumptions? In addition, state what further evidence, if any, would make the argument more sound and convincing or would make you better able to evaluate its conclusion.

What might weaken or strengthen the argument?

The argument states that adaptation by developing countries of the customs, practices, and beliefs of Western nations, in particular those of America, tends to distort and thereby threaten the cultural integrity of those countries. While I might agree with this statement in general, I find the argument unpersuasive because it is simply declarative. The premise follows the conclusion with providing any specifics or supporting data.

Information that would be helpful includes definitions. What is a "developing country"? Are all emerging countries alike? In fact, they are very dissimilar. Much of Eastern Europe, an area emerging from the economic practice of the USSR, still struggles in the shift to western capitalism. Yet much of Eastern Europe welcomes western culture including its technology, fast food, and cinema. These western "imports" graft onto the old imperial ways that were displaced by Russian communism.

Are the emerging countries in southern Africa the same as those in Eastern Europe? For that matter, is southern Africa like northern Africa? The continent is so large and varied that multiple cultures, political forms, and religions mix and mingle while others cautiously protect their discrete societies. Various Islamic cultures coexist and thrive in certain areas but not in other areas. Dictatorships and democratic forms of authority blossom in different places on the continent.

Furthermore, the landscape of "emerging countries" varies widely. In Eastern Europe, the topography is similar and so, therefore, are the exports to western countries. In contrast, the African continent contains deserts, lush forests, and plains. Exports from different African countries vary similarly. Parts of Africa are desert and export oil. The lush growth of southern Africa produces minerals and valuable stones. The forests and the plains are filled with wildlife. The protection of species that exist only in Africa is aided by the money supplied by tourism, especially from tourists from the West.

The argument contains only a premise in the first sentence and a conclusion in the second. In the intellectual space between the two lie unstated assumptions that undermine the conclusion that western culture is destructive. Although the conclusion certainly has great political import, it is not supported by any evidence.

Integrated Reasoning

→ NEW FOR 2012
→ OVERALL STRATEGIES
→ SAMPLE PROBLEMS AND STRATEGIES

On June 5, 2012, the GMAT exam changed from its well-known format to the Next Generation GMAT.

NEW FOR 2012

The new Integrated Reasoning section has been added to test your ability to decipher information and data from multiple sources and formats. This Barron's guide breaks down everything you need to know about the Next Generation GMAT, the new Integrated Reasoning section, and the strategies and methodologies needed to succeed on test day.

Section Details

The Integrated Reasoning section has a 30-minute time limit with 12 questions. Some of the questions may have several parts. A special online calculator is available for use on only this part of the GMAT. The Integrated Reasoning section will be scored separately from your GMAT score (from 200–800) and from your AWA score (from 0–6). This section will be scored on a scale from 1–8, in intervals of 1. There are no partial points given, which means that if a question has three Yes/No statements, you need to get all three correct in order to get credit. For more details on Integrated Reasoning scoring, go to *mba.com*.

The Integrated Reasoning section is designed to measure your ability to review data in multiple formats using various methods, to identify key issues and trends, to apply high-level reasoning, and to organize information in order to make an informed decision. For this, you will need to be comfortable with synthesizing information from charts, tables, graphs, spreadsheets, e-mails, and letters in paragraph form. As with the rest of the GMAT, you will not need prior business knowledge to answer Integrated Reasoning questions. The new Integrated Reasoning section can be best summarized as a blend of the GMAT Quantitative and Critical Reasoning sections along with some argumentative logic, thus the use of the term integrated.

Note that the Integrated Reasoning section is not computer adaptive like the quantitative and verbal sections, which become easier or more difficult in response to your performance. This means the questions are preselected, just like in a simple paper and pencil test. Therefore, you should expect a diverse mix of question types and difficulty levels.

OVERALL STRATEGIES

The Integrated Reasoning section requires some of the same skills you will use on the overall GMAT. It also has a similar structure and format. Therefore, you can apply many of the strategies you would use on the overall GMAT.

1. **INVEST TIME TO UNDERSTAND THE QUESTION:** For every GMAT problem, including the quantitative and verbal sections, you must ask yourself "What's going on?" before you dive into solving the question. Make sure you understand the question and the information given. Get a general sense of what the question is asking. Think about how you might set up your solution. Investing time up front to review the data and key insights before diving into the questions will save you from losing time by backtracking.

2. **AVOID THE TWO MOST COMMON ERRORS:** The most common errors that test takers make on the GMAT are misreading the question and making unnecessary calculation errors. Make sure you review the questions, the information, the passages, and the answer choices quickly but carefully. When you make calculations, be sure to keep your scratch work clean, structured, and error free.

3. **KNOW HOW EVERYTHING RELATES:** Try to get a sense of how all the information—variables, numbers, and text—relates to each other. The GMAC writers don't expect you to look at all the data in great detail. Therefore, look for certain themes or trends within the data that are obvious. Most of the information given in the questions tells you the "what." Your job is to figure out the "so what." Ask yourself, "What does this tell me?" and "Why is this so important?"

4. **YOU DON'T ALWAYS NEED THE CALCULATOR:** The Integrated Reasoning section provides a calculator, but that doesn't mean you should always use it. It is an awkward tool. Most of the time, you can set up your questions to keep its use to a minimum. Most GMAT math problems can be solved conceptually and with minimal calculations. Even though you can solve all quantitative problems with a step-by-step process, there are always shortcuts. Do some mental calculations, simplify your work, and estimate whenever possible. You will be surprised by how little you need the online calculator.

5. **DON'T SKIM, SYNTHESIZE INSTEAD:** Skimming will not help you in this section. You are being tested on your ability to analyze and synthesize the data. That doesn't mean you have look at every single detail. However, you do need to watch for important key words, note titles, headings, labels, and subject lines, along with units and key numbers.

6. **PRACTICE DATA SHUFFLING:** Since much of the navigation in Integrated Reasoning requires using tabs, scrolling, and sorting, you can practice much of this using spreadsheet software like Microsoft Excel. You can also try using a calculator on your computer for practice. Don't let the need to navigate slow you down.

7. **LEVERAGE CURRENT GMAT STRATEGIES:** Use the theory and strategies you learned in the Quantitative and Verbal sections of this book to help you. Many of the typical GMAT strategies use processes and methodologies that are transferable to the Integrated Reasoning section. You can apply similar skills to answering all the questions—quantitative analysis, algebra, deductive reasoning, argumentative logic and structure, identifying conclusions, and anticipating questions.

8. **LOOK FOR ALL THE HIDDEN CLUES:** The GMAT test developers like to hide clues to questions in many places. You need to know where these clues are. Start with the questions and answer choices themselves. They can give you an idea of where to look in a question and what to look for. You can also use your work from previous questions within a section; you can use your work cumulatively to solve the next problem. Don't forget to look within the charts, tables, graphs, and paragraphs. They contain key numbers, labels, and words that provide more insight to the problem than you might originally realize. Digest every piece of the puzzle. With practice, you will begin to know what you should look for and what you can ignore.

9. **YOU DON'T NEED TO MEMORIZE:** Since you are given so much data and information, the test writers at the GMAC cannot expect you to memorize everything, nor should you try. Devote your time and energy to understanding the problem, navigating effectively, outlining a solution path, and getting to the answer. If you need to refer back, the data is always available.

10. **CONFIDENCE IS KEY:** Just like with the rest of the GMAT, confidence goes a long way to your success. When you are confident, you look at problems as a fun challenge and have the determination to solve them correctly. When you lack confidence, you second-guess yourself and you spend too much time focused on the wrong things. You use many of the skills tested on the Integrated Reasoning section every day in your professional and personal lives. Approach problems knowing that the theory, structure, and strategies you have internalized will help you succeed on the Integrated Reasoning section and on the rest of the GMAT.

THE FOUR QUESTION TYPES

The new Integrated Reasoning section contains four new question types:

1. **GRAPHICS INTERPRETATION:** You will analyze a graphical image and then select options in a drop-down menu in order to create accurate statements.

2. **TABLE ANALYSIS:** You will receive a sortable table of information, similar to a spreadsheet, that you must analyze to answer questions in true/false, yes/no, or other formats.

3. **TWO-PART ANALYSIS:** You will receive a paragraph of information and then answer a question in a two-part format. This requires you to look at data in two different ways in order to solve the question.

4. **MULTI-SOURCE REASONING:** You are given two to three sources of information presented in various forms—including text, charts, and graphs—on tabbed pages. You then have to answer questions in either a yes/no format or in a select one out of five format.

Following are the four Integrated Reasoning question types, along with strategies and sample questions for each.

GRAPHICS INTERPRETATION

True to its name, this section will require you to interpret graphics. The basic idea is this:

Look at this graph. Understand what it is trying to say. Extract some key information.

You will be given a graphical image—scatter plot, graph with variables, Venn diagram, bar chart, statistical curve distribution, or pie chart—and some explanatory text. There will be several statements you will need to complete using choices from a drop-down menu.

TIP

On the actual GMAT, Graphics Interpretation questions will require you to use drop-down menus to choose your answer.

SKILLS TESTED

- Assimilating, analyzing, and interpreting data in graphical forms
- Identifying and extracting key information
- Interpreting past events and predicting future outcomes

Graphics Interpretation Strategies

1. **START WITH WHAT YOU KNOW:** As with any GMAT question, ask yourself "What's going on?" before attempting to answer. Invest the time to get the gist of the graph. Try to look at it from a high-level perspective and to understand the information it is trying to convey. Think of an appropriate title for the graph in your own words (IYOW) if none is given.

2. **MAKE SURE YOU CATCH EVERYTHING:** Now focus on the details. Look at any titles, axis labels, symbols, legends, or units of measurements given. Is the graph displaying data in thousands or millions, in inches or feet, and so on? Investing time up-front to understand the graph thoroughly will save you from having to analyze everything again later.

3. **IDENTIFY TRENDS AND RELATIONSHIPS:** Look for any key trends or relationships among the variables, the *x*-axis, and *y*-axis. Are there any direct or indirect relationships? Do certain areas of the graph have spikes, a greater concentration of points, or either a positive or a negative slope? This is where we interpret the data and extract the key information.

TIP

Try to express most GMAT problems in your own words (or IYOW). If you can express what's going on in your own words, you know the information. If you can't do this, you don't know this information. Using IYOW is a great way to test your understanding of the problem.

4. **USE THE STATEMENTS TO HELP YOU:** Just like in the rest of the GMAT, the answer choices can provide you with some great insights. If the statements talk about slope, familiarize yourself with the slopes of any lines shown on the graph. The statements will mention certain key words that are relevant to answering the question. If you identify enough, you will be able to "connect the dots" and solve the puzzle. In other words, you can piece together all the different aspects of the graph and what it is trying to say.

5. **ANTICIPATE THROUGHOUT THE QUESTION:** Throughout your first read of the material, try to anticipate what the relevant information is and what the questions are going to ask. Once you see the questions, you can try to figure out what the answer is before you open up the drop-down menu. It's a great confidence booster if you see the answer you anticipated in the drop-down menu. If you don't see your answer there, it's a good indicator that you may have made some oversights.

The following two graphs show economic data from 1999–2000.

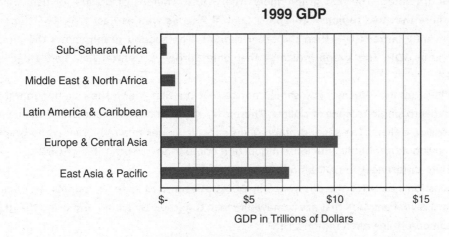

1999 GDP

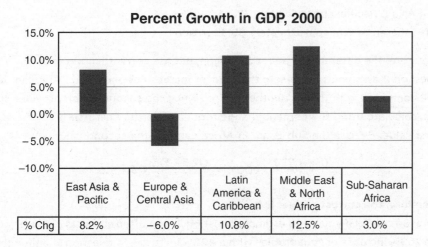

Percent Growth in GDP, 2000

	East Asia & Pacific	Europe & Central Asia	Latin America & Caribbean	Middle East & North Africa	Sub-Saharan Africa
% Chg	8.2%	−6.0%	10.8%	12.5%	3.0%

Complete each statement according to the information presented in the diagram.

1. In 1999, by approximately how much did the East Asia and Pacific GDP surpass Sub-Saharan Africa's GDP?

   (A) $4.5 trillion
   (B) $5.0 trillion
   (C) $6.0 trillion
   (D) $7.0 trillion

2. In the year 2000, the Middle East and North Africa's percent growth in GDP was approximately what percent greater than Sub-Saharan Africa's percent growth in GDP?

   (A) 225%
   (B) 317%
   (C) 367%
   (D) 417%

SOLUTION AND STRATEGY REVIEW

The first thing you should notice is that you are given two graphs, not one, but they are both related. The first graph shows the GDP in trillions of dollars for five regions. Also note that two regions—Europe & Central Asia as well as East Asia & Pacific—had significantly larger GDPs than the other regions. The second graph shows the percent change in GDP. This graph indicates that only Europe & Central Asia had a decrease in GDP.

When you look further, you should notice that the first graph shows a horizontal axis divided into single trillions of dollars. Therefore, you may have to estimate to the nearest half-trillion dollars. The second graph gives specific values in a table below the graph.

You should probably anticipate a question comparing growth rates of GDP or absolute differences in GDP among the regions.

Question 1 asks for the difference in GDP between two specific regions. The answer choices reveal answers that are somewhat close together. By estimating using the graph, we can determine each region's GDP.

East Asia & Pacific: approximately $7.4 trillion
Sub-Saharan Africa: approximately $0.33 trillion

Therefore, the difference is about $7 trillion **and the correct answer is D**.

Question 2 asks you to calculate the percent increase of one region's percent growth in GDP compared with that of another region. Since the second graph provides specific values, calculate using the percent change formula. Use the East Asia & Pacific value as the first value, *FV*. Use the Sub-Saharan Africa value as the second value, *PV*.

$$\frac{(FV - PV)}{PV} \times 100\% = \frac{(12.5 - 3)}{3} \times 3 = 316.7\%$$

Therefore, **the correct answer is B**.

Note: Be careful if you try to estimate question 2. Too often students confuse "double" with a 200% increase or "quadruple" with a 400% increase. In question 2, although 12.5% is a little over four times 3.0%, this actually means that it is a little over a 300% increase.

TABLE ANALYSIS

In this section, you will be required to analyze tables. The basic idea is this:

Look at this detailed table. Sort the information to answer statements about it.

You will be given a table or spreadsheet that has sorting ability, much like a Microsoft Excel worksheet. Some text will be included to explain the table. The questions will have varying types of statements—yes/no, true/false, would help to explain/would not help to explain, or inferable/not inferable. You will have to select one choice for each statement. Every column in the table is sortable either numerically or alphabetically.

SKILLS TESTED

- Assimilating, analyzing, and interpreting data tables
- Sifting through and organizing a mass of information
- Identifying trends and patterns
- Extracting meaningful information to make decisions
- Understanding how data can be used to satisfy certain conditions or support either a hypothesis or principle

Table Analysis: Strategies

1. **START WITH WHAT IS GIVEN:** Look at the table and the headings. Invest the time up-front to get the gist of the table. Get a sense of the data given, sorting options, rankings, columns, and highest and lowest items in the table. Think of an appropriate title for the table in your own words (IYOW) if none is given.

2. **USE THE QUESTIONS OR STATEMENTS TO HELP YOU FOCUS:** The questions will give you a good idea of what kind of information needs to be extracted from the table. Yes/no and true/false are usually easy to figure out. However, watch out for the more abstract "would help explain" questions. Ask yourself if sorting a particular column would point you toward a solution.

3. **IDENTIFY TRENDS AND RELATIONSHIPS:** Look for any key trends or relationships among the numbers given. Look at how the numbers or rankings change among columns. Do you see some obvious disparities? Are there direct, indirect, or inverse relationships? This is where you interpret the data and extract the key information. Do not spend an undue amount of time going through each piece of data. Rather, you need to get an overall sense of the table. Remember, you can always look back at the table for reference, so there is no need to memorize anything.

4. **DON'T OVERANALYZE; BE EFFICIENT:** These questions contain a lot of information. You can easily get lost on some of the larger spreadsheets and forget about the clock. If you practice sorting beforehand using a spreadsheet program, you can get a better understanding of how sorting works. When you look at numbers, you can estimate or use very rough numbers (for example, $23,846 is better thought of as $24k). Remember again that the questions will refer you to which columns to look at. So take the time to determine what would be the best sort to find the answer.

The table below displays data of the Best Picture Oscar winners from 1996–2010.

Movie	Year of Release	Month of Release	Cost to Produce (in millions $)	Rank of Cost	Box Office Gross (in millions $)	Rank at Box Office
The English Patient	1996	Nov.	$27	8	$64	12
Titanic	1997	Dec.	$200	1	$496	1
Shakespeare in Love	1998	Dec.	$25	9	$73	10
American Beauty	1999	Other	$15	11	$108	8
Gladiator	2000	Other	$103	2	$187	3
A Beautiful Mind	2001	Dec.	$58	5	$155	4
Chicago	2002	Dec.	$45	6	$134	5
The Lord of The Rings: The Return of The King	2003	Dec.	$94	3	$364	2
Million Dollar Baby	2004	Dec.	$30	7	$65	11
Crash	2005	Other	$7	15	$53	14
The Departed	2006	Other	$90	4	$132	6
No Country for Old Men	2007	Nov.	$25	9	$64	12
Slumdog Millionaire	2008	Nov.	$15	11	$98	9
The Hurt Locker	2009	Other	$15	11	$15	15
The King's Speech	2010	Nov.	$15	11	$114	7

For each of the following statements, select *True* if the statement can be shown to be true based on the information in the table. Otherwise, select *False*.

True False

◯ ◯ Best Picture winners have frequently been released very late in the year, often in December, but a recent trend has been to release Best Picture winners earlier in the year.

◯ ◯ Best Picture winners are always profitable at the box office.

◯ ◯ The median box office gross of Best Picture winners is greater than the average box office gross of Best Picture winners.

SOLUTION AND STRATEGY REVIEW

The first things you should notice are the column headings. In particular, the year of release and the month of release suggest that you may get a question on trends over time. Note also that month of release has only three options: December, November, and other. Columns are also included for both production cost and box office grosses. This may lead to a question on profitability. Lastly, since you are given rankings, you may encounter a statement that refers either to the ranking specifically or to the median.

The questions are true or false. One GMAT trick is to have double statements where you are given two pieces of information to prove true or false. The GMAT will often have one portion that is true while the other portion is false, so beware. Let's now look at the statements to help determine the path to a solution.

(i) The first statement discusses release date. Therefore, sort by either release year or release month. Since December is a key word in the statement, you should use the month of release column. Note that the question is also asking for a yearly trend, so your best sorting option is by year of release. December release dates happen in the early years. In the years past 2004, half the release months were November and the other half were other. Therefore, the trend described in the questions is correct. **The answer is True.**

(ii) The second statement is all about profitability, as you had anticipated! You can sort either by cost to produce or by box office gross. Every single movie was profitable EXCEPT *The Hurt Locker*. Therefore, **the answer is False**.

(iii) This statement refers to both the median and the average box office gross. So you should sort by box office rank or by box office gross. Since there are 15 items in the list, the median is at 8, which is *American Beauty*. Its box office gross was $108 million. Calculating the average will clearly take a long time, so there has to be an easier way. If you look at the top-ranked movies, *Titanic and Lord of the Rings: The Return of the King* made $496 million and $364 million, respectively. These two movies will skew the average higher than the median. **The answer is False.**

Note that you might not use all the data or columns, especially when the table is very large. That is why it's better to use the questions to determine your approach.

TWO-PART ANALYSIS

This section requires you to do two-part analysis. The basic idea is this:

Analyze a problem with two components and solve for two components.

You will be given a problem that is structured with two components. The question could be either a typical GMAT quantitative problem (two-variable, rate, or work problems), a verbal problem (two opinions on an issue, two separate aspects of research), or a combination of both. The problem will have two issues, variables, or aspects under consideration. The question will also have two components, usually as columns in a chart, with several possible answers in rows. These answer components may or may not be related. Your job is to select the one correct answer for each column.

SKILLS TESTED

- Solving complex or multilayered problems
- Recognizing relationships between two entities
- Solving simultaneous equations
- Thinking and reasoning
- Weighing trade-offs and making decisions with more than one aspect

Two-Part Analysis: Strategies

1. **START WITH WHAT YOU KNOW AND UNDERSTAND:** Write down what you know from the question, especially for multilayered or complex problems. This includes what you know and what is implied by the statements in the question. This is your starting point and helps you figure out what's going on before diving deeper.

TIP

Two-Part Analysis questions are similar to typical GMAT quantitative and verbal problems. Therefore, many of the strategies and theory you learn in the other sections of this book will apply to this question format.

2. **STRUCTURE WITH CHARTS OR DRAWINGS:** Typically, the more complex a GMAT problem is, the more important it is to add structure to it. Lay out the data in a more organized form or use a drawing to visualize the information. Using a structure also keeps your scratch work clean, makes your scratch work easy to follow, and helps you to extract key aspects of the problem.

3. **ALGEBRA IS YOUR BEST FRIEND:** In many of the more quantitative problems, algebra is a great tool. Algebra is the language of math. It can help you simplify the problem, understand what's going on, and unlock keys to the solution.

4. **DETERMINE THE KEY ISSUES:** In complex problems, several issues, aspects, or constraints are at play. Spend some time identifying and understanding what they are. Then you might be able to look at the answer choices and see which ones meet the question's criteria.

5. **PLUG AND PLAY:** Once you have a strong understanding of the problem, you can start trying some of the answer choices given. Many of the Two-Part Analysis problems have dependent variables. Plugging in one answer may lead to what the other answer should be. If the other answer choice is there, that is great. If not, try another answer choice and see if you can find a match.

TWO-PART ANALYSIS: SAMPLE PROBLEM

Mackintoshies, a raincoat company, sells three different types of raincoats: vinyl, wool, and polyester. Due to an economic downturn, the company has reduced its spending budget on materials to $250,000 for the next year. The company recently acquired 10,000 meters of vinyl fabric for $7 per yard. The best supplier price that Mackintoshies could find sells wool for $10 per yard and polyester for $8 per yard.

In the table below, determine the amount of wool and polyester that Mackinoshies should spend so that the total amount spent on materials is exactly $250,000. Choose only one option in each column.

Wool	Polyester	Number of Yards
○	○	4,000
○	○	6,000
○	○	9,000
○	○	12,000
○	○	15,000

SOLUTION AND STRATEGY REVIEW

Start by writing down everything you know, both direct and implied.

Coat types: vinyl, wool, and polyester
Budget: $250,000
Money recently spent: 10,000 yards of polyester at $7 per yard = $70,000 spent
Costs for wool and polyester: $10/yard and $8/yard, respectively
Amount left to spend: $250,000 – $70,000 = $180,000

This problem looks like an ideal one for your best friend algebra. Use algebra to create a cost equation.

Let W = the amount in yards of wool bought
Let P = the amount in yards of polyester bought
$$10W + 8P = \$180,000$$

Since you do not have another equation to solve this algebraically, your best bet is to look at the answer choices. You can solve either by inspection (looking at the numbers and see which pair fits) or by plugging answer choices into the cost equation. Remember that GMAT math typically works out quite cleanly, so the $10W$ is very easy to fit in. Note that any of the answer choices multiplied by 10 (as in the $10W$) would give a number that ends in 0,000. So a shortcut would be to find a number that also multiplies by 8 (as in the $8P$) to give four zeros. The only answer choice that would do that is 15,000. So try 15,000 as the amount of polyester bought.

$$8(15,000) + 10W = 180,000$$
$$120,000 + 10W = 180,000$$
$$10W = 60,000$$
$$W = 6,000$$

Since that answer is in the chart, it's clear. **The answer is 6,000 yards of wool and 15,000 yards of polyester.**

MULTI-SOURCE REASONING

For the final question type in the Integrated Reasoning section, you will be required to use multi-source reasoning. The basic idea here is:

Look at multiple sources of information, and pull the relevant data to solve problems.

You will be given two or three tabs that contain a large amount of information, either in text form (such as e-mails and research articles) or in table form. The idea is to give you more information than you need. Your job is to pull the relevant information from the sources and solve problems. Some of the more wordy problems resemble GMAT Reading Comprehension or lengthy Critical Reasoning questions. You may be required to use quantitative skills, verbal skills, or both. You will also have to use either deductive or inductive reasoning. Questions may be in a yes/no or a multiple-choice format.

SKILLS TESTED

- Assimilating voluminous amount of data and extracting relevant content
- Using both deductive and inductive reasoning
- Integrating various types of information from different sources to make a decision
- Dealing with information overload
- Using both quantitative and qualitative information simultaneously
- Analyzing a case study

Multi-Source Reasoning: Strategies

1. **DETERMINE THE SCOPE OF THE QUESTION:** First determine whether the question is more quantitative or verbal, as this will determine which strategies and tactics are appropriate for the question. If the question is more verbal, first think about what the key aspect or topic is of the entire case study. Then look at each tabbed section and identify its key aspect or topic. This will help you get a better understanding of the pieces of the puzzle and the puzzle as a whole. If the question is more quantitative, make sure you know what the basic objective of the question is and what variables are at play.

2. **DETERMINE THE "SO WHAT?":** Each section, particularly for the verbal-type questions, will have conclusions, inferences, and purposes from which you can extract deductions or use inductive reasoning. Think about what each section's purpose is and what the writer is trying to conclude. Again, you should do this both in context and in your own words (IYOW). Most of these questions will ask you to draw a conclusion, so understanding each section is key. The writer of each section will give you the "what," but you need to determine the "so what?"

3. **USE EACH QUESTION FOR DIRECTION:** Each question will give you a good idea of what issues or areas to focus on. The question should align with the scope and purpose you have already identified. If you are confused with all the information, you can first determine the main gist of the information and then look at the question. Depending on the question, you should be able to determine which section will be the best place to start.

4. **STRUCTURE YOUR INFORMATION:** Whether the question is qualitative, quantitative, or both, you will have to digest a lot of information. Write down the key pieces of information from each section, or create a chart that helps you sort out the issues or the math. Take the time to determine what would be the best tab to find the answer.

5. **LOOK AT THE STATEMENTS, AND ASK YOURSELF WHETHER THAT IS TRUE:** For every inference or conclusion you have to make, you will find support in the content. As a quick check, you can try two options. The first is to find the specific support from the statements. If you can find support, then you know the answer is correct. However, if you cannot find the support, the answer cannot be correct. The second option is to ask yourself whether the answer is true based on the statements. If you can find a plausible alternative inference, perhaps the statement is false or the answer is no.

E-mail 1: E-mail from **HR manager** to prospective employee

Oct 19, 2011, 4:45 P.M.

I have just spoken with the finance director, and we are pleased to offer you the position of Analyst, Financial Services within our organization. Your starting salary will be $55,000 prorated to the date that you start. Your full health and dental benefits will start within three months of your start date. I have attached a standard contract that outlines everything in our official offer.

We are anxious to get you going, so we are hoping you are willing to start right away this upcoming Monday, October 24, 2011. We look forward to your early confirmation so that we can start the paperwork before your first day.

If you have any questions, please do not hesitate to contact me.

E-mail 2: From **prospective employee** in response to HR manager's Oct 19, 2011, 4:45 P.M. message

Oct 21, 2011, 8:30 A.M.

Thank you so much for your offer. I am very pleased that you responded so promptly and are anxious to have me join your team. I want to ask for some more time to consider this offer, as I have been looking for a job externally over the past three months and now have other similar offers on the table.

Additionally, I would like to propose a later start date of November 14, 2011, because I would love to have some time to spend with my family on a vacation to celebrate the new position. My work-life balance is important to me since my wife and I had a baby last year and I have been working long hours over the past two years in my current role.

Lastly, I would like to ask for a higher starting base salary. The current industry rate, $55,000, is within the median range of salaries. However, your organization is well-known to be a Tier-1 company, so I would expect a salary more comparable to a top-quartile range. Additionally, I already have two years of experience in my current role as an analyst. I currently make $53,500 and thus would want a more senior role.

I look forward to your response.

TIP

On the actual GMAT, multiple documents (in this case, e-mails), will be in a document similar to an Excel document. You will be able to click back and forth between tabs containing different documents and sort information in multiple ways. However, for the sake of this book, the documents are presented one after another.

E-mail 3: E-mail from **HR manager** in response to the prospective employee's message.

Oct 21, 2:57 P.M.

Thank you for your e-mail. We understand your concerns and appreciate the time and energy you have put into your response.

At this time, I can offer you only a starting bonus of $6,000 if you start with us this coming Monday, October 24, 2011. I am authorized to also offer a new title of Senior Analyst, which will put you in the next higher salary grade, which will give you more room to grow with wage increases and bonuses. Finally, instead of our normal benefits package, I can offer additional room for more extended health and dental benefits, totaling approximately $2,000.

This offer is now final, conditional on your acceptance and nonnegotiable. We need to have a decision from you by Friday, October 21, 2011 at 5 P.M. Please confirm at your earliest convenience.

Consider each of the following statements. Does the information in the three sources support the inference as stated?

Yes	No	
◯	◯	The HR manager addressed the majority of the employee's demands.
◯	◯	The most important issue for the company is the starting date.
◯	◯	Both parties are in agreement over the starting salary and benefits.
◯	◯	If given similar offers from other companies, the prospective employee will likely favor a company that has a more flexible starting date.
◯	◯	If given similar offers from other companies, the prospective employee will likely not accept this current offer.

SOLUTION AND STRATEGY REVIEW

First, you should determine the basic gist of the question. This situation is basically a contract negotiation for employment. The person doing the hiring is negotiating the terms of the contract with the potential employee. More specifically, the first e-mail is the offer, which includes the title, salary, benefits, and start date. The second e-mail brings up issues surrounding the starting date and the salary. The third e-mail offers a starting bonus and extra benefits but remains firm on the starting date.

If you look at the purpose of each section, you can identify that the potential employee goes into some detail about the starting date. You can infer that this issue is quite important to him. He also mentions salary and puts together a cogent argument about his current salary, the industry, and his two years of experience.

What is really interesting is the last section. The person doing the hiring clearly has not directly addressed the potential hire's concerns and is not very flexible on the starting date.

You now have enough information and understanding to look at the questions.

(i) The employee's demands were starting time, base salary, and title. The HR manager offered a bonus, extra benefits, and a better title. Although there was accommodation on the job title, the HR manager did not meet the majority of the demands. **Therefore, the answer is No.**

(ii) The HR manager mentions expediting the process several times and has remained firm on the starting date, despite the employee's request. You can see key words such as "anxious," "early confirmation," and the entire last paragraph of the final e-mail saying that the offer was now "final." The company wants him to start right away. **Therefore, the answer is Yes.**

(iii) Although the HR manager offered extra benefits and the employee has needs for his new family, they are both still in disagreement over the starting salary. **Therefore, the answer is No.**

(iv) The key here is the "similar offers" from other companies. The employee has made it clear that a later starting date is important. If given the same offer, the employee "will likely" (another key phrase) accept an offer with a more favorable starting date. **Therefore, the answer is Yes.**

(v) This question is a little bit tougher, as you need to use some inductive reasoning here. The employee did mention that he was shopping around other offers. He also has been clear about the importance of a flexible starting date. Additionally, the HR manager has not addressed the potential employee's major concerns. Since other offers are at play, you can infer that he will "likely not" accept this offer. **Therefore, the answer is Yes.**

Note how important it is to understand the gist—subject, purpose, and conclusion—of the overall situation and each section. Understanding what drives each person and the main aspects of the case study are essential to doing well in this qualitative example of Multi-Source Reasoning.

Reading Comprehension | 6

→ **BASIC READING SKILLS**

→ **APPLYING BASIC READING SKILLS**

→ **PINPOINTING THE TOPIC SENTENCE**

→ **DETERMINING THE GENERAL THEME**

→ **FINDING LOGICAL RELATIONSHIPS**

→ **MAKING INFERENCES**

A large proportion of the GMAT is designed to test your ability to comprehend material contained in reading passages. The Reading Comprehension review is preparation for not only the Reading Comprehension questions on the test but also the Critical Reasoning questions. The Reading Comprehension questions do allow you to turn back to the passages when answering the questions. However, many of the questions may be based on what is *implied* in the passages, rather than on what is explicitly stated. Your ability to draw inferences from the material is critical to successfully completing these questions. It is also critical to your success on the Critical Reasoning questions, which test your ability to evaluate assumptions, inferences, and arguments.

In each case, success depends on the extent of your reading comprehension skills. The following discussion is designed to help you formulate an approach to reading passages that will enable you to better understand the material you will be asked to read on the GMAT. Practice exercises at the end of this chapter will give you an opportunity to try out this approach.

REMEMBER

Your answer may depend on what is implied in a passage rather than on explicit statements.

BASIC READING SKILLS

A critical reading skill to be developed is the ability to discover the central theme of a passage. By making yourself aware of what the entire passage is about, you are in a position to relate what you read to this central theme, logically picking out the main points and significant details as you go along. Although the manner in which the central theme is stated may vary from passage to passage, it can usually be found in the title (if one is presented), in the "topic sentence" of a paragraph in shorter passages, or, in longer passages, by reading several paragraphs.

Another essential skill is the capacity to organize mentally how the passage is put together and determine how each part is related to the whole. This is the skill you will have to use to the greatest degree on the GMAT, where you must pick out significant and insignificant factors, remember main details, and relate information you have read to the central theme.

In general, mastery of these basic skills will provide you with a solid basis for better reading comprehension wherein you will be able to read carefully to draw a conclusion from the material, decide the meanings of words and ideas presented and how they in turn affect the meaning of the passage, and recognize opinions and views that are expressed.

APPLYING BASIC READING SKILLS

The only ways to become adept at the basic reading skills are to practice using them as much as possible and to have a working knowledge of many words. In the same manner, making an effort to locate topic sentences, general themes, and specific details in material you read will enable you to improve your skills in these areas. The following drills will help. After you have read through them and answered the questions satisfactorily, you can try the longer practice exercises at the end.

PINPOINTING THE TOPIC SENTENCE

The term "topic sentence" is used to describe the sentence that gives the key to an entire paragraph. Usually the topic sentence is found in the beginning of a paragraph. However, there is no absolute rule. A writer may build the paragraph to a conclusion, putting the key sentence at the end. Here is an example in which the topic sentence is located at the beginning:

EXAMPLE 1

Line The world faces a serious problem of overpopulation. Right now many people
(2) starve from lack of adequate food. Efforts are being made to increase the rate of food production, but the number of people to be fed increases at a faster rate.

The idea is stated directly in the opening sentence. You know that the passage will be about "a serious problem of overpopulation." Like a heading or caption, the topic sentence sets the stage or gets your mind ready for what follows in that paragraph.

Before you try to locate the topic sentence in a paragraph you must remember that this technique depends upon reading and judgment. Read the whole passage first. Then try to decide which sentence comes closest to expressing the main point of the paragraph. Do not worry about the position of the topic sentence in the paragraph; look for the most important statement. Find the idea to which all the other sentences relate.

Try to identify the topic sentence in this passage:

During the later years of the American Revolution, the Articles of Confederation government was formed. This government suffered severely from a lack of power. Each state distrusted the others and gave little authority to

Line the central or federal government. The Articles of Confederation produced a

(5) government which could not raise money from taxes, prevent Indian raids, or force the British out of the United States.

What is the topic sentence? Certainly the paragraph is about the Articles of Confederation. However, is the key idea in the first sentence or in the second sentence? In this instance, the *second* sentence does a better job of giving you the key to this paragraph—the lack of centralized power that characterized the Articles of Confederation. The sentences that complete the paragraph relate more to the idea of "lack of power" than to the time when the government was formed. Don't assume that the topic sentence is always the first sentence of a paragraph. Try this:

There is a strong relation between limited education and low income. Statistics show that unemployment rates are highest among those adults who attended school the fewest years. Most jobs in a modern industrial society

Line require technical or advanced training. The best pay goes with jobs that

(5) demand thinking and decisions based on knowledge. A few people manage to overcome their limited education by personality or a "lucky break." However, studies of lifetime earnings show that the average high school graduate earns more than the average high school dropout, who in turns earns more than the average adult who has not finished eighth grade.

Here, the first sentence contains the main idea of the whole paragraph. One more example should be helpful:

They had fewer men available as soldiers. Less than one third of the railroads
Line and only a small proportion of the nation's industrial production was theirs.
(3)   For most of the war their coastline was blockaded by Northern ships. It is a
tribute to Southern leadership and the courage of the people that they were
not defeated for four years.

In this case you will note that the passage builds up to its main point. The topic
sentence is the last one. Practice picking out the topic sentences in other material
you read until it becomes an easy task.

DETERMINING THE GENERAL THEME

A more advanced skill is the ability to read several paragraphs and relate them to one general
theme or main idea. The procedure involves careful reading of the entire passage and deciding which idea is the central or main one. You can tell you have the right idea when it is most
frequent or most important, or when every sentence relates to it. As you read the next passage,
note the *underlined* parts.

True democracy means direct rule by the people. A good example can be
found in a modern town meeting in many small New England towns. All citizens aged 21 or over may vote. They not only vote for officials, but they also
Line get together to vote on local laws (or ordinances). The small size of the town
(5)   and the limited number of voters make this possible.
       In the cities, voters cast ballots for officials who get together to make the
laws. Because the voters do not make the laws directly, this system is called
indirect democracy or representative government. There is no problem of distance to travel, but it is difficult to run a meeting with hundreds of thousands
(10) of citizens.
       Representation of voters and a direct voice in making laws are more of a
problem in state or national governments. The numbers of citizens and the
distances to travel make representative government the most practical way
to make laws.

Think about the passage in general and the underlined parts in particular. Several
examples discuss voting for officials and making laws. In the first paragraph both of
these are done by the voters. The second paragraph describes representative government in which voters elect officials who make laws. The last paragraph emphasizes the problem of size and numbers and says that representative government is
more practical. In the following question, put all these ideas together.

The main theme of this passage is that

(A) the United States is not democratic
(B) citizens cannot vote for lawmakers
(C) representative government does not make laws
(D) every citizen makes laws directly
(E) increasing populations lead to less direct democracy

The answer is choice (E). Choices (B), (C), and (D) can be eliminated because they are not true of the passage. Choice (A) may have made you hesitate a little. The passage makes comments about *less direct* democracy, but it never says that representative government is *not democratic.*

The next three passages offer further practice in finding the main theme. Answer the question following each example and check the analysis to make sure you understand.

EXAMPLE 2

Skye, 13 miles off the northwest coast of Scotland, is the largest and most famous of the Hebrides. Yet fame has neither marred its natural beauty nor brought affectation to its inhabitants. The scene and the people are almost as
Line they were generations ago.
(5)   The first sight that impresses the visitor to Skye is its stark beauty. This is not beauty of the usual sort, for the island is not a lush green "paradise." It is, on the other hand, almost devoid of shrubbery. Mountains, moorlands, sky, and sea combine to create an overpowering landscape. Endless stretches of rocky hills dominate the horizon. Miles of treeless plains meet the eye. Yet this
(10) scene has a beauty all its own.
        And then cutting into the stark landscape are the fantastic airborne peaks of the Cuillins, rising into the clear skies above. The Cuillins are the most beloved mountains in Scotland and are frequently climbed. Their rugged, naked grandeur, frost-sculptured ridges and acute peaks even attracted Sir
(15) Edmund Hillary.

The main idea of this passage is

(A) the sky over Skye
(B) the lack of trees on Skye
(C) the natural beauty of Skye
(D) the lack of affectation on Skye
(E) the Cuillins in the skies of Skye

All of the answers have some truth to them. The problem is to find the best answer. Four of the choices are mentioned in the passage only by a small comment. But choice (C) is discussed throughout every part of the passage. The clue to the correct answer was how often the same theme was covered.

EXAMPLE 3

Trade exists for many reasons. No doubt it started from a desire to have something different. Men also realized that different men could make different products. Trade encouraged specialization, which led to improvement in Line quality.

(5)   Trade started from person to person, but grew to involve different towns and different lands. Some found work in transporting the goods or selling them. Merchants grew rich as the demand for products increased. Craftsmen were able to sell more products at home and abroad. People in general had a greater variety of things to choose.

(10)   The knowledge of new products led to an interest in the lands which produced them. More daring persons went to see other lands. Others stayed at home, but asked many questions of the travelers. As people learned about the products and the conditions in other countries, they compared them with their own. This often led to a desire for better conditions or a hope for a better

(15) life. Trade was mainly an economic force, but it also had other effects.

The general theme of the passage is how

(A) trade makes everyone rich
(B) trade divides the world
(C) products are made
(D) trade changes people's lives
(E) people find new jobs

This is not easy, as you may feel that all the choices are good. Most of them were mentioned in some part of the passage. However, you must select the best choice. If you had trouble, let us analyze the passage.

Paragraph one emphasizes a "desire" for "something different" and "improvement." The second paragraph mentions "found work," "merchants grew rich," "craftsmen . . . sell more," and "greater variety of things to choose." The third paragraph covers "interest in the lands," "compared them with their own," "desire for better conditions," and "better life." All these are evidence of the same general theme of how trade brings changes in the lives of people. *Choice (D) is the best answer.*

Choice (A) is tempting because of the comment on merchants getting rich. However, this idea is not found all through the passage. Choice (B) may catch the careless thinker. Trade does not divide the world, even though the passage talks about dividing jobs. Choice (C) is weak. Some comment is made about making products, but not in all parts of the passage. Choice (E) is weak for the same reason as choice (C).

EXAMPLE 4

The enormous problems of turning swamps and desert into fields and orchards, together with the ideal of share-and-share-alike, gave birth to the kibbutz.

Line In those days, the kibbutz member had to plow the fields with a rifle slung
(5) over his shoulder.

Today security is still a factor in the kibbutz. Shelters are furrowed into the ground along every walk among the shade trees, near the children's house, where all the young children of the kibbutz live, and near the communal dining room.

(10) But the swamps have been conquered, and the desert is gradually becoming green. And while kibbutz members once faced deprivation and a monotonous diet, today they reap the harvest of hard work and success.

One such kibbutz is Dorot, at the gateway to the Negev desert and typical of the average-size Israeli communal settlement.

(15) Life on the kibbutz has become more complex through growth and prosperity. While once the land barely yielded enough for a living, Dorot, like many other kibbutzim, now exports some of its crops. It also has become industrialized, another trend among these settlements. Dorot has a factory which exports faucets to a dozen countries, including the United States.

The main theme of this article is

(A) the manufacture of faucets is a sign of growth and prosperity in the kibbutz
(B) with the solving of agricultural problems the kibbutz has become a more complex society
(C) since security is a problem for the kibbutz, it has become industrialized
(D) Dorot is the prosperous gateway to the Negev desert
(E) kibbutzim are good places to live, although they are located in swamps and deserts

Choice (A) receives brief mention at the end of the passage. It is an idea in the passage, but certainly not the general idea of the passage. Choice (D) is the same kind of answer as choice (A)—it is too specific a fact. Choice (E) is unrelated to the passage. We now have choices (B) and (C) as possible answers. Choice (C) seems reasonable until you analyze it. Did the need for security *cause* the industrialization? Or are there better examples of how life has become more complex now that agricultural problems have been solved? The evidence leans more to choice (B).

In summary, in order to find the general theme:
1. Read at your normal speed.
2. Locate the topic sentence in each paragraph.
3. Note ideas that are frequent or emphasized.
4. Find the idea to which most of the passage is related.

FINDING LOGICAL RELATIONSHIPS

In order to understand fully the meaning of a passage, you must first look for the general theme and then relate the ideas and opinions found in the passage to this general theme. In this way, you can determine not only what is important but also how the ideas interrelate to form the whole. From this understanding, you will be better able to answer questions that refer to the passage.

As you read the following passages, look for general theme and supporting facts, words or phrases that signal emphasis or shift in thought, and the relation of one idea to another.

EXAMPLE 1

Candidates for election pay close attention to statements and actions that will make the voters see them favorably. In ancient Rome candidates wore pure white togas (the Latin word *candidatus* means "clothed in white") to indicate
Line that they were pure, clean, and above any "dirty work." However, it is interest-
(5) ing to note that such a toga was not worn after election.

In more modern history, candidates have allied themselves with political parties. Once a voter knows and favors the views of a certain political party, he may vote for anyone with that party's label. Nevertheless, divisions of opinion develop, so that today there is a wide range of candidate views in
(10) any major party.

1. The best conclusion to be drawn from the first paragraph is that after an election

    (A) all candidates are dishonest
    (B) candidates are less concerned with symbols of integrity
    (C) candidates do not change their ideas
    (D) officials are always honest
    (E) policies always change

You noted the ideas about a candidate in Rome. You saw the word "however" signal a shift in ideas or thinking. Now the third step rests with your judgment. You cannot jump to a conclusion; you must see which conclusion is reasonable or fair. Choices (A), (D), and (E) should make you wary. They say "all" or "always," which means without exception. The last sentence is not that strong or positive. Choices (B) and (C) must be considered. There is nothing in the paragraph that supports the fact that candidates do not change their ideas. This forces you into choice (B) as the only statement logically related to what the paragraph said.

2. A fair statement is that most candidates from the same political party today are likely to

    (A) have the same views
    (B) be different in every view
    (C) agree on almost all points
    (D) agree on some points and disagree on others
    (E) agree only by accident

Here again, the burden rests on your judgment after following ideas and word clues. The paragraph makes the point that there is a wide range of views. That eliminates choice (A). Choice (B) is not logical because the candidates would not likely be in the same party if they disagree on every view. The remaining choices are different degrees of agreement. Choice (E) is weak because candidates are too interested to arrive at agreement only by accident. The wide range mentioned seems to oppose choice (C) and favor choice (D) as a little more likely. You may say that choice (C) sounds pretty good. Again we stress that you *are picking the very best choice*, not just a good choice. That is what we mean by reflecting carefully on all possibilities and selecting the best available choice.

EXAMPLE 2

In 1812 Napoleon had to withdraw his forces from Russia. The armies had invaded successfully and reached the city of Moscow. There was no question of French army disloyalty or unwillingness to fight. As winter came, the Rus-

Line sian army moved out of the way, leaving a wasted land and burned buildings.

(5) Other conquered European nations seized upon Napoleon's problems in Russia as their chance to rearm and to break loose from French control.

According to the passage, it may be inferred that the main reason for Napoleon's withdrawal from Russia was the

(A) disloyalty of the French troops
(B) Russian winter
(C) burned buildings
(D) revolts in other countries
(E) Russian army

In this passage, only choice (A) is totally incorrect. Choice (E) is very weak because the Russian army was not able to stop the invasion. The choices narrow to which is the best of (B), (C), and (D). It seems that all three answers are supported by the passage. There needs to be some thought and judgment by you. Which of these could be overcome easily and which could be the strongest reason for Napoleon leaving Russia? The burned buildings could be overcome by the troops making other shelters. The Russian winter was severe and the army did not want to face it. However, marching out of Russia in the winter was also a great problem. Napoleon probably would have stayed in Moscow except for a more serious problem—the loss of the control he had established over most of Europe. Thus, answer (D) is best.

EXAMPLE 3

By 1915 events of World War I were already involving the United States and threatening its neutrality. The sinking of the British liner *Lusitania* in that year by a German submarine caused great resentment among Americans. Over a
Line hundred United States citizens were killed in the incident. President Wilson
(5) had frequently deplored the use of submarines by Germany against the United States. Since the United States was neutral, it was not liable to acts of war by another nation.

However, Wilson resolved to represent the strong feeling in the country (notably in the Midwest) and in the Democratic Party that United States neu-
(10) trality should be maintained. He felt that the United States should have "peace with honor," if possible.

There were also people, mostly in the East, who wanted to wage a preventive war against Germany. Such leaders as Theodore Roosevelt bitterly attacked Wilson as one who talked a great deal but did nothing.

(15) By 1917 Germany again used unrestricted submarine warfare and Wilson broke off relations with Germany. In February British agents uncovered the Zimmerman Telegram. This was an attempt by the German ambassador to Mexico to involve that nation in a war against the United States. And in March several American merchant ships were sunk by German submarines. His
(20) patience at an end, Wilson at last took the position of a growing majority of Americans and asked Congress to declare war on Germany. Thus, the United States entered World War I.

1. This passage tries to explain that

   (A) Wilson wanted the United States to go to war against Germany
   (B) Wilson tried to avoid war with Germany
   (C) Germany wanted the United States to enter the war
   (D) other nations were pressuring the United States to enter the war
   (E) Mexico was our main enemy

2. We can conclude from the passage that most citizens of the United States in 1917 were

   (A) totally opposed to war with Germany
   (B) in favor of war before Wilson was
   (C) willing to accept war after Wilson persuaded them
   (D) neutral
   (E) trying to avoid war

3. The last event in the series of happenings that led to a declaration of war against Germany was

   (A) the Zimmerman Telegram
   (B) attacks on U.S. merchant ships
   (C) Wilson's war message to Congress
   (D) a change in public opinion
   (E) the sinking of the *Lusitania*

In question 1, the key is to note Wilson's actions discussed in paragraph two. Near the end of the passage there is a phrase about "his patience at an end." This describes a man who was trying to avoid a conflict, as in answer choice (B).

Question 2 rests on two ideas. There was a change in the feeling of the American people about war. The other idea is that Wilson responded after he felt that they had changed. The phrase "took the position of a growing majority of Americans" tells us that Wilson followed the change in opinion, as in answer choice (B).

In question 3, you need to check the sequence of events. The declaration of war followed the president's request, so choice (C) is correct.

MAKING INFERENCES

An inference is assumed by the reader from something said by the writer. It is not stated directly. However, an inference must be true, not just likely or probable. It usually involves an opinion or viewpoint that the writer wants the reader to follow or assume. In another kind of inference, the reader figures out the author's opinion even though it is not stated. The clues are generally found in the manner in which facts are presented and in the choice of words and phrases. Opinion is revealed by the one-sided nature of a passage in which no opposing facts are given. It is shown further by "loaded" words that reveal the author's feelings.

It is well worth noting that opinionated writing is often more interesting than straight factual accounts. Some writers are very colorful, forceful, or amusing in presenting their views. You should understand that there is nothing wrong with reading opinion. You should read varied opinions, but know that they are opinions. Then make up your own mind.

Not every writer will insert an opinion obviously. However, you can get clues from how often the same idea is said (frequency), whether arguments are balanced on both sides (fairness), and the choice of wording (emotional or loaded words). Look for the clues in this next passage.

EXAMPLE 1

Slowly but surely the great passenger trains of the United States have been fading from the rails. Short-run commuter trains still rattle in and out of the cities. Between major cities you can still find a train, but the schedules are
Line becoming less frequent. The Twentieth Century Limited, The Broadway Lim-
(5) ited, and other luxury trains that sang along the rails at 60 to 80 miles an hour are no longer running. Passengers on other long runs complain of poor service, old equipment, and costs in time and money. The long-distance traveler today accepts the noise of jets, the congestion at airports, and the traffic between airport and city. A more elegant and graceful way is becoming only
(10) a memory.

1. With respect to the reduction of long-run passenger trains, this writer expresses

    (A) regret

    (B) pleasure

    (C) grief

    (D) elation

    (E) anger

Before you choose the answer, you must deduce what the writer's feeling is. He does not actually state his feeling, but clues are available so that you may infer what it is. Choices (B) and (D) are impossible, because he gives no word that shows he is pleased by the change. Choice (C) is too strong, as is choice (E). Choice (A) is the most reasonable inference to make. He is sorry to see the change. He is expressing regret.

2. The author seems to feel that air travel is

    (A) costly

    (B) slow

    (C) streamlined

    (D) elegant

    (E) uncomfortable

Here we must be careful because he says very little about air travel. However, his one sentence about it presents three negative or annoying points. The choice now becomes fairly clear. Answer (E) is correct.

EXAMPLE 2

When the United States was founded at the end of the eighteenth century, it was a small and weak country, made up mostly of poor farmers. Foreign policy, reflecting this domestic condition, stressed "no entangling alliances." The
Line State Department then had a staff of less than half a dozen persons, whose
(5) total salary was $6,600 (of which $3,500 went to the Secretary of State), and a diplomatic service budget (July, 1790) of $40,000. Militarily, too, the country was insignificant. The first United States army, soon after the American Revolution, was made up of one captain (John Doughty) and 80 men. Clearly, the United States did not consider itself a real power and was not taken seri-
(10) ously by the rest of the world.

It was not until immense changes took place *inside* the United States that the country began to play an important role in foreign affairs. By the beginning of the twentieth century, the United States had ceased to be a predominantly agricultural nation and had become an industrial one. Its population
(15) had grown to more than 30 times its original number. George Washington was president of 3,000,000 Americans; Theodore Roosevelt, of 100,000,000.

1. A country today cannot expect to play an important part in world affairs unless it

   I. has wealth
  II. has a large population
 III. is strong internally

  (A) I only
  (B) III only
  (C) I and II only
  (D) II and III only
  (E) I, II, and III

This is a slightly different style of question. You must look at each of the answer choices in I, II, and III. As you consider the passage and what it suggests, you note that each of the answer choices in I, II, and III make good sense. Therefore, answer choice (E) is the best answer because it includes all of the correct statements. Again, this is not designed to trick you. The purpose of such a question is to be sure that you have read all the choices.

2. The writer seems to think that a major factor in making the United States a world power was

  (A) industrialization
  (B) the passing of time
  (C) a change in government policies
  (D) the presidency of Theodore Roosevelt
  (E) the avoidance of entangling alliances

The passage does not answer the question directly. You must infer what is meant by the author. However, there is a clue in the author's comment that changes inside a country make a big difference in its foreign policy. The big internal changes noted are the growth of America's population and industrial power. By correctly interpreting the passage, you will be led to choice (A) for this question.

In Example 3 you will find three short statements by three different writers. The questions will require that you make inferences about each writer and then make comparisons of one against the other two.

EXAMPLE 3

Writer I

No nation should tolerate the slacker who will not defend his country in time of war. The so-called conscientious objector is a coward who accepts the benefits of his country but will not accept the responsibility. By shirking his fair share, he forces another person to assume an unfair burden.

Writer II

A democratic nation should have room for freedom of conscience. Religious training and belief may make a man conscientiously opposed to participation in war. The conscientious objector should be permitted to give labor service or some form of noncombat military duty. His beliefs should be respected.

Writer III

The rights of the conscientious objector should be decided by each individual. No government should dictate to any person or require him to endanger his life if the person, in conscience, objects. There need be no religious basis. It is enough for a free individual to think as he pleases and to reject laws or rules to which he conscientiously objects.

Line (5)
(10)
(15)

1. A balanced opinion on this subject is presented by

   (A) Writer I
   (B) Writer II
   (C) Writer III
   (D) all of the writers
   (E) none of the writers

2. We can conclude that the writer most likely to support a person who refuses any military service is

   (A) Writer I
   (B) Writer II
   (C) Writer III
   (D) all of the writers
   (E) none of the writers

3. An authoritarian person is most likely to agree with

   (A) Writer I
   (B) Writer II
   (C) Writer III
   (D) all of the writers
   (E) none of the writers

Look for clues in the language or choice of words that are loaded with feeling such as "slacker," "so-called," and "shirking" by Writer I and "dictate," "endanger," and "as he pleases" by Writer III. Compare them with the language used by Writer II. Then see if you can connect what these writers say with views you have heard or read. We are not asking you to accept any of these opinions. You are using your skill in reading what the writers think and adding it to your own knowledge. Then you make logical inferences. The correct answers are 1 (B), 2 (C), and 3 (A).

SUMMARY

Now that you have spent time reviewing the three basic skills—pinpointing the topic sentence, determining the general theme, and finding logical relationships—which you should master for better reading comprehension ability, try the three practice exercises that follow. Answers to these exercises appear on page 205. You should also try to spend time using this reading approach as you read other material not related to the GMAT.

The following three reading passages are similar to the Reading Comprehension passages found on the GMAT. You should read each one and then answer the questions that follow according to the directions. Remember that in Reading Comprehension sections you are permitted to refer to the passage while answering the questions.

EXERCISE A

TIME: 9 minutes

> DIRECTIONS: This part contains a reading passage. You are to read it carefully. When answering the questions, you *will* be able to refer to the passages. The questions are based on what is stated or *implied* in the passage. You have nine minutes to complete this part.

Recent years have seen an enormous expansion of interest in international comparisons of marketing systems. Much of this interest is an extension of the interest in international trade and business. It grows out of the desire of many American
Line companies to enlarge their operations overseas. What such companies want to know
(5) is how much of the marketing procedure they use at home can be applied abroad, how much must be modified and in what ways, how much must be avoided altogether, and what must be added that is not usable in the United States itself. The results of a comparative study of marketing systems may help to provide the needed information.

(10) What should we look for when we make thorough and comprehensive comparisons of marketing systems? First and most important is the search for generalizations (universals). We seek generalizations about marketing that can be applied in every society of which we have any knowledge. Whether generalizations of this scope are possible is one of the basic problems with which we have to deal in the study of
(15) marketing. Assuming that they are possible, we would like to know what they are and how to formulate them as accurately as possible.

In the absence of true universals, we look for limited generalizations. These will give us a basis for classifying countries according to their marketing systems. Perhaps we can find a basis for the differentiation of western from eastern countries,
(20) as well as between emerging and developed countries. Perhaps we can answer such questions as: "What significant differences are there between marketing in the United States and marketing in the developed countries of Western Europe?" "What similarities and differences are there between emerging and developed country marketing systems?"

Excerpted from: Reavis Cox, "The Search for Universals in Comparative Studies of Domestic Marketing Systems" in *American Marketing Association*, P. D. Bennett (ed.), *Marketing and Economic Development: Proceedings of the 1965 Fall Conference* (Chicago, 1965), pp. 143, 145.

1. The author of the passage is primarily concerned with accomplishing which of the following?

   (A) presenting a theory of marketing
   (B) describing a course of action
   (C) showing that there is growing interest in doing business abroad
   (D) defining what generalizations are
   (E) suggesting future directions for comparative marketing studies

2. It can be inferred from the passage that the author believes that

   (A) generalizations can be found in every society
   (B) comparative marketing studies can benefit business firms
   (C) there are significant differences between marketing systems
   (D) we have limited knowledge of emerging countries' marketing systems
   (E) information provided from comparative studies gives the background necessary to understand the performance of marketing systems

3. The author of the passage would most likely agree with which of the following?

   (A) Generalizations should not be made between countries with different marketing systems.
   (B) Searching for generalizations is a major problem for marketers.
   (C) Some generalization may enable characterizing countries by their stage of development.
   (D) A comparative study of marketing systems begins with a search for universals.
   (E) Comparative marketing studies are essential for firms wishing to enter new markets.

4. Which of the following titles best summarizes the content of the passage?

   (A) "In Search of True Universals"
   (B) "The Nature of Comparative Marketing Systems"
   (C) "The Search for Universals in Comparative Marketing Studies"
   (D) "A Functional Approach to the Study of Marketing Systems"
   (E) "A Comparative Approach to Marketing Systems"

5. The passage suggests that a comparative study of marketing systems

   (A) can determine whether marketing strategies need to be adapted or standardized
   (B) is limited because of methodological problems
   (C) can be applied only in countries in which we have any knowledge
   (D) may not be possible at all
   (E) will enable us to formulate

6. Which of the following can be inferred from lines 6–7 in the passage?

   (A) Marketing strategies that work in the United States may not succeed in other countries.
   (B) Marketing strategies cannot be standardized across countries.
   (C) One cannot generalize about different marketing systems.
   (D) It is imperative to search for universals before determining marketing strategies.
   (E) Some marketing strategies should be avoided in the United States.

EXERCISE B

TIME: 9 minutes

DIRECTIONS: This part contains a reading passage. You are to read it carefully. When answering the questions, you *will* be able to refer to the passages. The questions are based on what is stated or *implied* in the passage. You have nine minutes to complete this part.

Every person should be able to use his or her native language correctly. It only requires a little pain, a little care, a little study to enable one to do so, and the reward is great. All the words in the English language are divided into nine great classes.
Line These classes are called the Parts of Speech. They are Article, Noun, Adjective, Pro-
(5) noun, Verb, Adverb, Preposition, Conjunction and Interjection.

Of these, the noun is the most important, as all the others are more or less dependent upon it. A noun signifies the name of any person, place or thing, in fact, anything of which we can have either thought or idea.

There are two kinds of nouns, proper and common. Common nouns are names
(10) which belong in common like *man, woman, city*. Proper nouns distinguish individual members such as *John, Philadelphia, Mary*. In the former case *man* and *woman* are names which belong in common to the all humans, and *city* is also a name which is common to all large centers of population, but *John* and *Mary* signify a particular individual, while *Philadelphia* denotes a particular one from among the cities of
(15) the world.

Nouns are varied by person, number and gender. Person is that relation between the speaker, those addressed, and the subject under consideration. The persons are *first*, *second* and *third* and they represent respectively the speaker, the person addressed and the person or thing mentioned or under consideration.

(20) *Number* is the distinction of one from more than one. There are two numbers, singular and plural; the singular denotes one, the plural two or more. The plural is generally formed from the singular by the addition of *s* or *es*.

Gender has the same relation to nouns that sex has to individuals, but while there are only two sexes, there are four genders: masculine, feminine, neuter and "com-
(25) mon." The masculine gender denotes all those of the male kind, the feminine gender all those of the female kind, the neuter gender denotes inanimate things or whatever is without life, and the common gender is applied to animate beings, the sex of which for the time being is indeterminable, such as fish, mouse, bird, etc. Sometimes things which are without life as we conceive it are, by a *figure of speech called* personifica-
(30) tion, changed into either the masculine or feminine gender, as, for instance, we might say of the sun, *he* is rising; of the moon, *she* is setting.

An *article* is a word placed before a noun to show whether the latter is used in a particular or general sense. There are but two articles, *a* or *an* and *the*.

An *adjective* is a word which qualifies a noun, that is, which shows some distin-
(35) guishing mark or characteristic belonging to the noun.

Definitions

A *pronoun* is a word used for or instead of a noun to keep us from repeating the same noun too often. Pronouns, like nouns have number, gender and person. There are two kinds of pronouns, *personal* and *relative*. A *verb* is a word which signifies action
(40) or the doing of something. A verb is inflected by tense and mood and by number and person, though the latter two belong strictly to the subject of the verb. An *adverb* is a word which modifies a verb. A *preposition* serves to connect words and to show the relation between the objects which the words express. A *conjunction* is a word which joins words, phrases, clauses and sentences together. An *interjection* is a word which
(45) expresses surprise or some sudden emotion of the mind.

Excerpt from Chapter I of *How to Speak and Write Correctly* by Joseph Devlin

1. Which of the following titles best describes the content of the passage?

   (A) "The English Language"
   (B) "Parts of Speech"
   (C) "How to Speak and Write Correctly"
   (D) "The English Language in a Nutshell"
   (E) "Classification of English Words"

2. All of the following are used to present the author's view of the language EXCEPT

   (A) relative pronouns
   (B) gendered language
   (C) verb tenses
   (D) singular and plural
   (E) pronouns

3. The best description of the author's attitude toward the English language is

   (A) fastidious
   (B) objective
   (C) approving
   (D) hostile
   (E) ambivalent

4. The author mentions all of the following EXCEPT

   (A) four genders
   (B) style
   (C) nouns
   (D) adverbs
   (E) adjectives

5. The author provides information that would answer which of the following questions?

   (A) What is the definition of personification?
   (B) Why is it important to use language properly?
   (C) Why do words have gender?
   (D) Why are verbs best when they are active?
   (E) What perspective is best for a work of fiction?

EXERCISE C

TIME: 9 minutes

> DIRECTIONS: This part contains a reading passage. You are to read it carefully. When answering the questions, you *will* be able to refer to the passages. The questions are based on what is stated or *implied* in the passage. You have nine minutes to complete this part.

Man and nature were the culprits as Venice sank hopelessly—or so it seemed—into the 177 canals on which the city is built. While nature's work took ages, man's work was much quicker and more brutal. But now man is using his ingenuity to save
Line what he had almost destroyed. The sinking has been arrested and Venice should
(5) start rising again, like an oceanic phoenix from the canals.

The saving of Venice is the problem of the Italian Government, of course, but Venice is also a concern for Europe. And it happened that in the second half of 1975 Italy was in the chair of the European Council of Ministers. But the EC as such has no program for the salvation of Venice. "The Community is not a cultural community,"
(10) explained one Commission official. "There are some areas where it just does not have competence, the preservation of historical landmarks being one of them." So the efforts to save Venice have taken on a worldwide, rather than a Community-wide dimension.

Industrialization of the Porto Marghera area brought economic benefits to Ven-
(15) ice, but it also raped the city as growing air and water pollution began to take their toll on the priceless works of art and architecture. The danger of the imminent disappearance of Venice's cultural heritage was first brought to public attention in November 1966 when tides rose over six feet to flood Venice's canals and squares. Since then, various national and international organizations have sought ways and
(20) means to halt the destruction of the "queen of the Adriatic," though no one program has proved wholly satisfactory.

The US "Save Venice" group and the British "Venice in Peril" committee were formed to raise money for the restoration of priceless works of art and monuments. In 1967 the United Nations Educational, Scientific and Cultural Organization (UNESCO)
(25) took on the task of helping to save Venice by setting up a joint international advisory committee with the Italian Government. Such distant lands as Pakistan, no stranger to aid programs itself, joined in the effort, giving UNESCO a gift of 10,000 postage stamps for "Venice in Peril." Even a group of famous cartoonists felt moved to draw attention to the fact that "Venice must be saved" and organized an exhibit in 1973,
(30) with the Council of Europe in Strasbourg, France, and this year a ballet festival drew people and funds to Venice.

Though Venice, the city of bridge-linked islands, was built in the fifth century, the land on which it was built has been sinking "naturally" for a billion years. Movements of the earth's crust have caused the very slow and gradual descent of the Po
(35) Valley. And nature's forces aren't easily countered. Each year, Venice has been sinking about one millimeter into the lagoon which holds this Adriatic jewel. To add to Venice's peril, the slow melting of the polar cap causes the level of the sea to rise

another millimeter. If nothing is done to reverse nature's work, Venice is doomed to be another Atlantis, lost forever beneath the murky sea.

(40)   Man's part in the sink-Venice movement has been for reasons mainly economic. For the last 400 years, the population of Venice has been drifting toward the mainland to escape the isolation and inconvenience of living on a series of islets. Between 1951 and 1971, Venice lost 63,000 inhabitants. To curtail this migration, new, artificial land areas, on the Dutch model, were added to the old Venice. Venice's original
(45) builders had not been far-sighted enough and set the ground level at only a few inches above what they expected to be the maximum tides. The combination of reclaimed land and Porto Marghera industrialization have "squeezed" the lagoon until its waters have no place to go but . . . up.

     As Porto Marghera grows as an industrial port, and more and deeper channels
(50) are added for larger ships, currents become faster and dikes make the ravaging tides even more violent. The "acqua alta" has always been a problem for Venice, but with increased industrialization, flooding has become more frequent, sometimes occurring 50 times a year. Added to the violent "scirocco" that blows up to 60 miles an hour, Venice is rendered all the more vulnerable.

(55)   Yet Venice is not crumbling. Despite the visible decay caused by repeated floods and despite pollution that peels the stucco off the palazzi and eats away at their bottom-most steps, the structures are solid. The Rialto Bridge still stands safely on its ancient foundations supported by 6,000 piles.

     And something has been done to stop the damage done by water. Indeed, one
(60) simple measure has proved to work miracles. The ban on pumping from the thousands of artesian wells in and around the city—an easy source of water, but also a folly that caused a further descent of 5 millimeters a year—has been so effective that Venice should rise an inch in the next 20 years.

1. According to the passage, between 1951 and 1971, Venice lost approximately how many residents annually?

    (A) 475
    (B) 3,150
    (C) 6,300
    (D) 15,500
    (E) 63,000

2. The author's point of view is that Venice

    (A) cannot be saved from destruction
    (B) is in danger of imminent disappearance
    (C) is doomed to become another "Atlantis"
    (D) can be saved, but much work is necessary
    (E) must become a member of the EC

3. Which of the following conditions has *not* contributed to Venice's peril?

    (A) Movement of the earth's crust
    (B) Natural causes
    (C) Melting of the polar cap
    (D) Industrialization
    (E) Shipping on the canals

4. According to the passage, which of the following figures indicates the approximate year when Venice first began sinking?

    (A) 400 B.C.
    (B) A.D. 1400
    (C) A.D. 1966
    (D) A.D. 1970
    (E) None of the above

5. The author feels that Venice is an example of

    (A) a doomed city like Atlantis
    (B) uncontrolled conditions
    (C) a combination of natural and human destruction
    (D) international neglect
    (E) benign concern by international agencies

Answers and Analysis

EXERCISE A

1. **(B)** The author calls for a comparative study of marketing systems in the first paragraph and infers it in the last paragraph as well.
2. **(B)** The passage states that business firms wishing to expand their operations abroad need to know what marketing strategies to employ. If comparative marketing studies can provide some of the information needed to decision makers, businesses will be helped.
3. **(D)** This is stated in the second paragraph.
4. **(C)** This title summarizes the content of the passage.
5. **(A)** The passage suggests that adaptation or modification of marketing strategies can be decided upon through a comparative marketing study.
6. **(A)** It is not always known whether marketing strategies that are successful at home will be successful abroad. Note the part of the sentence that reads how much must be avoided altogether. This implies that what works at home may not work abroad.

EXERCISE B

1. **(D)** This passage does describe the English language. The other answers are either too specific or too broad.
2. **(C)** Although the passage discusses verbs, it does not mention verb tenses.
3. **(B)** Since the author uses few words that indicate emotion, the tone of the passage is best described as objective.
4. **(B)** The author discusses grammar, the parts of speech. There is no discussion of style— the art of writing.
5. **(A)** Paragraph 6 defines personification. *Sometimes things which are without life as we conceive it are, by a* figure of speech called *personification . . . .*

EXERCISE C

1. **(B)** 63,000 people were lost over a 20-year period (1951–1971), or approximately 3,150 annually.
2. **(D)** Venice can be saved, but much work is necessary. See lines 3–5.
3. **(E)** Answer (A) appears in lines 34–35, (B) in 33, (C) in 36–38, and (D) in lines 46–48. Choice (E) is not mentioned.
4. **(E)** In line 33 it is stated that the land on which Venice is situated has been sinking for a billion years.
5. **(C)** The theme is given in the first line and repeated in lines 34, 38–39, 40, 46–48, and 53.

Sentence Correction

7

→ **REVIEW OF COMMON ERRORS AND HOW TO AVOID THEM**
→ **STRATEGY FOR SELECTING THE CORRECT RESPONSE**

The Sentence Correction questions of the GMAT test your understanding of the basic rules of English grammar and usage. This chapter reviews those errors in grammar and usage that appear most frequently on the test.

On the GMAT you will be given sentences in which all or part of the sentence is underlined. You will then be asked to choose the best phrasing of the underlined part from five alternatives. (A) will always be the original phrasing.

EXAMPLE

Not having heard clearly, <u>the speaker was asked to repeat his statement.</u>

(A) the speaker was asked to repeat his statement.

(B) she asked the speaker to repeat again his statement.

(C) the speaker was asked to repeat his statement again.

(D) she asked the speaker to repeat his statement.

(E) she then asked the speaker again to repeat his statement.

Answer

(D) is the best choice.

REVIEW OF COMMON ERRORS AND HOW TO AVOID THEM

Since you need only *recognize* errors in grammar and usage for this part of the exam, this section of the book will review those errors most commonly presented in the GMAT and teach you *what to look for*. We will not review the *basic* rules of grammar, such as the formation and use of the different tenses and the passive voice, the subjective and objective cases of pronouns, the position of adjectives and adverbs, and the like. We assume that a candidate for the GMAT is familiar with basic grammar, and we will concentrate on error recognition based on that knowledge.

Verb Errors

1. ERRORS IN VERB TENSE

Check if the correct verb *tense* has been used in the sentence.

INCORRECT:	When I came home, the children still didn't finish dinner.
CORRECT:	When I came home, the children still hadn't finished dinner.
INCORRECT:	As we ate dinner, the phone rang.
CORRECT:	As we were eating dinner, the phone rang.

In REPORTED SPEECH, check that the rule of *sequence of tenses* has been observed.

INCORRECT:	She promised she will come.
CORRECT:	She promised she would come.
INCORRECT:	She said she doesn't know his phone number.
CORRECT:	She said she didn't know his phone number.
INCORRECT:	She claimed she has never been there.
CORRECT:	She claimed she had never been there.

2. ERRORS IN TENSE FORMATION

Check if the tense has been formed correctly. *Know* the past participle of irregular verbs!

INCORRECT:	He throwed it out the window.
CORRECT:	He threw it out the window.
INCORRECT:	Having just drank some water, I wasn't thirsty.
CORRECT:	Having just drunk some water, I wasn't thirsty.

3. ERRORS IN SUBJECT-VERB AGREEMENT

Check if the subject of the verb is singular or plural. Does the verb agree in number?
Multiple subjects will be connected by the word AND:

Ted, John, and I are going.

If a singular subject is separated by a comma from an accompanying phrase, *it remains singular.*

The bride, together with the groom and her parents, is receiving at the door.

INCORRECT:	There is many reasons why I can't help you.
CORRECT:	There are many reasons why I can't help you.
INCORRECT:	Sir Lloyd, accompanied by his wife, were at the party.
CORRECT:	Sir Lloyd, accompanied by his wife, was at the party.

INCORRECT:	His mastery of several languages and the social graces make him a sought-after dinner guest.
CORRECT:	His mastery of several languages and the social graces makes him a sought-after dinner guest.

4. ERRORS IN CONDITIONAL SENTENCES

In conditional sentences, the word *if* will NEVER be followed by the words *will* or *would*.

Here are the correct conditional forms:

FUTURE:	If I have time, I will do it tomorrow.
PRESENT:	If I had time, I would do it now.
PAST:	If I had had time, I would have done it yesterday.

Sentences using the words *when, as soon as, the moment*, etc., are formed like future conditionals:

I will tell him if I see him.
I will tell him when I see him.

The verb *to be* will ALWAYS appear as *were* in the present conditional:

If I were you, I wouldn't do that.
She wouldn't say so if she weren't sure.

NOTE: Not all sentences containing *if* are conditionals. When *if* appears in the meaning of *whether*, it may take the future:

I don't know if he will be there. (I don't know whether he will be there.)

INCORRECT:	If I would have known, I wouldn't have gone.
CORRECT:	If I had known, I wouldn't have gone.

INCORRECT:	You wouldn't be so tired if you weren't going to bed so late.
CORRECT:	You wouldn't be so tired if you didn't go to bed so late.

INCORRECT:	Call me the moment you will get home.
CORRECT:	Call me the moment you get home.

INCORRECT:	We could go to the beach if it wasn't so hot.
CORRECT:	We could go to the beach if it weren't so hot.

5. ERRORS IN EXPRESSIONS OF DESIRE

Unfulfilled desires are expressed by the form "_____ had hoped that _____ would (or *could*, or *might*) do _____ ."

I had hoped that I would pass the exam.

Expressions with *wish* are formed as follows:

PRESENT:	I wish I knew him.
FUTURE:	I wish you could (would) come.
PAST:	I wish he had come. (or could have come, would have come, might have come)

NOTE: As in conditionals, the verb *to be* will ALWAYS appear as *were* in the present: I wish she were here.

INCORRECT:	I wish I heard that story about him before I met him.
CORRECT:	I wish I had heard (or could have heard or would have heard) that story about him before I met him.

INCORRECT:	She wishes you will be on time.
CORRECT:	She wishes you could (or would) be on time.

6. ERRORS IN VERBS FOLLOWED BY VERB WORDS

The following list consists of words and expressions that are followed by a VERB WORD (the infinitive without the *to*):

ask	prefer	requirement
demand	recommend	suggest
desire	recommendation	suggestion
insist	require	urge

It is essential/imperative/important/necessary that . . .

INCORRECT:	She ignored the doctor's recommendation that she stops smoking.
CORRECT:	She ignored the doctor's recommendation that she stop smoking.

INCORRECT:	It is essential that you are on time.
CORRECT:	It is essential that you be on time.

INCORRECT:	He suggested that we should meet at the train.
CORRECT:	He suggested that we meet at the train.

7. ERRORS IN NEGATIVE IMPERATIVES

Note the two forms for negative imperatives:

A. Please don't do that.
B. Would you please not do that.

INCORRECT:	Would you please don't smoke here.
CORRECT:	Please don't smoke here.
	OR
	Would you please not smoke here.

8. ERRORS IN AFFIRMATIVE AND NEGATIVE AGREEMENT OF VERBS

Note the two correct forms for *affirmative* agreement:

A. I am an American and so is she.
B. I am an American and she is too.

A. Mary likes Bach and so does John.
B. Mary likes Bach and John does too.

A. My father will be there and so will my mother.
B. My father will be there and my mother will too.

INCORRECT:	I have seen the film and she also has.
CORRECT:	I have seen the film and so has she.
	OR
	I have seen the film and she has too.

Note the two correct forms for *negative* agreement:

A.   I'm not American and he isn't either.
B.   I'm not American and neither is he.

A.   Mary doesn't like Bach and John doesn't either.
B.   Mary doesn't like Bach and neither does John.

A.   My father won't be there and my mother won't either.
B.   My father won't be there and neither will my mother.

INCORRECT:	I haven't seen the film and she hasn't neither.
CORRECT:	I haven't seen the film and she hasn't either.
	OR
	I haven't seen the film and neither has she.

9. ERRORS OF INFINITIVES OR GERUNDS IN THE COMPLEMENT OF VERBS

Some verbs may be followed by either an infinitive or a gerund:

I love swimming at night.
I love to swim at night.

Other verbs, however, may require either one *or* the other for idiomatic reasons. Following is a list of the more commonly used verbs in this category:

Verbs requiring an INFINITIVE:

agree	fail	intend	promise
decide	hope	learn	refuse
expect	want	plan	

Verbs requiring a GERUND:

admit	deny	quit
appreciate	enjoy	regret
avoid	finish	risk
consider	practice	stop

Phrases requiring a GERUND:

approve of	do not mind	keep on
be better off	forget about	look forward to
can't help	insist on	think about
count on	get through	think of

INCORRECT:	I intend learning French next semester.
CORRECT:	I intend to learn French next semester.

INCORRECT:	I have stopped to smoke.
CORRECT:	I have stopped smoking.

INCORRECT:	We are looking forward to see you.
CORRECT:	We are looking forward to seeing you.

10. ERRORS IN VERBS REQUIRING **HOW** IN THE COMPLEMENT

The verbs KNOW, TEACH, LEARN, and SHOW require the word *HOW* before an infinitive in the complement.

INCORRECT:	She knows to drive.
CORRECT:	She knows how to drive.

INCORRECT:	I will teach you to sew.
CORRECT:	I will teach you how to sew.

11. ERRORS IN TAG ENDINGS

Check for *three* things in tag endings:

A. Does the ending use the *same person* as the sentence verb?

B. Does the ending use the *same tense* as the sentence verb?

C. If the sentence verb is positive, is the ending negative; if the sentence verb is negative, is the ending positive?

It's nice here, isn't it?
It isn't nice here, is it?
She speaks French, doesn't she?
She doesn't speak French, does she?
They'll be here tomorrow, won't they?
They won't be here tomorrow, will they?

EXCEPTIONS:

I'm right, aren't I?
We ought to go, shouldn't we?
Let's see, shall we?

NOTE: If there is a contraction in the sentence verb, make sure you know what the contraction stands for:

INCORRECT:	She's been there before, isn't she?
CORRECT:	She's been there before, hasn't she?

INCORRECT:	You'd rather go yourself, hadn't you?
CORRECT:	You'd rather go yourself, wouldn't you?

12. ERRORS IN IDIOMATIC VERB EXPRESSIONS

Following are a few commonly used idiomatic verb expressions. Notice whether they are followed by a verb word, a participle, an infinitive, or a gerund. Memorize a sample of each to check yourself when choosing an answer:

A. *must have* (*done*)—meaning "it is a logical conclusion"

They're late. They must have missed the bus.
There's no answer. They must have gone out.

B. *had better* (*do*)—meaning "it is advisable"

It's getting cold. You had better take your coat.
He still has fever. He had better not go out yet.

C. *used to* (*do*)—meaning "was in the habit of doing in the past"

I used to smoke a pack of cigarettes a day, but I stopped.
When I worked on a farm, I used to get up at 4:30 in the morning.

D. *to be used to*—meaning "to be accustomed to"

to get used to
}—meaning "to become accustomed to"
to become used to

The noise doesn't bother me; I'm used to studying with the radio on.
In America you'll get used to hearing only English all day long.

E. *make* someone *do*—meaning "force someone to do"
have someone *do*—meaning "cause someone to do"
let someone *do*—meaning "allow someone to do"

My mother made me take my little sister with me to the movies.
The teacher had us write an essay instead of taking an exam.
The usher didn't let us come in until the intermission.

F. *would rather*—meaning "would prefer"

I would rather speak to her myself.
I would rather not speak to her myself.

But if the preference is for someone *other than the subject* to do the action, use the PAST:

I would rather you spoke to her.
I would rather you didn't speak to her.

Pronoun Errors

1. ERRORS IN PRONOUN SUBJECT-OBJECT

Check if a pronoun is the SUBJECT or the OBJECT of a verb or preposition.

INCORRECT:	All of us—Fred, Jane, Alice, and me—were late.
CORRECT:	All of us—Fred, Jane, Alice, and I—were late.

INCORRECT:	How could she blame you and he for the accident?
CORRECT:	How could she blame you and him for the accident?

2. ERRORS WITH WHO AND WHOM

When in doubt about the correctness of WHO/WHOM, try substituting the subject/object of a simpler pronoun to clarify the meaning:

I don't know who/whom Sarah meant.

Try substituting *he/him*; then rearrange the clause in its proper order:

he/him Sarah meant / Sarah meant him

Now it is clear that the pronoun is the *object* of the verb *meant*, so *whom* is called for.

CORRECT: I don't know whom Sarah meant.

ANOTHER EXAMPLE:

There was a discussion as to who/whom was better suited.

Try substituting *she/her*:

she was better suited / her was better suited

Here the pronoun is the *subject* of the verb *suited*:

CORRECT: There was a discussion as to who was better suited.

3. ERRORS OF PRONOUN SUBJECT-VERB AGREEMENT

Check if the pronoun and its verb agree in number. Remember that the following are *singular:*

anyone	either	neither	what
anything	everyone	no one	whatever
each	everything	nothing	whoever

These are *plural:*

both	many	several	others
few			

INCORRECT: John is absent, but a few of the class is here.
CORRECT: John is absent but a few of the class are here.

INCORRECT: Everyone on the project have to come to the meeting.
CORRECT: Everyone on the project has to come to the meeting.

INCORRECT: Either of those dresses are suitable for the party.
CORRECT: Either of those dresses is suitable for the party.

INCORRECT: Neither of them are experts on the subject.
CORRECT: Neither of them is an expert on the subject.

NOTE: The forms "either . . . or" and "neither . . . nor" are singular and take a singular verb. For reasons of diction, however, if the noun immediately preceding the verb is plural, use a plural verb. An English speaker finds it difficult to pronounce a singular verb after a plural subject, as in ". . . they is coming," even though "they" is preceded by "Neither he nor . . . ."

Either his parents or he is bringing it.
Either he or his parents are bringing it.
Neither his parents nor he was there.
Neither he nor his parents were there.

4. ERRORS OF POSSESSIVE PRONOUN AGREEMENT

Check if possessive pronouns agree in *person* and *number*.

INCORRECT:	If anyone calls, take their name.
CORRECT:	If anyone calls, take his name.

INCORRECT:	Those of us who care should write to their congressman.
CORRECT:	Those of us who care should write to our congressman.

INCORRECT:	Some of you will have to come in their own cars.
CORRECT:	Some of you will have to come in your own cars.

5. ERRORS IN PRONOUNS AFTER THE VERB **TO BE**

TO BE is an intransitive verb and will always be followed by a subject pronoun.

INCORRECT:	It must have been her at the door.
CORRECT:	It must have been she at the door.

INCORRECT:	I wish I were him!
CORRECT:	I wish I were he!

INCORRECT:	He didn't know that it was me who did it.
CORRECT:	He didn't know that it was I who did it.

6. ERRORS IN POSITION OF RELATIVE PRONOUNS

A relative pronoun refers to the word preceding it. If the meaning is unclear, the pronoun is in the wrong position.

INCORRECT:	He could park right in front of the door, which was very convenient.

Since it was not the door which was convenient, the "which" is illogical in this position. In order to correct the sentence, it is necessary to rewrite it completely:

CORRECT:	His being allowed to park right in front of the door was very convenient.

INCORRECT:	The traffic was very heavy, which made me late.
CORRECT:	I was late because of the heavy traffic.

OR

The heavy traffic made me late.

7. ERRORS IN PARALLELISM OF IMPERSONAL PRONOUNS

In forms using impersonal pronouns, use *either* "one . . . one's/his or her" *or* "you . . . your."

INCORRECT:	One should take your duties seriously.
CORRECT:	One should take one's/ his or her duties seriously.

OR

You should take your duties seriously.

INCORRECT:	One should have their blood pressure checked regularly.
CORRECT:	One should have one's/ his or her blood pressure checked regularly.

OR

You should have your blood pressure checked regularly.

Adjective and Adverb Errors

1. ERRORS IN THE USE OF ADJECTIVES AND ADVERBS

Check if a word modifier is an ADJECTIVE or an ADVERB. Make sure the correct form has been used.

An ADJECTIVE describes a noun and answers the question, *What kind*?

She is a good cook. (What kind of cook?)

An ADVERB describes either a verb or an adjective and answers the question, *How*?

She cooks well. (She cooks how?)

This exercise is relatively easy. (How easy?)

Most adverbs are formed by adding *-ly* to the adjective.

EXCEPTIONS

Adjective	*Adverb*
early	early
fast	fast
good	well
hard	hard (*hardly* means *almost not*)
late	late (*lately* means *recently*)

INCORRECT:	I sure wish I were rich!
CORRECT:	I surely wish I were rich!

INCORRECT:	The young man writes bad.
CORRECT:	The young man writes badly.

INCORRECT:	He's a real good teacher.
CORRECT:	He's a really good teacher.

2. ERRORS OF ADJECTIVES WITH VERBS OF SENSE

The following verbs of sense are intransitive and are described by ADJECTIVES:

be	look	smell	taste
feel	seem	sound	

INCORRECT:	She looked very well.
CORRECT:	She looked very good.

NOTE: "He is well" is also correct in the meaning of "He is healthy" or in describing a person's well-being.

INCORRECT:	The food tastes deliciously.
CORRECT:	The food tastes delicious.

NOTE: When the above verbs are used as transitive verbs, modify with an adverb, as usual: She tasted the soup quickly.

3. ERRORS IN COMPARATIVES

A. Similar comparison

ADJECTIVE: She is as <u>pretty</u> as her sister.

ADVERB: He works as <u>hard</u> as his father.

B. Comparative (of two things)

ADJECTIVE: She is <u>prettier</u> than her sister.

She is more <u>beautiful</u> than her sister.

She is less <u>successful</u> than her sister.

ADVERB: He works <u>harder</u> than his father.

He reads more <u>quickly</u> than I.

He drives less <u>carelessly</u> than he used to.

NOTE 1: A pronoun following *than* in a comparison will be the *subject pronoun*:

You are prettier than she (is).
You drive better than he (does).

NOTE 2: In using comparisons, adjectives of one syllable, or of two syllables ending in -*y*, add -*er*: smart, smarter; pretty, prettier. Other words of more than one syllable use *more*: interesting, more interesting. Adverbs of one syllable add -*er*; longer adverbs use *more*: fast, faster; quickly, more quickly.

NOTE 3: The word *different* is followed by *from*:

You are <u>different</u> from me.

C. Superlative (comparison of more than two things)

ADJECTIVE: She is the <u>prettiest</u> girl in her class.

He is the most <u>successful</u> of his brothers.

This one is the least <u>interesting</u> of the three.

ADVERB: He plays the <u>best</u> of all.

He speaks the most <u>interestingly</u>.

He spoke to them the least <u>patronizingly</u>.

EXCEPTIONAL FORMS

good	better	best
bad	worse	worst
much/many	more	most
little	less	least

INCORRECT: This exercise is harder then the last one.

CORRECT: This exercise is harder than the last one.

INCORRECT: He works faster than her.

CORRECT: He works faster than she.

INCORRECT:	She is the more responsible person of the three.
CORRECT:	She is the most responsible person of the three.

INCORRECT:	She was much different than I expected.
CORRECT:	She was much different from what I expected.

INCORRECT:	This year I'll have littler free time.
CORRECT:	This year I'll have less free time.

4. ERRORS IN PARALLEL COMPARISONS

In parallel comparisons, check if the correct form has been used.

INCORRECT:	The more you practice, you will get better.
CORRECT:	The more you practice, the better you will get.

INCORRECT:	The earlier we leave, we will get there earlier.
CORRECT:	The earlier we leave, the earlier we will get there.

INCORRECT:	The busier you become, lesser time you have for reading.
CORRECT:	The busier you become, the less time you have for reading.

5. ERRORS OF ILLOGICAL COMPARATIVES

Check comparisons to make sure they *make sense*.

INCORRECT:	Alaska is bigger than any state in the United States.
CORRECT:	Alaska is bigger than any other state in the United States. (If Alaska were bigger than *any state*, it would be bigger than itself!)

INCORRECT:	That is the most important of any other reason.
CORRECT:	That is the most important reason.

INCORRECT:	Of the two books, this one is best.
CORRECT:	Of the two books, this one is better.

6. ERRORS OF IDENTICAL COMPARISONS

Something can be *the same as* OR *like* something else. Do not mix up the two forms.

INCORRECT:	Your dress is the same like mine.
CORRECT:	Your dress is like mine.

OR

Your dress is the same as mine.

7. ERRORS IN IDIOMS USING COMPARATIVE STRUCTURES

Some idiomatic terms are formed like comparatives, although they are not true comparisons:

as high as	as much as	as few as
as little as	as many as	

INCORRECT:	You may have to spend so much as two hours waiting.
CORRECT:	You may have to spend as much as two hours waiting.

INCORRECT:	It cost twice more than I thought it would.
CORRECT:	It cost twice as much as I thought it would.

8. ERRORS IN NOUN-ADJECTIVES

When a NOUN is used as an ADJECTIVE, treat it as an adjective. Do not pluralize or add *'s.*

INCORRECT:	You're talking like a two-years-old child!
CORRECT:	You're talking like a two-year-old child!

9. ERRORS IN MODIFYING COUNTABLE AND NONCOUNTABLE NOUNS

If a noun can be preceded by a number, it is a countable noun and will be modified by these words:

a few	many, more	some
few, fewer	number of	

If it cannot be preceded by a number, it is noncountable and will be modified by these words:

amount of	little, less	some
a little	much, more	

INCORRECT:	I was surprised by the large amount of people who came.
CORRECT:	I was surprised by the large number of people who came.

INCORRECT:	You need only a little eggs in this recipe.
CORRECT:	You need only a few eggs in this recipe.

Errors in Usage

1. ERRORS IN CONNECTORS

There are several ways of connecting ideas. Do not mix the different forms:

and	also	not only . . . but also
too	as well as	both . . . and

INCORRECT:	She speaks not only Spanish but French as well.
CORRECT:	She speaks Spanish and French.

She speaks Spanish. She also speaks French.
She speaks Spanish and French too.
She speaks not only Spanish but also French.
She speaks both Spanish and French.
She speaks Spanish as well as French.

2. ERRORS IN QUESTION WORD CONNECTORS

When a question word such as *when* or *what* is used as a connector, the clause that follows is *not* a question. Do not use the interrogative form.

INCORRECT:	Do you know when does the movie start?
CORRECT:	Do you know when the movie starts?

INCORRECT:	I don't know what is his name.
CORRECT:	I don't know what his name is.

INCORRECT:	Did he tell you why hasn't he come yet?
CORRECT:	Did he tell you why he hasn't come yet?

3. ERRORS IN PURPOSE CONNECTORS

The word *so* by itself means *therefore*.

It was too hot to study, so we went to the beach.

So that means *in order to* or *in order that*.

INCORRECT: We took a cab so we would be on time.

CORRECT: We took a cab so that we would be on time.

4. ERRORS WITH BECAUSE

It is incorrect to say: *The reason is because . . .* Use: *The reason is that . . .*

INCORRECT:	The reason he was rejected was because he was too young.
CORRECT:	The reason he was rejected was that he was too young.

OR

He was rejected because of his young age.

OR

He was rejected because he was too young.

5. ERRORS OF DANGLING MODIFIERS

An introductory verbal modifier should be directly followed by the noun or pronoun that it modifies. Such a modifier will start with a gerund or participial phrase and be followed by a comma. Look for the modified noun or pronoun *immediately* after the comma.

INCORRECT:	Seeing that the hour was late, it was decided to postpone the committee vote.
CORRECT:	Seeing that the hour was late, the committee decided to postpone the vote.
INCORRECT:	Unaccustomed to getting up early, it was difficult for him to get to work on time.
CORRECT:	Unaccustomed to getting up early, he found it difficult to get to work on time.
INCORRECT:	Wanting to get feedback, a questionnaire was handed out to the audience.
CORRECT:	Since the speaker wanted to get feedback, she handed out a questionnaire to the audience.

6. ERRORS IN PARALLEL CONSTRUCTION

In sentences containing a series of two or more items, check if the same form has been used for all the items in the series. Do *not* mix infinitives with gerunds, adjectives with participial phrases, or verbs with nouns.

INCORRECT:	The film was interesting, exciting, and it was made well.
CORRECT:	The film was interesting, exciting, and well made.
INCORRECT:	The purpose of the meeting is to introduce new members and raising money.
CORRECT:	The purpose of the meeting is to introduce new members and to raise money.
	OR
	The purpose of the meeting is introducing new members and raising money.
INCORRECT:	He died unloved, unknown, and without any money.
CORRECT:	He died unloved, unknown, and penniless.
INCORRECT:	He was popular because of his sense of humor, his intelligence, and he could get along with people.
CORRECT:	He was popular because of his sense of humor, his intelligence, and his ability to get along with people.
	OR
	He was popular because he had a sense of humor, was intelligent, and could get along with people.

7. ERRORS OF UNNECESSARY MODIFIERS

In general, the more simply an idea is stated, the better it is. An adverb or adjective can often eliminate extraneous words.

INCORRECT:	She drove in a careful way.
CORRECT:	She drove carefully.
INCORRECT:	The problem was difficult and delicate in nature.
CORRECT:	It was a difficult, delicate problem.

Beware of words with the same meaning in the same sentence.

INCORRECT:	The new innovations were startling.
CORRECT:	The innovations were startling.
INCORRECT:	Would you please repeat again what you said?
CORRECT:	Would you please repeat what you said?
INCORRECT:	He left more richer than when he came.
CORRECT:	He left richer than when he came.

Beware of general wordiness.

INCORRECT:	That depends on the state of the general condition of the situation.
CORRECT:	That depends on the situation.

8. ERRORS OF COMMONLY CONFUSED WORDS

Following are some of the more commonly misused words in English:

to lie	lied	lied	lying	to tell an untruth
to lie	lay	lain	lying	to recline
to lay	laid	laid	laying	to put down

(*Idiomatic* usage: LAY THE TABLE, put dishes, etc., on the table; CHICKENS LAY EGGS; LAY A BET, make a bet)

to rise	rose	risen	rising	to go up; to get up
to arise	arose	arisen	arising	to wake up; to get up

(*Idiomatic* usage: A PROBLEM HAS ARISEN, a problem has come up)

to raise	raised	raised	raising	to lift; bring up

(*Idiomatic* usage: TO RAISE CHILDREN, to bring up children; TO RAISE VEGETABLES, to grow vegetables; TO RAISE MONEY, to collect funds for a cause)

to set	set	set	setting	to put down

(*Idiomatic* usage: SET A DATE, arrange a date; SET THE TABLE, put dishes, etc., on the table; THE SUN SET, the sun went down for the night; TO SET THE CLOCK, to adjust the timing mechanism of a clock)

to sit	sat	sat	sitting	to be in or get into a sitting position

to let	let	let	letting	to allow; to rent
to leave	left	left	leaving	to go away

formerly—previously
formally—in a formal way

to affect—to influence (verb)
effect—result (noun)

INCORRECT:	He was laying in bed all day yesterday.
CORRECT:	He was lying in bed all day yesterday.
INCORRECT:	It had laid in the closet for a week before we found it.
CORRECT:	It had lain in the closet for a week before we found it.
INCORRECT:	The price of gas has raised three times last year.
CORRECT:	The price of gas rose three times last year.
	OR
	The price of gas was raised three times last year.
INCORRECT:	He raised slowly from his chair.
CORRECT:	He arose slowly from his chair.
INCORRECT:	We just set around the house all day.
CORRECT:	We just sat around the house all day.

INCORRECT:	His mother wouldn't leave him go with us.
CORRECT:	His mother wouldn't let him go with us.

INCORRECT:	All the men were dressed formerly.
CORRECT:	All the men were dressed formally.

INCORRECT:	My words had no affect on her.
CORRECT:	My words had no effect on her.

9. ERRORS OF MISUSED WORDS AND PREPOSITIONAL IDIOMS

A. in spite of; despite

The two expressions are synonymous; use *either* one *or* the other.

INCORRECT:	They came despite of the rain.
CORRECT:	They came in spite of the rain.
	OR
	They came despite the rain.

B. scarcely; barely; hardly

All three words mean *almost not at all*; do NOT use a negative with them.

INCORRECT:	I hardly never see him.
CORRECT:	I hardly ever see him.

INCORRECT:	He has scarcely no money.
CORRECT:	He has scarcely any money.

C. Note and memorize the prepositions in these common idioms:

agree/disagree with
approve/disapprove of
be afraid of
be ashamed of
be bored with
be conscious of
be equal to
be interested in
capable/incapable of
compare to (point out similarities between things of a different order)
compare with (point out differences between things of the same order)
dependent on
except for
in the habit of
independent of
next to
related to
similar to

D. Confusion of words that *sound alike*:

adapt—to change, to adjust
adept—skilled

advice—counsel (n.)
advise—to give advice (v.)

affect—to influence (v.)
effect—result (n.)

afflicted—stricken
inflicted—caused or imposed something negative

affront—to insult
confront—to face

alteration—a change
altercation—argument

allude—to refer to indirectly
elude—to evade

allusion—a reference to
illusion—unreal image
delusion—false belief

apprise—to let know
appraise—to estimate the value of

beside—near
besides—in addition

capital—money; punishable by death; large form of letter
Capitol—the U.S. house of legislature

caret—a mark used in proofreading
carat—unit of gem weight
carrot—an orange vegetable

censor—one who screens objectionable material
censure—condemnation

cite—to quote
sight—vision
site—location

coherent—intelligible
inherent—a naturally included quality

collaborate—to work together
corroborate—to confirm

command—to order
commend—to praise

compile—to collect
comply—to consent

complement—to make complete
compliment—to praise

continual—happening often
continuous—happening uninterruptedly

conscientious—diligent
conscious—aware; awake

credible—believable
creditable—worthy of credit or praise
credulous—believing anything

depredation—a robbing
deprecation—disapproval

detain—to keep or hold up
retain—to keep in possession; to remember

detracted—taken away from
distracted—diverted

devise—to create
revise—to change; to improve

devolve—to deliver from one possessor to another
evolve—to develop

discouraging—seeming to be with no chance of success
disparaging—belittling

disinterested—having nothing personal to gain; impartial
uninterested—having no interest in

elegant—graceful; refined; with good taste
eloquent—persuasive; fluent (speech or writing)

elicit—to draw out
illicit—unlawful

emigrant—one who leaves a country to settle in another
immigrant—one who comes to a new country to settle

eminent—famous; prominent
imminent—impending
immanent—universal

epaulet—a shoulder decoration (usually on a uniform)
epithet—a descriptive word or phrase

epic—a long poem dealing with heroic deeds
epoch—a period of time marked by noteworthy people or events

flouting—scorning
flaunting—showing off provocatively

foreword—introduction to a book
forward—toward the front

gorilla—an ape
guerrilla—a soldier of the underground

horde—a crowd
hoard—to store up a supply

human—belonging to the race of man
humane—kind

immoral—without a sense of morality
immortal—able to live forever

imply—to hint
infer—to conclude from a known fact

in—within
inn—a pub or hostel

incandescent—glowing
clandestine—secret

incite—to urge to action
insight—quality of perceptiveness

incorporate—to include; to merge
incarcerate—to imprison

incredible—unbelievable
incredulous—doubting

ingenious—clever
ingenuous—frank

irrelevant—having no bearing on a matter
irreverent—lacking respect

loath—reluctant
loathe—to hate

luxuriant—growing thickly; highly ornamented
luxurious—rich; having an aura of wealth

perpetuate—to cause to continue
perpetrate—to do (something evil)

persecute—to affflict constantly in order to injure
prosecute—to institute legal proceedings against

personal—private
personnel—employees

perspective—appearance as determined by distance and position
prospective—likely

precede—to come before
proceed—to continue

prescribe—to order; to advise (as medicine)
proscribe—to outlaw

principal—the amount of a debt; the head of a school
principle—a fundamental law

profuse—excessive
profess—to declare

prophecy—prediction (n.)
prophesy—to predict (v.)

relay—to convey; a race between teams
relate—to tell; to connect

repel—to reject
repeal—to cancel

respectful—showing regard for
respective—particular

rightly—with good reason
rightfully—having a lawful claim
righteously—acting in a virtuous way

ruminating—meditating
fulminating—shouting
culminating—ending

sensual—of the body
sensuous—appealing to the senses

staple—basic commodity; a pin holding papers together
stable—firm; a shed for horses

stationary—immobile
stationery—writing materials

supplement—to add to something
supplant—to forcefully replace

temerity—boldness
timidity—shyness

their—belonging to them
there—in that place
they're—they are

troop—a group of people
troupe—a company of singers, dancers, or actors

weigh—to measure the weight of
way—road
whey—a part of milk that is separated from the curds in cheese making

weather—atmospheric conditions
whether—if

wholesome—healthful
fulsome—disgusting because of excessiveness

Errors in Punctuation—Use of the Semicolon

1. ERRORS WITH TWO INDEPENDENT CLAUSES

A semicolon (;) is used to connect two independent clauses or sentences into one sentence. A semicolon is usually used when there is some connection between the two clauses. In the following example, the writer may want to contrast or compare the two athletes. How do you know when to use a semicolon? If you place a period between the two clauses, two independent sentences result.

INCORRECT: John is a baseball player, Fred is a football player.
CORRECT: John is a baseball player; Fred is a football player.

2. ERRORS WITH A CONJUNCTION

Do not use a semicolon when a conjunction (*but, and, while*) is between two independent clauses or sentences. Use a comma.

INCORRECT: John started the project; but Fred finished it.
CORRECT: John started the project, but Fred finished it.

3. ERRORS IN A LIST OF ITEMS

Do not use commas between several lists of items. Use a semicolon between lists that have their own commas.

INCORRECT: Bob went to Paris, Marseilles, and Lyons, France, Berlin, Bremen, and
              Munich, Germany, and St. Petersburg, Moscow, and Kirov, Russia.
CORRECT: Bob went to Paris, Marseilles, and Lyons, France; Berlin, Bremen, and
              Munich, Germany; and St. Petersburg, Moscow, and Kirov, Russia.

4. ERRORS WITH CONJUNCTIVE ADVERBS

Place a semicolon before the adverb when two independent clauses or sentences are joined by a conjunctive adverb (moreover, however, nevertheless, otherwise).

INCORRECT: John scored ten points, however, Fred scored twenty points.
CORRECT: John scored ten points; however, Fred scored twenty points.

The sentence correction review emphasizes the sorts of errors most commonly found on the GMAT exam. If you believe that you have good mastery of English grammar, you might take a practice test before spending time with the review. In any case, before you attempt a practice exercise, look at the strategy suggestions below and on page 230. After taking the practice exam, you will be able to identify those errors that you were not able to identify correctly. Then, find the relevant section in the review in order to learn how to remedy your mistakes.

STRATEGY FOR SELECTING THE CORRECT RESPONSE

The first step in the Sentence Correction part of the exam is to read the sentence carefully in order to spot an error of grammar or usage. Once you have found an error, eliminate choice (A) and ALL OTHER ALTERNATIVES CONTAINING THAT ERROR. Concentrate on the remaining alternatives to choose your answer. Do not select an alternative that has changed the *meaning* of the original sentence.

EXAMPLE 1

If I knew him better, <u>I would have insisted that he change</u> the hour of the lecture.

(A) I would have insisted that he change
(B) I would have insisted that he changed
(C) I would insist that he change
(D) I would insist for him to change
(E) I would have insisted him to change

Since we must assume the unmarked part of the sentence to be correct, this is a PRESENT CONDITIONAL sentence; therefore, the second verb in the sentence should read *I would insist.* Glancing through the alternatives, you can eliminate (A), (B), and (E). You are left with (C) and (D). Remember that the word *insist* takes a *verb word* after it. (C) is the only correct answer.

If you do not find any grammatical error in the underlined part, read the alternatives to see if one of them does not use a clearer or more concise style to express the same thing. Do not choose an alternative that changes the meaning of the original sentence.

EXAMPLE 2

The couple, who had been married recently, booked their honeymoon passage through an agent who lived near them.

(A) The couple, who had been married recently, booked their honeymoon passage through an agent who lived near them.

(B) The couple, who had been recently married, booked their honeymoon passage through an agent who lived not far from them.

(C) The newlyweds booked their honeymoon passage through a local agent.

(D) The newlyweds booked their passage through an agent that lived not far from them.

(E) The couple lived not far from the agent who through him they booked their passage.

Although (A), the original, has no real errors, (C) expresses the same thing more concisely, without distorting the original meaning of the sentence.

Remember: If you find no errors, and if you find that none of the alternatives improve the original, choose (A).

DIRECTIONS: This exercise consists of a number of sentences, in each of which some part or the whole is underlined. Each sentence is followed by five alternative versions of the underlined portion. Select the alternative you consider both most correct and most effective according to the requirements of standard written English. Answer (A) is the same as the original version; if you think the original version is best, select answer (A).

In considering the answer choices, be attentive to matters of grammar, diction, and syntax, as well as clarity, precision, and fluency. Do not select an answer that alters the meaning of the original sentence.

1. A good doctor inquires not only about his patients' physical health, but about their mental health too.

   (A) but about their mental health too
   (B) but their mental health also
   (C) but also he inquires about their mental health
   (D) but also about their mental health
   (E) but too about their mental health

2. Knowing that the area was prone to earthquakes, all the buildings were reinforced with additional steel and concrete.

   (A) Knowing that the area was prone to earthquakes,
   (B) Having known that the area was prone to earthquakes,
   (C) Since the area was known to be prone to earthquakes,
   (D) Since they knew that the area was prone to earthquakes,
   (E) Being prone to earthquakes,

3. John would never have taken the job if he had known what great demands it would make on his time.

   (A) if he had known
   (B) if he knew
   (C) if he had been knowing
   (D) if he knows
   (E) if he was knowing

4. Anyone wishing to enroll in the program should send in their applications before the fifteenth of the month.

   (A) send in their applications
   (B) send their applications in
   (C) send in their application
   (D) send their application in
   (E) send in his application

5. Start the actual writing only after having thoroughly researched your subject, organized your notes, and <u>you have planned an outline</u>.

    (A) you have planned an outline

    (B) planned an outline

    (C) you having planned an outline

    (D) an outline has been planned

    (E) an outline was planned

Answers and Analysis

1. **(D)** The connective *not only* MUST be accompanied by *but also*. Eliminate (A), (B), and (E). (C) repeats *he inquires* unnecessarily. (D) is correct.

2. **(C)** *All the buildings* couldn't have known that the area was prone to earthquakes. Since the unmarked part of the sentence must be assumed to be correct, eliminate all alternatives beginning with a dangling modifier: (A), (B), and (E). In (D) the word *they* is unclear. Where there is no definite subject, the passive is preferable. (C) is correct.

3. **(A)** This is a past conditional sentence. (A) is correct.

4. **(E)** *Anyone* is singular. At one glance eliminate every choice but (E).

5. **(B)** Here is a series of three verbs: having *researched, organized,* and *planned.* (B) is correct.

Critical Reasoning

8

- → **IDENTIFYING THE QUESTION**
- → **IDENTIFYING THE PREMISE AND CONCLUSION**
- → **PASSAGES THAT OMIT EITHER SOME PREMISES OR THE CONCLUSION**
- → **DEDUCTIVE AND INDUCTIVE ARGUMENTS**
- → **TYPES OF INDUCTIVE ARGUMENTS**
- → **DETERMINING THE LOGICAL SEQUENCE OF AN ARGUMENT**
- → **ANALYZING THE LOGICAL SEQUENCE OF AN ARGUMENT**
- → **ATTACKING THE ASSUMPTIONS OF AN ARGUMENT**
- → **FALLACIES**
- → **SOME FINAL HINTS**

The principal object of the critical reasoning questions in the GMAT is to test skills in constructing and evaluating arguments. An argument is a sequence of two or more phrases, clauses, sentences, or statements, one of which is a claim or conclusion, which follows the premises. For example:

"The ground was wet, so it must have been raining."

The first part of the sentence, "The ground was wet . . . ," is called a *premise*. The *conclusion* of the sentence, "it must have been raining," is based on the premise. Taken together, the premise and the conclusion form an *argument*. The method of reasoning in this example can be termed an *inference*. It is the inference that links the conclusion to the premise. Whether or not the argument and conclusion are valid is another question. In this case, the conclusion is not valid. The ground could have been wet for a variety of reasons, not necessarily connected with the weather.

TIP

Look for cue words. They identify premises.

IDENTIFYING THE QUESTION

After the student reads the problem, the first order of business is to identify the question being asked. This can often be demanding because the more difficult questions will be wordy, and as a result, confusing. It is therefore very important to isolate the question and read it carefully.

Be careful to discern between different language, such as which answer *yields significant information*, which inference *is supported by the problem the author is arguing*, or which assumption *will weaken or strengthen the conclusion*. Often the questions will ask the student to find the answer that does *NOT weaken* or *NOT strengthen* the conclusion.

Some questions will use the phrase *if true*. This does not direct the student to decide which of the 5 answers is true but, rather, to assume that all 5 are true. The task then is to choose the best possible answer assuming that all are true.

IDENTIFYING THE PREMISE AND CONCLUSION

In evaluating an argument and its strength and validity, the first step is to identify the components—the premise and conclusion. Some arguments in the GMAT may omit either some premises or the conclusion. You are then asked to provide one or the other.

Cue Words

Very often you will be helped in identifying the parts of an argument by the presence of cue words. Words such as "if," "given that," "since," "because," "for," "suppose," and "in view of" signal the presentation of evidence and reasons in support of a fact or claim. These cues identify premises. Conclusions, on the other hand, may often be preceded by words such as "thus," "hence," "so," and "therefore."

Without cue words, identifying and analyzing an argument become more difficult. For example, in conversation one might say:

"The roads were empty yesterday. It was Sunday."

This example seems to contain two simple assertions that do not necessarily constitute an argument. However, the juxtaposition of the two facts may indicate that one statement was intended to be a conclusion based on the fact stated in the other statement. In the example given, one is really saying:

"In view of the fact that it was Sunday, the roads were empty yesterday."

Fortunately, examples with no cue words at all are not common.

Position of Conclusion

Conclusions do not have to be at the end of an argument, as in the first example about wet streets and rain. Conclusions and premises may be reversed while the same meaning is conveyed. For example:

"David was talking during the lesson, so he didn't understand the teacher's instructions."
"David did not understand the teacher's instructions because he was talking during the lesson."

In both statements, the conclusion is "David did not understand the teacher's instructions."

Connecting Events to Draw Conclusions

Arguments frequently contain a number of premises and possibly more than one conclusion. Therefore, it is necessary to classify and connect things and events in order to analyze the arguments. To aid this analysis, think of events in terms of time sequence or causal relationships. For example:

"Sarah overslept, which caused her to be late leaving for school; therefore, she ran all the way, causing her to be out of breath."

Sometimes we predict future events, basing our prediction on regular sequences we have previously experienced. An example of such a sequence:

"The sun rose this morning. The sun rose yesterday. Therefore, it will rise tomorrow."

Note that we are not using our previous experience to prove anything, but rather applying our knowledge about what has happened before as a basis for our conclusion about what will happen in the future.

Determining What the Writer Is Trying to Prove

At first glance the analysis of some arguments looks difficult because of the absence of cue words. In these cases, ask yourself, "What is the writer trying to prove?" Once you have identified the main point of the argument, define it. Ask "How great a claim (or 'How limited a claim') is the author making?" "What precisely is the author talking about?" "What was the author's purpose in making the claim?"

To answer the first of these questions, look again for signal words—for instance "all," "none," "never," "always," "some," and "sometimes." There is a big difference, for example, between "all cars are red" and "some cars are red." The first statement is false. The second is most definitely true. Similarly, note the difference between "I have never seen him before" and "I have not seen him today."

Often the use of different verbs and adverbs can change the meaning of similar claims. Consider the first example used in this chapter: "The ground was wet, so it must have been raining." We can limit the claim by changing "must" to "probably." "The ground was wet. So it probably has been raining." The first statement stands more chance of being proven false. Anything else that can be shown to have made the ground wet limits the chance that it must have been the rain that caused the wetness. However, it could still have been raining, and there is always the probability, no matter how small, that it may have been.

Descriptive words, both nouns and adjectives, in a passage are also used to limit or expand claims made by another. Take the example:

"Teachers in New York deserve extra pay for the dangers they face in the classroom."

Here the claim is made about teachers; it cannot be extended (without further information) to members of any other occupation or to teachers from any other place except New York.

Another example:

"Prisoners in San Quentin rioted today because they were angry about their conditions."

The author's choice of the word "Prisoners" indicates merely that more than one prisoner rioted. Maybe all or maybe only some prisoners rioted. Note also that the author claims to know the reason for the riot—namely, that the prisoners were angry about their conditions and for no other reason. However, you cannot assume that just because an author states a reason for a claim, he or she is correct in that assumption. And if an author makes a claim about the cause of some event, he or she may either endorse or condemn it. Endorsement of a claim without any supporting evidence is not a substitute for proof.

The use of assumptions is vital in evaluating an argument. We have seen earlier that the conclusion of one argument can act as the premise for a further argument. In practice, we do not extend arguments indefinitely, but we stop at the conclusion we set out to prove, having begun from what seems to be a convenient and secure starting point. The strength of the argument depends on the legitimacy of its assumptions.

PASSAGES THAT OMIT EITHER SOME PREMISES OR THE CONCLUSION

Sometimes a passage will omit either a premise or the conclusion. If this occurs, you will be required to provide one or the other. Look at the following examples.

Missing Premises—Example 1

The recent increase in the employment rate was spurred on by predictions of high economic growth in the coming year. If major industries increase their exports, the employment rate will increase in the future.

Which of the following will strengthen the conclusion that the employment rate will increase?
(A) Exports of products from major companies will increase.
(B) Exports of products from major companies will decrease.
(C) Imports will increase.
(D) Tariffs will be imposed on U.S. exports.
(E) Predications stimulate trade.

(A) The premise in this passage states that the high employment rate was caused by predictions of high economic growth. The premise is followed by the conclusion that if major industries increase exports, the employment rate will increase. Is the conclusion valid? What evidence is given that exports affect the employment rate? There is no evidence provided in this example. What would strengthen the argument? The passage should provide evidence that demonstrates a connection between exports and economic growth. However, those predictions would not have affected the employment rate if the export of major industries had not increased. Now the argument is complete:

The recent increase in the employment rate was spurred on by predictions of high economic growth in the coming year. However, those predictions would not have affected the employment rate if it had not been for the increase of exports of major industries. If major industries increase their exports, the employment rate will increase in the future.

Missing Premise—Example 2

Mr. Smith has been accused of spying for a foreign country. An investigation by the Security Service has not found him guilty of breaches of security or of any connection with agents of the foreign country. Therefore, Mr. Smith is not a foreign spy.

Which of the following will strengthen the conclusion?
(A) The security services are accurate in their investigations 80 percent of the time.
(B) The particular foreign country that Mr. Smith represents has a very fine covert spy agency.
(C) The security services are generally accurate.
(D) If Mr. Smith was a foreign spy, the security services would have discovered it.
(E) The particular foreign country that Mr. Smith represents has accused Americans of spying.

(D) The premise in this example is that after a security investigation, Mr. Smith was cleared of the accusation of being a foreign spy. This implicit premise can be weakened very easily by adding another. Suppose we add the premise *the security services are accurate in their investigations 80 percent of the time*. What about the other 20 percent of the time? Perhaps Mr. Smith falls in the 20 percent category, so the conclusion that he is not a spy has been weakened.

On the other hand, the conclusion can be strengthened by adding the premise *if Mr. Smith was a foreign spy, the security services would have discovered this*.

Missing Conclusion—Example 1

A passenger in an air terminal is scanning the televised flight monitor to see the status of a flight from Paris to Copenhagen. The passenger scans all the flights listed on the monitor and finds no Paris/Copenhagen flight.

What is a possible conclusion? Someone might infer that the flight has been delayed or canceled or that not all flights are listed on that particular monitor. Any of these conclusions could follow from the premises if further evidence is provided.

Missing Conclusion—Example 2

Most Americans eat at fast-food establishments more than once a week and many researchers agree that such eating habits are the leading (if not primary) cause of obesity in the U.S. Obesity-related diseases such as diabetes and hypertension burden our healthcare system by billions of dollars every year. Whether through healthcare, insurance premiums, or state and federal taxes, you suffer the consequences even if you eat only healthful, home-cooked meals.

This passage has four premises:

1. **Most Americans eat at fast-food establishments more than once a week.**
2. **Researchers agree that such eating habits are the leading cause of obesity.**
3. **Obesity-related diseases burden the healthcare system by billions of dollars every year.**
4. **Even those who consume healthy meals will have to share the burden of healthcare costs.**

What can be concluded from the four premises? *A small tax should be levied on every high-calorie meal served at fast-food chains in this country.* Such a conclusion would not only offset obesity-related healthcare costs but force consumers to seek out more healthful options when looking for lunch.

What premises could weaken the above argument? *Only high-fat meals are a leading cause of obesity* or *researchers have found that lack of exercise is a major factor leading to obesity*.

DEDUCTIVE AND INDUCTIVE ARGUMENTS

An argument may be deductive or inductive, depending on how the conclusion follows or is inferred from the premises.

An argument may be defined as deductive if it is *impossible* for the conclusion to be false if all the premises are true. In other words, in a deductive argument, the premises necessitate the conclusion. An example of a deductive argument is:

All men are mortal.
Brian is a man.
Therefore, Brian is a mortal.

If both premises are true, then the conclusion follows automatically.

An argument is inductive if it is *improbable* that the conclusion is false if all premises are true. The premises do not necessitate but do make probable the conclusion. The conclusion may be false even if all the premises are true.

Determining if the conclusion in an argument has been arrived at through deductive reasoning or through inductive reasoning can often be discerned from the wording of the statement or sentence. Words such as "usually," "sometimes," and "generally," are usually signals of induction.

An example of an inductive argument is:

1. Freshmen usually find Economics I difficult.
2. Jones is a freshman.
3. Therefore, Jones finds Economics I difficult.

In the above statement, both premises are true. If the premises are true, does the conclusion automatically follow? No, because not all freshmen find Economics I difficult, and Jones may be one of the minority of freshmen who do not. The key word is usually a conditional term that makes the conclusion ("Therefore, Jones finds Economics I difficult") incorrect.

The distinction between deduction and induction should not be taken as a distinction between a good or superior way of arguing or reasoning and an inferior way. An inductive argument is not necessarily a bad argument. The two methods of argument serve different and complementary purposes. The distinction is in the manner by which a conclusion follows its premise(s).

TYPES OF INDUCTIVE ARGUMENTS

Inductive arguments may be based on examples, generalizations, analogy, causal connection; or other grounds for belief. We shall discuss a few types of inductive arguments.

Argument by Example

Arguing by example means inferring conclusions from specific cases or examples. The number of cases or examples used may vary from one to several. Example:

The U.S. gives billions of dollars in foreign aid to Balonia. Leaders of Balonia resent foreign aid. The U.S. should discontinue direct foreign aid to developing countries.

In the above argument, only one example—that of Balonia—was used as a premise for reaching the conclusion that foreign aid should be discontinued. If it could be shown that

Balonia is not a developing country, then one premise is false, and the argument and conclusion are invalid.

Assume for the moment that both premises are true. Is the conclusion then valid? Remember: only one example was given. One might argue that most developing countries welcome foreign aid and, therefore, that the single example given is irrelevant or atypical.

A typical critical reasoning question on the GMAT may ask you to select an answer that weakens an argument. In other words, you will be asked to select an answer that falsifies a premise or casts doubt on a generalization. One way to do this is to show that the specific example(s) given is (are) not typical or relevant and therefore cannot be the basis of a valid inductive argument in which examples are used to build a generalization.

Argument by Analogy

Arguing or reasoning by analogy consists of making a comparison between two similar cases, and inferring that what is true in one case is true in the other. A model for argument by analogy is as follows:

Example *A* is like (analogous to) example *B*.
A is different from *B* because of *C*.

This model may be illustrated by the following example.

Premise 1
The Conservative and Labor Parties support a viable economy, including economic growth, industrialization, a fair wage policy, and unrestricted immigration.

Premise 2
The Conservative Party endorsed free trade.

Conclusion
Therefore, the Labor Party will endorse free trade.

In premise 1, both *A* (Conservative Party) and *B* (Labor Party) have the same characteristics (economic growth, industrialization, fair wage policy, and unrestricted immigration). In premise 2, *A* (Conservative Party) takes on an additional characteristic, endorsing free trade. In the conclusion, comparison by analogy states that *B* (Labor Party) will also endorse free trade. This is an invalid argument by analogy. Even though the argument has shown that the two parties are similar in some ways, it does not necessarily follow that they are alike in other ways.

In some arguments there is a lack of similar shared characteristics. For example:

1. France and England have nearly the same population size.
2. France has fluoridated drinking water.
3. England will have fluoridated drinking water.

The problem in the above example is that there are not enough points of similarity between France and England to lead to the conclusion. Critical differences might involve income, drinking habits, attitudes toward medicine, and many other things.

Causal Arguing

In causal arguing, one infers that an act or factor (cause) produces a result (effect). This may be illustrated as:

Cause (Known)

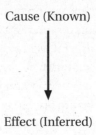

Effect (Inferred)

An *X* may be said to be a cause of *Y* if the occurrence of *X* is sufficient for the occurrence of *Y*. Whenever *X* occurs, *Y* follows, so that *X* determines *Y*. (Note here that factors other than *X* may also determine *Y* and that this does not alter the validity of the stated argument.)

DETERMINING THE LOGICAL SEQUENCE OF AN ARGUMENT

Having discussed types of arguments, we will now demonstrate in more detail how an argument can be identified and analyzed. You must be able to determine what the writer is trying to establish.

In order to identify an argument:

1. Find the conclusion first. This may be done by locating the cue that introduces the conclusion.
2. Find the premise(s). Again, locate the cue words (if present) that signal premises.
3. Determine if the premise(s) are true.
4. Determine the logical form of the argument.

A good way to check whether or not a conclusion follows from the premise(s) is to draw a Venn diagram, a device named after the British logician John Venn (1834–1923). A simplified form of the Venn diagram may consist of circles, one for each term of an argument. Take a simple argument:

"All weeds are plants; all daisies are weeds. Therefore, all daisies are plants."

We can now classify the various things (terms) in this argument and enclose each in a circle. Thus:

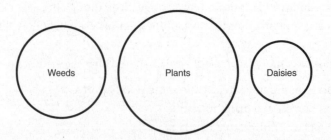

This deductive argument can be arranged to show the premises and conclusion, by showing that "daisies" are totally included in "weeds" and "weeds" are totally included in "plants."

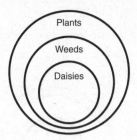

Since "daisies" are totally included in "plants," the conclusion of the argument is valid.

Venn diagrams can also be used to show if arguments are invalid. For example, take the argument:

"Because all dollars are money and all yen are money, then all dollars must be yen."

By placing dollars, money, and yen in circles and arranging them appropriately, we arrive at:

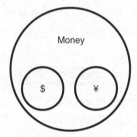

We can see that the conclusion—all dollars are yen—does not stand under scrutiny, since dollars and yen are not in the same small circle. All we can conclude is that both dollars and yen are money.

Using Venn Diagrams

Using examples, we shall now discuss the steps involved in using Venn diagrams to analyze the structure and logical sequence of an argument.

Study the following example.

1. All men are mortal.
2. Brian is a man.
3. Brian is a mortal.

STEP ONE

The first premise states that all men belong to a term which is called mortality. Therefore, we need one circle to represent the term and another circle for "men."

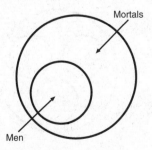

STEP TWO

The second premise states that Brian is a man. We draw a third circle for Brian. Brian's circle is within the circle of men.

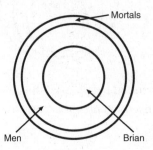

STEP THREE

Is the argument valid? Certainly, because we see that the conclusion—Brian is mortal—follows from the premises. Brian is in the "mortal" space, so he is mortal as well.

EXAMPLE

(1) Dr. Deutch's economics class is difficult.

(2) Dr. Jacque's economics class is difficult.

(3) Professor Sol's economics class is difficult.

(4) Therefore, all economic classes are difficult.

Step One. The first premise states that Dr. Deutch's economics class fits the term "difficult." This can be represented by two circles, one for the term "difficult," one for Dr. Deutch's class.

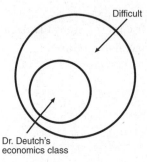

Step Two. Following step one, we are given two similar premises. We will add one circle for each.

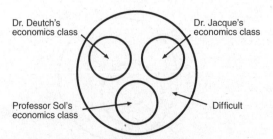

> **Step Three.** Does the conclusion "all economics classes are difficult" follow the premises? The argument is inductive since we do not know if the three economics classes represent all, 90%, or 20% of all economics classes. If we know that they represent all economics classes, we could conclude that the conclusion follows from its premises. Since we do not know this, the conclusion is invalid.

ANALYZING THE LOGICAL SEQUENCE OF AN ARGUMENT

Now that we have reviewed the use of cue words, the logical sequence of arguments, and the use of Venn diagrams to check the structure of an argument, let us apply these concepts to some examples.

The following conversation was held between two friends:

"I am a fervent supporter of the Republican Party and a member of its membership committee. However, I attended several meetings at a local branch of the Democratic Party because several of my office colleagues persuaded me to come along and because I like the ambiance and the refreshments that are served at these gatherings.

A fellow member of the Republican Party club heard that I had attended the Democratic meetings. He asked me whether I had switched my allegiance. When I explained that I had not, he said that a lot of people assumed that I had because anyone who attends several meetings of a political party must be a supporter of that party. I told my friend that I think he is wrong."

What is the reasoning shown in the conversation? Clearly, the member of the Republican Party believes that his friend is guilty by association. He claims that anyone who attends several meetings of a political party will be associated with the company that he (or she) keeps. What evidence is given for the claim? Searching the key words shows that "because" appears three times. First, in lines 3 and 4, it is used to explain why the person attends the Democratic Party meetings. Second, in line 8, "because" signals the important assumption that people attending meetings of a political party are presumed to be members of that party. The friend's reasoning is as follows:

1. Any person frequenting Democratic Party meetings is presumed to be a Democrat.
2. You are a person frequenting Democratic Party meetings.
3. *Therefore*, you are presumed to be a Democrat.

Is the reasoning logical? Let us check it with a Venn diagram. Three terms are evident: "Democrats," "persons frequenting Democratic Party meetings," and the subject "you." We draw a circle for each of these terms as explained above. The rule for putting the circles together is that the outermost circle contains the term that appears in a premise and the conclusion. That term is "Democrats." Next, the middle circle contains the term that appears in both premises. That term is "Persons frequenting Democratic Party meetings." Finally, the innermost circle contains the term that appears in the middle premise and the conclusion. That term is "you." Therefore, we may conclude that the person ("you") who frequents Democratic Party meetings will be *presumed* to belong to the term "Democrats."

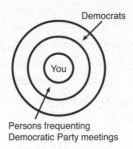

Democrats

You

Persons frequenting
Democratic Party meetings

Here's a question similar to one that appeared on a recent exam.

EXAMPLE

A weapons-smuggling incident recently took place in country Y. We all know that Y is a closed society. So Y's government must have known about the weapons.

Which of the following is an assumption that would make the conclusion above logically correct?

(A) If a government knows about a particular weapons-smuggling incident, it must have intended to use the weapons for its own purposes.

(B) If a government claims that it knew nothing about a particular weapons-smuggling incident, it must have known everything about it.

(C) If a government does not permit weapons to enter a country, it is a closed society.

(D) If a country is a closed society, its government has a large contingent of armed guards patrolling its borders.

(E) If a country is a closed society, its government has knowledge about everything that occurs in the country.

The only cue word in the above passage is "so," which signals a conclusion: Y's government must have known about the weapons. What evidence is available to buttress this conclusion? The first premise is that "Y is a closed society." Now the question is, How can we link the premise with its conclusion? We need a second premise, but we do not have it in the passage. Surely, a "weapons-smuggling incident" is not the linkage. Therefore, we have what is called a "hidden" premise, one that is not given but must be assumed. However, in passages of this sort, the "hidden" premise is usually one of the answer alternatives. In fact, the question stem asks us to find the alternative that would make the conclusion logically correct. That alternative is (E). The complete argument is:

1. If a country is a closed society, its government has knowledge.
2. Y is a closed society.
3. *Therefore*, Y's government must have known about the weapons.

Is the reasoning logical? Let us draw a Venn diagram. The terms are "country Y," "closed society," and "government has knowledge." Again, the outer circle contains the term found in a premise and the conclusion: "government has knowledge" ("must have known"). The middle circle contains the term found in both premises: "closed society." Finally, the inner-most circle contains the term found in the middle premise and the conclusion: "country Y." The Venn diagram shows that the reasoning is logical.

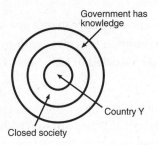

ATTACKING THE ASSUMPTIONS OF AN ARGUMENT

In the GMAT test, one often has to attack or find a fact that weakens an argument. The most effective way of doing this is to defeat the assumptions. Consider the following argument:

1. "Cooking classes take place on Tuesdays."
2. "Today is Tuesday."
3. "Therefore, cooking classes take place today."

We may be able to defeat this argument by analyzing the first premise. If we assume that cooking classes usually take place on a Tuesday, then there is a probability that if today is Tuesday it will be one of those Tuesdays when cooking classes are held, but this is obviously not certain. Premise (1) does not state that cooking classes take place every Tuesday; classes could be held every other Tuesday or every third Tuesday. Therefore, the third sentence, the conclusion of the argument *may* be false.

Often, the attack on the argument will not be so obvious because the assumptions on which the argument is built are hidden or concealed. Someone who is making a totally hon-est and correct argument will not explicitly acknowledge all of the assumptions he or she makes. These hidden assumptions may be open to attack. Bear this in mind, particularly if you are presented with an argument that seems logical and correct but that reaches a factu-ally impossible or absurd result. This could indicate the existence of hidden assumptions that make the argument invalid.

FALLACIES

As mentioned earlier, the thought process that links the premise of an argument to its conclu-sion is called an inference. Errors may occur in any part of the argumentation process. These errors in reasoning are called *fallacies* or *flaws*.

Logicians have been studying flaws since Aristotle considered them in his *On Sophistical Refutations*. He wrote:

> That some reasonings are genuine, while others seem to be so but are not, is evident. This happens with arguments as also elsewhere, through a certain likeness between the genuine and the sham.

A fallacy is a form of reasoning that is illogical or violates the rules of argumentation. A fallacy is, in other words, an argument that seems to be sound but is not.

Scholars differ on the classification of fallacies. We shall discuss the most common types of fallacies and those that appear most often on the GMAT.

Guilt by Association

One type of fallacy is guilt by association. Suppose that one proves that educator John Doe is a dues-paying member of the Association for Fairy Teeth (A.F.T.), a fact not denied by Doe. Suppose that three members of the association have been found to be subversives. An argument may be:

1. John Doe is a member of the A.F.T.
2. X, Y, and Z are members of the A.F.T. and are subversives.

Therefore, (3) John Doe is a subversive.

This argument involves an invalid induction from premise (2) to a (missing) premise: all members of the A.F.T. are subversives. This has not been proven in the argument. It is left for the reader to draw his or her own—in this case, fallacious—conclusion, namely, that John Doe is a subversive.

A Venn diagram may be helpful. The largest circle represents all members of the A.F.T. A small circle within the larger one represents the three A.F.T. members that are known subversives. We are told in the statements that X, Y, and Z are known subversives, but we are not told that it is known that they are the *only* subversives in the A.F.T. membership. Therefore, we have no way of knowing whether or not John Doe is a subversive. In terms of a Venn diagram, we have no way of knowing whether or not the circle representing subversives should represent more than three members or whether or not the John Doe circle should overlap a larger circle representing all subversives.

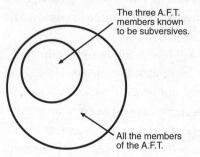

The three A.F.T. members known to be subversives.

All the members of the A.F.T.

Faulty Analogy

Another type of fallacy is that of faulty analogy. A faulty analogy assumes that things that are similar in one respect must be similar in other respects. In general, analogies may be a useful form of communication. They enable a speaker to convey concepts in terms already familiar to the audience. A statement such as "our civilization is flowering" may be helpful in making a point, but the generalization is faulty. May we conclude that civilizations are in need of fertilizer?

Suppose that an economist argues that a "tariff on textiles will help our textile industry, a tariff on steel will help the steel industry, a tariff on every imported product will benefit the economy."

The previous analogy may be stated as:

1. Tariffs on textiles benefit the textile industry.
2. Tariffs on steel benefit the steel industry.
Therefore (3), a tariff on every imported product benefits the economy.

A Venn diagram of the above argument is:

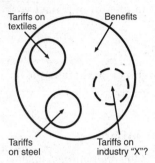

The analogy here assumes that because two industries benefit from tariffs, all others will also benefit. However, no proof for this argument is given.

Causal Fallacies

Some of the common causal fallacies are treating an insignificant relationship as a causal factor and assuming that a sequential relationship implies a causal relationship. That two events occur in sequence is not evidence of a causal relationship. For example, Herbert Hoover was elected President of the United States in 1928, an act followed by a recession in 1929. Did Hoover's policies cause the recession or were there other intervening factors? (There were.)

The following is an example of a causal fallacy.

Roni develops a rash whenever exposed to cactus weed. On his way home from a hike, he breaks out in a rash. Upon applying some ointment, he exclaims, "I must have brushed by cactus weed."

Roni's argument may be expanded as:

1. Rashes are caused by cactus weed.
2. I have a rash.
Therefore (3), I must have touched cactus weed.

Roni may be correct. However, other phenomena may have caused his rash: an allergy to certain food, contact with other plants, or many other things. Unless these can be ruled out, Roni's argument is fallacious.

POST HOC ERGO HOC ("AFTER THIS, ON ACCOUNT OF THIS")

One type of fallacy of causality is a fallacy termed *post hoc ergo hoc*. This is the proposition that because events follow one another, one causes the other.

Consider the following scenario. In one of a company's five sales districts, the advertising budget was increased 20 percent, while in the other four districts, advertising expenditure was unchanged. Sales increased in the first district by nearly 20 percent, while sales remained unchanged in the other four districts. Did the increased advertising cause the sales increase?

This argument is in the form:

1. Event Y followed event X
2. So X is the cause of Y

The inference is weak. Y may be affected by a third factor Z. For example, in the sales district with the increase, a major competitor may have withdrawn from the market.

Fallacies of Relevance

Fallacies of relevance involve arguments wherein one or more of the premises are irrelevant to the conclusion. Some examples are as follows.

AD HOMINEM (PERSONAL ATTACKS)

One type of fallacy of relevance is the *ad hominem* fallacy. In this type of fallacy, the person is attacked, not his or her argument. Attacking an opponent may well be easier than rebutting the merit of the argument. The role of the demagogue is to assassinate the character of his or her opponent, thereby casting doubt on his/her argument.

For example, an economics professor exclaims to her class: "Even a freshman knows that good economists don't necessarily have to be good mathematicians." Or, "Congressman Goodboy has argued eloquently in favor of increasing public spending in his district. Isn't he the same congressman who was accused of wasting taxpayers' money on new autobuses whose air conditioning systems didn't work?"

The fallacy in these examples is that arguments are not treated on their merit. The arguments follow the form:

1. Z asserts B.
2. Z would benefit if we accept B.
3. Z's assertion of B is insufficient to accept B as true.

This sort of argument attempts to show that B is not a reliable source because of some self-interest.

Another form of *ad hominem* argument is an appeal to the special position or vested interest of the person being argued with. Such arguments may include phrases such as "You, as members of the armed forces, can be counted on . . ." or "As a lover of the arts, you will be the first to agree that we need to raise taxes to support them."

Suppose that the listener does not agree to increased taxes. The argument then takes on the form:

1. You believe X (that taxes shouldn't be raised).
2. It is in your interest to reject X (your belief).
3. You should reject X.

The conclusion does not show that personal gain is evidence enough to reject the belief against increased taxes.

TU QUOQUE (YOU TOO)

This fallacy of relevance occurs when an argument is weakened by the assertion that its proponent is guilty by commission. A typical argument of this sort is, "You implore me not to drink, but you drink. Therefore, I can ignore your advice and do as I please." Here, the proponent's case is turned against him. This argument takes the form:

1. You assert not to do X.
2. But you do X.
3. I can ignore your advice not to do X.

The above argument is invalid because (2) is not relevant to the advice given. The behavior of the person giving the advice has nothing to do with the validity of the claim or advice.

Fallacies of Language (Ambiguity)

Ambiguity occurs when there are two or more meanings for a word, phrase, statement, or expression, especially when the meanings are easily confused. Another problem occurs when it is not clear in what context the meaning is being used. Words and expressions such as "democracy," "teamwork," "the American way," and "payoff" have different meanings to different people and may be used in different contexts. For example, is the United States government a democracy in the same sense as the Indian government? Does teamwork mean the same thing to Japanese and American workers? The only way to avoid ambiguity is to carefully define the meaning of words in context.

Let us look at some cases where ambiguity is used with intent to deceive or confuse.

Equivocation (Double Meaning)

The fallacy of equivocation occurs when words or phrases that have more than one meaning are used. An arguer using this fallacy relies on the fact that the audience fails to realize that some word or expression occurring more than once is used in different ways. The ambiguity may occur in both premises or in a premise and the conclusion. In the following for example, the structure of the argument is valid but an equivocation occurs.

1. Happiness is the end of life. (X is Y)
2. The end of life is death. (Y is Z)
3. So, happiness is death. (X is Z)

The fallacy is that the expression "end of life" has a different meaning in each premise. What has been asserted with one sense of the expression is then wrongly regarded as having been proved with respect to the other expression. An equivocation has been committed on the expression.

Amphiboly (Double Talk)

This fallacy results whenever there is ambiguity in sentence structure. For example:

"Can you spell backward?"

Most logic textbooks quote a story in Herodotus about Croesus and the oracle. Croesus asked the oracle what would be the outcome if he attacked Cyrus the Great of Persia. The oracle's reply was that, "He would destroy a great empire." Of course, the empire that was destroyed was his own. In both possible outcomes, the oracle would have been correct. Fallacies of these sorts can usually be corrected by changing the syntax or punctuation, as in the first example above: "Can you spell 'backwards'?"

Accent

The meaning of statements can change depending on which words are stressed. Placing stress on certain words can change the meaning from the original unaccented statement. See the folowing example:

"Throw away your food."
> to:

"Throw away your *food*." (instead of something else).
"*Throw away* your food." (instead of eating it?).
"Throw away *your* food." (instead of someone else's?).

SOME FINAL HINTS

Sherlock Holmes once said, "When you have eliminated the impossible, whatever remains, *however improbable,* must be the truth." Can this statement be a true guide to critical reasoning problems? When taking the test, be sure to relate the possible answers to the actual statements, without drawing on prior conceptions or possible misconceptions. Each of us perceives a thing in his or her own way, but critical reasoning problems can only have one solution.

Some final tactics to consider:

1. Never rule out the blatantly obvious; it may just be the only solution possible.
2. Never rule out the blatantly ridiculous; it could also be the only reasonable conclusion to be drawn from a specific set of criteria.
3. Always treat each conclusion in isolation since only one answer can be correct.
4. Look for absolute words that will likely invalidate the answer:

Always	All
Must	Complete
Everybody	Never

5. Look for the words that will likely validate the answer:

Usually	Can
Sometimes	Some
May	Most

SUMMARY

The key to mastering critical reasoning questions lies in understanding the structure of an argument. This understanding begins with the ability to identify premises and the conclusion. In addition, grasping the different sorts of arguments, *deductive* and *inductive*, is most helpful. Once these components of an argument are understood, the sequence of the components can be identified, as explained by the model shown on pages 240–241.

Math

9

→ **ARITHMETIC**

→ **ALGEBRA**

→ **GEOMETRY**

→ **TABLES AND GRAPHS**

→ **REVIEW OF FORMULAS**

→ **HINTS FOR ANSWERING MATH QUESTIONS**

The Problem-Solving and Data Sufficiency areas of the GMAT require a working knowledge of mathematical principles, including an understanding of the fundamentals of algebra, geometry, and arithmetic, and the ability to interpret graphs. The following review covers these areas thoroughly and if used properly, will prove helpful in preparing for the mathematical parts of the GMAT.

Read through the review carefully. You will notice that each topic is keyed for easy reference.

I. ARITHMETIC

I-1. INTEGERS

I-1.1

The numbers 1, 2, 3, . . . are called the positive integers. –1, –2, –3, . . . are called the negative integers. An integer is a positive or negative integer or the number 0. The term whole number is also used to describe an integer.

I-1.2

If the integer k divides m evenly, then we say m is divisible by k or k is a *factor* of m. For example, 12 is divisible by 4, but 12 is not divisible by 5. The factors of 12 are 1, 2, 3, 4, 6, and 12.

The term *divisor* is sometimes used instead of the term *factor*. Thus the divisors of 12 are 1, 2, 3, 4, 6, and 12.

If k and m are any positive integers, you can find integers q and r such that $m = qk + r$ with $0 \le r < k$. The integer q is called the *quotient*, and r is called the *remainder* when m is divided by k. If $r = 0$, then m is divisible by k.

If k is a factor of m, then there is another integer n such that $m = k \times n$; in this case, m is called a multiple of k.

Since $12 = 4 \times 3$, 12 is a multiple of both 4 and 3. For example, 5, 10, 15, and 20 are all multiples of 5, but 15 and 5 are not multiples of 10. Any integer is a multiple of each of its factors.

I-1.3

Any positive integer is divisible by itself and by 1. If p is a positive integer greater than 1, which has *only* p and 1 as factors, then p is called a *prime number*. 2, 3, 5, 7, 11, 13, 17, 19, and 23 are all primes. 14 is not a prime since it is divisible by 2 and by 7.

An integer that is divisible by 2 is called an *even* number; if an integer is not even, then it is an *odd* number. 2, 4, 6, 8, and 10 are even numbers, and 1, 3, 5, 7, and 9 are odd numbers.

If an integer is even, it can be written as $2k$ where k is an integer. If an integer is odd, it can be written as $2k + 1$ where k is an integer. These representations are useful when you are working problems that involve properties of even and/or odd numbers.

> **REMEMBER**
>
> **Any integer greater than 1 is a prime or can be written as a product of primes.**

EXAMPLE

Is the sum of two odd numbers even or odd?

Let m and p be two odd numbers. So $m = 2k + 1$ and $p = 2j + 1$, where k and j are integers. Then $m + p = 2k + 1 + 2j + 1 = 2k + 2j + 2 = 2(k + j + 1)$. Since $k + j + 1$ is an integer, $m + p$ is an even number. So the sum of any two odd numbers is always an even number.

You can use these ideas to summarize the properties of even and odd numbers with respect to addition, subtraction, and multiplication.

even ± even = even	odd ± odd = even	even ± odd = odd
even × even = even	odd × odd = odd	even × odd = even

If you divide an integer by another integer, the result may not be an integer. For example, 6/4 is not an integer.

A collection of integers is *consecutive* if each number is the successor of the integer which precedes it in the collection. For example, 7, 8, 9, and 10 are *consecutive*, but 7, 8, 10, 13 are not. 4, 6, 8, 10 are consecutive even numbers. 7, 11, 13, 17 are consecutive primes. 7, 13, 19, 23 are not consecutive primes since 11 is a prime between 7 and 13.

I-1.4

To write a number as a *product of prime factors*:

(STEP A) Divide the number by 2 if possible; continue to divide by 2 until the factor you get is not divisible by 2.

(STEP B) Divide the result from (A) by 3 if possible; continue to divide by 3 until the factor you get is not divisible by 3.

(STEP C) Divide the result from (B) by 5 if possible; continue to divide by 5 until the factor you get is not divisible by 5.

(STEP D) Continue the procedure with 7, 11, and so on, until all the factors are primes.

EXAMPLE

Express 24 as a product of prime factors.

STEP A 24 = 2 × 12, 12 = 2 × 6, 6 = 2 × 3 so 24 = 2 × 2 × 2 × 3. Since each factor (2 and 3) is prime, 24 = 2 × 2 × 2 × 3.

EXAMPLE

Express 252 as a product of primes.

STEP A 252 = 2 × 126, 126 = 2 × 63 and 63 is not divisible by 2, so 252 = 2 × 2 × 63.

STEP B 63 = 3 × 21, 21 = 3 × 7 and 7 is not divisible by 3. Since 7 is a prime, then 252 = 2 × 2 × 3 × 3 × 7 and all the factors are primes.

EXAMPLE

A class of 45 students will sit in rows with the same number of students in each row. Each row must contain at least 2 students and there must be at least 2 rows. A row is parallel to the front of the room. How many different arrangements are possible?

Since 45 = (the number of rows)(the number of students per row), the question can be answered by finding how many different ways to write 45 as a product of two positive integers each of which is larger than 1. (The integers must be larger than 1 since there must be at least 2 rows and at least 2 students per row.) So write 45 as a product of primes 45 = 3 × 15 = 3 × 3 × 5. Therefore 3 × 15, 5 × 9, 9 × 5, and 15 × 3 are the only possibilities. So, the correct answer is 4. The fact that a row is parallel to the front of the room means that 3 × 15 and 15 × 3 are different arrangements.

I–1.5

An integer, m, is a *common multiple* of two other integers k and j if it is a multiple of each of them. For example, 12 is a common multiple of 4 and 6, since $3 \times 4 = 12$ and $2 \times 6 = 12$. 15 is not a common multiple of 3 and 6, because 15 is not a multiple of 6.

An integer, k, is a *common factor* of two other integers m and n if k is a factor of m and k is a factor of n.

The *least common multiple* (L.C.M.) of two integers is the smallest integer that is a common multiple of both integers. To find the least common multiple of two numbers k and j:

STEP A Write k as a product of primes and j as a product of primes.

STEP B If there are any common factors *delete* them in *one* of the products.

STEP C Multiply the remaining factors; the result is the least common multiple.

Find the L.C.M. of 12 and 11.

(STEP A) $12 = 2 \times 2 \times 3$, $11 = 11 \times 1$.

(STEP B) There are no common factors.

(STEP C) The L.C.M. is $12 \times 11 = 132$.

EXAMPLE

Find the L.C.M. of 27 and 63.

(STEP A) $27 = 3 \times 3 \times 3$, $63 = 3 \times 3 \times 7$.

(STEP B) $3 \times 3 = 9$ is a common factor so delete it once.

(STEP C) The L.C.M. is $3 \times 3 \times 3 \times 7 = 189$.

You can find the L.C.M. of a collection of numbers in the same way except that if in step (B) the common factors are factors of more than two of the numbers, then delete the common factor in *all but one* of the products.

EXAMPLE

Find the L.C.M. of 27, 63, and 72.

(STEP A) $27 = 3 \times 3 \times 3$, $63 = 3 \times 3 \times 7$, $72 = 2 \times 2 \times 2 \times 3 \times 3$.

(STEP B) Delete 3×3 from two of the products.

(STEP C) The L.C.M. is $3 \times 7 \times 2 \times 2 \times 2 \times 3 \times 3 = 21 \times 72 = 1,512$.

EXAMPLE

It takes Eric 20 minutes to inspect a car. Jane only needs 15 minutes to inspect a car. If they both start inspecting cars at 9:00 A.M., what is the first time they will finish inspecting a car at the same time?

Since Eric will finish k cars after $k \times 20$ minutes and Jane will finish j cars after $j \times 15$ minutes, they will both finish inspecting a car at the same time when $k \times 20 = j \times 15$. Since k and j must be integers (they represent the number of cars finished), this question is asking you to find a common multiple of 20 and 15. The question asks for the first time they will finish at the same time, so you must find the least common multiple.

(STEP A) $20 = 4 \times 5 = 2 \times 2 \times 5$, $15 = 3 \times 5$

(STEP B) Delete 5 from one of the products.

(STEP C) So, the L.C.M. is $2 \times 2 \times 5 \times 3 = 60$.

So Eric and Jane will finish inspecting a car at the same time 60 minutes after they start, or at 10:00 A.M. (By that time, Eric will have inspected 3 cars and Jane will have inspected 4 cars.)

I-1.6

The numbers 0, 1, 2, 3, 4, 5, 6, 7, 8, and 9 are called *digits*. The number 132 is a three-digit number. In the number 132, 1 is the first or hundreds digit, 3 is the second or tens digit, and 2 is the last or units digit.

EXAMPLE

Find x if x is a two-digit number whose last digit is 2. The difference of the digits of x is 5.

The two digit numbers whose last digits are 2 are 12, 22, 32, 42, 52, 62, 72, 82, and 92. The difference of the digits of 12 is either 1 or –1 so 12 is not x. Since 7 – 2 is 5, x is 72.

I-2. FRACTIONS

I-2.1

A *fraction* is a number that represents a ratio or division of two numbers. A fraction is written in the form $\dfrac{a}{b}$. The number on the top, a, is called the numerator; the number on the bottom, b, is called the denominator. The denominator tells how many equal parts there are (for example, parts of a pie); the numerator tells how many of these equal parts are taken. For example, $\dfrac{5}{8}$ is a fraction whose numerator is 5 and whose denominator is 8; it represents taking 5 of 8 equal parts, or dividing 8 into 5.

A fraction with 1 as the denominator is the same as the whole number that is its numerator. For example, $\dfrac{12}{1}$ is 12, $\dfrac{0}{1}$ is 0.

If the numerator and denominator of a fraction are identical, the fraction represents 1. For example, $\dfrac{3}{3} = \dfrac{9}{9} = \dfrac{13}{13} = 1$. Any whole number, k, is represented by a fraction with a numerator equal to k times the denominator. For example, $\dfrac{18}{6} = 3$, and $\dfrac{30}{5} = 6$.

> **REMEMBER**
>
> A fraction cannot have 0 as a denominator since division by 0 is not defined.

I-2.2

MIXED NUMBERS

A *mixed number* consists of a whole number and a fraction. For example, $7\dfrac{1}{4}$ is a mixed number; it means $7 + \dfrac{1}{4}$ and $\dfrac{1}{4}$ is called the fractional part of the mixed number $7\dfrac{1}{4}$. Any mixed number can be changed into a fraction:

STEP A Multiply the whole number by the denominator of the fractional part.

STEP B Add the numerator of the fraction to the result of step (A).

STEP C Use the result of step (B) as the numerator and use the denominator of the fractional part of the mixed number as the denominator. This fraction is equal to the mixed number.

Write $7\frac{1}{4}$ as a fraction.

(STEP A) $4 \times 7 = 28$

(STEP B) $28 + 1 = 29$

(STEP C) So, $7\frac{1}{4} = \frac{29}{4}$.

A fraction whose numerator is larger than its denominator can be changed into a mixed number.

(STEP A) Divide the denominator into the numerator; the result is the whole number of the mixed number.

(STEP B) Put the remainder from step (A) over the denominator; this is the fractional part of the mixed number.

EXAMPLE

If a pizza pie has 8 pieces, how many pizza pies have been eaten at a party where 35 pieces were consumed?

Since there are 8 pieces in a pie, $\frac{35}{8}$ pies were eaten. To find the number of pies, we need to change $\frac{35}{8}$ into a mixed number.

(STEP A) Divide 8 into 35; the result is 4 with a remainder of 3.

(STEP B) $\frac{3}{8}$ is the fractional part of the mixed number.

So, $\frac{35}{8} = 4\frac{3}{8}$.

We can regard any whole number as a mixed number with 0 as the fractional part. For example, $\frac{18}{6} = 3$.

I-2.3

MULTIPLYING FRACTIONS

To multiply two fractions, multiply their numerators and divide this result by the product of their denominators.

REMEMBER

In calculations with mixed numbers, change the mixed numbers into fractions.

> **EXAMPLE**
>
> John saves $\frac{1}{3}$ of $240. How much does he save? $\frac{1}{3} \times \frac{240}{1} = \frac{240}{3}$ = $80, the amount John saves.

I–2.4

DIVIDING FRACTIONS

To divide one fraction (the dividend) by another fraction (the divisor), invert the divisor and multiply. To invert a fraction, turn it upside down; for example, if you invert $\frac{3}{4}$, the result is $\frac{4}{3}$. $\frac{4}{3}$ is called the *reciprocal* of $\frac{3}{4}$.

> **EXAMPLE**
>
> $$\frac{5}{6} \div \frac{3}{4} = \frac{5}{6} \times \frac{4}{3} = \frac{20}{18}$$

> **EXAMPLE**
>
> A worker makes a basket in $\frac{2}{3}$ of an hour. If the worker works for $7\frac{1}{2}$ hours, how many baskets will he make?
>
> We want to divide $\frac{2}{3}$ into $7\frac{1}{2}$, and $7\frac{1}{2} = \frac{15}{2}$, so we want to divide $\frac{15}{2}$ by $\frac{2}{3}$.
>
> Thus, $\frac{15}{2} \div \frac{2}{3} = \frac{15}{2} \cdot \frac{3}{2} = \frac{45}{4} = 11\frac{1}{4}$ baskets.

I–2.5

DIVIDING AND MULTIPLYING BY THE SAME NUMBER

If you multiply the numerator and denominator of a fraction by the same nonzero number, the fraction remains the same.

If you divide the numerator and denominator of any fraction by the same nonzero number, the fraction remains the same.

Consider the fraction $\frac{3}{4}$. If we multiply 3 by 10 and 4 by 10, then $\frac{30}{40}$ must equal $\frac{3}{4}$.

When we multiply fractions, if any of the numerators and denominators have a common factor (see Section I–1.2 for factors) we can divide each of them by the common factor and the fraction remains the same. This process is called *cancelling* and can be a great time-saver.

Multiply $\dfrac{4}{9} \times \dfrac{75}{8}$.

Since 4 is a common factor of 4 and 8, divide 4 and 8 by 4, getting $\dfrac{4}{9} \times \dfrac{75}{8} =$

$\dfrac{1}{9} \times \dfrac{75}{2}$. Since 3 is a common factor of 9 and 75, divide 9 and 75 by 3 to get

$\dfrac{1}{9} \times \dfrac{75}{2} = \dfrac{1}{3} \times \dfrac{25}{2}$.

So $\dfrac{4}{9} \times \dfrac{75}{8} = \dfrac{1}{3} \times \dfrac{25}{2} = \dfrac{25}{6}$.

This is denoted by striking or crossing out the appropriate numbers. For instance, the example would be written as $\dfrac{\overset{1}{\cancel{4}}}{\underset{3}{\cancel{9}}} \times \dfrac{\overset{25}{\cancel{75}}}{\underset{2}{\cancel{8}}} = \dfrac{1}{3} \times \dfrac{25}{2} = \dfrac{25}{6}$.

Since you want to work as fast as possible on the GMAT exam, cancel whenever you can.

I-2.6

EQUIVALENT FRACTIONS

Two fractions are equivalent or equal if they represent the same ratio or number. In the last section, you saw that if you multiply or divide the numerator and denominator of a fraction by the same nonzero number the result is equivalent to the original fraction. For example, $\dfrac{7}{8} = \dfrac{70}{80}$ since $70 = 10 \times 7$ and $80 = 10 \times 8$.

To find a fraction with a known denominator equal to a given fraction:

(STEP A) divide the denominator of the given fraction into the known denominator;

(STEP B) multiply the result of (A) by the numerator of the given fraction; this is the numerator of the required equivalent fraction.

Find a fraction with a denominator of 30 which is equal to $\dfrac{2}{5}$:

(STEP A) 5 into 30 is 6;

(STEP B) $6 \cdot 2 = 12$ so, $\dfrac{12}{30} = \dfrac{2}{5}$.

I-2.7

REDUCING A FRACTION TO LOWEST TERMS

A fraction has been reduced to lowest terms when the numerator and denominator have no common factors.

For example, $\frac{3}{4}$ is reduced to lowest terms, but $\frac{3}{6}$ is not because 3 is a common factor of 3 and 6.

For example, $\dfrac{\cancel{100}}{\cancel{150}} = \dfrac{2}{3}$. Since 2 and 3 have no common factors, $\frac{2}{3}$ is $\frac{100}{150}$ reduced to lowest

terms. A fraction is equivalent to the fraction reduced to lowest terms.

If you aren't sure if there are any common factors, write the numerator and denominator as products of primes. Then it will be easy to cancel any common factors.

$$\frac{63}{81} = \frac{3 \cdot 3 \cdot 7}{3 \cdot 3 \cdot 3 \cdot 3} = \frac{7}{9}$$

REMEMBER

To reduce a fraction to lowest terms, cancel all the common factors of the numerator and denominator. (Cancelling common factors will not change the value of the fraction.)

I-2.8

ADDING FRACTIONS

If the fractions have the same denominator, then the denominator is called a *common denominator*. Add the numerators, and use this sum as the new numerator with the common denominator as the denominator of the sum.

EXAMPLE

$$\frac{5}{12} + \frac{3}{12} = \frac{5+3}{12} = \frac{8}{12} = \frac{2}{3}$$

EXAMPLE

A box of light bulbs contains 24 bulbs. A worker replaces 17 bulbs in the shipping department and 13 bulbs in the accounting department. How many boxes of bulbs did the worker use?

The worker used $\frac{17}{24}$ of a box in the shipping department and $\frac{13}{24}$ of a box in the accounting department. So the total used was $\frac{17}{24} + \frac{13}{24} = \frac{30}{24} = 1\frac{1}{4}$ boxes.

If the fractions don't have the same denominator, you must first find a common denominator. There are many common denominators; the smallest one is called the *least common denominator*. For the first example, 12 is the least common denominator.

STEP A One way to get a common denominator is to multiply all the denominators.

For example, to find $\frac{1}{2} + \frac{2}{3} + \frac{7}{4}$, note that $2 \cdot 3 \cdot 4 = 24$ which is a common denominator.

STEP B Once you have found a common denominator, express each fraction as an equivalent fraction with the common denominator.

STEP C Add as you did for the case when the fractions had the same denominator.

EXAMPLE

$$\frac{1}{2} + \frac{2}{3} + \frac{7}{4} = ?$$

STEP A 24 is a common denominator.

STEP B $\frac{1}{2} = \frac{12}{24}, \frac{2}{3} = \frac{16}{24}, \frac{7}{4} = \frac{42}{24}.$

STEP C $\frac{1}{2} + \frac{2}{3} + \frac{7}{4} = \frac{12}{24} + \frac{16}{24} + \frac{42}{24} = \frac{12 + 16 + 42}{24} = \frac{70}{24} = \frac{35}{12}$

I-2.9

SUBTRACTING FRACTIONS

When the fractions have the same denominator, subtract the numerators and place the result over the denominator.

EXAMPLE

There are 5 tacos in a lunch box. Jim eats two of the tacos. What fraction of the original tacos are left in the lunch box?

Jim took $\frac{2}{5}$ of the original tacos, so $1 - \frac{2}{5}$ are left. Write 1 as $\frac{5}{5}$; then $\frac{5}{5} - \frac{2}{5} =$

$\frac{(5-2)}{5} = \frac{3}{5}.$

So, $\frac{3}{5}$ are left in the lunch box.

When the fractions have different denominators:

STEP A Find a common denominator.

STEP B Express the fractions as equivalent fractions with the same denominator.

STEP C Subtract.

$$\frac{3}{5} - \frac{2}{7} = ?$$

(STEP A) A common denominator is $5 \cdot 7 = 35$.

(STEP B) $\frac{3}{5} = \frac{21}{35}, \frac{2}{7} = \frac{10}{35}$.

(STEP C) $\frac{3}{5} - \frac{2}{7} = \frac{21}{35} - \frac{10}{35} = \frac{21-10}{35} = \frac{11}{35}$.

I-2.10

COMPLEX FRACTIONS

A fraction whose numerator and denominator are themselves fractions is called a *complex fraction*. For example $\frac{\frac{2}{3}}{\frac{4}{5}}$ is a complex fraction. A complex fraction can always be simplified by dividing the fraction.

$$\frac{2}{3} \div \frac{4}{5} = \frac{2}{3} \cdot \frac{5}{4} = \frac{1}{3} \cdot \frac{5}{2} = \frac{5}{6}$$

It takes $2\frac{1}{2}$ hours to get from Buffalo to Cleveland traveling at a constant rate of speed. What part of the distance is traveled in $\frac{3}{4}$ of an hour?

$$\frac{\frac{3}{4}}{2\frac{1}{2}} = \frac{\frac{3}{4}}{\frac{5}{2}} = \frac{3}{4} \cdot \frac{2}{5} = \frac{3}{2} \cdot \frac{1}{5} = \frac{3}{10} \text{ of the distance.}$$

I-3. DECIMALS

I-3.1

A collection of digits (the digits are 0, 1, 2, . . . 9) after a period (called the decimal point) is called a *decimal fraction*. For example, .503, .5602, .32, and .4 are all decimal fractions. A zero to the left of the decimal point is optional in a decimal fraction. So, 0.503 and .503 are equal.

Every decimal fraction represents a fraction. To find the fraction that a decimal fraction represents:

(STEP A) The denominator is $10 \times 10 \times 10 \times \ldots \times 10$. The number of copies of 10 is equal to the number of digits to the right of the decimal point.

(STEP B) The numerator is the number represented by the digits to the right of the decimal point.

EXAMPLE

What fraction does 0.503 represent?

(STEP A) There are 3 digits to the right of the decimal point, so the denominator is $10 \times 10 \times 10 = 1{,}000$.

(STEP B) The numerator is 503, so the fraction is $\dfrac{503}{1{,}000}$.

EXAMPLE

Find the fraction that .05732 represents.

(STEP A) There are five digits to the right of the decimal point, so the denominator is $10 \times 10 \times 10 \times 10 \times 10 = 100{,}000$.

(STEP B) The numerator is 5,732, so the fraction is $\dfrac{5{,}732}{100{,}000}$.

EXAMPLE

$$.3 = \frac{3}{10} = \frac{30}{100} = .30 = .30000 = \frac{30{,}000}{100{,}000} = .300000000 \ldots$$

REMEMBER

You can add any number of zeros to the right of a decimal fraction without changing its value.

I-3.2

We call the first position to the right of the decimal point the tenths place, since the digit in that position tells you how many tenths you should take. (It is the numerator of a fraction whose denominator is 10.) In the same way, we call the second position to the right the hundredths place, the third position to the right the thousandths, and so on. This is similar to the way whole numbers are expressed, since 568 means $5 \times 100 + 6 \times 10 + 8 \times 1$. The various digits represent different numbers depending on their position: the first place to the left of the decimal point represents units, the second place to the left represents tens, and so on.

The following diagram may be helpful:

T H O U S A N D S	H U N D R E D S	T E N S	O N E S	•	T E N T H S	H U N D R E D T H S	T H O U S A N D T H S

Thus, 5,342.061 means 5 thousands + 3 hundreds + 4 tens + 2 ones + 0 tenths + 6 hundredths + 1 thousandth.

I-3.3

A *decimal* is a whole number plus a decimal fraction; the decimal point separates the whole number from the decimal fraction. For example, 4,307.206 is a decimal that represents 4,307 added to the decimal fraction .206. A decimal fraction is a decimal with zero as the whole number.

I-3.4

A fraction whose denominator is a multiple of 10 is equivalent to a decimal. The denominator tells you the last place that is filled to the right of the decimal point. Place the decimal point in the numerator so that the last place to the right of the decimal point corresponds to the denominator. If the numerator does not have enough digits, add the appropriate number of zeros *before* the numerator.

EXAMPLE

Find the decimal equivalent of $\frac{5,732}{100}$.

Since the denominator is 100, you need two places to the right of the decimal point so, $\frac{5,732}{100}$ = 57.32.

What is the decimal equivalent of $\frac{57}{10,000}$?

The denominator is 10,000, so you need 4 decimal places to the right of the decimal point.

Since 57 only has two places, we add two zeros in front of 57; thus, $\frac{57}{10,000}$ = .0057.

Do not make the error of adding the zeros to the right of 57 instead of the left.

.5700 is $\frac{5,700}{10,000}$, not $\frac{57}{10,000}$.

I–3.5

ADDING DECIMALS

Decimals are much easier to add than fractions. To add a collection of decimals:

STEP A Write the decimals in a column with the decimal points vertically aligned.

STEP B Add enough zeros to the right of the decimal point so that every number has an entry in each column to the right of the decimal point.

STEP C Add the numbers in the same way as whole numbers.

STEP D Place a decimal point in the sum so that it is directly beneath the decimal points in the decimals added.

How much is 5 + 3.43 + 16.021 + 3.1?

STEP A
```
    5
    3.43
   16.021
 +  3.1
```

STEP B
```
    5.000
    3.430
   16.021
 +  3.100
```

STEP C
```
    5.000
    3.430
   16.021
 +  3.100
```

STEP D   27.551   The answer is 27.551.

EXAMPLE

If Mary has $.50, $3.25, and $6.05, how much does she have?

```
  $ .50
    3.25
+   6.05
  _____
  $9.80        So, Mary has $9.80.
```

I-3.6

SUBTRACTING DECIMALS

To subtract one decimal from another:

STEP A Put the decimals in a column so that the decimal points are vertically aligned.

STEP B Add zeros so that every decimal has an entry in each column to the right of the decimal point.

STEP C Subtract the numbers as you would whole numbers.

STEP D Place the decimal point in the result so that it is directly beneath the decimal points of the numbers you subtracted.

EXAMPLE

Solve 5.053 − 2.09.

STEP A
```
   5.053
 − 2.09
```

STEP B
```
   5.053
 − 2.090
```

STEP C
```
   5.053
 − 2.090
```

STEP D   2.963   The answer is 2.963.

EXAMPLE

If Joe has $12 and he loses $8.40, how much money does he have left?

Since $12.00 − $8.40 = $3.60, he has $3.60 left.

I–3.7

TIP

To multiply a decimal by 10, just move the decimal point to the right one place; to multiply by 100, move the decimal point two places to the right, and so on.

MULTIPLYING DECIMALS

Decimals are multiplied like whole numbers. *The decimal point of the product is placed so that the number of decimal places in the product is equal to the total of the number of decimal places in all of the numbers multiplied.*

EXAMPLE

What is (5.02)(.6)?

   (502)(6) = 3012. There were 2 decimal places in 5.02 and 1 decimal place in .6, so the product must have 2 + 1 = 3 decimal places. Therefore, (5.02)(.6) = 3.012.

EXAMPLE

If eggs cost $.06 each, how much should a dozen eggs cost?

   Since (12)(.06) = .72, a dozen eggs should cost $.72.

EXAMPLE

9,983.456 × 100 = 998,345.6

I–3.8

DIVIDING DECIMALS

To divide one decimal (the dividend) by another decimal (the divisor):

STEP A Move the decimal point in the divisor to the right until there is no decimal fraction in the divisor (this is the same as multiplying the divisor by a multiple of 10).

STEP B Move the decimal point in the dividend the same number of places to the right as you moved the decimal point in step (A).

STEP C Divide the result of (B) by the result of (A) as if they were whole numbers.

STEP D The number of decimal places in the result (quotient) should be equal to the number of decimal places in the result of step (B).

STEP E You may obtain as many decimal places as you wish in the quotient by adding zeros to the right in the dividend and then repeating step (C). For each zero you add to the dividend, you need one more decimal place in the quotient.

Divide .05 into 25.155.

(STEP A) Move the decimal point two places to the right in .05; the result is 5.

(STEP B) Move the decimal point two places to the right in 25.155; the result is 2515.5.

(STEP C) Divide 5 into 25155; the result is 5031.

(STEP D) Since there was one decimal place in the result of (B), the answer is 503.1.

(STEP E) There is no need to continue the division.

The work for this example might look like this:

$$\begin{array}{r} 503.1 \\ .05\overline{)25.155} \end{array}$$

You can always check division by multiplying.

$$(503.1)(.05) = 25.155 \text{ so our answer checks.}$$

If you write division as a fraction, the previous Example would be expressed as $\dfrac{25.155}{.05}$.

You can multiply both the numerator and denominator by 100 without changing the value of the fraction. So,

$$\frac{25.155}{.05} = \frac{25.155 \times 100}{.05 \times 100} = \frac{2515.5}{5.} .$$

So steps (A) and (B) always change the division of a decimal by a decimal into the division of a decimal by a whole number.

To divide a decimal by a whole number, divide them as if they were whole numbers. Then place the decimal point in the quotient so that the quotient has as many decimal places as the dividend.

$$\frac{100.11}{.8} = ?$$

(STEP A) Move the decimal point one place to the right in .8; the result is 8.

(STEP B) Move the decimal point one place to the right in 100.11; the result is 1001.1.

(STEP C) Divide 8 into 10011; the result is 1251, with a remainder of 3. Since the division is not exact, we use step (E).

(STEP D) The result must have four decimal places (1 from step (B) and 3 from step (E)), so the answer is 125.1375.

(STEP E) Add 3 zeros to the right of 1001.1 and repeat (C). So we divide 8 into 10011000; the result is 1251375.

The work for this example might look like this:

$$.8\overline{)100.11000}^{125.1375}$$

CHECK: (.8)(125.1375) = 100.11000 = 100.11 so this is correct.

EXAMPLE

If oranges cost 42¢ each, how many oranges can you buy for $2.52? Make sure the units are compatible, so 42¢ is $.42. Therefore, the number of oranges is

$$\frac{2.52}{.42} = \frac{252}{42} = 6.$$

EXAMPLE

Divide 5,637.6471 by 1,000.

The answer is 5.6376471, since to divide by 1,000 you move the decimal point 3 places to the left.

TIP

To divide a decimal by 10, move the decimal point to the left one place; to divide by 100, move the decimal point two places to the left, and so on.

I-3.9

CONVERTING A FRACTION INTO A DECIMAL

To convert a fraction into a decimal, divide the denominator into the numerator. For example, $\frac{3}{4} = \frac{3.00}{4} = .75$. Some fractions give a repeating decimal when you divide the denominator into the numerator, for example,

$\frac{1}{3} = .333\ldots$ where the three dots mean you keep on getting 3 with each step of division.

.333 . . . is a *repeating decimal.*

You should know the following decimal equivalents of fractions:

TIP

If a fraction has a repeating decimal, use the fraction in any computation.

$\frac{1}{100} = .01$	$\frac{1}{16} = .0625$	$\frac{1}{8} = .125$	$\frac{3}{8} = .375$	$\frac{3}{4} = .75$
$\frac{1}{50} = .02$	$\frac{1}{15} = .06\overline{6}$	$\frac{1}{6} = .16\overline{6}$	$\frac{2}{5} = .4$	$\frac{7}{8} = .875$
$\frac{1}{40} = .025$	$\frac{1}{12} = 0.83\overline{3}$	$\frac{1}{5} = .2$	$\frac{1}{2} = .5$	$\frac{3}{2} = 1.5$
$\frac{1}{25} = .04$	$\frac{1}{10} = .1$	$\frac{1}{4} = .25$	$\frac{5}{8} = .625$	
$\frac{1}{20} = .05$	$\frac{1}{9} = .\overline{111}$	$\frac{1}{3} = .33\overline{3}$	$\frac{2}{3} = .6\overline{6}$	

Any decimal with a bar above is a repeating decimal.

Barnes & Noble Booksellers #2891
1553 Almonesson Road
Deptford, NJ 08096
856-232-3123

STR:2891 REG:004 TRN:0144 CSHR:Daniel R

EDUCATOR   EXP: 11/25/2014

Renew Educator Card   T2
  (1 @ 0.00)   0.00
  Card#: XXXXXX3669
Mockingjay (Hunger Games Series #3)
  9780439023511   T1
  (1 @ 17.99) Educator 20% (3.60)
  (1 @ 14.39)   14.39
Barron's GMAT with CD-ROM, 17th Edition
  9781438073064   T1
  (1 @ 34.99) Educator 20% (7.00)
  (1 @ 27.99)   27.99

Subtotal   42.38
Sales Tax T1 (7.000%)   2.97
TOTAL   45.35
VISA   45.35
  Card#: XXXXXXXXXXXXX3743
  Expdate: XX/XX
  Auth: 443326
  Entry Method: Swiped

         Thanks for shopping at
              Barnes & Noble

101.29B   11/26/2012 04:37PM

              CUSTOMER COPY

Return Policy

<u>With a sales receipt or Barnes & Noble.com packing slip</u>, a full refund in the original form of payment will be issued from any Barnes & Noble Booksellers store for returns of undamaged NOOKs, new and unread books, and unopened and undamaged music CDs, DVDs, and audio books made within 14 days of purchase from a Barnes & Noble Booksellers store or Barnes & Noble.com with the below exceptions:

A store credit for the purchase price will be issued (i) for purchases made by check less than 7 days prior to the date of return, (ii) when a gift receipt is presented within 60 days of purchase, (iii) for textbooks, or (iv) for products purchased at Barnes & Noble College bookstores that are listed for sale in the Barnes & Noble Booksellers inventory management system.

Opened music CDs/DVDs/audio books may not be returned, and can be exchanged only for the same title and only if defective. NOOKs purchased from other retailers or sellers are returnable only to the retailer or seller from which they are purchased, pursuant to such retailer's or seller's return policy. Magazines, newspapers, eBooks, digital downloads, and used books are not returnable or exchangeable. Defective NOOKs may be exchanged at the store in accordance with the applicable warranty.

Returns or exchanges will not be permitted (i) after 14 days or without receipt or (ii) for product not carried by Barnes & Noble or Barnes & Noble.com.

Policy on receipt may appear in two sections.

Return Policy

<u>With a sales receipt or Barnes & Noble.com packing slip</u>, a full refund in the original form of payment will be issued from any Barnes & Noble Booksellers store for returns of undamaged NOOKs, new and unread books, and unopened and undamaged music CDs, DVDs, and audio books made within 14 days of purchase from a Barnes & Noble Booksellers store or Barnes & Noble.com with the below exceptions:

A store credit for the purchase price will be issued (i) for purchases made by check less than 7 days prior to the date of return, (ii) when a gift receipt is presented within 60 days of purchase, (iii) for textbooks, or (iv) for products purchased at Barnes & Noble College

What is $\frac{2}{9}$ of \$3,690.90?

Since the decimal for $\frac{2}{9}$ is .2222 . . . use the fraction $\frac{2}{9}$.

$\frac{2}{9} \times \$3,690.90 = 2 \times \$410.10 = \$820.20.$

I-4. PERCENTAGE

I-4.1

Percentage is another method of expressing fractions or parts of an object. Percentages are expressed in terms of hundredths, so 100% means 100 hundredths or 1, and 50% would be 50 hundredths or $\frac{1}{2}$.

A decimal is converted to a percentage by multiplying the decimal by 100. Since multiplying a decimal by 100 is accomplished by moving the decimal point two places to the right, *you convert a decimal into a percentage by moving the decimal point two places to the right.* For example, .134 = 13.4%.

If you wish to convert a percentage into a decimal, you divide the percentage by 100. There is a shortcut for this also. To divide by 100 you move the decimal point two places to the left.

Therefore, *to convert a percentage into a decimal, move the decimal point two places to the left.* For example, 24% = .24.

A fraction is converted into a percentage by changing the fraction to a decimal and then changing the decimal to a percentage. A percentage is changed into a fraction by first converting the percentage into a decimal and then changing the decimal to a fraction. *You should know the following fractional equivalents of percentages:*

$1\% = \frac{1}{100}$	$12\frac{1}{2}\% = \frac{1}{8}$	$40\% = \frac{2}{5}$	$80\% = \frac{4}{5}$	$133\frac{1}{3}\% = \frac{4}{3}$
$2\% = \frac{1}{50}$	$16\frac{2}{3}\% = \frac{1}{6}$	$50\% = \frac{1}{2}$	$83\frac{1}{3}\% = \frac{5}{6}$	$150\% = \frac{3}{2}$
$4\% = \frac{1}{25}$	$20\% = \frac{1}{5}$	$60\% = \frac{3}{5}$	$87\frac{1}{2}\% = \frac{7}{8}$	
$5\% = \frac{1}{20}$	$25\% = \frac{1}{4}$	$62\frac{1}{2}\% = \frac{5}{8}$	$100\% = 1$	
$8\frac{1}{3}\% = \frac{1}{12}$	$33\frac{1}{3}\% = \frac{1}{3}$	$66\frac{2}{3}\% = \frac{2}{3}$	$120\% = \frac{6}{5}$	
$10\% = \frac{1}{10}$	$37\frac{1}{2}\% = \frac{3}{8}$	$75\% = \frac{3}{4}$	$125\% = \frac{5}{4}$	

REMEMBER

When you compute with percentages, it is usually easier to change the percentages to decimals or fractions.

Note, for example, that $133\frac{1}{3}\% = 1.33\frac{1}{3} = 1\frac{1}{3} = \frac{4}{3}$.

A company has 6,435 bars of soap. If the company sells 20% of its bars of soap, how many bars of soap did it sell?

Change 20% into .2. Thus, the company sold $(.2)(6,435) = 1287.0 = 1,287$ bars of soap. An alternative method would be to convert 20% to $\frac{1}{5}$.

Then, $\frac{1}{5} \times 6,435 = 1,287$.

In a class of 60 students, 18 students received a grade of B. What percentage of the class received a grade of B?

$\frac{18}{60}$ of the class received a grade of B. $\frac{18}{60} = \frac{3}{10} = .3 = 30\%$, so 30% of the class received a grade of B.

If the population of Dryden was 10,000 in 1960 and the population of Dryden increased by 15% between 1960 and 1970, what was the population of Dryden in 1970?

The population increased by 15% between 1960 and 1970, so the increase was $(.15)(10,000)$ which is 1,500. The population in 1970 was $10,000 + 1,500 = 11,500$.

A quicker method: The population increased 15%, so the population in 1970 is 115% of the population in 1960. Therefore, the population in 1970 is 115% of 10,000 which is $(1.15)(10,000) = 11,500$.

I-4.2

INTEREST AND DISCOUNT

Two of the most common uses of percentages are in interest and discount problems.

The rate of interest is usually given as a percentage. The basic formula for interest problems is:

$$\text{INTEREST} = \text{AMOUNT} \times \text{TIME} \times \text{RATE}$$

You can assume the rate of interest is the annual rate of interest unless the problem states otherwise; so you should express the time in years.

EXAMPLE

How much interest will $10,000 earn in 9 months at an annual rate of 6%?

9 months is $\frac{3}{4}$ of a year and 6% = $\frac{3}{50}$, so using the formula, the interest is

$10,000 × $\frac{3}{4}$ × $\frac{3}{50}$ = $50 × 9 = $450.

EXAMPLE

What annual rate of interest was paid if $5,000 earned $300 in interest in 2 years?

Since the interest was earned in 2 years, $150 is the interest earned in one year.

$\frac{150}{5,000}$ = .03 = 3%, so the annual rate of interest was 3%.

The type of interest described above is called *simple interest*.

There is another method of computing interest called *compound interest*. In computing compound interest, the interest is periodically added to the amount (or principal) that is earning interest.

EXAMPLE

What will $1,000 be worth after three years if it earns interest at the rate of 5% compounded annually?

Compounded annually means that the interest earned during one year is added to the amount (or principal) at the end of each year. The interest on $1,000 at 5% for one year is $(1,000)(.05) = $50. So you must compute the interest on $1,050 (not $1,000) for the second year. The interest is $(1,050)(.05) = $52.50. Therefore, during the third year interest will be computed for $1,102.50. During the third year the interest is $(1,102.50)(.05) = $55.125 = $55.13. Therefore, after 3 years the original $1,000 will be worth $1,157.63.

If you calculated simple interest on $1,000 at 5% for three years, the answer would be $(1,000)(.05)(3) = $150. Therefore, using simple interest, $1,000 is worth $1,150 after 3 years. You earn more interest with compound interest.

You can assume that interest means simple interest unless a problem states otherwise. The basic formula for discount problems is:

DISCOUNT = COST × RATE OF DISCOUNT

EXAMPLE

What is the discount if a car that cost $3,000 is discounted 7%? The discount is $3,000 × .07 = $210 since 7% = .07.

If we know the cost of an item and its discounted price, we can find the rate of discount by using the formula

$$\text{rate of discount} = \frac{\text{cost} - \text{price}}{\text{cost}}$$

EXAMPLE

What was the rate of discount if a boat which cost $5,000 was sold for $4,800?

Using this formula, we find that the rate of discount equals

$$\frac{5,000 - 4,800}{5,000} = \frac{200}{5,000} = \frac{1}{25} = .04 = 4\%.$$

After an item has been discounted once, it may be discounted again. This procedure is called successive discounting.

EXAMPLE

A bicycle originally cost $100 and was discounted 10%. After three months it was sold after being discounted 15%. How much was the bicycle sold for?

After the 10% discount the bicycle was selling for $100(.90) = $90. An item which costs $90 and is discounted 15% will sell for $90(.85) = $76.50, so the bicycle was sold for $76.50.

Notice that if you added the two discounts of 10% and 15% and treated the successive discounts as a single discount of 25%, your answer would be that the bicycle sold for $75, which is incorrect. Successive discounts are *not* identical to a single discount of the sum of the discounts. The previous example shows that successive discounts of 10% and 15% are not identical to a single discount of 25%.

I–5. ROUNDING OFF NUMBERS

I–5.1

Many times an approximate answer can be found more quickly and may be more useful than the exact answer. For example, if a company had sales of $998,875.63 during a year, it is easier to remember that the sales were about $1 million.

Rounding off a number to a decimal place means finding the multiple of the representative of that decimal place that is closest to the original number. Thus, rounding off a number to the nearest hundred means finding the multiple of 100 that is closest to the original number. Rounding off to the nearest tenth means finding the multiple of $\frac{1}{10}$ that is closest to the original number.

After a number has been rounded off to a particular decimal place, all the digits to the right of that particular decimal place will be zero.

To round off a number to the *r*th decimal place:

(STEP A) Look at the digit in the place to the right of the *r*th place;

(STEP B) *If the digit is 4 or less, change all the digits in places to the right of the rth place to 0 to round off the number.*

(STEP C) *If the digit is 5 or more, add 1 to the digit in the rth place and change all the digits in places to the right of the rth place to 0 to round off the number.*

For example, the multiple of 100 that is closest to 5,342.1 is 5,300.

EXAMPLE

Round off 3.445 to the nearest tenth.

The digit to the right of the tenths place is 4, so 3.445 is 3.4 to the nearest tenth.

Most problems dealing with money are rounded off to the nearest hundredth or cent if the answer contains a fractional part of a cent. This is common business practice.

EXAMPLE

If 16 cookies cost $1.00, how much should three cookies cost?

Three cookies should cost $\frac{3}{16}$ of $1.00. Since $\frac{3}{16} \times 1 = .1875$, the cost would be $.1875. In practice, you would round it up to $.19 or 19¢.

Rounding off numbers can help you get quick, approximate answers. Since some questions require only rough answers, you can save time on the test by rounding off numbers.

EXAMPLE

If 5,301 of the 499,863 workers employed at the XYZ factory don't show up for work on Monday, about what percentage of the workers don't show up?

(A) 1
(B) 2
(C) 3
(D) 4
(E) 5

You can quickly see that the answer is (A) by rounding off both numbers to the nearest thousand before you divide, because $\frac{5,000}{500,000} = \frac{1}{100} = .01 = 1\%$. The exact answer is $\frac{5,301}{499,863} = .010604$, but it would take much longer to get an exact answer.

Round off 43.796 to the nearest tenth.

The place to the right of tenths is hundredths, so look in the hundredths place. Since 9 is bigger than 5, add 1 to the tenths place. Therefore, 43.796 is 43.8 rounded off to the nearest tenth.

If the digit in the *r*th place is 9 and you need to add 1 to the digit to round off the number to the *r*th decimal place, put a zero in the *r*th place and add 1 to the digit in the position to the left of the *r*th place. For example, 298 rounded off to the nearest 10 is 300; 99,752 to the nearest thousand is 100,000.

I-6. SIGNED NUMBERS

I-6.1

A number preceded by either a plus or a minus sign is called a *signed number*. For example, $+5$, -6, -4.2, and $+\frac{3}{4}$ are all signed numbers. If no sign is given with a number, a plus sign is assumed; thus, 5 is interpreted as $+5$.

Signed numbers can often be used to distinguish different concepts. For example, a profit of \$10 can be denoted by $+\$10$ and a loss of \$10 by $-\$10$. A temperature of 20 degrees below zero can be denoted $-20°$F.

I-6.2

Signed numbers are also called *directed numbers*. You can think of numbers arranged on a line, called a number line, in the following manner:

Take a line that extends indefinitely in both directions, pick a point on the line and call it 0, pick another point on the line to the right of 0 and call it 1. The point to the right of 1 which is exactly as far from 1 as 1 is from 0 is called 2, the point to the right of 2 just as far from 2 as 1 is from 0 is called 3, and so on. The point halfway between 0 and 1 is called $\frac{1}{2}$, the point halfway between $\frac{1}{2}$ and 1 is called $\frac{3}{4}$. In this way, you can identify any whole number or any fraction with a point on the line.

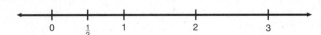

All the numbers that correspond to points to the right of 0 are called *positive numbers*. The sign of a positive number is $+$.

If you go to the left of zero the same distance as you did from 0 to 1, the point is called -1; in the same way as before, you can find -2, -3, $-\frac{1}{2}$, $-\frac{3}{2}$, and so on.

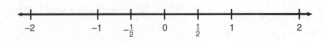

All the numbers that correspond to points to the left of zero are called *negative numbers*. Negative numbers are signed numbers whose sign is –. For example, –3, –5.15, –.003 are all negative numbers.

I–6.3

ABSOLUTE VALUE

The absolute value of a signed number is the distance of the number from 0. The absolute value of any nonzero number is *positive*. For example, the absolute value of 2 is 2; the absolute value of –2 is 2. The absolute value of a number a is denoted by $|a|$, so $|-2| = 2$. The absolute value of any number can be found by dropping its sign, $|-12| = 12$, $|4| = 4$. *Thus $|-a| = |a|$ for any number a.* The only number whose absolute value is zero is zero.

I–6.4

ADDING SIGNED NUMBERS

Case I. Adding numbers with the *same sign*:

(STEP A) The sign of the sum is the same as the sign of the numbers being added.

(STEP B) Add the absolute values.

(STEP C) Put the sign from step (A) in front of the number you obtained in step (B).

EXAMPLE

What is –2 + (–3.1) + (–.02)?

(STEP A) The sign of the sum will be –.

(STEP B) $|-2| = 2$, $|-3.1| = 3.1$, $|-.02| = .02$, and 2 + 3.1 + .02 = 5.12.

(STEP C) The answer is –5.12.

Case II. Adding two numbers with *different signs*:

(STEP A) The sign of the sum is the sign of the number that is largest in absolute value.

(STEP B) Subtract the absolute value of the number with the smaller absolute value from the absolute value of the number with the larger absolute value.

(STEP C) The answer is the number you obtained in step (B) preceded by the sign from part (A).

EXAMPLE

How much is –5.1 + 3?

(STEP A) The absolute value of – 5.1 is 5.1 and the absolute value of 3 is 3, so the sign of the sum will be –.

(STEP B) 5.1 is larger than 3, and 5.1 – 3 = 2.1.

(STEP C) The sum is –2.1.

Case III. Adding *more than two* numbers with *different signs*:

(STEP A) Add all the positive numbers; the result is positive (this is Case I).

(STEP B) Add all the negative numbers; the result is negative (this is Case I).

(STEP C) Add the result of step (A) to the result of step (B), by using Case II.

EXAMPLE

Find the value of 5 + 52 + (–3) + 7 + (–5.1).

(STEP A) 5 + 52 + 7 = 64.

(STEP B) –3 + (–5.1) = –8.1.

(STEP C) 64 + (–8.1) = 55.9, so the answer is 55.9.

EXAMPLE

If a store made a profit of $23.50 on Monday, lost $2.05 on Tuesday, lost $5.03 on Wednesday, made a profit of $30.10 on Thursday, and made a profit of $41.25 on Friday, what was its total profit (or loss) for the week? Use + for profit and – for loss.

The total is 23.50 + (–2.05) + (–5.03) + 30.10 + 41.25, which is 94.85 + (–7.08) = 87.77. So the store made a profit of $87.77.

I-6.5

SUBTRACTING SIGNED NUMBERS

When subtracting signed numbers:

(STEP A) Change the sign of the number you are subtracting (the subtrahend).

(STEP B) Add the result of step (A) to the number being subtracted from (the minuend) using the rules of the preceding section.

EXAMPLE

Subtract 4.1 from 6.5.

(STEP A) 4.1 becomes –4.1.

(STEP B) 6.5 + (–4.1) = 2.4.

EXAMPLE

What is 7.8 – (–10.1)?

(STEP A) –10.1 becomes 10.1.

(STEP B) 7.8 + 10.1 = 17.9.

So we subtract a negative number by adding a positive number with the same absolute value, and we subtract a positive number by adding a negative number of the same absolute value.

I-6.6

MULTIPLYING SIGNED NUMBERS

Case I. Multiplying two numbers:

(STEP A) Multiply the absolute values of the numbers.

(STEP B) If both numbers have the same sign, the result of step (A) is the answer—i.e., the product is positive. If the numbers have different signs, then the answer is the result of step (A) with a minus sign.

EXAMPLE

$(-5)(-12) = ?$

(STEP A) $5 \times 12 = 60$

(STEP B) Both signs are the same, so the answer is 60.

EXAMPLE

$(4)(-3) = ?$

(STEP A) $4 \times 3 = 12$

(STEP B) The signs are different, so the answer is –12.

TIP

You can remember the sign of the product in the following way:

$(-)(-) = +$
$(+)(+) = +$
$(-)(+) = -$
$(+)(-) = -$

Case II. Multiplying more than two numbers:

(STEP A) Multiply the first two factors using Case I.

(STEP B) Multiply the result of (A) by the third factor.

(STEP C) Multiply the result of (B) by the fourth factor.

(STEP D) Continue until you have used each factor.

EXAMPLE

$(-5)(4)(2)(-\frac{1}{2})(\frac{3}{4}) = ?$

(STEP A) $(-5)(4) = -20$

(STEP B) $(-20)(2) = -40$

(STEP C) $(-40)(-\frac{1}{2}) = 20$

(STEP D) $(20)(\frac{3}{4}) = 15$, so the answer is 15.

I-6.7

DIVIDING SIGNED NUMBERS

Divide the absolute values of the numbers; the sign of the quotient is determined by the same rules as you used to determine the sign of a product. Thus,

$$positive \div positive = positive$$
$$negative \div negative = positive$$
$$positive \div negative = negative$$
$$negative \div positive = negative$$

REMEMBER

The sign of the product or quotient is + if there are no negative factors or an even number of negative factors. The sign of the product or quotient is – if there are an odd number of negative factors.

EXAMPLE

Divide 53.2 by –4.

53.2 divided by 4 is 13.3. Since one of the numbers is positive and the other negative, the answer is –13.3.

EXAMPLE

$$\frac{-5}{-2} = \frac{5}{2} = 2.5$$

I-7. DESCRIPTIVE STATISTICS AND PROBABILITY

I-7.1

THE MEAN

The *average* or *arithmetic mean* of N numbers is the sum of the N numbers divided by N.

EXAMPLE

The scores for 9 students on a test were 72, 78, 81, 64, 85, 92, 95, 60, and 55. What was the average score of the students?

Since there are 9 students, the average is the total of all the scores divided by 9.

So, the average is $\frac{1}{9}$ of (72 + 78 + 81 + 64 + 85 + 92 + 95 + 60 + 55), which is $\frac{1}{9}$ of 682 or $75\frac{7}{9}$.

> ### EXAMPLE
>
> The temperature at noon in Coldtown, U.S.A. was 5°F on Monday, 10°F on Tuesday, 2°F below zero on Wednesday, 5°F below zero on Thursday, 0°F on Friday, 4°F on Saturday, and 1°F below zero on Sunday. What was the average temperature at noon for the week?
>
> Use negative numbers for the temperatures below zero. The average temperature is the average of 5, 10, –2, –5, 0, 4, and –1, which is
>
> $$\frac{5 + 10 + (-2) + (-5) + 0 + 4 + (-1)}{7} = \frac{11}{7} = 1\frac{4}{7}.$$
>
> Therefore, the average temperature at noon for the week is $1\frac{4}{7}$°F.

> ### EXAMPLE
>
> If the average annual income of 10 workers is $15,665 and two of the workers each made $20,000 for the year, what is the average annual income of the remaining 8 workers?
>
> The total income of all 10 workers is 10 times the average income, which is $156,650. The two workers made a total of $40,000, so the total income of the remaining 8 workers was $156,650 – $40,000 = $116,650. Therefore, the average annual income of the 8 remaining workers is $\frac{\$116,650}{8}$ = $14,581.25.

I-7.2

THE MEDIAN

If we arrange *N* numbers in order, the *median* is the middle number if *N* is odd and the average of the two middle numbers if *N* is even. In Example 1 above, the median score was 78, and in Example 2, the median temperature for the week was 0. Notice that the medians were different from the averages. In Example 3, we don't have enough data to find the median although we know the average.

The average and the median are examples of descriptive statistics. Other statistics that you should know are the *mode, range,* and *standard deviation*.

■ I-7.3

THE MODE

In a collection of numbers or measurements, the mode is the most frequent measurement in the collection.

TIP

In general the median and the average of a collection of numbers are different.

The number of defects in 12 different production runs were 2, 5, 10, 0, 5, 3, 4, 3, 2, 2, 0, and 0. The mode(s) of the defects are 2 and 0 since both 2 and 0 occurred 3 times in the set of defects.

A set can have more than one mode.

I-7.4

FREQUENCY DISTRIBUTIONS

A set of numbers is often summarized compactly by a frequency distribution. A frequency distribution for a set of measurements or numbers is a table that gives each value in the collection along with the number of times it occurs in the collection.

TIP

If you have a large data set, it is better to organize the data into a frequency distribution before starting calculations.

The number of defects in 12 different production runs were 2 , 5, 10, 0, 5, 3, 4, 3, 2, 2, 0, and 0. This data can be summarized in a frequency distribution as follows :

(i) The values that occur in the set in increasing order are 0, 2, 3, 4, 5, and 10.

(ii) The frequency of 0 is 3 since it occurs 3 times in the set. The frequency of 2 is 3 since it occurs 3 times in the set. The frequency of 3 is 2 since it occurs twice in the set. The frequency of 5 is 2 since it occurs twice in the set. Both 4 and 10 have frequency 1 since they occur only once in the set.

(iii) So the set can be summarized in a table:

Measurement	Frequency
0	3
2	3
3	2
4	1
5	2
10	1

Notice that the frequencies add up to 12, which is the number of measurements in the set.

Calculations are easier if the data are given in a frequency distribution.

Find the arithmetic mean, median, and mode of the set of defects in the 12 production runs given on page 252.

Finding the mean:

(i) Multiply each measurement by its frequency ($3 \times 0 = 0$, $3 \times 2 = 6$, $2 \times 3 = 6$, $1 \times 4 = 4$, $2 \times 5 = 10$, and $1 \times 10 = 10$).

(ii) Add the results obtained in step (i) ($0 + 6 + 6 + 4 + 10 + 10 = 36$).

(iii) Add the frequencies ($3 + 3 + 2 + 1 + 2 + 1 = 12$).

(iv) Divide the results of step (ii), which is the sum of the measurements, by the result of step (iii), which is number of measurements, to obtain the average ($\frac{36}{12} = 3$). So 3 is the average number of defects per production run for the set.

Finding the median:

(i) Find the number of measurements by adding the frequencies ($3 + 3 + 2 + 1 + 2 + 1 = 12$).

(ii) Find the location of the median in the ordered set. (The median will be the average of the sixth and seventh values.)

(iii) Since the frequency distribution gives the values in order, pick out the appropriate value(s) and calculate the median. (The sixth measurement is 2 and the seventh measurement is 3, so the median is $\frac{(2 + 3)}{2} = 2.5$.)

Finding the mode:

(i) Find the largest frequency (3 is the largest frequency).

(ii) The entries corresponding to the largest frequencies are the modes. (2 and 0 have frequencies of 3, so they are the modes.)

The *average or mean, median,* and *mode* are statistics that are used to estimate a "typical" or "most likely" measurement in a set. Another way of thinking about this idea is to say these statistics are used to estimate the center or middle of a collection of numbers.

I–7.5

RANGE AND STANDARD DEVIATION

In some situations we need to know the spread or dispersal of the values in a set. The *range* and *standard deviation* are two statistics used to measure how varied the measurements are.

Range. The range of a set of measurements is the difference of the largest and smallest measurements in the set.

Example: The range of defects in the production runs given in the previous section is $10 - 0 = 10$.

The range of a set of measurements depends only on the largest and smallest values in the set.

Standard Deviation. The standard deviation is a statistic used to measure the spread of a distribution that involves all the values in the set.

Example: Calculate the standard deviation of the set of defects in the 12 production runs.

(i) Find the mean of the set (we know the mean is 3).

(ii) Subtract the mean from each measurement; the results are called the deviations.

(iii) Square each deviation.

(iv) Add all the squares of the deviations. (Be sure to multiply the squared deviation by its frequency.)

(v) Divide by the number of measurements. (In other words, find the average of the squared deviations.)

(vi) Take the square root of the result of step (v). This is the standard deviation of the data.

We will calculate the standard deviation for the data. Much of the calculation can be done with the frequency distribution.

Measurement	Frequency	Deviation	Squared deviation
0	3	0 – 3	$(-3)^2 = 9$
2	3,	2 – 3	$(-1)^2 = 1$
3	2	3 – 3	$0^2 = 0$
4	1	4 – 3	$1^2 = 1$
5	2	5 – 3	$2^2 = 4$
10	1	10 – 3	$7^2 = 49$

(iv) The sum of the squared deviations is $3 \times 9 + 3 \times 1 + 2 \times 0 + 1 \times 1 + 2 \times 4 + 1 \times 49$, which is $27 + 3 + 0 + 1 + 8 + 49 = 88$.

(v) Divide 88 by 12 to get 7 and $\frac{1}{3}$.

(vi) The standard deviation is $\sqrt{7.333\ldots} = 2.708\ldots$

If one set has a smaller standard deviation than a second set, then the first set is less spread out than the second set.

If you multiply each number in a data set by the same constant to obtain a new data set, then the mean, median, mode, range, and standard deviation of the new set will be the statistics of the old set multiplied by the constant.

If you add the same constant to each number in a data set to obtain a new data set, then the mean, median, mode of the new set can be found by adding the constant to the mean, median, and mode of the original set.

However, the range and standard deviation will be unchanged since the new distribution has the same dispersal as the original distribution.

EXAMPLE

The compensation of the employees of the marketing department has a distribution with a mean of $51,000 and a standard deviation of $5,200. If every person in the department receives an increment of $1,000, find the mean and standard deviation of the compensations after the increments.

The mean is increased by $1,000, so the new mean is $51,000 + $1,000 = $52,000.

Since every compensation increased by $1,000 and the mean increased by $1,000, the deviations will be unchanged; so the standard deviation will remain $5,200.

EXAMPLE

The median of the daily high temperatures in a city for the month of June was 86° Fahrenheit with a range of 18° Fahrenheit. You can translate degrees Fahrenheit to degrees Celsius by the following formula:

$$\text{degrees Celsius} = \frac{5}{9}(\text{degrees Fahrenheit} - 32)$$

Find the median and the range of the daily high temperatures for June in degrees Celsius.

The median high temperature will be $\left(\frac{5}{9}\right)(86 - 32) = \left(\frac{5}{9}\right)(54) = 30°$ Celsius.

The range will be $\left(\frac{5}{9}\right)(18) = 10°$ Celsius. (Notice that you do not subtract 32 since adding or subtracting the same amount from each temperature will not change the range.)

REMEMBER

If you add the same constant to each number in a data set to get a new data set, then the range and standard deviation of the new data set will be the same as the range and standard deviation of the original data set.

I-7.6

DISCRETE PROBABILITY

Probability is a way to measure how likely an occurrence is. Probabilities are measured by assigning values from 0 to 1 inclusive. A probability assignment of 0 means something will "never" happen, a probability assignment of 1 means that something "always" happens.

The most common way of assigning probabilities is when each outcome is equally likely. If a question says a person is randomly chosen, that means each person has the same chance of being chosen. When outcomes are equally likely, then the probability of any particular outcome is 1 divided by the number of outcomes.

For example, think of a jar that contains 10 red and 5 blue marbles. You reach in and take a marble without looking. There are 15 marbles in the jar, so there are 15 different outcomes when you pick the marble. Since you did not look when you picked the marble, each marble should have the same chance of being picked, and so we assign $\frac{1}{15}$ as the probability that any particular marble is picked. Since there are 10 red marbles in the jar, the probability that a red marble is picked is $10 \times \left(\frac{1}{15}\right) = \frac{10}{15}$ or $\frac{2}{3}$. Since there are 5 blue marbles in the jar, the probability that a blue marble is picked is $5 \times \left(\frac{1}{15}\right) = \frac{5}{15}$ or $\frac{1}{3}$.

We let R stand for the outcome that the marble picked is red and $p(\text{R})$ stand for the probability that R occurs. So we showed $p(\text{R}) = \frac{10}{15}$ or $\frac{2}{3}$.

If B means that the marble picked was blue, then $p(\text{B}) = \frac{5}{15}$ or $\frac{1}{3}$.

If we picked a red marble from the jar and then picked a second marble without replacing the first marble, then the probability that the second marble is red if the first marble was red is $\frac{9}{14}$. The probability that the second marble is blue if the first marble was red is $\frac{5}{14}$.

Some simple facts that are useful when working with probability are the following:

1. The probability that an event does not happen is 1 minus the probability that the event does happen. This is often stated as *p(not A) = 1 – p(A)* (*not A* is also referred to as the negation of A.)

   For example, when we picked the marble from the jar, there were 10 red marbles and 5 nonred marbles in the jar, so *p*(not B) = the probability that the marble picked is not blue $= \frac{10}{15} = 1 - \left(\frac{5}{15}\right) = 1 - p(\text{B})$.

2. The probability that A is followed by B is the probability that A occurs times the probability that B occurs if A has occurred. This is often stated as *p(A and B) = p(A)p(B occurs if A occurred)*.

   For example, the probability that the first two marbles drawn are red is $\left(\frac{10}{15}\right) \times \left(\frac{9}{14}\right)$.

3. If two outcomes cannot both occur, they are called *disjoint*. If events are disjoint, the probability that both events occur is 0. This is stated as *p(A and B) = 0 if A and B are disjoint.*

   For example, the first marble picked is red and the first marble picked is blue are disjoint outcomes. However, the first marble is red and the second marble is blue are not disjoint outcomes since it is possible that the first marble is red and the second marble is blue.

4. To find the probability that at least one of two outcomes occurs, add the probabilities of each outcome and then subtract the probability that both outcomes occur. You subtract the probability that both occur since any outcome that has both occurring will be counted in the probability that the first occurs and again in the probability that the second occurs. This is stated as $p(A \text{ or } B) = p(A) + p(B) - p(A \text{ and } B)$.

EXAMPLE

One marble is picked from the jar, and without replacing the first marble in the jar a second marble is picked from the jar. What is the probability that the marbles are not the same color?

This can happen two different ways: red followed by blue and blue followed by red. The probability of red followed by blue is $\left(\dfrac{10}{15}\right) \times \left(\dfrac{5}{14}\right) = \dfrac{5}{21}$ and the probability of blue followed by red is $\left(\dfrac{5}{15}\right) \times \left(\dfrac{10}{14}\right) = \dfrac{5}{21}$. So the probability that the marbles are different colors is $\left(\dfrac{5}{21}\right) + \left(\dfrac{5}{21}\right) = \dfrac{10}{21}$.

EXAMPLE

One marble is picked from the jar and without replacing the first marble in the jar a second marble is picked from the jar. What is the probability that both marbles are the same color?

You could answer this by finding the probability of red followed by red and then the probability of blue followed by blue and adding the two results. However, a much easier way is to notice that the negation of (both marbles are the same color) is when the two marbles are different colors. So the probability that the two marbles are the same color is $1 - \left(\dfrac{10}{21}\right) = \dfrac{11}{21}$.

EXAMPLE

One marble is picked from the jar, and without replacing the first marble in the jar a second marble is picked from the jar. What is the probability that the second marble is blue?

The second marble is blue can happen in two different ways: (1) if the first marble is red and the second marble is blue or (2) if the first marble is blue and the second marble is blue.

The probability of red followed by blue is $\left(\dfrac{2}{3}\right) \times \left(\dfrac{5}{14}\right) = \dfrac{5}{21}$ and the probability of blue followed by blue is $\left(\dfrac{1}{3}\right) \times \left(\dfrac{4}{14}\right) = \dfrac{2}{21}$. So the probability that the second marble is blue is $\left(\dfrac{5}{21}\right) + \left(\dfrac{2}{21}\right) = \dfrac{7}{21} = \dfrac{1}{3}$.

One marble is picked from the jar, and without replacing the first marble in the jar a second marble is picked from the jar. What is the probability that at least one blue marble is picked?

Method 1 (Using property 1). The only way no blue marbles are picked is when both marbles are red. So the probability that at least one blue is picked is

$$1 - p(\text{both are red}) = 1 - \left[\left(\frac{2}{3}\right) \times \left(\frac{9}{14}\right)\right] = 1 - \left(\frac{3}{7}\right) = \frac{4}{7}.$$

Method 2 (Using property 4). Find the probability that the first marble is blue; then find the probability that the second marble is blue. If you add these two numbers, you will count the outcome blue followed by blue twice, so the correct answer is

$$p(\text{first is blue}) + p(\text{second is blue}) - p(\text{both are blue}) = \left(\frac{1}{3}\right) + \left(\frac{1}{3}\right) - \left(\frac{1}{3}\right) \times \left(\frac{4}{14}\right) =$$

$$\left(\frac{2}{3}\right) - \left(\frac{2}{21}\right) = \frac{12}{21} = \frac{4}{7}.$$

More examples of probability can be found in Section II–4—Counting Problems.

I–8. POWERS, EXPONENTS, AND ROOTS

I–8.1

If b is any number and n is a positive integer, b^n means the product of n factors, each of which is equal to b. Thus,

$b^n = b \times b \times b \times \cdots \times b$ where there are n copies of b.

If $n = 1$, there is only one copy of b so $b^1 = b$. Here are some examples:

$$2^5 = 2 \times 2 \times 2 \times 2 \times 2 = 32, \ (-4)^3 = (-4) \times (-4) \times (-4) = -64, \ \frac{3^2}{4} = \frac{3 \times 3}{4} = \frac{9}{4},$$

$$1^n = 1 \text{ for any } n, \ 0^n = 0 \text{ for any } n.$$

b^n is read as "b raised to the nth power." b^2 is read "b squared." b^2 is always greater than 0 (positive) if b is not zero, since the product of two negative numbers is positive. b^3 is read "b cubed." b^3 can be negative or positive.

You should know the following squares and cubes:

$1^2 = 1$	$6^2 = 36$	$11^2 = 121$	$1^3 = 1$
$2^2 = 4$	$7^2 = 49$	$12^2 = 144$	$2^3 = 8$
$3^2 = 9$	$8^2 = 64$	$13^2 = 169$	$3^3 = 27$
$4^2 = 16$	$9^2 = 81$	$14^2 = 196$	$4^3 = 64$
$5^2 = 25$	$10^2 = 100$	$15^2 = 225$	$5^3 = 125$

If you raise a fraction, $\frac{p}{q}$, to a power, then $\left(\frac{p}{q}\right)^n = \frac{p^n}{q^n}$. For example, $\left(\frac{5}{4}\right)^3 = \frac{5^3}{4^3} = \frac{125}{64}$.

If the value of an investment triples each year, what percent of its value today will the investment be worth in 4 years?

The value increases by a factor of 3 each year. Since the time is 4 years, there will be four factors of 3. So the investment will be worth $3 \times 3 \times 3 \times 3 = 3^4$ as much as it is today. $3^4 = 81$, so the investment will be worth 8,100% of its value today in four years.

I-8.2

EXPONENTS

In the expression b^n, b is called the *base* and n is called the *exponent*. In the expression 2^5, 2 is the base and 5 is the exponent. The exponent tells how many factors there are.

> The three basic formulas for problems involving exponents are:
> (A) $b^n \times b^m = b^{n+m}$
> (B) $a^n \times b^n = (a \cdot b)^n$
> (C) If $a^x = a^y$, then $x = y$, provided a is not 1
>
>   (A) and (B) are called *laws of exponents.*

What is 6^3?

$$\text{Since } 6 = 3 \times 2, \ 6^3 = 3^3 \times 2^3 = 27 \times 8 = 216.$$
$$\text{or}$$
$$6^3 = 6 \times 6 \times 6 = 216.$$

Find the value of $2^3 \times 2^2$.

Using (A), $2^3 \times 2^2 = 2^{(2+3)} = 2^5$ which is 32. You can check this, since $2^3 = 8$ and $2^2 = 4$; $2^3 \times 2^2 = 8 \times 4 = 32$.

I-8.3

NEGATIVE EXPONENTS

$b^0 = 1$ *for any nonzero number b.* If we want (A) to hold, then $b^n \times b^0$ should be b^{n+0}, which is b^n. So b^0 must be 1. For example, $3^0 = 1$. (NOTE: 0^0 is not defined.)

Using the law of exponents once more, you can define b^{-n} where n is a positive number. If (A) holds, $b^{-n} \times b^n = b^{-n+n} = b^0 = 1$, so $b^{-n} = \dfrac{1}{b^n}$. *Multiplying by b^{-n} is the same as dividing by b^n.*

| | EXAMPLE | |

$$2^{-3} = \frac{1}{2^3} = \frac{1}{8}$$

| | EXAMPLE | |

$$\left(\frac{1}{2}\right)^{-1} = \frac{1}{\frac{1}{2}} = 2$$

| | EXAMPLE | |

Find the value of $\dfrac{6^4}{3^3}$.

$$\frac{6^4}{3^3} = \frac{(3 \cdot 2)^4}{3^3} = \frac{3^4 \cdot 2^4}{3^3} = 3^4 \times 2^4 \times 3^{-3} = 3^4 \times 3^{-3} \times 2^4 = 3^1 \times 2^4 = 48.$$

I-8.4

ROOTS

If you raise a number d to the nth power and the result is b, then d is called the nth root of b, which is usually written $\sqrt[n]{b} = d$. Since $2^5 = 32$, then $\sqrt[5]{32} = 2$. The second root is called the square root and is written $\sqrt{}$; the third root is called the cube root. If you read the columns of the table in Section I–8.1 from right to left, you have a table of square roots and cube roots. For example, $\sqrt{225} = 15$; $\sqrt{81} = 9$; $\sqrt[3]{64} = 4$.

There are two possibilities for the square root of a positive number; the positive one is called the square root. Thus, we say $\sqrt{9} = 3$ although $(-3) \times (-3) = 9$.

Since the square of any nonzero number is positive, *the square root of a negative number is not defined as a real number.* Thus $\sqrt{-2}$ is not a real number. There are cube roots of negative numbers. $\sqrt[3]{-8} = -2$, because $(-2) \times (-2) \times (-2) = -8$.

You can also write roots as exponents; for example,

$$\sqrt[n]{b} = b^{\frac{1}{n}} \text{ ; so } \sqrt{b} = b^{\frac{1}{2}} , \sqrt[3]{b} = b^{\frac{1}{3}}.$$

Since you can write roots as exponents, formula (B) under Section I–8.2 is especially useful.

$$a^{\frac{1}{n}} \times b^{\frac{1}{n}} = (a \times b)^{\frac{1}{n}} \text{ or } \sqrt[n]{a \times b} = \sqrt[n]{a} \times \sqrt[n]{b}$$

This is the basic formula for simplifying square roots, cube roots, and so on. On the test you must state your answer in a form that matches one of the choices given.

EXAMPLE

$\sqrt{54}$ = ?

Since 54 = 9 × 6, $\sqrt{54} = \sqrt{9 \times 6} = \sqrt{9} \times \sqrt{6}$. Since $\sqrt{9} = 3$, $\sqrt{54} = 3\sqrt{6}$.

You cannot simplify by adding square roots unless you are taking square roots of the same number. For example,

$$\sqrt{3} + 2\sqrt{3} - 4\sqrt{3} = -\sqrt{3}, \text{ but } \sqrt{3} + \sqrt{2} \text{ is not equal to } \sqrt{5}.$$

EXAMPLE

Simplify $6\sqrt{12} + 2\sqrt{75} - 3\sqrt{98}$.

Since 12 = 4 × 3, $\sqrt{12} = \sqrt{4 \times 3} = \sqrt{4} \times \sqrt{3} = 2\sqrt{3}$; 75 = 25 × 3,

so $\sqrt{75} = \sqrt{25} \times \sqrt{3} = 5\sqrt{3}$; and 98 = 49 × 2, so $\sqrt{98} = \sqrt{49} \times \sqrt{2} = 7\sqrt{2}$.

Therefore, $6\sqrt{12} + 2\sqrt{75} - 3\sqrt{98} = 6 \times 2\sqrt{3} + 2 \times 5\sqrt{3} - 3 \times 7\sqrt{2} =$

$12\sqrt{3} + 10\sqrt{3} - 21\sqrt{2} = 22\sqrt{3} - 21\sqrt{2}$.

EXAMPLE

Simplify $27^{\frac{1}{3}} \times 8^{\frac{1}{3}}$.

$27^{\frac{1}{3}} = \sqrt[3]{27} = 3$ and $8^{\frac{1}{3}} = 2$, so $27^{\frac{1}{3}} \times 8^{\frac{1}{3}} = 3 \times 2 = 6$.

Notice that 6 is $\sqrt[3]{216}$ and $27^{\frac{1}{3}} \times 8^{\frac{1}{3}} = (27 \times 8)^{\frac{1}{3}} = 216^{\frac{1}{3}}$.

II–1. ALGEBRAIC EXPRESSIONS

II–1.1

Often it is necessary to deal with quantities that have a numerical value that is unknown. For example, we may know that Tom's salary is twice as much as Joe's salary. If we let the value of Tom's salary be called T and the value of Joe's salary be J, then T and J are numbers that are unknown. However, we do know that the value of T must be twice the value of J, or $T = 2J$.

T and $2J$ are examples of algebraic expressions. An algebraic expression may involve letters in addition to numbers and symbols; however, *in an algebraic expression a letter always stands for a number*. Therefore, you can multiply, divide, add, subtract, and perform other mathematical operations on a letter. Thus, x^2 would mean x times x. Some examples of algebraic expressions are: $2x + y$, $y^3 + 9y$, $z^3 - 5ab$, $c + d + 4$, $5x + 2y(6x - 4y + z)$. When letters or numbers are written together without any sign or symbol between them, multiplication is assumed. Thus, $6xy$ means 6 times x times y. $6xy$ is called a term; terms are separated by + or – signs. The expression $5z + 2 + 4x^2$ has three terms, $5z$, 2, and $4x^2$. Terms are often called monomials (mono = one). If an expression has more than one term, it is called a *polynomial* (poly = many). The letters in an algebraic expression are called *variables* or *unknowns*. When a variable is multiplied by a number, the number is called the *coefficient* of the variable. So, in the expression $5x^2 + 2yz$, the coefficient of x^2 is 5, and the coefficient of yz is 2.

II–1.2

SIMPLIFYING ALGEBRAIC EXPRESSIONS

It will also save time when you are working problems if you can change a complicated expression into a simpler one.

Case I. Simplifying expressions that don't contain parentheses:

(STEP A) Perform any multiplications or divisions before performing additions or subtractions. Thus, the expression $6x + y \div x$ means add $6x$ to the quotient of y divided by x. Another way of writing the expression would be $6x + \dfrac{y}{x}$. This is not the same as $\dfrac{6x + y}{x}$.

(STEP B) The order in which you multiply numbers and letters in a term does not matter. So, $6xy$ is the same as $6yx$.

(STEP C) The order in which you add terms does not matter; for instance, $6x + 2y - x = 6x - x + 2y$.

(STEP D) If there are roots or powers in any terms, you may be able to simplify the term by using the laws of exponents. For example, $5xy \cdot 3x^2y = 15x^3y^2$.

(STEP E) Combine like terms. *Like terms* (or similar terms) are terms that have exactly the same letters raised to the same powers. So x, $-2x$, $\dfrac{1}{3}x$ are like terms. For example, $6x - 2x + x + y$ is equal to $5x + y$. In combining like terms, you simply add or subtract the coefficients of the like terms, and the result is the coefficient of that term in the

---

REMEMBER

Since there are only five choices of an answer given for the test questions, you must be able to recognize algebraic expressions that are equal.

simplified expression. In the example given, the coefficients of x were $+6$, -2, and $+1$; since $6 - 2 + 1 = 5$ the coefficient of x in the simplified expression is 5.

(STEP F) Algebraic expressions that involve divisions or factors can be simplified by using the techniques for handling fractions and the laws of exponents. Remember dividing by b^n is the same as multiplying by b^{-n}.

EXAMPLE

$3x^2 - 4\sqrt{x} + \sqrt{4x} + xy + 7x^2 = ?$

(STEP D) $\sqrt{4x} = \sqrt{4}\sqrt{x} = 2\sqrt{x}$.

(STEP E) $3x^2 + 7x^2 = 10x^2$, $-4\sqrt{x} + 2\sqrt{x} = -2\sqrt{x}$.

The original expression equals $3x^2 + 7x^2 - 4\sqrt{x} + 2\sqrt{x} + xy$. Therefore, the simplified expression is $10x^2 - 2\sqrt{x} + xy$.

EXAMPLE

Simplify $\dfrac{21x^4y^2}{3x^6y}$.

(STEP F) $\dfrac{21}{3}x^4y^2x^{-6}y^{-1}$.

(STEP B) $7x^4x^{-6}y^2y^{-1}$.

(STEP D) $7x^{-2}y$, so the simplified term is $\dfrac{7y}{x^2}$.

EXAMPLE

Write $\dfrac{2x}{y} - \dfrac{4}{x}$ as a single fraction.

(STEP F) A common denominator is xy so $\dfrac{2x}{y} = \dfrac{2x \cdot x}{y \cdot x} = \dfrac{2x^2}{xy}$, and $\dfrac{4}{x} = \dfrac{4y}{xy}$.

Therefore, $\dfrac{2x}{y} - \dfrac{4}{x} = \dfrac{2x^2}{xy} - \dfrac{4y}{xy} = \dfrac{2x^2 - 4y}{xy}$.

Case II. Simplifying expressions that have parentheses:

The first rule is to perform the operations inside parentheses first. So $(6x + y) \div x$ means divide the sum of $6x$ and y by x. Notice that $(6x + y) \div x$ is different from $6x + y \div x$.

The main rule for getting rid of parentheses is the distributive law, which is expressed as $a(b + c) = ab + ac$. In other words, if any monomial is followed by an expression contained in a parenthesis, then *each* term of the expression is multiplied by the monomial. Once we have gotten rid of the parentheses, we proceed as we did in Case I.

REMEMBER

If an expression has more than one set of parentheses, remove the *inner parentheses first* and then work *out* through the rest of the parentheses.

$2x(6x - 4y + 2) = (2x)(6x) + (2x)(-4y) + (2x)(2) = 12x^2 - 8xy + 4x.$

EXAMPLE

$2x - (x + 6(x - 3y) + 4y) = ?$

To remove the inner parentheses we multiply $6(x - 3y)$ getting $6x - 18y$. Now we have $2x - (x + 6x - 18y + 4y)$, which equals $2x - (7x - 14y)$. Distribute the minus sign (multiply by –1), getting $2x - 7x - (-14y) = -5x + 14y$. Sometimes brackets are used instead of parentheses.

EXAMPLE

Simplify $-3x\left[\dfrac{1}{2}\left(3x - 2y\right) - 2(x(3 + y) + 4y)\right]$

$= -3x\left[\dfrac{1}{2}\left(3x - 2y\right) - 2(3x + xy + 4y)\right]$

$= -3x\left[\dfrac{3}{2}x - y - 6x - 2xy - 8y\right]$

$= -3x\left[-\dfrac{9}{2}x - 2xy - 9y\right]$

$= \dfrac{27}{2}x^2 + 6x^2y + 27xy.$

II–1.3

ADDING AND SUBTRACTING ALGEBRAIC EXPRESSIONS

Since algebraic expressions are numbers, they can be added and subtracted.

EXAMPLE

$(3x + 4y - xy^2) + (3x + 2x(x - y)) = ?$

The expression

$= (3x + 4y - xy^2) + (3x + 2x^2 - 2xy)$, removing the inner parentheses;

$= 6x + 4y + 2x^2 - xy^2 - 2xy$, combining like terms.

EXAMPLE

$(2a + 3a^2 - 4) - 2(4a^2 - 2(a + 4)) = ?$

It equals $(2a + 3a^2 - 4) - 2(4a^2 - 2a - 8)$, removing inner parentheses;

$= 2a + 3a^2 - 4 - 8a^2 + 4a + 16$, removing outer parentheses;

$= -5a^2 + 6a + 12$, combining like terms.

II–1.4

MULTIPLYING ALGEBRAIC EXPRESSIONS

When you multiply two expressions, you multiply *each term of the first by each term of the second.*

EXAMPLE

$(b - 4)(b + a) = b(b + a) - 4(b + a) = ?$

$= b^2 + ab - 4b - 4a.$

EXAMPLE

$(2h - 4)(h + 2h^2 + h^3) = ?$

$= 2h(h + 2h^2 + h^3) - 4(h + 2h^2 + h^3)$

$= 2h^2 + 4h^3 + 2h^4 - 4h - 8h^2 - 4h^3$

$= -4h - 6h^2 + 2h^4$, which is the product.

If you need to multiply more than two expressions, multiply the first two expressions, then multiply the result by the third expression, and so on until you have used each factor. Since algebraic expressions can be multiplied, they can be squared, cubed, or raised to other powers.

EXAMPLE

$(x - 2y)^3 = (x - 2y)(x - 2y)(x - 2y).$

Since $(x - 2y)(x - 2y)$

$= x^2 - 2yx - 2yx + 4y^2$

$= x^2 - 4xy + 4y^2,$

$(x - 2y)^3 = (x^2 - 4xy + 4y^2)(x - 2y)$

$= x(x^2 - 4xy + 4y^2) - 2y(x^2 - 4xy + 4y^2)$

$= x^3 - 4x^2y + 4xy^2 - 2x^2y + 8xy^2 - 8y^3$

$= x^3 - 6x^2y + 12xy^2 - 8y^3.$

The order in which you multiply algebraic expressions does not matter. Thus, $(2a + b)(x^2 + 2x) = (x^2 + 2x)(2a + b)$.

EXAMPLE

If a and b are two-digit numbers, and the last digit of a is 7 and the last digit of b is 8, what is the last digit of a times b?

The key to problems such as this is to think of a number in terms of its digits. So a must be written as $x7$, where x is a digit. This means $a = 10x + 7$. In the same way $b = 10y + 8$ for some digit y. So a times b is $(10x + 7)(10y + 8)$, which is $100xy + 80x + 70y + 56$. The digits x and y all are multiplied by 10 or 100 so they will not affect the units place. The only term that will affect the units place is 56. So the units digit or last digit of a times b is 6. This pattern works all the time and can be expressed by the following rule: the last digit of the product of two numbers is the last digit of the product of the last digits of the two numbers. For example, the last digit of 136 times 157 is 2 because the last digit of 6 times 7 is 2.

II–1.5

FACTORING ALGEBRAIC EXPRESSIONS

If an algebraic expression is the product of other algebraic expressions, then the expressions are called factors of the original expression. For instance, we claim that $(2h - 4)$ and $(h + 2h^2 + h^3)$ are factors of $-4h - 6h^2 + 2h^4$. We can always check to see if we have the correct factors by multiplying; so by the second Example in Section II–1.4 we see that our claim is correct. We need to be able to factor algebraic expressions in order to solve quadratic equations. It also can be helpful in dividing algebraic expressions.

First remove any monomial factor that appears in every term of the expression.

Some examples:

$3x + 3y = 3(x + y)$: 3 is a monomial factor.

$15a^2b + 10ab = 5ab(3a + 2)$: $5ab$ is a monomial factor.

$\frac{1}{2}hy - 3h^3 + 4hy = h\left(\frac{1}{2}y - 3h^2 + 4y\right), = h\left(\frac{9}{2}y - 3h^2\right)$: h is a monomial factor.

You may also need to factor expressions that contain squares or higher powers into factors that only contain linear terms. (Linear terms are terms in which variables are raised only to the first power.) The first rule to remember is that since $(a + b)(a - b) = a^2 + ba - ba - b^2 = a^2 - b^2$, the difference of two squares can always be factored.

REMEMBER

$a^2 - b^2 =$

$(a + b)(a - b)$

EXAMPLE

Factor $(9m^2 - 16)$.

$9m^2 = (3m)^2$ and $16 = 4^2$, so the factors are $(3m - 4)(3m + 4)$.

Since $(3m - 4)(3m + 4) = 9m^2 - 16$, these factors are correct.

Factor $x^4y^4 - 4x^2$.

$x^4y^4 = (x^2y^2)^2$ and $4x^2 = (2x)^2$, so the factors are $x^2y^2 + 2x$ and $x^2y^2 - 2x$.

You also may need to factor expressions that contain squared terms and linear terms, such as $x^2 + 4x + 3$. The factors will be of the form $(x + a)$ and $(x + b)$. Since $(x + a)(x + b) = x^2 + (a + b)x + ab$, you must look for a pair of numbers a and b such that $a \cdot b$ is the numerical term in the expression and $a + b$ is the coefficient of the linear term (the term with exponent 1).

Factor $x^2 + 4x + 3$.

You want numbers whose product is 3 and whose sum is 4. Look at the possible factors of 3 and check whether they add up to 4. Since $3 = 3 \times 1$ and $3 + 1$ is 4, the factors are $(x + 3)$ and $(x + 1)$. Remember to check by multiplying.

Factor $y^2 + y - 6$.

Since $- 6$ is negative, the two numbers a and b must be of opposite sign. Possible pairs of factors for $- 6$ are $- 6$ and $+1$, 6 and $- 1$, 3 and $- 2$, and $- 3$ and 2. Since $- 2 + 3 = 1$, the factors are $(y + 3)$ and $(y - 2)$. So $(y + 3)(y - 2) = y^2 + y - 6$.

Factor $a^3 + 4a^2 + 4a$.

Factor out a, so $a^3 + 4a^2 + 4a = a(a^2 + 4a + 4)$. Consider $a^2 + 4a + 4$; since $2 + 2 = 4$ and $2 \times 2 = 4$, the factors are $(a + 2)$ and $(a + 2)$. Therefore, $a^3 + 4a^2 + 4a = a(a + 2)^2$.

If the term with the highest exponent has a coefficient unequal to 1, divide the entire expression by that coefficient. For example, to factor $3a^3 + 12a^2 + 12a$, factor out a 3 from each term, and the result is $a^3 + 4a^2 + 4a$, which is $a(a + 2)^2$. Thus, $3a^3 + 12a^2 + 12a = 3a(a + 2)^2$.

There are some expressions that cannot be factored, for example, $x^2 + 4x + 6$. In general, if you can't factor something by using the methods given above, don't waste a lot of time on the question. Sometimes you may be able to check the answers given to find out what the correct factors are.

II-1.6

DIVISION OF ALGEBRAIC EXPRESSIONS

The main things to remember in division are:

1. When you divide a sum, you can get the same result by dividing each term and adding

quotients. For example, $\dfrac{9x + 4xy + y^2}{x} = \dfrac{9x}{x} + \dfrac{4xy}{x} + \dfrac{y^2}{x} = 9 + 4y + \dfrac{y^2}{x}$.

2. You can cancel common factors, so the results on factoring will be helpful. For example,

$\dfrac{x^2 - 2x}{x - 2} = \dfrac{x(x-2)}{x-2} = x.$

EXAMPLE

$\dfrac{2x + 2y + x^2 - y^2}{x + y} = ?$

$$\dfrac{2x + 2y + x^2 - y^2}{x + y} = \dfrac{2x + 2y}{x + y} + \dfrac{x^2 - y^2}{x + y}$$

$$= \dfrac{2(x + y)}{x + y} + \dfrac{(x - y)(x + y)}{x + y}$$

$$= 2 + x - y$$

You can also divide one algebraic expression by another using long division.

EXAMPLE

$(15x^2 + 2x - 4) \div (3x - 1) = ?$

$$
\begin{array}{r}
5x + 2 \\
3x - 1\overline{)15x^2 + 2x - 4} \\
\underline{15x^2 - 5x} \\
7x - 4 \\
\underline{6x - 2} \\
x - 2
\end{array}
$$

So, the answer is $5x + 2$ with a remainder of $x - 2$. You can check by multiplying,

$$(5x + 2)(3x - 1) = 15x^2 + 6x - 5x - 2$$
$$= 15x^2 + x - 2;$$

now add the remainder $x - 2$ and the result is $15x^2 + x - 2 + x - 2 = 15x^2 + 2x - 4$.

Division problems where you need to use properties of 1 and 2 are more likely than problems involving long division.

II-2. EQUATIONS

II-2.1

An *equation* is a statement that says two algebraic expressions are equal. $x + 2 = 3$, $4 + 2 = 6$, $3x^2 + 2x - 6 = 0$, $x^2 + y^2 = z^2$, $\frac{y}{x} = 2 + z$, and $A = LW$ are all examples of equations. We will refer to the algebraic expressions on each side of the equals sign as the left side and the right side of the equation. Thus, in the equation $2x + 4 = 6y + x$, $2x + 4$ is the left side and $6y + x$ is the right side.

II-2.2

If we assign specific numbers to each variable or unknown in an algebraic expression, then the algebraic expression will be equal to a number. This is called *evaluating* the expression. For example, if you evaluate $2x + 4y^2 + 3$ for $x = -1$ and $y = 2$, the expression is equal to $2(-1) + 4 \cdot 2^2 + 3 = -2 + 4 \cdot 4 + 3 = 17$.

EVALUATING ALGEBRAIC EXPRESSIONS

If we evaluate each side of an equation and the number obtained is the same for each side of the equation, then the specific values assigned to the unknowns are called a *solution of the equation*. Another way of saying this is that the choices for the unknowns satisfy the equation.

EXAMPLE

Consider the equation $2x + 3 = 9$.

If $x = 3$, then the left side of the equation becomes $2 \cdot 3 + 3 = 6 + 3 = 9$, so both sides equal 9, and $x = 3$ is a solution of $2x + 3 = 9$. If $x = 4$, then the left side is $2 \cdot 4 + 3 = 11$. Since 11 is not equal to 9, $x = 4$ is not a solution of $2x + 3 = 9$.

EXAMPLE

Consider the equation $x^2 + y^2 = 5x$.

If $x = 1$ and $y = 2$, then the left side is $1^2 + 2^2$ which equals $1 + 4 = 5$. The right side is $5 \cdot 1 = 5$; since both sides are equal to 5, $x = 1$ and $y = 2$ is a solution.

If $x = 5$ and $y = 0$, then the left side is $5^2 + 0^2 = 25$ and the right side is $5 \cdot 5 = 25$, so $x = 5$ and $y = 0$ is also a solution.

If $x = 1$ and $y = 1$, then the left side is $1^2 + 1^2 = 2$ and the right side is $5 \cdot 1 = 5$. Therefore, since $2 \neq 5$, $x = 1$ and $y = 1$ is not a solution.

There are some equations that *do not have any solutions that are real numbers*. Since the square of any real number is positive or zero, the equation $x^2 = -4$ does not have any solutions that are real numbers.

EQUIVALENCE

One equation is *equivalent* to another equation, if they have exactly the same solutions. The basic idea in solving equations is to transform a given equation into an equivalent equation whose solutions are obvious.

> The two main rules for solving equations are:
>
> (STEP A) If you add or subtract the same algebraic expression to or from each side of an equation, the resulting equation is equivalent to the original equation.
>
> (STEP B) If you multiply or divide both sides of an equation by the same nonzero algebraic expression, the resulting equation is equivalent to the original equation.

The most common type of equation is the linear equation with only one unknown. $6z = 4z - 3$, $3 + a = 2a - 4$, $3b + 2b = b - 4b$, are all examples of linear equations with only one unknown.

Using (A) and (B), you can solve a linear equation in one unknown in the following way:

1. Group all the terms that involve the unknown on one side of the equation and all the terms that are purely numerical on the other side of the equation. This is called *isolating the unknown.*
2. Combine the terms on each side.
3. Divide each side by the coefficient of the unknown.

EXAMPLE

Solve $6x + 2 = 3$ for x.

1. Using (A) above, subtract 2 from each side of the equation. Then $6x + 2 - 2 = 3 - 2$ or $6x = 3 - 2$.

2. $6x = 1$.

3. Divide each side by 6. Therefore, $x = \frac{1}{6}$.

You should always check your answer in the original equation.

CHECK: Since $6\left(\frac{1}{6}\right) + 2 = 1 + 2 = 3$, $x = \frac{1}{6}$ is the solution.

REMEMBER

If you square each side of an equation, you may get false solutions.

EXAMPLE

Solve $3x + 15 = 3 - 4x$ for x.

1. Add $4x$ to each side and subtract 15 from each side;

   $3x + 15 - 15 + 4x = 3 - 15 - 4x + 4x$.

2. $7x = -12$.

3. Divide each side by 7, so $x = \dfrac{-12}{7}$ is the solution.

CHECK: $3\left(\dfrac{-12}{7}\right) + 15 = \dfrac{-36}{7} + 15 = \dfrac{69}{7}$ and $3 - 4\left(\dfrac{-12}{7}\right) = 3 + \dfrac{48}{7} = \dfrac{69}{7}$.

If you do the same thing to each side of an equation, the result is still an equation but it may not be equivalent to the original equation. Be especially careful if you square each side of an equation. For example, $x = -4$ is an equation; square both sides and you get $x^2 = 16$, which has both $x = 4$ and $x = -4$ as solutions.

If the equation you want to solve involves square roots, get rid of the square roots by squaring each side of the equation. Remember to check your answer since squaring each side does not always give an equivalent equation.

> **TIP**
>
> **Always check your answer in the original equation.**

EXAMPLE

Solve $\sqrt{4x + 3} = 5$.

Square both sides: $\left(\sqrt{4x + 3}\right)^2 = 4x + 3$ and $5^2 = 25$, so the new equation is $4x + 3 = 25$. Subtract 3 from each side to get $4x = 22$ and now divide each side by 4. The solution is $x = \dfrac{22}{4} = 5.5$. Since $4(5.5) + 3 = 25$ and $\sqrt{25} = 5$, $x = 5.5$ is a solution to the equation $\sqrt{4x + 3} = 5$.

If an equation involves fractions, multiply through by a common denominator and then solve. Check your answer to make sure you did not multiply or divide by zero.

EXAMPLE

Solve $\dfrac{3}{a} = 9$ for a.

Multiply each side by a: the result is $3 = 9a$. Divide each side by 9, and you obtain $\dfrac{3}{9} = a$ or $a = \dfrac{1}{3}$. Since $\dfrac{3}{\frac{1}{3}} = 3 \cdot 3 = 9$, $a = \dfrac{1}{3}$ is a solution.

II-2.4

SOLVING TWO EQUATIONS IN TWO UNKNOWNS

You may be asked to solve two equations in two unknowns. Use one equation to solve for one unknown in terms of the other; now change the second equation into an equation in only one unknown, which can be solved by the methods of the preceding section.

EXAMPLE

Solve for x and y: $\begin{cases} \dfrac{x}{y} = 3 \\ 2x + 4y = 20. \end{cases}$

The first equation gives $x = 3y$. Using $x = 3y$, the second equation is $2(3y) + 4y = 6y + 4y$ or $10y = 20$, so $y = \dfrac{20}{10} = 2$. Since $x = 3y$, $x = 6$.

CHECK: $\dfrac{6}{2} = 3$, and $2 \cdot 6 + 4 \cdot 2 = 20$, so $x = 6$ and $y = 2$ is a solution.

EXAMPLE

If $2x + y = 5$ and $x + y = 4$, find x and y.

Since $x + y = 4$, $y = 4 - x$, so $2x + y = 2x + 4 - x = x + 4 = 5$ and $x = 1$. If $x = 1$, then $y = 4 - 1 = 3$. So, $x = 1$ and $y = 3$ is the solution.

CHECK: $2 \cdot 1 + 3 = 5$ and $1 + 3 = 4$.

The equations directly above are an example of a system of 2 linear equations in 2 unknowns. The method of solving 2 equations that we used in these examples is called *substitution*. You can use substitution to solve any linear system in 2 unknowns.

Sometimes we can solve two equations by adding them or by subtracting one from the other. If we subtract $x + y = 4$ from $2x + y = 5$ in the second Example, we have $x = 1$. This method is called the *addition* method. However, the substitution method will work in cases when the addition method does not work.

II-2.5

SOLVING QUADRATIC EQUATIONS

If the terms of an equation contain squares of the unknown as well as linear terms, the equation is called *quadratic*. Some examples of quadratic equations are $x^2 + 4x = 3$, $2z^2 - 1 = 3z^2 - 2z$, and $a + 6 = a^2 + 6$.

To solve a quadratic equation:

(STEP A) Group all the terms on one side of the equation so that the other side is *zero*.

(STEP B) Combine the terms on the nonzero side.

(STEP C) Factor the expression into linear expressions.

(STEP D) Set the linear factors equal to zero and solve.

The method depends on the fact that if a product of expressions is zero then at least one of the expressions must be zero.

EXAMPLE

Solve $x^2 + 4x = -3$.

(STEP A) $x^2 + 4x + 3 = 0$

(STEP C) $x^2 + 4x + 3 = (x + 3)(x + 1) = 0$

(STEP D) So $x + 3 = 0$ or $x + 1 = 0$. Therefore, the solutions are $x = -3$ and $x = -1$.

CHECK: $(-3)^2 + 4(-3) = 9 - 12 = -3$

$(-1)^2 + 4(-1) = 1 - 4 = -3$, so $x = -3$ and $x = -1$ are solutions.

A quadratic equation will usually have 2 different solutions, but it is possible for a quadratic to have only one solution or even no real solution.

EXAMPLE

If $2z^2 - 1 = 3z^2 - 2z$, what is z?

(STEP A) $0 = 3z^2 - 2z^2 - 2z + 1$

(STEP B) $z^2 - 2z + 1 = 0$

(STEP C) $z^2 - 2z + 1 = (z - 1)^2 = 0$

(STEP D) $z - 1 = 0$ or $z = 1$

CHECK: $2 \cdot 1^2 - 1 = 2 - 1 = 1$ and $3 \cdot 1^2 - 2 \cdot 1 = 3 - 2 = 1$, so $z = 1$ is a solution.

Equations that may not look like quadratics may be changed into quadratics.

EXAMPLE

Find a if $a - 3 = \dfrac{10}{a}$.

Multiply each side of the equation by a to obtain $a^2 - 3a = 10$, which is quadratic.

(STEP A) $a^2 - 3a - 10 = 0$

(STEP C) $a^2 - 3a - 10 = (a - 5)(a + 2)$

(STEP D) So $a - 5 = 0$ or $a + 2 = 0$

Therefore, $a = 5$ and $a = -2$ are the solutions.

CHECK: $5 - 3 = 2 = \dfrac{10}{5}$ so $a = 5$ is a solution. $-2 - 3 = -5 = \dfrac{10}{-2}$ so $a = -2$ is a solution.

You can also solve quadratic equations by using the *quadratic formula*. The quadratic formula states that the solutions of the quadratic equation

$$ax^2 + bx + c = 0 \text{ are } x = \frac{1}{2a}\left[-b + \sqrt{b^2 - 4ac}\right] \text{ and } x = \frac{1}{2a}\left[-b - \sqrt{b^2 - 4ac}\right]$$

This is usually written $x = \frac{1}{2a}\left[-b \pm \sqrt{b^2 - 4ac}\right]$

Use of the quadratic formula would replace some steps.

EXAMPLE

Find x if $x^2 + 5x = 12 - x^2$.

(STEP A) $x^2 + 5x + x^2 - 12 = 0$

(STEP B) $2x^2 + 5x - 12 = 0$

So $a = 2$, $b = 5$, and $c = -12$. Therefore, using the quadratic formula, the

solutions are $\frac{1}{4}\left[-5 \pm \sqrt{25 - 4 \cdot 2 \cdot (-12)}\right] = \frac{1}{4}\left[-5 \pm \sqrt{25 + 96}\right] = \frac{1}{4}\left[-5 \pm \sqrt{121}\right]$.

So, we have $x = \frac{1}{4}[-5 \pm 11]$. The solutions are $x = \frac{3}{2}$ and $x = -4$.

CHECK:

$$\left(\frac{3}{2}\right)^2 + 5 \cdot \frac{3}{2} = \frac{9}{4} + \frac{15}{2} = \frac{39}{4} = 12 - \left(\frac{3}{2}\right)^2 \quad (-4)^2 + 5(-4) = 16 - 20 = -4 = 12 - 16 = 12 - (-4)^2$$

NOTE: If $b^2 - 4ac$ is negative, then the quadratic equation $ax^2 + bx + c = 0$ has no real solutions because negative numbers do not have real square roots.

The quadratic formula will always give you the solutions to a quadratic equation. If you can factor the equation, factoring will usually give you the solution in less time.

II-3. WORD PROBLEMS

II–3.1

The general method for solving word problems is to translate them into algebraic problems. The quantities you are seeking are the unknowns, which are usually represented by letters. The information you are given in the problem is then turned into equations. Words such as "is," "was," "are," and "were" mean equals, and words like "of" and "as much as" mean multiplication.

TIP

Remember, you want to answer as many questions as you can in the time given. So factor if you can. If you don't see the factor immediately, then use the formula.

A coat was sold for $75. The coat was sold for 150% of the cost of the coat. How much did the coat cost?

You want to find the cost of the coat. Let $C be the cost of the coat. You know that the coat was sold for $75 and that $75 was 150% of the cost. So $75 = 150% of $C or $75 = 1.5C$.

Solving for C you get $C = \dfrac{75}{1.5} = 50$, so the coat cost $50.

CHECK: $(1.5)\$50 = \$75$.

Tom's salary is 125% of Joe's salary; Mary's salary is 80% of Joe's salary. The total of all three salaries is $61,000. What is Mary's salary?

Let M = Mary's salary, J = Joe's salary, and T = Tom's salary. The first sentence says $T = 125\%$ of J or $T = \dfrac{5}{4}J$, and $M = 80\%$ of J or $M = \dfrac{4}{5}J$. The second sentence says that $T + M + J = \$61,000$.

Using the information from the first sentence, $T + M + J = \dfrac{5}{4}J + \dfrac{4}{5}J + J =$

$\dfrac{25}{20}J + \dfrac{16}{20}J + J = \dfrac{61}{20}J$. So, $\dfrac{61}{20}J = 61,000$; solving for J you have

$J = \dfrac{20}{61} \times 61,000 = 20,000$.

Therefore, $T = \dfrac{5}{4} \times \$20,000 = \$25,000$ and $M = \dfrac{4}{5} \times \$20,000 = \$16,000$.

CHECK: $\$25,000 + \$16,000 + \$20,000 = \$61,000$. So Mary's salary is $16,000.

Steve weighs 25 pounds more than Jim. The combined weight of Jim and Steve is 325 pounds. How much does Jim weigh?

Let S = Steve's weight in pounds and J = Jim's weight in pounds. The first sentence says $S = J + 25$, and the second sentence becomes $S + J = 325$. Since $S = J + 25$, $S + J = 325$ becomes $(J + 25) + J = 2J + 25 = 325$. So $2J = 300$ and $J = 150$. Therefore, Jim weighs 150 pounds.

CHECK: If Jim weighs 150 pounds, then Steve weighs 175 pounds and $150 + 175 = 325$.

A carpenter is designing a closet. The floor will be in the shape of a rectangle whose length is 2 feet more than its width. How long should the closet be if the carpenter wants the area of the floor to be 15 square feet?

The area of a rectangle is length times width, usually written $A = LW$, where A is the area, L is the length, and W is the width. We know $A = 15$ and $L = 2 + W$. Therefore, $LW = (2 + W)W = W^2 + 2W$; this must equal 15. So we need to solve $W^2 + 2W = 15$ or $W^2 + 2W - 15 = 0$. Since $W^2 + 2W - 15$ factors into $(W + 5)(W - 3)$, the only possible solutions are $W = -5$ and $W = 3$. Since W represents a width, -5 cannot be the answer; therefore the width is 3 feet. The length is the width plus two feet, so the length is 5 feet. Since $5 \times 3 = 15$, the answer checks.

II–3.2

DISTANCE PROBLEMS

A common type of word problem is a distance or velocity problem. The basic formula is:

$$\text{DISTANCE TRAVELED} = \text{SPEED} \times \text{TIME}$$

The formula is abbreviated $d = st$. Velocity or rate are other names for speed.

A train travels at an average speed of 50 miles per hour for $2\frac{1}{2}$ hours and then travels at a speed of 70 miles per hour for $1\frac{1}{2}$ hours. How far did the train travel in the entire 4 hours?

The train traveled for $2\frac{1}{2}$ hours at an average speed of 50 miles per hour, so it traveled $50 \times \frac{5}{2} = 125$ miles in the first $2\frac{1}{2}$ hours. Traveling at a speed of 70 miles per hour for $1\frac{1}{2}$ hours, the distance traveled will be equal to $s \times t$ where $s = 70$ m.p.h. and $t = 1\frac{1}{2}$, so the distance is $70 \times \frac{3}{2} = 105$ miles. Therefore, the total distance traveled is $125 + 105 = 230$ miles.

> ### EXAMPLE
>
> The distance from Cleveland to Buffalo is 200 miles. A train takes $3\frac{1}{2}$ hours to go from Buffalo to Cleveland and $4\frac{1}{2}$ hours to go back from Cleveland to Buffalo. What was the average speed of the train for the round trip from Buffalo to Cleveland and back?
>
> The train took $3\frac{1}{2} + 4\frac{1}{2} = 8$ hours for the trip. The distance of a round trip is $2(200) = 400$ miles. Since $d = st$ then 400 miles $= s \times 8$ hours. Solve for s and you have $s = \dfrac{400 \text{ miles}}{8 \text{ hours}} = 50$ miles per hour. Therefore, the average speed is 50 miles per.hour.

The speed in the formula is the average speed. If you know that there are different speeds for different lengths of time, then you must use the formula more than once, as we did in the Example on page 276.

II-3.3

WORK PROBLEMS

In this type of problem you can always assume all workers in the same category work at the same rate. The main idea is: If it takes k workers 1 hour to do a job, then *each worker does $\frac{1}{k}$ of the job in an hour* or works at the rate of $\frac{1}{k}$ of the job per hour. If it takes m workers h hours to finish a job, then each worker does $\frac{1}{m}$ of the job in h hours or does $\frac{1}{h}$ of $\frac{1}{m}$ in an hour. Therefore, each worker *works at the rate of $\frac{1}{mh}$ of the job per hour.*

> ### EXAMPLE
>
> If 5 workers take an hour to dig a ditch, how long should it take 12 workers to dig a ditch of the same type?
>
> Since 5 workers took an hour, each worker does $\frac{1}{5}$ of the job in an hour. So 12 workers will work at the rate of $\frac{12}{5}$ of the job per hour. Thus if T is the time it takes for 12 workers to do the job, $\frac{12}{5} \times T = 1$ job and $T = \frac{5}{12} \times 1$, so $T = \frac{5}{12}$ hours or 25 minutes.

Worker A takes 8 hours to do a job. Worker B takes 10 hours to do the same job. How long should it take worker A and worker B working together, but independently, to do the same job?

Worker A works at a rate of $\frac{1}{8}$ of the job per hour, since he takes 8 hours to finish the job. Worker B finished the job in 10 hours, so he works at a rate of $\frac{1}{10}$ of the job per hour. Therefore, if they work together they should complete $\frac{1}{8} + \frac{1}{10} = \frac{18}{80} = \frac{9}{40}$, so they work at a rate of $\frac{9}{40}$ of the job per hour together. So if T is the time it takes them to finish the job, $\frac{9}{40}$ of the job per hour $\times$ T hours must equal 1 job. Therefore, $\frac{9}{40} \times T = 1$ and $T = \frac{40}{9} = 4\frac{4}{9}$ hours.

There are two taps, tap 1 and tap 2, in a keg. If both taps are opened, the keg is drained in 20 minutes. If tap 1 is closed and tap 2 is open, the keg will be drained in 30 minutes. If tap 2 is closed and tap 1 is open, how long will it take to drain the keg?

Tap 1 and tap 2 together take 20 minutes to drain the keg, so together they drain the keg at a rate of $\frac{1}{20}$ of the keg per minute. Tap 2 takes 30 minutes to drain the keg by itself, so it drains the keg at the rate of $\frac{1}{30}$ of the keg per minute. Let r be the rate at which tap 1 will drain the keg by itself. Then $\left(r + \frac{1}{30}\right)$ of the keg per minute is the rate at which both taps together will drain the keg, so $r + \frac{1}{30} = \frac{1}{20}$. Therefore, $r = \frac{1}{20} - \frac{1}{30} = \frac{1}{60}$, and tap 1 drains the keg at the rate of $\frac{1}{60}$ of the keg per minute, so it will take 60 minutes or 1 hour for tap 1 to drain the keg if tap 2 is closed.

II–4. COUNTING PROBLEMS

II–4.1

An example of one type of counting problem is: Fifty students signed up for both English and Math. Ninety students signed up for either English or Math. If 25 students are taking English but not taking Math, how many students are taking Math but not taking English?

In these problems, "either . . . or . . ." means you can take both, so the people taking both are counted among the people taking either Math or English.

You must avoid counting the same people twice in these problems. The formula is:

the number taking English or Math =
the number taking English + the number taking Math – the number taking both.

You have to subtract the number taking both subjects since they are counted once with those taking English and counted again with those taking Math.

A person taking English is either taking Math or not taking Math, so there are 50 + 25 = 75 people taking English, 50 taking English and Math, and 25 taking English but not taking Math. Since 75 are taking English, 90 = 75 + number taking Math – 50; so there are 90 – 25 = 65 people taking Math. 50 of the people taking Math are taking English so 65 – 50 or 15 are taking Math but not English.

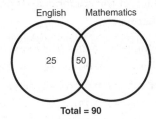

Total = 90

The figure shows what is given. Since 90 students signed up for English or Mathematics, 15 must be taking Mathematics but not English.

EXAMPLE

In a survey, 60% of those surveyed owned a car and 80% of those surveyed owned a TV. If 55% owned both a car and a TV, what percent of those surveyed owned a car or a TV or both?

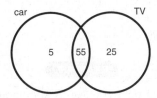

The basic formula is:

   people who own a car or a TV = people who own a car + people who own a TV – people who own both a car and a TV.

So the people who own a car or a TV = 60% + 80% – 55% = 85%. Therefore, 85% of the people surveyed own either a car or a TV.

If we just add 60% and 80% the result is 140% which is impossible. This is because the 55% who own both are counted twice.

This example could also be solved using probability. Let TV represent the outcome that the person surveyed owned a TV, so the probability that TV occurs is 80% = .8 or p(TV) = .8. In the same way let C stand for the outcome that the person surveyed owned a car, so p(C) = .6. You are told that p(C and TV) = .55.

The question asks you to find the probability that at least one of C and TV occurs. So p(C or TV) = p(C) + p(TV) – p(C and TV) = .6 + .8 – .55 = .85. Therefore, 85 percent of the people surveyed owned a car or a TV or both, and the probability that a person surveyed owned a car or a TV or both is 85 percent.

This type of problem can involve three or more groups. The basic principle remains to avoid counting the same person more than once.

EXAMPLE

Seventy students are enrolled in Math, English, or German. Forty students are in Math, 35 are in English, and 30 are in German. Fifteen students are enrolled in all three of the courses. How many of the students are enrolled in exactly two of the courses: Math, English, and German?

If we add 40, 35, and 30, the people enrolled in exactly two of the courses will be counted twice and the people in all three courses will be counted three times. So if we let N stand for the number enrolled in exactly two courses, then we have the equation $70 = 40 + 35 + 30 - N - 2(15) = 75 - N$. Therefore, N is $75 - 70 = 5$. So there are 5 students enrolled in exactly two of the three courses.

II–4.2

If an event can happen in m different ways, and each of the m ways is followed by a second event that can occur in k different ways, then the first event can be followed by the second event in $m \cdot k$ different ways. This is called *the fundamental principle of counting*.

EXAMPLE

If there are 3 different roads from Syracuse to Binghamton and 4 different roads from Binghamton to Scranton, how many different routes are there from Syracuse to Scranton that go through Binghamton?

There are 3 different ways to go from Syracuse to Binghamton. Once you are in Binghamton, there are 4 different ways to get to Scranton. So using the fundamental principle of counting, there are $3 \times 4 = 12$ different ways to get from Syracuse to Scranton going through Binghamton.

EXAMPLE

A club has 20 members. They are electing a president and a vice-president. How many different outcomes of the election are possible? (Assume the president and vice-president must be different members of the club.)

There are 20 members, so there are 20 choices for president. Once a president is chosen, there are 19 members left who can be vice-president. So, there are $20 \cdot 19 = 380$ different possible outcomes of the election.

The number of different ways that you can choose 2 people from the group of 20 *where the order matters* is called the number of *permutations* of 20 objects taken 2 at a time. The number of permutations of 20 objects taken 2 at a time is denoted by $P(20, 2)$. So this example can be answered by calculating $P(20, 2) = 20 \times 19 = 380$. You can see that the order matters by looking at a typical outcome and deciding if changing the order that you pick the people makes the outcome different. For example, the outcome Mary is president and Tom is vice-president is different from the outcome Tom is president and Mary is vice-president even though both outcomes involve the same two people being chosen.

In general, $P(n, k) = (n)(n-1)(n-2)\dots(n-k+1)$ is the number of permutations of n objects taken k at a time. For example, $P(10, 4) = 10 \times 9 \times 8 \times 7 = 5{,}040$.

EXAMPLE

How many ways can you arrange an English book, a math book, a history book, and a biology book on a shelf?

There are 4 choices for the first book, 3 choices for the next book, 2 choices for the third book, and only 1 choice for the fourth (or last) book. So there are $4 \times 3 \times 2 \times 1 = 24$ different ways to shelve the books. $4 \times 3 \times 2 \times 1$ is called *4 factorial* and is denoted 4!

Since math followed by biology is not the same as biology followed by math, this example asks you to find $P(4, 4) = 4 \times 3 \times 2 \times 1$.

EXAMPLE

There are 2 box seat tickets and 3 general admission tickets to a concert for 5 friends, Amy, Bob, Cary, Doug, and Ed. If they give the tickets out randomly, what is the probability that Amy and Cary will get the box seat tickets?

There are 5! ways to give out the tickets. There are $2 \times 1 \times 3!$ ways to give out the tickets where Amy and Cary get the box seats. (Think of the first two tickets as the box seat tickets.) Then the probability of Amy and Cary getting the tickets is $(2 \times 1 \times 3 \times 2 \times 1)/(5 \times 4 \times 3 \times 2 \times 1) = 1/10$.

Sometimes the order does not matter when you are choosing k objects from a group of n objects. Consider the following example and contrast it with the last Example on page 280.

EXAMPLE

A club has 20 members, and they are choosing 2 members to attend a conference. How many different ways can they choose the 2 members?

The order does not matter since choosing Mary and then Tom gives the same outcome as choosing Tom and then Mary. In both cases, Mary and Tom will attend the conference. Since there are 20×19 ways to choose 2 people if the order mattered and the same 2 people can be chosen in 2×1 different ways, the number of different 2 person groups is $(20 \times 19)/(2 \times 1) = 190$.

The number of different ways that you can choose 2 people from the group of 20 *where the order does not matter* is called the number of *combinations* of 20 objects taken 2 at a time. The number of combinations of 20 objects taken 2 at a time is denoted by $C(20, 2)$.

In general, $C(n, k) = (n)(n-1)(n-2)...(n-k+1)/k!$ You can also use $C(n, k) = P(n, k)/k!$ to find the number of combinations of n objects taken k at a time. For example,

$$C(10, 4) = (10 \times 9 \times 8 \times 7)/(4 \times 3 \times 2 \times 1) = 5,040/24 = 210.$$

EXAMPLE

There are 5 male applicants and 4 female applicants for 3 jobs. Since all the applicants are considered to be equally qualified, 3 of the applicants will be chosen randomly from the 9 applicants. What is the probability that 2 females and 1 male will be chosen for the 3 jobs?

The order does not matter since choosing X, Y, and Z gives the same result as choosing Z, Y, and X. The number of different ways to choose the 3 applicants is $C(9, 3) = (9 \times 8 \times 7 \times 6 \times 5 \times 4)/(3 \times 2 \times 1) = 84$. Since the 3 jobs are filled by randomly picking 3 of the applicants, the probability of any particular group of 3 being chosen is 1/84. There are $C(5, 1)$ ways to pick 1 male from the 5 males and $C(3, 2)$ ways to pick 2 females from the 3 females. So the number of ways to pick 1 male and 2 females for the 3 jobs is $C(5, 1)\,C(3, 2) = (5/1)(3 \times 2)/(2 \times 1) = 15$. So the probability that 1 male and 2 females are chosen for the 3 jobs is 15/84 or 5/28.

II-5. RATIO AND PROPORTION

II-5.1

RATIO

The ratio of a to b is written as $a : b = \dfrac{a}{b} = a \div b$. We can handle ratios as fractions, since a ratio is a fraction. In the ratio $a : b$, a and b are called the *terms* of the ratio.

Since $a : b$ is a fraction, b can never be zero. The fraction $\dfrac{a}{b}$ is usually different from the fraction $\dfrac{b}{a}$ $\left(\text{for example, } \dfrac{3}{2} \text{ is not the same as } \dfrac{2}{3}\right)$ *so the order of the terms in a ratio is important.*

EXAMPLE

If an orange costs 20¢ and an apple costs 12¢, what is the ratio of the cost of an orange to the cost of an apple?

The ratio is $\dfrac{20¢}{12¢} = \dfrac{5}{3}$ or 5 : 3. Notice that the ratio of the cost of an apple to the cost of an orange is $\dfrac{12¢}{20¢} = \dfrac{3}{5}$ or 3 : 5. So the order of the terms is important.

A ratio is a number, so if you want to find the ratio of two quantities they must be expressed in the same units.

What is the ratio of 8 inches to 6 feet?

Change 6 feet into inches. Since there are 12 inches in a foot, 6 feet = 6 × 12 inches = 72 inches. So the ratio is $\frac{8 \text{ inches}}{72 \text{ inches}} = \frac{1}{9}$ or 1 : 9.

If you regard ratios as fractions, the units must cancel out. In the Example above, if you did not change units the ratio would be $\frac{8 \text{ inches}}{6 \text{ feet}} = \frac{4 \text{ inches}}{3 \text{ feet}}$, which is not a number.

If two numbers measure different quantities, their quotient is usually called a *rate*. For example, $\frac{50 \text{ miles}}{2 \text{ hours}}$, which equals 25 miles per hour, is a rate of speed.

II–5.2

PROPORTION

A proportion is a statement that two ratios are equal. For example, $\frac{3}{12} = \frac{1}{4}$ is a proportion; it could also be expressed as 3 : 12 = 1 : 4 or 3 : 12 :: 1 : 4.

In the proportion $a : b = c : d$, the terms on the outside (a and d) are called the *extremes*, and the terms on the inside (b and c) are called the *means*. Since $a : b$ and $c : d$ are ratios, b and d are both different from zero, so $bd \neq 0$. Multiply each side of $\frac{a}{b} = \frac{c}{d}$ by bd; you get $(bd)\left(\frac{a}{b}\right) = ad$ and $(bd)\left(\frac{c}{d}\right) = bc$. Since $bd \neq 0$, the proportion is equivalent to the equation $ad = bc$. This is usually expressed in the following way:

In a proportion, the product of the extremes is equal to the product of the means.

Find x if $\frac{4}{5} = \frac{10}{x}$.

In the proportion $\frac{4}{5} = \frac{10}{x}$, 4 and x are the extremes and 5 and 10 are the means, so $4x = 5 \cdot 10 = 50$. Solve for x and we get $x = \frac{50}{4} = 12.5$.

Finding the products ad and bc is also called *cross multiplying the proportion*: $\frac{a}{b} \times \frac{c}{d}$. So cross multiplying a proportion gives two equal numbers. The proportion $\frac{a}{b} = \frac{c}{d}$ is read "a is to b as c is to d."

Two numbers are in the ratio 5 : 4 and their difference is 10. What is the larger number?

Let m and n be the two numbers. Then $\dfrac{m}{n} = \dfrac{5}{4}$ and $m - n = 10$. Cross multiply the proportion and you get $5n = 4m$ or $n = \dfrac{4}{5}m$. So $m - n = m - \dfrac{4}{5}m = \dfrac{1}{5}m = 10$ and $m = 50$, which means $n = \dfrac{4}{5} \cdot 50 = 40$. Therefore, the larger number is 50.

CHECK: $\dfrac{50}{40} = \dfrac{5}{4}$ and $50 - 40 = 10$.

Two variables, a and b, are *directly proportional* if they satisfy a relationship of the form $a = kb$, where k is a number. The distance a car travels in two hours and its average speed for the two hours are directly proportional, since $d = 2s$ where d is the distance and s is the average speed expressed in miles per hour. Here $k = 2$. Sometimes the word *directly* is omitted, so the expression "a and b are proportional" means $a = kb$.

If m is proportional to n and $m = 5$ when $n = 4$, what is the value of m when $n = 18$?

There are two different ways to work the problem.

I. Since m and n are directly proportional, $m = kn$; and $m = 5$ when $n = 4$, so $5 = k \cdot 4$, which means $k = \dfrac{5}{4}$. Therefore, $m = \dfrac{5}{4}n$. So when $n = 18$, $m = \dfrac{5}{4} \cdot 18 = \dfrac{90}{4} = 22.5$.

II. Since m and n are directly proportional, $m = kn$. If n' is some value of n, then the value of m corresponding to n' we will call m', and $m' = kn'$. So $\dfrac{m}{n} = k$ and $\dfrac{m'}{n'}$ therefore, $\dfrac{m}{n} = \dfrac{m'}{n'}$, is a proportion. Since $m = 5$ when $n = 4$, $\dfrac{m}{n} = \dfrac{5}{4} = \dfrac{m'}{18}$. Cross multiply and we have $4m' = 90$ or $m' \dfrac{90}{4} = 22.5$.

If two quantities are proportional, you can always set up a proportion in this manner.

If a machine makes 3 yards of cloth in 2 minutes, how many yards of cloth will the machine make in 50 minutes?

The amount of cloth is proportional to the time the machine operates.

Let y be the number of yards of cloth the machine makes in 50 minutes; then

$$\frac{2 \text{ minutes}}{50 \text{ minutes}} = \frac{3 \text{ yards}}{y \text{ yards}}, \text{ so } \frac{2}{50} = \frac{3}{y}.$$

Cross multiply and you have $2y = 150$, so $y = 75$. Therefore, the machine makes 75 yards of cloth in 50 minutes.

Since a ratio is a number, the units must cancel; so put the numbers that measure the same quantity in the same ratio.

EXAMPLE

How many ounces are there in $4\frac{3}{4}$ pounds?

Let x be the number of ounces in $4\frac{3}{4}$ pounds. Since there are 16 ounces in a

pound, $\frac{x \text{ ounces}}{16 \text{ ounces}} = \frac{4\frac{3}{4} \text{ pounds}}{1 \text{ pound}}$. Cross multiply to get $x = 16 \cdot 4\frac{3}{4} = 16 \cdot \frac{19}{4} = 76$;

so $4\frac{3}{4}$ pounds = 76 ounces.

You can always change units by using a proportion. You should know the following measurements:

LENGTH:	1 foot = 12 inches
	1 yard = 3 feet
AREA:	1 square foot = 144 square inches
	1 square yard = 9 square feet
TIME:	1 minute = 60 seconds
	1 hour = 60 minutes
	1 day = 24 hours
	1 week = 7 days
	1 year = 52 weeks
MONEY:	1 dollar = 100 cents

REMEMBER

Any two units of measurement of the same quantity are directly proportional.

On a map, it is $2\frac{1}{2}$ inches from Harrisburg to Gary. The actual distance from Harrisburg to Gary is 750 miles. What is the actual distance from town A to town B if they are 4 inches apart on the map?

Let d miles be the distance from A to B; then $\dfrac{2\frac{1}{2} \text{ inches}}{4 \text{ inches}} = \dfrac{750 \text{ miles}}{d \text{ miles}}$.

Cross multiply and we have $\left(2\frac{1}{2}\right)d = 4 \times 750 = 3,000$, so $d = \dfrac{2}{5} \times 3,000 = 1,200$.

Therefore, the distance from A to B is 1,200 miles. Problems like this one are often called *scale problems*.

Two variables, a and b, are *indirectly proportional* or *inversely proportional* if they satisfy a relationship of the form $k = ab$, where k is a number. So the average speed of a car and the time it takes the car to travel 300 miles are indirectly proportional, since $st = 300$ where s is the speed and t is the time.

m is indirectly proportional to n and $m = 5$ when $n = 4$. What is the value of m when $n = 18$?

Since m and n are indirectly proportional, $m \cdot n = k$, and $k = 5 \cdot 4 = 20$ because $m = 5$ when $n = 4$. Therefore, $18m = k = 20$, so $m = \dfrac{20}{18} = \dfrac{10}{9}$ when $n = 18$.

Other examples of indirect proportion are work problems (see Section II–3.3).

> If two quantities are directly proportional, then when one increases, the other increases. If two quantitites are indirectly proportional, when one quantity increases, the other decreases.

II–5.3

It is also possible to compare three or more numbers by a ratio. The numbers A, B, and C are in the ratio $2 : 4 : 3$ means $A : B = 2 : 4$, $A : C = 2 : 3$, and $B : C = 4 : 3$. The order of the terms is important: $A : B : C$ is read A is to B is to C.

What is the ratio of Tom's salary to Martha's salary to Anne's salary if Tom makes $15,000, Martha makes $12,000, and Anne makes $10,000?

The ratio is $15,000 : 12,000 : 10,000$ which is the same as $15 : 12 : 10$. You can cancel a factor that appears in *every* term.

The angles of a triangle are in the ratio 5 : 4 : 3. How many degrees are there in the largest angle?

The sum of the angles in a triangle is 180°. If the angles are $a°$, $b°$, and $c°$, then $a + b + c = 180$, and $a : b : c = 5 : 4 : 3$. You could find b in terms of a, since $\frac{a}{b} = \frac{5}{4}$, and c in terms of a, since $\frac{a}{c} = \frac{5}{3}$, and then solve the equation for a.

A quicker method for this type of problem is:

1. Add all the numbers: $5 + 4 + 3 = 12$

2. Use each number as the numerator of a fraction whose denominator is the result of step (1), getting $\frac{5}{12}, \frac{4}{12}, \frac{3}{12}$.

3. Each quantity is the corresponding fraction (from step 2) of the total.

Thus, $a = \frac{5}{12}$ of 180 or 75, $b = \frac{4}{12}$ of 180 or 60, and $c = \frac{3}{12}$ of 180 or 45.

So the largest angle is 75°.

CHECK: $75 : 60 : 45 = 5 : 4 : 3$ and $75 + 60 + 45 = 180$.

II-6. SEQUENCES AND PROGRESSIONS

II-6.1

A *sequence* is an ordered collection of numbers. For example, 2, 4, 6, 8, 10, . . . is a sequence. 2, 4, 6, 8, 10 are called the *terms* of the sequence. We identify the terms by their position in the sequence; so 2 is the first term, 8 is the 4th term, and so on. The dots mean the sequence continues; you should be able to figure out the succeeding terms. In the example, the sequence is the sequence of even integers, and the next term after 10 would be 12.

EXAMPLE

What is the eighth term of the sequence 1, 4, 9, 16, 25, . . . ?

Since $1^2 = 1$, $2^2 = 4$, $3^2 = 9$, the sequence is the sequence of squares of integers, so the eighth term is $8^2 = 64$.

Sequences are sometimes given by a rule that defines an entry (usually called the n-th entry) in terms of previous entries of the sequence.

EXAMPLE

If a sequence is defined by the rule $a_n = (a_{n-1} - 3)^2$, what is a_4 (the fourth term of the sequence) if a_1 is 1?

Since a_1 is 1, a_2 is $(1 - 3)^2 = (-2)^2 = 4$. So a_3 is $(4 - 3)^2 = (1)^2 = 1$. Therefore, a_4 is $(1 - 3)^2 = 4$.

II–6.2

An *arithmetic progression* is a sequence of numbers with the property that the *difference* of any two consecutive numbers is always the same. The numbers 2, 6, 10, 14, 18, 22, . . . constitute an arithmetic progression, since each term is 4 more than the term before it. 4 is called the common difference of the progression.

If d is the common difference and a is the first term of the progression, then the nth term will be $a + (n - 1)d$. So a progression with common difference 4 and initial term 5 will have $5 + 6(4) = 29$ as its 7th term. You can check your answer. The sequence would be 5, 9, 13, 17, 21, 25, 29, . . . so 29 is the seventh term.

A sequence of numbers is called a *geometric progression* if the *ratio* of consecutive terms is always the same. So 3, 6, 12, 24, 48, . . . is a geometric progression since $\frac{6}{3} = 2 = \frac{12}{6} = \frac{24}{12} = \frac{48}{24}$, ... *The nth term of a geometric progression is* ar^{n-1} where a is the first term and r is the common ratio. If a geometric progression started with 2 and the common ratio was 3, then the fifth term should be $2 \cdot 3^4 = 2 \cdot 81 = 162$. The sequence would be 2, 6, 18, 54, 162, . . . so 162 is indeed the fifth term of the progression.

We can quickly add up the first n terms of a geometric progression that starts with a and has common ratio r. *The formula for the sum of the first n terms is* $\frac{ar^n - a}{r - 1}$ when $r \neq 1$. (If $r = 1$ all the terms are the same so the sum is *na*.)

EXAMPLE

Find the sum of the first 7 terms of the sequence 5, 10, 20, 40, ...

Since $\frac{10}{5} = \frac{20}{10} = \frac{40}{20} = 2$, the sequence is a geometric sequence with common ratio 2. The first term is 5, so $a = 5$ and the common ratio is 2. The sum of the first seven terms means $n = 7$, thus the sum is $\frac{5 \cdot 2^7 - 5}{2 - 1} = 5(2^7 - 1) = 5(128 - 1) = 5 \cdot 127 = 635$.

CHECK: The first seven terms are 5, 10, 20, 40, 80, 160, 320, and 5 + 10 + 20 + 40 + 80 + 160 + 320 = 635.

II–7. INEQUALITIES

II–7.1

A number is positive if it is greater than 0, so 1, $\frac{1}{1,000}$, and 53.4 are all positive numbers. Positive numbers are signed numbers whose sign is +. If you think of numbers as points on a number line (see Section I–6.2), positive numbers correspond to points to the right of 0.

A number is negative if it is less than 0. $-\frac{4}{5}$, –50, and –.0001 are all negative numbers.

Negative numbers are signed numbers whose sign is –. Negative numbers correspond to points to the left of 0 on a number line.

Zero is the only number that is neither positive nor negative.

$a > b$ means the number a is greater than the number b; that is, $a = b + x$ where x is a positive number. If we look at a number line, $a > b$ means a is to the right of b. $a > b$ can also be read as b is less than a, which is also written $b < a$. For example, $-5 > -7.5$ because $-5 = -7.5 + 2.5$ and 2.5 is positive.

The notation $a \leq b$ means a is less than or equal to b, or b is greater than or equal to a. For example, $5 \geq 4$; also $4 \geq 4$. $a \neq b$ means a is not equal to b.

EXAMPLE

Which is larger, $\dfrac{13}{16}$ or $\dfrac{31}{40}$?

A common denominator is 80. $\dfrac{13}{16} = \dfrac{65}{80}$, and $\dfrac{31}{40} = \dfrac{62}{80}$; since $65 > 62$,

$\dfrac{65}{80} > \dfrac{62}{80}$, so $\dfrac{13}{16} > \dfrac{31}{40}$.

REMEMBER

If you need to know whether one fraction is greater than another fraction, put the fractions over a common denominator and compare the numerators.

II–7.2

Inequalities have certain properties that are similar to equations. We can talk about the left side and the right side of an inequality, and we can use algebraic expressions for the sides of an inequality. For example, $6x < 5x + 4$. A value for an unknown *satisfies an inequality*, if when you evaluate each side of the inequality the numbers satisfy the inequality. So if $x = 2$, then $6x = 12$ and $5x + 4 = 14$ and since $12 < 14$, $x = 2$ satisfies $6x < 5x + 4$. Two inequalities are equivalent if the same collection of numbers satisfies both inequalities.

The following basic principles are used in work with inequalities:

(STEP A) Adding the same expression to *each* side of an inequality gives an equivalent inequality (written $a < b \leftrightarrow a + c < b + c$ where $\leftrightarrow$ means equivalent).

(STEP B) Subtracting the same expression from *each* side of an inequality gives an equivalent inequality ($a < b \leftrightarrow a - c < b - c$).

(STEP C) Multiplying or dividing *each* side of an inequality by the same *positive* expression gives an equivalent inequality ($a < b \leftrightarrow ca < cb$ for $c > 0$).

(STEP D) Multiplying or dividing each side of an inequality by the same *negative* expression *reverses* the inequality ($a < b \leftrightarrow ca > cb$ for $c < 0$).

(STEP E) If both sides of an inequality have the same sign, inverting both sides of the inequality *reverses* the inequality.

$$0 < a < b \leftrightarrow 0 < \frac{1}{b} < \frac{1}{a}$$

$$a < b < 0 \leftrightarrow \frac{1}{b} < \frac{1}{a} < 0$$

(STEP F) If two inequalities are of the same type (both greater or both less), adding the respective sides gives the same type of inequality.

$$(a < b \text{ and } c < d, \text{ then } a + c < b + d)$$

Note that the inequalities are *not* equivalent.

(STEP G) If $a < b$ and $b < c$ then $a < c$.

Find the values of x for which $5x - 4 < 7x + 2$.

Using principle (B) subtract $5x + 2$ from each side, so $(5x - 4 < 7x + 2) \leftrightarrow$ $-6 < 2x$. Now use principle (C) and divide each side by 2, so $-6 < 2x \leftrightarrow -3 < x$.

So any x greater than -3 satisfies the inequality. It is a good idea to make a spot check. -1 is > -3; let $x = -1$ then $5x - 4 = -9$ and $7x + 2 = -5$. Since $-9 < -5$, the answer is correct for at least the particular value $x = -1$.

TIP

Don't forget to reverse inequalities if you multiply or divide by a negative number.

Some inequalities are not satisfied by any real number. For example, since $x^2 \geq 0$ for all x, there is no real number x such that $x^2 < -9$.

You may be given an inequality and asked whether other inequalities follow from the original inequality. You should be able to answer such questions by using principles (A) through (G).

If there is any property of inequalities you can't remember, try out some specific numbers. If $x < y$, then what is the relation between $-x$ and $-y$? Since $4 < 5$ but $-5 < -4$, the relation is probably $-x > -y$, which is true by (D).

EXAMPLE

Find the values of a that satisfy $a^2 + 1 > 2a + 4$.

We will solve this using an alternate method:

(STEP A) Group all terms on one side, so that the other side will be 0. The result is $a^2 - 2a + 1 - 4 = a^2 - 2a - 3 > 0$.

(STEP B) Find all values of the variable that make the expression equal 0.

Since $a^2 - 2a - 3 = (a - 3)(a + 1)$, the result is $a = 3$ and $a = -1$. So the only possible solutions are: $a > 3$, $-1 < a < 3$, and $a < -1$.

TIP

Don't forget that when you multiply an inequality by a negative number, the inequality is reversed.

(STEP C) Choose points other than those found in (B), and check whether the points are solutions. If $a = 0$, then $a^2 - 2a - 3 = -3$, which is less than 0, so $-1 < a < 3$ is not a solution. If $a = 4$, then $a^2 - 2a - 3 = 5$, which is greater than 0, so $a > 3$ is a solution. Use $a = -2$ to see that $a < -1$ is also a solution. So the solutions are $a > 3$ and $a < -1$.

This method is quicker for solving inequalities that are not linear.

III–1. ANGLES

III–1.1

If two straight lines meet at a point they form an *angle*. The point is called the *vertex* of the angle and the lines are called the *sides* or *rays* of the angle. The sign for angle is ∠ and an angle can be denoted in the following ways:

STEP A ∠*ABC* where *B* is the vertex, *A* is a point on one side, and *C* a point on the other side.

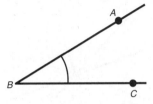

STEP B ∠*B* where *B* is the vertex.

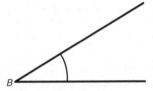

STEP C ∠1 or ∠*x* where *x* or 1 is written inside the angle.

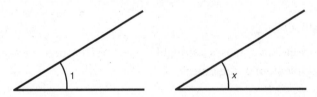

Angles are usually measured in degrees. We say that an angle equals *x* degrees, when its measure is *x* degrees. Degrees are denoted by °. An angle of 50 degrees is 50°. 60′ = 1°, 60″ = 1′ where ′ is read minutes and ″ is read seconds.

III–1.2

Two angles are *adjacent* if they have the same vertex and a common side and one angle is not inside the other.

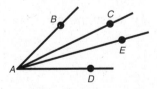

∠*BAC* and ∠*CAD* are adjacent, but ∠*CAD* and ∠*EAD* are not adjacent.

Where two lines intersect at a point, they form 4 angles. The angles opposite each other are called vertical angles. ∠1 and ∠3 are vertical angles. ∠2 and ∠4 are vertical angles.

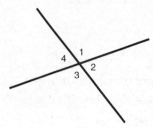

Vertical angles are equal,

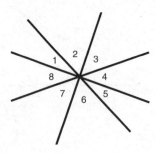

so, ∠1 = ∠5, ∠2 = ∠6, ∠3 = ∠7, ∠4 = ∠8.

III–1.3

A straight angle is an angle whose sides lie on a straight line. *A straight angle equals 180°.*

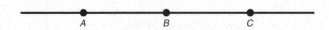

∠*ABC* is a straight angle.

If the sum of two adjacent angles is a straight angle, then the angles are *supplementary* and each angle is the supplement of the other.

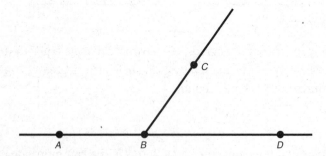

∠*ABC* and ∠*CBD* are supplementary.

If an angle of *x*° and an angle of *y*° are supplements, then *x* + *y* = 180.

If two supplementary angles are equal, they are both *right angles*. A right angle is half of a straight angle. A right angle = 90°.

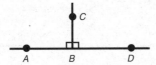

∠ABC = ∠CBD and they are both right angles. A right angle is denoted by ∟. When 2 lines intersect and all four of the angles are equal, then each of the angles is a right angle.

If the sum of two adjacent angles is a right angle, then the angles are *complementary* and each angle is the complement of the other.

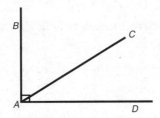

∠BAC and ∠CAD are complementary.

If an angle of $x°$ and an angle of $y°$ are complementary, then $x + y = 90$.

EXAMPLE

If the supplement of angle x is three times as much as the complement of angle x, how many degrees is angle x?

Let d be the number of degrees in angle x; then the supplement of x is $(180 - d)°$, and the complement of x is $(90 - d)°$. Since the supplement is 3 times the complement, $180 - d = 3(90 - d) = 270 - 3d$, which gives $2d = 90$, so $d = 45$.

Therefore, angle x is 45°.

If an angle is divided into two equal angles by a straight line, then the angle has been bisected and the line is called the *bisector* of the angle.

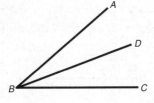

BD bisects ∠ABC; so ∠ABD = ∠DBC.

An *acute angle* is an angle less than a right angle. An obtuse angle is an angle greater than a right angle, but less than a straight angle.

$\angle 1$ is an acute angle, and $\angle 2$ is an obtuse angle.

III–2. LINES

III–2.1

A line is understood to be a straight line. A line is assumed to extend indefinitely in both directions. *There is one and only one line between two distinct points.* There are two ways to denote a line:

1. by a single letter: ℓ is a line;

2. by two points on the line: *AB* is a line.

A *line segment* is the part of a line between two points called *endpoints*. A line segment is denoted by its endpoints.

AB is a line segment. If a point *P* on a line segment is equidistant from the endpoints, then *P* is called the *midpoint* of the line segment.

P is the midpoint of *AB* if the length of *AP* = the length of *PB*. Two line segments are equal if their lengths are equal; so *AP* = *PB* means the line segment *AP* has the same length as the line segment *PB*. When a line segment is extended indefinitely in one direction, it is called a ray. A ray has one endpoint.

AB is a ray that has *A* as its endpoint.

III-2.2

P is a *point of intersection* of two lines if *P* is a point that is on both of the lines. *Two different lines cannot have more than one point of intersection*, because there is only one line between two points.

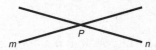

P is the point of intersection of *m* and *n*. We also say *m and n intersect at P*.

Two lines are parallel if they do not intersect no matter how far they are extended.

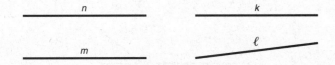

m and *n* are parallel, but *k* and *l* are not parallel since if *k* and *l* are extended they will intersect. Parallel lines are denoted by the symbol ∥; so *m* ∥ *n* means *m* is parallel to *n*.

If two lines are parallel to a third line, then they are parallel to each other.

If a third line intersects two given lines, it is called a *transversal*. A transversal and the two given lines form eight angles. The four inside angles are called *interior* angles. The four outside angles are called *exterior* angles. If two angles are on opposite sides of the transversal they are called *alternate* angles.

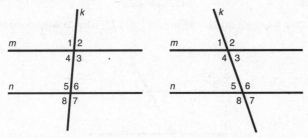

k is a transversal of the lines *m* and *n*. Angles 1, 2, 7, and 8 are the exterior angles, and angles 3, 4, 5, and 6 are the interior angles. ∠4 and ∠6 are an example of a pair of alternate angles. ∠1 and ∠5, ∠2 and ∠6, ∠3 and ∠7, and ∠4 and ∠8 are pairs of *corresponding* angles.

If two parallel lines are intersected by a transversal then:

1. Alternate interior angles are equal.
2. Corresponding angles are equal.
3. Interior angles on the same side of the transversal are supplementary.

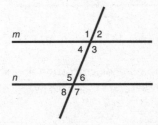

If we use the fact that vertical angles are equal, we can replace "interior" by "exterior" in 1. and 3.

m is parallel to *n* implies:

1. ∠4 = ∠6 and ∠3 = ∠5

2. ∠1 = ∠5, ∠2 = ∠6, ∠3 = ∠7, and ∠4 = ∠8

3. ∠3 + ∠6 = 180° and ∠4 + ∠5 = 180°

The reverse is also true. Let *m* and *n* be two lines that have *k* as a transversal.

1. If a pair of alternate interior angles are equal, then *m* and *n* are parallel.

2. If a pair of corresponding angles are equal, then *m* and *n* are parallel.

3. If a pair of interior angles on the same side of the transversal are supplementary, then *m* is parallel to *n*.

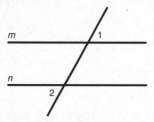

If ∠3 = ∠5, then *m* ∥ *n*. If ∠4 = ∠6 then *m* ∥ *n*. If ∠2 = ∠6 then *m* ∥ *n*. If ∠3 + ∠6 = 180°, then *m* ∥ *n*.

EXAMPLE

If *m* and *n* are two parallel lines and angle 1 is 60°, how many degrees is angle 2?

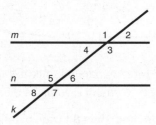

Let ∠3 be the vertical angle equal to angle 2.

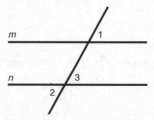

∠3 = ∠2. Since *m* and *n* are parallel, corresponding angles are equal. Since ∠1 and ∠3 are corresponding angles, ∠1 = ∠3. Therefore, ∠1 = ∠2, and ∠2 equals 60° since ∠1 = 60°.

III-2.3

When two lines intersect and all four of the angles formed are equal, the lines are said to be *perpendicular*. If two lines are perpendicular, they are the sides of right angles whose vertex is the point of intersection.

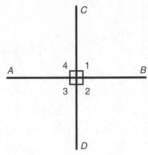

AB is perpendicular to *CD*, and angles 1, 2, 3, and 4 are all right angles. ⊥ is the symbol for perpendicular; so $AB \perp CD$.

If two lines in a plane are perpendicular to the same line, then the two lines are parallel.

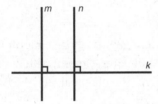

$m \perp k$ and $n \perp k$ imply that $m \parallel n$.

If *any one* of the angles formed when two lines intersect is a right angle, then the lines are perpendicular.

III-3. POLYGONS

A *polygon* is a closed figure in a plane that is composed of line segments that meet only at their endpoints. The line segments are called sides of the polygon, and a point where two sides meet is called a *vertex* (plural *vertices*) of the polygon.

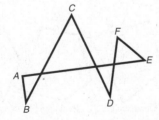

ABCDEF is not a polygon since the line segments intersect at points that are not endpoints.

Some examples of polygons are:

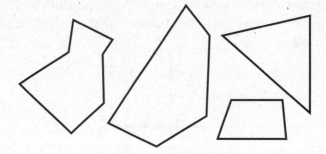

A polygon is usually denoted by the vertices given in order.

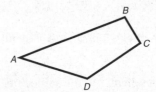

ABCD is a polygon.

A *diagonal* of a polygon is a line segment whose endpoints are nonadjacent vertices. The *altitude* from a vertex *P* to a side is the line segment with endpoint *P*, which is perpendicular to the side. In the diagram below, *AC* is a diagonal, and *CE* is the altitude from *C* to *AD*.

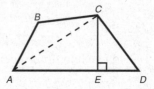

Polygons are classified by the number of angles or sides they have. A polygon with three angles is called a *triangle*; a four-sided polygon is a *quadrilateral*; a polygon with five angles is a *pentagon*; a polygon with six angles is a *hexagon*; an eight-sided polygon is an *octagon*. The number of angles is always equal to the number of sides in a polygon, so a six-sided polygon is a hexagon. The term *n*-gon refers to a polygon with *n* sides.

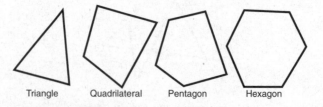

If the sides of a polygon are all equal in length and if all the angles of a polygon are equal, the polygon is called a *regular* polygon.

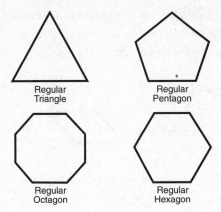

Regular
Triangle

Regular
Pentagon

Regular
Octagon

Regular
Hexagon

If the corresponding sides and the corresponding angles of two polygons are equal, the polygons are *congruent*. Congruent polygons have the same size and the same shape:

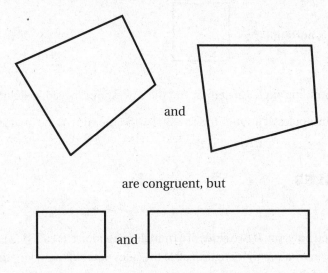

and

are congruent, but

and

are not congruent

In figures for problems on congruence, sides with the same number of strokes through them are equal.

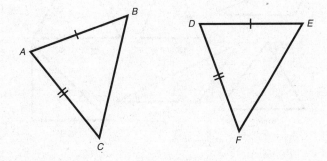

This figure indicates that *AB* = *DE* and *AC* = *DF*.

If all the corresponding angles of two polygons are equal and the lengths of the corresponding sides are proportional, the polygons are said to be *similar*. Similar polygons have the same shape but need not be the same size.

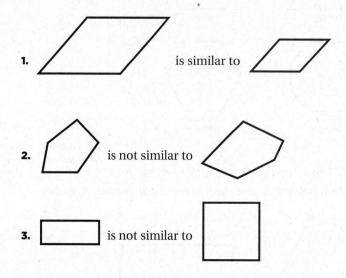

1. is similar to

2. is not similar to

3. is not similar to

In 3. the corresponding angles are equal, but the corresponding sides are not proportional.

The sum of all the angles of an *n*-gon is $(n-2)180°$. So the sum of the angles in a hexagon is $(6-2)180° = 720°$.

III–4. TRIANGLES

III–4.1

A *triangle* is a 3-sided polygon. If two sides of a triangle are equal, it is called *isosceles*. If all three sides are equal, it is an *equilateral* triangle. If all of the sides have different lengths, the triangle is *scalene*. When one of the angles in a triangle is a right angle, the triangle is a *right triangle*. If one of the angles is obtuse we have an *obtuse triangle*. If all the angles are acute, the triangle is an *acute triangle*.

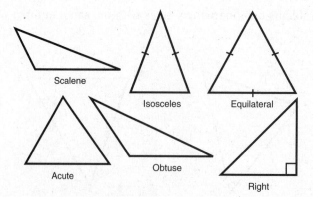

Scalene

Isosceles   Equilateral

Acute   Obtuse   Right

The symbol for a triangle is △; so △*ABC* means a triangle whose vertices are *A*, *B*, and *C*.

The sum of the lengths of any two sides of a triangle must be longer than the remaining side.

If two angles in a triangle are equal, then the lengths of the sides opposite the equal angles are equal. If two sides of a triangle are equal, then the angles opposite the two equal sides are equal. In an equilateral triangle all the angles are equal and each angle = 60°. If each of the angles in a triangle is 60°, then the triangle is equilateral.

REMEMBER

The sum of the angles in a triangle is 180°.

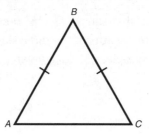

If $AB = BC$, then $\angle BAC = \angle BCA$.

If one angle in a triangle is larger than another angle, the side opposite the larger angle is longer than the side opposite the smaller angle. If one side is longer than another side, then the angle opposite the longer side is larger than the angle opposite the shorter side.

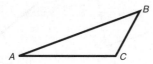

$AB > AC$ implies $\angle BCA > \angle ABC$.

If the side of a triangle is extended, then the resulting exterior angle is greater than either of the opposite and interior angles. So in the triangle above, if we had extended the side AC beyond C to a point D, then the angle BCD would be greater than the angle BAC and greater than the angle ABC.

In a right triangle, the side opposite the right angle is called the *hypotenuse*, and the remaining two sides are called *legs*.

REMEMBER

The Pythagorean theorem states that the square of the length of the hypotenuse is equal to the sum of the squares of the lengths of the legs.

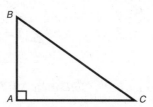

$(BC)^2 = (AB)^2 + (AC)^2$

If $AB = 4$ and $AC = 3$ then $(BC)^2 = 4^2 + 3^2 = 25$ so $BC = 5$. If $BC = 13$ and $AC = 5$, then $13^2 = 169 = (AB)^2 + 5^2$. So $(AB)^2 = 169 - 25 = 144$ and $AB = 12$.

If the lengths of the three sides of a triangle are a, b, and c and $a^2 + b^2 = c^2$, then the triangle is a right triangle where c is the length of the hypotenuse.

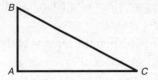

If $AB = 8$, $AC = 15$, and $BC = 17$, then since $17^2 = 8^2 + 15^2$, $\angle BAC$ is a right angle.

Three positive integers (a, b, c) that satisfy $a^2 + b^2 = c^2$ are called a *Pythagorean triple* since they can be thought of as the lengths of the three sides of a right triangle. So $(3, 4, 5)$, $(5, 12, 13)$, and $(8, 15, 17)$ are all examples of Pythagorean triples.

III-4.2

CONGRUENCE

Two triangles are congruent if two pairs of corresponding sides and the corresponding *included* angles are equal. This is called *Side-Angle-Side* and is denoted by S.A.S.

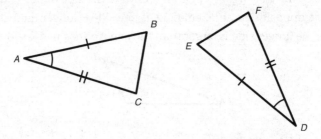

$AB = DE$, $AC = DF$, and $\angle BAC = \angle EDF$ imply that $\triangle ABC \cong \triangle DEF$. $\cong$ means congruent.

Two triangles are congruent if two pairs of corresponding angles and the corresponding *included* sides are equal. This is called *Angle-Side-Angle* or A.S.A.

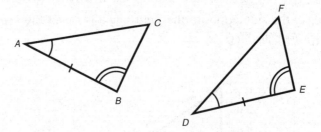

If $AB = DE$, $\angle BAC = \angle EDF$, and $\angle CBA = \angle FED$ then $\triangle ABC \cong \triangle DEF$.

If all three pairs of corresponding sides of two triangles are equal, then the triangles are congruent. This is called *Side-Side-Side* or S.S.S.

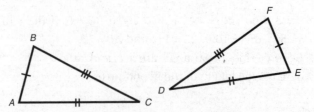

$AB = EF$, $AC = ED$, and $BC = FD$ imply that $\triangle ABC \cong \triangle EFD$.

Because of the Pythagorean Theorem, if any two corresponding sides of two right triangles are equal, the third sides are equal and the triangles are congruent.

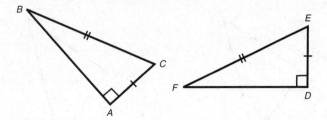

$AC = DE$ and $BC = EF$ imply $\triangle ABC \cong \triangle DFE$.

In general, if two corresponding sides of two triangles are equal, we cannot infer that the triangles are congruent.

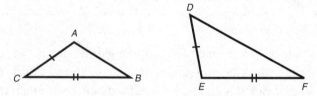

$AC = DE$ and $CB = EF$, but the triangles are not congruent.

If two sides of a triangle are equal, then the altitude to the third side divides the triangle into two congruent triangles.

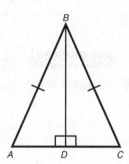

$AB = BC$ and $BD \perp AC$ imply $\triangle ADB \cong \triangle CDB$.

Therefore, $\angle ABD = \angle CBD$, so BD bisects $\angle ABC$. Since $AD = DC$, D is the midpoint of AC so BD is the median from B to AC. A *median* is the segment from a vertex to the midpoint of the side opposite the vertex.

If *AB* = 4, *AC* = 4.5, and *BC* = 6, ∠*BAC* = ∠*EDF*, *DE* = 4, and *DF* = 4.5, what is *EF*?

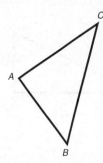 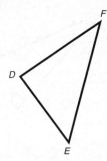

Since two pairs of corresponding sides (*AB* and *DE*, *AC* and *DF*) and the corresponding included angles (∠*BAC*, ∠*EDF*) are equal, the triangles *ABC* and *DEF* are congruent by S.A.S. Therefore, *EF* = *BC* = 6.

The altitude from any vertex of an equilateral triangle will divide the equilateral triangle into two congruent right triangles with angles of 30°, 60°, and 90°. Such right triangles are often called 30-60-90 triangles. It is important to know that in such a right triangle, the length of the side opposite the 30° angle is $\frac{1}{2}$ the length of the hypotenuse. This is true because the altitude will bisect the base of the equilateral triangle and the base is equal to the hypotenuse of the 30-60-90 triangle. By using the Pythagorean Theorem, you can see that the length of the other leg of the right triangle (the side opposite the 60° angle) will be $\left(\frac{1}{2}\right)(\sqrt{3})$ the length of the hypotenuse.

ABC is an equilateral triangle with the length of *BC* equal to 6 and *AD* is perpendicular to *BC*. What is the length of *AD*?

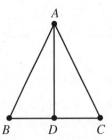

Since triangles *ABD* and *ADC* are congruent right triangles, *BD* = *DC* and each has length $\left(\frac{1}{2}\right)(6)$= 3. (You can also say that angle *BAD* is 30°, so *BD* is $\frac{1}{2}$ of *BA* and equals 3.) Since $AB^2 = AD^2 + BD^2$, we have $6^2 = AD^2 + 3^2$. So $AD^2 = 36 - 9 = 27$. Therefore $AD = \sqrt{27} = \sqrt{9}\sqrt{3} = 3\sqrt{3}$. You can also use the properties of the 30-60-90 triangle to get $AD = (\sqrt{3}/2)6 = 3\sqrt{3}$.

In an isosceles right triangle, two of the angles will equal each other. These triangles are often called 45-45-90 right triangles.

In such a triangle, the two legs are equal. Using the Pythagorean theorem shows that the length of each leg is $(1/\sqrt{2})$ the length of the hypotenuse.

III–4.3

SIMILARITY

Two triangles are similar if all three pairs of corresponding angles are equal. Since the sum of the angles in a triangle is 180°, it follows that if two corresponding angles are equal, the third angles must be equal.

If you draw a line that passes through a triangle and is parallel to one of the sides of the triangle, the triangle formed is similar to the original triangle.

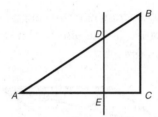

If $DE \parallel BC$ then $\triangle ADE \sim \triangle ABC$. The symbol ~ means similar.

EXAMPLE

A man 6 feet tall casts a shadow 4 feet long; at the same time a flagpole casts a shadow that is 50 feet long. How tall is the flagpole?

The man with his shadow and the flagpole with its shadow can be regarded as the pairs of corresponding sides of two similar triangles.

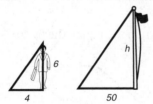

Let h be the height of the flagpole. Since corresponding sides of similar triangles are proportional, $\dfrac{4}{50} = \dfrac{6}{h}$. Cross multiply, getting $4h = 6 \cdot 50 = 300$; so $h = 75$. Therefore, the flagpole is 75 feet high.

III-5. QUADRILATERALS

A *quadrilateral* is a polygon with four sides. The sum of the angles in a quadrilateral is 360°. If both sets of opposite sides of a quadrilateral are parallel, the figure is a *parallelogram*.

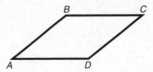

ABCD is a parallelogram.

In a parallelogram:

1. Opposite sides are equal.
2. Opposite angles are equal.
3. All diagonals divide the parallelogram into two congruent triangles.
4. The diagonals bisect each other. (A line *bisects* a line segment if it intersects the segment at the midpoint of the segment.)

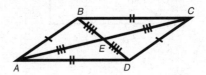

ABCD is a parallelogram.

1. $AB = DC$, $BC = AD$.
2. $\angle BCD = \angle BAD$, $\angle ABC = \angle ADC$.
3. $\triangle ABC \cong \triangle ADC$, $\triangle ABD \cong \triangle CDB$.
4. $AE = EC$ and $BE = ED$.

If *any* of the statements 1., 2., 3., and 4. are true for a quadrilateral, then the quadrilateral is a parallelogram.

If all of the sides of a parallelogram are equal, the figure is called a *rhombus*.

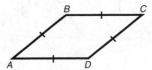

ABCD is a rhombus.

The diagonals of a rhombus are perpendicular.

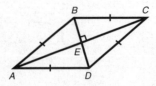

$BD \perp AC$; $\angle BEC = \angle CED = \angle AED = \angle AEB = 90°$.

If all the angles of a parallelogram are right angles, the figure is a *rectangle*.

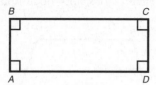

ABCD is a rectangle.

Since the sum of the angles in a quadrilateral is 360°, if *all* the angles of a quadrilateral are equal then the figure is a rectangle. The diagonals of a rectangle are equal. The length of a diagonal can be found by using the Pythagorean Theorem.

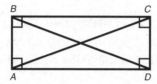

If *ABCD* is a rectangle, $AC = BD$ and $(AC)^2 = (AD)^2 + (DC)^2$.

If all the sides of a rectangle are equal, the figure is a *square*.

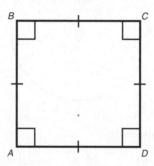

ABCD is a square.

If all the angles of a rhombus are equal, the figure is a square. The length of the diagonal of a square is $\sqrt{2}\,s$ where *s* is the length of a side.

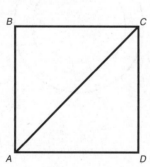

In square *ABCD*, $AC = (\sqrt{2})AD$.

A quadrilateral that has two parallel sides and two sides that are not parallel is called a *trapezoid*. The parallel sides are called *bases*, and the nonparallel sides are called *legs*.

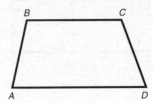

If *BC* ∥ *AD* then *ABCD* is a trapezoid; *BC* and *AD* are the bases.

III-6. CIRCLES

A *circle* is a figure in a plane consisting of all the points that are the same distance from a fixed point called the *center* of the circle. A line segment from any point on the circle to the center of the circle is called a *radius* (plural: *radii*) of the circle. All radii of the same circle have the same length.

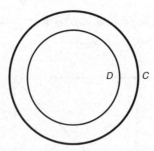

This circle has center *P* and radius *AP*.

A circle is denoted by a single letter, usually its center. Two circles with the same center are *concentric*.

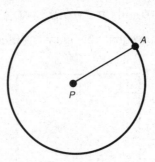

C and *D* are concentric circles.

A line segment whose endpoints are on a circle is called a *chord*. A chord that passes through the center of the circle is a *diameter*. A diameter divides a circle into two congruent halves that are called *semicircles*.

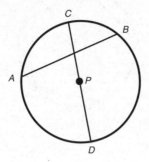

P is the center of the circle.

AB is a chord and *CD* is a diameter.

A diameter that is perpendicular to a chord bisects the chord.

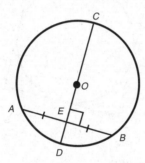

O is the center of this circle and $AB \perp CD$; then $AE = EB$.

If a line intersects a circle at one and only one point, the line is said to be a *tangent* to the circle. The point common to a circle and a tangent to the circle is called the *point of tangency*. The radius from the center to the point of tangency is perpendicular to the tangent.

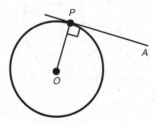

AP is tangent to the circle with center *O*. *P* is the point of tangency and $OP \perp PA$.

A polygon is *inscribed* in a circle if all of its vertices are points on the circle.

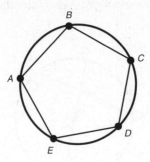

ABCDE is an inscribed pentagon.

A polygon *circumscribes* a circle if each side of the polygon is tangent to the circle.

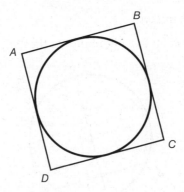

ABCD is a circumscribed quadrilateral.

An angle whose vertex is a point on a circle and whose sides are chords of the circle is called an *inscribed angle*. An angle whose vertex is the center of a circle and whose sides are radii of the circle is called a *central angle*.

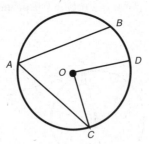

∠*BAC* is an inscribed angle.

∠*DOC* is a central angle.

An *arc* is a part of a circle.

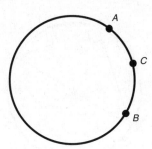

ACB is an arc. Arc *ACB* is written $\overset{\frown}{ACB}$.

If two letters are used to denote an arc, they represent the smaller of the two possible arcs. So $\overset{\frown}{AB} = \overset{\frown}{ACB}$.

An arc can be measured in degrees. The entire circle is 360°; thus an arc of 120° would be $\frac{1}{3}$ of a circle.

A central angle is equal in measure to the arc it intercepts.

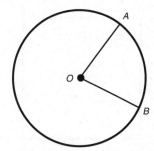

$\angle AOB = \overset{\frown}{AB}$

An inscribed angle is equal in measure to $\frac{1}{2}$ the arc it intercepts.

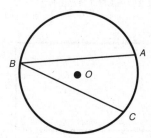

$\angle ABC = \frac{1}{2} \overset{\frown}{AC}$

An angle inscribed in a semicircle is a *right angle*.

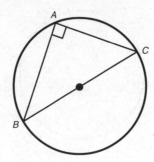

If *BC* is a diameter, then ∠*BAC* is inscribed in a semicircle; so ∠*BAC* = 90°.

III-7. AREA AND PERIMETER

III-7.1

The area *A* of a square equals s^2, where *s* is the length of a side of the square. Thus, $A = s^2$.

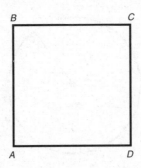

If *AD* = 5 inches, the area of square *ABCD* is 25 square inches.

The area of a rectangle equals length times width; if *L* is the length of one side and *W* is the length of a perpendicular side, then the area *A* = *LW*.

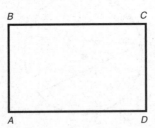

If *AB* = 5 feet and *AD* = 8 feet, then the area of rectangle *ABCD* is 40 square feet.

The area of a parallelogram is base × height; $A = bh$, where b is the length of a side and h is the length of an altitude to that side.

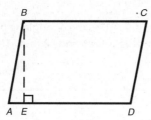

If $AD = 6$ yards and $BE = 4$ yards, then the area of the parallelogram $ABCD$ is $6 \cdot 4$ or 24 square yards.

The area of a trapezoid is the (average of the bases) × height. $A = \dfrac{(b_1 + b_2)}{2} h$ where b_1 and b_2 are the lengths of the parallel sides and h is the length of an altitude to one of the bases.

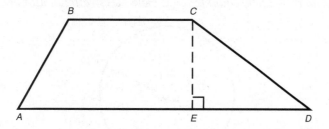

If $BC = 3$ miles, $AD = 7$ miles, and $CE = 2$ miles, then the area of trapezoid $ABCD$ is $\dfrac{(3+7)}{2} \cdot 2 = 10$ square miles.

The area of a triangle is $\dfrac{1}{2}$(base × height); $A = \dfrac{1}{2} bh$, where b is the length of a side and h is the length of the altitude to that side.

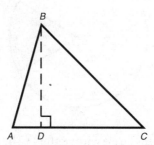

If $AC = 5$ miles and $BD = 4$ miles, then the area of the triangle is $\dfrac{1}{2} \times 5 \times 4 = 10$ square miles.

Since the legs of a right triangle are perpendicular to each other, the area of a right triangle is one-half the product of the lengths of the legs.

If the lengths of the sides of a triangle are 5 feet, 12 feet, and 13 feet, what is the area of the triangle?

Since $5^2 + 12^2 = 25 + 144 = 169 = 13^2$, the triangle is a right triangle and the legs are the sides with lengths 5 feet and 12 feet. Therefore, the area is $\frac{1}{2} \times 5 \times 12 = 30$ square feet.

If we want to find the area of a polygon that is not of a type already mentioned, we break the polygon up into smaller figures such as triangles or rectangles, find the area of each piece, and add these to get the area of the given polygon.

The area of a circle is πr^2 where r is the length of a radius. Since $d = 2r$ where d is the length of a diameter, $A = \pi\left(\dfrac{d}{2}\right)^2 = \pi\dfrac{d^2}{4}$. π is a number that is approximately $\dfrac{22}{7}$ or 3.14; however, *there is no fraction that is exactly equal to π. π is called an irrational number.*

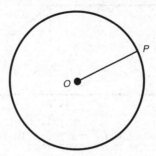

If $OP = 2$ inches, then the area of the circle with center O is $\pi 2^2$ or 4π square inches. The portion of the plane bounded by a circle and a central angle is called a *sector* of the circle.

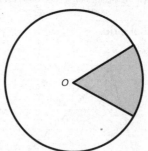

The shaded region is a sector of the circle with center O. The area of a sector with central angle $n°$ in a circle of radius r is $\dfrac{n}{360}\pi r^2$.

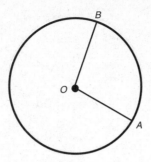

If $OB = 4$ inches and $\angle BOA = 100°$, then the area of the sector is $\dfrac{100}{360}\pi \cdot 4^2 = \dfrac{5}{18} \cdot 16\pi$ $= \dfrac{40}{9}\pi$ square inches.

III-7.2

The *perimeter* of a polygon is the sum of the lengths of the sides.

EXAMPLE 1

What is the perimeter of a regular pentagon whose sides are 6 inches long?

A pentagon has 5 sides. Since the pentagon is regular, all sides have the same length, which is 6 inches. Therefore, the perimeter of the pentagon is 5 × 6, which equals 30 inches or 2.5 feet.

The *perimeter of a rectangle* is $2(L + W)$ where L is the length and W is the width.

The *perimeter of a square* is $4s$ where s is the length of a side of the square.

The *perimeter of a circle* is called the *circumference* of the circle. The *circumference of a circle* is πd or $2\pi r$, where d is the length of a diameter and r is the length of a radius.

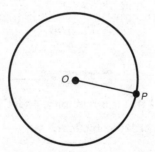

If O is the center of a circle and $OP = 5$ feet, then the circumference of the circle is $2 \times 5\pi$ or 10π feet.

The length of an arc of a circle is $\left(\dfrac{n}{360}\right)\pi d$ where the central angle of the arc is $n°$.

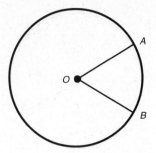

If O is the center of a circle where $OA = 5$ yards and $\angle AOB = 60°$, then the length of arc AB is $\dfrac{60}{360}\pi \times 10 = \dfrac{10}{6}\pi = \dfrac{5}{3}\pi$ yards.

EXAMPLE 2

How far will a wheel of radius 2 feet travel in 500 revolutions? (Assume the wheel does not slip.)

The diameter of the wheel is 4 feet; so the circumference is 4π feet. Therefore, the wheel will travel $500 \times 4\pi$ or $2{,}000\pi$ feet in 500 revolutions.

III–8. VOLUME AND SURFACE AREA

III–8.1

The volume of a rectangular solid or box is length times width times height.

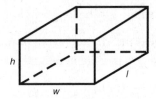

$$V = lwh$$

EXAMPLE 1

What is the volume of a box that is 5 feet long, 4 feet wide, and 6 feet high?

The volume is $5 \times 4 \times 6$ or 120 cubic feet.

If each of the faces of a rectangular solid is a congruent square, then the solid is a *cube*. The volume of a cube is the length of a side (or edge) cubed.

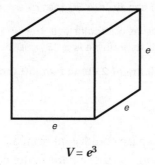

$$V = e^3$$

If the side of a cube is 4 feet long, then the volume of the cube is 4^3 or 64 cubic feet.

This solid is a circular cylinder. The top and the bottom are congruent circles. Most tin cans are circular cylinders. The volume of a circular cylinder is the product of the area of the circular base and the height.

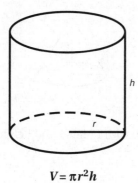

$$V = \pi r^2 h$$

EXAMPLE 2

A circular pipe has a diameter of 10 feet. A gallon of oil has a volume of 2 cubic feet. How many gallons of oil can fit into 50 feet of the pipe?

Think of the 50 feet of pipe as a circular cylinder on its side with a height of 50 feet and a radius of 5 feet. Its volume is $\pi \cdot 5^2 \cdot 50$ or $1{,}250\pi$ cubic feet.

Since a gallon of oil has a volume of 2 cubic feet, 50 feet of pipe will hold $\dfrac{1250\pi}{2}$ or 625π gallons of oil.

A *sphere* is the set of points in space equidistant from a fixed point called the center. The length of a segment from any point on the sphere to the center is called the radius of the sphere. *The volume of a sphere of radius r is $\dfrac{4}{3}\pi r^3$.*

The volume of a sphere with radius 3 feet is $\dfrac{4}{3}\pi 3^3 = 36\pi$ cubic feet.

This solid is a right circular cone with radius r and height h. The volume of the cone is $\left(\dfrac{1}{3}\right)\pi r^2 h.$

III-8.2

The surface area of a rectangular prism is $2LW + 2LH + 2WH$ where L is the length, W is the width, and H is the height.

EXAMPLE

If a roll of wallpaper covers 30 square feet, how many rolls are needed to cover the walls of a rectangular room 10 feet long by 8 feet wide by 9 feet high? There are no windows in the room.

We have to cover the surface area of the walls, which equals $2(10 \times 9 + 8 \times 9)$ or $2(90 + 72)$ or 324 square feet. (Note that the product omits the area of the floor or the ceiling.) Since a roll covers 30 square feet, we need $\frac{324}{30} = 10\frac{4}{5}$ rolls.

The surface area of a cube is $6e^2$ where e is the length of an edge.

The area of the circular part of a cylinder is called the lateral area. The lateral area of a cylinder is $2\pi rh$, since if we unroll the circular part, we get a rectangle whose dimensions are the circumference of the circle and the height of the cylinder. The total surface area is the lateral surface area plus the areas of the circles on top and bottom, so the total surface area is $2\pi rh + 2\pi r^2$.

EXAMPLE

How much tin is needed to make a tin can in the shape of a circular cylinder whose radius is 3 inches and whose height is 5 inches?

The area of both the bottom and top is $\pi \cdot 3^2$ or 9π square inches. The lateral area is $2\pi \cdot 3 \cdot 5$ or 30π square inches. Therefore, we need $9\pi + 9\pi + 30\pi$ or 48π square inches of tin.

III-9. COORDINATE GEOMETRY

In coordinate geometry, every point in the plane is associated with an ordered pair of numbers called *coordinates*. Two perpendicular lines are drawn; the horizontal line is called the x-axis and the vertical line is called the y-axis. The point where the two axes intersect is called the *origin*. Both of the axes are number lines with the origin corresponding to zero (see Section I–6.2). Positive numbers on the x-axis are to the right of the origin, negative numbers to the left. Positive numbers on the y-axis are above the origin, negative numbers below the origin. The coordinates of a point P are (x, y) if P is located by moving x units along the x-axis from the origin and then moving y units up or down.

REMEMBER

The distance along the *x*-axis is always given first.

The numbers in parentheses are the coordinates of the point. Thus "$P = (3, 2)$" means that the coordinates of P are (3, 2). *The distance between the point with coordinates (r, s) and the point with coordinates (a, b) is $\sqrt{(r-a)^2+(s-b)^2}$.* You should be able to answer most questions by using the distance formula.

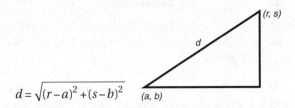

$$d = \sqrt{(r-a)^2+(s-b)^2}$$

EXAMPLE

Is *ABCD* a parallelogram?

$A = (3, 2)$, $B = (1, -2)$, $C = (-2, 1)$, $D = (1, 5)$. The length of *AB* is $\sqrt{(3-1)^2+(2-(-2))^2} = \sqrt{2^2+4^2} = \sqrt{20}$. The length of *CD* is $\sqrt{(-2-1)^2+(1-5)^2} = \sqrt{(-3)^2+(-4)^2} = \sqrt{25}$.

Therefore, $AB \neq CD$, so *ABCD* cannot be a parallelogram, since in a parallelogram the lengths of opposite sides are equal.

You can often use coordinate geometry to solve problems that do not appear to involve coordinates.

EXAMPLE

City A is 5 miles north of City B and City C is 12 miles west of City B. How far is it between City A and City C?

Set up a coordinate axis with City B at the origin, east-west as the *x* axis, and north-south as the *y* axis, as in the diagram.

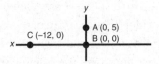

Then City A has coordinates (0, 5) and City C has coordinates (–12, 0). So the distance from A to C is the square root of (–12 – 0)² + (5 – 0)² or $\sqrt{144+25} = \sqrt{169}$, which is 13. So the answer is 13 miles.

Geometry problems occur frequently in the data sufficiency questions. *If you are not provided with a diagram, draw one for yourself.* Think of any conditions that will help you answer the question; perhaps you can see how to answer a different question that will lead to an answer to the original question. It may help to draw in some diagonals, altitudes, or other auxiliary lines in your diagram.

III-10 FUNCTIONS

III-10.1

A *function* is a rule where each object in a collection of objects, called the *domain*, is associated with one and only one element of a collection of objects, called the *range*. In almost all questions you will see on the GMAT, the objects will be numbers.

The object in the domain is often called the input of the function. The object the input is associated with is often called the output. Another way to think of the function concept is to say that for every input in its domain, a function associates one and only one output. The range is the set of all outputs.

Many functions are given by a formula such as $f(x) = 3x - 2$. When a function is given by a formula, the formula describes what number to associate with an arbitrary number x.

EXAMPLE

If a function is given by the rule $f(x) = 3x - 2$, what number is associated with a domain of 4? (This number is denoted as $f(4)$.)

The formula $f(x) = 3x - 2$ means that for any number x, the function produces the resulting number by multiplying x by 3 and then subtracting 2 from the result. So $f(4)$ is 3 times 4 minus 2, or 10. So the function associates 10 to the input 4, or $f(4) = 10$.

EXAMPLE

If a function is given by the rule $f(x) = 3x - 2$, what numbers, if any, are associated with an output of 4?

Since $f(x) = 3x - 2$ this question asks if $f(x) = 4$ has any solutions. So we need to find the solutions to the equation $3x - 2 = 4$. Solving this equation gives $3x = 6$, or $x = 2$. So the only number associated with a range of 4 is 2.

Notice that both Examples above involve the same function, but the questions are not the same. In the first Example, you are given an input and asked to find the output. In the second Example, you are given an output and asked to find an input.

Functions are used to describe many quantities. For example, the profit of a company is a function of the number of items it sells; the speed of a car is a function of the time since a trip started; the price of a gallon of gasoline is a function of the time since January 1, 2008; and so forth.

Functions may also be described by a table, such as the table below. It shows the diameter of a tree as a function of the tree's height above the ground.

Height (ft.)	10	20	30	40	50	60
Diameter (in.)	40	35	31	26	19	10

If we describe this function by $d(h)$ = the diameter of the tree at height h, then $d(10) = 40$, $d(20) = 35$, $d(30) = 31$, $d(40) = 26$, $d(50) = 19$, and $d(60) = 10$.

In this example, the domain of the function d is {10, 20, 30, 40, 50, 60}. The range of d is {10, 19, 26, 31, 35, 40}. When a function is given by a formula, you may assume the domain of the function is all real numbers or all real numbers that can be used in the formula.

EXAMPLE

What is the domain of the function given by the rule $f(x) = \dfrac{1}{(x - 2)}$?

The domain is all real numbers except 2. When $x = 2$, then $x - 2$ is 0. You can't divide by 0.

Sequences (see Section II-6) can be thought of as functions whose domain is the set of positive integers.

III-10.2

Functions can be graphed using coordinate geometry. A point (x, y) is a point on the graph of a function f if $y = f(x)$. The graph of the function f is the set of all points on the graph of f. This graph is usually called the graph of f.

EXAMPLE

The graph of the diameter of the tree given in the previous section would consist of the set of 6 points {(10, 40), (20, 35), (30, 31), (40, 26), (50, 19), (60, 10)}. The graph appears below.

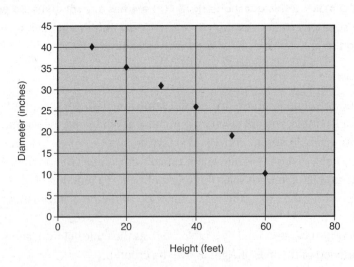

The most common type of function is a linear function. Linear functions are functions given by a formula of the type $f(x) = mx + b$, where m and b can be any real number. These functions are called linear because their graphs are straight lines.

The number m is called the *slope* of the line. The number b is called the *y-intercept* of the line.

The slope indicates the tilt or slant of the line. A line with a positive slope increases as you move to the right along the horizontal axis. (The line tilts up.) A line with a negative slope decreases as you move to the right along the horizontal axis. (The line tilts down.)

The slope of a line can also be thought of as the *rate of change of the output with respect to the input*. This idea can be useful in word problems. For example, if the distance, D, a car has traveled after t hours is given by the linear function $D = 40t + 2$ miles, then the slope is 40 and the rate of change of D (distance) with respect to t (time) is 40 miles per hour. So the slope describes the speed of the car.

The number b is called the *y*-intercept because the line crosses the *y*-axis at the point $(0, b)$.

In some problems, you may want to find the *x-intercept*, which is where the graph hits the *x*-axis. The *x*-intercept for the line $y = mx + b$ is found by solving $0 = mx + b$ for x.

A basic problem that you should be able to solve is to find the equation of the straight line that connects two given points, (x_1, y_1) and (x_2, y_2).

STEP A Calculate the slope as the change in y divided by the change in x.

$$m = \frac{(y_2 - y_1)}{(x_2 - x_1)}$$

STEP B Use one of the given points and solve for b. For example, $y_1 = mx_1 + b$, so $b = y_1 - mx_1$.

STEP C The equation of the line is $y = mx + b$.

EXAMPLE

Find the equation of the straight line that passes between $(1, 4)$ and $(-2, 10)$.

STEP A The slope is $m = \frac{(10 - 4)}{(-2 - 1)} = \frac{6}{(-3)} = -2$. So the equation is $y = -2x + b$.

STEP B Using the first point, we have $4 = -2(1) + b$, which gives $b = 4 + 2 = 6$.

STEP C So the equation is $y = -2x + 6$.

The graph of the linear function $f(x) = -2x + 6$ shows a straight line.

Another type of function that may appear is a quadratic or second-degree function. These are functions given by formulas of the form $f(x) = ax^2 + bx + c$, where a, b, and c are any real numbers.

If f is the function given by the formula $f(x) = x^2 + 3x - 4$, find $f(-2)$, $f(0)$, $f(3)$, and sketch the graph of f.

The table below gives several values of $f(x)$.

x	$f(x)$
−6	14
−4	0
−2	−6
0	−4
3	14

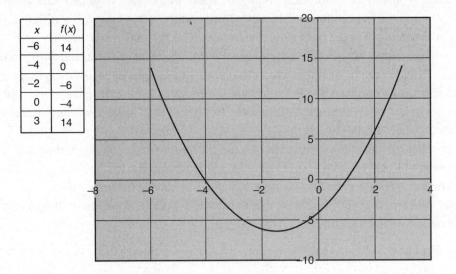

This is the graph of the function $f(x) = x^2 + 3x - 4$. This shape is called a *parabola*. Parabolas can be more or less narrow than the example shown above. They can also look like this shape turned upside down. All quadratic functions will have a parabola for their graph if a, the coefficient of x^2, is not zero.

IV-1. TABLES
General Hints

1. Make sure to look at the *entire* table or graph.

2. Figure out what *units* the table or graph is using. Make sure to express your answer in the correct units.

3. Look at the possible answers before calculating. Since many questions only call for an approximate answer, it may be possible to round off (see Section I–5), saving time and effort.

4 Don't confuse decimals and percentages. If the units are percentages, then an entry of .2 means .2%, which is equal to .002.

5. In inference questions, only the information given can be used.

6. See if the answer makes sense.

The table below gives the height and weight of 12 newborn infants.

Height (inches)	Weight (pounds)
21	10.2
10	3.3
15	5.6
18	9
20	11
19	8.2
18	9.5
23	12.1
14	5
16	5.9
17	5.8
20	8.9

1. What is the difference in weight between the tallest and shortest infants?

   (A) 13 pounds
   (B) 12.1 pounds
   (C) 8.8 pounds
   (D) 6.9 pounds
   (E) 3.3 pounds

   The correct answer is (C), which is obtained by subtracting 3.3 (the weight of the shortest—10 inches—infant) from 12.1 (the weight of the tallest—23 inches—infant). It is important to answer the question that is asked. Choice (A) is 23 – 10, but that gives the difference in height of the tallest and shortest infants. Choices (B) and (E) are the weights of the tallest and shortest infants, but the question asked for the *difference* in weight.

The data in the table above may also be presented as a *scatter plot*. In a scatter plot, each infant is represented by a point whose first coordinate is the infant's height and whose second coordinate is the infant's weight. The scatter plot for the data in the table is shown below.

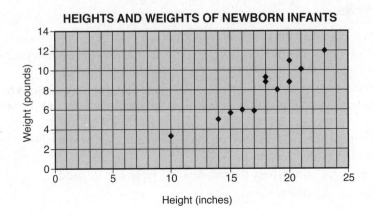

HEIGHTS AND WEIGHTS OF NEWBORN INFANTS

Using coordinate geometry, you can answer questions about the table from the scatter plot.

2. How many of the infants weighed more than 7 pounds?

   (A) 4
   (B) 5
   (C) 6
   (D) 7
   (E) 8

   The correct answer is (D). Since weight is the second coordinate, simply count the points that are above the horizontal line $y = 7$.

3. Which of the statements can be inferred from the data on the scatter plot?

   I.   None of the infants weighed 4 pounds.
   II. If one infant was taller than another infant, then the taller weighed more than the shorter infant.
   III. All of the infants weighed less than 13 pounds.

   (A) I only
   (B) III only
   (C) I and III only
   (D) II and III only
   (E) I, II, and III

   The correct choice is (C). II is false since the infant who is 19 inches tall weighs less than the infants who are 18 inches tall. Since no points have a second coordinate equal to 4, I is true. Since all the points have second coordinates less than 13, III is true.

IV-2. CIRCLE GRAPHS

Circle graphs are used to show how various sectors share in the whole. Circle graphs are sometimes called pie charts. Circle graphs often show the percentage of each sector. The area of each sector also indicates the percentage of each sector.

EXPENDITURES OF GENERAL INDUSTRIES
(by major categories)

2000 ($3,087 million)

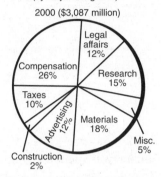

2010 ($4,851 million)

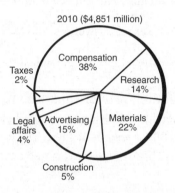

(Refer to the graph above to answer the following questions.)

1. The amount spent on materials in 2000 was 120% of the amount spent on

   (A) research in 2000
   (B) compensation in 2000
   (C) advertising in 2010
   (D) materials in 2010
   (E) legal affairs in 2000

   When using circle graphs to find ratios of various sectors, don't find the amounts each sector received and then the ratio of the amounts. Find the *ratio of the percentages*, which is much quicker. In 2000, 18% of the expenditures were for materials. We want x where 120% of x = 18%; so x = 15%. Any category that received 15% of 2000 expenditures gives the correct answer, but only one of the five choices is correct. Here, the answer is (A) since research received 15% of the expenditure in 2000. Check the 2000 answers first since you need look only at the percentages, which can be done quickly. Notice that (C) is incorrect, since 15% of the expenditures for 2010 is different from 15% of the expenditures for 2000.

2. The fraction of the total expenditures for 2000 and 2010 spent on compensation was about

(A) $\frac{1}{5}$

(B) $\frac{1}{4}$

(C) $\frac{1}{3}$

(D) $\frac{3}{7}$

(E) $\frac{1}{2}$

In 2000, 26% of $3,087 million was spent on compensation and in 2010 compensation received 38% of $4,851 million. The total expenditures for 2000 and 2010 are $(3,087 + 4,851) million. So the exact answer is $\frac{[(.26)(3,087)+(.38)(4,851)]}{(3,087+4,851)}$. Actually calculating the answer will waste a lot of time. Look at the answers and think for a second.

We are taking a weighted average of 26% and 38%. To find a weighted average, we multiply each value by a weight and divide by the total of all the weights. Here 26% is given a weight of 3,087 and 38% a weight of 4,851. The following general rule is often useful in average problems: The average or weighted average of a collection of values can *never* be:

1. less than the smallest value in the collection, or
2. greater than the largest value in the collection.

Therefore, the answer to the question must be greater than or equal to 26% and less than or equal to 38%.

Since $\frac{1}{5}$ = 20% and $\frac{1}{4}$ = 25%, which are both less than 26%, neither (A) nor (B) can

be the correct answer. Since $\frac{3}{7}$ = $42\frac{6}{7}$% and $\frac{1}{2}$ = 50%, which are both greater than

38%, neither (D) nor (E) can be correct. Therefore, by elimination, (C) is the correct answer.

In inference questions involving circle graphs, *do not compare different percentages.* For example, the 15% spent on research in 2000 is not the same amount as the 15% spent on advertising in 2010.

IV-3. LINE GRAPHS

Line graphs are used to show how a quantity changes continuously. Very often the quantity is measured as time changes. If the line goes up, the quantity is increasing; if the line goes down, the quantity is decreasing; if the line is horizontal, the quantity is not changing. To measure the height of a point on the graph, use your note board as a straight edge.

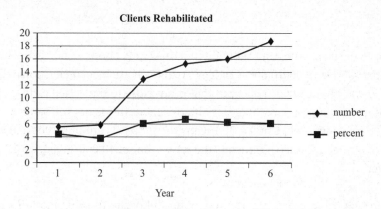

Clients Rehabilitated

Number (in thousands) and percent of all disability clients reported as rehabilitated by state agency

Year	1	2	3	4	5	6
Percent	4.4	3.9	6.2	6.9	6.5	6.3

(Refer to the graph and table above to answer the following questions.)

1. Between year 1 and year 6, the largest number of disability clients rehabilitated was in year
   (A) 1
   (B) 3
   (C) 4
   (D) 5
   (E) 6

The answer is (E) since the highest point on the number graph is at year 6.

2. In year 2, this state agency had about how many disability clients?
   (A) 3,900
   (B) 6,000
   (C) 100,000
   (D) 150,000
   (E) 200,000

3.9% of all disability clients were rehabilitated in year 2 and there were about 6,000 disability clients rehabilitated that year. So if T was the total number of disability clients that year, then 3.9% of T is about 6,000. Since 4% is $\frac{1}{25}$, then T is about $25 \times 6,000 = 150,000$. So (D) is the correct answer.

3. The ratio of the number of clients rehabilitated in year 6 to the number of clients rehabilitated in year 2 is about

(A) 1:3

(B) 1:1

(C) 3:2

(D) 3:1

(E) 6:1

In year 6, about 19,000 clients were rehabilitated. In year 2, about 6,000 clients were rehabilitated. So the ratio is 19,000/6,000. Choices (A) and (B) are incorrect. Choice (C) would mean the ratio was about 9,000/6,000, but that is not close to the actual ratio. So (C) is incorrect. (Note: the ratio of percentages is about 3:2, but this is not the same as the ratio of the numbers rehabilitated.) Choice (E) means the ratio was about 36,000/6,000, so that choice is incorrect. Choice (D) means the ratio is about 18,000/6,000, so (D) is the correct answer.

4. Between year 2 and year 5, the number of disability clients rehabilitated

(A) decreased by about 100%

(B) stayed about the same

(C) increased by about 150%

(D) increased by about 167%

(E) increased by about 250%

The increase between year 5 and year 2 was about 16,000 – 6,000 = 10,000. Since there were 6,000 disability patients who were rehabilitated in year 2, the number increased by $10,000/6,000 = \frac{5}{3}$, which is about 167%. So (D) is the correct choice.

TIP

Use your note board to compare bars that are not adjacent to each other.

IV-4. BAR GRAPHS

Quantities can be compared by the height or length of a bar in a bar graph. A bar graph can have either vertical or horizontal bars. You can compare different quantities or the same quantity at different times.

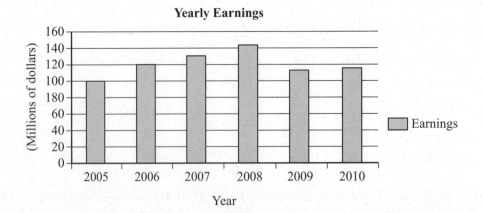

(Refer to the graph above to answer these questions.)

1. The yearly change in earnings of the largest magnitude for the years shown was
   (A) from 2005 to 2006
   (B) from 2006 to 2007
   (C) from 2007 to 2008
   (D) from 2008 to 2009
   (E) from 2009 to 2010

The correct answer is (D) since it is the only change that is wider than one unit on the vertical axis. To evaluate the change in yearly earnings, simply look at the difference in height of adjacent bars. (Since the question asks for the magnitude, a decrease is not considered as a negative number.)

2. During the time period shown (2005 to 2010), yearly earnings
   (A) decreased by about 15%
   (B) decreased by about 5%
   (C) stayed about the same
   (D) increased by about 15%
   (E) increased by about 40%

(D) is the correct choice. In 2005, yearly earnings were about 100. In 2010, the yearly earnings were around 115. So yearly earnings increased by about 15. Since the yearly earnings were 100 at the start, yearly earnings increased by about $\frac{15}{100}$ = 15%.

3. Which of the following statements about yearly earnings from 2005 to 2010 can be inferred from the graph above?

   I. Yearly earnings increased in every year from 2005 to 2010.
   II. Yearly earnings were never less than 90 million dollars between 2005 and 2010.
   III. Yearly earnings in some years between 2005 and 2010 were greater than 150 million dollars.

   (A) I only
   (B) II only
   (C) I and II only
   (D) II and III only
   (E) I, II, and III

(B) is correct. I is false since earnings decreased from 2008 to 2009. II is true since all of the bars are above 90. III is false since none of the bars are above 150.

REVIEW OF FORMULAS

(Numbers next to the formulas refer to the section where the formula is discussed.)

Interest = Amount × Time × Rate	I–4
Discount = Cost × Rate of Discount	I–4
Price = Cost × (100% – Rate of Discount)	I–4
$x^2 - y^2 = (x + y)(x - y)$	II–1
$x = \dfrac{1}{2a}\,[-b \pm \sqrt{b^2 - 4ac}\,]$ (quadratic formula)	II–2
Distance = Speed × Time	II–3
$a^2 + b^2 = c^2$ when a and b are the legs and c is the hypotenuse of a right triangle (Pythagorean Theorem)	III–4
Diameter of a circle = 2 × Radius	III–6
Area of a square = s^2	III–7
Area of a rectangle = LW	III–7
Area of a triangle = $\dfrac{1}{2}bh$	III–7
Area of a circle = πr^2	III–7
Area of a parallelogram = bh	III–7
Area of a trapezoid = $\dfrac{1}{2}(b_1 + b_2)h$	III–7
Circumference of a circle = πd	III–7
Perimeter of a square = $4s$	III–7
Perimeter of a rectangle = $2(L + W)$	III–7
Volume of a box = lwh	III–8
Volume of a cube = e^3	III–8
Volume of a cylinder = $\pi r^2 h$	III–8
Volume of a sphere = $\dfrac{4}{3}\pi r^3$	III–8
Surface area of a box = $2LW + 2LH + 2WH$	III–8

Surface area of a cube $= 6e^2$ III–8

Surface area of a cylinder $= 2\pi rh + 2\pi r^2$ III–8

Distance between points (x,y) and (a,b) is $\sqrt{(x-a)^2+(y-b)^2}$ III–9

The following are always equal:

Any two radii of the same circle.

The two sides opposite equal angles of a triangle.

The two angles opposite equal sides of a triangle.

Opposite angles formed by intersecting lines.

Alternate angles formed by parallel lines.

The four sides of a square.

The three sides of an equilateral triangle.

Opposite sides (and angles) of a parallelogram.

The sides (and angles) of any regular polygon.

Corresponding angles of similar polygons.

All right angles.

The square of the hypotenuse and the sum of the squares of two remaining sides of a right triangle.

The difference of two squares and the product of the sum and difference of their square roots.

The following are always right angles:

Any angle whose measure is 90 degrees.

Angles formed by perpendicular lines.

Any of four equal angles formed by the intersection of two lines.

Any angle that is equal to its supplement.

All angles of a square, rectangle, or cube.

Any angle inscribed in a semi-circle.

The angle formed by a circle's radius and tangent.

The angle opposite the longest side of a right triangle.

The angles between north, south, east, and west.

Angle between the base and height of a triangle.

Angle between the base and height of a cylinder.

The angle between floor and wall or ceiling and wall.

If any of the following properties hold, two triangles are congruent:

Two corresponding angles and the corresponding included sides are equal.

Two corresponding sides and the corresponding included angles are equal.

All three corresponding sides are equal.

Two right triangles that have any two corresponding sides equal.

HINTS FOR ANSWERING MATH QUESTIONS

1. Make sure you answer the question you are asked to answer.
2. Look at the answers before you start to work out a problem; you can save a lot of time.
3. Don't waste time on superfluous computations.
4. Estimate whenever you can to save time.
5. Budget your time so you can try all the questions. (Check the time box frequently.)
6. Don't make extra assumptions on inference questions.
7. Work efficiently; don't waste time worrying during the test.
8. Make sure you express your answer in the units asked for.
9. On data sufficiency questions, don't do any more work than is necessary. *(Don't solve the problem; you only have to know that the problem can be solved.)*

Problem-Solving

10

→ **MULTISTEP PROBLEMS**

→ **ARITHMETIC PROBLEMS**

→ **BASIC ALGEBRA PROBLEMS**

→ **GEOMETRY PROBLEMS**

→ **TACTICS**

The quantitative test contains 2 types of questions, problem-solving and data sufficiency. This chapter will help you understand problem-solving questions and how to succeed with this type of question. The next chapter will discuss data sufficiency questions.

According to the GMAT, the questions in the Quantitative Section are designed to test your knowledge of:

1. Basic mathematical skills
2. Understanding of mathematical concepts
3. The ability to reason quantitatively and solve quantitative problems

You will encounter very few problems that simply test your basic mathematical skills. Some of the problem-solving questions will involve your understanding of mathematical concepts. Many problems will require you to integrate different mathematical ideas or translate a verbal problem into a mathematical problem in order to find the solution.

MULTISTEP PROBLEMS

Most problem-solving questions require more than one step in order to obtain the correct answer. We will call such problems multistep problems. The next two questions illustrate the difference between a one-step problem and a multistep problem.

Answer the following two questions that involve the area of a rectangle. The answers and analyses of each question follow the questions.

TIP

If you know only the basic mathematical skills, you will do poorly on problem–solving questions. You must be able to apply math skills.

Find the area (in square feet) of a rectangle that is 10 feet wide and 12 feet long.

(A) 22

(B) 44

(C) 60

(D) 120

(E) 144

(D) The area of a rectangle is the length times the width. So the area of the rectangle is 10 feet $\times$ 12 feet = 120 square feet.

How many nonoverlapping 6-inch by 6-inch square tiles will it take to cover a rectangular floor that is 10 feet wide and 12 feet long?

(A) 120

(B) 240

(C) 480

(D) 960

(E) 3,600

(C) We know that the area of a rectangle is the length times the width and the area of a square is the length of a side squared. You can use several ways to calculate this answer. However, the main idea is to make sure that you use comparable units. The following describes three different ways to solve the problem.

First, you can convert everything to inches. Each square is 6^2 = 36 square inches. The width of the rectangle is 12 $\times$ 10 = 120 inches and the length of the rectangle is 12 $\times$ 12 = 144 inches. So the area of the rectangle is 120 $\times$ 144 = 17,280 square inches. Divide 17,280 by 36 to obtain 480; so the answer is 480 tiles. This is a simple way to solve the problem. However, since you will not have a calculator for the exam, performing the multiplications and division may be time consuming.

Second, you can convert all the dimensions into feet. Each tile is $\frac{1}{2}$ foot on each side, so the area is $\frac{1}{2} \times \frac{1}{2} = \frac{1}{4}$ square feet. The area of the rectangle is 12 $\times$ 10 = 120 square feet. Since 120 divided by $\frac{1}{4}$ is 480, the correct answer is 480 tiles. This method is simpler than converting everything into inches, but it involves fractions.

Third, since you want the number of tiles, simply change the dimensions into tiles. Since 6 inches is $\frac{1}{2}$ of a foot, we can say that the width of the rectangle, which is 10 feet, is 20 tiles. The length of the rectangle, which is 12 feet, is 24 tiles. So we can think of the floor as a rectangular area that is 20 tiles by 24 tiles, which has an area of 20 $\times$ 24 = 480 tiles. Notice that since each side of a tile is 6 inches, the tiles will fit the length and width with no overlap.

To answer the first Example, all you need to know is the formula for the area of a rectangle and substitute the given values into the formula. This type of question will almost never appear on the exam. In contrast, the second Example illustrates a typical problem-solving question that appears on the exam. The second Example requires you to be able to solve a problem like the first Example.

In the second Example, not only must you know how to calculate the area of a rectangle but you also need to translate verbal concepts into mathematical relations and to change units of measurements correctly. This is an example of a multistep problem.

Most of the problems on the Quantitative Section are multistep problems.

How Difficult Are the Problem-Solving Questions?

The problem-solving questions on the GMAT are designed to test your knowledge of

1. Arithmetic
2. Basic algebra
3. Well-known ideas of geometry

We will look closely at examples from each of these three categories of mathematics that may occur in problem-solving questions on the GMAT. We will investigate in detail a mathematical concept from each of these three branches. We will also solve several different types of questions that may appear on the exam that deal with these concepts.

Work through the following examples from each of the three categories given above. The examples will include problems of varying difficulty.

ARITHMETIC PROBLEMS

The following examples all involve basic ideas of arithmetic.

One or two straightforward questions may involve calculation. The following question is an example of an EASY question.

EXAMPLE

What is $0.01 + (0.02)^2 + (0.03)^3$?

(A) 0.0104027
(B) 0.010427
(C) 0.14
(D) 0.1427
(E) 0.149

(B) This is a simple calculation but you must be able to keep track of decimal places. Since $(0.02)^2 = 0.0004$ and $(0.03)^3 = 0.000027$, the answer is $0.01 + 0.0004 + 0.000027$, which is 0.010427.

More difficult questions involve understanding the concepts behind a calculation. The next 2 questions are more typical GMAT questions that involve understanding elementary arithmetic concepts such as multiplication and division.

The following question is of AVERAGE difficulty.

EXAMPLE

If a and b are digits and the product of the two-digit numbers $(1a)$ and $(b2) = 132$, then $a + b$ is

(A) 1

(B) 2

(C) 3

(D) 4

(E) 5

(B) To solve this question, you need to understand the concept of place value and how it relates to multiplication. The two-digit number $(1a)$ is equal to $1(10) + a$. The two-digit number $(b2)$ is equal to $b(10) + 2$. So $(1a)(b2) = (10 + a)(10b + 2) = 100b + 20 + 10ab + 2a = 100b + 10(2 + ab) + 2a$, which is equal to 132. So $2a$ is the digit in the units place and must equal 2. Therefore $a = 1$. The equation now becomes $100b + 10(2 + b) + 2 = 132$, which has 3 in the tens position so $2 + b = 3$. This means $b = 1$. Therefore $a + b = 1 + 1 = 2$. We can check and see that $1a = 11$, $b2 = 12$, and $(11)(12) = 132$.

Some questions will require you to choose the correct collection of answers. The following question requires a conceptual understanding of division. This question is MORE CHALLENGING than the previous question.

EXAMPLE

If p and q are integers and p divided by q is 20.15, then which of the following integers is a possible value for the remainder when p is divided by q?

   I. 15

   II. 5

   III. 3

(A) I only

(B) I and II only

(C) I and III only

(D) II and III only

(E) I, II, and III

(C) Remember that when we divide p by q, we mean that $p = qk + r$ where k and r are integers and the remainder, r, satisfies $0 \le r < q$. Dividing each side of this equation by q gives us $p/q = k + r/q$ where k is an integer and $0 \le r/q < 1$. Since $p/q = 20.15$, we know that $k = 20$ and $r/q = 0.15$. So $r/q = 15/100$, which gives us that $q = 100r/15$. We need r and q to be integers. Now check each possibility. If $r = 15$, then $q = 100$, so 15 is a possible remainder. If $r = 5$, then $q = 100(5/15)$, which is NOT an integer. So 5 is not a possible remainder. If $r = 3$, then $q = 100(3/15) = 20$, which is an integer. So 3 is a possible remainder. Therefore only I and III are possible values for the remainder and (C) is the correct answer.

Now we will look at this problem again and see if there are some simple ways to improve your chances of guessing the correct answer.

STEP A Writing 0.15 as 15/100 means that when you divide p by 100 the remainder is 15. So the correct answer must have 15 as a possibility. This means you can eliminate any choice that does not include I, so you can eliminate choice (D). For example, if $p = 2015$ and $q = 100$, then $p/q = 20.15$ and the remainder is 15.

STEP B Reducing the fraction 15/100 to 3/20 means that when you divide p by 20, the reminder is 3. (If $p = 403$, then $p/20 = 20.15$.) So the correct choice must include 3 as a possible remainder. Therefore you can eliminate any choice that does not include III. So we now know the correct answers must include I and III. This means the only possible answers are (C) and (E). You now have a 50/50 chance of guessing the correct answer.

BASIC ALGEBRA PROBLEMS

The following questions all involve the same algebraic concept: solving linear equations in 2 unknowns. (See Math Section II-2.4 for details.) These 3 questions illustrate some of the many different ways questions can be asked about this topic.

In general, you need one equation to find one unknown, two equations to find two unknowns, three equations to find three unknowns, and so on. However, many different questions can be constructed that go beyond this general idea.

The first question is a straightforward question requiring the solution of 2 linear equations in 2 unknowns. However, it asks for a combination of the unknowns. This question is BELOW AVERAGE in difficulty.

EXAMPLE

If $x + y = 2$ and $3x - y = 10$, then $2x + y$ is

(A) –1

(B) 3

(C) 5

(D) 6

(E) 7

(C) If you add the two equations, you get $4x = 12$, which you can solve to obtain $x = 3$. Substitute $x = 3$ into the first equation to get $3 + y = 2$ or $y = -1$. Be careful to answer the question that is asked. To finish the question, calculate $2x + y = 2(3) - 1 = 5$. If you have time, you should check your answers. Since $3 + (-1) = 2$ and $3(3) - (-1) = 10$, $x = 3$ and $y = -1$ are correct.

A few GMAT questions are as straightforward as the example above. However, many questions require a deeper understanding of the concept.

The next question requires you to understand how some questions involving 2 unknowns can be answered if you are given only a single equation. This question is of AVERAGE difficulty.

EXAMPLE

If $x - y = 2$, then the value of $-4x + 4y =$
(A) -8
(B) 0
(C) 2
(D) 8
(E) cannot be determined

(A) The key to this problem is to observe that the two expressions in the question are related. Since $-4(x - y) = -4x + 4y$ and $x - y = 2$ then $-4x + 4y = -4(2) = -8$. Notice that although you are given 2 unknowns and only one equation, you can solve for this particular combination of unknowns. If you are not careful, you might incorrectly choose (E).

Several questions on the exam will involve simple mathematical concepts but will not be written as simple equations or formulas. You must be able to translate some verbal information into mathematical language before you can solve the problem. The next question is an example of a problem that involves translating verbal information into a math problem. This problem is of AVERAGE difficulty.

EXAMPLE

Last year, an investment fund had $\frac{2}{3}$ of its assets in equities, which yielded 10%, and had $\frac{1}{3}$ of its assets in bonds, which yielded 5%. The fund's total yield last year was $150,000. How much money (in dollars) did the fund have invested in bonds last year?
(A) 100,000
(B) 150,000
(C) 600,000
(D) 1,000,000
(E) 2,000,000

(C) If the fund had E invested in equities and B invested in bonds, then the total yield last year was $0.1E + 0.05B$, which equals 150,000. Since $\frac{2}{3}$ of the assets were in equities and $\frac{1}{3}$ of the assets were in bonds, $E = 2B$ so $0.1E + 0.05B = 0.1(2B) + 0.05B = 0.25B = 150,000$. Solving for B gives $B = 600,000$. This is a simple example of a problem, that involves straightforward math ideas. However, you must be able to interpret the given information into mathematics. (This is a simple example of a word problem.)

Occasionally problems such as this may involve different units, so be sure to read the question carefully. For example, if the previous question had asked how many million dollars did the fund have in bonds, the answer would have been 0.6, not 600,000.

GEOMETRY PROBLEMS

The following questions all involve the same geometric concept: analyzing triangles.

The following question is BELOW AVERAGE in difficulty.

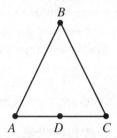

In triangle *ABC*, the length of *AB* is 6 and the length of *BC* is 6. Point *D* is on line segment *AC,* and the length of *AD* = the length of *CD*. How many degrees is angle *ADB*?

(A) 30

(B) 45

(C) 60

(D) 90

(E) 120

(D) The triangles *ADB* and *CDB* are congruent since all corresponding sides are the same length (SSS). This follows since *BD* is a side in both triangles and we are told that *AB* = *BC* and *AD* = *CD*. So angle *ADB* and angle *CDB* must be equal. Since *ADC* is a straight line, the sum of the angles is 180 degrees. So angle *ADB* equals 90 degrees.

The following question is of AVERAGE difficulty.

Triangle *A* has sides with lengths 5, 12, and 13 and Triangle *B* has sides with lengths 8, 15, and 17. Which of the following statements are true?

  I. Triangles *A* and *B* are similar.

 II. Triangles *A* and *B* are congruent.

 III. Triangles *A* and *B* are right triangles.

(A) I only

(B) II only

(C) III only

(D) I and III only

(E) I, II, and III

(C) Since one of the choices involves right triangles and you are given the lengths of the sides, the first thing you should do is use the Pythagorean Theorem to see if any of the triangles are right triangles. Since $5^2 + 12^2 = 25 + 144 = 169 = 13^2$, triangle A is a right triangle. Since $8^2 + 15^2 = 64 + 225 = 289 = 17^2$ triangle B is a right triangle. So III is true. At this point, we can eliminate choices (A) and (B). If this is all you know you should guess one of the three remaining choices. The corresponding sides of congruent triangles must be the same length. Since none of the sides of triangle A have the same length as any side of triangle B, the triangles cannot be congruent, and II is false. So we can eliminate choice (E). The only possible choices are (C) and (D). The ratio of the lengths of corresponding sides of similar triangles must be the same. Since the ratio of the smallest sides, 5/8, is not equal to the ratio of the largest sides, 13/17, the triangles are not similar. So I is not true, which means that (C) is the correct answer.

The next question uses coordinate geometry and is ABOVE AVERAGE in difficulty.

EXAMPLE

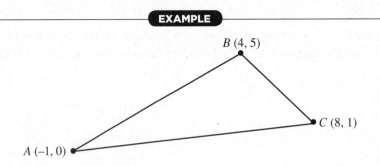

The coordinates of point A are $(-1, 0)$. The coordinates of point B are $(4, 5)$. The coordinates of point C are $(8, 1)$. The area of triangle ABC is

(A) $4\sqrt{2}$

(B) 9

(C) 16

(D) 20

(E) 45

(D) The area of a triangle is $\frac{1}{2}$ base times altitude, but you must use the coordinates to find the lengths of the sides of the triangle. The length of AC is $\sqrt{((8-(-1))^2 + (1-0)^2)}$ $= \sqrt{82}$. The length of AB is $\sqrt{((4-(-1))^2 + (5-0)^2)} = \sqrt{50}$. The length of BC is $\sqrt{((8-4)^2 + (1-5)^2)} = \sqrt{32}$. Since $82 = 50 + 32$, the Pythagorean Theorem tells us that ABC is a right triangle with AB perpendicular to BC. So we will use BC as the base and AB as the altitude. The area is $\frac{1}{2}\sqrt{50}\sqrt{32} = \frac{1}{2}(5\sqrt{2})(4\sqrt{2}) = \frac{1}{2}(5)(4)(2) = 20$.

This question requires you to use coordinates to find the lengths of the sides of the triangle as well as simplify square roots.

Several GMAT questions require you to use concepts from different branches of mathematics in order to solve the problem. For example, the next question requires understanding the solutions of 2 linear equations in 2 unknowns in a geometric sense. The solution to each linear equation represents all the points on a line. The solution to 2 linear equations in 2 unknowns represents the intersection of the 2 lines represented by the equations.

This question is ABOVE AVERAGE in difficulty.

EXAMPLE

The two lines $x + y = 2$ and $2x + 2y = 4$ intersect at

(A) there are no points where the lines intersect

(B) a single point

(C) two points

(D) all the points on one line

(E) all the points in a plane

(D) This question tests whether you understand the geometry of lines and how this relates to solving 2 equations in 2 unknowns. Since the two equations are multiples of each other because $2(x + y = 2)$ is $2x + 2y = 4$, they represent the same line. So their intersection is that same line.

You should now have an idea of how problem-solving problems are constructed and the different ways that a mathematical idea can be tested.

TACTICS

The list below provides general tactics for the quantitative test, followed by specific mathematical pitfalls to avoid.

1. Budget your time to be sure you finish the test.
2. Carefully read the question and be sure to answer the question that is asked.
3. Don't perform unnecessary calculations.
4. Look at the answer choices before you start to work on a problem.
5. Don't waste time on a problem you can't complete. Instead, use intelligent guessing and move on. Remember that you should finish the test.
6. Use your laminated note board to work out problems and copy and mark up diagrams.
7. You can use the edge of the note board as a ruler.
8. Check your work if you can.
9. If a problem involves units, keep track of the units. Make sure that your answer has the correct units.
10. Use numerical values to find or check answers that involve formulas and variables.
11. Translate the information you are given into numerical or algebraic equations to start working a problem.

Mathematical Pitfalls

1. Always remember that x or y can be negative, especially if you need to know whether x is "larger than" or "smaller than" something.

2. Always remember that there are both positive and negative solutions to $x^2 = a$ for any positive number a.

3. Always remember that $\sqrt{(a+b)}$ and $\sqrt{a} + \sqrt{b}$ are not the same.

4. In diagrams, angles that look like right angles are not right angles unless the problem states that they are right angles. The same is true for lines that look like parallel lines.

PROBLEM-SOLVING TIPS

When you work the practice exams, be sure to read through the analysis as you check the answer. Many times, the answer explains the strategy for solving the problem and/or gives methods to improve your score by intelligent guessing. By the time you finish the practice exercises, you should feel confident that you will be able to work the problem-solving questions on the GMAT exam.

Try these examples. Then check the answers and analysis.

1. If $x - y = 2$ then the value of $-4x + y$ is
   (A) −8
   (B) −2
   (C) 2
   (D) $x + y$
   (E) cannot be determined

2. The line chart below gives the earnings in thousands of dollars for each of the last 5 years for company A, company B, and company C.

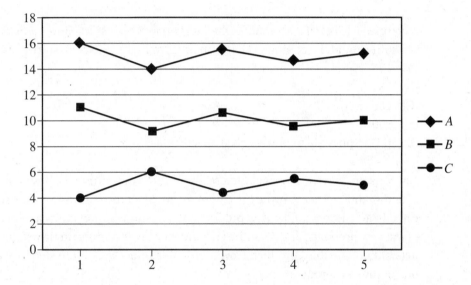

   Which of the following statements about the earnings of these companies for the last 5 years are true?

   I. The median earnings of company A are about the same as the median earnings of company B.
   II. The mean earnings of company A are about three times the mean earnings of company C.
   III. The standard deviation of the earnings of company A is about the same as the standard deviation of the earnings of company C.

   (A) none
   (B) II only
   (C) III only
   (D) II and III only
   (E) I, II, and III

3. If $x \le y \le 2$ and $0.4 \le s \le t \le 3$, then the largest possible value of $\dfrac{(x+y)}{(s+t)}$ is

(A) 2

(B) 3

(C) 4

(D) 5

(E) 6

4. If $x + y = 2$ and $-4x - 4y = -8$, then the value of x is

(A) −4

(B) 0

(C) 2

(D) 8

(E) cannot be determined

5. A company sells $100 - 0.5x$ shirts when it charges $\$x$ per shirt. How many dollars per shirt should the company charge in order to make $5,000 on shirt sales?

(A) 10

(B) 50

(C) 100

(D) 200

(E) It is impossible to make $5,000 on shirt sales.

6. 100 consumers were shown commercials for three new products: Brand X, Brand Y, and Brand Z. After viewing the commercials, 90 of the consumers were interested in at least one of the new products, 15 consumers were interested in all three of the new products, and 45 of the consumers were interested in two of the products but not the third product. How many consumers were interested in exactly one of the new products?

(A) 10

(B) 20

(C) 30

(D) 40

(E) 45

7. A right circular cone is inscribed in a hemisphere so that the base of the cone coincides with the base of the hemisphere. The ratio of the volume of the cone to the volume of the hemisphere is

Note: The volume of a hemisphere of radius $r = \dfrac{1}{2}\left(\dfrac{4}{3}\right)\pi r^3$ and the volume of a cone with radius r and height h is $\left(\dfrac{1}{3}\right)\pi r^2 h$.

(A) 1:3

(B) 1:2

(C) $1:\sqrt{2}$

(D) 1:1

(E) 2:1

8. What percent of the integers greater than or equal to 21 and less than 41 are prime numbers?

   (A) 4
   (B) 5
   (C) 15
   (D) 20
   (E) 25

9. If n is a prime integer, which of the following is NOT possible for the remainder when n^2 is divided by 10?

   (A) 1
   (B) 4
   (C) 5
   (D) 7
   (E) 9

10. The width of a rectangle is 10 meters, and the area of the rectangle is equal to the area of a square whose side is 4 meters. What is the length (in meters) of the rectangle?

    (A) 1
    (B) 1.4
    (C) 1.6
    (D) 2
    (E) 2.6

11. A house cost Ms. Jones C dollars in 2002. Three years later, she sold it for 25% more than she paid for it. She has to pay a tax of 50% of the gain. (The gain is the selling price minus the cost.) How much tax must Ms. Jones pay?

    (A) $\dfrac{1}{24}C$

    (B) $\dfrac{C}{8}$

    (C) $\dfrac{C}{4}$

    (D) $\dfrac{C}{2}$

    (E) $0.6C$

12. 8% of the bottles that a company has are green. 15% of the company's green bottles are sold in convenience stores. What percent of the company's bottles are green and sold in convenience stores?

    (A) 1.2
    (B) 6.4
    (C) 8
    (D) 12
    (E) 15

13. If n and p are both odd numbers, which of the following must be an even number?
  (A) $n + p$
  (B) np
  (C) $2n + p$
  (D) $n + p + 1$
  (E) $np + 2$

14. It costs g cents per mile for gasoline and m cents a mile for all other costs to drive a car. What is the cost in dollars to drive a car 1,000 miles? (1 dollar = 100 cents)
  (A) $\dfrac{(g+m)}{100}$
  (B) $g + m$
  (C) $10g + 10m$
  (D) $100g + 100m$
  (E) $1{,}000g + 1{,}000m$

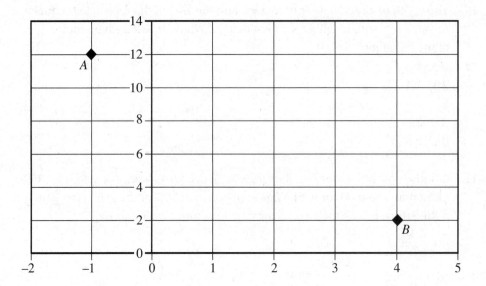

15. The coordinates of point A are $(-1, 12)$. The coordinates of point B are $(4, 2)$. Find the length of the line segment that connects A to B.
  (A) 5
  (B) $5\sqrt{2}$
  (C) 10
  (D) $5\sqrt{5}$
  (E) $10\sqrt{3}$

16. If x and y are real numbers, let $S(x, y) = x^2 - y^2$. Then $S(3, S(3, 4)) =$
    (A) −40
    (B) −7
    (C) 40
    (D) 49
    (E) 56

17. What is the area of figure *ABEDC*? *ABDC* is a rectangle and *BDE* is an isosceles right triangle.

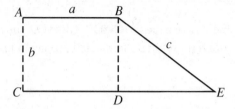

    (A) ab
    (B) ab^2
    (C) $b(a + \dfrac{b}{2})$
    (D) cab
    (E) $\left(\dfrac{1}{2}\right)bc$

18. In 2007, a house sold for $200,000. Three years later, the house sold for $136,000. The selling price of the house decreased by what percent in the three years?
    (A) 32
    (B) 47
    (C) 64
    (D) 68
    (E) 136

19. If $x + y = 6$ and $3x - y = 4$, then $x - y$ is equal to
    (A) −5
    (B) −1
    (C) 2.5
    (D) 4
    (E) 6

Use the following table for question 20.

Taxable Income (in dollars)	Tax (in dollars)
0–20,000	1% of taxable income
20,000–40,000	200 + 2% of taxable income over 20,000
40,000–60,000	600 + 3% of taxable income over 40,000
60,000–80,000	1,200 + 4% of taxable income over 60,000
80,000–100,000	2,000 + 5% of taxable income over 80,000
More than 100,000	3,000 + 6% of taxable income over 100,000

20. Your taxable income last year was $105,000. This year your taxable income is $125,000. How much more (in dollars) will you pay in taxes this year than last year?
   (A) 200
   (B) 400
   (C) 1,200
   (D) 1,800
   (E) 3,300

21. If $x + y > 5$ and $x - y > 3$, which of the following gives all possible values of x and only the possible values of x?
   (A) $x > 3$
   (B) $x > 4$
   (C) $x > 5$
   (D) $x < 5$
   (E) $x < 3$

22. If $x^2 + 2x - 8 = 0$, then x is either –4 or
   (A) – 2
   (B) –1
   (C) 0
   (D) 2
   (E) 8

23. If the average of the 6 numbers {2, 2, 7, 9, 10, x} is 4.5, what is the value of x?
   (A) –3
   (B) –1
   (C) 0
   (D) 3
   (E) 27

24. A sack of corn weighs 12 pounds, and a sack of wheat weighs 16 pounds. A store has an inventory of sacks of corn and sacks of wheat. 25% of the sacks are corn and the rest are wheat. What is the average weight (in pounds) of all the sacks in the store's inventory?

    (A) 12
    (B) 13
    (C) 14
    (D) 15
    (E) 16

25. If $x = \dfrac{5}{4} + \dfrac{4}{5}$, then

    (A) $x \le 1.5$
    (B) $1.5 < x \le 1.75$
    (C) $1.75 < x \le 2$
    (D) $2 < x \le 2.25$
    (E) $x > 2.25$

ANSWERS and ANALYSIS

The boldface letter following each number is the correct answer. The numbers in parentheses at the end of each analysis refer to the sections of the Math chapter that explain the necessary math principles.

1. **(E)** If $x - y = 2$, then $y = x - 2$. So $-4x + y = -4x + x - 2 = -3x - 2$, but this is not a value since $3x - 2$ will vary as x varies. For example, $x = 1$ and $y = -1$ as well as $x = 2$ and $y = 0$ are both solutions to $x - y = 2$. In the first case, $-4x + y = -5$ and $-4x + y = -8$ in the second case. In this problem, since $x - y$ is not a multiple of $-4x + y$, you need another equation to solve the problem. (II-2)

2. **(D)** This question asks you to compare basic statistics for the three companies. You could spend a lot of time reading the values of the earnings for each company for each year from the graph, calculating the mean, median, and standard deviation for each company, and finally comparing the statistics. However, the quick and easy way to attack this problem is to use a geometric understanding of these statistics. The median is the middle value of the set of earnings. So the median of A is about 15 (the median of A must be between 14 and 16). The median of B is about 10 (the median of B must be between 9 and 11). So I is false. The mean earnings of A should be about 15 and the mean earnings of C should be about 5, so II is true. The standard deviation is the spread around the mean. Since the deviations of A are roughly $+1, -1, +0.5, -0.5$, and 0 and the deviations of C are about $-1, +1, -0.5, +0.5$, and 0, both A and C have about the same standard deviation. So III is true. (Note: Don't waste time actually calculating the standard deviation. Since all the deviations are the same, you know the standard deviation will be the same.) So only II and III are true. (I-7)

3. **(D)** In order to make the quotient as large as possible, make the numerator as large as possible and the denominator as small as possible. So make x and y both 2 and s and t both 0.4. This will give $\frac{(x+y)}{(s+t)} = \frac{(2+2)}{(0.4+0.4)} = \frac{4}{.8} = 5$. (II-7)

4. **(E)** Since one equation is a multiple of the other, we can only say that $x = 2 - y$. So if $x = 2$ and $y = 0$, both equations are satisfied. If $x = 0$ and $y = 2$, both equations are satisfied. So although it appears that you have 2 equations in 2 unknowns, you actually have the same equation twice and therefore don't have enough information to solve for x. (II-2)

5. **(C)** The amount of money the company makes on shirt sales is (the number of shirts sold)(price per shirt), which is $(100 - 0.5x)\, x = -0.5x^2 + 100x$. So you need to solve the equation $-0.5x^2 + 100x = 5{,}000$. Subtract 5,000 from each side of the equation to obtain $-0.5x^2 + 100x - 5{,}000 = 0$. Divide each side of the equation by -0.5 to obtain $x^2 - 200x + 10{,}000 = 0$. Since $x^2 - 200x + 10{,}000 = (x - 100)^2$, the correct answer is $x = 100$.

   If you are able to find that $-0.5x^2 + 100x$ is the amount of money made on shirt sales, then you can check each answer to find the correct answer. If $x = 10$, then $-0.5x^2 + 100x$ is 950. If $x = 50$, then $-0.5x^2 + 100x$ is 3,750. If $x = 100$, then $-0.5x^2 + 100x$ is 5,000.

   If $x = 200$, then $-0.5x^2 + 100x$ is 0. So the correct answer is (C). (II-1, II-3)

6. **(C)** The number of consumers interested in at least one product = the number interested in exactly one of the new products + the number interested in exactly two of the new products + the number interested in exactly three of the new products. By using the information given, we have 90 = the number interested in exactly one product + 45 + 15. Solving this equation for the number of consumers interested in exactly one of the new products is $90 - 15 - 45 = 30$. (II-4)

7. **(B)** Look at the diagram below. You should sketch a similar diagram to help you solve the problem.

   The volume of a hemisphere of radius r is $\frac{1}{2}\left(\frac{4}{3}\right)\pi r^3$ and the volume of a cone with radius r and height h is $\left(\frac{1}{3}\right)\pi r^2 h$. Since the base of the cone and the base of the hemisphere coincide, they both have the same radius. Since the cone is inscribed in the hemisphere, the height of the cone and the radius of the hemisphere are the same. So if r is the radius of the hemisphere, the volume of the cone is $\left(\frac{1}{3}\right)\pi r^2 r$ or $\left(\frac{1}{3}\right)\pi r^3$. Therefore, the ratio is $\left[\dfrac{\left(\frac{1}{3}\right)\pi r^3}{\left(\frac{2}{3}\right)\pi r^3}\right] = \frac{1}{2}$ or 1:2. (III-8)

8. **(D)** To decide whether an integer is prime, divide it by all the primes less than the integer's square root. If none of these primes divide the integer, then the integer is a prime. For numbers less than 41 since $7^2 = 49$, you need to divide only by 2, 3, and 5. All the even numbers are not primes since they are divisible by 2, so this leaves 21, 23, 25, 27, 29, 31, 33, 35, 37, and 39 as possible primes (Note: 41 is not less than 41). Since 21, 27, 33, and 39 are divisible by 3, they are not prime. Only 23, 25, 29, 31, 35, and 37 are left as possible primes. 25 and 35 are divisible by 5, so the only primes between 21 and 40 are 23, 29, 31, and 37. There are 20 integers that are greater than or equal to 21 and less than 41, so 4 of these 20 integers are prime. The question asks for the percentage of prime numbers, which is $\frac{4}{20} = 0.20 = 20\%$. (I-1)

9. **(D)** The easiest way to solve this problem is simply to take some prime numbers, square them, and divide by 10. Since 2 is a prime and $2^2 = 4$, choice (B) is incorrect. Likewise since 3, 5, and 11 are primes and $3^2 = 9$, $5^2 = 25$, and $11^2 = 121$, choices (A), (C), and (E) are incorrect. So the only choice left is (D).

    You can show this is true algebraically by looking at the primes larger than 2 as numbers of the form $10k + 1$ or $10k + 3$ or $10k + 5$ or $10k + 7$ or $10k + 9$. (No primes other than 2 are even, so no primes can be written as $10k + 2$ or $10k + 4$, and so on.) If we expand $(10k + 1)^2$ as $100k^2 + 20k + 1$ and divide by 10, we see that the remainder is 1. In the same way, primes of the form $10k + 3$ will have a remainder of 9 when squared and divided by 10. Primes of the form $10k + 5$ will have a remainder of 5 when squared and divided by 10. Primes of the form $10k + 7$ will have a remainder of 9 when squared and divided by 10. Primes of the form $10k + 9$ will have a remainder of 1 when squared and divided by 10. So (D) is the correct choice. (I-1)

10. **(C)** The area of the square is $4^2 = 16$. Since the area of the rectangle is length times width, you need to solve the equation $10 \times$ width = 16. Divide each side of the equation by 10 to get width = 1.6. (II-2, III-7)

11. **(B)** Ms. Jones sold the house for 125% of C or $\left(\frac{5}{4}\right)C$. Thus the gain is $\left(\frac{5}{4}\right)C - C = \left(\frac{1}{4}\right)C$. She must pay a tax of 50% of $\left(\frac{1}{4}\right)C$ or $\frac{1}{2}$ of $\left(\frac{1}{4}\right)C$. Therefore, the tax is $\left(\frac{1}{8}\right)C$. Notice that the three years has nothing to do with the problem. Sometimes a question may contain unnecessary information. (I-2, I-4)

12. **(A)** 15% of the green bottles were sold in convenience stores. Since 8% of the company's bottles are green, 15% of 8% of the bottles are green and sold in convenience stores. Since $(0.15)(0.08) = 0.0120$, which is 1.2%, the correct answer is (A). (I-4)

13. **(A)** Since n and p are odd, you can think of n as $2k + 1$ and p as $2j + 1$. Then $n + p = 2k + 2j + 2 = 2(k + j + 1)$, which is an even number, so (A) is correct. If we use the same method, we see that $np = (2k + 1)(2j + 1) = 4kj + 2k + 2j + 1 = 2(2kj + k + j) + 1$, which is odd not even. So (B) is not correct. In the same way you can see that (C), (D), and (E) are not correct.

You could also solve this problem or eliminate some choices by simply choosing 2 odd numbers for n and p. For example, if $n = 3$ and $p = 5$, then $n + p = 3 + 5 = 8$, which is even, so (A) is possible. (This does not show that (A) is correct since n and p could be other odd numbers.) $3 \times 5 = np = 15$, which is odd. So (B) is not correct. $2(3) + 5 = 2n + p = 11$, which is odd. So (C) is not correct. $3 + 5 + 1 = n + p + 1 = 9$, which is odd. So (D) is not correct. $3 \times 5 + 2 = np + 2 = 17$ is odd. So (E) is not correct. So (A) is the correct choice. (I-1)

14. **(C)** It costs $g + m$ cents to drive the car 1 mile, so it costs $1,000(g + m)$ cents to drive the car 1,000 miles. However, the question asks for the cost in dollars. So you must divide $1,000 (g + m)$ cents by 100, which is $10 (g + m) = 10g + 10m$ dollars. So (C) is the correct answer. (II-1)

15. **(D)** The length of the line segment is $\sqrt{((-1-4)^2 + (12-2)^2)} = \sqrt{(25+100)} = \sqrt{125}$. Since this is not one of the given answers you need to simplify $\sqrt{125}$, which is $\sqrt{(25 \times 5)} = \sqrt{25}\sqrt{5} = 5\sqrt{5}$. (I-8, III-9)

16. **(A)** Use the definition to calculate $S(3, 4) = 3^2 - 4^2 = 9 - 16 = -7$. So $S(3, S(3, 4))$ is $S(3, -7)$, which is $3^2 - (-7)^2 = 9 - 49 = -40$. (II-1, III-10)

17. **(C)** The area of a rectangle is length times width. So the area of rectangle $ABDC$ is ab. The area of a triangle is $\frac{1}{2}$ base times altitude. Since triangle BDE is an isosceles right triangle, the base and the altitude are both b. So the area of triangle BDE is $\left(\frac{1}{2} \right)b^2$. Thus the area of the figure is $ab + \left(\frac{1}{2} \right)b^2$, which is equal to $b(a + \frac{b}{2})$. You must know how to simplify algebraic expressions in order to express the answer as one of the given choices. (II-1, III-7)

18. **(A)** In three years, the selling price of the house decreased by $200,000 - $136,000 = $64,000. Since the original selling price was $200,000, the percentage of decrease is $\frac{64,000}{200,000} \times 100 = 0.32 \times 100 = 32\%$. (I-4)

19. **(B)** Add the two equations to obtain $4x = 10$. So $x = 2.5$. Since $x + y = 2.5 + y = 6$, y must be 3.5. So $x - y = 2.5 - 3.5 = -1$. (II-2)

20. **(C)** When your taxable income was $105,000, you paid $3,000 + $0.06(105,000 - 100,000) = $3,000 + $0.06(5,000) = $3,000 + $300 = $3,300. If your taxable income is $125,000, then the tax you will pay is $3,000 + $0.06 (125,000 - 100,000) = $3,000 + $1,500 = $4,500. So you will pay $4,500 - $3,300 = $1,200 more in taxes this year. A faster method is to notice that since both taxable incomes were over $100,000, the $20,000 increase in your taxable income will be taxed at 6%. So your tax will increase by 0.06 ($20,000) = $1,200. (I-4, IV-1)

21. **(B)** Since both inequalities have the same sign, you can add the two inequalities and obtain $2x > 8$, which is equivalent to $x > 4$.

Another method is to graph the two lines $x + y = 5$ and $x - y = 3$. These lines meet at $x = 4$ and $y = 1$. Since the solutions to both inequalities are the region to the right of this point, $x > 4$ is the correct choice. (II-7)

22. **(D)** You can factor $x^2 + 2x - 8$ into $(x - 2)$ $(x + 4)$. So if x is either 2 or -4, then $x^2 + 2x - 8 = 0$ and (D) is the correct choice. If you have time, you can substitute each choice into the expression $x^2 + 2x - 8$ and eliminate choices. For example, if $x = -2$, then $x^2 + 2x - 8 = (-2)^2 + 2(-2) - 8 = 4 - 4 - 8 = -8$, so (A) is not correct, etc. (II-1, II-2)

23. **(A)** If the average of the 6 numbers is 4.5, then the sum of the numbers is $6 \times 4.5 = 27$. So $2 + 2 + 7 + 9 + 10 + x = 30 + x = 27$. Solve for x to obtain $x = -3$. (I-7)

24. **(D)** Let x be the number of sacks of corn and y be the number of sacks of wheat. Since 75% of the sacks are wheat and 25% of the sacks are corn, we know $y = 3x$. We need to find the total weight of all the sacks and divide by $x + y$ to find the average weight of all the sacks. The total weight (in pounds) of the corn is $12x$ and the total weight (in pounds) of the wheat is $16y$. So the total weight is $12x + 16y$. Thus, the average weight is $\frac{(12x + 16y)}{(x + y)}$. Since $y = 3x$, the average weight is

$$\frac{(12x + 16(3x))}{(x + 3x)} = \frac{60x}{4x} = 15 \text{ pounds. So (D) is the correct choice. (I-7)}$$

25. **(D)** Since $\frac{5}{4} = \frac{25}{20}$ and $\frac{4}{5} = \frac{16}{20}$, we have $\frac{5}{4} + \frac{4}{5} = \frac{(25 + 16)}{20} = \frac{41}{20} = 2$ and $\frac{1}{20}$, which is 2.05. So the correct choice is (D). (I-2, I-3, II-7)

Data Sufficiency

11

→ **STRATEGY**
→ **USING EXAMPLES**
→ **INTELLIGENT GUESSING**
→ **LOGICAL REASONING**

In this section we investigate data sufficiency questions. The quantitative section of the GMAT is composed of a mix of data sufficiency and problem-solving questions. In a data sufficiency question, you will be asked a question and then given two additional statements. You must decide whether the additional statements give enough information in order to answer the given question.

According to the GMAT, the data sufficiency questions in the Quantitative Section are designed to measure your ability to

1. Analyze a quantitative problem
2. Recognize which information is relevant
3. Determine at what point there is sufficient information to solve a problem

Since these questions are not testing the same skills as problem-solving questions, they require you to use a different strategy.

The first and most important part of this strategy is to read and understand the directions for these problems. Unlike the directions for problem-solving questions, the directions for data sufficiency questions are complex. You need to read the directions over carefully and understand them before you can answer these types of questions. The directions follow.

DIRECTIONS: Each of the following problems has a question and two statements that are labeled (1) and (2). Use the data given in (1) and (2) together with other available information (such as the number of hours in a day, the definition of *clockwise*, mathematical facts, etc.) to decide whether the statements are *sufficient* to answer the question. Then fill in space

(A) If you can get the answer from **(1) ALONE** but not from **(2)** alone

(B) If you can get the answer from **(2) ALONE** but not from **(1)** alone

(C) If you can get the answer from **BOTH (1)** and **(2) TOGETHER** but not from (1) alone or (2) alone

(D) If **EITHER** statement **(1) ALONE OR** statement **(2) ALONE** suffices

(E) If you **CANNOT** get the answer from statements (1) and (2) **TOGETHER** but need even more data

All numbers used in this section are real numbers.

A figure given for a problem is intended to provide information consistent with that in the question, but not necessarily with the additional information contained in the statements.

All figures lie in the plane unless you are told otherwise.

Figures are drawn as accurately as possible; straight lines may not appear straight on the screen.

Here is an EASY data sufficiency problem.

EXAMPLE

Is x greater than zero?

(1) $x^4 - 16 = 0$

(2) $x^3 - 8 = 0$

(B) STATEMENT (1) alone is not sufficient since $x^4 - 16 = 0$ has two solutions. The first solution, $x = 2$, is greater than 0. The second, $x = -2$, is less than 0. STATEMENT (2) alone is sufficient since the only solution to the equation $x^3 = 8$ is 2.

STRATEGY

The previous example is easier than most of the data sufficiency questions on the GMAT. The best way to attack data sufficiency problems is with a strategy. Learning and applying this strategy to data sufficiency problems is the best way to solve these problems. The strategy depends on answering three straightforward questions in order. If you answer all three questions, you will always arrive at the correct answer. In addition, if you can answer one or two of the questions, you will be able to eliminate at least one answer and guess intelligently.

Ask yourself these three questions:

I. Is STATEMENT (1) alone sufficient to answer the question?

II. Is STATEMENT (2) alone sufficient to answer the question?

III. Are STATEMENTS (1) and (2) together sufficient to answer the question?

Try to answer questions I, II, and III in order. In many cases, you will not have to answer all three questions to arrive at the correct answer.

If the answer to I is YES and the answer to II is NO, then the correct choice is (A).

If the answer to I is YES and the answer to II is YES, then the correct choice is (D).

If the answer to I is NO and the answer to II is YES, then the correct choice is (B).

If the answer to I is NO, the answer to II is NO, and the answer to III is YES, then the correct choice is (C).

If the answer to I is NO, the answer to II is NO, and the answer to III is NO, then the correct choice is (E).

The chart below illustrates the strategy. To use the chart, simply start at the top. By answering YES or NO, move down the chart until you arrive at the correct choice.

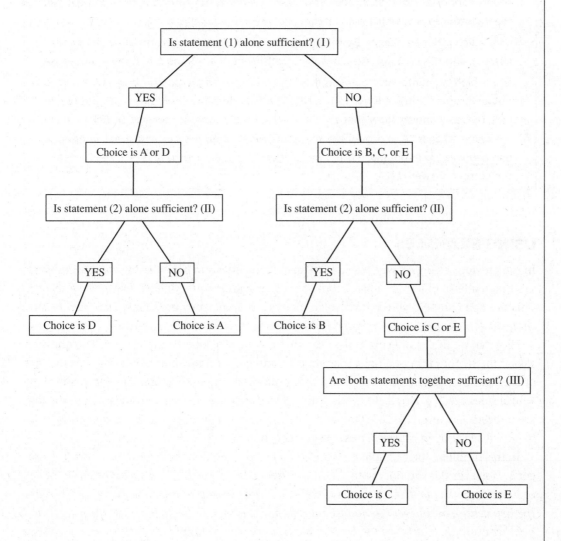

Working a Problem Using the Strategy

The following question is an example of an EASY data sufficiency question.

EXAMPLE

Is the hypotenuse of a right triangle an integer? The legs of the right triangle are *a* and *b*.

(1) *a* is a positive integer.

(2) *b* is a positive integer.

(E) The Pythagorean Theorem tells you that the hypotenuse is the square root of $a^2 + b^2$. So the question asks if you have sufficient data to conclude whether or not the square root of $a^2 + b^2$ is an integer. STATEMENT (1) alone is not sufficient. If $a = 3$ and $b = 4$, the hypotenuse is 5, which is an integer. However, if $a = 3$ and $b = 2$, the hypotenuse is $\sqrt{13}$, which is not an integer. So the answer to I is NO, and the only possible choices are (B), (C), and (E). STATEMENT (2) alone is not sufficient. If $a = 3$ and $b = 4$, the hypotenuse is 5, which is an integer. However, if $a = 3$ and $b = 2$, the hypotenuse is $\sqrt{13}$, which is not an integer. So the answer to II is NO. The only possible choices are (C) and (E). In fact, these examples show that STATEMENTS (1) and (2) together are not sufficient since we found integers *a* and *b* where the hypotenuse is an integer and other integers *a* and *b* where the hypotenuse is not an integer. So the answer to III is NO, which means the correct answer is (E).

USING EXAMPLES

In the previous example, we were able to answer the question by assigning some simple values that made STATEMENT (1) and/or STATEMENT (2) true and then trying to answer the question. This method can help you quickly solve many data sufficiency problems. *However, be sure that you don't jump to an incorrect conclusion when you are using examples.*

How can we find simple examples? Let's look at the previous example again. The question asks if the hypotenuse of a right triangle is an integer, and the statements say that the legs of the right triangle are integers. The most common example of a right triangle is a triangle whose sides are 3, 4, and 5. So it is possible that the hypotenuse is an integer when the legs are integers. However, if one leg is 3 and the other leg is an integer that is not 4, such as 2, the hypotenuse is not an integer. Thus, the correct choice is (E).

In this problem, the example $a = 3$ and $b = 4$ let you find that the hypotenuse was the integer 5. However this did not mean that the correct choice was (C). *The fact that some choices of* a *and* b *make the hypotenuse an integer does not mean that all choices of* a *and* b *make the hypotenuse an integer. We found one example that made the hypotenuse an integer and another example that made the hypotenuse a noninteger. This means that the correct choice is (E).*

INTELLIGENT GUESSING

Remember that you only have a limited amount of time for each section of the test and your score will be lower if you do not complete the section. So if you are not able to figure out the answer to a question in the time you have budgeted for it, you need to make an intelligent guess and move on to the next question.

The strategy enables you to eliminate some choices if you can answer any of these three questions:

    I. Is STATEMENT (1) alone sufficient?

    II. Is STATEMENT (2) alone sufficient?

    III. Are STATEMENTS (1) and (2) together sufficient?

Even if you cannot answer all three questions and complete the strategy, you can eliminate some choices and make an intelligent guess. The following cases illustrate how to use the three questions to make an intelligent guess even if you can answer only one of the three questions. (You can also visualize these ideas as moving down the chart that illustrates the strategy by answering each of the questions.)

If you can answer I and the answer to I is YES and if you cannot answer II and III, then only (A) and (D) are possible. So guess one of those two choices.

If you can answer I and the answer to I is NO and if you cannot answer II and III, then only (B), (C), and (E) are possible. So guess one of those three choices.

If you can answer II and the answer to II is YES and if you cannot answer I and III, then only (B) and (D) are possible. So guess one of those two choices.

If you can answer II and the answer to II is NO and if you cannot answer I and III, then only (A), (C), and (E) are possible. So guess one of those three choices.

If you can answer III and the answer to III is YES and if you cannot answer I or II, then only (A), (B), (C), or (D) are possible. So guess one of these four choices.

If you can answer III and the answer to III is NO, then the answer is (E).

If you can answer I and II and the answer to both of these questions is NO, but you can't answer III, then the only possibilities are (C) or (E). So guess one of these two choices.

> ### YOU CAN SOLVE THE PROBLEM IF THE ANSWER IS NO
>
> Do not confuse answering the question with showing that the answer to the question must be YES. If the information given means that you can show that the statement is false, then you have enough information to answer the question.

Here is an example that is ABOVE AVERAGE in difficulty.

EXAMPLE

If a and b are the legs of a right triangle, is the hypotenuse of the right triangle an integer?

(1) $a = 2$

(2) b is a positive integer

(C) The hypotenuse of the triangle is $\sqrt{(a^2 + b^2)}$. STATEMENT (1) alone is not sufficient. If $b = \sqrt{5}$, the hypotenuse is $\sqrt{(4 + 5)} = 3$, which is an integer. If $b = 2$, the hypotenuse is $\sqrt{(4 + 4)} = \sqrt{8}$, which is not an integer. STATEMENT (2) alone is not sufficient. If $b = 4$ and $a = 3$, the hypotenuse is an integer. If $b = 4$ and $a = 1$, then the hypotenuse is not an integer. STATEMENTS (1) and (2) together are sufficient to answer the question since the hypotenuse is $\sqrt{(b^2 + 4)}$, which is never an integer. If $b = 1$ or $b = 2$, the hypotenuse is not an integer since $\sqrt{5}$ and $\sqrt{8}$ are not integers. For any positive integer $b \geq 3$, we know $b^2 < b^2 + 4 < b^2 + 2b + 1 = (b + 1)^2$, which means that the square root of $b^2 + 4$ is greater than the integer b and less than the integer $b + 1$. So the hypotenuse can never be an integer. So the answer to the question "Is the hypotenuse an integer?" is NO. Thus STATEMENTS (1) and (2) together are sufficient to answer the question.

The previous two examples can be categorized as YES/NO questions. In these types of questions, you are not calculating a numerical value. You only have to decide whether or not you can answer YES or answer NO. Remember that if the answer is NO, you can answer the question just as in the previous example.

The mathematical knowledge required for data sufficiency questions is the same as for problem-solving questions. Both types of questions require knowledge of

1. Arithmetic
2. Elementary algebra
3. Commonly known concepts of geometry

The previous two examples involved concepts from geometry (the Pythagorean Theorem) and arithmetic (integers and square roots.) The next three examples involve algebra.

The next problem is an example of a data sufficiency problem where you are asked to calculate a numerical value. These types of problems are not the same as YES/NO problems, but we will use the same strategy as we did before. The strategy works for any data sufficiency problem.

The following question is BELOW AVERAGE in difficulty.

EXAMPLE

What is the value of $2x + y$?

(1) $x + y = 2$

(2) $2x - y = 2$

(C) This is a straightforward question. In general you need two linear equations in two unknowns to find the unknowns. STATEMENT (1) alone is not sufficient since $x = 1$, $y = 1$ and $x = 2$, $y = 0$ are both solutions to STATEMENT (1) but give different values for $2x + y$. In the same way STATEMENT (2) alone is not sufficient since $x = 2$, $y = 2$ and $x = 1$, $y = 0$ are both solutions to STATEMENT (2) but give different values for $2x + y$. So (C) and (E) are the only possible answers. By using STATEMENTS (1) and (2) together, you can solve for x and y and then calculate $2x + y$. So (C) is the correct choice. **If you actually calculate x and y and then calculate $2x + y$, you are just wasting time that you could use to work on other problems.**

NEVER WASTE TIME CALCULATING THE EXACT ANSWER TO DATA SUFFICIENCY QUESTIONS. ONCE YOU KNOW YOU CAN FIND THE ANSWER, YOU CAN PICK THE CORRECT CHOICE.

The next 2 questions depend on the same topic of solving 2 linear equations in 2 unknowns but require a deeper understanding of the topic in order to make the correct choice.

The next question is ABOVE AVERAGE in difficulty.

EXAMPLE

What is the value of $2x + y$?

(1) $x + y = 2$

(2) $4x + 2y = 6$

(B) This is more difficult than the previous question although they both appear to be the same type of question. STATEMENT (1) alone is not sufficient since $x = 1$, $y = 1$ and $x = 2$, $y = 0$ are both solutions to STATEMENT (1) but give different values for $2x + y$. However, STATEMENT (2) alone is sufficient since $4x + 2y = 2(2x + y)$. So $2x + y = \frac{1}{2}(6) = 3$. Thus (B) is the correct choice. A common mistake is to decide you need both STATEMENTS (1) and (2) in order to find x and y. However, you are asked about $2x + y$. You can find the value of $2x + y$ using only one equation since $2x + y$ is a multiple of $4x + 2y$.

The following question is ABOVE AVERAGE in difficulty.

EXAMPLE

What is the value of x?

(1) $x - 2y = 3$

(2) $-2x + 4y = -6$

(E) Since STATEMENT (1) and STATEMENT (2) are multiples of each other ($-2x + 4y = -2(x - 2y)$), they will have exactly the same solutions. So $x = 1$, $y = -1$ and $x = 3$, $y = 0$ are both solutions to STATEMENTS (1) and (2). Therefore STATEMENTS (1) and (2) together are not sufficient to determine the value of x. Notice that if you did not analyze this problem carefully, you might choose (C) since it looks like there are 2 different equations. You could jump to the conclusion that using both these equations will let you find x.

The next example involves geometry and is ABOVE AVERAGE in difficulty.

EXAMPLE

Are two triangles congruent?

(1) Both triangles are right triangles.

(2) Both triangles have the same perimeter.

(E) STATEMENT (1) is not sufficient since lots of right triangles are not congruent. For example, a triangle with sides 3, 4, and 5 is a right triangle and a triangle with sides 5, 12, and 13 is a right triangle. Since all of the corresponding sides are not the same length, the triangles are not congruent. (If you take any two triangles with sides 3, 4, and 5, they are congruent right triangles.) So even if you cannot go any further, you know that the only possible answers are (B), (C), or (E).

STATEMENT (2) alone is not sufficient since a right triangle with sides 3, 4, and 5, and an equilateral triangle with sides 4, 4, and 4 have the same perimeter but are not congruent. So you can eliminate (B). The only possibilities are (C) or (E).

You need to decide if two right triangles with the same perimeter must be congruent in order to complete the problem. You can think of the perimeter as a piece of string that will be the outside of the triangle. You form a triangle by placing the string over 3 pegs that are the vertices of the triangle. You can form different (noncongruent) right triangles with the same length of string by moving the pegs, so there are right triangles with the same perimeter that are not congruent. Therefore STATEMENTS (1) and (2) together are not sufficient and the correct choice is (E). The idea of stretching or shrinking the sides of a triangle helped you to investigate geometric properties of these triangles. This concept can help you visualize problems and their solutions.

NOTE: Thinking of the perimeter as a piece of string makes it easier to see that two different right triangles can have the same perimeter. You could work this as an algebra problem as is done in the following paragraph. However, doing so will take more time. You could use that time to work on other problems.

Here is an algebraic solution that uses the 3, 4, 5 right triangle, which has a perimeter of 12. Any other right triangle with a perimeter of 12 will have sides a, b, and $(12 - a - b)$ that satisfy $(12 - a - b)^2 = a^2 + b^2$. Let $a = 2$ so that the triangle is not congruent to the 3, 4, 5 right triangle. Then $(12 - a - b)^2 = (10 - b)^2$, which must equal $2^2 + b^2$. So $100 - 20b + b^2 = 4 + b^2$, which means $20b = 96$ or $b = 4.8$. So the right triangle with sides 2, 4.8, 5.2 has a perimeter of 12 but is not congruent to the 3, 4, 5 right triangle. Finding this example took much longer to work out than thinking geometrically.

LOGICAL REASONING

A problem may simply test your reasoning ability. In all data sufficiency problems, **DO NOT MAKE EXTRA ASSUMPTIONS**. This is particularly important in problems that involve reasoning.

The following problem is AVERAGE in difficulty.

────── **EXAMPLE** ──────

Plane X flies at r miles per hour from A to B. Plane Y flies at s miles per hour from B to A. Both planes take off at the same time. Which plane flies at a faster rate? C is between A and B.

(1) C is closer to A than it is to B.

(2) Plane X flies over C before plane Y flies over C.

(E) STATEMENT (1) alone is obviously not sufficient. STATEMENT (2) alone is also insufficient. So the only possible choices are (C) or (E). If STATEMENTS (1) and (2) are both true, C is closer to A. Additionally, if plane X is flying faster than plane Y, plane X will certainly fly over C before plane Y. However, if plane X flies slower than plane Y and C is very close to A, plane X will still fly over C before plane Y does. Thus, STATEMENTS (1) and (2) together are not sufficient.

The following problem is BELOW AVERAGE in difficulty.

────── **EXAMPLE** ──────

How many bacteria are in a test tube now?

(1) There were 100 bacteria in the test tube 1 week ago.

(2) The number of bacteria in the test tube doubles every 12 hours.

(C) STATEMENT (1) alone is not sufficient since you are not given any information that describes whether or not the number of bacteria changes. STATEMENT (2) alone is not sufficient since you need to know how many bacteria there are at some starting time to use the doubling property. STATEMENTS (1) and (2) together give enough information to find the answer since you have a starting value and a method to calculate all future values. You should not waste time actually calculating the answer.

PRACTICE EXERCISES

Now work out the following examples. Then check your answers and make sure you understand the analysis of each question.

1. Find the value of the expression $x^3 y - \left(\dfrac{x^3}{y} \right)$.

   (1) $x = 2$
   (2) $y = 1$

2. If x is a two-digit number (so $x = ba$ with b and a digits), what is the last digit a of x?

   (1) The number $3x$ is a three-digit number whose last digit is a.
   (2) The digit a is less than 7.

3. Is the number $\dfrac{N}{3}$ an odd integer? (You may assume that $\dfrac{N}{3}$ is an integer.)

   (1) $N = 3K$ where K is an integer.
   (2) $N = 6J + 3$ where J is an integer.

4. How many families in Jaytown own exactly two phones?

   (1) 150 families in Jaytown own at least one telephone.
   (2) 45 families in Jaytown own at least three telephones.

5. Is the line PQ parallel to the line SR?

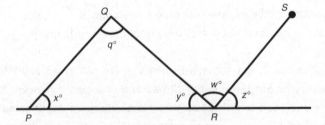

   (1) $w = q$
   (2) $y = z$

6. What is the value of $x^3 - y^3$?

   (1) $x^6 - y^6 = 0$
   (2) $y = 0$

7. How much does John weigh? Tim weighs 200 pounds.

   (1) Tim's weight plus Moe's weight is equal to John's weight.
   (2) John's weight plus Moe's weight is equal to twice Tim's weight.

8. Which triangle, ADE or AEC, has the larger area? $ABCD$ is a rectangle.

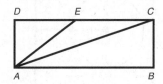

   (1) DE is longer than EC.
   (2) AC is longer than AE.

9. $ABCDEFGH$ is a cube. What is the length of the line segment AG?

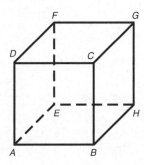

   (1) The length of the line segment AB is 4 inches.
   (2) The area of the square $BCGH$ is 16 square inches.

10. Is the integer K an odd integer?

    (1) $K = 3M$ where M is an integer.
    (2) $K = 6J$ where J is an integer.

11. What was the value of the sales of the ABC Company in 2000?

    (1) The sales of the ABC Company increased by $100,000 each year from 1990 to 2000.
    (2) The value of the sales of the ABC Company doubled between 1990 and 2000.

12. Is x greater than 2? (You may assume y is not equal to zero.)

    (1) $\left(\dfrac{x}{y}\right)$ is greater than 2.

    (2) $\left(\dfrac{1}{y}\right)$ is less than 1.

13. How many gallons of a chemical can be stored in a cylindrical tank if the radius of the tank is 15 feet? One gallon is equal to 231 cubic inches.

    (1) The height of the tank is 20 feet.
    (2) The temperature is 60 degrees Fahrenheit.

14. Is the area of the circle with center O larger than the area of the region outside the circle and inside the square $ABCD$? The straight line OEF is parallel to AB.

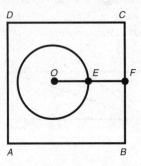

    (1) $OE < \left(\dfrac{1}{4}\right) AB$

    (2) $EF < \left(\dfrac{1}{4}\right) AB$

15. If $x^6 - y^6 = 0$, what is the value of $x^3 - y^3$?

    (1) x is positive.
    (2) y is greater than 1.

16. A jar is filled with 60 marbles. All the marbles in the jar are either red or green. What is the smallest number of marbles that must be drawn from the jar in order to be certain that a red marble is drawn?

    (1) The ratio of red marbles to green marbles is 2:1.
    (2) There are 20 green marbles in the jar.

17. Is k an odd integer?

    (1) k is divisible by 3.
    (2) The square root of k is an integer divisible by 3.

18. Mr. Parker made $20,000 in 2007. What is Mr. Parker's average yearly income for the three years from 2007 to 2009?
    (1) He made 10% more in each year than he did in the previous year.
    (2) His total combined income for 2008 and 2009 was $46,200.

19. . A right triangle has legs a and b. Is the hypotenuse of the right triangle an integer?
N is a positive integer greater than 1.

(1) $a = N^2 - 1$
(2) $b = 2N$

20. At 7 o'clock, how many people are on line to buy tickets at a theater box office?

(1) People are getting on the line at the rate of 2 people per minute at 7 o'clock.
(2) People are buying tickets and leaving the line at the rate of 4 people every 2 minutes at 7 o'clock.

21. How many of the numbers x, y, and z are positive? x, y, and z are all less than 30.

(1) $x + y + z = 61$
(2) $x + y = 35$

22. Point P is the center of circle O. Q and R are points on circle O. Point Q has coordinates (3, 4). Is point S, which has coordinates (–5, 6), on circle O?

(1) The coordinates of R are (2, 1).
(2) The coordinates of P are (–1, 1).

23. What percentage of the integers greater than 1,000 and less than the positive integer N are prime?

(1) N is a square
(2) $N = 10,000,000$

Answers and Analysis

The letter following each number is the correct answer.

1. **(B)** If STATEMENT (1) is true, then $x^3 y - \left(\dfrac{x^3}{y}\right)$ is equal to $8y - \left(\dfrac{8}{y}\right)$, but the value of y is

needed to find the value of the expression. Therefore, STATEMENT (1) alone is not sufficient. So the answer to question I is NO, and the only possible choices are (B), (C), or (E). If STATEMENT (2) alone is true, then $x^3 y - \left(\dfrac{x^3}{y}\right)$ is equal to $x^3 1 - \left(\dfrac{x^3}{1}\right)$, which is

equal to 0. Therefore, STATEMENT (2) alone is sufficient, and the answer to question II is YES. So the correct choice is B.

This problem illustrates the need to be careful. You might quickly infer that a value for x and a value for y are both needed and INCORRECTLY answer (C). To understand the problem, you need to simplify the expression by factoring out an x^3 from each

term. So $x^3 y - \left(\dfrac{x^3}{y}\right)$ is equal to $x^3 (y - \left(\dfrac{1}{y}\right))$, which is equal to 0 if $x = 0$ or if $y - \left(\dfrac{1}{y}\right) = 0$.

Thus, the expression's value is determined if $x = 0$ or if $y = 1$; otherwise, you need both a value for x and a value for y. (II-2)

2. **(E)** If STATEMENT (1) is true, then since $x = ba$, $3x = 3(10b + a) = 30b + 3a$. Now, because b is multiplied by 10 in the expression for $3x$, the final digit of $3x$ must be the final digit of $3a$. Since a is a digit, $0 \leq a \leq 9$, which implies $0 \leq 3a \leq 27$. So for the last digit of $3a$ to be equal to a, $3a$ must equal a or $10 + a$ or $20 + a$. If $a = 3a$, then $a = 0$. If $10 + a = 3a$, then $10 = 2a$ or $a = 5$. If $20 + a = 3a$, then $20 = 2a$ or $a = 10$, but since 10 is not a digit this is not possible. So if (1) is true, then a is 0 or 5, and (1) alone is not sufficient. Thus the answer to question I is NO, and the only possible choices are (B), (C), or (E).

   Now since 26 and 25 are both two-digit numbers whose last digits are less than 7, STATEMENT (2) alone is not sufficient. So the answer to question II is NO, and the only possible choices are (C) or (E). Also, since (2) does not allow us to choose between 0 and 5, STATEMENTS (1) and (2) together are not sufficient, so the correct choice is (E).

   Many people would be able to see that STATEMENT (2) alone would be insufficient but might not be able to decide whether (1) is sufficient. You can use the strategy to make an intelligent guess. Since (2) alone is not sufficient, the answer to question II on the decision tree is NO. Since choices (B) and (D) need an answer of YES to II, the only possible choices are (A), (C), or (E). Since you can eliminate two choices, it is worthwhile to guess. (I-1)

3. **(B)** STATEMENT (1) alone is not sufficient since then $\dfrac{N}{3} = \dfrac{(3K)}{3} = K$. Now if $K = 1$, then $\dfrac{N}{3} = 1$, which is odd, but if $K = 2$, then $\dfrac{N}{3} = 2$, which is even. So the answer to question I is NO, and the only possible choices are B, C, or E.

   STATEMENT (2) alone is sufficient since then $\dfrac{N}{3} = \dfrac{(6J + 3)}{3} = 2J + 1$, which is always odd since J is an integer. So the answer to question II is YES, and the correct choice is (B). (I-1)

4. **(E)** If you use STATEMENTS (1) and (2) together, you can deduce that $150 - 45 = 105$ families own at least one telephone and less than three telephones. However, since this is the total of families with one phone and families with two phones, we cannot find the number of families with exactly two phones. So (1) and (2) together are not sufficient. Thus, the answer to question III is NO, and the correct choice is (E). (II-4)

5. **(A)** Since w and q are alternate interior angles, if STATEMENT (1) is true then PQ is parallel to SR. So (1) alone is sufficient. Thus, the answer to question I is YES and the only possible choices are (A) and (D).

   STATEMENT (2) alone is not sufficient since the line RS can be moved so that y is still equal to z but PQ and RS are not parallel. (See the diagram below.)

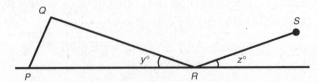

   Therefore, the answer to question II is NO, and the correct choice is (A). (III-2)

6. **(C)** If STATEMENT (1) alone is true, then since $x^6 - y^6$ can be factored into $(x^3 + y^3)(x^3 - y^3)$, either $x^3 + y^3 = 0$ or $x^3 - y^3 = 0$. So (1) alone is not sufficient, and the answer to question I is NO. Thus, the only possible choices are (B), (C), or (E).

   STATEMENT (2) alone is insuffficient since if $y = 0$, then $x^3 - y^3 = x^3$, and we have no value for x. So the answer to question II is NO, and the only possible choices are (C) or (E).

   If (1) and (2) are both true, then we can deduce that x and y must both be equal to zero, which is sufficient. Thus, the answer to question III is YES, and the correct choice must be (C). (II-1, II-2)

7. **(C)** Let J, M, and T stand for the weights of John, Moe, and Tim respectively. We need to find J and we know $T = 200$. STATEMENT (1) gives the equation $200 + M = J$, but since we don't know M, (1) alone is not sufficient.

   STATEMENT (2) alone gives the equation $J + M = 2T = 400$, and since we don't know M, (2) alone is insufficient.

   However, if we use STATEMENTS (1) and (2) together, then we have two linear equations in two unknowns, which we know can be solved to find J and M.

   NOTE: Don't waste time actually solving the equations. You only have to decide if there is enough information to answer the question; you don't have to compute the actual answer. (II-2, II-3)

8. **(A)** Since the area of a triangle is $\left(\frac{1}{2}\right)$(altitude)(base) and since both triangles have DA as an altitude, if the base (DE) of triangle ADE is larger than the base (EC) of triangle AEC, then the area of ADE is larger than the area of AEC. So STATEMENT (1) alone is sufficient, and the answer to question I is YES.

   STATEMENT (2) alone is not sufficient since for any point E between D and C (2) will be true, but, depending on whether E is closer to D or C, a different triangle will have the larger area. So the answer to question II is NO, and the correct choice is (A). (III-4, III-5)

9. **(D)** By using the distance formula (Pythagorean Theorem) you could find the length of AG if you knew the lengths of AH and GH (or if you knew the lengths of AC and CG or many other combinations). If you knew the lengths of AB and BH, then you could find the length of AH. Thus, it is sufficient to know the lengths of AB, BH, and GH. Since $ABCDEFGH$ is a cube, AB, BH, and GH all have the same length since they are all edges of the cube. So it is sufficient to know the length of an edge of the cube. Now STATEMENTS (1) and (2) are equivalent since the area of a square face of the cube is 16 if and only if the length of an edge is 4. Therefore, (1) alone and (2) alone are sufficient, and the correct choice is (D).

   Notice that, if you knew that (1) and (2) are equivalent, then the only possible choices are (D) or (E), so you can make an intelligent guess. (III-8)

10. **(B)** STATEMENT (2) alone is sufficient since if (2) is true, then $K = 2(3J)$, which means that K is even. Note this is sufficient to answer the question even though the answer is NO.

    STATEMENT (1) alone is not sufficient since if M is even, then K is even, but if M is odd, then K is odd. (I-1)

11. **(C)** STATEMENT (1) alone is insufficient since we don't know the sales for any year. Thus, the answer to question I is NO. Therefore, the only possible choices are (B), (C), or (E).

STATEMENT (2) alone is not sufficient since we don't know the value of the sales in 1990. So the answer to question II is NO, and the only possible choices are (C) and (E).

Using (1), we can calculate the change in sales from 1990 to 2000, and then by using (2), we can find the value of the sales in 2000. Therefore, the answer to question III is YES, and the correct choice is (C). (II-3)

12. **(E)** Since $x = 3$, $y = 1$, and $x = 1$, $y = \left(\frac{1}{3}\right)$ both make STATEMENT (1) true, but (1) alone is not sufficient. So the answer to question I is NO, and the only possible choices are (B), (C), or (E).

STATEMENT (2) alone is obviously not sufficient since it gives no information about x. Thus, the answer to question II is NO, and the only possible choices are (C) or (E). (Note: Even if you can't answer question I for this problem, you should be able to answer question II, and you would be able to guess either (A), (C), or (E).)

Now if y were positive, we could use STATEMENT (2) to deduce that $y > 1$ and then (1) would imply that $x > 2$. However, negative values of y can also satisfy (2) (for example, $y = -1$) and then (1) would have solutions with $x < 2$. So (1) and (2) together are not sufficient, and the answer to question III is NO. Thus the correct choice is (E). (II-7)

13. **(A)** STATEMENT (1) alone is sufficient since it will allow you to compute the volume of the tank in cubic feet. To actually find the answer, you would then change cubic feet into gallons using the fact that 231 cubic inches is one gallon. However, do not perform the calculation since it will only waste time.

Since using STATEMENT (2) alone will not allow you to find the volume of the tank, the correct answer is (A). (III-8)

14. **(A)** The area of the circle plus the area of the region outside the circle and inside the square is equal to the area of the square, which is $(AB)^2$. Thus, if you can determine whether one area is larger (or smaller) than $\left(\frac{1}{2}\right)(AB)^2$, that is sufficient.

STATEMENT (1) alone is sufficient since the area of the circle is $\pi(OE)^2$, and if (1) holds, then $\pi(OE)^2 < \pi\left(\left(\frac{1}{4}\right)AB\right)^2 = \left(\frac{\pi}{16}\right)(AB)^2$. But since $\frac{\pi}{16}$ is less than $\left(\frac{1}{2}\right)$, we can answer the question. So the answer to question I is YES, and the only possible choices are (A) or (D).

STATEMENT (2) alone is not sufficient since (2) does not give any information about the radius of the circle. Note: You might think that $OE + EF = \left(\frac{1}{2}\right)AB$; however, that requires the additional information that O is also the center of the square, which is NOT given. So the answer to question II is NO, and the correct choice is (A). (III-6)

15. **(C)** The key to solving this problem is to relate $x^3 - y^3$ to the information $x^6 - y^6 = 0$. If you think of $x^6 - y^6$ as $(x^3)^2 - (y^3)^2$, then you can factor the equation into $(x^3 - y^3)(x^3 + y^3) = 0$. So if $x^3 + y^3$ is not zero, then $x^3 - y^3$ must be zero. Thus STATEMENTS (1) and (2) together are sufficient because they imply that $x^3 + y^3$ is greater than zero.

    However, (1) alone or (2) alone is not sufficient because the cube of a negative number is negative. We could have $x^3 + y^3$ equal zero, and then the value of $x^3 - y^3$ may not be determined. For example, $x = 1$, $y = 1$ and $x = 1$, $y = -1$ show (1) alone is not sufficient, and $x = 2$, $y = 2$ and $x = -2$, $y = 2$ show (2) alone is not sufficient. (II-1, II-2)

16. **(D)** If there are x red marbles and y green marbles in the jar, then you could choose y marbles in a row that were all green. However, $y + 1$ marbles must contain at least one red marble. So it is sufficient to know the number of red marbles and the number of green marbles. Since you are given that $x + y = 60$, STATEMENT (2) is obviously sufficient. Also STATEMENT (1) is sufficient since it implies that $x = 2y$, which enables you to find x and y. Therefore, the correct answer choice is (D). (I-7)

17. **(E)** STATEMENT (1) is insufficient since 9 (which is odd) and 6 (which is even) are both divisible by 3. STATEMENT (2) is also insufficient since 81 is odd and $\sqrt{81} = 9$ is divisible by 3 but 36 is even and $\sqrt{36} = 6$ is divisible by 3. 81 and 36 are also divisible by 3, so (1) and (2) together are still insufficient. (I-7)

18. **(D)** To find Mr. Parker's average income, find his total income for the years 2007 through 2009 and then divide the total income by 3.

    STATEMENT (1) alone is sufficient. Since we know his income for 2007, we can find his income in 2008 and 2009 by using STATEMENT (1). Therefore, we can find the total income. STATEMENT (2) alone is sufficient. Add the combined income from 2008 and 2009 to the income from 2007 (which is given) to find the total income.

    Therefore, either STATEMENT (1) alone or STATEMENT (2) alone is sufficient. (I-7)

19. **(C)** This is an example of a harder data sufficiency problem. The Pythagorean Theorem tells you that the hypotenuse is the square root of $a^2 + b^2$. So the question asks if you have sufficient data to conclude whether or not the square root of $a^2 + b^2$ is an integer. STATEMENT (1) alone is not sufficient because if you let $N = 2$, then $a = 3$. If $b = 4$, the hypotenuse is 5, which is an integer. However, if $a = 3$ and $b = 2$, the hypotenuse is $\sqrt{13}$, which is not an integer. STATEMENT (2) alone is also not sufficient. If you let $N = 2$, then $b = 4$. If $a = 3$, the hypotenuse is an integer. However, if $a = 1$, the hypotenuse is $\sqrt{17}$, which is not an integer. At this point, just by looking at an example, you know that the only possibilities are (C) or (E). So if you can't go any farther, guess one of these choices.

    Assuming both (1) and (2) are true, we have $a^2 + b^2 = (N^2 - 1)^2 + (2N)^2$. Expand and collect terms. We have $N^4 - 2N^2 + 1 + 4N^2 = N^4 + 2N^2 + 1$, which is $(N^2 + 1)^2$. So the hypotenuse is $(N^2 + 1)$, which is an integer. Therefore (C) is the answer.

    NOTE: If you assumed that STATEMENTS (1) and (2) were true and expanded, you could see that the hypotenuse is an integer. So (C) is a possible correct choice. However, you must rule out that STATEMENT (1) by itself or STATEMENT (2) by itself could be sufficient in order to know that (C) is the correct choice. (III-4)

20. **(E)** Both STATEMENTS (1) and (2) tell you how the line is changing at 7 o'clock. However, you need information about the length of the line at some time. For example, if 100 people were on line, STATEMENTS (1) and (2) could be true. However, both STATEMENTS (1) and (2) could also be true if 50 people were on line. So STATEMENTS (1) and (2) together are not sufficient to answer the question. (II-3)

21. **(A)** STATEMENT (1) alone is sufficient. Since all the numbers are less than 30, all three must be positive for their sum to be larger than 60.

    STATEMENT (2) alone is insufficient. It implies that x and y are positive but gives no information about z. (II-7)

22. **(B)** STATEMENT (1) is not sufficient since an infinite number of circles can be drawn through Q and R. Since you have no information about P, which is the center of circle O, you can't decide whether S is on circle O. STATEMENT (2) alone is sufficient since it allows you to calculate the distance from P to Q, which must be the radius of circle O. Then you can calculate the distance from P to S. If it is equal to the radius of O, S is on the circle. Remember: You do not need to perform these calculations. (III-6, III-9)

23. **(B)** Since several different positive integers are square and greater than 1,000, such as 10,000 or 40,000, STATEMENT (1) is obviously not sufficient. Since you can decide whether any positive integer is a prime, STATEMENT (2) alone is sufficient. So the correct choice is (B). It would take a long, long time to decide whether each integer between 1,000 and 10,000,000 is a prime, but you only have to decide if you could solve the problem. How long it would take is irrelevant. (I-1)

Sample
TESTS

Sample Test 1 with Answers and Analysis

→ TEST

→ ANSWERS

→ ANALYSIS

→ EVALUATING YOUR SCORE

ANSWER SHEET
Sample Test 1

INTEGRATED REASONING SECTION

1. i. Ⓐ Ⓑ Ⓒ Ⓓ
   ii. Ⓐ Ⓑ Ⓒ Ⓓ

2.

Could Be Classified	Could Not Be Classified	Animal
○	○	Penguin
○	○	Flamingo
○	○	Flying Squirrel
○	○	Pterodactyl
○	○	Eagle

3.

Yes	No
○	○
○	○
○	○

4.

Yes	No
○	○
○	○
○	○
○	○

5. Ⓐ Ⓑ Ⓒ Ⓓ Ⓔ

6.

Either Day	Neither Day	Speaker
○	○	Branson, male, U.K.
○	○	Robinson, female, U.K.
○	○	D'Agostino, female, Brazil
○	○	Miller, female, Canada
○	○	Soares, male, India

7. i. Ⓐ Ⓑ Ⓒ Ⓓ
   ii. Ⓐ Ⓑ Ⓒ Ⓓ

8. Ⓐ Ⓑ Ⓒ Ⓓ Ⓔ

9.

True	False
○	○
○	○
○	○

10. i. Ⓐ Ⓑ Ⓒ Ⓓ
    ii. Ⓐ Ⓑ Ⓒ Ⓓ

11.

True	False
○	○
○	○
○	○

12.

Would Help Explain	Would Not Help Explain
○	○
○	○
○	○

ANSWER SHEET
Sample Test 1

QUANTITATIVE SECTION

1. Ⓐ Ⓑ Ⓒ Ⓓ Ⓔ   11. Ⓐ Ⓑ Ⓒ Ⓓ Ⓔ   21. Ⓐ Ⓑ Ⓒ Ⓓ Ⓔ   31. Ⓐ Ⓑ Ⓒ Ⓓ Ⓔ
2. Ⓐ Ⓑ Ⓒ Ⓓ Ⓔ   12. Ⓐ Ⓑ Ⓒ Ⓓ Ⓔ   22. Ⓐ Ⓑ Ⓒ Ⓓ Ⓔ   32. Ⓐ Ⓑ Ⓒ Ⓓ Ⓔ
3. Ⓐ Ⓑ Ⓒ Ⓓ Ⓔ   13. Ⓐ Ⓑ Ⓒ Ⓓ Ⓔ   23. Ⓐ Ⓑ Ⓒ Ⓓ Ⓔ   33. Ⓐ Ⓑ Ⓒ Ⓓ Ⓔ
4. Ⓐ Ⓑ Ⓒ Ⓓ Ⓔ   14. Ⓐ Ⓑ Ⓒ Ⓓ Ⓔ   24. Ⓐ Ⓑ Ⓒ Ⓓ Ⓔ   34. Ⓐ Ⓑ Ⓒ Ⓓ Ⓔ
5. Ⓐ Ⓑ Ⓒ Ⓓ Ⓔ   15. Ⓐ Ⓑ Ⓒ Ⓓ Ⓔ   25. Ⓐ Ⓑ Ⓒ Ⓓ Ⓔ   35. Ⓐ Ⓑ Ⓒ Ⓓ Ⓔ
6. Ⓐ Ⓑ Ⓒ Ⓓ Ⓔ   16. Ⓐ Ⓑ Ⓒ Ⓓ Ⓔ   26. Ⓐ Ⓑ Ⓒ Ⓓ Ⓔ   36. Ⓐ Ⓑ Ⓒ Ⓓ Ⓔ
7. Ⓐ Ⓑ Ⓒ Ⓓ Ⓔ   17. Ⓐ Ⓑ Ⓒ Ⓓ Ⓔ   27. Ⓐ Ⓑ Ⓒ Ⓓ Ⓔ   37. Ⓐ Ⓑ Ⓒ Ⓓ Ⓔ
8. Ⓐ Ⓑ Ⓒ Ⓓ Ⓔ   18. Ⓐ Ⓑ Ⓒ Ⓓ Ⓔ   28. Ⓐ Ⓑ Ⓒ Ⓓ Ⓔ
9. Ⓐ Ⓑ Ⓒ Ⓓ Ⓔ   19. Ⓐ Ⓑ Ⓒ Ⓓ Ⓔ   29. Ⓐ Ⓑ Ⓒ Ⓓ Ⓔ
10. Ⓐ Ⓑ Ⓒ Ⓓ Ⓔ   20. Ⓐ Ⓑ Ⓒ Ⓓ Ⓔ   30. Ⓐ Ⓑ Ⓒ Ⓓ Ⓔ

VERBAL SECTION

1. Ⓐ Ⓑ Ⓒ Ⓓ Ⓔ   12. Ⓐ Ⓑ Ⓒ Ⓓ Ⓔ   23. Ⓐ Ⓑ Ⓒ Ⓓ Ⓔ   34. Ⓐ Ⓑ Ⓒ Ⓓ Ⓔ
2. Ⓐ Ⓑ Ⓒ Ⓓ Ⓔ   13. Ⓐ Ⓑ Ⓒ Ⓓ Ⓔ   24. Ⓐ Ⓑ Ⓒ Ⓓ Ⓔ   35. Ⓐ Ⓑ Ⓒ Ⓓ Ⓔ
3. Ⓐ Ⓑ Ⓒ Ⓓ Ⓔ   14. Ⓐ Ⓑ Ⓒ Ⓓ Ⓔ   25. Ⓐ Ⓑ Ⓒ Ⓓ Ⓔ   36. Ⓐ Ⓑ Ⓒ Ⓓ Ⓔ
4. Ⓐ Ⓑ Ⓒ Ⓓ Ⓔ   15. Ⓐ Ⓑ Ⓒ Ⓓ Ⓔ   26. Ⓐ Ⓑ Ⓒ Ⓓ Ⓔ   37. Ⓐ Ⓑ Ⓒ Ⓓ Ⓔ
5. Ⓐ Ⓑ Ⓒ Ⓓ Ⓔ   16. Ⓐ Ⓑ Ⓒ Ⓓ Ⓔ   27. Ⓐ Ⓑ Ⓒ Ⓓ Ⓔ   38. Ⓐ Ⓑ Ⓒ Ⓓ Ⓔ
6. Ⓐ Ⓑ Ⓒ Ⓓ Ⓔ   17. Ⓐ Ⓑ Ⓒ Ⓓ Ⓔ   28. Ⓐ Ⓑ Ⓒ Ⓓ Ⓔ   39. Ⓐ Ⓑ Ⓒ Ⓓ Ⓔ
7. Ⓐ Ⓑ Ⓒ Ⓓ Ⓔ   18. Ⓐ Ⓑ Ⓒ Ⓓ Ⓔ   29. Ⓐ Ⓑ Ⓒ Ⓓ Ⓔ   40. Ⓐ Ⓑ Ⓒ Ⓓ Ⓔ
8. Ⓐ Ⓑ Ⓒ Ⓓ Ⓔ   19. Ⓐ Ⓑ Ⓒ Ⓓ Ⓔ   30. Ⓐ Ⓑ Ⓒ Ⓓ Ⓔ   41. Ⓐ Ⓑ Ⓒ Ⓓ Ⓔ
9. Ⓐ Ⓑ Ⓒ Ⓓ Ⓔ   20. Ⓐ Ⓑ Ⓒ Ⓓ Ⓔ   31. Ⓐ Ⓑ Ⓒ Ⓓ Ⓔ
10. Ⓐ Ⓑ Ⓒ Ⓓ Ⓔ   21. Ⓐ Ⓑ Ⓒ Ⓓ Ⓔ   32. Ⓐ Ⓑ Ⓒ Ⓓ Ⓔ
11. Ⓐ Ⓑ Ⓒ Ⓓ Ⓔ   22. Ⓐ Ⓑ Ⓒ Ⓓ Ⓔ   33. Ⓐ Ⓑ Ⓒ Ⓓ Ⓔ

WRITING ASSESSMENT

Time: 30 minutes

ANALYSIS OF AN ARGUMENT

> DIRECTIONS: Write a clear, logical, and well-organized response to the following argument. Your response should be in the form of a short essay, following the conventions of standard written English. On the CAT, your answer should be the equivalent of an essay that would fill three pages of lined 8½″ × 11″ paper. If you are taking a paper test, write legibly. Essays that are illegible or that are written on a topic other than the one outlined in the question will not be scored.

The installation of electronic high-speed scanning devices at the entrances and exits of toll roads will obviate the need for toll booths. Automobiles will have scanner-sensitive license plates—like the bar codes on consumer packaged products—so that the scanner devices will record the license numbers of cars entering and exiting the toll road. Car owners will be billed monthly by the highway authorities.

Discuss how logically persuasive you find the above argument. In presenting your point of view, analyze the sort of reasoning used and supporting evidence. In addition, state what further evidence, if any, would make the argument more sound and convincing or would make you better able to evaluate its conclusion.

STOP

ON THE ACTUAL GMAT,
AFTER YOU HAVE CONFIRMED YOUR ANSWER,
YOU CANNOT RETURN TO IT.

INTEGRATED REASONING SECTION

Time: 30 minutes

12 questions

This section consists of four types of questions: Graphics Interpretation, Table Analysis, Two-part Analysis, and Multi-Source Reasoning.

> DIRECTIONS: The new Integrated Reasoning section consists of four question types. Some require the use of both quantitative and verbal skills. Others involve the use of graphics, tables, or text material. The questions also use various response formats.
>
> For each question, review the text, graphic, or text material provided and respond to the task that is presented. *Note: An onscreen calculator is available in this section on the actual test.*

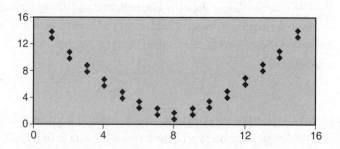

1. The scatter plot above shows the relationship between two variables.

   Complete each statement according to the information presented in the diagram.

   i. Which of the following statements is the only one that can be said to be true based on the chart?

   (A) The slope is positive.
   (B) The relationship is strong.
   (C) The slope is negative.
   (D) The slope is linear.

   ii. If you plotted the absolute difference between the two variables at each point in the chart, what slope would the graph have?

   (A) a positive slope
   (B) a slope of zero
   (C) a negative slope
   (D) a parabolic slope

2. Birds are a class of vertebrate animals. Birds (class Aves) are a more homogeneous group than many other vertebrate classes, such as mammals. Birds possess very distinct characteristics. The top two are as follows:

(i) **The beak or bill** is a bony, toothless structure that extends from the jawbone. It is used primarily for eating, grooming, and feeding young.

(ii) **The wings**, which are a pair of forelimbs, are uniquely adapted for flying.

Based on the information above and ignoring all other characteristics of birds, which of the following could be classified as a "Bird" and which could not?

Could Be Classified	Could Not Be Classified	Animal
◯	◯	Penguin
◯	◯	Flamingo
◯	◯	Flying squirrel
◯	◯	Pterodactyl
◯	◯	Eagle

3. The table below displays data concerning UltraMart stores in Canada.

Store Number	City	Province	# of Employees	Grocery Section
3145	Concord	Ontario	27	N
3004	Brandon	Manitoba	28	N
3149	Mascouche	Quebec	31	N
3122	Belleville	Ontario	36	N
3065	Orleans	Ontario	38	N
3148	Levis	Quebec	42	N
3007	Brossard	Quebec	44	N
3134	Kanata	Ontario	44	N
3063	North Bay	Ontario	48	N
3097	Sudbury	Ontario	48	N
3140	Saint Bruno	Quebec	49	N
3000	Agincourt	Ontario	50	N
3080	Rosemere	Quebec	53	N
3642	St. Constant	Quebec	55	N
3046	La Salle	Quebec	59	N
3090	St. Jean	Quebec	59	Y
3161	Oshawa	Ontario	60	Y
3039	Joliette	Quebec	61	Y
3044	Kirkland	Quebec	64	Y
3189	Laval	Quebec	65	Y
3047	Laval	Quebec	66	N
3146	St. Foy	Quebec	66	Y
3053	Markham	Ontario	68	Y
3084	Saskatoon	Saskatchewan	68	Y
3135	Brampton	Ontario	70	N
3195	Richmond Hill	Ontario	70	Y
3130	Brampton	Ontario	72	Y
3186	Pickering	Ontario	72	Y
3054	Meadowvale	Ontario	77	Y
3159	Scarborough	Ontario	79	Y
3125	Gatineau	Quebec	80	Y
3131	Ottawa	Ontario	82	Y
3111	Scarborough	Ontario	83	N
3051	London	Ontario	84	N
3029	Edmonton	Alberta	86	Y
3656	Montreal	Quebec	86	Y
3635	Scarborough	Ontario	87	Y
3043	Kingston	Ontario	88	Y
3012	Calgary	Alberta	98	N
3074	Quebec City	Quebec	98	Y
3050	London	Ontario	99	Y
3119	Winnipeg	Manitoba	102	Y
3654	Mississauga	Ontario	103	N
3055	Mississauga	Ontario	107	Y
3009	Calgary	Alberta	112	Y
3106	Toronto	Ontario	119	Y
3165	Montreal	Quebec	121	Y
3105	Toronto	Ontario	128	N
3740	Toronto	Ontario	131	Y
3031	Etobicoke	Ontario	142	Y

For each of the following statements, select *Yes* if the statement can be shown to be true based on the information in the table. Otherwise, select *No*.

Yes No

◯ ◯ The median number of employees in a store in Quebec is higher than the median number of employees in a store in Ontario.

◯ ◯ If a store has less than 60 employees, it does not have enough resources to support a grocery section.

◯ ◯ More than seven cities have at least two stores.

Questions 4 and 5 refer to the following articles.

Article 1: From an environmental journal

February 28—Given the global increase of deforestation, some experts predict that in 50 years, Earth may lose over 20% of wildlife species to extinction. In addition, the destruction of forests provokes further global warming. CO_2 levels are predicted to rise by 100% in the same time period, which could have disastrous effects. Lastly, the loss of trees in an area also decreases the amount of water within that region, thus affecting the world's water supply. Governments and industry have failed to put sufficient restrictions and regulations in place. Although recycling programs have made a significant dent in reducing paper use, there is still much more work to be done. However, one of the challenges is that many citizens vote down proposals for recycling program expansion or regulations on industry.

Article 2: Interview with a well-known scientist

March 6—Dr. James Finnegan, special advisor to the New York City Mayor's Program on Environment Sustainability, has been most critical of the forest industry, which continually hires and utilizes aggressive lobbyists to ensure that expanded recycling program proposals are defeated. He advises that without a significant increase in recycling programs, the rate of global warming could soon quadruple in the next generation.

"It's true that most voters keep rejecting costly measures to reduce paper and lumber usage, such as more aggressive 'reduce, reuse, and recycle' programs. Worse yet, CEOs are unsurprisingly going to avoid taking huge risks for unpopular policies among their key stockholders. However, if something isn't done soon, by 2060, a bottle of water may become so expensive that only the rich can afford it as a luxury item."

Article 3: From a forestry magazine

April 2—The price of bottled water over the last two decades has increased by 200% as a decrease in supply has met with an increased demand. Despite an increase in recycled paper products available to the public, most paper companies charge a premium for them. This has encouraged some companies to exploit many large natural water resources around the world. This has also motivated many companies to continue using nonrecycled paper products. Several American environmental groups have expressed concern that certain pulp and paper companies choose the economics of extraction and manufacturing over the well-being of the ecosystem. Some North American scientists have called for an increase in regulations to protect deforestation and water sources. However, companies from both industries caution that this may dramatically increase the cost of both recycled paper and fresh water.

4. Consider each of the following statements. Does the information in the three articles support the inferences as stated?

    Yes No

    ○ ○ Deforestation is the most significant cause of increasing CO_2 levels in the atmosphere.

    ○ ○ Citizens tend to vote down environmentally friendly proposals due to the strong lobbying of the forestry industry.

    ○ ○ Dr. James Finnegan would prefer to pass legislation to regulate the forestry industry than legislation to regulate the bottled-water industry.

    ○ ○ Business leaders in environmentally affected industries may not always agree with science experts on environmental sustainability.

---

5. Each of the following is true based on the passage EXCEPT:

    (A) at least 15% of Earth's wildlife species may become extinct within 50 years.

    (B) a bottle of water will cost the same as a bottle of premium vodka by the year 2060.

    (C) bottled water has doubled in price over the past 20 years.

    (D) for most consumers, recycled paper can cost more to purchase than nonrecycled paper.

    (E) CO_2 levels are expected to double before the end of the 21st century.

An organization of technology leaders is arranging a two-day business conference in California that will bring together the top minds in leadership and development from around the world. The conference organizers want to get a diverse range of speakers for the event. Each day will have six speakers. To reflect the global diversity, one day will have a majority of international speakers (i.e., not from North America) and the other day will have a majority of female speakers. Neither day should have more than 2 speakers from the same country unless they are from the United States. So far, 10 speakers have already booked. The list of speakers for each day, including the speaker's country of origin, is as follows:

Day 1 (Majority International)	Day 2 (Majority Female)
Smith, female, U.K.	Fiorina, female, U.S.A.
Dalton, female, U.K.	Godin, male, U.S.A.
Xiang, male, China	Rodrigues, male, Brazil
Sharma, male, Spain	Hayek, female, Mexico
Robbins, male, U.S.A.	Valentino, female, Brazil

6. Select a speaker who could be added to the schedule for either day. Then select a speaker who could not be added to either day. Make only two selections, one in each column.

Either Day	Neither Day	Speaker
○	○	Branson, male, U.K.
○	○	Robinson, female, U.K.
○	○	D'Agostino, female, Brazil
○	○	Miller, female, Canada
○	○	Soares, male, India

Question 7 refers to the following graphs and information.

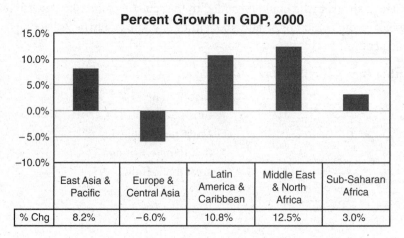

Graph 1

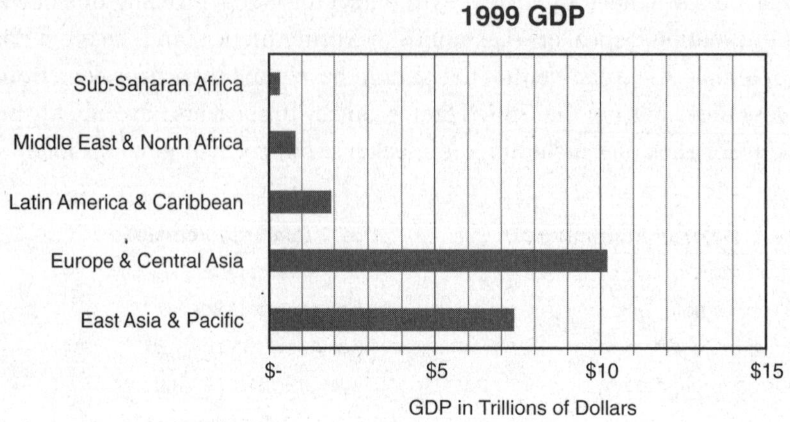

1999 GDP

GDP in Trillions of Dollars

Graph 2

Percent Growth in GDP, 2000

	East Asia & Pacific	Europe & Central Asia	Latin America & Caribbean	Middle East & North Africa	Sub-Saharan Africa
% Chg	8.2%	−6.0%	10.8%	12.5%	3.0%

7. Complete each statement according to the information presented in the diagram.

i. What is the approximate dollar amount by which Europe and Central Asia's GDP increased from 1999 to 2000?

(A) −$610 billion
(B) −$439 billion
(C) −$6 billion
(D) $610 billion

ii. Which is closest to the combined growth in GDP in 2000 for all five regions?

(A) −3%
(B) 0%
(C) 4%
(D) 8%

Sally is the head of the party planning committee for Dinder Mufflin. She takes her job very seriously. She loves to plan each office party and personalize it for the specific employee. Sally buys her party supplies from the Big Blast Boxstore.

Sally makes her purchases monthly to take advantage of Big Blast Boxstore's end-of-the-month clearance sales. Depending on the number of birthdays and the birthday person's party preferences, Sally plans accordingly.

Big Blast Boxstore Price List

Party Supply	Packaging	Cost
Ribbon	8 feet rolls, 6 per package	$8.00
Streamers	10 feet rolls, 10 per package	$6.00
Balloons	20 balloons per bag	$4.00
Goodie bags	24 bags per package	$12.00

Big Blast Boxstore Monthly Clearance Sale Discounts

Amount Spent	Ribbon	Streamers	Balloons	Goodie Bags
$30–$50	$15.00	$10.00	$5.00	None
Over $50	$25.00	$20.00	$10.00	$10.00

8. Which of the following options would result in the lowest cost?

   (A) August has 3 birthdays. Sally needs 180 feet of ribbon, 300 feet of streamers, 50 balloons, and 100 goodie bags.

   (B) February has 3 birthdays. Sally needs 300 feet of ribbon, 200 feet of streamers, 30 balloons, and 60 goodie bags.

   (C) September has 4 birthdays. Sally needs 300 feet of ribbon, 300 feet of streamers, 150 balloons, and 120 goodie bags.

   (D) December has 5 birthdays. Sally needs 360 feet of ribbon, 400 feet of streamers, 100 balloons, and 30 goodie bags.

   (E) April has 6 birthdays. Sally needs 336 feet of ribbon, 900 feet of streamers, 260 balloons, and 120 goodie bags

9. Answer the following True or False statements.

   True   False

   ◯   ◯   If Sally was able to put leftover party supplies in storage, it would be cheaper to purchase 9 packages of streamers and 7 packages of ribbon instead of 8 packages of streamers and 6 packages of ribbon.

   ◯   ◯   It is cheaper for Sally to purchase 300 feet of ribbon and 900 feet of streamers than to purchase 144 goodie bags and 24 balloons.

   ◯   ◯   In order to get the maximum discount possible from purchasing all four products, Sally needs to spend at least $222.00.

The scatter plot below charts the test scores for an English exam and a math exam for 22 students in Mrs. Rosenblatt's class.

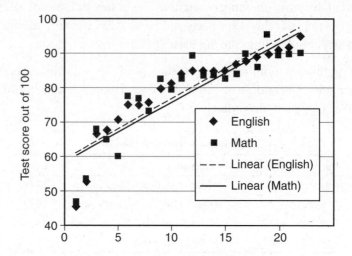

10. Complete each statement according to the information given by the graph.

i. How does the slope of the regression line for the English exam compare with the slope of the regression line for the math exam?

(A) The slope of the regression line for the English exam is greater than the regression line for the math exam.

(B) The slope of the regression line for the English exam is less than the regression line for the math exam.

(C) The slope of the regression line for the English exam is equal to the regression line for the math exam.

(D) The slope of the regression line for the English exam is undefined and cannot be compared with the slope of the regression line for the math exam.

ii. How do Mrs. Rosenblatt's students tend to score in math as compared with English?

(A) They tend to score better in math than in English.

(B) They tend to score worse in math than in English.

(C) They tend to score the same in math than in English.

(D) Since each student is an individual, the scores of the entire class cannot be compared with each other.

Questions 11 and 12 refer to the following table.

The table below shows data for the major types of sliced deli cheeses.

Type of Sliced Deli Cheese	Share of Market (lb.)	Change in Sales vs. Last Year (lb.)	Change in % Volume (lb.)	Share of Market ($)	Sales vs. Last Year ($)	Change in % Volume ($)
King Light Swiss	0	–17,489	–100	0	–168,120	–100
King Light Havarti	0	–17,893	–100	0	–172,403	–100
King Havarti	0	–22,860	–100	0	–218,829	–100
King Swiss	0	–27,648	–100	0	–265,065	–100
Kruger Mozzarella	16.2	8,547	4.2	14.7	124,537	7.6
King Swiss w/Zipper	11.5	64,852	74	11.9	641,205	81
Kruger Swiss	7.4	–10,292	–9.5	8.5	–58,444	–5.4
King Swiss Light w/Zipper	6.8	38,301	73.1	7.9	428,774	81.3
Aggio Jarlsberg	4.5	1,345	2.3	6.3	55,857	7.9
King Mozzarella w/Zipper	4.1	25,302	85.3	3.8	224,430	94.3
Davinci Swiss w/Zipper	3.4	44,729	NA	4.0	485,913	NA
Kruger Cheddar Mild	2.9	27,184	247.3	1.6	136,576	258
Davinci Havarti	2.7	26,911	290.2	3.2	292,398	320
Davinci Part Skim Mozzarella	2.6	7,797	29.2	2.4	92,119	45.4
Davinci Provolone	2.3	13,019	73.7	2.5	146,653	98.3
Norway Jarlsberg	2.1	361	1.3	1.8	7,186	3.5
Norway Jarlsberg Light	2.0	7,584	40.6	2.8	107,464	45.8
Kruger Part Skim Mozzarella	1.9	–14,941	–37.3	1.7	–121,058	–36.7
King Provolone w/Zipper	1.6	13,236	176	1.8	143,205	188
King Havarti w/Zipper	1.6	10,326	90.7	1.7	103,554	103
King Raclette w/Zipper	1.3	4,205	33.3	1.7	55,905	37.2

11. Consider each of the following statements. For each statement, indicate whether the statement is true or false based on the information provided in the table.

True	False	
◯	◯	Cheddar and mozzarella cheese slices have a higher in-store price point than Swiss or Havarti cheese slices.
◯	◯	Swiss cheese slices accounted for more dollar sales than any other type of cheese slice.
◯	◯	King's cheese slices have had the largest overall absolute growth per pound since last year.

12. For each of the following statements, select *Would help explain* if it would, if true, help explain some of the information in the table. Otherwise select *Would not help explain*.

Would Help Explain	Would Not Help Explain	
◯	◯	Consumers tend to prefer cheese slices packages with zippers versus packages with no zipper.
◯	◯	King discontinued some of their SKU's (stock keeping units) and replaced them with products that were packaged with zippers.
◯	◯	Light cheese slices are more expensive to manufacture than regular cheese slices.

STOP

QUANTITATIVE SECTION

Time: 75 minutes

37 questions

This section consists of two types of questions: Problem Solving and Data Sufficiency.

Problem Solving

DIRECTIONS: Solve each of the following problems; then indicate the correct answer.

NOTE: A figure that appears with a problem is drawn as accurately as possible so as to provide information that may help in answering the question.

Numbers in this test are real numbers.

Data Sufficiency

DIRECTIONS: Each of the following problems has a question and two statements that are labeled (1) and (2). Use the data given in (1) and (2) together with other available information (such as the number of hours in a day, the definition of *clockwise*, mathematical facts, etc.) to decide whether the statements are *sufficient* to answer the question. Then fill in space

(A) If you can get the answer from **(1) ALONE** but not from (2) alone

(B) If you can get the answer from **(2) ALONE** but not from (1) alone

(C) If you can get the answer from **BOTH (1)** and **(2) TOGETHER** but not from (1) alone or (2) alone

(D) If **EITHER** statement **(1) ALONE OR** statement **(2) ALONE** suffices

(E) If you **CANNOT** get the answer from statements (1) and (2) **TOGETHER** but need even more data

All numbers used in this section are real numbers.

A figure given for a problem is intended to provide information consistent with that in the question, but not necessarily with the additional information contained in the statements.

All figures lie in the plane unless you are told otherwise.

Figures are drawn as accurately as possible; straight lines may not appear straight on the screen.

1. How many books are on the bookshelf?

    (1) The bookshelf is 12 feet long.

    (2) The average weight of each book is 1.2 pounds.

2. The equation of a straight line containing the points (10,100) and (15, 60) is

    (A) $y = -8x + 180$

    (B) $y = 8x - 180$

    (C) $y = (\frac{1}{8})x + 7.5$

    (D) $y = -8x - 180$

    (E) $y = (-\frac{1}{8})x + 22.5$

3. If $f(x) = x^3 - 4$ and $f(y) = 4$, then y is equal to

    (A) 0

    (B) $2^{\frac{1}{3}}$

    (C) $\sqrt{2}$

    (D) 2

    (E) 3

4. In triangle *ABC*, find *z* if *AB* = 5 and *y* = 40.

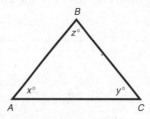

    (1) *BC* = 5

    (2) The bisector of angle *B* is perpendicular to *AC*.

5. How far is it from town *A* to town *B*? Town *C* is 12 miles east of town *A*.

    (1) Town *C* is south of town *B*.
    (2) It is 9 miles from town *B* to town *C*.

6. If $x + y + z + w = 15$, then at least k of the numbers x, y, z, w must be positive, where k is

    (A) 0
    (B) 1
    (C) 2
    (D) 3
    (E) 4

7. Is there a route from *A* to *C* that passes through *B* and is more than 8 miles long?

    (1) Two roads from *A* to *B* are at least 5 miles long.
    (2) Three roads from *B* to *C* are at least 5 miles long.

8. If you test 2 different lightbulbs from a box of 100 bulbs that contains 1 defective bulb what is the probability that both lightbulbs that you test are defective?

    (A) 0
    (B) 0.0001
    (C) $\dfrac{1}{9,900}$
    (D) 0.01
    (E) $\dfrac{1}{99}$

9. A company can sell $100x$ machine parts if it charges $10 - 0.1x$ dollars for each machine part. How many machine parts can the company sell if it charges $4.00 for each machine part?

    (A) 6
    (B) 9.6
    (C) 60
    (D) 960
    (E) 6,000

(A) If you can get the answer from (1) **ALONE** but not from (2) alone

(B) If you can get the answer from (2) **ALONE** but not from (1) alone

(C) If you can get the answer from **BOTH (1)** and **(2) TOGETHER** but not from (1) alone or (2) alone

(D) If **EITHER** statement **(1) ALONE OR** statement **(2) ALONE** suffices

(E) If you **CANNOT** get the answer from statements (1) and (2) **TOGETHER** but need even more data

10. A car goes 15 miles on a gallon of gas when it is driven at 50 miles per hour. When the car is driven at 60 miles per hour it only goes 80 percent as far. How many gallons of gas will it take to travel 120 miles driving at 60 miles per hour?

(A) 2

(B) 6.4

(C) 8

(D) 9.6

(E) 10

11. Train X leaves New York at 1 A.M. and travels east at a speed of x miles per hour. If train Z leaves New York at 2 A.M. and travels east, at what rate of speed in miles per hour will train Z have to travel in order to catch train X at exactly 5:30 A.M.?

(A) $\left(\dfrac{5}{6}\right)x$

(B) $\left(\dfrac{9}{8}\right)x$

(C) $\left(\dfrac{6}{5}\right)x$

(D) $\left(\dfrac{9}{7}\right)x$

(E) $\left(\dfrac{3}{2}\right)x$

12. A company makes a profit of 6 percent on its first $1,000 of sales each day, and 5 percent on all sales in excess of $1,000 for that day. How many dollars in profit will the company make on a day when sales are S dollars if S is greater than 1,000?

(A) $0.05S$

(B) $0.06S$

(C) 110

(D) $10 + 0.05S$

(E) $60 + 0.05S$

13. Is x an even integer? Assume n and p are integers.

    (1) $x = (n + p)^2$
    (2) $x = 2n + 10p$

14. What is the value of x?

    (1) $\dfrac{x}{y} = 3$
    (2) $x - y = 9$

15. Two different holes, hole A and hole B, are put in the bottom of a full water tank. If the water drains out through the holes, how long will it be before the tank is empty?

    (1) If only hole A is put in the bottom, the tank will be empty in 24 minutes.
    (2) If only hole B is put in the bottom, the tank will be empty in 42 minutes.

16. How many pounds of fertilizer that is 10 percent nitrogen must be added to 12 pounds of fertilizer that is 20 percent nitrogen so that the resulting mixture is 18 percent nitrogen?

    (A) 3
    (B) 6
    (C) 12
    (D) 24
    (E) 48

17. What is the probability that there is exactly 1 defective pen in a box of pens?

    (1) The probability that all the pens in the box are not defective is 96 percent.
    (2) The probability that there is more than 1 defective pen in the box is 3 percent.

18. The line t passes through the lines l and k and forms the angles u, v, x, y, a, b, c, and d. Is line l parallel to line k?

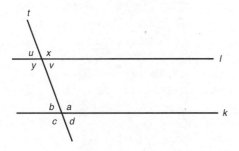

    (1) $x = u$
    (2) $u = a$

19.   Is there a route from *A* to *C* that passes through *B* and is more than 11 miles long?

(1)   Two roads from *A* to *B* are at least 5 miles long.
(2)   Three roads from *B* to *C* are at least 5 miles long.

20.   Let $g(x) = 4^x$. If $g(a) = 32$, then *a* is

(A)   2
(B)   2.33
(C)   2.5
(D)   2.75
(E)   3

21.   In the figure, angles *A, B, C, D, E, F, G, H* are all 90° and $AB = AH = EF = DE$. Also, $BC = CD = HG$ and the Cartesian coordinates of *A*, *C*, and *E* are (1, 2), (2, 5), and (5, 4), respectively. What is the area of figure *ABCDEFG*?

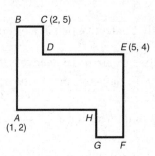

(A)   6
(B)   7
(C)   8
(D)   10
(E)   12

22. When an automobile is driven at 70 miles per hour, it uses 0.06 gallon of gas per mile. When the car is driven at 50 miles per hour, it uses 0.04 gallon of gas per mile. Which of the following relations are *possible* between the gallons of gas used per mile and the speed at which the car is driven?

   I. They are directly proportional.
   II. They are indirectly proportional.
  III. They are linearly related.

(A) only I
(B) only II
(C) only III
(D) I and III
(E) I, II, and III

23. The points A and C are on the line l. Is line segment AB greater than line segment BC?

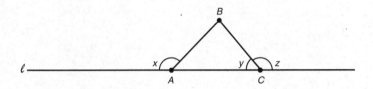

(1) Angle x is greater than angle y.
(2) Angle z is greater than angle x.

24. Is x positive?

(1) $x^2 + 10x > 0$
(2) $3^x > 1$

25.

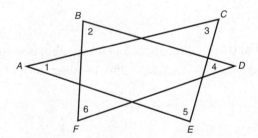

The sum of angles 1, 2, 3, 4, 5, and 6 is

(A) 180°
(B) 360°
(C) 480°
(D) 540°
(E) 720°

26. If $a + 2b = 6$ and $ab = 4$ what is $\dfrac{2}{a} + \dfrac{1}{b}$?

  (A) $\dfrac{1}{2}$

  (B) 1

  (C) $\dfrac{3}{2}$

  (D) 2

  (E) $\dfrac{5}{2}$

27. Ms. Jones has twice as much invested in stocks as in bonds. Last year, the stock investments paid 7.5 percent of their value and the bonds paid 10 percent of their value. If the total that both investments paid last year was $1,000, how much did Ms. Jones have invested in stocks?

  (A) $3,636

  (B) $4,000

  (C) $7,500

  (D) $8,000

  (E) $10,000

28. A pair of skis originally cost $160. After a discount of x percent, the skis were discounted y percent. Do the skis cost less than $130 after the discounts?

  (1) $x = 20$
  (2) $y = 15$

29. Is $xy < 0$?

  (1) $\dfrac{1}{x} < \dfrac{1}{y}$

  (2) $x > 0$

30. What is the mean (average) number of defective pens in a box of pens? The probability that there is exactly 1 defective pen in a box is 1 percent.

    (1) The probability that all the pens in the box are not defective is 96 percent.
    (2) The probability that there is more than 1 defective pen in the box is 3 percent.

31. Two-thirds of the roads from *A* to *B* are at least 5 miles long, and $\frac{1}{4}$ of the roads from *B* to *C* are at least 5 miles long. If you randomly pick a road from *A* to *B* and then randomly pick a road from *B* to *C*, what is the probability that at least one of the roads you pick is at least 5 miles long?

    (A) $\frac{1}{6}$

    (B) $\frac{1}{4}$

    (C) $\frac{2}{3}$

    (D) $\frac{3}{4}$

    (E) $\frac{11}{12}$

32. *ABC* and *AED* are triangles with *BC* and *ED* perpendicular to *AB*. Find the length of *ED* if the area of *ABC* is 16.

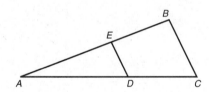

    (1) *AB* = 8
    (2) *AE* = 5

33. There are 30 socks in a drawer. Sixty percent of the socks are red, and the rest are blue. What is the minimum number of socks that must be taken from the drawer without looking in order to be certain that at least 2 blue socks have been chosen?

    (A) 2
    (B) 3
    (C) 14
    (D) 19
    (E) 20

34. Are two triangles congruent?

    (1) Both triangles are right triangles.
    (2) Both triangles have the same perimeter.

35. *C* is a circle with center *D* and radius 2. *E* is a circle with center *F* and radius *R*. Are there any points that are on both *E* and *C*?

    (1) The distance from *D* to *F* is $1 + R$.
    (2) $R = 3$.

36. *ABC* and *AED* are triangles with *BC* parallel to *ED*. Find the area of *BCDE* if the area of *ABC* is 16.

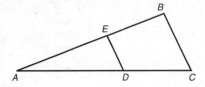

    (1) $BC = 8$
    (2) $ED = 5$

37. A car traveled 75 percent of the way from town *A* to town *B* at an average speed of 50 miles per hour. The car travels at an average speed of *S* miles per hour for the remaining part of the trip. The average speed for the entire trip was 40 miles per hour. What is *S*?

(A) 10
(B) 20
(C) 25
(D) 30
(E) 37.5

STOP

ON THE ACTUAL GMAT,
AFTER YOU HAVE CONFIRMED YOUR ANSWER,
YOU CANNOT RETURN TO IT.

VERBAL SECTION

Time: 75 minutes

41 questions

Reading Comprehension

DIRECTIONS: This section contains three reading passages. You are to read each one carefully. When answering the questions, you *will* be allowed to refer back to the passages. The questions are based on what is *stated* or *implied* in each passage.

Critical Reasoning

DIRECTIONS: For each question in this section, choose the best answer from among the listed alternatives.

Sentence Correction

DIRECTIONS: This part of the section consists of a number of sentences, in each of which some part or the whole is underlined. Each sentence is followed by five alternative versions of the underlined portion. Select the alternative you consider both most correct and most effective according to the requirements of standard written English. Answer (A) is the same as the original version; if you think the original version is best, select answer (A).

In considering the answer choices, be attentive to matters of grammar, diction, and syntax, as well as clarity, precision, and fluency. Do not select an answer that alters the meaning of the original sentence.

1. Lavoisier, the 18th-century scientist, became more influential and famous than most of his contemporaries because not only did he discover and isolate many of the chemical elements but he also gave them names that both described the element in terms of its power and function and came to be accepted by other scientists in subsequent generations.

    Which of the following can be inferred from the above passage?

    (A) Lavoisier strived for fame and influence in the 18th century.
    (B) All elements found in the 18th century were named after Lavoisier.
    (C) Some of the elements that Lavoisier isolated were given names that described their properties.
    (D) Lavoisier was the most influential and famous scientist of his time.
    (E) Lavoisier became famous only because the names that he gave the chemicals became accepted.

2. The disaster that followed the earthquake in Armenia was tragic and serious, not just because of the fatalities and injuries, but because such widespread and severe damage was avoidable. The earthquake was less than 6 on the open-ended Richter scale, but its effects and aftermath matched the scene of events after much stronger quakes. What caused the casualty figures to reach such horrendous heights was that the buildings in the area were generally of a design that could not be expected to withstand anything more than a minor tremor.

    Which of the following statements can best be inferred from the passage?

    (A) People were not killed and injured by the earthquake, but by the falling masonry.
    (B) Resources should be invested in predicting the location, incidence, and strength of earthquakes.
    (C) Emergency evacuation procedures should be introduced in areas where earthquakes tend to occur frequently.
    (D) It would be better if earthquakes occurred only in areas far away from large centers of population.
    (E) The rescue aid provided by international organizations and other countries after the earthquake will hopefully improve relations.

3. In 1896, Henri Bequerel found that uranium salts emitted penetrating radiations similar to those which Roentgen produced only a year earlier with a gas discharge tube.

    (A) similar to those which Roentgen
    (B) like those which Roentgen
    (C) similar to those that Roentgen had
    (D) similar to them that Roentgen
    (E) similar to those Roentgen

4. Unless they reverse present policies immediately, the world may suffer permanent damage from the unregulated use of pesticides.

    (A) Unless they reverse present policies
    (B) Unless present policies are reversed
    (C) Unless present policies will be reversed
    (D) If it will not reverse present policies
    (E) If present policies will not be reversed

5. John wanted to have gone to the movies.

    (A) wanted to have gone
    (B) had wanted to have gone
    (C) wanted to go
    (D) wanted to have went
    (E) had wanted to have went

Questions 6–9 are based on the following passage.

Despite the early protectionist moves, such as introducing steel tariffs, the Bush administration has pushed hard for trade liberalization in the past few years. In contrast, the European Union has appeared divided and ineffective. Its trade com-
Line missioner, Peter Mandelson, has so far failed to persuade skeptical member states
(5) that the benefits of new export markets will outweigh the costs of allowing greater competition at home, especially in agriculture. Though some members, notably Britain and other north Europeans, favor a more liberal approach, it has proved all but impossible to get agreement from France and other more protected economies with vociferous farmers. Europe's general position has been to refuse any more low-
(10) ering of agricultural barriers until poorer countries agree to liberalize trade in goods and services.

Nor is the G20 group of developing nations giving much impetus to the talks. Led by India and Brazil, the G20 is refusing to negotiate without deeper concessions on agriculture. India, with its large population, may turn out to be a big problem. Its
(15) government worries that competition from Chinese factories and American farms represents too great a threat, while gaining more access to world markets is only of limited attraction.

Other poor countries are also unsure what they would gain. There is general talk of hopeful prospects for poor farmers gaining greater access to rich-world markets.
(20) But the benefits will not flow evenly from rich to poor. The World Bank estimates that removing current agricultural distortions would produce a general benefit of more than $300 billion a year. Relative to national income, poor countries would enjoy a third more of this benefit than rich, industrialized ones. However, nearly half of that benefit would come from reforms by the developing countries themselves,
(25) something governments might do anyway were it not for the serious problem of the political pain the reforms are bound to cause.

6. It can be inferred from the passage that a removal of agricultural distortions would provide gains to poor countries of approximately

    (A) $300 billion per year.
    (B) $500 billion per year.
    (C) $400 billion per year.
    (D) $200 billion per year.
    (E) The sum cannot be determined from the passage.

7. According to the passage, the main concern of the Indian government is to

    (A) penetrate Chinese consumer markets.
    (B) reduce barriers to the sale of its farm produce.
    (C) impose more restrictive trade policies.
    (D) improve its bargaining position.
    (E) penetrate new overseas markets.

8. The author states that the American government is

    (A) liberalizing its foreign trade policy.
    (B) sensitive to the demands of third-world countries.
    (C) becoming more protectionist.
    (D) refusing to negotiate with developing countries.
    (E) ignoring the needs of third-world countries.

9. The passage provides support for the proposition that achieving an agreement at the latest round of trade talks seems doubtful because

    (A) the EU trade commissioner has failed to persuade India and China to liberalize exports of farm produce.
    (B) America's fast-track negotiating authority is soon to expire.
    (C) poorer countries refuse to lower agricultural barriers until developed countries open their markets to manufactured goods.
    (D) both the EU and G20 groups are unsure of the gains that might accrue from an agreement.
    (E) Britain and France are steadfastly against a new agreement.

10. Scientists believe they have discovered the wreck of the *USS Harvard*, sunk by Japanese torpedoes during World War II. Their conclusions are drawn from underwater searches by mini-submarines of the area about 4 miles west of Midway Island in the Pacific Ocean during what started out as offshore oil platform accident procedures. There are some military historians that are skeptical about the scientists' claim, on the basis that sophisticated sonar equipment has not identified the ship as, indeed, the *Harvard*.

Which of the following, if true, would weaken the historians' arguments?

(A) Thorough searching by divers and bathyscopes has not located the wreck.
(B) Three other ships were sunk in this area during World War II.
(C) The ship's last known position was 20 miles east of Midway.
(D) The use of sonar only enables the user to identify the shape and dimension of a wreck.
(E) It is not known whether the *Harvard* suffered much structural damage before being sunk.

11. In Great Britain, the problem of violence among spectators at soccer games has become more and more serious, with hardly a weekend passing without many arrested and many injured from among those who supposedly came to see a sport.

Many suggestions have been made to combat this problem, most of them involving the introduction of more restrictions on the freedom of the crowds. Increased police presence at all games, enclosing supporters of opposing teams in pens, preventing the two groups from coming into contact with each other, and the use of membership cards with photographs that must be presented in order to gain access have all been tried.

What is needed now is a deterrent factor. Increased fines, Saturday afternoon detention centers, and even jail terms must be introduced speedily and rigorously if we are going to solve this problem.

Which of the following, if true, would most strengthen the present view of the writer?

(A) The British Government has just passed legislation outlawing alcoholic drink to be sold at or brought into soccer matches.
(B) Last week there were 36 arrested and 50 injured in fighting among the top soccer matches. This was an increase of 25% over the figures for the previous week.
(C) The soccer clubs should do more to encourage families to attend their games by improving facilities and making special enclosures.
(D) Violence is on the increase at soccer matches, and the authorities must get tougher.
(E) Closed-circuit television has been set up to monitor trouble-making elements in the crowd.

12. <u>Either you transfer the data that was demanded</u> or file a report explaining why you did not submit the overall annual figures.

   (A) Either you transfer the data that was demanded
   (B) You either transfer the data, which was demanded,
   (C) You either transfer the data that were demanded
   (D) Either you transfer the data, which was demanded,
   (E) Either you transfer the data, which were demanded,

13. <u>On entering the stadium, cheers greeted them</u> as a sign of universal approval of their great achievement.

   (A) On entering the stadium, cheers greeted them
   (B) On entering the stadium, they were greeted by cheers
   (C) While entering the stadium, cheers greeted them
   (D) On entering the stadium cheers greeted them
   (E) On entering the stadium: cheers greeted them

14. The set of propositions <u>which was discussed by the panel have been</u> published in the society journal.

   (A) which was discussed by the panel have been
   (B) which were discussed by the panel have been
   (C) that was discussed by the panel has been
   (D) which were discussed by the panel has been
   (E) which was discussed, by the panel, has been

Questions 15–18 are based on the following passage.

Freud's methods have fallen from favor in recent decades, but science historians say that his investigation of the unconscious more than a century ago stands as a revolutionary achievement that still informs many therapists' understanding of
Line memory, trauma, and behavior.
(5)   Freud's drawings were serious science. In the latter part of the 19th century, German researchers considered drawing to be instrumental to scientific discovery, both as a way to capture the microscopic detail of nerve cells, for example, and to illustrate theories of how the brain might work, said Lynn Gamwell, curator of the exhibit and director of the Art Museum at the State University of New York at
(10) Binghamton. "Einstein once said that when he thought about science, he thought visually, he thought in pictures, and this appears to be the case with Freud," said Dr. Gamwell, a professor of science history.
     Freud's drawings tell a story in three acts, from biology to psychology, from the microscope to the couch. The first, from Freud's college years into his mid-twenties,
(15) took place in laboratories, where he examined the nervous systems of crayfish and lamprey, among other animals. The 21 drawings from this period would look familiar to anyone who used a microscope in high school but on deeper inspection betray compulsive detail.

(20) At the time these drawings appeared, many neurologists presumed the body was somehow mirrored in the brain, perhaps altered in form but recognizable, intact. Freud said the brain worked differently; that is, fibers and cells "contain the body periphery in the same way as a poem contains the alphabet, in a complete arrangement" based on a body part's function, not its location. Later research supported Freud's contention.

15. In the late 19th century, it was believed that drawings were important to scientific discovery because they

(A) helped researchers relax during times of stress.
(B) were the only way to study basic functions.
(C) illustrated how the brain functions.
(D) helped to determine gender.
(E) were more accurate than photographs.

16. According to the passage, Freud began his career as a

(A) neurologist.
(B) psychologist.
(C) biologist.
(D) laboratory assistant.
(E) artist.

17. The passage suggests that in a career change, Freud switched from anatomy to a study of

(A) brain functions.
(B) unconscious behavior.
(C) neuropathology.
(D) nervous systems.
(E) pathology.

18. The best possible title for the passage is

(A) *Freud as an Artist.*
(B) *On the Structure of Nerve Fibers.*
(C) *From Microscope to Couch.*
(D) *Elementary Psychoanalysis.*
(E) *From Dissection to Introspection.*

19. There are three main factors that control the risks of becoming dependent on drugs. These factors are the type of drug, the personality of the individual, and the circumstances in which the drug is taken. Indeed, it could be said that the majority of the adult population have taken alcohol, yet few have become dependent on it. Also, many strong drugs that have been used for medical purposes have not caused the patient to become addicted.

   However, it can be demonstrated that people who have taken drugs for fun are more likely to become dependent on the drug. The dependence is not always physiological but may remain psychological, although the effects are still essentially the same. Those at greatest risk appear to be personalities that are psychopathic, immature, or otherwise unstable.

   Psychological dependence is very strong with heroin, morphine, cocaine, and amphetamines. Physiological dependence is great with heroin and morphine, but less with amphetamines, barbiturates, and alcohol.

   Which of the following conclusions can be drawn from the text?

   (A) One cannot become addicted to certain drugs if one has a strong personality.
   (B) Taking drugs for "kicks" increases the possibility of becoming dependent on drugs.
   (C) Psychological dependence is greatest with heroin.
   (D) Alcohol is a safe drug since very few people become dependent on it.
   (E) Long-term use of certain drugs for medical purposes does not cause addiction.

20. In 1985 there were 20 deaths from automobile accidents per 1,000 miles traveled. A total of 20,000 miles were traveled via automobiles in 1985. In the same year, 800 people died in airplane crashes and 400 people were killed in train disasters. A statistician concluded from these data alone that it was more dangerous to travel by plane, train, and automobile, in that order.

   Which of the following refutes the statistician's conclusion?

   (A) There is no common denominator by which to compare the number of deaths resulting from each mode of travel.
   (B) Road conditions were not stated.
   (C) More people travel by car than any other mode of transport; therefore, the probability of a car accident is greater.
   (D) The number of plane flights and train trips is not stated.
   (E) The probability of being killed in a train disaster and as a result of a car crash is the same.

21. From a letter to the commercial editor of a newspaper: Your article of January 9 drew attention to the large deficit in Playland's balance of payments that has worsened over the past three years. Yet, you favor the recent trade treaty signed between Playland and Workland. That treaty results in a lowering of our import duties that will flood us with Workland's goods. This will only exacerbate our balance of trade. How can you be in favor of the treaty?

Which of the following considerations would weaken the letter writer's argument?

(A) import diversion versus import creation
(B) prices paid by importers versus prices paid by consumers
(C) economic goals versus political goals
(D) duties levied increase government revenue
(E) free trade versus protectionism

22. In 1930, there were, on the average 10 deaths at birth (infant mortality) per 10,000 population. By 1940 there were 8.5, and by 1950, 7.0. Today there are 5.5 deaths at birth per 10,000 population, and it is anticipated that the downward trend will continue.

Each of the following, if true, would help to account for this trend EXCEPT

(A) Medical care is more widespread and available.
(B) More effective birth control methods have been implemented.
(C) Sanitary conditions have improved.
(D) The number of pediatricians per 10,000 population has increased.
(E) Midwifery has declined in favor of medical doctors.

23. Product shipments of household appliances are expected to rise to $17 billion next year, an average annual increase of 8.0 percent over the past five years. The real growth rate, after allowing for probable price increases, is expected to be about 4.3 percent each year, resulting in shipments this year of $14 billion in 1987 dollars.

Each of the following, if true, could help to account for this trend EXCEPT

(A) Consumer spending for durable products has increased.
(B) The number of new households has increased.
(C) Consumer disposable income has increased.
(D) The consumer price of electricity has decreased.
(E) The life of durable products has increased.

24. In this particular job we have discovered that <u>to be diligent is more important than being bright</u>.

(A) to be diligent is more important than being bright
(B) for one to be diligent is more important than being bright
(C) diligence is more important than brightness
(D) being diligent is more important than to be bright
(E) by being diligent is more important than being bright

25. No one but <u>him could have told them that the thief was I</u>.

    (A) him could have told them that the thief was I
    (B) he could have told them that the thief was I
    (C) he could have told them that the thief was me
    (D) him could have told them that the thief was me
    (E) he could have told them the thief was me

26. Products that have well-known brands generally command premium prices when produced in developed countries. The same branded products manufactured in third-world, low-image countries, however, are perceived to be inferior, even though manufacturing processes can be effectively transferred to less developed countries resulting in the same quality products. Paradoxically, the same branded products produced in a low image country have to be discounted.

Which of the following, if true, explains the paradox above?

    (A) Workers in low-image countries lack the skills to make quality products.
    (B) Country image is perceived by consumers to be more important than brand name.
    (C) Companies do not reveal where their products are manufactured, thus confusing consumers.
    (D) Workers in third-world countries work longer hours for lower pay than in developed countries.
    (E) Brand names have become less important to consumers when comparing competing products.

27. Before the middle of the 14th century, there were no universities north of Italy, except in France and England. By the end of the 15th century, there were 23 universities in this region, from Louvain and Mainz to Rostock, Cracow, and Bratislava, and the number of universities in Europe as a whole had more than doubled.

Given the above information, which of the following statements is correct?

    (A) Until the age of university expansion in the 15th century, there were perhaps 11 universities in the whole of Europe.
    (B) South of Italy there were 23 universities in the 14th century.
    (C) In the 13th century, France and England were the only countries in Europe with universities.
    (D) After the great age of university expansion in the 14th and 15th centuries, France and England were not the only northern European countries to have such centers of learning.
    (E) Italy was the cradle of university expansion.

28. After a careful evaluation of the circumstances surrounding the incident, we decided that we <u>neither have the authority nor</u> the means to cope with the problem.

    (A) neither have the authority nor
    (B) neither have authority or
    (C) have neither the authority nor
    (D) have neither the authority or
    (E) have not either the authority nor

29. <u>Everyone of us have understood that without him helping us</u> we would not have succeeded in our program over the past six months.

    (A) Everyone of us have understood that without him helping us
    (B) Everyone of us has understood that without his helping us
    (C) Everyone of us have understood that without his help
    (D) Everyone of us has understood that without him helping us
    (E) Every single one of us have understood that without him helping us

30. On the African continent, the incidence of vitamin <u>deficiencies correlates positively with</u> the level of solar radiation

    (A) deficiencies correlates positively with
    (B) deficiencies correlate positively with
    (C) deficiencies, correlate positively with,
    (D) deficiencies correlate positively to
    (E) deficiencies correlates positively to

31. The dominant beliefs of ancient Rome centered on a passion for order even in the face of evidence to the contrary, the Roman theory of a Ptolemaic universe, the absolute right of emperors, <u>parliament, and that Earth being the center of the universe kept the cosmic order of the universe.</u>

    (A) parliament, and that Earth being the center of the universe kept the cosmic order of the universe.
    (B) the parliament, and that Earth being the center of the universe kept the cosmic order of the universe.
    (C) parliamentary law, and an Earth-centered cosmic order.
    (D) parliament, and that Earth had been the center of the universe.
    (E) parliamentary law, and that Earth was the center of the universe.

32. <u>If they would have taken greater care</u> in the disposal of the nuclear waste, the disaster would not have occurred.

   (A) If they would have taken greater care
   (B) Unless they took greater care
   (C) Had they not taken greater care
   (D) If they had taken greater care
   (E) If they took greater care

33. <u>Neither the judge nor I am ready to announce who the winner is.</u>

   (A) Neither the judge nor I am ready to announce who the winner is.
   (B) Neither the judge nor I are ready to announce who the winner is.
   (C) Neither the judge nor I are ready to announce who is the winner.
   (D) Neither the judge nor I am ready to announce who is the winner.
   (E) Neither I or the judge are ready to announce who is the winner.

34. One major obligation of the social psychologist is to provide his own discipline, the other social sciences, and interested laymen with conceptual tools that will increase the range and the reliability of their understanding of social phenomena. Beyond that, responsible government officials are today turning more frequently to the social scientist for insights into the nature and solution of the problems with which they are confronted.

   The above argument assumes that

   (A) social psychologists must have a strong background in other sciences as well as their own.
   (B) a study of social psychology should be a part of the curriculum of government officials.
   (C) the social scientist has an obligation to provide the means by which social phenomena may be understood by others.
   (D) social phenomena are little understood by those outside the field of social psychology.
   (E) a good social psychologist is obligated principally by the need to solve interdisciplinary problems.

35. Administrators and executives are members of the most stable occupation.

The stability mentioned in the above statement could be dependent on each of the following factors *except*

(A) training and skills.
(B) nature of the occupation.
(C) professional status.
(D) relatively high income.
(E) rate of mobility.

36. Between 1979 and 1983, the number of unincorporated, self-employed women increased five times faster than the number of self-employed men and more than three times faster than the number of women wage-and-salary workers. Part-time self-employment among women increased more than full-time self-employment.

Each of the following, if true, could help to account for this trend EXCEPT

(A) Owning a business affords flexibility to combine work and family responsibilities.
(B) The proportion of women studying business administration courses has grown considerably.
(C) There are more self-employed women than men.
(D) Unincorporated service industries have grown by 300 percent over the period; the ratio of women to men in this industry is three to one.
(E) The financial reward of having a second wage earner in the household has taken on increased significance.

37. <u>More than any animal</u>, the wolverine exemplifies the unbridled ferocity of "nature red in tooth and claw."

(A) More than any animal,
(B) More than any other animal,
(C) More than another animal,
(D) Unlike any animal,
(E) Compared to other animals,

Questions 38–41 are based on the following passage.

Lord Kelvin's claim for a recognition of the fact that in organic nature scientific thought is compelled to accept the idea of some kind of directive power, and his statement that biologists are coming once more to a firm acceptance of a vital
Line principle, drew from several distinguished men of science retorts heated enough to
(5) prove beyond a doubt the gulf between the two main divisions of evolutionists. It will be well, perhaps, for the benefit of readers who have not followed the history of the theory of evolution during its later developments, to state in a few words what these two main divisions are. All evolutionists agree that the differences between species are caused by the accumulation and transmission of variations, but they do
(10) not agree as to the causes to which the variations are due.

The view held by the older evolutionists, Buffon, Erasmus, Darwin, and Lamarck, who have been followed by many modern thinkers, including Herbert Spencer and Butler, is that the variations occur mainly as the result of effort and design; the opposite view is that the variations occur merely as the result of chance. The former is
(15) sometimes called the theological view, because it recognizes the presence in organic nature of design, whether it be called creative power, directive force, directivity, or vital principle; in the latter view the existence of design is absolutely negated.

—Excerpt from the introduction by R. A. Streatfeild in *Essays on Life, Art and Science* by Samuel Butler

38. The author implies Lord Kelvin believes that evolution is

(A) a vital principle.
(B) a heated theory.
(C) caused by variations.
(D) caused by God.
(E) a result of chance.

39. A possible title that best expresses the meaning of the passage would be

(A) *The Evolutionary Ideas of Lord Kelvin*
(B) *The Evolution of Evolution*
(C) *Understanding Organic Nature*
(D) *Lord Kelvin, Buffon, Erasmus, Darwin, Lamarck, Spencer, and Butler's Concepts of Evolution*
(E) *Evolution: Chance Versus Design*

40. According to the passage,

    (A) the discussion between evolutionary theorists is rooted in cause and effect.
    (B) the study of biology is necessary to understand evolution.
    (C) a later generation, as opposed to earlier evolutionary theorists, held that the differences in species are caused by the accumulation of variations.
    (D) Kelvin believed that evolution is chance.
    (E) biologists agree that evolution involves an accretion of changes.

41. The author of the passage suggests that

    (A) the discussion is scientifically objective.
    (B) the discussion is emotional.
    (C) there is general agreement between early and later evolutionary theorists.
    (D) the passage will explain evolution to readers.
    (E) evolution must be explained theologically.

STOP

ON THE ACTUAL GMAT,
AFTER YOU HAVE CONFIRMED YOUR ANSWER,
YOU CANNOT RETURN TO IT.

INTEGRATED REASONING SECTION

1. i. B

ii. B

2.

Could Be Classified	Could Not Be Classified	Animal
○	●	Penguin
●	○	Flamingo
○	●	Flying Squirrel
●	○	Pterodactyl
●	○	Eagle

3.

Yes	No
○	●
○	●
●	○

4.

Yes	No
○	●
○	●
○	●
●	○

5. B

6.

Either Day	Neither Day	Speaker
○	●	Branson, male, U.K.
○	○	Robinson, female, U.K.
○	○	D'Agostino, female, Brazil
●	○	Miller, female, Canada
○	○	Soares, male, India

7. i. A

ii. B

8. B

9.

True	False
●	○
●	○
○	●

10. i. A

ii. B

11.

True	False
○	●
●	○
○	●

12.

Would Help Explain	Would Not Help Explain
●	○
●	○
○	●

ANSWER KEY
Sample Test 1

QUANTITATIVE SECTION

1. E	**11.** D	**21.** D	**31.** D
2. A	**12.** D	**22.** C	**32.** C
3. D	**13.** B	**23.** B	**33.** E
4. D	**14.** C	**24.** B	**34.** E
5. C	**15.** C	**25.** B	**35.** C
6. B	**16.** A	**26.** C	**36.** C
7. C	**17.** C	**27.** D	**37.** C
8. A	**18.** C	**28.** A	
9. E	**19.** E	**29.** C	
10. E	**20.** C	**30.** E	

VERBAL SECTION

1. C	**12.** C	**23.** E	**34.** C
2. A	**13.** B	**24.** C	**35.** E
3. C	**14.** D	**25.** A	**36.** C
4. B	**15.** C	**26.** B	**37.** B
5. C	**16.** C	**27.** D	**38.** D
6. E	**17.** A	**28.** C	**39.** E
7. B	**18.** C	**29.** B	**40.** E
8. A	**19.** B	**30.** A	**41.** B
9. D	**20.** A	**31.** C	
10. D	**21.** A	**32.** D	
11. B	**22.** B	**33.** A	

SELF-SCORING GUIDE
Analytical Writing

Evaluate your essay (or have a friend or teacher evaluate it for you) on the following basis. Read your essay completely, paying special attention to its logical organization and use of examples and facts to buttress its claims or position. Assign a holistic score between 0 and 6, using the scale below.

6 OUTSTANDING

Cogent, well-articulated analysis of the issue or critique of the argument. Develops a position with insightful reasons and persuasive examples. Well organized. Superior command of language and variety of syntax. Only minor flaws in grammar, usage, and mechanics.

5 STRONG

Well-developed analysis or critique. Develops a position with well-chosen examples or reasons. Generally well organized. Clear control of language and variety of syntax. Minor flaws in grammar, usage, and mechanics.

4 ADEQUATE

Competent analysis or critique. Develops a position with relevant reasons or examples. Adequately organized. Adequate control of language, but may lack syntactic variety. May have some flaws in grammar, usage, and mechanics.

3 LIMITED

Competent but clearly flawed analysis or critique. Vague or limited in developing a position. Poorly organized. Weak in using relevant examples or reasons. Language used imprecisely or lacking in sentence variety. Contains major errors or frequent minor errors in grammar, usage, and mechanics.

2 SERIOUSLY FLAWED

Serious weaknesses in analysis and organization. Unclear or seriously limited in presenting or developing a position. Disorganized. Few relevant examples or reasons. Frequent serious problems in language and sentence structure. Numerous errors in grammar, usage, or mechanics that interfere with meaning.

1 FUNDAMENTALLY DEFICIENT

Little evidence of ability to organize and develop a coherent response to issue or argument. Severe and persistent errors in language and sentence structure. Pervasive pattern of errors in grammar, usage, and mechanics that severely interfere with meaning.

0 UNSCORABLE

Illegible or not written on the assigned topic.

ANSWERS EXPLAINED
Integrated Reasoning Section

1. i. (B) If you look at the scatter plot, you can see a distinct relationship between the two curved lines. Assuming that one variable is always a little bit more than the other variable at each point on the graph, the relationship is very strong. Even if you assume that one variable is larger than the other at some of the points and vice versa for the rest, the relationship is still strong given that the distance apart appears small and constant. Therefore, the correct answer is **B**.

ii. (B) The absolute difference between the variables at each point in the chart is constant. Therefore, the graph would be plotted along the same number across, resulting in a straight line. Since the question doesn't say which variable is plotted on the x-axis and which is plotted on the y-axis, the only possible answer of the choices given is zero. Note that if "an undefined slope" was one of the choices instead of "a slope of zero," an undefined slope would be correct. Therefore, the answer is **B**.

2. (Could Not Be Classified, Could Be Classified, Could Not Be Classified, Could Be Classified, Could Be Classified)
(i) Although the penguin has the appropriate beak, its forelimbs are not adapted for flying as described in the second criterion. Therefore a penguin **could not be classified** as a bird.
(ii) The flamingo matches both criteria given: having a beak or bill and having wings adapted for flying. Therefore a flamingo **could be classified** as a bird.
(iii) The flying squirrel's forelimbs could technically be said to have been adapted for flying. However, the flying squirrel clearly does not have a beak as defined in the first criterion. Therefore a flying squirrel **could not be classified** as a bird.
(iv) The pterodactyl matches both criteria given: having a beak or bill and having wings adapted for flying. Therefore a pterodactyl **could be classified** as a bird.
(v) The eagle matches both criteria given: having a beak or bill and having wings adapted for flying. Therefore an eagle **could be classified** as a bird.

3. (No, No, Yes)
(i) First you need to determine the median number of employees per stores in Quebec. If you sort the chart by province, you can see that Quebec has 16 stores. Then if you sort by number of employees, you can see that the 8th and 9th largest numbers are 61 and 64, respectively. Therefore the median is 62.5. If you look quickly at the Ontario stores, you can count 27 of them. Just by going down the chart, which is already sorted by number of employees, you can quickly estimate that the median is within a group of Ontario stores with numbers of employees in the 70s. More specifically, the median is the 14th number, which is 77. Therefore the answer is **No**.
(ii) If you sort by number of employees, you can see that the St. Jean store has 59 employees and also has a grocery section. Therefore the answer is **No**.
(iii) If you sort by city, you will find more than 7 cities that have either two or three locations. Therefore the answer is **Yes**.

4. (No, No, No, Yes)

(i) Article 1 does mention that deforestation affects CO_2 emissions. However, no direct link is given in any article suggesting that deforestation is the only or the major cause of increasing CO_2 levels. Therefore the answer is **No**.

(ii) Both articles 1 and 2 cite that citizens vote down some environmental proposals. There is also mention of aggressive lobbying by the forestry industry. However, no direct link between the lobbying and voters striking down environment proposals is provided. Lobbying may be a strong cause but is not necessarily the main reason. Therefore the answer is **No**.

(iii) Dr. Finnegan mentions both the forestry industry and bottled-water industry in article 2. However, there is no mention of where his focus is or whether he would support one type of legislation over another. Therefore the answer is **No**.

(iv) Both articles 2 and 3 imply that scientists, one of whom is Dr. Finnegan, have opinions that differ from those of leaders of both industries. So you can say that the two parties may not always agree. Therefore the answer is **Yes**.

5. (B)

This question is a bit tougher because you are looking for support in the articles for four of the answer choices. Only one answer is not supported by the articles. Answer choice A is fine because article 1 mentions 20% of wildlife may become extinct. Answer choice C is supported because article 3 mentions that the price has actually tripled over the past two decades. Answer choice D is supported in article 3. Answer choice E is supported by article 1 since levels are expected to double in 50 years, which is still within the 21st century. Only answer choice B is not supported since there is no mention of vodka. Article 2 does mention that bottled water may have a premium price as a luxury item, but no specifics are given in the passage. Therefore the answer choice is **B**.

6. (Miller, Branson)

This problem has 3 constraints.

- Four or more international speakers are needed on Day 1.
- Four or more female speakers are needed on Day 2.
- No more than two speakers from the same country can appear on either day.

Day 1 already has four international speakers, but two are from the U.K. Therefore the only constraint that applies is that you cannot add speakers from the U.K. on Day 1. This constraint eliminates Branson and Robinson from Day 1.

Day 2 already has three female speakers. In addition, two speakers are from the U.S.A. and two are from Brazil. Therefore, you cannot add any speakers who are male, from the U.S.A., or from Brazil. These constraints eliminate Branson, D'Agostino, and Soares.

Therefore Branson can attend on neither day and Miller can attend on either day.

7. i. (A)

Graph 1 shows that Europe and Central Asia's GDP in 1999 was approximately $10 trillion. Graph 2 shows that Europe and Central Asia's growth in 2000 was –6.0%. The increase in GDP is approximately:

$$\$10 \text{ trillion} \times -0.06 = -\$0.6 \text{ trillion}$$

This amount, which converts to –$600 billion, is close to –$610 billion. Therefore the answer is **A**.

ii. (B) You already know from question 7. i. that Europe and Central Asia's GDP decreased by approximately $600 billion. Graph 1 shows that East Asia and Pacific have the only other significant GDP, approximately $7.5 trillion. Use the information from graph 2 and the calculator to determine the increase in GDP in 2000 for East Asia and Pacific:

$$\$7.5 \text{ trillion} \times 0.082 = \$0.62 \text{ trillion}$$

This GDP increase for East Asia and Pacific almost matches the GDP decrease for Europe and Central Asia, so they cancel out each other. You can estimate Latin America GDP growth to be approximately $0.2 trillion. Similarly, Middle East and North Africa have an approximate GDP growth of $0.1 trillion. The increase in GDP for Sub-Saharan Africa is insignificant. This total increase of approximately $0.3 trillion in GDP for all five regions, which is a little over $20 trillion, works out to approximately 1.5% growth. Therefore the closest answer is **B**.

8. **(B)** First notice how the answer choices vary. Then determine which products have a greater effect on the total cost. Goodie bags are far more expensive and have the smallest discounts, so answer choices C and E are likely to be quite high, especially since the ribbon and streamer amounts are also quite high. Next notice how many feet of ribbon and streamers are in each package. The ribbon package yields 48 feet of ribbon, while the streamer package yields 100 feet of streamers. Calculate the costs for the other answer choices:

A: ($8 × 4) + ($6 × 3) + ($4 × 3) + ($12 × 5) = $122 subtotal
$122 – ($15 ribbon discount + $10 goodie bag discount) = $97 total

B: ($8 × 7) + ($6 × 2) + ($4 × 2) + ($12 × 3) = $112 subtotal
$112 – $25 ribbon discount = $87 total

D: ($8 × 8) + ($6 × 4) + ($4 × 5) + ($12 × 2) = $132 subtotal
$132 – $25 ribbon discount = $107 total

Therefore the answer is **B**.

9. **(True, True, False)**
(i) At first glance, this problem doesn't seem to make sense. However, the trick is to consider the discounts given for large-scale spending. Since 9 packages of streamers cost $54, a $20 discount is given. This results in a total cost of only $34. In contrast, 8 packages of streamers cost $48 before the $10 discount is applied. The total cost for 8 packages of streamers is $38. Similarly, 7 packages of ribbons cost $56 minus the $25 discount, resulting in a total cost of only $31. In contrast, 6 packages of ribbons cost $48 before the $10 discount is applied. The total cost for 6 packages of ribbons is $38. Add the amounts:

9 streamers plus 7 ribbons: $34 + $31 = $65
8 streamers plus 6 ribbons: $38 + $33 = $71

Therefore the answer is **True**.

(ii) Calculate the cost of buying 300 feet of ribbon plus 900 feet of streamers and the cost of purchasing 144 goodie bags plus 24 balloons.

300 feet of ribbon: 7 packages × $8 = $56 subtotal
$56 – $25 discount = $31 total
900 feet of streamers: 9 packages × $6 = $54 subtotal
$54 – $20 discount = $34 total
300 feet of ribbon plus 900 feet of streamers: $31 + $34 = $65
144 goodie bags: 6 packages × $12 = 72 subtotal
$72 – $10 discount = $62 total

At this point, you can stop since you know a package of balloons will cost $4 and take the price of goodie bags and balloons above the price of the ribbons and streamers. Therefore the answer is **True**.

(iii) To get the maximum discount from all four products, Sally needs to spend more than $50 for each product. She would need:

- 7 packages of ribbons totaling $56
- 9 packages of streamers totaling $54
- 13 packages of balloons totaling $52
- 5 packages of goodie bags totaling $60

The total cost looks like it would be $222. Wait! Do not forget to include the discounts. When the discounts kick in, the total amount that Sally has to spend is reduced by $25 + $20 + $10 + $10 = $65. Therefore the total amount Sally spends is $157 and the answer is **False**.

10. **i. (A)** The regression lines for both math and English scores are very close to each other. However, you can see from the scatter plot that the dotted regression line (English) has a steeper slope than the solid regression line (math). Therefore the slope for the English score regression line is greater than the slope for the Math score regression line. The answer is **A**.

ii. (B) The easiest way to solve this is by looking at the scatter plot and counting how often a square (math) is above a diamond (English). Excluding the points where the square and diamond are too close to tell, you can find at least 13 diamonds that are higher than squares. This represents more than half of the 22 students. Therefore the students tend to score worse in math than in English. The answer is **B**.

11. **(False, True, False)**
(i) It's important to learn how to use the data given. In order to determine the in-store price points, look at the share of market in pounds (lb.) and the share of market in dollars ($). Calculate the average price per pound ($/lb.) just by dividing share in dollars by share in pounds. Determine the price per pound of the four cheeses:

Kruger Cheddar Mild: $\frac{\$1.60}{2.9 \text{ lb.}} = \$0.55/\text{lb.}$ Kruger Swiss: $\frac{\$8.50}{7.4 \text{ lb.}} = \$1.15/\text{lb.}$

Kruger Mozzarella: $\frac{\$14.70}{16.2 \text{ lb.}} = \$0.91/\text{lb.}$ Davinci Havarti: $\frac{\$3.20}{2.7 \text{ lb.}} \$1.86/\text{lb.}$

Both cheddar and mozzarella give values of less than $1/lb. Both Swiss and Havarti give values higher than $1/lb. Looking at the other examples of these cheeses would show the same relationship. Therefore the cheddar and mozzarella are not higher priced than the Swiss and Havarti. The answer is **False**.

(ii) The best way to figure this out is by sorting by the share of market ($). You can use the calculator to add up all the shares by dollar for Swiss cheese products:

$$11.9 + 8.5 + 7.9 + 4.0 = 32.3$$

The only other competitor would be mozzarella. Add up the shares by dollar for mozzarella:

$$14.7 + 5.9 + 3.8 + 2.4 + 1.7 = 28.5$$

Therefore the answer is **True**.

(iii) The easiest way to determine King's cheese slices growth per pound is to sort by product. Then look at the change in sales vs. last year (lb.). Instead of using the calculator for a long list of numbers, just estimate. Try matching up the negative and positive values for King brand products. You should be able to estimate a little less than 70,000 lb. Now do the same for Davinci products. You will get a ballpark figure of around 90,000 lb. for Davinci. This should be enough information for you to answer the question with confidence. The answer is **False**.

12. **(Would Help Explain, Would Help Explain, Would Not Help Explain)**
(i) If you sort by change in % volume ($), you will see that most of the zippered packages are at the top of the list. This suggests a trend where consumers favor packages with zippers and would help to explain the statement. Therefore the answer is **Would Help Explain** the statement.
(ii) If you sort by change in % volume (lb.) or by change in % volume ($), you will notice four King products that have decreased by 100%. This would imply that they were discontinued. You may also notice that the same flavors were replaced by packages with zippers. Therefore the table **Would Help Explain** the statement.
(iii) The table does show that the price per pound of light cheese (e.g., King Swiss Light w/ Zipper) is higher than the price per pound of regular cheese (e.g., King Swiss w/ Zipper). However, no information is given regarding the manufacturing costs of any of the sliced cheeses. Therefore the table **Would Not Help Explain** the statement.

Quantitative Section

(Roman numerals at the end of each answer refer to the section of Chapter 9 in which the appropriate math principle is discussed.)

---

1. How many books are on the bookshelf?

(1) The bookshelf is 12 feet long.
(2) The average weight of each book is 1.2 pounds.

(E) STATEMENT (1) would be sufficient if there were information about the width of each book. Since STATEMENT (2) gives information only about the *weight* of each book, both statements together are not sufficient. (III-1) ★☆☆

---

2. The equation of a straight line containing the points (10,100) and (15, 60) is

(A) $y = -8x + 180$
(B) $y = 8x - 180$
(C) $y = (\frac{1}{8})x + 7.5$
(D) $y = -8x - 180$
(E) $y = (-\frac{1}{8})x + 22.5$

(A) The slope of the line is ★☆☆
$\frac{(y_1 - y_2)}{(x_1 - x_2)}$, which is $\frac{(100-60)}{(10-15)} = \frac{40}{-5} = -8$.
So the equation of the line is $y = -8x + b$. Use either point to find b. Using (10,100), we have $100 = y = -8x + b = -8(10) + b$, so $100 = -80 + b$, which gives us $b = 180$. So the equation of the line is $y = -8x + 180$. (III-10)

---

3. If $f(x) = x^3 - 4$ and $f(y) = 4$, then y is equal to

(A) 0
(B) $2^{\frac{1}{3}}$
(C) $\sqrt{2}$
(D) 2
(E) 3

(D) Since $f(y) = y^3 - 4$ and $f(y) = 4$, we know ★☆☆
that $y^3 - 4 = 4$. Solve the equation for y, which gives $y^3 = 8$, and so $y = 2$. (II-2, III-10)

★☆☆ **4.** In triangle *ABC*, find *z* if *AB* = 5 and *y* = 40.

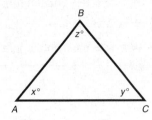

(1) *BC* = 5

(2) The bisector of angle *B* is perpendicular to *AC*.

(D) STATEMENT (1) alone is sufficient since *BC* = *AB* implies *x* = *y* = 40. Since the sum of the angles in a triangle is 180°, *z* must equal 100. STATEMENT (2) alone is sufficient. Let *D* be the point where the bisector of angle *B* meets *AC*. Then according to (2), triangle *BDC* is a right triangle. Since angle *y* is 40°, the remaining angle in triangle *BDC* is 50° and equals $\frac{1}{2}z$; so *z* = 100. (III-4)

★☆☆ **5.** How far is it from town *A* to town *B*? Town *C* is 12 miles east of town *A*.

(1) Town *C* is south of town *B*.

(2) It is 9 miles from town *B* to town *C*.

(C) STATEMENT (2) alone is insufficient since you need to know what direction town *B* is from town *C*.

STATEMENT (1) alone is insufficient since you need to know how far it is from town *B* to town *C*.

Using both STATEMENTS (1) and (2), *A*, *B*, and *C* form a right triangle with legs of 9 miles and 12 miles. The distance from town *A* to town *B* is the hypotenuse of the triangle, so the distance from town *A* to town *B* is $\sqrt{9^2 + 12^2}$ = 15 miles. (III-4, III-9)

★☆☆ **6.** If *x* + *y* + *z* + *w* = 15, then at least *k* of the numbers *x*, *y*, *z*, *w* must be positive, where *k* is

(A) 0

(B) 1

(C) 2

(D) 3

(E) 4

(B) If three of the numbers are negative, then as long as the fourth is greater than the absolute value of the sum of the other three, the sum of all four is positive. For example, (−50) + (−35) + (−55) + 155 = 15. (I-6)

★★☆ **7.** Is there a route from *A* to *C* that passes through *B* and is more than 8 miles long?

(1) Two roads from *A* to *B* are at least 5 miles long.

(2) Three roads from *B* to *C* are at least 5 miles long.

(C) STATEMENT (1) alone is not sufficient since you have no information about the distance from *B* to *C*. STATEMENT (2) alone is not sufficient since you have no information about the distance from *A* to *B*. The two statements together are sufficient since they show that there are at least six routes from *A* to *C* that pass through *B* and are at least 10 miles long. (II-4)

8. If you test 2 different lightbulbs from a box of 100 bulbs that contains 1 defective bulb what is the probability that both lightbulbs that you test are defective?

(A) 0

(B) 0.0001

(C) $\dfrac{1}{9,900}$

(D) 0.01

(E) $\dfrac{1}{99}$

(A) Since the question says you test 2 *different* bulbs and there is only 1 defective bulb in the box, there is no possibility that both bulbs will be defective. (I-7)

---

9. A company can sell $100x$ machine parts if it charges $10 - 0.1x$ dollars for each machine part. How many machine parts can the company sell if it charges $4.00 for each machine part?

(A) 6

(B) 9.6

(C) 60

(D) 960

(E) 6,000

(E) If the company sells the parts for $4.00 each, then $4 = 10 - 0.1x$. Solve $4 = 10 - 0.1x$ for x. The result is $x = 60$. The company will sell $100x$ parts; so they will sell $100(60) = 6,000$ machine parts. (III-10)

---

10. A car goes 15 miles on a gallon of gas when it is driven at 50 miles per hour. When the car is driven at 60 miles per hour it only goes 80 percent as far. How many gallons of gas will it take to travel 120 miles driving at 60 miles per hour?

(A) 2

(B) 6.4

(C) 8

(D) 9.6

(E) 10

(E) Let x be the number of miles the car travels on a gallon of gas when driven at 60 mph. Then 80 percent of 15 is x; so $(0.80)(15) = x$ and $x = 12$. So it will take $\dfrac{120}{12} = 10$ gallons of gas to travel 120 miles at 60 mph. Notice that many of the other choices correspond to misconceptions.

If you divide $\dfrac{120}{15}$, you get 8, which is choice (C), but this is the number of gallons needed to travel 120 miles at 50 mph. If you take 80 percent of 8 gallons, you get choice (B), and if you take 120 percent of 8, you get choice (D). So the fact that your answer matches one of the given choices does not mean it is correct. (I-4, II-3)

★★☆ **11.** Train X leaves New York at 1 A.M. and travels east at a speed of x miles per hour. If train Z leaves New York at 2 A.M. and travels east, at what rate of speed in miles per hour will train Z have to travel in order to catch train X at exactly 5:30 A.M.?

(A) $\left(\dfrac{5}{6}\right)x$

(B) $\left(\dfrac{9}{8}\right)x$

(C) $\left(\dfrac{6}{5}\right)x$

(D) $\left(\dfrac{9}{7}\right)x$

(E) $\left(\dfrac{3}{2}\right)x$

(D) By 5:30 A.M. train X will have traveled $(4\frac{1}{2})x$ miles. So train Z must travel $(4\frac{1}{2})x$ miles in $3\frac{1}{2}$ hours. The average rate of speed necessary is $\dfrac{4\frac{1}{2}x}{3\frac{1}{2}}$ which equals $\left(\dfrac{9}{7}\right)x$.

(II-1, II-3)

★★☆ **12.** A company makes a profit of 6 percent on its first \$1,000 of sales each day, and 5 percent on all sales in excess of \$1,000 for that day. How many dollars in profit will the company make on a day when sales are S dollars if S is greater than 1,000?

(A) $0.05S$
(B) $0.06S$
(C) 110
(D) $10 + 0.05S$
(E) $60 + 0.05S$

(D) Since S is greater than 1,000, the profit is 6 percent of \$1,000 plus 5 percent of $(S-1,000)$ dollars, which is $\$60 + (0.05S - 50)$ dollars. Therefore, the profit equals $(10 + 0.05S)$ dollars. (II-3)

★★☆ **13.** Is x an even integer? Assume n and p are integers.

(1) $x = (n + p)^2$
(2) $x = 2n + 10p$

(B) An even integer is an integer divisible by 2. Since $2n + 10p$ is $2(n + 5p)$, using STATEMENT (2) lets you deduce that x is even. STATEMENT (1) by itself is not sufficient. If n were 2 and p were 3, $(n + p)^2$ would be 25, which is not even, but by choosing n to be 2 and p to be 4, $(n + p)^2$ is 36, which is even. (I-1)

14. What is the value of x?

(1) $\dfrac{x}{y} = 3$

(2) $x - y = 9$

(C) STATEMENT (1) alone implies $x = 3y$. Since there is no more information about y, STATEMENT (1) alone is insufficient.

    STATEMENT 2 alone gives $x = 9 + y$ but there is no information about y, so STATEMENT (2) alone is not sufficient.

    STATEMENTS (1) and (2) together are sufficient. If $x = 9 + y$ and $x = 3y$, then $3y = 9 + y$, which gives $y = \dfrac{9}{2}$; so $x = (3)\left(\dfrac{9}{2}\right) = \dfrac{27}{2}$. (II-2)

★★☆

---

15. Two different holes, hole A and hole B, are put in the bottom of a full water tank. If the water drains out through the holes, how long will it be before the tank is empty?

(1) If only hole A is put in the bottom, the tank will be empty in 24 minutes.

(2) If only hole B is put in the bottom, the tank will be empty in 42 minutes.

(C) In each minute, hole A drains $\dfrac{1}{24}$ of the tank according to STATEMENT (1). Since we have no information about B, STATEMENT (1) alone is not sufficient. In each minute, hole B drains $\dfrac{1}{42}$ of the tank according to STATEMENT (2), but STATEMENT (2) gives no information about hole A. So STATEMENT (2) alone is not sufficient. If we use STATEMENTS (1) and (2), then both holes together will drain $\dfrac{1}{24} + \dfrac{1}{42}$ or $\dfrac{11}{168}$ of the tank each minute. Therefore, it will take $\dfrac{168}{11}$ or $15\dfrac{3}{11}$ minutes for the tank to empty.

So STATEMENTS (1) and (2) together are sufficient, but neither statement alone is sufficient. (*Note*: Don't bother working out how long it will take to drain the tank.) (II-3)

★★☆

---

16. How many pounds of fertilizer that is 10 percent nitrogen must be added to 12 pounds of fertilizer that is 20 percent nitrogen so that the resulting mixture is 18 percent nitrogen?

(A) 3
(B) 6
(C) 12
(D) 24
(E) 48

(A) Let x pounds be the amount of 10 percent nitrogen fertilizer that is needed. Then the amount of nitrogen in the mixture will be 10% of x + 20% of 12 = $0.1x + 2.4$. The percentage of nitrogen in the mixture will be $\dfrac{(0.1x + 2.4)}{(x + 12)}$, which must equal 0.18. Solve this equation for x by multiplying each side by $x + 12$ to obtain

$$0.1x + 2.4 = 0.18(x + 12)$$
$$= 0.18x + 2.16$$
$$2.4 - 2.16 = 0.18x - 0.1x$$
$$0.24 = 0.08x$$
$$x = \dfrac{(0.24)}{(0.8)} = 3 \qquad \text{(II-2)}$$

★★☆

★★☆ **17.** What is the probability that there is exactly 1 defective pen in a box of pens?

(1) The probability that all the pens in the box are not defective is 96 percent.

(2) The probability that there is more than 1 defective pen in the box is 3 percent.

(C) STATEMENT (1) alone is not sufficient since we can only deduce that 100% – 96% = 4% is the probability that there is *at least 1* defective pen in the box. STATEMENT (2) alone is not sufficient since we can only deduce that 100% – 3% = 97% is the probability that there are 0 or 1 defective pen in the box. Using STATEMENTS (1) and (2) together, we can see that 4% – 3% = 1% is the probability that there is exactly 1 defective pen in the box. (I-7)

★★☆ **18.** The line t passes through the lines l and k and forms the angles u, v, x, y, a, b, c, and d. Is line l parallel to line k?

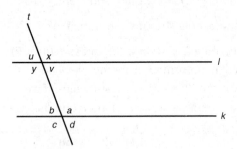

(1) $x = u$

(2) $u = a$

(C) STATEMENT (1) alone is not sufficient since it tells you that l and t are perpendicular but gives no information about t and k. STATEMENT (2) alone is not sufficient. If the angles u and a are right angles, then l and k are parallel; but if the angles are not right angles, then the lines are not parallel. STATEMENTS (1) and (2) together are sufficient since together they prove that l and k are parallel. (III-2)

★★☆ **19.** Is there a route from A to C that passes through B and is more than 11 miles long?

(1) Two roads from A to B are at least 5 miles long.

(2) Three roads from B to C are at least 5 miles long.

(E) STATEMENT (1) alone is not sufficient since you have no information about the distance from B to C. STATEMENT (2) alone is not sufficient since you have no information about the distance from A to B. The two statements together are not sufficient. For instance if the longest road from A to B is 5.2 miles long and the longest road from B to C was 5.6 miles long, then the longest route from A to C through B is 10.8 miles. But if the longest road from A to B is 7 miles long and the longest road from B to C is 5.6 miles long, then the longest route from A to C through B is 12.6 miles. (II-4)

20. Let $g(x) = 4^x$. If $g(a) = 32$, then a is

(A) 2
(B) 2.33
(C) 2.5
(D) 2.75
(E) 3

(C) We must solve $4^a = 32$. The key to this problem is the fact that 4 and 32 are both powers of 2, and so we can rewrite the equation as $4^a = (2^2)^a = 2^{2a} = 32 = 2^5$. So $2a$ must equal 5 since $2^x = 2^y$ if and only if $x = y$. Solve $2a = 5$ to obtain $a = 2.5$.

Another method: Since $4 = 16$, we have $2(4^2) = 32$. Since $2 = \sqrt{4} = 4^{\frac{1}{2}}$, $32 = (4^2)(4^{0.5}) = 4^{2.5}$. (I-8)

★★☆

---

21. In the figure, angles A, B, C, D, E, F, G, H are all 90° and $AB = AH = EF = DE$. Also, $BC = CD = HG$ and the Cartesian coordinates of A, C, and E are (1, 2), (2, 5), and (5, 4), respectively. What is the area of figure $ABCDEFG$?

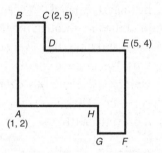

(A) 6
(B) 7
(C) 8
(D) 10
(E) 12

(D) Since the angle at B is 90°, the coordinates of B are (1, 5), so $AB = 3$ and $BC = 1$. To find the area, break the figure into three smaller figures by extending the line CD until it meets AH at point J and extending line GH until it meets DE at point K. Then the area sought is the sum of the areas of $ABCJ$, $JDKH$, and $KEFG$. All three figures are rectangles because all their angles are 90°. The area of $ABCJ$ is 3×1 since AB is 3 and BC is 1. The area of $JDKH$ is $JD \times JH$. Since the coordinates of D, J, and K are (2, 4), (2, 2), and (4, 4), respectively, the area of $JDKH$ is $2 \times 2 = 4$. Finally, since $EF = AB = 3$ and $KE = 1$, the area of $EFGK$ is $3 \times 1 = 3$. Therefore, the area of the figure is $3 + 4 + 3 = 10$. (III-9)

★★☆

★★☆ **22.** When an automobile is driven at 70 miles per hour, it uses 0.06 gallon of gas per mile. When the car is driven at 50 miles per hour, it uses 0.04 gallon of gas per mile. Which of the following relations are *possible* between the gallons of gas used per mile and the speed at which the car is driven?

   I.   They are directly proportional.
  II.   They are indirectly proportional.
 III.   They are linearly related.

  (A) only I
  (B) only II
  (C) only III
  (D) I and III
  (E) I, II, and III

(C) Let G be the gallons of gas per mile and S be the speed at which the car is driven. The two quantities G and S are directly proportional if $G = kS$ for some constant k. So if G and S are directly proportional, then $70 = k(0.06)$ and $50 = k(0.04)$. Solve both equations for k. The first equation gives $k = \dfrac{70}{0.06}$, but the second equation gives $k = \dfrac{50}{0.04}$, which is not equal to $\dfrac{70}{0.06}$. So G and S are not directly proportional, and I is impossible. The two quantities G and S are indirectly proportional if $GS = k$ for some constant k. So $70(0.06)$ and $50(0.04)$ should both equal k. Since $50(0.04)$ is not equal to $70(0.06)$, G and S are not indirectly proportional, and II is impossible. Since two points determine a straight line, it is possible for G and S to be linearly related. You can find the equation of the line through the two points (70, 0.06) and (50, 0.04). *Don't waste time doing this. You already know enough to answer the question, so don't spend any more time on the problem.* Therefore, the correct answer is III only. (II-5, III-10)

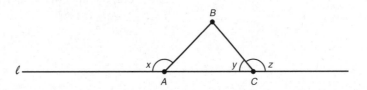

★★☆ **23.** The points A and C are on the line l. Is line segment AB greater than line segment BC?

  (1) Angle x is greater than angle y.
  (2) Angle z is greater than angle x.

(B) STATEMENT (1) is always true since the exterior angle of one vertex is equal to the sum of the other two interior angles of a triangle. So STATEMENT (1) alone is not sufficient. STATEMENT (2) alone is sufficient since it implies that angle BAC is greater than angle BCA. This implies that the side opposite angle BAC (which is BC) is greater than the side opposite angle BCA (which is AB.) (III-4)

24. Is x positive?

    (1) $x^2 + 10x > 0$

    (2) $3^x > 1$

(B) Since $x^2 + 10x = x(x + 10)$, STATEMENT (1) is true for $x > 0$ or $x < -10$. So STATEMENT (1) alone is not sufficient. STATEMENT (2) alone is sufficient since $3^0 = 1$ and as x increases 3^x increases. (I-8, II-2)

★★☆

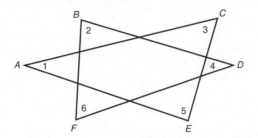

25. The sum of angles 1, 2, 3, 4, 5, and 6 is

    (A) 180°

    (B) 360°

    (C) 480°

    (D) 540°

    (E) 720°

(B) Since *ACE* is a triangle with angles 1, 3, and 5, the sum of angles 1, 3, and 5 is 180°. Since *BDF* is a triangle with angles 2, 4, and 6, the sum of angles 2, 4, and 6 is 180°. So the sum of angles 1, 2, 3, 4, 5, and 6 is 180° + 180° = 360°. (III-3, III-4)

★★★

26. If $a + 2b = 6$ and $ab = 4$ what is $\dfrac{2}{a} + \dfrac{1}{b}$?

    (A) $\dfrac{1}{2}$

    (B) 1

    (C) $\dfrac{3}{2}$

    (D) 2

    (E) $\dfrac{5}{2}$

(C) Convert $\dfrac{2}{a} + \dfrac{1}{b}$ into a single fraction.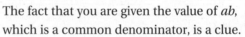

The fact that you are given the value of ab, which is a common denominator, is a clue.

So $\dfrac{2}{a} + \dfrac{1}{b} = \dfrac{(2b+a)}{ab} = \dfrac{6}{4} = \dfrac{3}{2}$. (I-2, II-2)

★★★

★★★ **27.** Ms. Jones has twice as much invested in stocks as in bonds. Last year, the stock investments paid 7.5 percent of their value and the bonds paid 10 percent of their value. If the total that both investments paid last year was $1,000, how much did Ms. Jones have invested in stocks?

(A) $3,636
(B) $4,000
(C) $7,500
(D) $8,000
(E) $10,000

(D) Let S be the amount invested in stocks and B be the amount invested in bonds. Then $0.75S + 0.1B = 1,000$ and $S = 2B$. So $0.075(2B) + .1B = .25B = 1000$, which means that $B = \dfrac{1,000}{0.25}$ or $B = \$4,000$. Finally, $S = 2B$; so $S = \$8,000$. (II-2, II-3)

★★★ **28.** A pair of skis originally cost $160. After a discount of x percent, the skis were discounted y percent. Do the skis cost less than $130 after the discounts?

(1) $x = 20$
(2) $y = 15$

(A) Since 80 percent of $160 = \$128$, we know that after the first discount the skis cost less than $130. Any further discount will only lower the price. So (1) alone is sufficient. STATEMENT (2) alone is not sufficient since if x were 10 percent, (2) would tell us the price is less than $130; but if x were 1 percent, (2) would imply that the price is greater than $130. (II-3)

★★★ **29.** Is $xy < 0$?

(1) $\dfrac{1}{x} < \dfrac{1}{y}$

(2) $x > 0$

(C) STATEMENT (1) alone is not sufficient; x could be negative or positive with y positive, and (1) would be true.

· STATEMENT (2) alone is not sufficient since it gives no information about y.

STATEMENT (1) and (2) together are sufficient. If $x > 0$, then (1) implies y is > 0; so $xy > 0$. (II-7)

30. What is the mean (average) number of defective pens in a box of pens? The probability that there is exactly 1 defective pen in a box is 1 percent.

(1) The probability that all the pens in the box are not defective is 96 percent.

(2) The probability that there is more than 1 defective pen in the box is 3 percent.

(E) We need to know the probability of each number of defective pens to calculate the mean. STATEMENT (1) alone is not sufficient since we can only deduce that 100% − 97% = 3% is the probability that *there are more than 1* defective pen in the box. STATEMENT (2) alone is not sufficient since more than 1 could mean 2, 3, and so on. Using STATEMENTS (1) and (2) together, we still don't have the information needed to calculate the mean. (I-7)

★★☆

---

31. Two-thirds of the roads from A to B are at least 5 miles long, and $\frac{1}{4}$ of the roads from B to C are at least 5 miles long. If you randomly pick a road from A to B and then randomly pick a road from B to C, what is the probability that at least one of the roads you pick is at least 5 miles long?

(A) $\dfrac{1}{6}$

(B) $\dfrac{1}{4}$

(C) $\dfrac{2}{3}$

(D) $\dfrac{3}{4}$

(E) $\dfrac{11}{12}$

(D) Two-thirds of your choices for the road from A to B are at least 5 miles long. One-third of your choices of the road from A to B are less than 5 miles long, but for these choices $\frac{1}{4}$ of your choices from B to C will be at least 5 miles long. So $\frac{2}{3} + \left(\frac{1}{3}\right)\left(\frac{1}{4}\right) = \frac{9}{12} = \frac{3}{4}$ of your choices will give at least one road that is at least 5 miles long.

Another method: Let E be the event that the road from A to B is at least 5 miles long and let F be the event that the road from B to C is at least 5 miles long. The question asks for the probability of the union of E and $F [(P(E \cup F)]$, which is equal to $P(E) + P(F) - P(E \cap F)$.

This is $\frac{2}{3} + \frac{1}{4} - \left(\frac{2}{3}\right)\left(\frac{1}{4}\right) = \frac{9}{12} = \frac{3}{4}$. (I-7)

★★★

★★★ **32.** *ABC* and *AED* are triangles with *BC* and *ED* perpendicular to *AB*. Find the length of *ED* if the area of *ABC* is 16.

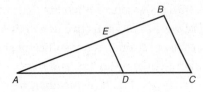

(1) *AB* = 8
(2) *AE* = 5

(C) STATEMENT (1) alone is not sufficient since *ED* can be moved inside the triangle *ABC* without changing *AB*. STATEMENT (2) is insufficient because *BC* can be moved and its length changed without changing STATEMENT (2). Since *BC* and *ED* are perpendicular to the same line, they are parallel. So the triangles *AED* and *ABC* are similar, and so
$$\frac{ED}{BC} = \frac{AE}{AB} = \frac{5}{8}$$ using STATEMENT (1) and STATEMENT (2). Using the fact that the area of *ABC* is 16 will let you find that the altitude from *C* to *AB* (which is *BC*) has length 4. Since $\frac{ED}{BC} = \frac{5}{8}$ you can find *ED* so STATEMENTS (1) and (2) together are sufficient. (III-4, III-7)

★★★ **33.** There are 30 socks in a drawer. Sixty percent of the socks are red, and the rest are blue. What is the minimum number of socks that must be taken from the drawer without looking in order to be certain that at least 2 blue socks have been chosen?

(A) 2
(B) 3
(C) 14
(D) 19
(E) 20

(E) The key word in this problem is *certain*. If you pick only 2 socks, you might get a pair of blue socks, but this is not certain. If the question asked for a pair of socks the same color, then after only 3 socks have been picked, 2 socks will have to be the same color—but the 2 socks might be red. Since 60 percent of the 30 socks, or 18 socks, are red, it is possible, although unlikely, that you could pick 18 reds and only 1 blue after 19 picks. However, if you pick 20 socks, you will get at least 2 blue socks. So the correct choice is (E). (I-7, II-4)

★★★ **34.** Are two triangles congruent?

(1) Both triangles are right triangles.
(2) Both triangles have the same perimeter.

(E) A triangle with sides of lengths 3, 4, and 5 is a right triangle since $3^2 + 4^2 = 5^2$, and its perimeter is 12. A triangle with sides of lengths 2, 4.8, and 5.2 also has a perimeter of 12. And since $2^2 + (4.8)^2 = (5.2)^2$, it too is a right triangle. Therefore, two triangles can satisfy STATEMENTS (1) and (2) yet not be congruent. On the other hand, any pair of congruent right triangles satisfies STATEMENTS (1) and (2). Thus, STATEMENTS (1) and (2) together are not sufficient to answer the question. (III-4)

35. *C* is a circle with center *D* and radius 2. *E* is a circle with center *F* and radius *R*. Are there any points that are on both *E* and *C*?

(1)   The distance from *D* to *F* is 1 + *R*.
(2)   *R* = 3.

(C) STATEMENT (2) alone is not sufficient since we must know how close the circles are and we know only the radius of each circle.

STATEMENT (1) alone is not sufficient. If *R* is less than 0.5, then the circle with center *F* is completely inside the circle with center *D*, and so there are no points on both circles.

STATEMENTS (1) and (2) together are sufficient since STATEMENT (2) means that *R* is greater than 0.5. The centers of the two circles are closer than the sum of the radii. (So we can form a triangle with *DF* as one side and the two other sides with lengths 2 and *R*, respectively; but this means that the third vertex of the triangle will be on both circle *E* and circle *C*.) (III-4, III-6)

---

36. *ABC* and *AED* are triangles with *BC* parallel to *ED*. Find the area of *BCDE* if the area of *ABC* is 16.

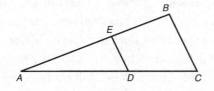

(1)   *BC* = 8
(2)   *ED* = 5

(C) Since *ED* can be moved inside the triangle, which will change the area of *BCDE* without changing STATEMENT (1), STATEMENT (1) alone is not sufficient. STATEMENT (2) by itself is insufficient since it gives no information about the other three sides of *BCDE*. Since *ED* and *BC* are parallel, triangles *ABC* and *AED* are similar, and the ratio of corresponding sides such as $\frac{ED}{BC}$ will be $\frac{5}{8}$ using STATEMENTS (1) and (2). Since the triangles are similar, their altitudes from *A* to *ED* and from *A* to *BC* must also have the same ratio, $\frac{5}{8}$, which means that the ratio of the area of *AED* to the area of *ABC* is $\left(\frac{5}{8}\right)\left(\frac{5}{8}\right) = \frac{25}{64}$. Since you are given the area of *ABC*, you can find the area of *AED*. Subtract the area of *AED* from the area of *ABC* to get the area of *BCDE*. (*Note:* Don't bother to do the calculations because you only have to decide if there is enough information to solve the problem.) (III-4, III-7)

★★★   **37.** A car traveled 75 percent of the way from town A to town B at an average speed of 50 miles per hour. The car travels at an average speed of S miles per hour for the remaining part of the trip. The average speed for the entire trip was 40 miles per hour. What is S?

(A) 10
(B) 20
(C) 25
(D) 30
(E) 37.5

(C) This problem can be worked out by some complicated algebra if you let D be the distance between the towns and let T be the total time of the trip. However, it is much easier to work it out if you simply choose a convenient number for the distance. So assume the distance between town A and town B is 1,000 miles. Then 75 percent of the distance is 750 miles, so the car traveled for $\frac{750}{50} = 15$ hours at 50 mph. If the car averaged 40 mph for the entire trip, then the entire trip took $\frac{1,000}{40} = 25$ hours. So the car must have taken $25 - 15 = 10$ hours for the part of the trip it traveled at S miles per hour. It traveled $1,000 - 750 = 250$ miles at S miles per hour, so S is $\frac{250}{10} = 25$. A common mistake is to solve the equation $0.75(50) + 0.25S = 40$ for S. This approach would be correct if the car traveled 75 percent of the time at 50 miles per hour and 25 percent of the time at S miles per hour. However, you are given that the car traveled 75 percent of the distance at 50 miles per hour and since speed changes the time it takes to travel a certain distance, 75 percent of the distance will not be 75 percent of the time. (II-2, II-3)

Verbal Section

1. Lavoisier, the 18th-century scientist, became more influential and famous than most of his contemporaries because not only did he discover and isolate many of the chemical elements but he also gave them names that both described the element in terms of its power and function and came to be accepted by other scientists in subsequent generations.

Which of the following can be inferred from the above passage?

(A) Lavoisier strived for fame and influence in the 18th century.
(B) All elements found in the 18th century were named after Lavoisier.
(C) Some of the elements that Lavoisier isolated were given names that described their properties.
(D) Lavoisier was the most influential and famous scientist of his time.
(E) Lavoisier became famous only because the names that he gave the chemicals became accepted.

(C) That Lavoisier strived for fame and influence may be a statement of fact, but not one that may be concluded from the passage. We learn from the passage only that he became famous and influential; therefore, choice (A) is inappropriate. Certainly, some of the elements discovered in the 1700s were named after Lavoisier, as can be learned from the passage, but not all of them. Therefore, choice (B) is also not appropriate. Choice (D) can be ruled out because of the presence in the passage of the key words "more influential . . . than most of his contemporaries" and not, as choice (D) states, "the most influential . . . scientist of his time." There is a comparison between Lavoisier and the other scientists, but that is as far as the passage goes. Choice (E) is not appropriate because the passage does not give as fact that the names he allocated to the chemicals he discovered were accepted as the only reason for his subsequent fame. The word *only* rules it out. Choice (C) correctly states the conclusion, which can be drawn from the passage and is, therefore, the appropriate answer.

★★★ **2.** The disaster that followed the earthquake in Armenia was tragic and serious, not just because of the fatalities and injuries, but because such widespread and severe damage was avoidable. The earthquake was less than 6 on the open-ended Richter scale, but its effects and aftermath matched the scene of events after much stronger quakes. What caused the casualty figures to reach such horrendous heights was that the buildings in the area were generally of a design that could not be expected to withstand anything more than a minor tremor.

Which of the following statements can best be inferred from the passage?

(A) People were not killed and injured by the earthquake, but by the falling masonry.

(B) Resources should be invested in predicting the location, incidence, and strength of earthquakes.

(C) Emergency evacuation procedures should be introduced in areas where earth-quakes tend to occur frequently.

(D) It would be better if earthquakes occurred only in areas far away from large centers of population.

(E) The rescue aid provided by international organizations and other countries after the earthquake will hopefully improve relations.

(A) The main inference in the whole paragraph is that an earthquake by itself—that is, a movement of the earth's crust that on the surface is felt as a series of sudden jerks—will not necessarily cause human casualties. It is only when quakes occur in heavily populated areas wherein there are many buildings and the buildings collapse that people are injured and killed by being hit by falling bricks and masonry. (A), there-fore, is the appropriate answer. The proposal in choice (B), however laudable, does not emanate from the passage. Choice (C) proposes another alternative measure that can-not be inferred from the passage. (D) presents an opinion with which probably nobody would disagree, but again, this view is not taken from the text. (E) can be ruled out for the same reason: It is not contained in and cannot be inferred from the passage.

★★★ **3.** In 1896, Henri Bequerel found that uranium salts emitted penetrating radiations <u>similar to those which Roentgen</u> produced only a year earlier with a gas discharge tube.

(A) similar to those which Roentgen

(B) like those which Roentgen

(C) similar to those that Roentgen had

(D) similar to them that Roentgen

(E) similar to those Roentgen

(C) The past perfect tense *had produced* is required in this sentence to show that Roentgen's work preceded that of Bequerel.

4. Unless they reverse present policies immediately, the world may suffer permanent damage from the unregulated use of pesticides.

(A) Unless they reverse present policies
(B) Unless present policies are reversed
(C) Unless present policies will be reversed
(D) If it will not reverse present policies
(E) If present policies will not be reversed

(B) Choice (A) suffers from the use of the ambiguous pronoun *they*. It is not clear whom *they* is supposed to refer to. The use of the future tense in choices (C), (D), and (E) is incorrect.

---

5. John wanted to have gone to the movies.

(A) wanted to have gone
(B) had wanted to have gone
(C) wanted to go
(D) wanted to have went
(E) had wanted to have went

(C) The sequence of tenses is incorrect. According to the meaning of the sentence, John's wanting comes *before*, not *after*, John's going.

The passage for questions 6–9 appears on page 434.

---

6. It can be inferred from the passage that a removal of agricultural distortions would provide gains to poor countries of approximately

(A) $300 billion per year.
(B) $500 billion per year.
(C) $400 billion per year.
(D) $200 billion per year.
(E) The sum cannot be determined from the passage.

(E) See paragraph 3. The passage states that "relative to national income, poor countries would enjoy a third more of this benefit than, rich, industrialized ones." The key to the answer are the words <u>relative to national</u> income. Thus, the benefits, but not the actual sums, would be valued on a relative basis, compared with national income. However, the passage does not show the national incomes, so calculating an absolute amount is not possible.

---

7. According to the passage, the main concern of the Indian government is to

(A) penetrate Chinese consumer markets.
(B) reduce barriers to the sale of its farm produce.
(C) impose more restrictive trade policies.
(D) improve its bargaining position.
(E) penetrate new overseas markets.

(B) The Indian government, like many other "poorer" countries, wants developed countries to reduce barriers to imports of farm produce. See paragraph 2.

★☆☆   **8.** The author states that the American government is

     (A) liberalizing its foreign trade policy.
     (B) sensitive to the demands of third-world countries.
     (C) becoming more protectionist.
     (D) refusing to negotiate with developing countries.
     (E) ignoring the needs of third-world countries.

     (A) The answer is given in line 2 of the first paragraph.

★★★   **9.** The passage provides support for the proposition that achieving an agreement at the latest round of trade talks seems doubtful because

     (A) the EU trade commissioner has failed to persuade India and China to liberalize exports of farm produce.
     (B) America's fast-track negotiating authority is soon to expire.
     (C) poorer countries refuse to lower agricultural barriers until developed countries open their markets to manufactured goods.
     (D) both the EU and G20 groups are unsure of the gains that might accrue from an agreement.
     (E) Britain and France are steadfastly against a new agreement.

     (D) Paragraphs 1 and 3 illustrate that both some EU countries and the G20 group of developing nations are unsure of the costs and gains resulting from a new trade agreement. Note that (C) is just the opposite of what is contained in the passage, as found at the end of the first paragraph.

★★★   **10.** Scientists believe they have discovered the wreck of the *USS Harvard*, sunk by Japanese torpedoes during World War II. Their conclusions are drawn from underwater searches by mini-submarines of the area about 4 miles west of Midway Island in the Pacific Ocean during what started out as offshore oil platform accident procedures. There are some military historians that are skeptical about the scientists' claim, on the basis that sophisticated sonar equipment has not identified the ship as, indeed, the *Harvard*.

Which of the following, if true, would weaken the historians' arguments?

     (A) Thorough searching by divers and bathyscopes has not located the wreck.
     (B) Three other ships were sunk in this area during World War II.
     (C) The ship's last known position was 20 miles east of Midway.
     (D) The use of sonar only enables the user to identify the shape and dimension of a wreck.
     (E) It is not known whether the *Harvard* suffered much structural damage before being sunk.

(D) The statement in choice (A) would strengthen the historians' arguments, so (A) is incorrect. The additional information provided in statement (B) could also be used to strengthen the historians' argument since, if there is a wreck of a ship in the location in question, it may not be that of the *Harvard* but rather could be that of any of several ships known to have been sunk in the area during the War. Therefore, (B) is inappropriate. The statement in (E) does not help to determine whether what has been found is or is not a wreck or whether it is or is not the *Harvard*; it is not relevant to the argument, and therefore (E) is incorrect. The fact that the *Harvard's* last known position was not close to the area where the wreck has been found may strengthen the historians' conclusion. It certainly does not weaken their argument. To weaken the historians' argument most effectively, counterevidence that shows that their method of investigation or study produces results that are inconclusive must be provided. Statement (D) does this. It points out shortcomings in the method employed—that is, sonar equipment—thereby making the conclusions reached more tenuous. This is the statement that would most effectively weaken the historians' arguments, and thus (D) is the correct answer.

---

11. In Great Britain, the problem of violence among spectators at soccer games has become more and more serious, with hardly a weekend passing without many arrested and many injured from among those who supposedly came to see a sport.

    Many suggestions have been made to combat this problem, most of them involving the introduction of more restrictions on the freedom of the crowds. Increased police presence at all games, enclosing supporters of opposing teams in pens, preventing the two groups from coming into contact with each other, and the use of membership cards with photographs that must be presented in order to gain access have all been tried.

    What is needed now is a deterrent factor. Increased fines, Saturday afternoon detention centers, and even jail terms must be introduced speedily and rigorously if we are going to solve this problem.

    Which of the following, if true, would most strengthen the present view of the writer?

    (A) The British Government has just passed legislation outlawing alcoholic drink to be sold at or brought into soccer matches.
    (B) Last week there were 36 arrested and 50 injured in fighting among the top soccer matches. This was an increase of 25% over the figures for the previous week.
    (C) The soccer clubs should do more to encourage families to attend their games by improving facilities and making special enclosures.
    (D) Violence is on the increase at soccer matches, and the authorities must get tougher.
    (E) Closed-circuit television has been set up to monitor trouble-making elements in the crowd.

(B) The question asks which statement would most strengthen the present view of the writer. Choice (D) is simply a summation of the author's opinion and is not necessarily likely to strengthen his view. While the writer may agree with the sentiments expressed in (C), it by itself will not reinforce his views. Choices (D) and (C), therefore, cannot be correct. What will harden the author's viewpoint is learning more facts that are not to his liking. Presumably, the developments noted in (A) and (E) will meet with his approval and are therefore not appropriate. On the other hand, the information conveyed by (B) will serve to increase his anger and resolve and strengthen his present view. (B), therefore, is the appropriate answer.

★★☆ **12.** <u>Either you transfer the data that was demanded</u> or file a report explaining why you did not submit the overall annual figures.

(A) Either you transfer the data that was demanded
(B) You either transfer the data, which was demanded,
(C) You either transfer the data that were demanded
(D) Either you transfer the data, which was demanded,
(E) Either you transfer the data, which were demanded,

(C) Choice (C) correctly uses *were* and begins with *you*, placing *either* closer to *or*. Choices (A), (B), (D), and (E) are incorrect. Data is a plural noun, so the singular *was* is incorrect.

★☆☆ **13.** <u>On entering the stadium, cheers greeted them</u> as a sign of universal approval of their great achievement.

(A) On entering the stadium, cheers greeted them
(B) On entering the stadium, they were greeted by cheers
(C) While entering the stadium, cheers greeted them
(D) On entering the stadium cheers greeted them
(E) On entering the stadium: cheers greeted them

(B) Choices (A), (C), (D), and (E) all say that the *cheers* are entering the stadium. A participial phrase at the beginning of a sentence must be followed by the word it modifies.

★★★ **14.** The set of propositions <u>which was discussed by the panel have been</u> published in the society journal.

(A) which was discussed by the panel have been
(B) which were discussed by the panel have been
(C) that was discussed by the panel has been
(D) which were discussed by the panel has been
(E) which was discussed, by the panel, has been

(D) Choice (D) is correct since it uses the singular verbs *was* and *has* with the singular noun *set*.

The passage for questions 15–18 appears on page 437.

15. In the late 19th century, it was believed that drawings were important to scientific discovery because they

   (A) helped researchers relax during times of stress.

   (B) were the only way to study basic functions.

   (C) illustrated how the brain functions.

   (D) helped to determine gender.

   (E) were more accurate than photographs.

(C) See paragraph 2. Drawings were considered instrumental to scientific discovery to illustrate how the brain functions.

16. According to the passage, Freud began his career as a

   (A) neurologist.

   (B) psychologist.

   (C) biologist.

   (D) laboratory assistant.

   (E) artist.

(C) Freud started his career as a biologist. Evidence of this is given in the third paragraph.

17. The passage suggests that in a career change, Freud switched from anatomy to a study of

   (A) brain functions.

   (B) unconscious behavior.

   (C) neuropathology.

   (D) nervous systems.

   (E) pathology.

(A) Although Freud eventually studied unconscious behavior, his career change was from descriptive anatomy to a focus on brain functions (paragraph 4).

18. The best possible title for the passage is

   (A) *Freud as an Artist.*

   (B) *On the Structure of Nerve Fibers.*

   (C) *From Microscope to Couch.*

   (D) *Elementary Psychoanalysis.*

   (E) *From Dissection to Introspection.*

(C) The microscope represents the biologist's tool, while the couch is the psychoanalyst's tool. These illustrate the career change that Freud made.

ANSWERS EXPLAINED

19. There are three main factors that control the risks of becoming dependent on drugs. These factors are the type of drug, the personality of the individual, and the circumstances in which the drug is taken. Indeed, it could be said that the majority of the adult population have taken alcohol, yet few have become dependent on it. Also, many strong drugs that have been used for medical purposes have not caused the patient to become addicted.

However, it can be demonstrated that people who have taken drugs for fun are more likely to become dependent on the drug. The dependence is not always physiological but may remain psychological, although the effects are still essentially the same. Those at greatest risk appear to be personalities that are psychopathic, immature, or otherwise unstable.

Psychological dependence is very strong with heroin, morphine, cocaine, and amphetamines. Physiological dependence is great with heroin and morphine, but less with amphetamines, barbiturates, and alcohol.

Which of the following conclusions can be drawn from the text?

(A) One cannot become addicted to certain drugs if one has a strong personality.
(B) Taking drugs for "kicks" increases the possibility of becoming dependent on drugs.
(C) Psychological dependence is greatest with heroin.
(D) Alcohol is a safe drug since very few people become dependent on it.
(E) Long-term use of certain drugs for medical purposes does not cause addiction.

(B) Although a strong personality might have some resistance to the psychological dependence factors of drug use, it cannot be stated with any certainty that a strong personality can prevent physiological dependence. In this way, (A) is not a reasonable conclusion.

Psychological dependence on heroin is greater than that of drugs such as alcohol and marijuana, but it is not stated to be the greatest since psychological dependence is also great with cocaine and amphetamines. There is no conclusive evidence in the text to support this view. (C) is not, therefore, a reasonable conclusion.

A safe drug implies no danger of addiction, and since it cannot be shown that there is no danger of addiction to alcohol, statement (D) is also not valid.

Although short-term use of certain drugs for medical purposes rarely produces dependence, long-term use of certain drugs often causes physiological dependence; in this respect (E) is not a valid assumption.

(B) is the only conclusion that can probably be true. Statistics show that many hard-drug addicts and regular users started their habit by taking drugs for "kicks." Also the search for drugs to be used for kicks almost inevitably causes exposure to localities where harder and more addictive drugs are available, thus increasing the chances of attempting more addictive drugs for kicks. The passage states that the circumstances in which the drug is taken is one factor controlling the risk of becoming dependent and also that it can be demonstrated that people who have taken drugs for fun are more likely to become dependent on the drug.

20. In 1985 there were 20 deaths from automobile accidents per 1,000 miles traveled. A total of 20,000 miles were traveled via automobiles in 1985. In the same year, 800 people died in airplane crashes and 400 people were killed in train disasters. A statistician concluded from these data alone that it was more dangerous to travel by plane, train, and automobile, in that order.

★★★

Which of the following refutes the statistician's conclusion?

(A) There is no common denominator by which to compare the number of deaths resulting from each mode of travel.
(B) One year is insufficient to reach such a conclusion.
(C) More people travel by car than any other mode of transport; therefore, the probability of a car accident is greater.
(D) The number of plane flights and train trips is not stated.
(E) The probability of being killed in a train disaster and as a result of a car crash is the same.

(A) Note that the casualty figure for automobile deaths is given as the ratio of number of deaths to miles traveled. In order to make a comparison with other modes of transport, the same denominator (miles traveled) would have to be used.

---

21. From a letter to the commercial editor of a newspaper: Your article of January 9 drew attention to the large deficit in Playland's balance of payments that has worsened over the past three years. Yet, you favor the recent trade treaty signed between Playland and Workland. That treaty results in a lowering of our import duties that will flood us with Workland's goods. This will only exacerbate our balance of trade. How can you be in favor of the treaty?

★★★

Which of the following considerations would weaken the letter writer's argument?

(A) import diversion versus import creation
(B) prices paid by importers versus prices paid by consumers
(C) economic goals versus political goals
(D) duties levied increase government revenue
(E) free trade versus protectionism

(A) If the treaty results in increased Workland exports to Playland at the expense of local producers (import creation), Playland's balance of payments will show a larger deficit. If, however, increased Workland exports to Playland merely replace imports from other countries (import diversion), the trade balance will not change. Alternative (C) is a second-best consideration; that is, that political objectives supersede economic goals. The remaining alternatives have no bearing on Playland's balance of trade.

★☆☆ **22.** In 1930, there were, on the average 10 deaths at birth (infant mortality) per 10,000 population. By 1940 there were 8.5, and by 1950, 7.0. Today there are 5.5 deaths at birth per 10,000 population, and it is anticipated that the downward trend will continue.

Each of the following, if true, would help to account for this trend *except*

(A) Medical care is more widespread and available.
(B) More effective birth control methods have been implemented.
(C) Sanitary conditions have improved.
(D) The number of pediatricians per 10,000 population has increased.
(E) Midwifery has declined in favor of medical doctors.

(B) There is no association between birth control and infant mortality. Birth control can prevent pregnancies but not death after birth.

★★★ **23.** Product shipments of household appliances are expected to rise to $17 billion next year, an average annual increase of 8.0 percent over the past five years. The real growth rate, after allowing for probable price increases, is expected to be about 4.3 percent each year, resulting in shipments this year of $14 billion in 1987 dollars.

Each of the following, if true, could help to account for this trend *except*

(A) Consumer spending for durable products has increased.
(B) The number of new households has increased.
(C) Consumer disposable income has increased.
(D) The consumer price of electricity has decreased.
(E) The life of durable products has increased.

(E) Choices (A), (B), (C), and (D) may all increase the demand for household appliances. The answer is Choice (E) because demand should be lower if appliances last longer.

★★★ **24.** In this particular job we have discovered that <u>to be diligent is more important than being bright</u>.

(A) to be diligent is more important than being bright
(B) for one to be diligent is more important than being bright
(C) diligence is more important than brightness
(D) being diligent is more important than to be bright
(E) by being diligent is more important than being bright

(C) Comparisons must be parallel: *diligence* matches brightness. *Being bright* in choices (A) and (B) does not match *to be diligent*. Choice (D) matches *being diligent* to *to be bright*. Choice (E) matches *by being diligent* to *being bright*.

25. No one but <u>him could have told them that the thief was I.</u>

    (A) him could have told them that the thief was I

    (B) he could have told them that the thief was I

    (C) he could have told them that the thief was me

    (D) him could have told them that the thief was me

    (E) he could have told them the thief was me

(A) *But* in this sentence means *except*, which is always followed by the object *him* rather than the subject *he.* The verb *was* needs the subject *I.*

---

26. Products that have well-known brands generally command premium prices when produced in developed countries. The same branded products manufactured in third-world, low-image countries, however, are perceived to be inferior, even though manufacturing processes can be effectively transferred to less developed countries resulting in the same quality products. Paradoxically, the same branded products produced in a low image country have to be discounted.

    Which of the following, if true, explains the paradox above?

    (A) Workers in low-image countries lack the skills to make quality products.

    (B) Country image is perceived by consumers to be more important than brand name.

    (C) Companies do not reveal where their products are manufactured, thus confusing consumers.

    (D) Workers in third-world countries work longer hours for lower pay than in developed countries.

    (E) Brand names have become less important to consumers when comparing competing products.

(B) The statement mentions that manufacturing processes can be transferred to third-world countries resulting in the production of same quality products. Thus, the paradox is explained by the fact that consumers rely more on country image than a product's well-known brand name when making a purchase. Choice (A) is incorrect because even if it is true that workers in low-image countries lack the skills to make quality products, the products are discounted because consumers perceive them to be inferior for whatever reason. Choice (C) is wrong because if consumers do not know where products are manufactured, products carrying a well-known brand name would not have to be discounted. Choice (D) may be true, but it does not explain why consumers perceive products made in third world countries to be inferior. Choice (E) is incorrect because even if brand names have become less important, it does not explain why in some countries they are sold at premium prices, while in others at discounted prices.

ANSWERS EXPLAINED

★★☆ **27.** Before the middle of the 14th century, there were no universities north of Italy, except in France and England. By the end of the 15th century, there were 23 universities in this region, from Louvain and Mainz to Rostock, Cracow, and Bratislava, and the number of universities in Europe as a whole had more than doubled.

Given the above information, which of the following statements is correct?

(A) Until the age of university expansion in the 15th century, there were perhaps 11 universities in the whole of Europe.

(B) South of Italy there were 23 universities in the 14th century.

(C) In the 13th century, France and England were the only countries in Europe with universities.

(D) After the great age of university expansion in the 14th and 15th centuries, France and England were not the only northern European countries to have such centers of learning.

(E) Italy was the cradle of university expansion.

(D) The passage states that university expansion—north of Italy and outside France and England—took place between the mid-14th century and the end of the 15th century. There is nothing in the passage about the number of universities in the whole of Europe, so we have no way of knowing if (A) is correct. Statement (B) is not substantiated by what is in the passage—namely, that "by the end of the 15th century, there were 23 universities" in a wide region. There is nothing in the passage that states that France and England were the only countries with universities in the 13th century, so (C) is not appropriate. Similarly, nothing in the passage states or implies that Italy was the cradle of university expansion (E).

★★☆ **28.** After a careful evaluation of the circumstances surrounding the incident, we decided that we <u>neither have the authority nor</u> the means to cope with the problem.

(A) neither have the authority nor

(B) neither have authority or

(C) have neither the authority nor

(D) have neither the authority or

(E) have not either the authority nor

(C) The idiom *neither . . . nor* refers to *authority* and *means* and must precede them directly.

★☆☆ **29.** <u>Everyone of us have understood that without him helping us</u> we would not have succeeded in our program over the past six months.

(A) Everyone of us have understood that without him helping us

(B) Everyone of us has understood that without his helping us

(C) Everyone of us have understood that without his help

(D) Everyone of us has understood that without him helping us

(E) Every single one of us have understood that without him helping us

(B) *Everyone* is singular and requires the singular *has*. Choices (A), (D), and (E) incorrectly used *him* rather than the possessive pronoun *his*.

---

30. On the African continent, the incidence of vitamin <u>deficiencies correlates positively with</u> the level of solar radiation

    (A) deficiencies correlates positively with
    (B) deficiencies correlate positively with
    (C) deficiencies, correlate positively with,
    (D) deficiencies correlate positively to
    (E) deficiencies correlates positively to

(A) The idiom is *correlates with*, not *correlates to*. The subject of this sentence is the singular *incidence*. Therefore the verb must be the singular *correlates*.

---

31. The dominant beliefs of ancient Rome centered on a passion for order even in the face of evidence to the contrary, the Roman theory of a Ptolemaic universe, the absolute right of emperors, <u>parliament, and that Earth being the center of the universe kept the cosmic order of the universe.</u>

    (A) parliament, and that Earth being the center of the universe kept the cosmic order of the universe.
    (B) the parliament, and that Earth being the center of the universe kept the cosmic order of the universe.
    (C) parliamentary law, and an Earth-centered cosmic order.
    (D) parliament, and that Earth had been the center of the universe.
    (E) parliamentary law, and that Earth was the center of the universe.

(C) All aspects of the list must be parallel. Since the list begins with *a Ptolemaic universe*, everything must be either a noun or a noun phrase. Therefore, any sentence that uses a verb phrase such as *being the center, had been*, or *was the center* is incorrect.

---

32. <u>If they would have taken greater care</u> in the disposal of the nuclear waste, the disaster would not have occurred.

    (A) If they would have taken greater care
    (B) Unless they took greater care
    (C) Had they not taken greater care
    (D) If they had taken greater care
    (E) If they took greater care

(D) *Would not have occurred* requires *if they had*.

---

33. <u>Neither the judge nor I am ready to announce who the winner is.</u>

    (A) Neither the judge nor I am ready to announce who the winner is.
    (B) Neither the judge nor I are ready to announce who the winner is.
    (C) Neither the judge nor I are ready to announce who is the winner.
    (D) Neither the judge nor I am ready to announce who is the winner.
    (E) Neither I or the judge are ready to announce who is the winner.

(A) Choice (A) correctly uses *I am.* Choices (B), (C), and (E) incorrectly use *I are.* Choices (C), (D), and (E) use the awkward construction *who is the winner* instead of *who the winner is.*

★★★   **34.** One major obligation of the social psychologist is to provide his own discipline, the other social sciences, and interested laymen with conceptual tools that will increase the range and the reliability of their understanding of social phenomena. Beyond that, responsible government officials are today turning more frequently to the social scientist for insights into the nature and solution of the problems with which they are confronted.

The above argument assumes that

(A) social psychologists must have a strong background in other sciences as well as their own.
(B) a study of social psychology should be a part of the curriculum of government officials.
(C) the social scientist has an obligation to provide the means by which social phenomena may be understood by others.
(D) social phenomena are little understood by those outside the field of social psychology.
(E) a good social psychologist is obligated principally by the need to solve interdisciplinary problems.

(C) The statement refers to the social psychologist's obligation to provide a wide range of people—those in his own discipline, other social scientists, laymen, and government officials—with the tools to understand social phenomena. Alternative (E) might be a correct assumption if it was not linked to inter-disciplinary problems. Alternatives (A), (B), and (D) are incorrect assumptions.

★★☆   **35.** Administrators and executives are members of the most stable occupation.

The stability mentioned in the above statement could be dependent on each of the following factors *except*

(A) training and skills.
(B) nature of the occupation.
(C) status.
(D) relatively high income.
(E) rate of mobility.

(E) The factors listed in (A), (B), (C), and (D) all affect occupational mobility. The rate of turnover (E) is another way of measuring mobility; it is not an explanatory variable, or, in other words, it is not a factor that affects stability or mobility.

36. Between 1979 and 1983, the number of unincorporated, self-employed women increased five times faster than the number of self-employed men and more than three times faster than the number of women wage-and-salary workers. Part-time self-employment among women increased more than full-time self-employment.

Each of the following, if true, could help to account for this trend *except*

(A) Owning a business affords flexibility to combine work and family responsibilities.
(B) The proportion of women studying business administration courses has grown considerably.
(C) There are more self-employed women than men.
(D) Unincorporated service industries have grown by 300 percent over the period; the ratio of women to men in this industry is three to one.
(E) The financial reward of having a second wage earner in the household has taken on increased significance.

(C) Even if it were true that there are more self-employed women than men (C), this does not explain why this number increased five times faster than the number of men. Choice (A) supports the argument by showing that it has become more convenient for women to be self-employed. Choice (B) gives a means to that end. Choice (D) provides evidence to support the claim, and (E) is an example of a motivating factor that induced more women to work.

37. More than any animal, the wolverine exemplifies the unbridled ferocity of "nature red in tooth and claw."

(A) More than any animal,
(B) More than any other animal,
(C) More than another animal,
(D) Unlike any animal,
(E) Compared to other animals,

(B) Choice (B) includes the necessary word *other*, which makes the comparison correct. Choice (D) changes the meaning of the sentence by its implication that the wolverine is *not* an animal.

The passage for questions 38–41 appears on page 445.

38. The author implies Lord Kelvin believes that evolution is

(A) a vital principle.
(B) a heated theory.
(C) caused by variations.
(D) caused by God.
(E) a result of chance.

(D) The first paragraph explains that Kelvin's understanding of evolution is that it needs a *directive power*, which is a reference to God.

39. A possible title that best expresses the meaning of the passage would be

(A) *The Evolutionary Ideas of Lord Kelvin*
(B) *The Evolution of Evolution*
(C) *Understanding Organic Nature*
(D) *Lord Kelvin, Buffon, Erasmus, Darwin, Lamarck, Spencer, and Butler's Concepts of Evolution*
(E) *Evolution: Chance Versus Design*

(E) This title is specific to the entire passage, but not too general. Choices (A), (C), and (D) are too specific. These titles do not encompass the entire passage. Choice (B) is too general.

★★☆ **40.** According to the passage,

(A) the discussion between evolutionary theorists is rooted in cause and effect.
(B) the study of biology is necessary to understand evolution.
(C) a later generation of evolutionary theorists includes Herbert Spencer and Butler.
(D) Kelvin believed that evolution is chance.
(E) biologists agree that evolution involves an accretion of changes.

(E) The first paragraph states that both schools of evolutionists agree that *differences between species are caused by the accumulation and transmission of variations.* Choice (C) is incorrect because both generations held this belief.

★★★ **41.** The author of the passage suggests that

(A) the discussion is scientifically objective.
(B) the discussion is emotional.
(C) there is general agreement between early and later evolutionary theorists.
(D) the passage will explain evolution to readers.
(E) evolution must be explained theologically.

(B) In the first paragraph, the author states that the reaction of the scientific community to the concept of intelligent design drew heated *retorts.*

EVALUATING YOUR SCORE

Tabulate your score for the Quantitative and Verbal sections of the Sample Test according to the directions on pages 11–12 and record the results in the Self-Scoring Table below. Then find your rating for each score on the Self-Scoring Scale and record it in the appropriate blank.

SELF-SCORING TABLE

Section	Score	Rating
Quantitative		
Verbal		

SELF-SCORING SCALE—RATING

Section	Poor	Fair	Good	Excellent
Quantitative	0–15	15–25	26–30	31–37
Verbal	0–15	15–25	26–30	31–41

Study again the Review sections covering material in Sample Test 1 for which you had a rating of FAIR or POOR. Then go on to Sample Test 2. Find your approximate GMAT score by using the scoring table on the next page.

*Important note: Up-to-date scoring guidelines for the Integrated Reasoning section can be found at *mba.com*.

SCORING TABLE

Add the number of correct answers on the Quantitative test and the number of correct answers on the Verbal test to find **T**, your total number of correct answers.

T should be a number less than or equal to 78. Find your equivalent scaled score in the table below.

Again, this table refers to Quantitative and Verbal scores only. For specifics on Integrated Reasoning scoring, go to *mba.com*.

T	Score	T	Score	T	Score	T	Score
78	800	59	660	40	510	21	370
77	790	58	650	39	500	20	360
76	790	57	640	38	490	19	350
75	780	56	630	37	490	18	340
74	770	55	620	36	480	17	340
73	760	54	620	35	470	16	330
72	760	53	610	34	460	15	320
71	750	52	600	33	460	14	310
70	740	51	590	32	450	13	300
69	730	50	580	31	440	12	290
68	720	49	580	30	430	11	280
67	720	48	570	29	430	10	270
66	710	47	560	28	420	9	260
65	700	46	550	27	410	8	250
64	690	45	550	26	400	7	240
63	690	44	540	25	400	6	230
62	680	43	530	24	390	5	220
61	670	42	520	23	380	4	210
60	660	41	520	22	370	<4	200

*All scoring in this table is an approximation.

Sample Test 2 with Answers and Analysis

→ TEST
→ ANSWERS
→ ANALYSIS
→ EVALUATING YOUR SCORE

ANSWER SHEET
Sample Test 2

INTEGRATED REASONING SECTION

1. i. Ⓐ Ⓑ Ⓒ Ⓓ

ii. Ⓐ Ⓑ Ⓒ Ⓓ

2.

Amount Needed to Spend on New Hires	Amount Each Student Expects to Make	Amount in $
○	○	0
○	○	720
○	○	1,080
○	○	1,920
○	○	2,560
○	○	3,840

3.

Would Help Explain	Would Not Help Explain
○	○
○	○
○	○

4. Ⓐ Ⓑ Ⓒ Ⓓ Ⓔ

5.

True	False
○	○
○	○
○	○

6.

Yes	No
○	○
○	○
○	○

7.

Would Definitely be Part of the Optimite Program	Would Definitely NOT be Part of the Optimite Program
○	○
○	○
○	○
○	○
○	○

8. Ⓐ Ⓑ Ⓒ Ⓓ Ⓔ

9. i. Ⓐ Ⓑ Ⓒ Ⓓ Ⓔ

ii. Ⓐ Ⓑ Ⓒ Ⓓ Ⓔ

10. i. Ⓐ Ⓑ Ⓒ Ⓓ

ii. Ⓐ Ⓑ Ⓒ Ⓓ

11.

True	False
○	○
○	○
○	○

12. Ⓐ Ⓑ Ⓒ Ⓓ Ⓔ

ANSWER SHEET
Sample Test 2

QUANTITATIVE SECTION

1. Ⓐ Ⓑ Ⓒ Ⓓ Ⓔ   11. Ⓐ Ⓑ Ⓒ Ⓓ Ⓔ   21. Ⓐ Ⓑ Ⓒ Ⓓ Ⓔ   31. Ⓐ Ⓑ Ⓒ Ⓓ Ⓔ
2. Ⓐ Ⓑ Ⓒ Ⓓ Ⓔ   12. Ⓐ Ⓑ Ⓒ Ⓓ Ⓔ   22. Ⓐ Ⓑ Ⓒ Ⓓ Ⓔ   32. Ⓐ Ⓑ Ⓒ Ⓓ Ⓔ
3. Ⓐ Ⓑ Ⓒ Ⓓ Ⓔ   13. Ⓐ Ⓑ Ⓒ Ⓓ Ⓔ   23. Ⓐ Ⓑ Ⓒ Ⓓ Ⓔ   33. Ⓐ Ⓑ Ⓒ Ⓓ Ⓔ
4. Ⓐ Ⓑ Ⓒ Ⓓ Ⓔ   14. Ⓐ Ⓑ Ⓒ Ⓓ Ⓔ   24. Ⓐ Ⓑ Ⓒ Ⓓ Ⓔ   34. Ⓐ Ⓑ Ⓒ Ⓓ Ⓔ
5. Ⓐ Ⓑ Ⓒ Ⓓ Ⓔ   15. Ⓐ Ⓑ Ⓒ Ⓓ Ⓔ   25. Ⓐ Ⓑ Ⓒ Ⓓ Ⓔ   35. Ⓐ Ⓑ Ⓒ Ⓓ Ⓔ
6. Ⓐ Ⓑ Ⓒ Ⓓ Ⓔ   16. Ⓐ Ⓑ Ⓒ Ⓓ Ⓔ   26. Ⓐ Ⓑ Ⓒ Ⓓ Ⓔ   36. Ⓐ Ⓑ Ⓒ Ⓓ Ⓔ
7. Ⓐ Ⓑ Ⓒ Ⓓ Ⓔ   17. Ⓐ Ⓑ Ⓒ Ⓓ Ⓔ   27. Ⓐ Ⓑ Ⓒ Ⓓ Ⓔ   37. Ⓐ Ⓑ Ⓒ Ⓓ Ⓔ
8. Ⓐ Ⓑ Ⓒ Ⓓ Ⓔ   18. Ⓐ Ⓑ Ⓒ Ⓓ Ⓔ   28. Ⓐ Ⓑ Ⓒ Ⓓ Ⓔ
9. Ⓐ Ⓑ Ⓒ Ⓓ Ⓔ   19. Ⓐ Ⓑ Ⓒ Ⓓ Ⓔ   29. Ⓐ Ⓑ Ⓒ Ⓓ Ⓔ
10. Ⓐ Ⓑ Ⓒ Ⓓ Ⓔ   20. Ⓐ Ⓑ Ⓒ Ⓓ Ⓔ   30. Ⓐ Ⓑ Ⓒ Ⓓ Ⓔ

VERBAL SECTION

1. Ⓐ Ⓑ Ⓒ Ⓓ Ⓔ   12. Ⓐ Ⓑ Ⓒ Ⓓ Ⓔ   23. Ⓐ Ⓑ Ⓒ Ⓓ Ⓔ   34. Ⓐ Ⓑ Ⓒ Ⓓ Ⓔ
2. Ⓐ Ⓑ Ⓒ Ⓓ Ⓔ   13. Ⓐ Ⓑ Ⓒ Ⓓ Ⓔ   24. Ⓐ Ⓑ Ⓒ Ⓓ Ⓔ   35. Ⓐ Ⓑ Ⓒ Ⓓ Ⓔ
3. Ⓐ Ⓑ Ⓒ Ⓓ Ⓔ   14. Ⓐ Ⓑ Ⓒ Ⓓ Ⓔ   25. Ⓐ Ⓑ Ⓒ Ⓓ Ⓔ   36. Ⓐ Ⓑ Ⓒ Ⓓ Ⓔ
4. Ⓐ Ⓑ Ⓒ Ⓓ Ⓔ   15. Ⓐ Ⓑ Ⓒ Ⓓ Ⓔ   26. Ⓐ Ⓑ Ⓒ Ⓓ Ⓔ   37. Ⓐ Ⓑ Ⓒ Ⓓ Ⓔ
5. Ⓐ Ⓑ Ⓒ Ⓓ Ⓔ   16. Ⓐ Ⓑ Ⓒ Ⓓ Ⓔ   27. Ⓐ Ⓑ Ⓒ Ⓓ Ⓔ   38. Ⓐ Ⓑ Ⓒ Ⓓ Ⓔ
6. Ⓐ Ⓑ Ⓒ Ⓓ Ⓔ   17. Ⓐ Ⓑ Ⓒ Ⓓ Ⓔ   28. Ⓐ Ⓑ Ⓒ Ⓓ Ⓔ   39. Ⓐ Ⓑ Ⓒ Ⓓ Ⓔ
7. Ⓐ Ⓑ Ⓒ Ⓓ Ⓔ   18. Ⓐ Ⓑ Ⓒ Ⓓ Ⓔ   29. Ⓐ Ⓑ Ⓒ Ⓓ Ⓔ   40. Ⓐ Ⓑ Ⓒ Ⓓ Ⓔ
8. Ⓐ Ⓑ Ⓒ Ⓓ Ⓔ   19. Ⓐ Ⓑ Ⓒ Ⓓ Ⓔ   30. Ⓐ Ⓑ Ⓒ Ⓓ Ⓔ   41. Ⓐ Ⓑ Ⓒ Ⓓ Ⓔ
9. Ⓐ Ⓑ Ⓒ Ⓓ Ⓔ   20. Ⓐ Ⓑ Ⓒ Ⓓ Ⓔ   31. Ⓐ Ⓑ Ⓒ Ⓓ Ⓔ
10. Ⓐ Ⓑ Ⓒ Ⓓ Ⓔ   21. Ⓐ Ⓑ Ⓒ Ⓓ Ⓔ   32. Ⓐ Ⓑ Ⓒ Ⓓ Ⓔ
11. Ⓐ Ⓑ Ⓒ Ⓓ Ⓔ   22. Ⓐ Ⓑ Ⓒ Ⓓ Ⓔ   33. Ⓐ Ⓑ Ⓒ Ⓓ Ⓔ

WRITING ASSESSMENT

Time: 30 minutes

ANALYSIS OF AN ARGUMENT

> DIRECTIONS: Write a clear, logical, and well-organized response to the following argument. Your response should be in the form of a short essay, following the conventions of standard written English. On the CAT, your answer should be the equivalent of an essay that would fill three pages of lined 8$\frac{1}{2}$″ × 11″ paper. If you are taking a paper test, write legibly. Essays that are illegible or that are written on a topic other than the one outlined in the question will not be scored.

Requiring school uniforms will save families money. Students will not pressure their parents to buy clothes some families cannot afford.

Discuss how logically persuasive you find the above argument. Does the argument include inferred assumptions? In presenting your point of view, analyze the sort of reasoning used and supporting evidence. In addition, state what further evidence, if any, would make the argument more sound and convincing or would make you better able to evaluate its conclusion. What might weaken or strengthen the argument?

ON THE ACTUAL GMAT,
AFTER YOU HAVE CONFIRMED YOUR ANSWER,
YOU CANNOT RETURN TO IT.

INTEGRATED REASONING SECTION

Time: 30 minutes

12 questions

This section consists of four types of questions: Graphics Interpretation, Table Analysis, Two-part Analysis, and Multi-Source Reasoning.

> **DIRECTIONS:** The new Integrated Reasoning section consists of four question types. Some require the use of both quantitative and verbal skills. Others involve the use of graphics, tables, or text material. The questions also use various response formats.
>
> For each question, review the text, graphic, or text material provided and respond to the task that is presented. *Note: An onscreen calculator is available in this section on the actual test.*

Question 1 refers to the following information and graph.

1. The graph below charts the cumulative frequency of height (in inches) of college basketball players at USC in 2002.

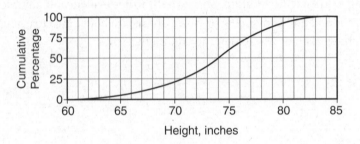

Answer each question according to the information presented in the diagram.

i. What is the range of heights within the third quartile?

(A) 3 inches
(B) 4 inches
(C) 5 inches
(D) Cannot be determined

ii. Approximately what percentage of players is within 6 inches of the median height?

(A) 66.7%
(B) 75%
(C) 83.3%
(D) 90%

2. The painting company Youth Pro Painters has just hired ten students this year for the 12-week summer season. Their target is to paint 1,200 houses over the summer. On average, ten students can paint four houses in 16 hours. Each student painter makes $8 per hour and is expected to work 40 hours per week.

In the table below, identify how much money the company needs to spend on additional hires in order to meet its objective. Also identify the amount of money each student can expect to make in half the summer. Choose only one option in each column.

Amount Needed to Spend on New Hires	Amount Each Student Expects to Make	Amount in $
◯	◯	0
◯	◯	720
◯	◯	1,080
◯	◯	1,920
◯	◯	2,560
◯	◯	3,840

3. The table below shows data for the percentage of the eligible population subgroups attending school.

Country	Kindergarten	Primary School	Secondary School	Post-Secondary
Argentina	71	95	90	54
Bolivia	59	91	79	38
Chile	56	88	88	22
Columbia	62	98	95	60
Paraguay	67	86	77	45
Peru	32	81	68	19
Ecuador	45	93	65	21

For each of the following statements, select *Would help explain* if it would, if true, help explain some of the information in the table. Otherwise select *Would not help explain*.

Would Help Explain	Would Not Help Explain	
◯	◯	In South America, kindergartens are not as available as are primary schools.
◯	◯	Peru has a larger rural and agricultural population than the other countries, and most of the farms are maintained by the families that live on them.
◯	◯	Parents in Argentina value education more than parents in the other South American countries shown in the chart do.

Questions 4–6 refer to the following documents.

Document 1:

Curlypro, a hair product manufacturing company based in Chicago, is evaluating expansion options for its product line. The company has two plants that are currently operating at full capacity. Management has finalized its top three production plant options.

Nanning, the capital of Guangxi Province in Southern China
This 30,000-square-foot plant has the capacity to produce and deliver 1,500 crates per month. The plant manager has asked for a three-year commitment and a minimum order of 1,000 crates per month. Curlypro has some concerns about shipping costs and time, but this would be an issue only if shipping the minimum amount for all three years.

Chennai, India
This 20,000-square-foot plant features a large capacity of 2,500 crates per month. The plant manager requires a three-year commitment and a minimum order of 1,000 crates per month. Similar to the Nanning plant, this plant may have prohibitive shipping costs and timing. The primary concern is that the region's reputation for underage factory workers might instigate a consumer backlash. The plant manager assures us that they do not hire anyone under the age of 18.

Sandusky, Ohio
This 18,000-square-foot plant has a capacity of 1,200 crates per month. Both Curlypro and the Sandusky plant are eager to have American workers supply the company as this will have great marketing appeal. They can also take advantage of some government assistance that will allow the Sandusky plant to require only a one-year contract and no minimum order size.

Document 2:

Curlypro produces two main products—Curlypro shampoo and Curlypro conditioner. Sales have grown substantially in the past two years. Curlypro estimates sales for the current year will reach 400 crates per month for each product line.

The current forecast for sales in the next three years is approximately a 25% to 50% increase each year for both lines. Although all the plants have significant capacity, Curlypro management wants to make the right investment for the long term. They are leaning toward the Sandusky plant due to its flexibility and the chance to keep production within the country.

Document 3:

Market research has suggested that Curlypro should launch two new lines of hair products—a Curlypro 2-in-1 shampoo/conditioner and a Curlypro dandruff control shampoo. Management is very eager to take advantage of the current success and rising brand awareness. Forecasts for the sales of each new product line are 200 crates per month, with a growth rate of 100% in year two and 50% in year three.

4. What is the difference in three-year sales forecasts for Curlypro between the most optimistic and most pessimistic forecasts, including launching either both new product lines or neither?

    (A) 1,137.5 crates per month
    (B) 2,025 crates per month
    (C) 2,337.5 crates per month
    (D) 2,800 crates per month
    (E) 3,137.5 crates per month

---

5. Answer the following true or false statements.

    True   False

    ◯   ◯   If each crate sold generates $1,000 in profit, if Curlypro decides to work with the Chinese plant, if the shipping costs increase by $100,000 total, and if Curlypro's sales equal the most pessimistic forecast, net monthly profits will be over $1 million in year 1.

    ◯   ◯   Curlypro would sell more units overall in the first year if it launched both new products, even with the most pessimistic forecast of its current product lines, than if it continued to produce only two products and sold them at the most optimistic forecast.

    ◯   ◯   If Curlypro chose the Chennai plant and the subsequent negative public perception caused the sales increase to be 25% lower than the most optimistic sales forecast, launching one new product line would not entirely offset this loss over three years.

---

6. For each of the following scenarios, determine if the selected plant will have enough capacity to manage the production demands of Curlypro. Select *Yes* if the plant will have sufficient capacity. Otherwise, select *No*.

    Yes   No

    ◯   ◯   Nanning plant, year 2: Assuming Curlypro's most pessimistic forecast and the introduction of the 2-in-1 shampoo/conditioner in the second year

    ◯   ◯   Sandusky plant, year 2: Assuming Curlypro's most optimistic forecast and no new product launches

    ◯   ◯   Chennai plant, year 1: Assuming Curlypro's most optimistic forecast and the launch of both new product lines in year 1

Questions 7 and 8 refer to the following excerpt from a fictitious education report about a fictitious new school program called Optimite.

The new Optimite program has found considerable success in eastern Europe over the past two years. Two school boards in the North Shore have now called for its experimental introduction in North Chicago. The program is complex, requiring a classroom size of 60 students in grade 11. Within an Optimite class would be three teachers working simultaneously. The Optimite objective is to have collaborative learning on site via case studies and matches, physical and mental challenges, and high-level discussions. Students are encouraged to research and discuss social, political, and economic topics and to use advanced technology tools in the classroom. Optimite also requires a diverse student body of cultural and socioeconomic backgrounds, with no majority of any distinct group. Students will be evaluated before participating and again after a two-semester trial. They will be tested on skills such as leadership, innovation, quantitative analysis, verbal reasoning, and communication.

7. Based on the description in the excerpt, which of the following activities would definitely be part of the fictitious Optimite program? Which of the following activities would definitely not be part of the program? Make only two selections, one in each column.

Would Definitely Be Part of the Optimite Program	Would Definitely Not Be Part of the Optimite Program	
○	○	Capoeira martial arts
○	○	Delivering a presentation on business ethics
○	○	A case competition
○	○	A field trip to a museum of marine biology
○	○	Moderated debate on local politics

8. Which of the following issues would not be a concern to the school board in order to launch the Optimite program?

(A) Classroom size and technology resources
(B) Transportation of students to the location
(C) Finding enough students to meet the diversity requirements
(D) Maintaining a teacher-student ratio below the state standard of 24 students per teacher
(E) Finding enough qualified instructors to teach the program

Question 9 refers to the following Venn diagram and information.

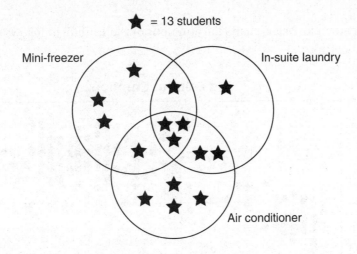

★ = 13 students

Mini-freezer

In-suite laundry

Air conditioner

9. Refer to the Venn diagram above. Each ★ represents 13 student residents living in New College dormitories. The student dormitories have minifreezers, in-suite laundry, air conditioners, or a combination. Complete each statement according to the information presented in the diagram.

i. If one student resident is selected at random from the New College dormitories, what is the probability that the student will have in-suite laundry?

(A) 2 out of 5
(B) 7 out of 15
(C) 3 out of 5
(D) 2 out of 3
(E) 7 out of 10

ii. If a student resident has air conditioning in the dormitory, what is the probability that the student will also have a minifreezer?

(A) 1 out of 10
(B) 1 out of 3
(C) 3 out of 10
(D) 2 out of 5
(E) 1 out of 2

Question 10 refers to the following scatter plot and information.

The scatter plot below charts the eruptions of Old Faithful in Yellowstone National Park.

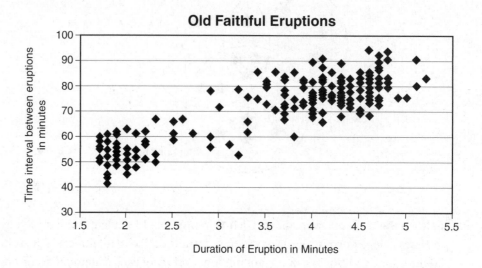

10. Complete each statement according to the information given by the graph.

i. Approximately how much time occurs between eruptions of Old Faithful?

(A) It's not possible to predict
(B) Every 55 minutes
(C) Every 80 minutes
(D) Either every 55 minutes or every 80 minutes

ii. Which of the following is closest to the length of the average duration of Old Faithful eruptions?

(A) 2 minutes
(B) 2.5 minutes
(C) 3.5 minutes
(D) 4.5 minutes

Questions 11 and 12 refer to the following table.

The table below shows data for revenues and profits of the top 13 companies globally in 2010.

Company	Revenues ($ billions)	Revenue Rank	% Change in Revenue Since 2009	Profits ($ billions)	% Change in Profits Since 2009
Wal-Mart Stores, Inc.	421.8	1	3.3	16.4	14.3
Exxon Mobil	354.7	2	24.6	30.5	58.0
Chevron	196.3	3	20.1	19.0	81.5
ConocoPhillips	185.0	4	32.6	11.4	133.8
Fannie Mae	153.8	5	429.2	-14.0	n/a*
General Electric	151.6	6	-3.3	11.6	5.6
Berkshire Hathaway	136.2	7	21.1	13.0	61.0
General Motors	135.6	8	29.6	6.2	n/a*
Bank of America Corp.	134.2	9	-10.8	-2.2	-135.7
Ford Motor	129.0	10	9.0	6.6	141.5
Hewlett-Packard	126.0	11	10.0	8.8	14.4
AT&T	124.6	12	1.3	19.9	58.5
J.P. Morgan Chase & Co.	115.5	13	-0.1	17.4	48.1

*n/a means that the actual number could not be calculated due to a negative profit change value in 2008

11. Consider each of the following statements. For each statement, indicate whether the statement is true or false based on the information provided in the table.

True False

○ ○ The amount of revenue growth of the top five ranked companies combined is greater than that of the rest of the companies in the list.

○ ○ The median profit amount is larger than the difference between the average of the top six profitable companies and the bottom six profitable companies.

○ ○ If Fannie Mae's percentage change in revenue dropped by 95% in 2010 and assuming operation costs remain constant, Fannie Mae should become profitable by 2010.

12. If stock market value was based on only the average rank of three values—percentage change in revenue, total profit amount, and percentage change in profit—which company would be the best one to invest in?

(A) Wal-Mart Stores, Inc.
(B) Berkshire Hathaway
(C) Fannie Mae
(D) Exxon Mobil
(E) ConocoPhillips

ON THE ACTUAL GMAT,
AFTER YOU HAVE CONFIRMED YOUR ANSWER,
YOU CANNOT RETURN TO IT.

QUANTITATIVE SECTION

Time: 75 minutes

37 questions

This section consists of two types of questions: Problem Solving and Data Sufficiency.

Problem Solving

DIRECTIONS: Solve each of the following problems; then indicate the correct answer.

NOTE: A figure that appears with a problem is drawn as accurately as possible so as to provide information that may help in answering the question.

Numbers in this test are real numbers.

Data Sufficiency

DIRECTIONS: Each of the following problems has a question and two statements that are labeled (1) and (2). Use the data given in (1) and (2) together with other available information (such as the number of hours in a day, the definition of *clockwise*, mathematical facts, etc.) to decide whether the statements are *sufficient* to answer the question. Then fill in space

(A) If you can get the answer from **(1) ALONE** but not from (2) alone

(B) If you can get the answer from **(2) ALONE** but not from (1) alone

(C) If you can get the answer from **BOTH (1)** and **(2) TOGETHER** but not from (1) alone or (2) alone

(D) If **EITHER** statement **(1) ALONE OR** statement **(2) ALONE** suffices

(E) If you **CANNOT** get the answer from statements (1) and (2) **TOGETHER** but need even more data

All numbers used in this section are real numbers.

A figure given for a problem is intended to provide information consistent with that in the question, but not necessarily with the additional information contained in the statements.

All figures lie in the plane unless you are told otherwise.

Figures are drawn as accurately as possible; straight lines may not appear straight on the screen.

1. It takes 30 days to fill a laboratory dish with bacteria. If the size of the bacteria colony doubles each day, how long did it take for the bacteria to fill one half of the dish?

   (A) 10 days
   (B) 15 days
   (C) 24 days
   (D) 29 days
   (E) 29.5 days

2. If the ratio of the areas of two squares is 2 : 1, then the ratio of the perimeters of the squares is

   (A) $1 : 2$
   (B) $1 : \sqrt{2}$
   (C) $\sqrt{2} : 1$
   (D) $2 : 1$
   (E) $4 : 1$

3. Let p and n be positive integers with $p < n$. If the legs of a right triangle are $n^2 - p^2$ and $2np$ then the hypotenuse of the right triangle is

   (A) $n + p$
   (B) $n^4 + 2n^2p^2 + p^4$
   (C) $(n + p)^2$
   (D) $n^2 + p^2$
   (E) cannot be determined

4. Is x greater than zero?

   (1) $x^4 - 16 = 0$
   (2) $x^3 - 8 = 0$

SAMPLE TEST 2

5. If both conveyer belt *A* and conveyer belt *B* are used, they can fill a hopper with coal in 1 hour. How long will it take for conveyer belt *A* to fill the hopper without conveyer belt *B*?

    (1) Conveyer belt *A* moves twice as much coal as conveyer belt *B*.

    (2) Conveyer belt *B* would take 3 hours to fill the hopper without conveyer belt *A*.

6. There are three types of tickets available for a concert: orchestra, which cost $12 each; balcony, which cost $9 each; and box, which cost $25 each. There were *P* orchestra tickets, *B* balcony tickets, and *R* box tickets sold for the concert. Which of the following expressions gives the percentage of ticket proceeds due to the sale of orchestra tickets?

    (A) $100 \times \dfrac{P}{(P+B+R)}$

    (B) $100 \times \dfrac{12P}{(12P+9B+25R)}$

    (C) $\dfrac{12P}{(12P+9B+25R)}$

    (D) $100 \times \dfrac{(9B+25R)}{(12P+9B+25R)}$

    (E) $100 \times \dfrac{(12P+9B+25R)}{(12P)}$

7. City *B* is 5 miles east of city *A*. City *C* is 10 miles southeast of city *B*. Which of the following is the closest to the distance from city *A* to city *C*?

    (A) 11 miles
    (B) 12 miles
    (C) 13 miles
    (D) 14 miles
    (E) 15 miles

8. There are 30 socks in a drawer. What is the probability that if 2 socks are picked from the drawer without looking both socks are blue?

    (1) 40 percent of the socks in the drawer are blue.

    (2) The ratio of blue socks to red socks in the drawer is 2 : 1.

9. If $3x - 2y = 8$, then $4y - 6x$ is

    (A) -16
    (B) -8
    (C) 8
    (D) 16
    (E) cannot be determined

10. It costs 10¢ a kilometer to fly and 12¢ a kilometer to drive. If you travel 200 kilometers, flying x kilometers of the distance and driving the rest, then the cost of the trip in dollars is

    (A) 20
    (B) 24
    (C) $24 - 2x$
    (D) $24 - .02x$
    (E) $2,400 - 2x$

11. Is y larger than 1?

    (1) y is larger than 0.
    (2) $y^2 - 4 > 0$.

12. A worker is hired for 6 days. He is paid $2 more for each day of work than he was paid for the preceding day of work. How much was he paid for the first day of work?

    (1) His total wages for the 6 days were $150.
    (2) He was paid 150 percent of his first day's pay for the sixth day.

13. Let $*y$ be the operation given by $*y = \dfrac{4}{y} - y$. Which of the following statements are true?

    I.   If $0 < y$, then $*y$ is negative.
    II. If $0 < y < z$, then $*y > *z$.
    III. If $0 < y$, then $y(*y)$ is less than 5.

    (A) I only
    (B) II only
    (C) III only
    (D) II and III only
    (E) I, II, and III

14. A car originally sold for $3,000. After a month, the car was discounted x percent, and a month later the car's price was discounted y percent. Is the car's price after the discounts less than $2,600?

   (1) $y = 10$
   (2) $x = 15$

15. How likely is a bird to be classified as positive?

   (1) 80 percent of birds with avian flu are classified as positive.
   (2) 5 percent of birds without avian flu are classified as positive.

16. If the area of a square increases by 69 percent, then the side of the square increases by

   (A) 13%
   (B) 30%
   (C) 39%
   (D) 69%
   (E) 130%

17. Which of the following statements can be inferred from the table?

Distribution of Work Hours in a Factory

Number of Workers		Number of Hours Worked
20		45–50
15		40–44
25		35–39
16		30–34
4		0–29
80	TOTAL	3,100

   I.   The average number of hours worked per worker is less than 40.
   II. At least 3 workers worked more than 48 hours.
   III. More than half of all the workers worked more than 40 hours.

   (A) I only
   (B) II only
   (C) I and II only
   (D) I and III only
   (E) I, II, and III

18. When a truck travels at 60 miles per hour, it uses 30 percent more gasoline to travel any distance than it does when it travels at 50 miles per hour. The truck can travel 20 miles on a gallon of gas if it is traveling at 50 miles per hour. The truck has only 10 gallons of gas and is 160 miles from its destination. It takes 20 minutes for the truck to stop for gas. How long will it take the truck to reach its final destination if it is driven at 60 miles per hour?

(A) 160 minutes
(B) 180 minutes
(C) 190 minutes
(D) 192 minutes
(E) 195 minutes

19. Company A owns 40 percent of the stock in the XYZ Corporation. Company B owns 15,000 shares. Company C owns all the shares not owned by company A or B. How many shares of stock does company A own if company C has 25 percent more shares than company A?

(A) 45,000
(B) 50,000
(C) 60,000
(D) 75,000
(E) 90,000

20. How many squares with sides $\frac{1}{2}$ inch long are needed to cover a rectangle that is 4 feet long and 6 feet wide?

(A) 24
(B) 96
(C) 3,456
(D) 13,824
(E) 14,266

21. How much cardboard will it take to make an open cubical box with no top?

    (1) The area of the bottom of the box is 4 square feet.
    (2) The volume of the box is 8 cubic feet.

22. Is the integer x divisible by 3?

    (1) The last digit in x is 3.
    (2) $x + 5$ is divisible by 6.

23. Is the figure $ABCD$ a rectangle?

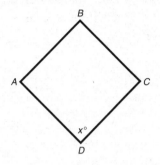

    (1) $x = 90$
    (2) $AB = CD$

24. A sequence of numbers is given by the rule $a_n = (a_{n-1})^2$. What is a_5?

    (1) $a_1 = -1$
    (2) $a_3 = 1$

25. In a group of people solicited by a charity, 30 percent contributed $40 each, 45 percent contributed $20 each, and the rest contributed $12 each. What percentage of the total contributed came from people who gave $40?

    (A) 25%
    (B) 30%
    (C) 40%
    (D) 45%
    (E) 50%

26. A trapezoid *ABCD* is formed by adding the isosceles right triangle *BCE* with base 5 inches to the rectangle *ABED*, where *DE* is *t* inches. What is the area of the trapezoid in square inches?

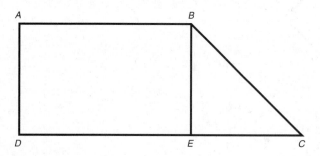

(A) $5t + 12.5$
(B) $5t + 25$
(C) $2.5t + 12.5$
(D) $(t + 5)^2$
(E) $t^2 + 25$

27. A manufacturer of jam wants to make a profit of $75 when it sells 300 jars of jam. It costs 65¢ each to make the first 100 jars of jam and 55¢ each to make each jar after the first 100. What price should it charge for the 300 jars of jam?

(A) $75
(B) $175
(C) $225
(D) $240
(E) $250

28. A car traveled 75 percent of the distance from town *A* to town *B* by traveling for *T* hours at an average speed of *V* miles per hour. The car traveled at an average speed of *S* miles per hour for the remaining part of the trip. Which of the following expressions represents the time the car traveled at *S* miles per hour?

(A) $\dfrac{VT}{S}$

(B) $\dfrac{VS}{4T}$

(C) $\dfrac{4VT}{3S}$

(D) $\dfrac{3S}{VT}$

(E) $\dfrac{VT}{3S}$

29. How much is John's weekly salary?

(1) John's weekly salary is twice as much as Fred's weekly salary.
(2) Fred's weekly salary is 40 percent of the total of Chuck's weekly salary and John's weekly salary.

30. Find $x + 2y$.

(1) $x + y = 4$
(2) $2x + 4y = 12$

31. Is angle *BAC* a right angle?

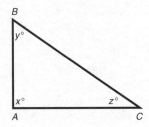

(1) $x = 2y$
(2) $y = 1.5z$

32. If a, b, and c are digits, is $a + b + c$ a multiple of 9? A digit is one of the integers 0, 1, 2, 3, 4, 5, 6, 7, 8, 9.

    (1) The three-digit number abc is a multiple of 9.
    (2) $(a \times b) + c$ is a multiple of 9.

33. In Teetown 50 percent of the people have blue eyes and blond hair. What percent of the people in Teetown have blue eyes but do not have blond hair?

    (1) 70 percent of the people in Teetown have blond hair.
    (2) 60 percent of the people in Teetown have blue eyes.

34. Thirty-six identical chairs must be arranged in rows with the same number of chairs in each row. Each row must contain at least 3 chairs, and there must be at least 3 rows. A row is parallel to the front of the room. How many different arrangements are possible?

    (A) 2
    (B) 4
    (C) 5
    (D) 6
    (E) 10

35. Which of the following solids has the largest volume? (*Figures are not drawn to scale.*)

   I.   A cylinder of radius 5 millimeters and height 11 millimeters

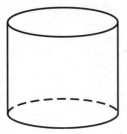

   II.   A sphere of radius 6 millimeters (the volume of a sphere of radius r is $\frac{4}{3}\pi r^3$)

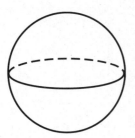

   III.   A cube with edge of 9 millimeters.

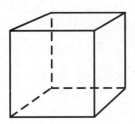

(A) I
(B) II
(C) III
(D) I and II
(E) II and III

36. The pentagon *ABCDE* is inscribed in a circle with center *O*. How many degrees is angle *ABC*?

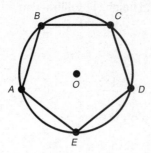

   (1) The pentagon *ABCDE* is a regular pentagon, which means that all sides are the same length and all interior angles are the same size.
   (2) The radius of the circle is 5 inches.

37. Is $k^2 + k - 2 > 0$?

   (1) $k < 1$
   (2) $k > -1$

ON THE ACTUAL GMAT,
AFTER YOU HAVE CONFIRMED YOUR ANSWER,
YOU CANNOT RETURN TO IT.

VERBAL SECTION

Time: 75 minutes
41 questions

Reading Comprehension

DIRECTIONS: This section contains three reading passages. You are to read each one carefully. When answering the questions, you *will* be allowed to refer back to the passages. The questions are based on what is *stated* or *implied* in each passage.

Critical Reasoning

DIRECTIONS: For each question in this section, choose the best answer from among the listed alternatives.

Sentence Correction

DIRECTIONS: This part of the section consists of a number of sentences, in each of which some part or the whole is underlined. Each sentence is followed by five alternative versions of the underlined portion. Select the alternative you consider both most correct and most effective according to the requirements of standard written English. Answer (A) is the same as the original version; if you think the original version is best, select answer (A).

In considering the answer choices, be attentive to matters of grammar, diction, and syntax, as well as clarity, precision, and fluency. Do not select an answer that alters the meaning of the original sentence.

1. Farmers in the North have observed that heavy frost is usually preceded by a full moon. They are convinced that the full moon somehow generates the frost.

   Which of the following, if true, would weaken the farmers' conviction?

   (A) The temperature must fall below 10 degrees Celsius (50 degrees Fahrenheit) for frost to occur.
   (B) Absence of a cloud cover cools the ground, which causes frost.
   (C) Farmers are superstitious.
   (D) No one has proven that the moon causes frost.
   (E) Farmers are not experts in meteorology.

2. Professor Tembel told his class that the method of student evaluation of teachers is not a valid measure of teaching quality. Students should fill out questionnaires at the end of the semester when courses have been completed.

   Which of the following, if true, provides support for Professor Tembel's proposal?

   (A) Professor Tembel received low ratings from his students.
   (B) Students filled out questionnaires after the midterm exam.
   (C) Students are interested in teacher evaluation.
   (D) Teachers are not obligated to use the survey results.
   (E) Student evaluation of teachers is voluntary.

3. If she was to decide to go to college, I, for one, would recommend that she plan to go to Yale.

   (A) If she was to decide to go to college,
   (B) If she were to decide to go to college,
   (C) Had she decided to go to college,
   (D) In the event that she decides to go to college,
   (E) Supposing she was to decide to go to college,

4. Except for you and I, everyone brought a present to the party.

   (A) Except for you and I, everyone brought
   (B) With exception of you and I, everyone brought
   (C) Except for you and I, everyone had brought
   (D) Except for you and me, everyone brought
   (E) Except for you and me, everyone had brought

Questions 5–8 are based on the following passage.

The domestic economy expanded in a remarkably vigorous and steady fashion.
. . . The resurgence in consumer confidence was reflected in the higher proportion
of incomes spent for goods and services and the marked increase in consumer will-
ingness to take on installment debt. A parallel strengthening in business psychology
was manifested in a stepped-up rate of plant and equipment spending and a gradual
pickup in outlays for inventory. Confidence in the economy was also reflected in the
strength of the stock market and in the stability of the bond market. . . . For the year
as a whole, consumer and business sentiment benefited from rising public expectations that a resolution of the conflict in Vietnam was in prospect and that East-West
tensions were easing.

The United States balance of payments deficit declined sharply. Nevertheless, by
any other test, the deficit remained very large, and there was actually a substantial
deterioration in our trade account to a sizable deficit, almost two thirds of which was
with Japan. . . .

The underlying task of public policy for the year ahead—and indeed for the longer run—remained a familiar one: to strike the right balance between encouraging
healthy economic growth and avoiding inflationary pressures. With the economy
showing sustained and vigorous growth, and with the currency crisis highlighting
the need to improve our competitive posture internationally, the emphasis seemed
to be shifting to the problem of inflation. The Phase Three program of wage and
price restraint can contribute to dampening inflation. Unless productivity growth
is unexpectedly large, however, the expansion of real output must eventually begin
to slow down to the economy's larger run growth potential if generalized demand
pressures on prices are to be avoided. Indeed, while the unemployment rates of a bit
over five percent were still too high, it seems doubtful whether the much lower rates
of four percent and below often cited as appropriate definitions of full employment
do in fact represent feasible goals for the United States economy—unless there are
improvements in the structure of labor and product markets and public policies
influencing their operation. There is little doubt that overall unemployment rates
can be brought down to four percent or less, for a time at least, by sufficient stimula-
tion of aggregate demand. However, the resultant inflationary pressures have in the
past proved exceedingly difficult to contain.

5.   The passage was most likely published in a

   (A)   popular magazine
   (B)   general newspaper
   (C)   science journal
   (D)   financial journal
   (E)   textbook

6. Confidence in the economy was expressed by all of the following EXCEPT

    (A)   a strong stock market
    (B)   a stable bond market
    (C)   increased installment debt
    (D)   increased plant and equipment expenditures
    (E)   rising interest rates

7. According to the passage, a major problem is how to

    (A)   sustain economic growth
    (B)   improve labor productivity
    (C)   balance growth with low inflation
    (D)   stimulate demand
    (E)   avoid large increases in imports

8. The passage mentions each of the following indicators of economic growth EXCEPT

    (A)   increased installment debt
    (B)   a decline in the balance of payments deficit
    (C)   consumer spending for goods and services
    (D)   a rise in business confidence
    (E)   business spending for inventories

9. When one reads the poetry of the seventeenth century, you find a striking contrast between the philosophy of the Cavalier poets such as Suckling and the attitude of the Metaphysical poets such as Donne.

    (A)   When one reads the poetry of the seventeenth century, you find
    (B)   When you read the poetry of the seventeenth century, one finds
    (C)   When one reads the poetry of the seventeenth century, he finds
    (D)   If one reads the poetry of the 17th century, you find
    (E)   As you read the poetry of the 17th century, one finds

10. Because of his broken hip, John Jones has not and possibly never will be able to run the mile again.

    (A)   has not and possibly never will be able to run
    (B)   has not and possibly will never be able to run
    (C)   has not been and possibly never would be able to run
    (D)   has not and possibly never would be able to run
    (E)   has not been able to run and possibly never will be able to run

SAMPLE TEST 2

11. The President of country "X" lobbied for passage of his new trade bill, which would liberalize trade with industrialized countries such as Japan, members of the European Union, and Canada. It is known that increased trade among countries leads to faster economic growth due to increased employment and lower product prices. Increased trade also allows countries to produce products and services more efficiently.

Each of the following, if true, could account for the above, EXCEPT

(A) Employment in country "X."
(B) Labor unions have petitioned the President to provide more local jobs.
(C) The trade agreement could bring a *quid pro quo* on pending negotiations.
(D) Economists claimed that the passage of the bill would increase the country's trade deficit.
(E) It was politically desirable for a trade bill at the present time.

12. If we are doomed to have local drug rehabilitation centers—and society has determined that we are—then society ought to pay for them.

Which of the following, if true, would weaken the above argument?

(A) Drug rehabilitation centers are too expensive to be locally funded.
(B) Many neighborhood groups oppose rehabilitation centers.
(C) Drug rehabilitation centers are expensive to maintain.
(D) Drug addicts may be unwilling to receive treatment.
(E) A government committee has convinced many groups that local rehabilitation centers are ineffective.

Questions 13–16 are based on the following passage.

These huge waves wreak terrific damage when they crash on the shores of distant lands or continents. Under a perfectly sunny sky and from an apparently calm sea, a wall of water may break twenty or thirty feet high over beaches and waterfronts,
Line crushing houses and drowning unsuspecting residents and bathers in its path.
(5)   How are these waves formed? When a submarine earthquake occurs, it is likely to set up a tremendous amount of shock, disturbing the quiet waters of the deep ocean. This disturbance travels to the surface and forms a huge swell in the ocean many miles across. It rolls outward in all directions, and the water lowers in the center as another swell looms up. Thus, a series of concentric swells are formed similar to
(10) those made when a coin or small pebble is dropped into a basin of water. The big difference is in the size. Each of the concentric rings of basin water traveling out toward the edge is only about an inch across and less than a quarter of an inch high. The swells in the ocean are sometimes nearly a mile wide and rise to several multiples of ten feet in height.
(15)   Many of us have heard about these waves, often referred to by their Japanese name of "tsunami." For ages they have been dreaded in the Pacific, as no shore has been free from them. An underwater earthquake in the Aleutian Islands could start a swell that would break along the shores and cause severe damage in the southern part of

Chile in South America. These waves travel hundreds of miles an hour, and one can
(20) understand how they would crash as violent breakers when caused to drag in the shallow waters of a coast.

Nothing was done about tsunamis until after World War II. In 1947 a particularly bad submarine earthquake took place south of the Aleutian Islands. A few hours later, people bathing in the sun along the quiet shores of Hawaii were dashed to
(25) death and shore-line property became a mass of shambles because a series of monstrous, breaking swells crashed along the shore and drove far inland. Hundreds of lives were lost in this catastrophe, and millions upon millions of dollars' worth of damage was done.

13. One surprising aspect of the waves discussed in the passage is the fact that they

   (A) are formed in concentric patterns
   (B) often strike during clear weather
   (C) arise under conditions of cold temperature
   (D) are produced by deep swells
   (E) may be forecast scientifically

14. It can be inferred that nothing was done about tsunamis until after World War II because

   (A) little was known about how tsunamis were formed
   (B) no damage was reported until after World War II
   (C) it was not known how to protect against them
   (D) the damage to life and property in Hawaii was severe
   (E) the United States had the means to invest in a solution to the tsunami problem

15. It is believed that the waves are caused by

   (A) seismic changes
   (B) concentric time belts
   (C) atmospheric conditions
   (D) underwater earthquakes
   (E) storms

16. A possible title for the passage could be

   (A) *How Submarine Waves Are Formed*
   (B) *How to Locate Submarine Earthquakes*
   (C) *Underwater Earthquakes*
   (D) *"Tsunami" Waves*
   (E) *How to Prevent Submarine Earthquakes*

17. <u>Had I realized how close</u> I was to failing, I would not have gone to the party.

   (A) Had I realized how close
   (B) If I would have realized
   (C) Had I had realized how close
   (D) When I realized how close
   (E) If I realized how close

18. <u>The football team's winning it's first game of the season</u> excited the student body.

   (A) The football team's winning it's first game of the season
   (B) The football team having won it's first game of the season
   (C) The football team's having won it's first game of the season
   (D) The football team's winning its first game of the season
   (E) The football team winning it's first game of the season

19. Anyone interested in the use of computers can learn much <u>if you have access to</u> a state-of-the-art microcomputer.

   (A) if you have access to
   (B) if he has access to
   (C) if access is available to
   (D) by access to
   (E) from access to

20. <u>No student had ought to be put into a situation where</u> he has to choose between his loyalty to his friends and his duty to the class.

   (A) No student had ought to be put into a situation where
   (B) Students ought to not be put into a situation where
   (C) No student should be put into a situation when
   (D) Students should be put into a situation in which
   (E) No student should be put into a situation where

21. <u>Being that I am realist</u>, I could not accept her statement that supernatural beings had caused the disturbance.

   (A) Being that I am realist,
   (B) Because I am a realist,
   (C) Just like I am a realist,
   (D) Being as I am a realist,
   (E) Realist that I am,

22. Surviving this crisis is going to take everything we've got. In addition to . . . massive retraining, we may also need subsidies—direct or channeled through the private sector—for a radically expanding service sector. Not merely things like environmental clean-up, but basic human services. (Alvin Toffler, *Previews and Premises* (New York: Bantam Books, 1985), p. 57.)

Which of the following statements is inconsistent with the above?

(A) Subsidies are needed to overcome the crisis.
(B) Environmental controls will be loosened.
(C) The service sector is going to expand to such an extent that many more workers will be needed.
(D) The private sector may play a role in retraining workers.
(E) Before the crisis can end, an environmental clean-up will have to take place.

23. Per-capita income last year was $25,000. Per-capita income is calculated by dividing total aggregate cash income by the total population. Real median income for families headed by a female, with no husband present, was $29,000. Therefore, women wage-earners earned more than the national average.

Which of the following would, if true, weaken the above conclusion?

(A) Per-capita income is calculated in real terms.
(B) In 99 percent of the cases, families headed by a female included no other wage-earner.
(C) Average income is not significantly different from median income.
(D) The overall average and per-capita income were the same.
(E) Only a small proportion of the total wage earners are women family heads.

Questions 24–27 are based on the following passage.

I decided to begin the term's work with the short story since that form would be the easiest for [the police officers], not only because most of their reading up to then had probably been in that genre, but also because a study of the reaction of people
Line to various situations was something they relied on in their daily work.
(5)   The officer must remain neutral and clearly try to present a picture of the facts, while the artist usually begins with a preconceived message or attitude which is then transmitted through the use of carefully selected details of action described in words intended to provoke associations and emotional reactions in the reader. Only at the end of the term did the officer point out to me that he and his men also
(10) try to evaluate the events they describe and that their description of a sequence of events must of necessity be structured and colored by their understanding of what has taken place.

The policemen's reactions to events and characters in the stories were surprisingly unprejudiced . . . . They did not object to writers whose stories had to do with (15) their protagonist's rebellion against society's accepted values. Nor did stories in which the strong father becomes the villain and in which our usual ideals of manhood are turned around offend them. The many hunters among my students readily granted the message in those hunting tales in which sensitivity triumphs over male aggressiveness, stories that show the boy becoming a man because he fails to (20) shoot the deer, goose, or catbird. The only characters they did object to were those they thought unrealistic. As the previous class had done, this one also excelled in interpreting the ways in which characters reveal themselves, subtly manipulate and influence each other; they, too, understood how the story usually saves its insight, its revelation, for the end.

(25) This almost instinctive grasp of the writing of fiction was revealed when the policemen volunteered to write their own short stories. . . . They not only took great pains with plot and character, but with style and language. The stories were surprisingly well written, revealing an understanding of what a solid short story must contain: the revelation of character, the use of background description and language to create (30) atmosphere and mood, the need to sustain suspense and yet make each event as it occurs seem natural, the insight achieved either by the characters in the story or the reader or both.

24. According to the passage, compared with the artist, the policeman is

   (A) ruled by action, not words
   (B) factual and not fanciful
   (C) neutral and not prejudiced
   (D) stoic and not emotional
   (E) aggressive and not passive

25. The author implies that policemen reacted to story events and characters

   (A) dispassionately
   (B) according to a policeman's stereotyped image
   (C) like dilettantes
   (D) with a dislike of defiant heroes
   (E) with prejudice

26. To which sort of characters did the hunters object?

   (A) unrealistic
   (B) emotional
   (C) sordid
   (D) timid
   (E) aggressive

27. The information in the passage indicates that the author believes which of the following best describes policemen as literature students:

(A) They are no different from other students.
(B) Their reactions to characters in stories are naïve.
(C) They glorify the ideal of manhood.
(D) They tend to admire American virtues of hard work and effort.
(E) Their short stories are taken from on the job experiences.

28. Foreign investment is composed of direct investment transactions (investment in plant, equipment, and land) and securities investment transactions. Throughout the post-World War II period, net increases in U.S. direct investment in Europe (funds outflows) exceeded net new European direct investment in the U.S.

Each of the following, if true, could help to account for this trend EXCEPT

(A) Land values in Europe were increasing at a faster rate than in the United States.
(B) Duties on imported goods in Europe were higher than those imposed by the United States.
(C) The cost of labor (wages) was consistently lower in Europe than in the United States.
(D) Labor mobility was much higher in the United States than in Europe.
(E) Corporate liquidity was lower in Europe than in the United States.

29. Most large retail stores hold sales in the month of January. The original idea of price reduction campaigns in January became popular when it was realized that sales of products would generally slow down following the Christmas rush, were it not for some incentive. The lack of demand could be solved by the simple solution of reducing prices.

There is now an increasing tendency among major department stores in large urban centers to have their "January sales" begin before Christmas, some time before the end of the calendar year. The idea behind this trend is to endeavor to sell the maximum amount of stock at a profit, even if that may not be at the maximum profit.

Which of the following conclusions cannot be drawn from the above?

(A) The incidence of "early" January sales results in the lower holdings of stocks with the corollary of lower stock holding costs.
(B) Demand is a function of price; as you lower price, demand increases.
(C) Major stores seem to think it makes sense to have the January sales campaigns pre-Christmas.
(D) It is becoming less popular to start the January sales in the New Year.
(E) The major department stores do not worry as much about profit maximization as they do about sales maximization.

30. The reason I came late to class today is because the bus broke down.

   (A) I came late to class today is because
   (B) why I came late to class today is because
   (C) I was late to school today is because
   (D) that I was late to school today is because
   (E) I came late to class today is that

31. The grocer hadn't hardly any of those kind of canned goods.

   (A) hadn't hardly any of those kind
   (B) hadn't hardly any of those kinds
   (C) had hardly any of those kind
   (D) had hardly any of those kinds
   (E) had scarcely any of those kind

32. Having stole the money, the police searched the thief.

   (A) Having stole the money, the police searched the thief.
   (B) Having stolen the money, the thief was searched by the police.
   (C) Having stolen the money, the police searched the thief.
   (D) Having stole the money, the thief was searched by the police.
   (E) Being that he stole the money, the police searched the thief.

33. The child is neither encouraged to be critical or to examine all the evidence for his opinion.

   (A) neither encouraged to be critical or to examine
   (B) neither encouraged to be critical nor to examine
   (C) either encouraged to be critical or to examine
   (D) encouraged either to be critical nor to examine
   (E) not encouraged either to be critical or to examine

34. The process by which the community influence the actions of its members is known as social control.

   (A) influence the actions of its members
   (B) influences the actions of its members
   (C) had influenced the actions of its members
   (D) influences the actions of their members
   (E) will influence the actions of its members

35. Of the world's largest external-debt countries in 1999, three had the same share of world external-debt as they had in 1990. These three countries may serve as examples of countries that succeeded in holding steady their share of world external-debt.

Which of the following, if true, would most seriously undermine the idea that these countries serve as examples as described above?

(A) Of the three countries, two had a much larger share of world external-debt in 1995 than in 1999.
(B) Some countries strive to reduce their share of world external-debt, not keep it steady.
(C) The three countries have different rates of economic growth.
(D) The absolute value of debt of the three countries is different.
(E) Some countries are more concerned with internal budgets than with external debt.

36. The director of the customs service suggested that customs taxes on automobiles will not be reduced as planned by the government because of the high incidence of traffic accidents last year.

Which of the above statements weakens the argument above?

I. Although the traffic accident rate last year was high, it was not appreciably higher than previous years and anyway, compulsory insurance covered most physical damage to automobiles and property.
II. A Commerce Department report showed that the demand for automobiles was highly inelastic. That is, as dealers lowered their prices, sales did not increase appreciably.
III. A study by the Economics Department at Classics University found that most traffic accidents had been caused by human error although it also concluded that an inadequate road network contributed to at least 40 percent of passenger injuries.

(A) I, but not II and not III.
(B) II, but not I and not III.
(C) I and III, but not II.
(D) II and III, but not I.
(E) I, II, and III.

37. Significant beneficial effects of smoking occur primarily in the area of mental health, and the habit originates in a search for contentment. The life expectancy of our people has increased greatly in recent years; it is possible that the relaxation and contentment and enjoyment produced by smoking has lengthened many lives. Smoking is beneficial.

Which of the following, if true, weakens the above conclusion?

(A) Mental health can be improved by many means.
(B) The government earns millions of dollars from the tobacco tax and tens of thousands of civilians are employed in the tobacco industry.
(C) The evidence cited in the statement covers only one example of the effects of cigarette smoking.
(D) Life expectancy has been extended due to better medical care.
(E) Not everyone enjoys life.

38. An economist was quoted as saying that the Consumer Price Index (CPI) will go up next month because of a recent increase in the price of fruit and vegetables.

Which of the following cannot be inferred from the statement?

(A) The cost of fruits and vegetables has risen sharply.
(B) Consumers have decreased their consumption of fruits and vegetables.
(C) The cost of fruit and vegetables is a major item in the CPI.
(D) Food cost changes are reflected quickly in the CPI.
(E) Other items that make up the CPI have not significantly decreased in price.

39. At a political rally at Jefferson Stadium, candidate Smith exclaimed: "Nearly everyone at the rally is behind me. It looks like I am going to be elected."

On which unstated assumption does Smith's conclusion rely?

(A) Smith's opponent also appeared at the rally.
(B) The rally was attended by almost all the residents of Smith's constituency.
(C) Smith's constituency will continue to vote for him, and his opponent does not have more supporters than those who attended the rally and will vote for Smith.
(D) Smith was supported by the local mayor.
(E) People always vote their emotions.

40. Depending on skillful suggestion, argument is seldom used in advertising.

(A) Depending on skillful suggestion, argument is seldom used in advertising.
(B) Argument is seldom used by advertisers, who depend instead on skillful suggestion.
(C) Skillful suggestion is depended on by advertisers instead of argument.
(D) Suggestion, which is more skillful, is used in place of argument by advertisers.
(E) Instead of suggestion, depending on argument is used by skillful advertisers.

41. In a famous experiment by Pavlov, when a dog smelled food, it salivated. Subsequently, a bell was rung whenever food was placed near the dog. After a number of trials, only the bell was rung, whereupon the dog would salivate even though no food was present.

Which of the following conclusions may be drawn from the above experiment?

(A) Dogs are easily fooled.
(B) Dogs are motivated only by the sound of a bell.
(C) The ringing of a bell was associated with food.
(D) A conclusion cannot be reached on the basis of one experiment.
(E) Two stimuli are stronger than one.

ON THE ACTUAL GMAT,
AFTER YOU HAVE CONFIRMED YOUR ANSWER,
YOU CANNOT RETURN TO IT.

INTEGRATED REASONING SECTION

1. **i.** A

   ii. B

2.

Amount Needed to Spend on New Hires	Amount Each Student Expects to Make	Amount in $
●	○	0
○	○	720
○	○	1,080
○	●	1,920
○	○	2,560
○	○	3,840

3.

Would Help Explain	Would Not Help Explain
●	○
●	○
○	●

4. C

5.

True	False
○	●
●	○
●	○

6.

Yes	No
●	○
○	●
●	○

7.

Would Definitely be Part of the Optimite Program	Would Definitely NOT be Part of the Optimite Program
○	○
○	○
●	○
○	●
○	○

8. D

9. **i.** B

   ii. D

10. **i.** D

    ii. C

11.

True	False
●	○
○	●
●	○

12. D

ANSWER KEY
Sample Test 2

QUANTITATIVE SECTION

1. D	11. C	21. D	31. C
2. C	12. D	22. B	32. A
3. D	13. D	23. E	33. B
4. B	14. B	24. D	34. C
5. D	15. E	25. E	35. B
6. B	16. B	26. A	36. A
7. D	17. A	27. E	37. C
8. A	18. B	28. E	
9. A	19. C	29. E	
10. D	20. D	30. B	

VERBAL SECTION

1. B	12. E	23. E	34. B
2. B	13. B	24. C	35. A
3. B	14. D	25. A	36. B
4. D	15. D	26. A	37. D
5. D	16. A	27. A	38. B
6. E	17. A	28. D	39. C
7. C	18. D	29. A	40. B
8. B	19. B	30. E	41. C
9. C	20. E	31. D	
10. E	21. B	32. B	
11. D	22. B	33. E	

SELF-SCORING GUIDE
Analytical Writing

Evaluate your essay (or have a friend or teacher evaluate it for you) on the following basis. Read your essay completely, paying special attention to its logical organization and use of examples and facts to buttress its claims or position. Assign a holistic score between 0 and 6, using the scale below.

6 OUTSTANDING

Cogent, well-articulated analysis of the issue or critique of the argument. Develops a position with insightful reasons and persuasive examples. Well organized. Superior command of language and variety of syntax. Only minor flaws in grammar, usage, and mechanics.

5 STRONG

Well-developed analysis or critique. Develops a position with well-chosen examples or reasons. Generally well organized. Clear control of language and variety of syntax. Minor flaws in grammar, usage, and mechanics.

4 ADEQUATE

Competent analysis or critique. Develops a position with relevant reasons or examples. Adequately organized. Adequate control of language, but may lack syntactic variety. May have some flaws in grammar, usage, and mechanics.

3 LIMITED

Competent but clearly flawed analysis or critique. Vague or limited in developing a position. Poorly organized. Weak in using relevant examples or reasons. Language used imprecisely or lacking in sentence variety. Contains major errors or frequent minor errors in grammar, usage, and mechanics.

2 SERIOUSLY FLAWED

Serious weaknesses in analysis and organization. Unclear or seriously limited in presenting or developing a position. Disorganized. Few relevant examples or reasons. Frequent serious problems in language and sentence structure. Numerous errors in grammar, usage, or mechanics that interfere with meaning.

1 FUNDAMENTALLY DEFICIENT

Little evidence of ability to organize and develop a coherent response to issue or argument. Severe and persistent errors in language and sentence structure. Pervasive pattern of errors in grammar, usage, and mechanics that severely interfere with meaning.

0 UNSCORABLE

Illegible or not written on the assigned topic.

ANSWERS EXPLAINED
Integrated Reasoning Section

1. i. (A) The third quartile of the graph is the area between 50% and 75%. If you look at the graph, you can see where the line crosses the *x*-axis at 50% and at 75%. At 50%, the *x*-axis is at 74 inches. At 75%, the *x*-axis is at 77 inches. This gives you the range of heights:

$$77 - 74 = 3$$

Therefore, the answer is **A**.

ii. (B) From question 1, you know that the median height, or 50% of all the players, is 74 inches. Since you need to look at all players within 6 inches of that height, you should look at the graph between 68 inches and 80 inches. At 68 inches, the line is approximately halfway between 0% and 25%. At 80 inches, the line is approximately halfway between 75% and 100%. This represents about 75% of all the players. Therefore, the answer is **B**.

2. ($0, $1,920)

(i) This is a three-tiered rate problem that tracks the number of painters, houses, and hours. Since the question asks for how many new people you need to hire, let's first calculate how many hours are required to build 1,200 houses.

10 students paint 4 houses in 16 hours ÷ 10 students paint 1,200 houses in 4,800 hours

From this you know that Youth Pro Painters needs 4,800 student painter hours to complete 1,200 houses. Since there are 12 weeks in the summer and 40 working hours in a week, you can calculate how many students are needed.

$$4{,}800 \text{ hours} \div 40 \text{ hours/week} \div 12 \text{ weeks} = 10 \text{ students}$$

The company has just enough students to paint 1,200 houses, so the total amount needed to spend on additional hires is **$0**.

(ii) To calculate the amount of money each student can make in half the summer, first calculate the amount each student will earn during the summer.

$$40 \text{ hr/week} \times 12 \text{ weeks} \times \$8.00/\text{hr} = \$3{,}840$$

To determine how much each student makes in half the summer, divide by 2. The answer is **$1,920**.

3. (Would help explain, Would help explain, Would not help explain)

(i) This can be easily found by sorting through either the primary school column or kindergarten column. The kindergarten column ranges from 71 to 32 while the primary school column ranges from 98 to 81. This chart would help explain that kindergartens are not offered as much as are primary schools. The answer is **would help explain**.

(ii) If you look at the data from the table for Peru, you can see a much lower percentage for both kindergarten and post-secondary education compared with primary and secondary. If you sort the primary and secondary school numbers, you can also see that Peru ranks among the bottom. This could suggest that farming families are keeping children away from school. Therefore, the answer is **would help explain**.

(iii) You could associate the data in the chart with where education is more valued by its country's citizens. However, when you check on Argentina and how it ranks, it is the highest in the kindergarten column and is second in the other three columns. Columbia ranks first in the other three columns. Thus the table could not help you infer anything about Argentinean parents. Therefore, the answer is **would not help explain**.

4. **(C)** The best way to sort out all the information here is with a chart. In fact, if you look at the question first, you might decide to set up a chart with all the detailed information while reading the documents. Then you can reference the chart when answering the question.

| | Two Current Product Lines (crates per month) | | New Product Lines (crates per month) | |
	Pessimistic	Optimistic	2-in-1	Dandruff
Year 0	800	800	0	0
Year 1	1,000	1,200	200	200
Year 2	1,250	1,800	400	400
Year 3	1,562.5	2,700	600	600

Most pessimistic forecast without new product launches: 1,562.5

Most optimistic forecast with new product launches: $2,700 + 1,200 = 3,900$

Find the difference: $3,900 - 1,562.5 = 2,337.5$

Therefore, the answer is **C**.

5. **(False, True, True)**

(i) Since you are looking at only year 1 and just the existing product line, you can calculate this using the information you already organized in the chart from question 5. Sales are 1,000 units × $1,000 per crate, giving you $1 million monthly. Since the shipping costs are $100,000, this brings our overall profit down to $900,000 monthly. Therefore, the answer is **false**.

(ii) Since you are looking at only year 1, you can break down this question into each scenario. Again, using a chart would help you organize the data.

Scenario 1: Pessimistic, 25% growth, 2 new product launches:

$$800 \times 1.25 + 200 + 200 = 1,400 \text{ crates}$$

Scenario 2: Optimistic, 50% growth, no new product launches:

$$800 \times 1.5 = 1,200 \text{ crates}$$

Scenario 1 does sell more units than scenario 2. Therefore, the answer is **true**.

(iii) In this case, the question is much easier if you use a chart. You also need to understand that the 25% decrease due to the negative perception affects just the sales increase, not the total sales.

	Two Current Product Lines (crates per month)		One New Product Line
	Total Optimistic Sales	With 25% Decrease	
Year 0	800	n/a	0
Year 1	1,200	1,100	200
Year 2	1,650	1,512.5*	400
Year 3	2,079.7	600	

*At this point, you may notice that the cumulative percentage increase is 37.5% per year for the current product lines. So you can easily calculate year 3.

As you can see, the total sales of the one new product line over three years are 1,200 crates. The total growth of the current lines over three years is 2,080 − 800 = 1,280. Therefore, launching one new product will not "entirely" offset the launch (even though it's pretty close). The answer is **true**.

6. **(Yes, No, Yes)**

(i) From the chart you created for question 5, you can extract the second-year pessimistic forecast and the new product launch of just one product in one year.

$$1,250 + 200 = 1,450$$

Nanning's capacity is 1,500 crates per month. Therefore, the answer is **yes**.

(ii) Similar to part (i), you can extract the second-year optimistic forecast from the chart you created for question 5, which is 1,800 crates per month. Sandusky's capacity is 1,200 crates per month. Therefore, the answer is **no**.

(iii) Again, you can use the chart you created for question 5 to extract the optimistic forecast for year 1 and two new product launches for the first year.

$$1,200 + 200 + 200 = 1,600$$

Chennai's capacity is 2,500 crates per month. Therefore, the answer is **yes**.

7. **(A case competition, A field trip to a museum of marine biology)**

This challenging question gives us a considerable amount of multilayered information. Some of it is useful, and some of it is not. You need to know the difference. The question is trying to get you to focus on the key support that is necessary to make the conclusion.

At first glance, many of the answers seem possible, but the key here is to find what must be true based on the passage. Capoeira martial arts, delivering a presentation on business ethics, and moderated debate on local politics are all quite possible given the scope of the Optimite program. However, they are all too specific. It's equally possible that the program would have alternative physical challenges, presentations, or debates. Having a case competition, generally speaking, is the only activity that must be part of the program since the passage says "case studies and matches." Therefore, **a case competition** would definitely be part of the program.

A field trip to a museum of marine biology would not be part of the program for two reasons. The first is that the Optimite program focuses on learning "on site." The second is that the description does not mention science. Therefore, **a field trip to a museum of marine biology** would definitely **not** be part of the program.

8. (D) In this question, four of the answer choices would be issues of concern to the school board.

Choice A is a concern since the program has a class size of 60 and requires advanced technology tools in the classroom.

Choice B is a concern because of the diversity of the eligible students and the preexisting concern of getting all the students to school.

Choice C is a concern because it may be difficult to find 60 diverse and talented students.

Choice E is a concern for two reasons. First, like any new program, Optimite will require teachers to learn the new curriculum. Second, the format is different than that in traditional classrooms. Optimite uses a "team" teaching structure. It's possible that some teachers may not want to get involved.

Since the Optimite program requires three teachers for 60 students, it thus has a ratio of 20 students per teacher. This is already under the standard of 24 students per teacher. The correct answer is **D**.

9. i. (B) This is a hard Venn diagram because it consists of three circles. The process to review and analyze the chart is the same as if it consisted of two, though. Determine the total number of residents with laundry and the total number of residents. There are 7 stars in the laundry circle and the total number of stars in the Venn diagram is 15. The probability is 7 out of 15. Therefore, the answer is **B**.

ii. (D) For this question, you need to consider only those residents with air conditioning. The circle for air conditioning contains 10 stars. The number of stars with air conditioning that also have minifreezers is 3 + 1 = 4. This gives us a probability of 4 out of 10 or 2 out of 5. Therefore, the answer is **D**.

10. i. (D) This is among the more tricky scatter plot distributions because it is bimodal, which means that the data suggest two distinct areas or patterns of Old Faithful's eruptions. The first significant section is on the bottom left, and the second significant section is on the top right. Since the answer choices are looking at eruption intervals, you can approximately determine two separate ones: 55 minutes and 80 minutes. Therefore, the answer is **D**.

ii. (C) This question is also challenging because you need to use weighted averages to determine the duration of the average eruption. You certainly don't need to count all the plot points, but you can see that more are in the top right section than in other sections. Therefore, the average will be closer to the right side of the x-axis. If the average of the plots at the bottom left section is approximately 2 minutes and at the top right section is between 4 and 4.5 minutes, the weighted average should be more than 3 or 3.25 minutes. The only answer that fits these criteria is 3.5 minutes. Therefore, the answer is **C**.

11. (True, False, True)

(i) This question requires you to extrapolate new information—revenue growth. Rather than using the calculator to create an entirely new column, you should try to estimate whenever possible. If you look at the top two companies, Wal-Mart and Exxon Mobil, they have much higher revenues than the rest. In addition, Exxon

Mobil's growth is substantial. In addition, Fannie Mae is in the top five. Since its revenue grew 429.2%, that would mean a revenue growth of over 80% of the total revenue, or over $120 billion. This would far outweigh the rest of the companies, two of which had negative growth. Therefore, the answer is **true**.

(ii) First, you need to sort the profit column. The median number is General Electric at $11.6 billion. Again, it is quicker to use ballpark numbers. The top half's average would be approximately $20 billion. The bottom half's average would be quite low because of the combined –$16.2 billion of Fannie Mae and Bank of America. This will bring the average profit of the bottom half to approximately $2 to $5 billion. The difference between the top half and the bottom half will be much greater than $11.6 billion. Therefore, the answer is **false**.

(iii) This question requires you extrapolate from the table. Fannie Mae's revenue change was about 430%. (Remember you don't need to use specific numbers here.) A 95% drop would give you a little over a 20% revenue increase for 2010/2011. Since Fannie Mae's profit loss was $14 billion and its operating costs are the same, you can calculate how much new revenue it will earn. Since 20% of $150 billion is $30 billion, Fannie Mae would have to earn profits. Therefore, the answer is **true**.

12. **(D)** The definition given here of a good value stock is based on only the first three columns containing numbers. So you need to sort through each column quickly and find the best company in which to invest. When you sort the column "% Change in Revenue Since 2009," you see that Fannie Mae comes out on top. However, you can eliminate it since the other two columns will decrease Fannie Mae's value significantly. Of the other four answer choices, Exxon Mobil, ConocoPhillips, and Berkshire Hathaway rank in the top five.

At this point, a quick way to solve this problem is to create a chart to track the ranks. The more complicated a question is and the more information you are dealing with, the more important it is that you add structure to the problem. Charts are a great way to do this.

Company	% Change in Revenue	Profit	% Change in Profit	Average Rank
Exxon Mobil	4	1	6	11/3
ConocoPhillips	2	8	2	12/3
Berkshire Hathaway	5	6	STOP!	

Once you get to the percent change in profit for Berkshire Hathaway, you can stop filling in the chart. This is because even if Berkshire Hathaway ranks number one in percentage change in profit (it does not), its average rank would still be greater than that of Exxon Mobil. You could have also quickly added Wal-Mart if you had thought to chart this whole question out at the beginning of this section. However, it would not have ranked high. Therefore, the answer is **D**.

Quantitative Section

(Roman numerals at the end of each answer refer to the section of Chapter 9 in which the appropriate math principle is discussed.)

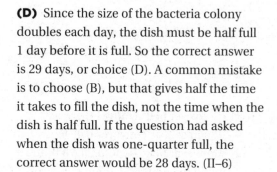

1. It takes 30 days to fill a laboratory dish with bacteria. If the size of the bacteria colony doubles each day, how long did it take for the bacteria to fill one half of the dish?

   (A) 10 days
   (B) 15 days
   (C) 24 days
   (D) 29 days
   (E) 29.5 days

   (D) Since the size of the bacteria colony doubles each day, the dish must be half full 1 day before it is full. So the correct answer is 29 days, or choice (D). A common mistake is to choose (B), but that gives half the time it takes to fill the dish, not the time when the dish is half full. If the question had asked when the dish was one-quarter full, the correct answer would be 28 days. (II–6) ★★★

2. If the ratio of the areas of two squares is 2 : 1, then the ratio of the perimeters of the squares is

   (A) 1 : 2
   (B) 1 : $\sqrt{2}$
   (C) $\sqrt{2}$: 1
   (D) 2 : 1
   (E) 4 : 1

   (C) If s and t denote the sides of the two squares, then $s^2 : t^2 = 2 : 1$. Thus, $\left(\dfrac{s}{t}\right)^2 = \dfrac{2}{1}$ and $\dfrac{s}{t} = \dfrac{\sqrt{2}}{1}$. Since the ratio of the perimeters is $4s : 4t = s : t$, (C) is the correct answer. (II-5, III-7) ★★☆

3. Let p and n be positive integers with $p < n$. If the legs of a right triangle are $n^2 - p^2$ and $2np$ then the hypotenuse of the right triangle is

   (A) $n + p$
   (B) $n^4 + 2n^2p^2 + p^4$
   (C) $(n + p)^2$
   (D) $n^2 + p^2$
   (E) cannot be determined

   (D) The Pythagorean Theorem states that $a^2 + b^2 = c^2$ where a and b are the legs and c is the hypotenuse of any right triangle. So the hypotenuse is the square root of $(n^2 - p^2)^2 + (2np)^2$. Expanding each part gives $n^4 - 2n^2p^2 + p^4 + 4n^2p^2 = n^4 + 2n^2p^2 + p^4 = (n^2 + p^2)^2$. So the hypotenuse is $(n^2 + p^2)$.

   NOTE: There are some deceptive choices. Choice (B) is the square of the hypotenuse. Choice (C) is $(n + p)^2$, which is not the same as $(n^2 + p^2)$. (II-1, III-4) ★★★

ANSWERS EXPLAINED

★★☆ **4.** Is x greater than zero?

(1) $x^4 - 16 = 0$

(2) $x^3 - 8 = 0$

(B) $x^3 - 8 = 0$ has only $x = 2$ as a real solution. And 2 is greater than 0, so STATEMENT (2) alone is sufficient.

Since $x = 2$ and $x = -2$ are both solutions of $x^4 - 16 = 0$, STATEMENT (1) alone is not sufficient. (II-2)

★★☆ **5.** If both conveyer belt A and conveyer belt B are used, they can fill a hopper with coal in 1 hour. How long will it take for conveyer belt A to fill the hopper without conveyer belt B?

(1) Conveyer belt A moves twice as much coal as conveyer belt B.

(2) Conveyer belt B would take 3 hours to fill the hopper without conveyer belt A.

(D) STATEMENT (1) is sufficient since it implies that conveyer belt A loads $\frac{2}{3}$ of the hopper while conveyer belt B loads only $\frac{1}{3}$ with both working. Since conveyer belt A loads $\frac{2}{3}$ of the hopper in an hour, it will take $1 \div \left(\frac{2}{3} \right)$ or 1.5 hours to fill the hopper by itself.

STATEMENT (2) is also sufficient since it implies that conveyer belt B fills $\frac{1}{3}$ of the hopper in 1 hour. Thus, conveyer belt A loads $\frac{2}{3}$ in 1 hour, and that means conveyer belt A would take 1.5 hours by itself. (II-3)

★★★ **6.** There are three types of tickets available for a concert: orchestra, which cost $12 each; balcony, which cost $9 each; and box, which cost $25 each. There were P orchestra tickets, B balcony tickets, and R box tickets sold for the concert. Which of the following expressions gives the percentage of ticket proceeds due to the sale of orchestra tickets?

(A) $100 \times \dfrac{P}{(P+B+R)}$

(B) $100 \times \dfrac{12P}{(12P+9B+25R)}$

(C) $\dfrac{12P}{(12P+9B+25R)}$

(D) $100 \times \dfrac{(9B+25R)}{(12P+9B+25R)}$

(E) $100 \times \dfrac{(12P+9B+25R)}{(12P)}$

(B) First find an expression for the proceeds from orchestra tickets, which is $12P$. Next, find an expression for the total proceeds, which is $12P + 9B + 25R$. So $\dfrac{12P}{(12P+9B+25R)}$ gives the part of the total proceeds due to the sale of orchestra tickets. However, this is not a percentage. You need to multiply this expression by 100 to get a percentage. So the correct choice is (B). (I-4, II-3)

7. City *B* is 5 miles east of city *A*. City *C* is 10 miles southeast of city *B*. Which of the following is the closest to the distance from city *A* to city *C*?

(A) 11 miles
(B) 12 miles
(C) 13 miles
(D) 14 miles
(E) 15 miles

(D) Set up a coordinate system with *A* at (0, 0). Then *B* is at (5, 0). Since *C* is southeast of *B*, then *BCD* is an isosceles right triangle whose hypotenuse is 10 miles. So $BD^2 + CD^2 = 10^2 = 100$ and $BD = CD$, so $BD^2 = 50$. Therefore, $BD = \sqrt{50} = \sqrt{25}\sqrt{2} = 5\sqrt{2}$. So the coordinates of *C* are $(5 + 5\sqrt{2}, -5\sqrt{2})$. Remember, the distance between two points whose coordinates are (*x*, *y*) and (*a*, *b*) is $\sqrt{(x-a)^2+(y-b)^2}$. So the distance from *A* to *C* is the square root of $(5 + 5\sqrt{2})^2 + (-5\sqrt{2})^2$. You can work with these numbers, but it will be messy. It is much faster to use the fact that $\sqrt{2}$ is about 1.4. Remember, the question asks for only an approximate answer. So $5\sqrt{2}$ is about 7; thus, the distance is the square root of $(5 + 7)^2 + (-7)^2$. This is equal to the square root of 144 + 49 or 193. *Do not try to find the square root of this number if you don't know it.* Simply square each answer and see which is closest to 193. Since $14^2 = 196$, the correct choice is 14 miles or (D). (III-9)

★★★

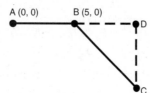

8. There are 30 socks in a drawer. What is the probability that if 2 socks are picked from the drawer without looking both socks are blue?

(1) 40 percent of the socks in the drawer are blue.
(2) The ratio of blue socks to red socks in the drawer is 2 : 1.

(A) If 40 percent of the socks are blue, then we can see that there are 12(.4 × 30) blue socks in the drawer. So the probability that both socks are blue is $\left(\frac{12}{30}\right)\left(\frac{11}{29}\right)$ and STATEMENT 1 is sufficient.

STATEMENT 2 is not sufficient since it does not tell us how many blue socks are in the drawer. You don't know that all the socks are either red or blue because there could be socks of other colors in the drawer. (I-7)

★★☆

★★☆ **9.** If $3x - 2y = 8$, then $4y - 6x$ is

(A) −16
(B) −8
(C) 8
(D) 16
(E) cannot be determined

(A) $4y - 6x = -2(3x - 2y) = -2(8) = -16$. (II-2)

★★☆ **10.** It costs 10¢ a kilometer to fly and 12¢ a kilometer to drive. If you travel 200 kilometers, flying x kilometers of the distance and driving the rest, then the cost of the trip in dollars is

(A) 20
(B) 24
(C) $24 - 2x$
(D) $24 - .02x$
(E) $2,400 - 2x$

(D) Since the total distance is 200 kilometers, of which you fly x kilometers, you drive $(200 - x)$ kilometers. Therefore, the cost is $10x + (200 - x)12$, which is $10x - 12x + 2,400$ or $2,400 - 2x$ cents. The answer in dollars is obtained by dividing by 100, which is $(24 - .02x)$ dollars. (II-1)

★★☆ **11.** Is y larger than 1?

(1) y is larger than 0.
(2) $y^2 - 4 > 0$.

(C) (2) alone is not sufficient since both $y = 3$ and $y = -3$ satisfy $y^2 - 4 > 0$. (1) alone is not sufficient, since $\frac{1}{2}$ is larger than 0 but less than 1, while 3 is larger than 0 and larger than 1. If $y^2 - 4 > 0$, then either y is >2 or $y < -2$. If (1) and (2) both hold, then y must be >2, which is >1. (II-7)

★★☆ **12.** A worker is hired for 6 days. He is paid $2 more for each day of work than he was paid for the preceding day of work. How much was he paid for the first day of work?

(1) His total wages for the 6 days were $150.
(2) He was paid 150 percent of his first day's pay for the sixth day.

(D) Let x be the amount he was paid the first day. Then he was paid $x + 2$, $x + 4$, $x + 6$, $x + 8$, and $(x + 10)$ dollars for the succeeding days. (1) alone is sufficient since the total he was paid is $(6x + 30)$ dollars, and we can solve $6x + 30 = 150$ (to find that he was paid $20 for the first day). (2) alone is also sufficient. He was paid $(x + 10)$ dollars on the sixth day, so (2) means that $(1.5)x = x + 10$ (which is the same as $x = 20$). (II-6)

13. Let $*y$ be the operation given by $*y = \dfrac{4}{y} - y$. Which of the following statements are true?

   I. If $0 < y$, then $*y$ is negative.
   II. If $0 < y < z$, then $*y > *z$.
   III. If $0 < y$ then $y(*y)$ is less than 5.

   (A) I only
   (B) II only
   (C) III only
   (D) II and III only
   (E) I, II, and III

(D) I is not true for all positive y since $*1 = 4 - 1 = 3$, which is not negative. The question asks which statements are true for *all positive y*, not just some positive y.

II is true since if $0 < y < z$, then $\dfrac{4}{y} > \dfrac{4}{z}$ and

$-y > -z$, so $\left(\dfrac{4}{y}\right) - y$ is $> \left(\dfrac{4}{z}\right) - z$. So $*y > *z$.

Since $y(*y) = y\left[\left(\dfrac{4}{y}\right) - y\right] = 4 - y^2$, which is

less than 5 for any positive y, III is always true. So the correct answer is (D). (II-7)

---

14. A car originally sold for \$3,000. After a month, the car was discounted x percent, and a month later the car's price was discounted y percent. Is the car's price after the discounts less than \$2,600?

   (1) $y = 10$
   (2) $x = 15$

(B) Since 85 percent of \$3,000 is \$2,550, (2) alone is sufficient. (1) alone is not sufficient since if x were 5 percent, (1) would tell us that the price of the car is less than \$2,600. But if x were 1 percent, (1) would imply that the price of the car is greater than \$2,600. (I-4)

---

15. How likely is a bird to be classified as positive?

   (1) 80 percent of birds with avian flu are classified as positive.
   (2) 5 percent of birds without avian flu are classified as positive.

(E) Even assuming (1) and (2), you would still need to know what percentage of birds have avian flu in order to answer the question. Since that information is not available, both statements together are not sufficient. (I-7)

---

16. If the area of a square increases by 69 percent, then the side of the square increases by

   (A) 13%
   (B) 30%
   (C) 39%
   (D) 69%
   (E) 130%

(B) If A_1 denotes the increased area and A the original area, then $A_1 = 1.69A$ since A_1 is A increased by 69 percent. Thus, $s_1^2 = A_1 = 1.69A = 1.69s^2$, where s_1 is the increased side and s the original side. Since the square root of 1.69 is 1.3, we have $s_1 = 1.3s$ so s is increased by .3 or 30 percent. (I-4)

17. Which of the following statements can be inferred from the table?

Distribution of Work Hours in a Factory

Number of Workers		Number of Hours Worked
20		45–50
15		40–44
25		35–39
16		30–34
4		0–29
80	TOTAL	3,100

I. The average number of hours worked per worker is less than 40.

II. At least 3 workers worked more than 48 hours.

III. More than half of all the workers worked more than 40 hours.

(A) I only
(B) II only
(C) I and II only
(D) I and III only
(E) I, II, and III

(A) I can be inferred since the average number of hours worked is $\frac{3,100}{80} = 38.75$, which is less than 40. II cannot be inferred since there is no information given beyond the fact that 20 workers worked between 45 and 50 hours. Since only 35 workers worked 40 or more hours, III cannot be inferred. (IV-1)

18. When a truck travels at 60 miles per hour, it uses 30 percent more gasoline to travel any distance than it does when it travels at 50 miles per hour. The truck can travel 20 miles on a gallon of gas if it is traveling at 50 miles per hour. The truck has only 10 gallons of gas and is 160 miles from its destination. It takes 20 minutes for the truck to stop for gas. How long will it take the truck to reach its final destination if it is driven at 60 miles per hour?

(A) 160 minutes
(B) 180 minutes
(C) 190 minutes
(D) 192 minutes
(E) 195 minutes

(B) To calculate the driving time, simply divide 160 miles by 60 miles per hour to obtain $2\frac{2}{3}$ hours, or 160 minutes. However, you need to decide whether or not the truck must stop for gasoline. At a speed of 60 miles per hour, the truck will use 30 percent more fuel, so it will need 1.3 gallons to travel 20 miles. Thus x (the amount of fuel needed to travel 160 miles) must satisfy the proportion $\frac{160}{20} = \frac{x}{1.3}$ or $x = 8(1.3) = 10.4$ gallons. So, if the truck is driven at 60 miles per hour, it will have to stop for gas since it has only 10 gallons. Therefore, the total time needed is $160 + 20 = 180$ minutes. (II-3)

A N S W E R S   E X P L A I N E D

19. Company *A* owns 40 percent of the stock in the XYZ Corporation. Company *B* owns 15,000 shares. Company *C* owns all the shares not owned by company *A* or *B*. How many shares of stock does company *A* own if company *C* has 25 percent more shares than company *A*?

(A) 45,000
(B) 50,000
(C) 60,000
(D) 75,000
(E) 90,000

(C) If company *C* owns 25 percent more than company *A* and *A* owns 40 percent of XYZ Corporation, then company *C* must own $1.25 \times .4 = .5$, or 50 percent of XYZ Corporation. Since *B* owns all that *A* and *C* do not own, then *B* must own $100\% - 40\% - 50\% = 10\%$.

If 10 percent of the shares is 15,000 shares, then there must be 150,000 shares in XYZ Corporation. Since company *A* owns 40 percent, it owns $150,000 \times 0.40 = 60,000$ shares. So (C) is the correct answer. Remember: Always answer the question asked. If you picked (D), you found only how many shares company *C* owns. (I-4, II-2)

★★★

---

20. How many squares with sides $\frac{1}{2}$ inch long are needed to cover a rectangle that is 4 feet long and 6 feet wide?

(A) 24
(B) 96
(C) 3,456
(D) 13,824
(E) 14,266

(D) The area of the rectangle is $4 \times 6 = 24$ square feet. Since 1 square foot is 144 square inches, the area of the rectangle is 3,456 square inches. Each square has an area of $\left(\frac{1}{2}\right)^2$ or $\frac{1}{4}$ square inches. Therefore, the number of squares needed $= 3,456 \div \frac{1}{4} = 3,456 \times 4 = 13,824$. (III-7)

★★★

---

21. How much cardboard will it take to make an open cubical box with no top?

(1) The area of the bottom of the box is 4 square feet.
(2) The volume of the box is 8 cubic feet.

(D) Since there are a bottom and 4 sides, each a congruent square, the amount of cardboard needed will be $5e^2$, where *e* is the length of an edge of the box. So we need to find *e*.

(1) alone is sufficient. Since the area of the bottom is e^2, (1) means $e^2 = 4$ with $e = 2$ feet. (2) alone is also sufficient. Since the volume of the box is e^3, (2) means $e^3 = 8$ and $e = 2$ feet. (III-8)

★★☆

★★★ **22.** Is the integer x divisible by 3?

(1) The last digit in x is 3.
(2) $x + 5$ is divisible by 6.

(B) STATEMENT (1) is not sufficient. If x is 33, then (1) is true and x is divisible by 3, but if x is 23, then (1) is true but x is not divisible by 3.

STATEMENT (2) is sufficient. According to (2) there must be an integer k such that $x + 5 = 6k$, so x is $6k - 5$. But this means that x divided by 3 will be $2k - \left(\dfrac{5}{3} \right)$, so x is not divisible by 3. So (B) is the correct choice. (I-1)

★★☆ **23.** Is the figure $ABCD$ a rectangle?

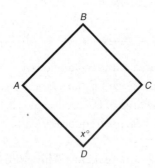

(1) $x = 90$
(2) $AB = CD$

(E) If $ABCD$ has the pairs of opposite sides equal and each angle is 90°, then it is a rectangle. But there are many quadrilaterals that have two opposite sides equal with one angle a right angle. For example, the figure below has $AB = DC$ and $x = 90$, but it is not a rectangle. Therefore, (1) and (2) together are insufficient. (III-5)

★★☆ **24.** A sequence of numbers is given by the rule $a_n = (a_{n-1})^2$. What is a_5?

(1) $a_1 = -1$
(2) $a_3 = 1$

(D) (2) alone is sufficient since if $a_3 = 1$, then $a_4 = (a_3)^2 = 1^2 = 1$; then $a_5 = (a_4)^2 = 1^2 = 1$. (1) alone is also sufficient. If $a_1 = -1$, then $a_2 = (a_1)^2 = 1$ and $a_3 = (a_2)^2 = 1$, but $a_3 = 1$ is given by (2), which we know is sufficient. (II-6)

25. In a group of people solicited by a charity, 30 percent contributed $40 each, 45 percent contributed $20 each, and the rest contributed $12 each. What percentage of the total contributed came from people who gave $40?

(A) 25%
(B) 30%
(C) 40%
(D) 45%
(E) 50%

(E) Those who gave $12 were 25 percent (100% − 30% − 45% = 25%) of the group. Let x, y, and z stand for the number of people who contributed $40, $20, and $12, respectively. Then, the total number of people (n) who contributed is $x + y + z = n$. The total amount (T) contributed is

$$\$40x + \$20y + \$12z = T$$

Since 30 percent contributed $40, we know that $x = .3n$; in the same way, we know that $y = .45n$ and $z = .25n$. Therefore, the total contributed was

$$
\begin{aligned}
T &= \$40(.3n) &+ \$20(.45n) &+ \$12(.25n) \\
&= 12n &+ 9n &+ 3n \\
&= 24n
\end{aligned}
$$

The amount contributed by those who gave $40 was, therefore,

$$\$40\,(.3n) = 12n$$

So the percentage contributed by the $40 donors is $100(12n/24n)$ or 50 percent. (II-2)

★★★

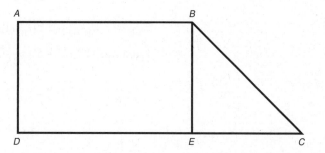

26. A trapezoid *ABCD* is formed by adding the isosceles right triangle *BCE* with base 5 inches to the rectangle *ABED*, where *DE* is t inches. What is the area of the trapezoid in square inches?

(A) $5t + 12.5$
(B) $5t + 25$
(C) $2.5t + 12.5$
(D) $(t + 5)^2$
(E) $t^2 + 25$

(A) The area of trapezoid *ABCD* equals the area of rectangle *ABED*, which is $t \times 5$ (since $BE = BC = 5$), plus the area of triangle *BEC*, which is $\dfrac{(5 \times 5)}{2}$. The answer is thus $5t + 12.5$. (III-7)

★★☆

★☆☆ **27.** A manufacturer of jam wants to make a profit of $75 when it sells 300 jars of jam. It costs 65¢ each to make the first 100 jars of jam and 55¢ each to make each jar after the first 100. What price should it charge for the 300 jars of jam?

(A) $75
(B) $175
(C) $225
(D) $240
(E) $250

(E) The selling price of the jars should equal cost plus $75. The cost of making 300 jars = (100)65¢ + (200)55¢ = $65 + $110 = $175. So the selling price should be $175 + $75 or $250. (II-3)

★★★ **28.** A car traveled 75 percent of the distance from town A to town B by traveling for T hours at an average speed of V miles per hour. The car traveled at an average speed of S miles per hour for the remaining part of the trip. Which of the following expressions represents the time the car traveled at S miles per hour?

(A) $\dfrac{VT}{S}$

(B) $\dfrac{VS}{4T}$

(C) $\dfrac{4VT}{3S}$

(D) $\dfrac{3S}{VT}$

(E) $\dfrac{VT}{3S}$

(E) You need to find the total distance traveled in order to find the total time. Since the car traveled $V \times T$ miles when it averaged V miles per hour, then VT is 75 percent of the total distance. Therefore, the total distance traveled is $\dfrac{VT}{.75} = \dfrac{4VT}{3}$.

The distance that was traveled at S miles per hour is the total distance minus the distance at V miles per hour, which is

$$\left(\frac{4}{3}\right)VT - VT = \frac{VT}{3}$$

So the time spent traveling at S miles per hour was $(VT)/3 \div S = \dfrac{VT}{3S}$. (II-3)

★★☆ **29.** How much is John's weekly salary?

(1) John's weekly salary is twice as much as Fred's weekly salary.
(2) Fred's weekly salary is 40 percent of the total of Chuck's weekly salary and John's weekly salary.

(E) Let J, F, and C stand for the weekly salaries of John, Fred, and Chuck. (1) says $J = 2F$, and (2) says $F = .4(C + J)$. Since there is no information given about the value of C or F, we cannot deduce the value of J. Therefore, (1) and (2) together are insufficient. (II-3)

30. Find $x + 2y$.

    (1) $x + y = 4$

    (2) $2x + 4y = 12$

(B) STATEMENT (2) alone is sufficient. $2x + 4y = 2(x + 2y)$, so if $2x + 4y = 12$, then $2(x + 2y) = 12$ and $x + 2y = 6$.

    STATEMENT (1) alone is insufficient. If you use only STATEMENT (1), then you can get $x + 2y = x + y + y = 4 + y$, but there is no information on the value of y. (II-2)

★★☆

---

31. Is angle *BAC* a right angle?

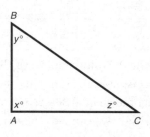

    (1) $x = 2y$

    (2) $y = 1.5z$

(C) Since the sum of the angles in a triangle is 180°, $x + y + z = 180$. Using STATEMENT (1) alone, we have $2y + y + z = 3y + z = 180$, which is insufficient to determine y or z.

    Using STATEMENT (2) alone, we have $x + 1.5z + z = x + 2.5z = 180$, which is not sufficient to determine x or z.

    However, if we use both STATEMENTS (1) and (2) we obtain $3y + z = 4.5z + z = 5.5z = 180$, so $z = \frac{2}{11}$ of 180. Now $y = \frac{3}{2}$ of z, so $y = \frac{3}{11}$ of 180, and $x = \frac{6}{11}$ of 180. Therefore, angle *BAC* is not a right angle and STATEMENTS (1) and (2) are sufficient. (II-2, III-4)

★★☆

---

32. If a, b, and c are digits, is $a + b + c$ a multiple of 9? A digit is one of the integers 0, 1, 2, 3, 4, 5, 6, 7, 8, 9.

    (1) The three-digit number *abc* is a multiple of 9.

    (2) $(a \times b) + c$ is a multiple of 9.

(A) The three-digit number *abc* is $(100 \times a) + (10 \times b) + c$. If *abc* is a multiple of 9, then there is an integer k such that $k9 = (100 \times a) + (10 \times b) + c$. Divide this equation by 9 and you have

$$k = \left[\left(\frac{100}{9}\right) \times a\right] + \left[\left(\frac{10}{9}\right) \times b\right] + \frac{c}{9}$$

$$= \left[11a + \left(\frac{a}{9}\right)\right] + \left[b + \left(\frac{b}{9}\right)\right] + \frac{c}{9}$$

$$= 11a + b + \left(\frac{a}{9}\right) + \left(\frac{b}{9}\right) + \left(\frac{c}{9}\right)$$

$$= 11a + b + \left[\left(\frac{a+b+c}{9}\right)\right]$$

So (1) alone is sufficient. (2) is not sufficient since choosing $a = 0 = b$ and $c = 9$ makes (2) valid and $a + b + c$ is 9, but choosing $a = 4 = b$ and $c = 2$ also makes (2) valid with $a + b + c$ equal to 10. (I-1)

★★★

★★☆ **33.** In Teetown 50 percent of the people have blue eyes and blond hair. What percent of the people in Teetown have blue eyes but do not have blond hair?

(1) 70 percent of the people in Teetown have blond hair.

(2) 60 percent of the people in Teetown have blue eyes.

(B) STATEMENT (2) alone is sufficient. 60 percent of the people have blue eyes and 50 percent of the people have blue eyes and blond hair, so 60% − 50% = 10% of the people have blue eyes but do not have blond hair.

STATEMENT (1) alone is not sufficient. Using STATEMENT (1) alone we can only find out how many people have blond hair and do not have blue eyes, in addition to what is given. (II-4)

★★★

34. Thirty-six identical chairs must be arranged in rows with the same number of chairs in each row. Each row must contain at least 3 chairs, and there must be at least 3 rows. A row is parallel to the front of the room. How many different arrangements are possible?

(A) 2
(B) 4
(C) 5
(D) 6
(E) 10

(C) Let c be the number of chairs in a row and r be the number of rows. Since each row must have the same number of chairs, c times r must equal 36. We need to know how many ways we can write 36 as a product of two integers each greater than or equal to 3, since each way to write 36 corresponds to an acceptable arrangement of the room. (c must be greater than or equal to 3 since each row must contain at least 3 chairs. In the same way, r must be greater than or equal to 3 because there must be at least 3 rows.) Writing 36 as a product of primes, we obtain $36 = 2 \times 18 = 2 \times 2 \times 9 = 2 \times 2 \times 3 \times 3$. So 36 can be written as 1×36, 2×18, 3×12, 4×9, 6×6, 9×4, 12×3, 18×2, and 36×1. Of these possibilities, five (3×12, 4×9, 6×6, 9×4, and 12×3) satisfy the requirements. Therefore, there are five arrangements. (I-1)

35. Which of the following solids has the largest volume? (*Figures are not drawn to scale.*)

I. A cylinder of radius 5 millimeters and height 11 millimeters

II. A sphere of radius 6 millimeters (the volume of a sphere of radius r is $\frac{4}{3}\pi r^3$)

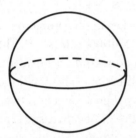

III. A cube with edge of 9 millimeters.

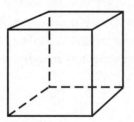

(A) I
(B) II
(C) III
(D) I and II
(E) II and III

(B) The volume of the cube is $9 \times 9 \times 9 = 729$ cubic millimeters. The sphere has volume $\frac{4}{3}\pi 6 \times 6 \times 6 = 288\pi$. Since π is greater than 3, 288π is greater than 729. The volume of the cylinder is $5 \times 5 \times 11\pi = 275\pi$. So the sphere has the largest volume.

You can save a lot of time in doing this problem if you do not change π to a decimal and then multiply the answers out. (III-8)

★★★

★★★ **36.** The pentagon *ABCDE* is inscribed in a circle with center *O*. How many degrees is angle *ABC*?

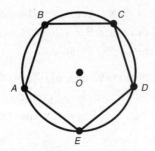

(1) The pentagon *ABCDE* is a regular pentagon, which means that all sides are the same length and all interior angles are the same size.

(2) The radius of the circle is 5 inches.

(A) The sum of the angles of the pentagon is 540°. [The sum of the angles of a polygon with *n* sides that is inscribed in a circle is $(n-2)180°$.]

STATEMENT (1) alone is sufficient. If the polygon is regular, all angles are equal, and so angle *ABC* is $\frac{1}{5}$ of 540° or 108°.

STATEMENT (2) alone is insufficient because the radius of the circle does not give any information about the angles of the pentagon. (III-3)

★★★ **37.** Is $k^2 + k - 2 > 0$?

(1) $k < 1$
(2) $k > -1$

(C) The key to this problem is to factor $k^2 + k - 2$ into $(k+2)(k-1)$. The product of the two expressions is positive if and only if both expressions have the same sign. When (1) holds, then $k-1$ is negative, but $k+2$ can be positive or negative, so (1) alone is not sufficient. When (2) holds, then $k+2$ is positive, but $k-1$ can be positive or negative, so (2) alone is not sufficient. However, if both (1) and (2) are true, then k is between -1 and 1 and, so $k+2$ is positive and $k-1$ is negative, which means $(k+2)(k-1)$ is negative. This is sufficient to answer the question. (II-1)

Verbal Section

1. Farmers in the North have observed that heavy frost is usually preceded by a full moon. They are convinced that the full moon somehow generates the frost.

Which of the following, if true, would weaken the farmers' conviction?

(A) The temperature must fall below 10 degrees Celsius (50 degrees Fahrenheit) for frost to occur.

(B) Absence of a cloud cover cools the ground, which causes frost.

(C) Farmers are superstitious.

(D) No one has proven that the moon causes frost.

(E) Farmers are not experts in meteorology.

(B) The argument represents a fallacy in causality. Absence of cloud cover enables the moon to be seen. And, it is the absence of cloud cover—not a full moon—that causes the ground to cool and produce frost. Answer choice (A) may be a necessary but insufficient condition for frost to occur; that is, there may be an absence of frost even below 10 degrees Celsius. Farmers may be superstitious, but there is nothing in the statement that links superstition with the farmers' conviction (alternative C). Alternative (D) is inappropriate because, even if true, it could not change the farmers' convictions. Farmers do not have to be experts in meteorology (E) to hold a conviction.

2. Professor Tembel told his class that the method of student evaluation of teachers is not a valid measure of teaching quality. Students should fill out questionnaires at the end of the semester when courses have been completed.

Which of the following, if true, provides support for Professor Tembel's proposal?

(A) Professor Tembel received low ratings from his students.

(B) Students filled out questionnaires after the midterm exam.

(C) Students are interested in teacher evaluation.

(D) Teachers are not obligated to use the survey results.

(E) Student evaluation of teachers is voluntary.

(B) The question concerns Professor Tembel's proposal to improve the validity of the method used to measure teacher quality. Alternative (B) supports the proposal. Students relate only partial experience with a teacher if the questionnaires are completed at midterm. Alternative (A) suggests that Professor Tembel's motive for questioning the present evaluation method stems from his low ratings. It is questionable whether handing out questionnaires at the end of the semester would improve his ratings. Alternatives (C), (D), and (E) are not related to the validity of the evaluation method.

★★☆   **3.** If she was to decide to go to college, I, for one, would recommend that she plan to go to Yale.

    (A) If she was to decide to go to college,
    (B) If she were to decide to go to college,
    (C) Had she decided to go to college,
    (D) In the event that she decides to go to college,
    (E) Supposing she was to decide to go to college,

    (B) The sentence correctly uses the simple past tense. Choices (A) and (C) use incorrect tenses. Choices (D) and (E) change the meaning.

★★☆   **4.** Except for you and I, everyone brought a present to the party.

    (A) Except for you and I, everyone brought
    (B) With exception of you and I, everyone brought
    (C) Except for you and I, everyone had brought
    (D) Except for you and me, everyone brought
    (E) Except for you and me, everyone had brought

    (D) This corrects the error in the case of the pronoun. Choice (E) corrects the error in case but introduces an error in tense.

The passage for questions 5–8 appears on page 515.

★★☆   **5.** The passage was most likely published in a

    (A) popular magazine
    (B) general newspaper
    (C) science journal
    (D) financial journal
    (E) textbook

    (D) This passage deals with the economy and economic policy. Note that Choice (E) is too vague. An economic policy textbook might have been a correct answer if it had been an alternative.

★★☆   **6.** Confidence in the economy was expressed by all of the following EXCEPT

    (A) a strong stock market
    (B) a stable bond market
    (C) increased installment debt
    (D) increased plant and equipment expenditures
    (E) rising interest rates

    (E) All of the others can be found in paragraph 1.

7. According to the passage, a major problem is how to ★★☆

    (A) sustain economic growth
    (B) improve labor productivity
    (C) balance growth with low inflation
    (D) stimulate demand
    (E) avoid large increases in imports

(C) See paragraph 3. The task is to obtain high economic growth without stimulating high inflation.

---

8. The passage mentions each of the following indicators of economic growth EXCEPT ★★☆

    (A) increased installment debt
    (B) a decline in the balance of payments deficit
    (C) consumer spending for goods and services
    (D) a rise in business confidence
    (E) business spending for inventories

(B) All of the indicators are mentioned in the first paragraph of the passage except the decline in the balance of payments deficit. The decline, although mentioned in the passage, was not an indicator of economic growth.

---

9. When one reads the poetry of the seventeenth century, you find a striking contrast between the philosophy of the Cavalier poets such as Suckling and the attitude of the Metaphysical poets such as Donne. ★★☆

    (A) When one reads the poetry of the seventeenth century, you find
    (B) When you read the poetry of the seventeenth century, one finds
    (C) When one reads the poetry of the seventeenth century, he finds
    (D) If one reads the poetry of the 17th century, you find
    (E) As you read the poetry of the 17th century, one finds

(C) The improper use of the pronouns *one* and *you* is corrected in Choice (C).

---

10. Because of his broken hip, John Jones <u>has not and possibly never will be able to run</u> the mile again. ★★☆

    (A) has not and possibly never will be able to run
    (B) has not and possibly will never be able to run
    (C) has not been and possibly never would be able to run
    (D) has not and possibly never would be able to run
    (E) has not been able to run and possibly never will be able to run

(E) The omission of the past participle *been* is corrected in Choice (E).

★★☆ **11.** The President of country "X" lobbied for passage of his new trade bill, which would liberalize trade with industrialized countries such as Japan, members of the European Union, and Canada. It is known that increased trade among countries leads to faster economic growth due to increased employment and lower product prices. Increased trade also allows countries to produce products and services more efficiently.

Each of the following, if true, could account for the above, EXCEPT

(A) Employment in country "X."
(B) Labor unions have petitioned the President to provide more local jobs.
(C) The trade agreement could bring a *quid pro quo* on pending negotiations.
(D) Economists claimed that the passage of the bill would increase the country's trade deficit.
(E) It was politically desirable for a trade bill at the present time.

(D) All of the facts except (D) would be consonant with the President's actions. Fact (D) would be against passage of such a bill.

★★☆ **12.** If we are doomed to have local drug rehabilitation centers—and society has determined that we are—then society ought to pay for them.

Which of the following, if true, would weaken the above argument?

(A) Drug rehabilitation centers are too expensive to be locally funded.
(B) Many neighborhood groups oppose rehabilitation centers.
(C) Drug rehabilitation centers are expensive to maintain.
(D) Drug addicts may be unwilling to receive treatment.
(E) A government committee has convinced many groups that local rehabilitation centers are ineffective.

(E) The argument is in the form of a conditional syllogism: (1) *If* we must have drug rehabilitation centers, *then* society ought to pay for them. (2) We must have drug rehabilitation centers. (3) Society ought to pay for them. Alternative (E) falsifies the minor premise 2. Whether or not neighborhood groups oppose the centers (B) or drug addicts will go to them to receive treatment (D) is not relevant to the argument concerning who will pay for them. The level of government funding (A) or the amount of expense (C) are not mentioned in the passage and are not relevant to the argument. However, a government statement that local rehabilitation centers are ineffective would seriously weaken the premise upon which the argument rests.

The passage for questions 13–16 appears on page 517.

★★☆ **13.** One surprising aspect of the waves discussed in the passage is the fact that they

(A) are formed in concentric patterns
(B) often strike during clear weather
(C) arise under conditions of cold temperature
(D) are produced by deep swells
(E) may be forecast scientifically

(B) Paragraph 1 says, "Under a perfectly sunny sky and from an apparently calm sea . . . ." None of the other answer choices is particularly surprising.

---

14. It can be inferred that nothing was done about tsunamis until after World War II because

(A) little was known about how tsunamis were formed
(B) no damage was reported until after World War II
(C) it was not known how to protect against them
(D) the damage to life and property in Hawaii was severe
(E) the United States had the means to invest in a solution to the tsunami problem

(D) Most of the passage deals with the technical details about how tsunamis are formed. In the third and fourth paragraphs, the author mentions the damage caused by them, first in Chile and then in Hawaii. There is no explicit reference why nothing was done about tsunamis until after World War II. So we can infer either that it was because of the severe damage caused in Hawaii that only the United States had the means to invest in a solution. Note that although the damage in Hawaii was severe, answer choice (D), it was also severe in Chile (line 17). So the event in Hawaii must have motivated the United States to invest in a solution.

---

15. It is believed that the waves are caused by

(A) seismic changes
(B) concentric time belts
(C) atmospheric conditions
(D) underwater earthquakes
(E) storms

(D) Paragraph 2 says, "How are those waves formed? When a submarine earthquake occurs . . . ."

---

16. A possible title for the passage could be

(A) *How Submarine Waves Are Formed*
(B) *How to Locate Submarine Earthquakes*
(C) *Underwater Earthquakes*
(D) *"Tsunami" Waves*
(E) *How to Prevent Submarine Earthquakes*

(A) See the first line in paragraph 2. Choice (B) is incorrect because the passage never explains how to locate a submarine earthquake. Choices (C) and (D) are incorrect because although the passage broadly addresses underwater earthquakes and the tsunami that may result, the correct answer more specifically addresses how the earthquakes form. Choice (E) is incorrect because prevention of underwater earthquakes is not discussed.

17. <u>Had I realized how close</u> I was to failing, I would not have gone to the party.

    (A) Had I realized how close

    (B) If I would have realized

    (C) Had I had realized how close

    (D) When I realized how close

    (E) If I realized how close

(A) Choice (B) is incorrect because *if I would have* indicates an action that did not happen in the past. Choice (C) is awkward and wordy. Choice (D) creates an illogical sentence. *When* indicates certainty, which is illogical in a conditional sentence, *if I would not have.* Choice (E) uses the simple past tense to describe one action that occurred before another.

★★★ **18.** <u>The football team's winning it's first game of the season</u> excited the student body.

    (A) The football team's winning it's first game of the season

    (B) The football team having won it's first game of the season

    (C) The football team's having won it's first game of the season

    (D) The football team's winning its first game of the season

    (E) The football team winning it's first game of the season

(D) Choices (A), (B), (C), and (E) all use the contraction for *it is (it's)* rather than the possessive *its.*

★★☆ **19.** Anyone interested in the use of computers can learn much <u>if you have access to</u> a state-of-the-art microcomputer.

    (A) if you have access to

    (B) if he has access to

    (C) if access is available to

    (D) by access to

    (E) from access to

(B) Choice (A) uses the incorrect pronoun *he* to modify *anyone.* Choices (C), (D), and (E) are awkward.

★★☆ **20.** <u>No student had ought to be put into a situation where</u> he has to choose between his loyalty to his friends and his duty to the class.

    (A) No student had ought to be put into a situation where

    (B) Students ought to not be put into a situation where

    (C) No student should be put into a situation when

    (D) Students should be put into a situation in which

    (E) No student should be put into a situation where

(E) This corrects the error in tense and in the use of adjective or adverbial clauses in the other answers.

21. <u>Being that I am realist</u>, I could not accept her statement that supernatural beings had caused the disturbance.

(A) Being that I am realist,

(B) Because I am a realist,

(C) Just like I am a realist,

(D) Being as I am a realist,

(E) Realist that I am,

(B) It uses correct grammar to establish that because the speaker is a realist, he or she could not accept supernatural beings as a cause of the disturbance. In choice (A), *being that* is not idiomatic. *Just like* in choice (C) is both awkward and not idiomatic. In choice (D), *being as* is not idiomatic. Choice (E) is awkward.

---

22. Surviving this crisis is going to take everything we've got. In addition to . . . massive retraining, we may also need subsidies—direct or channeled through the private sector—for a radically expanding service sector. Not merely things like environmental clean-up, but basic human services. (Alvin Toffler, *Previews and Premises* (New York: Bantam Books, 1985), p. 57.)

Which of the following statements is inconsistent with the above?

(A) Subsidies are needed to overcome the crisis.

(B) Environmental controls will be loosened.

(C) The service sector is going to expand to such an extent that many more workers may be needed.

(D) The private sector may play a role in retraining workers.

(E) Before the crisis can end, an environmental clean-up will have to take place.

(B) The "crisis" that is alluded to in the statement refers to a need for environmental clean-up and basic human services (the latter mentioned in alternative (E)). In order to provide these services more workers will be needed (C), many of whom will have to be retrained. This retraining will have to be financed by subsidies (A), which may be provided by the private sector (D). Alternative (B) is inconsistent with the statement that calls for more environmental controls (clean-up), not less.

---

23. Per-capita income last year was $25,000. Per-capita income is calculated by dividing total aggregate cash income by the total population. Real median income for families headed by a female, with no husband present, was $29,000. Therefore, women wage-earners earned more than the national average.

Which of the following would, if true, weaken the above conclusion?

(A) Per-capita income is calculated in real terms.

(B) In 99 percent of the cases, families headed by a female included no other wage-earner.

(C) Average income is not significantly different from median income.

(D) The overall average and per-capita income were the same.

(E) Only a small proportion of the total wage earners are women family heads.

(E) Total per-capita income includes salaries and wages earned by women. In order to determine if women wage-earners earned more than the overall average, the salaries of all women—not just women heading families with no husband present—would have to be calculated separately. Alternative (E) states that women family heads are not representative of all women wage earners. Thus, the conclusion in the statement is a fallacy of relevance or representativeness. All other alternatives would buttress the conclusion.

The passage for questions 24–27 appears on page 520.

★★☆ **24.** According to the passage, compared with the artist, the policeman is

    (A) ruled by action, not words
    (B) factual and not fanciful
    (C) neutral and not prejudiced
    (D) stoic and not emotional
    (E) aggressive and not passive

(C) The correct answer is given in paragraph 2. Policemen must be neutral and present the facts, while the "artist usually begins with a preconceived message or attitude," i.e., prejudiced. Although artists are *emotional*, no mention is made that policemen are stoic, as in choice (D).

★★★ **25.** The author implies that policemen reacted to story events and characters

    (A) dispassionately
    (B) according to a policeman's stereotyped image
    (C) like dilettantes
    (D) with a dislike of defiant heroes
    (E) with prejudice

(A) See the first line in paragraph 2, which states that the police officer's view is as neutral as possible.

★★☆ **26.** To which sort of characters did the hunters object?

    (A) unrealistic
    (B) emotional
    (C) sordid
    (D) timid
    (E) aggressive

(A) According to the third paragraph of the passage, it was the hunters who objected to unrealistic characters.

27. The information in the passage indicates that the author believes which of the following best describes policemen as literature students: ★ ★ ☆

(A) They are no different from other students.
(B) Their reactions to characters in stories are naïve.
(C) They glorify the ideal of manhood.
(D) They tend to admire American virtues of hard work and effort.
(E) Their short stories are taken from on the job experiences.

(A) Policemen reacted like regular students of literature. This can be inferred from the discussion at the end of paragraph 2 and in paragraph 3. Their reactions were "unprejudiced" (line 14), and they "excelled" (line 21).

---

28. Foreign investment is composed of direct investment transactions (investment in plant, equipment, and land) and securities investment transactions. Throughout the post-World War II period, net increases in U.S. direct investment in Europe (funds outflows) exceeded net new European direct investment in the U.S. ★ ★ ☆

Each of the following, if true, could help to account for this trend EXCEPT

(A) Land values in Europe were increasing at a faster rate than in the United States.
(B) Duties on imported goods in Europe were higher than those imposed by the United States.
(C) The cost of labor (wages) was consistently lower in Europe than in the United States.
(D) Labor mobility was much higher in the United States than in Europe.
(E) Corporate liquidity was lower in Europe than in the United States.

(D) Land values were higher in Europe, attracting U.S. capital (A); higher duties on U.S. exports to Europe (B) brought a substitution of foreign production for U.S. exports; lower labor costs in Europe (C) meant it was cheaper to produce there. Higher liquidity (E) in the U.S. provided the capital for foreign investment. Only (D) is irrelevant as an explanation of direct investment.

ANSWERS EXPLAINED

★★★ **29.** Most large retail stores hold sales in the month of January. The original idea of price reduction campaigns in January became popular when it was realized that sales of products would generally slow down following the Christmas rush, were it not for some incentive. The lack of demand could be solved by the simple solution of reducing prices.

There is now an increasing tendency among major department stores in large urban centers to have their "January sales" begin before Christmas, some time before the end of the calendar year. The idea behind this trend is to endeavor to sell the maximum amount of stock at a profit, even if that may not be at the maximum profit.

Which of the following conclusions cannot be drawn from the above?

(A) The incidence of "early" January sales results in the lower holdings of stocks with the corollary of lower stock holding costs.

(B) Demand is a function of price; as you lower price, demand increases.

(C) Major stores seem to think it makes sense to have the January sales campaigns pre-Christmas.

(D) It is becoming less popular to start the January sales in the New Year.

(E) The major department stores do not worry as much about profit maximization as they do about sales maximization.

(A) A number of points are made in the paragraph, and a number of conclusions can be drawn. One is (B), the simple law of economics—that demand varies with price. Also, since it is stated that there is now an increasing tendency to have the January sales in December, it must be becoming less popular to start the sales in January itself. Therefore, the conclusions in (C) and (D) can be drawn, and so choices (C) and (D) are not appropriate. Further, the hypothesis in (C) and also in (E) can be inferred from what is stated in the paragraph about the stores' policies on end-of-year sales. Answer choice (A) introduces a new idea that may be correct and valid, but which cannot be inferred or concluded from what is stated in the paragraph; (A), therefore is the correct answer.

★★★ **30.** The reason <u>I came late to class today is because</u> the bus broke down.

(A) I came late to class today is because

(B) why I came late to class today is because

(C) I was late to school today is because

(D) that I was late to school today is because

(E) I came late to class today is that

(E) The correct idiom is *the reason that*. Therefore, choices (A) and (B) are incorrect. Choice (C) is awkward. Choice (D) redundantly uses both *the reason that* and *because*. Choice (E) misplaces *that*, incorrectly separating it from the first part of the idiom, the reason.

31. The grocer <u>hadn't hardly any of those kind</u> of canned goods. ★★☆

(A) hadn't hardly any of those kind
(B) hadn't hardly any of those kinds
(C) had hardly any of those kind
(D) had hardly any of those kinds
(E) had scarcely any of those kind

(D) Choice (D) corrects the double negative (*hadn't hardly*) in choices (A) and (B). Choice (C) and (E) uses the plural *those* with the singular *kind*.

---

32. <u>Having stole the money, the police searched the thief.</u> ★★★

(A) Having stole the money, the police searched the thief.
(B) Having stolen the money, the thief was searched by the police.
(C) Having stolen the money, the police searched the thief.
(D) Having stole the money, the thief was searched by the police.
(E) Being that he stole the money, the police searched the thief.

(B) *Having stolen the money* correctly modifies the agent of that action, *the thief.* Choice (C) incorrectly has the *police* stealing the money. Choices (A) and (D) use the incorrect verb *stole.* Choice (E) uses the unidiomatic *being that.*

---

33. The child is <u>neither encouraged to be critical or to examine</u> all the evidence for ★★★
his opinion.

(A) neither encouraged to be critical or to examine
(B) neither encouraged to be critical nor to examine
(C) either encouraged to be critical or to examine
(D) encouraged either to be critical nor to examine
(E) not encouraged either to be critical or to examine

(E) This question involves two aspects of correct English. *Neither* should be followed by *nor*; *either* by *or.* Choices A and D are, therefore, incorrect. The words *neither . . . nor* and *either . . . or* should be placed before the two items being discussed—*to be critical* and *to criticize.* Choice E meets both requirements.

---

34. The process by which the community <u>influence the actions of its members</u> is known as ★☆☆
social control.

(A) influence the actions of its members
(B) influences the actions of its members
(C) had influenced the actions of its members
(D) influences the actions of their members
(E) will influence the actions of its members

(B) The singular subject, *community*, uses the singular verb, *influences.* Choice (A) is therefore incorrect. Choices (C) and (E) both use incorrect verb tenses. Choice (D) uses the plural pronoun *their* to modify the singular noun *community.*

ANSWERS EXPLAINED

★★★ **35.** Of the world's largest external-debt countries in 1999, three had the same share of world external-debt as they had in 1990. These three countries may serve as examples of countries that succeeded in holding steady their share of world external-debt.

Which of the following, if true, would most seriously undermine the idea that these countries serve as examples as described above?

(A) Of the three countries, two had a much larger share of world external-debt in 1995 than in 1999.

(B) Some countries strive to reduce their share of world external-debt, not keep it steady.

(C) The three countries have different rates of economic growth.

(D) The absolute value of debt of the three countries is different.

(E) Some countries are more concerned with internal budgets than with external debt.

(A) Two of the three countries actually experienced shifts in their share of world external-debt from 1990 to 1999, hardly an example of stability. Answer choice (B) may be true for some countries, but it does not weaken the statement. Answer choices (C) and (D) skirt the issues: rates of economic growth and absolute debt are not related to external debt in the statement. Answer choice (E) may be so, but the example in the statement deals with external, not internal, debt.

★★★ **36.** The director of the customs service suggested that customs taxes on automobiles will not be reduced as planned by the government because of the high incidence of traffic accidents last year.

Which of the above statements weakens the argument above?

I. Although the traffic accident rate last year was high, it was not appreciably higher than previous years and anyway, compulsory insurance covered most physical damage to automobiles and property.

II. A Commerce Department report showed that the demand for automobiles was highly inelastic. That is, as dealers lowered their prices, sales did not increase appreciably.

III. A study by the Economics Department at Classics University found that most traffic accidents had been caused by human error although it also concluded that an inadequate road network contributed to at least 40 percent of passenger injuries.

(A) I, but not II and not III.

(B) II, but not I and not III.

(C) I and III, but not II.

(D) II and III, but not I.

(E) I, II, and III.

(B) The argument addresses custom taxes, which, if lowered, would cause the purchase of more cars. Option II weakens the argument by stating the demand for cars is *inelastic*. Neither option I nor option III addresses the number of cars on the road.

Option III asserts human error as the cause for accidents, which is irrelevant to the customs tax. Option I deals with the number of accidents rather than the implication that lower custom taxes will cause more cars to be on the road.

---

37. Significant beneficial effects of smoking occur primarily in the area of mental health, and the habit originates in a search for contentment. The life expectancy of our people has increased greatly in recent years; it is possible that the relaxation and contentment and enjoyment produced by smoking has lengthened many lives. Smoking is beneficial.

★★★

Which of the following, if true, weakens the above conclusion?

(A) Mental health can be improved by many means.
(B) The government earns millions of dollars from the tobacco tax and tens of thousands of civilians are employed in the tobacco industry.
(C) The evidence cited in the statement covers only one example of the effects of cigarette smoking.
(D) Life expectancy has been extended due to better medical care.
(E) Not everyone enjoys life.

(D) Choice (D) questions the assumption of a relationship between smoking, mental health, and life expectancy. While mental health can be improved by many means, it does not preclude cigarette smoking. Choices (B) and (C) do not address the relation between smoking and mental halth. Choice (E) has no relation to the argument.

---

38. An economist was quoted as saying that the Consumer Price Index (CPI) will go up next month because of a recent increase in the price of fruit and vegetables.

★★★

Which of the following cannot be inferred from the statement?

(A) The cost of fruits and vegetables has risen sharply.
(B) Consumers have decreased their consumption of fruits and vegetables.
(C) The cost of fruit and vegetables is a major item in the CPI.
(D) Food cost changes are reflected quickly in the CPI.
(E) Other items that make up the CPI have not significantly decreased in price.

(B) The claim in the statement is that the CPI will go up. The reasoning behind the claim is based on the premise that the cost of fruit and vegetables has risen sharply (A). Since these commodities are major items in the CPI (C) and because food cost changes are reflected quickly in the index (D), the index will go up. A premise that could weaken the claim might be (E) if other items included in the index and weighted at least as much decreased in price, thus offsetting the cost increases for fruits and vegetables. However, alternative (E) gives evidence to the contrary. Alternative (B) may not be inferred. If consumers reduced consumption of fruits and vegetables, the prices of these items would be expected to drop. In any case, the rate of consumption cannot be inferred.

ANSWERS EXPLAINED

★★☆ **39.** At a political rally at Jefferson Stadium, candidate Smith exclaimed: "Nearly everyone at the rally is behind me. It looks like I am going to be elected."

On which unstated assumption does Smith's conclusion rely?

(A) Smith's opponent also appeared at the rally.

(B) The rally was attended by almost all the residents of Smith's constituency.

(C) Smith's constituency will continue to vote for him, and his opponent does not have more supporters than those who attended the rally and voted for Smith.

(D) Smith was supported by the local mayor.

(E) People always vote their emotions.

(C) Smith assumes that all those who attended the rally will continue to support him and that those voters who support his opponent do not outnumber those that support Smith. Choice (A) would have weakened Smith's conclusion. If his opponent were present, that opponent's supporters might also have attended. A single endorsement in choice (D), although important, does not necessarily lead to victory. Choice (E), *emotions*, has nothing to do with Smith's conclusion that he will win.

★★☆ **40.** Depending on skillful suggestion, argument is seldom used in advertising.

(A) Depending on skillful suggestion, argument is seldom used in advertising.

(B) Argument is seldom used by advertisers, who depend instead on skillful suggestion.

(C) Skillful suggestion is depended on by advertisers instead of argument.

(D) Suggestion, which is more skillful, is used in place of argument by advertisers.

(E) Instead of suggestion, depending on argument is used by skillful advertisers.

(B) The correct choice eliminates the misplaced modifier. Choice (B) also clearly states, using few words, that advertisers do not use argument. In choice (A), the first clause awkwardly and illogically states that *argument* depends on *skillful suggestion*. This first clause contains both a misplaced modifier and a dangling participle. Choice (C) corrects the illogical modifier. However, it uses *is depended on by*, which is both awkward and wordy. Choice (D) corrects the misplaced modifier but uses the awkward and wordy *is used in place of*. Choice (E) changes the intended meaning.

★☆☆ **41.** In a famous experiment by Pavlov, when a dog smelled food, it salivated. Subsequently, a bell was rung whenever food was placed near the dog. After a number of trials, only the bell was rung, whereupon the dog would salivate even though no food was present.

Which of the following conclusions may be drawn from the above experiment?

(A) Dogs are easily fooled.

(B) Dogs are motivated only by the sound of a bell.

(C) The ringing of a bell was associated with food.

(D) A conclusion cannot be reached on the basis of one experiment.

(E) Two stimuli are stronger than one.

(C) In this experiment, the dog was conditioned to associate the ringing of a bell with food. Therefore, when the dog heard the bell, it expected to be fed, even though it could not smell food. Alternative (A) cannot be inferred. Alternatives (B) and (D) are incorrect, and there is no proof for (E).

EVALUATING YOUR SCORE

Tabulate your score for each section of the Sample Test according to the directions on pages 11–12 and record the results in the Self-Scoring Table below. Then find your rating for each score on the Self-Scoring Scale and record it in the appropriate blank.

SELF-SCORING TABLE

Section	Score	Rating
Quantitative		
Verbal		

SELF-SCORING SCALE—RATING

Section	Poor	Fair	Good	Excellent
Quantitative	0–15	15–25	26–30	31–37
Verbal	0–15	15–25	26–30	31–41

Study again the Review sections covering material in Sample Test 2 for which you had a rating of FAIR or POOR. Then go on to Sample Test 3. Find your approximate GMAT score by using the scoring table on the next page.

*Important note: Up-to-date scoring guidelines for the Integrated Reasoning section can be found at *mba.com*.

SCORING TABLE

Add the number of correct answers on the Quantitative test and the number of correct answers on the Verbal test to find **T**, your total number of correct answers.

T should be a number less than or equal to 78. Find your equivalent scaled score in the table below.

Again, this table refers to Quantitative and Verbal scores only. For specifics on Integrated Reasoning scoring, go to *mba.com*.

T	Score	T	Score	T	Score	T	Score
78	800	59	660	40	510	21	370
77	790	58	650	39	500	20	360
76	790	57	640	38	490	19	350
75	780	56	630	37	490	18	340
74	770	55	620	36	480	17	340
73	760	54	620	35	470	16	330
72	760	53	610	34	460	15	320
71	750	52	600	33	460	14	310
70	740	51	590	32	450	13	300
69	730	50	580	31	440	12	290
68	720	49	580	30	430	11	280
67	720	48	570	29	430	10	270
66	710	47	560	28	420	9	260
65	700	46	550	27	410	8	250
64	690	45	550	26	400	7	240
63	690	44	540	25	400	6	230
62	680	43	530	24	390	5	220
61	670	42	520	23	380	4	210
60	660	41	520	22	370	<4	200

Sample Test 3 with Answers and Analysis

→ **TEST**
→ **ANSWERS**
→ **ANALYSIS**
→ **EVALUATING YOUR SCORE**

ANSWER SHEET
Sample Test 3

INTEGRATED REASONING SECTION

1. i. Ⓐ Ⓑ Ⓒ Ⓓ
  ii. Ⓐ Ⓑ Ⓒ Ⓓ

2.

Stanley and Gene Would Agree	Stanley and Gene Would NOT Agree
◯	◯
◯	◯
◯	◯

3.

Would Help Explain	Would Not Help Explain
◯	◯
◯	◯
◯	◯
◯	◯

4.

Yes	No
◯	◯
◯	◯
◯	◯

5. Ⓐ Ⓑ Ⓒ

6.

Fragile Items Sent Separately from Non-fragile Items	All Items Sent via Fragile Shipping
◯	◯
◯	◯
◯	◯

7.

Total Number of Possible Project Teams	Total Number of Ways to Rank Employees
◯	◯
◯	◯
◯	◯
◯	◯
◯	◯

8. i. Ⓐ Ⓑ Ⓒ Ⓓ
  ii. Ⓐ Ⓑ Ⓒ Ⓓ

9.

True	False
◯	◯
◯	◯
◯	◯
◯	◯

10. i. Ⓐ Ⓑ Ⓒ Ⓓ
  ii. Ⓐ Ⓑ Ⓒ Ⓓ

11.

True	False
◯	◯
◯	◯
◯	◯

12.

Time for All Three to Fill the Pool Together	Time it Will Take for Karen to Fill Half of the Pool
◯	◯
◯	◯
◯	◯
◯	◯
◯	◯

ANSWER SHEET
Sample Test 3

QUANTITATIVE SECTION

1. Ⓐ Ⓑ Ⓒ Ⓓ Ⓔ   11. Ⓐ Ⓑ Ⓒ Ⓓ Ⓔ   21. Ⓐ Ⓑ Ⓒ Ⓓ Ⓔ   31. Ⓐ Ⓑ Ⓒ Ⓓ Ⓔ
2. Ⓐ Ⓑ Ⓒ Ⓓ Ⓔ   12. Ⓐ Ⓑ Ⓒ Ⓓ Ⓔ   22. Ⓐ Ⓑ Ⓒ Ⓓ Ⓔ   32. Ⓐ Ⓑ Ⓒ Ⓓ Ⓔ
3. Ⓐ Ⓑ Ⓒ Ⓓ Ⓔ   13. Ⓐ Ⓑ Ⓒ Ⓓ Ⓔ   23. Ⓐ Ⓑ Ⓒ Ⓓ Ⓔ   33. Ⓐ Ⓑ Ⓒ Ⓓ Ⓔ
4. Ⓐ Ⓑ Ⓒ Ⓓ Ⓔ   14. Ⓐ Ⓑ Ⓒ Ⓓ Ⓔ   24. Ⓐ Ⓑ Ⓒ Ⓓ Ⓔ   34. Ⓐ Ⓑ Ⓒ Ⓓ Ⓔ
5. Ⓐ Ⓑ Ⓒ Ⓓ Ⓔ   15. Ⓐ Ⓑ Ⓒ Ⓓ Ⓔ   25. Ⓐ Ⓑ Ⓒ Ⓓ Ⓔ   35. Ⓐ Ⓑ Ⓒ Ⓓ Ⓔ
6. Ⓐ Ⓑ Ⓒ Ⓓ Ⓔ   16. Ⓐ Ⓑ Ⓒ Ⓓ Ⓔ   26. Ⓐ Ⓑ Ⓒ Ⓓ Ⓔ   36. Ⓐ Ⓑ Ⓒ Ⓓ Ⓔ
7. Ⓐ Ⓑ Ⓒ Ⓓ Ⓔ   17. Ⓐ Ⓑ Ⓒ Ⓓ Ⓔ   27. Ⓐ Ⓑ Ⓒ Ⓓ Ⓔ   37. Ⓐ Ⓑ Ⓒ Ⓓ Ⓔ
8. Ⓐ Ⓑ Ⓒ Ⓓ Ⓔ   18. Ⓐ Ⓑ Ⓒ Ⓓ Ⓔ   28. Ⓐ Ⓑ Ⓒ Ⓓ Ⓔ
9. Ⓐ Ⓑ Ⓒ Ⓓ Ⓔ   19. Ⓐ Ⓑ Ⓒ Ⓓ Ⓔ   29. Ⓐ Ⓑ Ⓒ Ⓓ Ⓔ
10. Ⓐ Ⓑ Ⓒ Ⓓ Ⓔ   20. Ⓐ Ⓑ Ⓒ Ⓓ Ⓔ   30. Ⓐ Ⓑ Ⓒ Ⓓ Ⓔ

VERBAL SECTION

1. Ⓐ Ⓑ Ⓒ Ⓓ Ⓔ   12. Ⓐ Ⓑ Ⓒ Ⓓ Ⓔ   23. Ⓐ Ⓑ Ⓒ Ⓓ Ⓔ   34. Ⓐ Ⓑ Ⓒ Ⓓ Ⓔ
2. Ⓐ Ⓑ Ⓒ Ⓓ Ⓔ   13. Ⓐ Ⓑ Ⓒ Ⓓ Ⓔ   24. Ⓐ Ⓑ Ⓒ Ⓓ Ⓔ   35. Ⓐ Ⓑ Ⓒ Ⓓ Ⓔ
3. Ⓐ Ⓑ Ⓒ Ⓓ Ⓔ   14. Ⓐ Ⓑ Ⓒ Ⓓ Ⓔ   25. Ⓐ Ⓑ Ⓒ Ⓓ Ⓔ   36. Ⓐ Ⓑ Ⓒ Ⓓ Ⓔ
4. Ⓐ Ⓑ Ⓒ Ⓓ Ⓔ   15. Ⓐ Ⓑ Ⓒ Ⓓ Ⓔ   26. Ⓐ Ⓑ Ⓒ Ⓓ Ⓔ   37. Ⓐ Ⓑ Ⓒ Ⓓ Ⓔ
5. Ⓐ Ⓑ Ⓒ Ⓓ Ⓔ   16. Ⓐ Ⓑ Ⓒ Ⓓ Ⓔ   27. Ⓐ Ⓑ Ⓒ Ⓓ Ⓔ   38. Ⓐ Ⓑ Ⓒ Ⓓ Ⓔ
6. Ⓐ Ⓑ Ⓒ Ⓓ Ⓔ   17. Ⓐ Ⓑ Ⓒ Ⓓ Ⓔ   28. Ⓐ Ⓑ Ⓒ Ⓓ Ⓔ   39. Ⓐ Ⓑ Ⓒ Ⓓ Ⓔ
7. Ⓐ Ⓑ Ⓒ Ⓓ Ⓔ   18. Ⓐ Ⓑ Ⓒ Ⓓ Ⓔ   29. Ⓐ Ⓑ Ⓒ Ⓓ Ⓔ   40. Ⓐ Ⓑ Ⓒ Ⓓ Ⓔ
8. Ⓐ Ⓑ Ⓒ Ⓓ Ⓔ   19. Ⓐ Ⓑ Ⓒ Ⓓ Ⓔ   30. Ⓐ Ⓑ Ⓒ Ⓓ Ⓔ   41. Ⓐ Ⓑ Ⓒ Ⓓ Ⓔ
9. Ⓐ Ⓑ Ⓒ Ⓓ Ⓔ   20. Ⓐ Ⓑ Ⓒ Ⓓ Ⓔ   31. Ⓐ Ⓑ Ⓒ Ⓓ Ⓔ
10. Ⓐ Ⓑ Ⓒ Ⓓ Ⓔ   21. Ⓐ Ⓑ Ⓒ Ⓓ Ⓔ   32. Ⓐ Ⓑ Ⓒ Ⓓ Ⓔ
11. Ⓐ Ⓑ Ⓒ Ⓓ Ⓔ   22. Ⓐ Ⓑ Ⓒ Ⓓ Ⓔ   33. Ⓐ Ⓑ Ⓒ Ⓓ Ⓔ

WRITING ASSESSMENT

Time: 30 minutes

ANALYSIS OF AN ARGUMENT

> DIRECTIONS: Write a clear, logical, and well-organized response to the following argument. Your response should be in the form of a short essay, following the conventions of standard written English. On the CAT, your answer should be the equivalent of an essay that would fill three pages of lined 8½″ × 11″ paper. If you are taking a paper test, write legibly. Essays that are illegible or that are written on a topic other than the one outlined in the question will not be scored.

Women are more fashion-conscious than men. Women's clothing styles change every year, forcing them to update their wardrobes so as not to appear behind the times.

Discuss how logically persuasive you find the above argument. In presenting your point of view, analyze the sort of reasoning used and supporting evidence. Are there inferred assumptions? In addition, state what further evidence, if any, would make the argument more sound and convincing or would make you better able to evaluate its conclusion. What might weaken or strengthen the argument?

ON THE ACTUAL GMAT,
AFTER YOU HAVE CONFIRMED YOUR ANSWER,
YOU CANNOT RETURN TO IT.

INTEGRATED REASONING SECTION

Time: 30 minutes

12 questions

This section consists of four types of questions: Graphics Interpretation, Table Analysis, Two-part Analysis, and Multi-Source Reasoning.

> **DIRECTIONS:** The new Integrated Reasoning section consists of four question types. Some require the use of both quantitative and verbal skills. Others involve the use of graphics, tables, or text material. The questions also use various response formats.
>
> For each question, review the text, graphic, or text material provided and respond to the task that is presented. *Note: An onscreen calculator is available in this section on the actual test.*

Question 1 refers to the following information and graph.

1. The following graph charts the market share of the top motorcycle companies in 2003 and 2004.

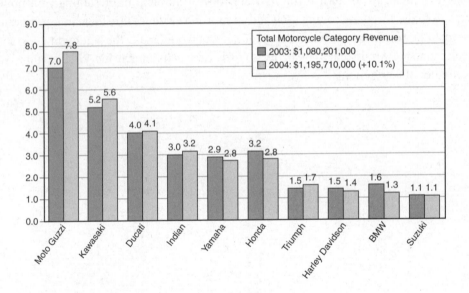

Complete each statement according to the information presented in the diagram.

i. Which company has seen the largest share percentage increase?

(A) Moto Guzzi

(B) Kawasaki

(C) Indian

(D) Triumph

ii. How do the majority of the motorcycle companies compare with the growth of the entire motorcycle market?

(A) Most motorcycle companies are outpacing the growth of the entire motorcycle market.

(B) Most motorcycle companies are not keeping up with the growth of the entire motorcycle market.

(C) Most motorcycle companies are on par with the growth of the entire motorcycle market.

(D) None of the above.

---

2. Read the opinions of Stanley and Gene. Then answer the question below.

Stanley: It is clear to both of us that one of the biggest societal issues in our country is our aging population. Baby boomers and most elderly people prefer to avoid living in climates that are unpleasant, particularly those with extreme temperatures. One of the benefits of living in our country is that we have coastal regions where the climate is generally mild and temperate. Ergo, we can expect populations in these areas to grow while other areas in our country will probably experience population declines.

Gene: I think you are wrong. Areas of our country where the climate is harsh are usually characterized by relatively low living costs. There are, of course, a few exceptions. However, low living costs are an influential factor for seniors and retirees who have little savings and live on fixed incomes. This important issue will not likely be solved by our government in the short term.

Which of the following statements would Stanley and Gene agree on and which would they disagree about? Choose only one option in each column.

Stanley and Gene Would Agree	Stanley and Gene Would Disagree	
◯	◯	Statement 1: Regions that are characterized by harsh climates are likely to see population declines in the future.
◯	◯	Statement 2: The reason for the population shift toward coastal areas and away from other regions is economic.
◯	◯	Statement 3: Coastal regions are affordable places for seniors and retirees to live.
◯	◯	Statement 4: Seniors and retirees dislike cold weather.
◯	◯	Statement 5: The aging population is a noteworthy issue that needs to be addressed in our country.

Questions 3 and 4 refer to the following information and table.

The table below displays data on the top-grossing live performances over a three-month period in 2010.

Concert	Show Type	Average Box Office Gross per City	Box Office Rank	Average Ticket Price	Ticket Price Rank
Cirque du Soleil—"Michael Jackson: The Immortal"	Performance art	$2,362,502	1	$109.98	2
Kanye West/Jay-Z	Rap/R&B	$1,902,032	2	$112.94	1
Cirque du Soleil—"Dralion"	Performance art	$1,148,681	3	$64.08	6
Cirque du Soleil—"Quidam"	Performance art	$912,283	4	$64.65	5
Bob Seger & The Silver Bullet Band	Rock	$753,644	5	$73.39	4
Trans-Siberian Orchestra	Classical	$618,135	6	$52.29	10
Jason Aldean	Country	$592,300	7	$44.11	16
Brad Paisley	Country	$586,414	8	$52.70	9
Blake Shelton	Country	$367,522	9	$48.17	11
Jeff Dunham	Comedy	$346,408	10	$46.76	13
Miranda Lambert	Country	$314,295	11	$45.15	14
Lady Antebellum	Country	$294,995	12	$44.54	15
Eric Church	Country	$263,628	13	$34.51	18
Rain—"A Tribute To The Beatles"	Rock	$189,572	14	$47.50	12
Rise Against	Rock	$148,490	15	$34.03	19
The String Cheese Incident	Rock	$147,062	16	$39.19	17
"Mythbusters"	Theatre	$144,212	17	$53.09	8
Mannheim Steamroller	Classical	$138,470	18	$56.66	7
"Winter Jam"—Skillet	Rock—Christian	$136,638	19	$11.04	20
Salute to Vienna	Classical	$132,574	20	$78.87	3

3. For each of the following statements, select *Would help explain* if it would, if true, help explain some of the information in the table. Otherwise select *Would not help explain.*

Would Help Explain	Would Not Help Explain	
○	○	Consumers generally spend less on a concert featuring one solo artist.
○	○	The live theater industry (e.g., Broadway) generates less overall revenue than the classical music concert industry.
○	○	Country music concert ticket prices are more expensive than rock music concert ticket prices.

4. For each of the following statements, select *Yes* if the statement can be shown to be true based on the information in the table. Otherwise, select *No.*

Yes	No	
○	○	The top Cirque du Soleil concerts cumulatively grossed more than twice as much money per city than that of the top country music concerts.
○	○	The median average ticket price is greater than the average ticket price of all of the top rock concerts.
○	○	Salute to Vienna did not have the smallest average audience per city.

Brochure page 1

BodyBliss Spa in Reno, Nevada, makes an assortment of specialty aromatherapy massage oils for clients all across North America. They have created five main types:

(1) Standard—A mixture of five essential oils (lavender, ylang ylang, rose, patchouli, and sage) shipped in 12 × 150 mL bottles. Total cost is $14.99. This package does not require any special shipping.

(2) Energy—A specialized mixture of invigorating oils (cypress, ginger, and grapefruit) shipped in 20 × 200 mL bottles. Total cost is $24.99. This package requires special fragile shipping.

(3) Exotic—A unique blend of imported oils (jojoba, borage, and rosehip) shipped in a 1.2-liter bottle. Total cost is $39.99. This package requires special fragile shipping.

(4) Signature—A BodyBliss Spa exclusive blend (sandalwood, avocado, apricot, and sunflower) shipped in 10 × 50 mL bottles. Total cost is $59.99. This package requires special fragile shipping.

(5) Combo—An assorted mix of the above BodyBliss Spa's lines as well as a set of 10 aromatherapy candles. This assortment is shipped together in a large package, some of which requires fragile packaging and some that does not. Total cost is $149.99.

Brochure page 2

BodyBliss Spa uses the shipper IPC (International Packers Corporation) to deliver all their orders.

IPC costs:

(1) IPC regular shipping: $50 plus $0.10 per each mL

(2) IPC fragile shipping: $80 plus $0.15 per each mL

(3) IPC express shipping: (2–4 days vs. the normal 2–4 weeks): $100 extra

Brochure page 3

If any order is a hybrid order (i.e., it contains both items that require fragile shipping and items that do not require fragile shipping), BodyBliss gives customers a choice of shipping methods.

(1) All items, regardless of type, will be sent via fragile shipping.

(2) Items requiring fragile shipping will be sent via fragile shipping, and all other items will be sent separately via regular shipping.

If a customer places a hybrid order, the BodyBliss Spa associate will confirm the customer's shipping choice. The associate will also assure the customer that no damage will occur when shipping fragile and nonfragile items together.

5. If a woman in Idaho has a total of $750 to spend on a BodyBliss Spa order, which of the following orders could she afford, including the cost of shipping?

(A) Ten standard packs

(B) Four signature blends

(C) The combo pack

---

6. For each of the following hybrid orders, which shipping option will be less expensive?

Fragile Items Sent Separately from Nonfragile Items	All Items Sent via Fragile Shipping	Order
○	○	Fifteen energy assortments requiring fragile shipping and five standard assortments not requiring fragile shipping
○	○	Ten exotic assortments requiring fragile shipping and ten standard assortments not requiring fragile shipping
○	○	Five signature assortments requiring fragile shipping and fifteen standard assortments not requiring fragile shipping

7. The company Jagua is hiring a consulting firm to work on a change management project for the organization. Jagua management's goal is to streamline some of the internal processes involved in running the organization. As part of the project, the consulting firm has asked Jagua to give them a list of eight people from whom to select five members to join the project team. Jagua selected Annie, Bobby, Charles, Deanna, Edward, Frank, George, and Helen as the prime candidates. After the consulting firm interviewed the candidates, it was revealed that Helen and Charles had a previous romantic relationship that ended a few months ago. They requested not to be selected for the same team.

Based on the information above, determine the total number of possible project teams that the consulting firm could create. Additionally, determine how many possible ways the consulting firm could rank the eight employees in terms of preference (regardless of Helen's and Charles's requests). Make only two selections, one in each column.

Total Number of Possible Project Teams	Total Number of Ways to Rank the Employees	Amount
○	○	$\dfrac{8!}{5!}$
○	○	$\dfrac{8!}{(5!3!)} - \dfrac{6!}{(3!3!)}$
○	○	$\dfrac{8!}{5!} - \dfrac{6!}{3!}$
○	○	$\dfrac{(8!-5!)}{3!}$
○	○	$8!$

8.   The graph below charts the film length of 15 Best Picture winners at the Academy Awards along with the film's month of release.

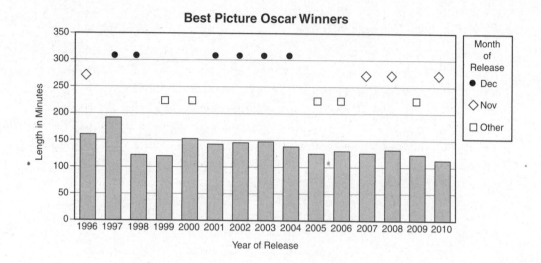

Complete each statement according to the information presented in the diagram.

(i) Approximately how much longer was the average length of a Best Picture movie in the latter portion of the 1990s than the average length of a Best Picture movie in the 2000s?

(A)   5 minutes
(B)   15 minutes
(C)   25 minutes
(D)   35 minutes

(ii) By extrapolating from the graph, which of the following is a possible trend?

(A)   Best Picture films are being released earlier in the year and are getting shorter in length.
(B)   Best Picture films need to be less than 150 minutes in length in order to win.
(C)   No film released in December can win Best Picture anymore.
(D)   Best Picture films are being released earlier in the year and are shorter due to lower budgets.

9. Read the four e-mails. Then identify the statements that follow as either *True* or *False*.

E-mail 1: Frank Smythe, an owner of several boats

April 21, 5:55 P.M.

Dear Mr. and Mrs. Smith,

Thanks so much for coming by to see our fleet of sailboats on sale at the yacht club today. We hope that you enjoyed your visit and tour. It seemed like you were most interested in the 24-foot yacht *Santa Maria*. We hope you are willing to make an offer on the *Santa Maria*. As I mentioned, the selling price is $120,000. We can have the boat ready to sail within two weeks of purchase. The timing is perfect since the warm season will be upon us shortly. Please let me know if you have any questions. Hope to hear from you soon.

Frank

E-mail 2: Herb Smith, responding to Frank's e-mail

April 23, 10:47 A.M.

Dear Frank,

We appreciate the follow-up. My wife Peggy and I had a great time checking out your impressive fleet of boats. I appreciated the special attention you gave us in answering our questions as we are both "newbies" at yachting. We are definitely interested, and the boat we purchase will make an excellent gift to myself for my retirement! Unfortunately, your price is a bit out of our range. Cost is a big issue, and we were hoping to spend no more than $90,000. Since we have a lot of time, perhaps we can find the option that works best for us. I did like the *Santa Maria*, especially because it was in good condition and the less work I have to do on the boat the better. I am willing to negotiate 10-15% higher, but that is the best I can do. What can you do for us?

Thanks,

Herb

E-mail 3: Frank Smythe, responding to Herb's e-mail

```
April 23, 11:34 A.M.

Dear Herb,

I'm sure we can work out something! I'll be honest with you—
boats are in big demand, and I typically sell them between
90% and 125% of the original retail price. I have another
person who is interested in this boat, but I like you guys
better. I'll tell you what I can do. If we can finalize a sale
within two weeks, I can knock down the price by 10% and throw
in a full paint job with any color you want. Additionally, I can
offer three two-hour sailboat lessons ($1,500 value).  What do
you think of that?

Frank
```

E-mail 4: Herb Smith, responding to Frank's e-mail

```
April 25, 4:42 P.M.

Dear Frank,

I truly appreciate your offer. I just spoke with my wife, and
our only hesitation is the time rush. We initially got into this
thinking to explore it over the next few months, and you are
offering me something pretty decent now! I'm going to work on my
wife a bit more on this (she needs a bit more convincing, haha)
and get back to you after this weekend. I'll want to talk to my
kids as well since they'll likely want to use it in the summer.

Thanks,

Herb
```

True	False	
◯	◯	Herb is likely the primary decision maker for purchasing a new boat.
◯	◯	Herb is more anxious to buy this boat than Frank is to sell it.
◯	◯	If Peggy tells Herb that she thinks the paint job is worth $5,000 to her and that she appreciates the sailing lessons, Herb will likely accept the offer.
◯	◯	For Herb, taking the time to get the right yacht by July is more important than the final price.

10. The bubble graph below charts the average starting salary at MBA schools on the *x*-axis, median GMAT score on the *y*-axis, and relative reputation with the bubble size.

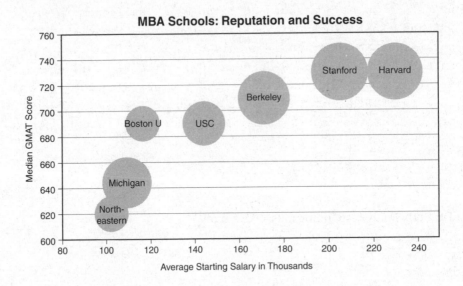

Complete each statement according to the information given by the graph.

(i) What is the relationship between median GMAT score and average starting salary?

(A) Positive
(B) Negative
(C) Inversely proportional
(D) Cannot be determined

(ii) "All MBA schools need to have a high average starting salary and a high median GMAT score in order to achieve a strong reputation." Which of the following describes this statement?

(A) The truth of the statement depends on several factors.
(B) The statement is true.
(C) The statement is false.
(D) The truth of the statement cannot be determined.

11. The table below shows data for a select group of countries, including population, number of theaters, and number of tourists.

Country	Population	# of Theaters	# of People per Theater	Visiting Tourists (in millions)	Tourists per Population (ratio)
Australia	22,864,922	519	44,056	5.89	0.026
Brazil	192,376,496	790	243,515	5.16	0.003
Canada	34,745,000	656	52,965	16.10	0.046
Egypt	81,712,000	165	495,224	14.05	0.017
Germany	81,831,000	1,854	44,138	24.22	0.030
Italy	60,776,531	2,068	29,389	43.63	0.072
Mexico	112,336,538	792	141,839	22.40	0.020
Russian Federation	143,030,106	563	254,050	20.27	0.014
Spain	46,196,278	1,052	43,913	52.68	0.114
Turkey	74,724,269	314	237,975	27.00	0.036
United Kingdom	62,300,000	659	94,537	28.13	0.045
United States of America	313,224,000	6,356	49,280	59.75	0.019

Consider each of the following statements. For each statement, indicate whether the statement is true or false based on the information provided in the table.

True False

○   ○   Tourism in Europe is larger than tourism in the Americas (North and South).

○   ○   The five most populated countries in the chart have less than double all the theaters in the rest of the countries in the chart combined.

○   ○   The top five countries with the highest tourists per population ratios do not include any countries that place in the top five countries with the highest number of people per theater.

12. Tony, Carl, and Karen work at a local swimming pool. One of their operational responsibilities is to drain the pool, clean it, and then fill it. Tony can fill a pool with a hose in x hours. Carl can fill a pool with a hose in y hours. Karen can fill a pool with a hose in z hours.

Based on the information above, determine the time all three take to fill the pool together. If all three stop filling the pool when it is halfway full, how long does Karen take to fill the rest of the pool by herself? Make only two selections, one in each column.

Time for all Three to Fill the Pool Together	Time for Karen to Fill Half the Pool	Amount of Time
◯	◯	$\dfrac{z}{2}$
◯	◯	$\dfrac{xyz}{(yz + xz + xy)}$
◯	◯	$\dfrac{(yz + xz + xy)}{2xyz}$
◯	◯	$\dfrac{2z}{3}$
◯	◯	$\dfrac{3z}{(x + y + z)}$

STOP

QUANTITATIVE SECTION

Time: 75 minutes

37 questions

This section consists of two types of questions: Problem Solving and Data Sufficiency.

Problem Solving

DIRECTIONS: Solve each of the following problems; then indicate the correct answer.

NOTE: A figure that appears with a problem is drawn as accurately as possible so as to provide information that may help in answering the question.

Numbers in this test are real numbers.

Data Sufficiency

DIRECTIONS: Each of the following problems has a question and two statements that are labeled (1) and (2). Use the data given in (1) and (2) together with other available information (such as the number of hours in a day, the definition of *clockwise*, mathematical facts, etc.) to decide whether the statements are *sufficient* to answer the question. Then fill in space

(A) If you can get the answer from **(1) ALONE** but not from (2) alone

(B) If you can get the answer from **(2) ALONE** but not from (1) alone

(C) If you can get the answer from **BOTH (1)** and **(2) TOGETHER** but not from (1) alone or (2) alone

(D) If **EITHER** statement **(1) ALONE OR** statement **(2) ALONE** suffices

(E) If you **CANNOT** get the answer from statements (1) and (2) **TOGETHER** but need even more data

All numbers used in this section are real numbers.

A figure given for a problem is intended to provide information consistent with that in the question, but not necessarily with the additional information contained in the statements.

All figures lie in the plane unless you are told otherwise.

Figures are drawn as accurately as possible; straight lines may not appear straight on the screen.

(A) If you can get the answer from **(1) ALONE** but not from **(2)** alone

(B) If you can get the answer from **(2) ALONE** but not from **(1)** alone

(C) If you can get the answer from **BOTH (1)** and **(2) TOGETHER** but not from (1) alone or (2) alone

(D) If **EITHER** statement **(1) ALONE OR** statement **(2) ALONE** suffices

(E) If you **CANNOT** get the answer from statements (1) and (2) **TOGETHER** but need even more data

1. Water has been poured into an empty rectangular tank at the rate of 5 cubic feet per minute for 6 minutes. The length of the tank is 4 feet and the width is $\frac{1}{2}$ of the length. How deep is the water in the tank?

    (A)   7.5 inches
    (B)   3 feet 7.5 inches
    (C)   3 feet 9 inches
    (D)   7 feet 6 inches
    (E)   30 feet

2. If x, y, z are chosen from the three numbers -3, $\frac{1}{2}$, and 2, what is the largest possible value of the expression $\left(\frac{x}{y}\right)z^2$?

    (A) $-\frac{3}{8}$
    (B)   16
    (C)   24
    (D)   36
    (E)   54

3. A survey of n people found that 60 percent preferred brand A. An additional x people were surveyed who all preferred brand A. Seventy percent of all the people surveyed preferred brand A. Find x in terms of n.

    (A) $\frac{n}{6}$
    (B) $\frac{n}{3}$
    (C) $\frac{n}{2}$
    (D) n
    (E) $3n$

4. Is *x* greater than *y*?

    (1) $3x = 2k$

    (2) $k = y^2$

5. Is *ABCD* a parallelogram?

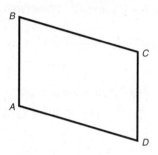

    (1) $AB = CD$

    (2)   *AB* is parallel to *CD*

6. The hexagon *ABCDEF* is regular. That means all its sides are the same length and all its interior angles are the same size. Each side of the hexagon is 2 feet. What is the area of the rectangle *BCEF*?

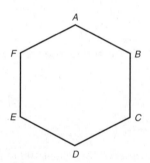

    (A)   4 square feet

    (B) $4\sqrt{3}$ square feet

    (C)   8 square feet

    (D) $4 + 4\sqrt{3}$ square feet

    (E)   12 square feet

7. In Motor City 90 percent of the population own a car, 15 percent own a motorcycle, and everybody owns one or the other or both. What is the percentage of motorcycle owners who own cars?

    (A)   5%

    (B)   15%

    (C) $33\frac{1}{3}\%$

    (D)   50%

    (E)   90%

8. Jim's weight is 140 percent of Marcia's weight. Bob's weight is 90 percent of Lee's weight. Lee weighs twice as much as Marcia. What percentage of Jim's weight is Bob's weight?

(A) $64\frac{2}{7}$

(B) $77\frac{7}{9}$

(C) 90

(D) $128\frac{4}{7}$

(E) $155\frac{5}{9}$

9. What is the two-digit number whose first digit is a and whose second digit is b? The number is greater than 9.

(1) $2a + 3b = 11a + 2b$

(2) The two-digit number is a multiple of 19.

10. A chair originally cost $50.00. The chair was offered for sale at 108 percent of its cost. After a week, the price was discounted 10 percent and the chair was sold. The chair was sold for

(A) $45.00

(B) $48.60

(C) $49.00

(D) $49.50

(E) $54.00

11. k is a positive integer. Is k a prime number?

(1) No integer between 2 and $\sqrt{k}$, inclusive, divides k evenly.

(2) No integer between 2 and $\frac{k}{2}$, inclusive, divides k evenly, and k is greater than 5.

12. Towns A and C are connected by a straight highway that is 60 miles long. The straight-line distance between town A and town B is 50 miles, and the straight-line distance from town B to town C is 50 miles. How many miles is it from town B to the point on the highway connecting towns A and C that is closest to town B?

(A) 30
(B) 40
(C) $30\sqrt{2}$
(D) 50
(E) 60

13. A worker is paid x dollars for the first 8 hours he works each day. He is paid y dollars per hour for each hour he works in excess of 8 hours. During one week he works 8 hours on Monday, 11 hours on Tuesday, 9 hours on Wednesday, 10 hours on Thursday, and 9 hours on Friday. What is his average daily wage in dollars for the 5-day week?

(A) $x + 1.4y$
(B) $2x + y$
(C) $\dfrac{(5x + 8y)}{5}$
(D) $8x + 1.4y$
(E) $5x + 7y$

14. A club has 8 male and 8 female members. The club is choosing a committee of 6 members. The committee must have 3 male and 3 female members. How many different committees can be chosen?

(A) 112,896
(B) 3,136
(C) 720
(D) 112
(E) 9

15. The towns A, B, and C lie on a straight line. C is between A and B. The distance from A to B is 100 miles. How far is it from A to C?

(1) The distance from A to B is 25 percent more than the distance from C to B.

(2) The distance from A to C is $\dfrac{1}{4}$ of the distance from C to B.

16. A club has 10 male and 5 female members. Each member of the club writes his/her name on a ticket, and the tickets are deposited in a box. The club chooses 2 members to go to a national meeting by drawing 2 tickets from the box. What is the probability that both members picked for the trip are female?

    (A) $\dfrac{2}{21}$

    (B) $\dfrac{1}{10}$

    (C) $\dfrac{2}{7}$

    (D) $\dfrac{5}{15}$

    (E) $\dfrac{2}{5}$

17. The distribution of scores on a math test had a mean of 82 percent with a standard deviation of 5 percent. The score that is exactly 2 standard deviations above the mean is

    (A) 72%
    (B) 82%
    (C) 92%
    (D) 95%
    (E) cannot be determined

18. What is the value of $x - y$?

    (1) $x + 2y = 6$
    (2) $x = y$

19. The number of eligible voters is 100,000. How many eligible voters voted?

    (1) 63 percent of the eligible men voted.
    (2) 67 percent of the eligible women voted.

20. A motorcycle costs $2,500 when it is brand new. At the end of each year it is worth 80 percent of what it was worth at the beginning of the year. What is the motorcycle worth when it is 3 years old?

    (A) $1,000
    (B) $1,200
    (C) $1,280
    (D) $1,340
    (E) $1,430

21. Which of the following inequalities is the solution to the inequality $7x - 5 < 12x + 18$?

    (A) $x < -\dfrac{13}{5}$

    (B) $x > -\dfrac{23}{5}$

    (C) $x < -\dfrac{23}{5}$

    (D) $x > \dfrac{23}{5}$

    (E) $x < \dfrac{23}{5}$

22. The hexagon *ABCDEF* is inscribed in the circle with center *O*. What is the length of *AB*?

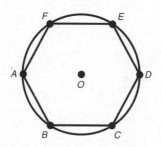

    (1) The radius of the circle is 4 inches.
    (2) The hexagon is a regular hexagon. That means all its sides are the same length and all its interior angles are the same size.

23. What was the percentage of defective items produced at a factory?

(1) The total number of defective items produced was 1,234.

(2) The ratio of defective items to nondefective items was 32 to 5,678.

24. On a list of people's ages the tabulator made an error that resulted in 20 years being added to each person's age. Which of the following statements is true?

I. The mean of the listed ages and the mean of the actual ages are the same.

II. The standard deviation of the listed ages and the actual ages are the same.

III. The range of the listed ages and the actual ages are the same.

(A) only II

(B) I and II

(C) I and III

(D) II and III

(E) I, II, and III

25. Is ABC a right triangle? $AB = 5$; $AC = 4$.

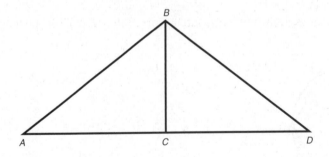

(1) $BC = 3$

(2) $AC = CD$

26. Did the price of energy rise last year?

    (1) If the price of energy rose last year, then the price of food would rise this year.
    (2) The price of food rose this year.

27. Mary, John, and Karen ate lunch together. Karen's meal cost 50 percent more than John's meal, and Mary's meal cost $\frac{5}{6}$ as much as Karen's meal. If Mary paid $2 more than John, how much was the total that the three of them paid?

    (A) $28.33
    (B) $30.00
    (C) $35.00
    (D) $37.50
    (E) $40.00

28. A group of 49 consumers were offered a chance to subscribe to three magazines: A, B, and C. Thirty-eight of the consumers subscribed to at least one of the magazines. How many of the 49 consumers subscribed to exactly two of the magazines?

    (1) Twelve of the 49 consumers subscribed to all three of the magazines.
    (2) Twenty of the 49 consumers subscribed to magazine A.

29. If a and b are digits and the sum of the numbers 2a3, b31, and 431 is 925 as shown

$$
\begin{array}{r}
2a3 \\
b31 \\
+\ 431 \\
\hline
925
\end{array}
$$

    then the value of $a - b$ is

    (A) −4
    (B) 2
    (C) 4
    (D) 6
    (E) 10

30. If the angles of a triangle are in the ratio 1 : 2 : 2, the triangle

    (A) is isosceles
    (B) is obtuse
    (C) is a right triangle
    (D) is equilateral
    (E) has one angle greater than 80°

31. How much was a certain Rembrandt painting worth in January 1991?

    (1) In January 1997 the painting was worth $2 million.
    (2) Over the ten years 1988–1997 the painting increased in value by 10 percent each year.

32. A sequence of numbers $a_1, a_2, a_3, \ldots$ is given by the rule $a_n^2 = a_{n+1}$. Does 3 appear in the sequence?

    (1) $a_1 = 2$
    (2) $a_3 = 16$

33. A wall with no windows is 11 feet high and 20 feet long. A large roll of wallpaper costs $25 and will cover 60 square feet of wall. A small roll of wallpaper costs $6 and will cover 10 square feet of wall. What is the least cost for enough wallpaper to cover the wall?

    (A) $75
    (B) $99
    (C) $100
    (D) $120
    (E) $132

34. A jar is filled with 60 marbles. All the marbles in the jar are either red or green. What is the smallest number of marbles that must be drawn from the jar in order to be certain that a red marble is drawn?

    (1) The ratio of red marbles to green marbles is 3 : 1.
    (2) There are 15 green marbles in the jar.

35. Is $\dfrac{1}{x}$ greater than $\dfrac{1}{y}$?

    (1) x is greater than 1.
    (2) x is less than y.

36. Plane X flies at r miles per hour from A to B. Plane Y flies at S miles per hour from B to A. Both planes take off at the same time. Which plane flies at a faster rate? Town C is between A and B.

    (1) C is closer to A than it is to B.
    (2)   Plane X flies over C before plane Y.

37. Is $\dfrac{x}{12} > \dfrac{y}{40}$?

    (1) $10x > 3y$
    (2) $12x < 4y$

STOP

ON THE ACTUAL GMAT,
AFTER YOU HAVE CONFIRMED YOUR ANSWER,
YOU CANNOT RETURN TO IT.

VERBAL SECTION

Time: 75 minutes

41 questions

Reading Comprehension

DIRECTIONS: This section contains three reading passages. You are to read each one carefully. When answering the questions, you *will* be allowed to refer back to the passages. The questions are based on what is *stated* or *implied* in each passage.

Critical Reasoning

DIRECTIONS: For each question in this section, choose the best answer from among the listed alternatives.

Sentence Correction

DIRECTIONS: This part of the section consists of a number of sentences, in each of which some part or the whole is underlined. Each sentence is followed by five alternative versions of the underlined portion. Select the alternative you consider both most correct and most effective according to the requirements of standard written English. Answer (A) is the same as the original version; if you think the original version is best, select answer (A).

In considering the answer choices, be attentive to matters of grammar, diction, and syntax, as well as clarity, precision, and fluency. Do not select an answer that alters the meaning of the original sentence.

Questions 1–4 are based on the following passage.

The main burden of assuring that the resources of the federal government are well managed falls on relatively few of the five million men and women whom it employs. Under the department and agency heads there are 8,600 political, career, military,
Line and foreign service executives—the top managers and professionals—who exert
(5) major influence on the manner in which the rest are directed and utilized. Below their level there are other thousands with assignments of some managerial significance, but we believe that the line of demarcation selected is the best available for our purposes in this attainment.

There is no complete inventory of positions or people in federal service at this
(10) level. The lack may be explained by separate agency statutes and personnel systems, diffusion among so many special services, and absence of any central point (short of the President himself) with jurisdiction over all upper-level personnel of the government.

Top Presidential appointees, about 500 of them, bear the brunt of translating the
(15) philosophy and aims of the current administration into practical programs. This group includes the secretaries and assistant secretaries of cabinet departments, agency heads and their deputies, heads and members of boards and commissions with fixed terms, and chiefs and directors of major bureaus, divisions, and services. Appointments to many of these politically sensitive positions are made on recom-
(20) mendation by department or agency heads, but all are presumably responsible to Presidential leadership.

One qualification for office at this level is that there be no basic disagreement with Presidential political philosophy, at least so far as administrative judgments and actions are concerned. Apart from the bi-partisan boards and commissions, these
(25) men are normally identified with the political party of the President, or are sympathetic to it, although there are exceptions.

1. According to the author, no complete inventory exists of positions in the three highest levels of government because

    (A) no one has bothered to count them
    (B) computers cannot handle all the data
    (C) no one is responsible for completing the project
    (D) the President has never requested such information
    (E) the Classification Act prohibits such a census

2. It may be inferred from the passage that top Presidential appointees have as their central responsibility

   (A) the prevention of politically motivated interference with the actions of their agencies
   (B) the monitoring of government actions on behalf of the President's own political party
   (C) developing courses of action following administration objectives
   (D) investigating charges of corruption within the government
   (E) maintaining adequate controls over the rate of government spending

3. One exception to the general rule that top Presidential appointees must be in agreement with the President's political philosophy may be found in

   (A) most cabinet-level officers
   (B) members of the White House staff
   (C) bi-partisan boards and commission
   (D) those offices filled by patronage
   (E) offices requiring scientific or technical expertise

4. The primary purpose of the passage is to

   (A) describe the qualifications for Presidential appointees
   (B) show how policy makers are selected
   (C) distinguish among different levels of federal service employees
   (D) describe who are the major influences among federal employees
   (E) show why the federal government is well managed

5. Richard is a terrible driver. He has had at least five traffic violations in the past year.

   Which of the following can be said about the above claim?

   (A) This is an example of an argument that is directed against the source of the claim rather than the claim itself.
   (B) The statement is fallacious because it contains an illegitimate appeal to authority.
   (C) The above argument obtains its strength from a similarity of two compared situations.
   (D) The argument is built upon an assumption that is not stated but rather is concealed.
   (E) In the above statement, there is a shifting in the meaning of terms, causing a fallacy of ambiguity.

6. The exchange rate is the ruling official rate of exchange of dollars for other currencies. It determines the value of American goods in relation to foreign goods. If the dollar is devalued in terms of other currencies, American exports (which are paid for in dollars) become cheaper to foreigners and American imports (paid for by purchasing foreign currency) become more expensive to holders of dollars.

What conclusion can be drawn from the above?

(A) There are certain disadvantages for the United States economy attached to devaluation.
(B) The prospect of devaluation results in a speculative outflow of funds.
(C) By encouraging exports and discouraging imports, devaluation can improve the American balance of payments.
(D) The difference between imports and exports is called the Trade Gap.
(E) It is possible that inflation neutralizes the beneficial effects of devaluation.

7. <u>Although I calculate that he will be here</u> any minute, I cannot wait much longer for him to arrive.

(A) Although I calculate that he will be here
(B) Although I reckon that he will be here
(C) Because I calculate that he will be here
(D) Although I think that he will be here
(E) Because I am confident that he will be here

8. <u>The fourteen-hour day not only has been reduced</u> to one of ten hours but also, in some lines of work, to one of eight or even six.

(A) The fourteen-hour day not only has been reduced
(B) Not only the fourteen-hour day has been reduced
(C) Not the fourteen-hour day only has been reduced
(D) The fourteen-hour day has not only been reduced
(E) The fourteen-hour day has been reduced not only

9. In the human body, platelets promote blood clotting by clumping together. Aspirin has been found to prevent clotting by making platelets less sticky. Research has now shown that heart attacks and strokes caused by blood clots could be avoided by taking one aspirin a day. Statistics show that the incidence of second heart attacks has been reduced by 21% and overall mortality rates by 15% as a result of taking aspirin.

Unfortunately, the drug has several unpleasant side effects, including nausea, gastric bleeding, and, in severe cases, shock. In children, it has been linked to Reye's Syndrome, a rare, but occasionally fatal, childhood illness.

On balance, however, for men aged 40 and over, an aspirin a day may present an excellent prophylactic measure for a disease that affects 1.5 million Americans yearly and claims the lives of about 540,000.

Which of the following conclusions can most properly be drawn from the information above?

(A) All people should take an aspirin a day to prevent heart attacks.
(B) Painkillers prevent heart attacks.
(C) Smokers can safely continue smoking, provided that they take at least one aspirin a day.
(D) The majority of people suffering second subsequent cardiac arrests could have been saved by taking an aspirin a day.
(E) Aspirin can be used to reduce mortality rates in patients who have already suffered heart attacks.

10. In the past, to run for one's country in the Olympics was the ultimate achievement of any athlete. Nowadays, an athlete's motives are more and more influenced by financial gain, and consequently we do not see our best athletes in the Olympics, which is still only for amateurs.

Which of the following will most weaken the above conclusion?

(A) The publicity and fame that can be achieved by competing in the Olympics draws the best amateur athletes, who then become more "marketable" by agents and potential sponsors.
(B) The winning of a race is not as important as participating.
(C) There is a widely held belief that our best Olympic athletes already receive enough in terms of promotion and sponsorship.
(D) It has been suggested that professional athletes should be allowed to compete in the games.
(E) Athletics as an entertainment is like any other entertainment job and deserves a financial reward.

11. <u>We want the teacher to be him</u> who has the best rapport with the students.

    (A) We want the teacher to be him
    (B) We want the teacher to be he
    (C) We want him to be the teacher
    (D) We desire that the teacher be him
    (E) We anticipate that the teacher will be him

12. <u>If she were to win the medal</u>, I for one would be disturbed.

    (A) If she were to win the medal,
    (B) If she was to win the medal,
    (C) If she wins the medal,
    (D) If she is the winner of the medal,
    (E) In the event that she wins the medal,

13. The function of a food technologist in a large marketing chain of food stores is to ensure that all foodstuffs that are offered for sale in the various retail outlets meet certain standard criteria for nonperishability, freshness, and fitness for human consumption.

    It is the technologist's job to visit the premises of suppliers and food producers (factory or farm), inspect the facilities, and report thereon. Her responsibility also includes receiving new products from local and foreign suppliers and performing exhaustive quality control testing on them. Finally, she should carry out surprise spot-checks on goods held in the marketing chain's own warehouses and stores.

What conclusion can best be drawn from the preceding paragraph?

    (A) A university degree in food technology is a necessary and sufficient condition for becoming a food technologist.
    (B) Imported products, as well as home-produced goods, must be rigorously tested.
    (C) The food technologist stands between the unhygienic producer and the unsuspecting consumer.
    (D) Home-produced foodstuffs are safer to eat than goods imported from abroad because they are subject to more regular and closer inspection procedures.
    (E) Random checking of the quality of goods stored on the shelves in a foodstore is the best way of ensuring that foodstuffs of an inferior quality are not purchased by the general public.

14. The scouts were told <u>to take an overnight hike, pitch camp, prepare dinner, and that they should be in bed by 9 P.M.</u>

(A) to take an overnight hike, pitch camp, prepare dinner, and that they should be in bed by 9 P.M.

(B) to take an overnight hike, to pitch camp, to prepare dinner, and that they should be in bed by 9 P.M.

(C) to take an overnight hike, pitch camp, prepare dinner, and be in bed by 9 P.M.

(D) to take an overnight hike, pitching camp, preparing dinner and going to bed by 9 P.M.

(E) to engage in an overnight hike, pitch camp, prepare dinner, and that they should be in bed by 9 P.M.

Questions 15–18 are based on the following passage.

In the past, American colleges and universities were created to serve a dual purpose—to advance learning and to offer a chance to become familiar with bodies of knowledge already discovered to those who wished it. To create and to impart, Line these were the hallmarks of American higher education prior to the most recent, (5) tumultuous decades of the twentieth century. The successful institution of higher learning had never been one whose mission could be defined in terms of providing vocational skills or as a strategy for resolving societal problems. In a subtle way Americans believed postsecondary education to be useful, but not necessarily of immediate use. What the student obtained in college became beneficial in later (10) life—residually, without direct application in the period after graduation.

Another purpose has now been assigned to the mission of American colleges and universities. Institutions of higher learning—public or private—commonly face the challenge of defining their programs in such a way as to contribute to the service of the community.

(15) One need only be reminded of the change in language describing the two-year college to appreciate the new value currently being attached to the concept of a service-related university. The traditional two-year college has shed its pejorative "junior" college label and is generally called a "community" college, a clearly value-laden expression representing the latest commitment in higher education.

(20) This novel development is often overlooked. Educators have always been familiar with those parts of the two-year college curriculum that have a "service" or vocational orientation. Knowing this, otherwise perceptive commentaries on American postsecondary education underplay the impact of the attempt of colleges and universities to relate to, if not resolve, the problems of society. Whether the subject (25) under review is student unrest, faculty tenure, the nature of the curriculum, the onset of collective bargaining, or the growth of collegiate bureaucracies, in each instance the thrust of these discussions obscures the larger meaning of the emergence of the service-university in American higher education. Even the highly regarded critique of Clark Kerr, formerly head of the Carnegie Foundation, which set the parameters of (30) academic debate around the evolution of the so-called "multiversity," failed to take account of this phenomenon.

Taken together the attrition rate (from known and unknown causes) was 48 percent, but the figure for regular students was 36 percent while for Open Admissions categories it was 56 percent. The most important statistics, however, relate to

(35) the findings regarding Open Admissions students, and these indicated as a projection that perhaps as many as 70 percent would not graduate from a unit of the City University.

15. The academic debate mentioned in line 30 concerning the role of the so-called "multiversity" did not consider which of the following?

(A) Student unrest
(B) Social problems
(C) Community college enrollments
(D) Open admissions
(E) Community service

16. According to the passage, the purpose of American higher education in the past was *not* to

(A) advance learning
(B) solve societal problems
(C) impart knowledge
(D) provide useful knowledge
(E) prepare future managers

17. According to the author, one of the recent, important changes in higher education is

(A) student representation on college boards
(B) faculty tenure requirements
(C) curriculum updates
(D) service-education concepts
(E) cost constraints

18. According to the passage, American secondary education

(A) is geared to help solve social problems
(B) has become more useful in the long run
(C) has a relatively low attrition rate
(D) is known for its emphasis on vocational skills
(E) pioneered distance learning

19. The <u>government's failing to keep it's pledges</u> will earn the distrust of all the other nations in the alliance.

(A) government's failing to keep it's pledges
(B) government failing to keep it's pledges
(C) government's failing to keep its pledges
(D) government failing to keep its pledges
(E) governments failing to keep their pledges

20. Most students like to read <u>these kind of books</u> during their spare time.

(A) these kind of books
(B) these kind of book
(C) this kind of book
(D) this kinds of books
(E) those kind of books

21. In the normal course of events, <u>John will graduate high school and enter</u> college in two years.

(A) John will graduate high school and enter
(B) John will graduate from high school and enter
(C) John will be graduated from high school and enter
(D) John will be graduated from high school and enter into
(E) John will have graduated high school and enter

22. The daily journey from his home to his office takes John Bond on average an hour and 35 minutes by car. A friend has told him of a different route that is longer in mileage, but will only take an hour and a quarter on average, because it contains stretches of roads where it is possible to drive at higher speeds.

   John Bond's only consideration apart from the time factor is the cost, and he calculates that his car will consume 10% less gasoline if he takes the suggested new route. John decides to take the new route for the next two weeks as an experiment.

If the above were the only other considerations, which one of the following may have an effect on the decision John has made?

(A) Major road work is begun on the shorter (in distance) route, which holds up traffic for an extra 10 minutes. The project will take six months, but after it, the improvements will allow the journey to be made in half an hour less than at present.
(B) There is to be a strike at local gas stations and the amount of gasoline drivers may purchase may be rationed.
(C) John finds a third route that is slightly longer than his old route, but shorter than the suggested route.
(D) The old route passes the door of a work colleague, who without a ride, would have to go to work by bus.
(E) None of the above.

23. This year the Consumer Price Index, a measure of inflation, was 6 percent, while last year it was only 4 percent. Analysts conclude from these figures that inflation is on an upward trend and we can expect that it will be even higher next year.

Which of the following statements, if true, could most weaken the analysts' prediction?

(A) Inflation in other countries with similar economies is not predicted to increase in the future.
(B) The price of natural gas, a major component of the Consumer Price Index, rose by 8 percent year this year, owing to a temporary decrease in its supply.
(C) Increases in inflation can be predicted on the basis of two years' experience.
(D) The cost of production of most products has increased over the last five years.
(E) The ability of labor unions to force employers to increase wages has been a recurring phenomenon.

24. Although the Internet is a vital source of information, research has shown that headquarters executives of global companies obtain as much as two-thirds of the information about competitors they need from personal sources. Headquarters executives generally acknowledge that company managers overseas are the people who know best what is going on in their areas. Therefore, they are the best source of information needed for strategic planning.

Which of the following, if true, would weaken the above conclusion?

(A) In many global companies, both personal sources of information and the Internet are used.
(B) In many global companies, one-third of the information collected comes from personal sources.
(C) Strategic planning requires collecting information about all aspects of the market including consumer behavior.
(D) Overseas company managers only collect information relevant to their local operations.
(E) It is difficult to judge the accuracy of information available on the Internet.

Questions 25–30 are based on the following passage.

For those of a certain age and educational background, it is hard to think of higher education without thinking of ancient institutions. Some universities are a venerable age—the University of Bologna was founded in 1088 and Oxford University in
Line 1096—and many of them have a strong sense of tradition. The truly old ones make
(5) the most of their pedigrees, and those of a more recent vintage work hard to create an aura of antiquity.

And yet these tradition-loving (or -creating) institutions are currently ending a thunderstorm of changes so fundamental that some say the very idea of the university is being challenged. Universities are experimenting with new ways of funding
(10) (most notably through student fees), forging partnerships with private companies, and engaging in mergers and acquisitions. Such changes are tugging at the ivy's roots.

This is happening for four reasons. The first is the democratization of higher education—"massification," in the language of the educational profession. In the rich world, massification has been going on for some time. The proportion of adults with
(15) higher educational qualifications in the OECD countries almost doubled between 1975 and 2000, from 22 percent to 41 percent. But most of the rich countries are still struggling to digest this huge growth in numbers. And now massification is spreading to the developing world. China doubled its student population in the late 1990s, and India is trying to follow suit.

(20) The second reason is the rise of the knowledge economy. The world is in the grips of a "soft revolution" in which knowledge is replacing physical resources as the main driver of economic growth. The OECD calculates that between 1985 and 1997, the contribution of knowledge-based industries to total value added increased from 51 percent to 59 percent in Germany and from 45 percent to 51 percent in Britain. The
(25) best companies are now devoting at least a third of their investment to knowledge-intensive intangibles, such as R&D, licensing, and marketing. Universities are among the most important engines of the knowledge economy. Not only do they produce the brain workers who man it, they also provide much of its backbone, from laboratories to libraries to computer networks.

(30) The third factor is globalization. The death of distance is transforming academia just as radically as it is transforming business. The number of people from OECD countries studying abroad has doubled over the past 20 years, to 1.9 million; universities are opening campuses all around the world; and a growing number of countries are trying to turn higher education into an export industry.

(35) The fourth is competition. Traditional universities are being forced to compete for students and research grants, and private companies are trying to break into a sector that they regard as "the new health care." The World Bank calculates that global spending on higher education amounts to $300 billion a year, or 1 percent of global economic output. There are more than 80 million students worldwide, and 3.5 mil-
(40) lion people are employed to teach them or look after them.

25. Changes in tradition-oriented universities' education are caused by

   (A) increased enrollments
   (B) globalization
   (C) online education
   (D) more qualified students
   (E) lack of resources

26. The best possible title for the passage is

   (A) *Massification*
   (B) *The Business of Education*
   (C) *The Decline of Tradition-Loving Universities*
   (D) *Downfall of Academic Dogma*
   (E) *Globalization of Higher Education*

27. The passage suggests that mass higher education is forcing universities to become

    (A) more democractic
    (B) better managed
    (C) more liberal
    (D) more teaching oriented
    (E) more competitive

28. According to the passage, younger universities try to

    (A) compete with older ones
    (B) create an image like that of more traditional universities
    (C) diversify their student bodies
    (D) rely less on outside financing
    (E) diversify income sources

29. The author states that universities react to the challenges facing them by

    (A) making curriculum more relevant to societal needs
    (B) entering alliances in order to survive
    (C) creating distance learning programs
    (D) encouraging donations from the public
    (E) becoming more democratic

30. The passage states that in business terms, higher education has become

    (A) more profitable
    (B) an export industry
    (C) better managed
    (D) bottom-line oriented
    (E) customer oriented

31. The owners of a local supermarket have decided to make use of three now-redundant checkout counters. They believe that they will attract those customers who lately have been put off by the long checkout lines during the mid-morning and evening rush hours. The owners have concluded that in order to be successful, the increased revenue from existing and added counters will have to be more than the increase in maintenance costs for the added counters.

The underlying goal of the owners can be summarized thus:

    (A) To improve services to all customers.
    (B) To attract people who have never been to the store.
    (C) To make use of the redundant counters.
    (D) To keep maintenance costs on the added counters as low as possible.
    (E) To increase monthly profits.

32. The cost of housing in many parts of the United States has become so excessive that many young couples, with above-average salaries, can only afford small apartments. Mortgage commitments are so huge that they cannot consider the possibility of starting a family. A new baby would probably mean either the mother or father giving up a well-paid position. The lack of or great cost of child-care facilities precludes the return of both parents to work.

Which of the following adjustments could practically be made to the situation described above that would allow young couples to improve their housing prospects?

(A) Encourage couples to remain childless.
(B) Encourage couples to have one child only.
(C) Encourage couples to postpone starting their families until a later age than previously acceptable to society.
(D) Encourage young couples to move to cheaper areas of the United States.
(E) Encourage fathers to remain at home while mothers return to work.

33. With the exception of Frank and I, everyone in the class finished the assignment before the bell rang.

(A) Frank and I, everyone in the class finished
(B) Frank and me, everyone in the class finished
(C) Frank and me, everyone in the class had finished
(D) Frank and I, everyone in the class had finished
(E) Frank and me everyone in the class finished

34. Many middle-class individuals find that they cannot obtain good medical attention, despite they need it badly.

(A) despite they need it badly
(B) despite they badly need it
(C) in spite of they need it badly
(D) however much they need it
(E) therefore, they need it badly

35. Unless new reserves are found soon, the world's supply of coal is being depleted in such a way that with demand continuing to grow at present rates, reserves will be exhausted by the year 2050.

Which of the following, if true, will most weaken the above argument?

(A) There has been a slowdown in the rate of increase in world demand for coal over the last 5 years from 10% to 5%.
(B) It has been known for many years that there are vast stocks of coal under Antarctica that have yet to be economically exploited.
(C) Oil is being used increasingly in place of coal for many industrial and domestic uses.
(D) As coal resources are depleted, more and more marginal supplies, which are more costly to produce and less efficient in use, are being mined.
(E) None of the above.

36. In accordance with their powers, many state authorities are introducing fluoridation of drinking water. This follows the conclusion of 10 years of research that the process ensures that children and adults receive the required intake of fluoride that will strengthen teeth. The maximum level has been set at one part per million. However, there are many who object, claiming that fluoridation removes freedom of choice.

Which of the following will best weaken the claim of the proponents of fluoridation?

(A) Fluoridation over a certain prescribed level has been shown to lead to a general weakening of teeth.
(B) There is no record of the long-term effects of drinking fluoridated water.
(C) The people to be affected by fluoridation claim that they have not had sufficient opportunity to voice their views.
(D) Fluoridation is only one part of general dental health.
(E) Water already contains natural fluoride.

37. <u>When one eats in this restaurant, you often find</u> that the prices are high and that the food is poorly prepared.

   (A) When one eats in this restaurant, you often find
   (B) When you eat in this restaurant, one often finds
   (C) As you eat in this restaurant, you often find
   (D) If you eat in this restaurant, you often find
   (E) When one ate in this restaurant, he often found

38. Ever since the bombing, there has been much opposition <u>from they who maintain that it was an unauthorized war.</u>

   (A) from they who maintain that it was an unauthorized war
   (B) from they who maintain that it had been an unauthorized war
   (C) from those who maintain that it was an unauthorized war
   (D) from they maintaining that it was unauthorized
   (E) from they maintaining that it had been unauthorized

39. <u>I am not to eager to go to this play because it did not get good reviews.</u>

   (A) I am not to eager to go to this play because it did not get good reviews.
   (B) Because of its poor reviews, I am not to eager to go to this play.
   (C) Because of its poor revues, I am not to eager to go to this play.
   (D) I am not to eager to go to this play because the critics did not give it good reviews.
   (E) I am not too eager to go to this play because of its poor reviews.

40. In 1980, global service exports totaled about $370 billion, approximately 20 percent of world trade. Still, no coherent system of rules, principles, and procedures exists to govern trade in services.

   Which of the following best summarizes the argument?

   (A) Regulatory systems lag behind reality.
   (B) A regulatory system ought to reflect the importance of service exports.
   (C) World trade totaled $1850 billion in 1980.
   (D) Service trade legislation is a veritable wasteland.
   (E) While trade legislation exists, it is uncoordinated.

41. <u>We had decided that the emphasis would be placed on the results that might</u> <u>be attained.</u>

   (A) We had decided that the emphasis would be placed on the results that might be attained.
   (B) We decided that the emphasis had been placed on the results that might be attained.
   (C) We decided to emphasize the results which we might attain.
   (D) We decided to emphasize the results that we attain.
   (E) We decided that the emphasis be placed on the results we might attain.

STOP

ON THE ACTUAL GMAT,
AFTER YOU HAVE CONFIRMED YOUR ANSWER,
YOU CANNOT RETURN TO IT.

INTEGRATED REASONING SECTION

1. i. D

ii. D

2.

Stanley and Gene Would Agree	Stanley and Gene Would NOT Agree
○	●
○	○
○	○
○	○
●	○

3.

Would Help Explain	Would Not Help Explain
●	○
○	●
○	●

4.

Yes	No
○	●
●	○
○	●

5. B

6.

Fragile Items Sent Separately from Non-fragile Items	All Items Sent via Fragile Shipping
●	○
●	○
●	○

7.

Total Number of Possible Project Teams	Total Number of Ways to Rank Employees
○	○
●	○
○	○
○	○
○	●

8. i. C

ii. A

9.

True	False
●	○
○	●
○	○
○	●

10. i. A

ii. C

11.

True	False
●	○
●	○
○	●

12.

Time for All Three to Fill the Pool Together	Time it Will Take for Karen to Fill Half of the Pool
○	●
●	○
○	○
○	○
○	○

ANSWER KEY
Sample Test 3

QUANTITATIVE SECTION

1.	C	11.	D	21.	B	31.	C
2.	D	12.	B	22.	C	32.	D
3.	B	13.	A	23.	B	33.	B
4.	E	14.	B	24.	D	34.	D
5.	C	15.	D	25.	A	35.	C
6.	B	16.	A	26.	E	36.	E
7.	C	17.	C	27.	B	37.	A
8.	D	18.	B	28.	E		
9.	A	19.	E	29.	C		
10.	B	20.	C	30.	A		

VERBAL SECTION

1.	C	12.	A	23.	B	34.	D
2.	C	13.	C	24.	C	35.	E
3.	C	14.	C	25.	B	36.	B
4.	C	15.	E	26.	B	37.	C
5.	D	16.	B	27.	E	38.	C
6.	C	17.	D	28.	B	39.	E
7.	D	18.	B	29.	B	40.	B
8.	E	19.	C	30.	B	41.	E
9.	E	20.	C	31.	E		
10.	A	21.	B	32.	C		
11.	B	22.	C	33.	C		

SELF-SCORING GUIDE
Analytical Writing

Evaluate your essay (or have a friend or teacher evaluate it for you) on the following basis. Read your essay completely, paying special attention to its logical organization and use of examples and facts to buttress its claims or position. Assign a holistic score between 0 and 6, using the scale below.

6 OUTSTANDING

Cogent, well-articulated analysis of the issue or critique of the argument. Develops a position with insightful reasons and persuasive examples. Well organized. Superior command of language and variety of syntax. Only minor flaws in grammar, usage, and mechanics.

5 STRONG

Well-developed analysis or critique. Develops a position with well-chosen examples or reasons. Generally well organized. Clear control of language and variety of syntax. Minor flaws in grammar, usage, and mechanics.

4 ADEQUATE

Competent analysis or critique. Develops a position with relevant reasons or examples. Adequately organized. Adequate control of language, but may lack syntactic variety. May have some flaws in grammar, usage, and mechanics.

3 LIMITED

Competent but clearly flawed analysis or critique. Vague or limited in developing a position. Poorly organized. Weak in using relevant examples or reasons. Language used imprecisely or lacking in sentence variety. Contains major errors or frequent minor errors in grammar, usage, and mechanics.

2 SERIOUSLY FLAWED

Serious weaknesses in analysis and organization. Unclear or seriously limited in presenting or developing a position. Disorganized. Few relevant examples or reasons. Frequent serious problems in language and sentence structure. Numerous errors in grammar, usage, or mechanics that interfere with meaning.

1 FUNDAMENTALLY DEFICIENT

Little evidence of ability to organize and develop a coherent response to issue or argument. Severe and persistent errors in language and sentence structure. Pervasive pattern of errors in grammar, usage, and mechanics that severely interfere with meaning.

0 UNSCORABLE

Illegible or not written on the assigned topic.

ANSWERS EXPLAINED

Integrated Reasoning Section

1. **i. (D)** The share percentage increase can be quickly found by taking the 2004 results and dividing by the 2003 results. At a quick glance, you should see that you should focus on Moto Guzzi and on Triumph. If you look at Moto Guzzi, the change in share is 0.8, which is more than 10% of its 2003 share of 7.0. Similarly, Triumph's share increase of 0.2 is 10% more than its 2003 share of 1.5.

$$0.8 \div 7.0 = 0.114$$
$$0.2 \div 1.5 = 0.133$$

Triumph has the largest percentage share increase. Therefore, the answer is **D**.

ii. (D) The growth of the market is 10.1%. Most test takers will see that only Triumph and Moto Guzzi have share growth above 10.1%. However, share growth is not the same thing as revenue growth. There is no way to know the revenue growths of the companies. Therefore, the answer is **D**.

2. **(Statement 5, Statement 1)**

The scope of this question is the aging population. The two friends discuss a variety of topics: population decline and growth, climates, cost of living, finances, and government action. However, you need to notice exactly how Gene is responding to Stanley's argument. Stanley's main point is that the elderly do not like bad climates and thus would move to coastal regions, which have better climates for them. Stanley brings up the financial aspect as the key influencer for where the elderly choose to live.

Statement 1 is essentially Stanley's argument, with which Gene disagrees. Therefore, it is the point on which both parties disagree.

Statement 2 is not helpful because it suggests that the shift to coastal areas is due to economic reasons. This topic is not argued by either Stanley or Gene.

Statement 3 is incorrect because the conversation offers no proof that coastal regions are affordable for the elderly.

Statement 4 is wrong because there is no mention that the "extreme temperatures" are either hot or cold. This is a good example of how we need to keep our assumptions from influencing our answers.

Statement 5 is correct because both Stanley and Gene say that the aging population is an "important" or the "biggest" issue.

Stanley and Gene would agree on **Statement 5**. Stanley and Gene would disagree about **Statement 1**.

3. **(Would help explain, Would not help explain, Would not help explain)**

(i) If you sort the table by box office gross, the top six either feature more than one performer or is a band. If you sort the table by average ticket price, you will see that most of the top prices are for groups, orchestras, or bands. Therefore, the answer is **would help explain**.

(ii) This question is tricky. The table does not give enough information on what is defined as a "live theater industry" show. Is Cirque du Soleil part of this or not? What about the comedy show? You do have information about the top three classical music concerts but not about the entire industry. Therefore, you do not have sufficient information. The answer is **would not help explain**.

(iii) You can sort either by average ticket price or by performance type. Sorting by performance type is probably easier. A quick glance of the country music concert ticket prices shows a range between $35 and $53. If you look at the rock concerts, Bob Seger's concert had an average ticket price of $73.39, which is higher than the range of country music ticket prices. Therefore, the answer is **would not help explain**.

4. (No, Yes, No)

(i) Estimate the total gross sales for Cirque du Soleil and for the country music concerts.

Cirque du Soleil: $1.1 million + $0.9 million + $2.3 million = $4.3 million
Country music: $250K + $600K + $300K + $300K + $350K + $600K = $2.4 million

The estimated $2.4 million for country music is over half of Cirque du Soleil's estimated box office receipts of $4.3 million. Therefore, the answer is **no**.

(ii) To find the median average ticket price, just sort by the "average ticket price" column and look for the two middle numbers. The table lists even number of concerts, so you need to take the average of the two middle numbers. The median is approximately $50. Now sort by the "show type" column to see the ticket prices for rock concerts. Only one value is above $50, but this is offset by the $11 "Winter Jam" ticket price. The rest would clearly bring the average well below $50. Therefore, the answer is **yes**.

(iii) This question requires you to look at two columns together—"average box office gross per city" and "average ticket price"—and then divide to calculate the audience size. There are too many values for you to calculate the audience size of each concert, so you need to use some insight here. Remember that GMAT math is meant to be quite clean, so there will be some obvious possible answers.

First you should sort by box office gross. The first thing you should look at is Salute to Vienna since the question directed you there already. It is at the bottom of the list but it has a very high ticket price. Use ballpark numbers to calculate the number of people in the audience.

$$\$132,000 \div \$79 = 1,670$$

The only other obvious candidate is Mannheim Steamroller, but it has a larger gross and smaller ticket price. At this point, you can stop. However, if you are still not sure, you can do a check of a country music concert and one of the top five shows. You will find that they are not even close. Salute to Vienna does indeed have the smallest audience, therefore the answer is **no**.

5. (B)
First look at the questions, as they are clearly computationally demanding. For quantitative multisource reasoning questions, such as question 5, it's a good idea to sort your information in a chart. Be sure to use simple numbers.

	Standard	Energy	Exotic	Signature	Combo
Cost	$15	$25	$40	$60	$150
Size (mL)	1,800	4,000	1,200	500	7,500
Regular shipping*	$50 + $0.10/mL				
Fragile shipping	$80 + $0.15/mL				
Express shipping	$100 extra				

*Note: Only standard can have regular shipping.

Use the chart to break these calculations down easily.

Ten standard packs: $(10 \times \$15) + \$50 + (\$0.10 \times 1{,}800 \times 10) = \$2{,}000$

Four signatures blends: $(4 \times \$60) + \$80 + (\$0.15 \times 500 \times 4) = \$620$

At this point, you can stop since there can be only one correct answer. Additionally, if you look at the chart above, the sheer size of the combo pack will increase the cost significantly. Therefore, the answer is **B**.

6. **(Ship separately, Ship separately, Ship Separately)**

	Standard	Energy	Exotic	Signature	Combo
Cost	15	25	40	60	150
Size (mL)	1,800	4,000	1,200	500	7,500
Regular shipping*	$50 + $0.10/mL				
Fragile shipping	$80 + $0.15/mL				
Express shipping	$100 extra				

*Note: Only standard can have regular shipping.

(i) This question looks very time consuming. Therefore, you should think of a shortcut to answer it. The real question here is if the separated regular shipping is more costly than shipping the entire order via fragile shipping. For the first example, you should look at the cost of just the order with regular shipping.

$$5 \text{ standard: } (5 \times \$15) + \$50 + (5 \times 1{,}800 \times \$0.10) = \$1{,}025$$

If you were to include the standard order in the fragile shipping of the energy order, the incremental cost would increase by $0.05/mL and would decrease by $50 for the upfront shipping cost that you would no longer be paying. So if the cost of $0.05/mL is greater than $50, then you should stick with the separated shipping.

$$\$0.05 \times 5 \times 1{,}800 = \$450$$

This is way too much, therefore you should **ship separately**.

(ii) The second statement has 10 standard orders. The incremental cost for shipping via fragile shipping will again be greater. Therefore, you should **ship separately**.

(iii) The third statement has 15 standard orders. Again, the incremental cost for shipping via fragile shipping will be greater. Therefore, you should **ship separately**.

7. $(\frac{8!}{(5!3!)} - \frac{6!}{(3!3!)}, 8!)$

Despite all the text, this is a quantitative combination problem. Here is what you know for each problem.

(i) Total number of possible project teams:

- Need to create a team of 5 people (K)
- There are 8 candidates (N)
- Order does not matter, so it's a combination (not a permutation) problem
- 2 people do not want to be on the same team

The best way to set this up is first calculate the number of ways to create a team of 5 from 8 with no constraint and then subtract the number of ways that violate the constraint.

Total number of ways without constraint: $_NC_K = _8C_5 = \dfrac{8!}{(5!3!)}$

To find the total number of ways with the constraint, put the couple on the team. There are now 2 people on the team, leaving you to fill 3 spots using 6 people.

Total number of ways with constraint: $_NC_K = _6C_3 = \dfrac{6!}{(3!3!)}$

The total number of possible project teams is the difference, $_8C_5 - _6C_3 = \dfrac{8!}{(5!3!)} - \dfrac{6!}{(3!3!)}$

(ii) Total number of ways to rank the employees (ignoring office politics):

- Need to rank 8 people
- Order matters
- There is no selection

This is a simple form of calculating an arrangement. The total number of ways to rank the employees is **8!**

8. **i. (C)** The graph indicates that the average length of the four movies from the latter portion of the 1990s is approximately 150 minutes. Because the y-axis has intervals of 50, the best you can estimate is half of that interval, which is 25. The movies from the 2000s are mostly a little bit above or a little bit below the midway mark between 100 and 150. Therefore, you can estimate their average length to be approximately 125 minutes. The difference in average length is approximately 25 minutes. The correct answer is **C**.

ii. (A) Choice B is not possible since there are three Best Picture movies longer than 150 minutes.

Choice C is wrong because you cannot say for certain that a movie released in December won't win the Best Picture award. You can only extrapolate a possibility. Choice D is wrong because no information is provided that suggests that lower budgets are an issue.

The graph shows a definite trend toward both shorter films and an earlier release month. Therefore, the correct answer is **A**.

9. **(True, False, True, False)**

Before you attempt to answer, you should identify the scope or basic gist of each question. This is an e-mail exchange between a buyer and seller of a yacht. The two people are trying to negotiate on price, but there are other aspects to consider, including lessons, time of purchase, condition of the boat, and customer service.

(i) You need to infer based on the passages. Herb is the primary communicator to the seller. He has also mentioned that this boat is a "gift" for his retirement, not his wife's. Although he does refer to trying to convince his wife, he is clearly the primary influencer and purchaser. Therefore, the answer is **true**.

(ii) Herb has inferred that his timeline is not as aggressive as Frank's. You also know that Frank has offered an incentive for completing the sale within two weeks. Finally, if you note the time stamps on the e-mails, Frank has sent both his responses within an hour of his last communication with Herb. Herb, on the other hand, responds in a couple of days. You can deduce that Frank, not Herb, is more anxious to complete the transaction. Therefore, the answer is **false**.

(iii) Based on the information, Herb's highest purchase price is 15% greater than $90,000, which is $103,500. Frank's lowest price is 10% less than $120,000, which is $108,000. The two men are only $4,500 apart. Herb's tone in his last e-mail suggests he is very tempted to agree based on key phrases such as "truly," "only hesitation is the time rush," and "pretty decent." He is also implying that his kids could use the boat over the summer, which means he is now thinking about buying the boat well before July. Herb's wife Peggy, who "needs a bit more convincing," is willing to admit that the paint job adds $5,000 to the value. Finally, the couple likely appreciates the $1,500 value of the lessons since they have mentioned they are "newbies" at yachting. Therefore, you can deduce from the statement and the rest of the e-mails that Herb will accept. The answer is **true**.

(iv) Herb has mentioned that "cost is a big issue." He has also shifted his position closer to accepting Frank's latest offer. From this you can infer that the final price is not more important than Herb taking his time to decide whether or not to purchase the boat. Therefore, the answer is **false**.

10. i. (A) This is a bubble graph, which is usually used to track three different things. In this case, it is plotting GMAT median scores, average starting salaries, and school reputation.

As the median GMAT increases, so does the average starting salary. Therefore, this is a positive relationship. The correct choice is **A**.

ii. (C) Michigan has a low starting salary and low median GMAT, yet it has a strong reputation. Therefore, you can say the statement is false. Second, another key word in the statement is "all." The graph charts several schools, not all of them. You may be inclined to select D. However, given the statement as is, it is false. The correct choice is **C**.

11. (True, True, False)

(i) If you sort the table by visiting tourists, a large majority of the top tourist destinations are in Europe (except for the U.S.). Therefore, the answer is **true**.

(ii) First sort the table by population. Then look at the number of theaters in the top five most populated countries. Use ballpark numbers to estimate

$$6.4K + 0.8K + 0.6K + 0.8K + 1.9K = 10,500 \text{ theaters}$$

For the rest of the countries, you can estimate about 5,400 theaters. The top five populated countries have less than double the theaters of the rest of the countries combined. Therefore, the answer is **true**.

(iii) First sort the table by tourists per population ratio. Note that the top five countries are Spain, Italy, Canada, U.K., and Turkey. Now sort the number of people per theater. Check if any of the countries stay in the top five. You should see that Turkey is still there. Therefore, the answer is **false**.

12. $\left(\dfrac{xyz}{(yz + xz + xy)}, \dfrac{z}{2}\right)$

(i) This is a rate problem. The standard formula for solving this type of rate problem is the following.

$$\frac{1}{A} + \frac{1}{B} = \frac{1}{\text{Duo}}$$

The term A is the amount of time needed for person A to do a task. The term B is the amount of time needed for person B to do that same task. The word duo is the time needed for persons A and B to work together to do that same task. This formula is cumulative. That means if a third person is added, another term can be added to the equation.

$$\frac{1}{A} + \frac{1}{B} + \frac{1}{C} = \frac{1}{\text{Trio}}$$

If you input the variables given in the question, you get the following.

$$\frac{1}{x} + \frac{1}{y} + \frac{1}{z} = \frac{1}{\text{Trio}}$$

To solve this equation, find a common denominator for the three fractions on the left.

$$\frac{(yz + xz + xy)}{xyz} = \frac{1}{\text{Trio}}$$

Therefore, the time all three take to fill the pool is the inverse, $\dfrac{xyz}{(yz + xz + xy)}$.

(ii) Once the pool is half full, only half a pool is left to fill. The time Karen takes to fill the rest of the pool by herself is simply the time she takes to fill the entire pool divided by 2.

The time for Karen to fill half the pool is $\dfrac{z}{2}$.

Quantitative Section

(Roman numerals at the end of each answer refer to the section of Chapter 9 in which the appropriate math principle is discussed.)

1. Water has been poured into an empty rectangular tank at the rate of 5 cubic feet per minute for 6 minutes. The length of the tank is 4 feet and the width is $\frac{1}{2}$ of the length.

How deep is the water in the tank?

(A) 7.5 inches
(B) 3 feet 7.5 inches
(C) 3 feet 9 inches
(D) 7 feet 6 inches
(E) 30 feet

(C) The volume of water that has been poured into the tank is 5 cubic feet per minute for 6 minutes, or 30 cubic feet. The tank is rectangular, so its volume is length times width times height, with the answer in cubic units. The width is $\frac{1}{2}$ the length, or $\frac{1}{2}$ of 4 feet, which is 2 feet. The volume, which we already know is 30 cubic feet, is, therefore, 4 feet × 2 feet × the height. The height (depth of the water in the tank) is, therefore, $\frac{30}{8} = 3\frac{3}{4}$ feet = 3 feet 9 inches. (III-8)   ★★☆

2. If x, y, z are chosen from the three numbers -3, $\frac{1}{2}$, and 2, what is the largest possible value of the expression $\left(\frac{x}{y}\right)z^2$?

(A) $-\frac{3}{8}$
(B) 16
(C) 24
(D) 36
(E) 54

(D) Since -3 has the largest absolute value of the three given numbers, using z as -3 will make z^2 as large as possible. Since $\frac{x}{y}$ is a quotient, to make it as large as possible use the smallest positive number for y and the largest positive number for x. So if you use $x = 2$ and $y = \frac{1}{2}$, then $\frac{x}{y}$ is as large as possible. Therefore, the largest value of the expression is $\frac{2}{\frac{1}{2}}(-3)^2 = 4(9) = 36$. (I-2).   ★★★

★★★ **3.** A survey of n people found that 60 percent preferred brand A. An additional x people were surveyed who all preferred brand A. Seventy percent of all the people surveyed preferred brand A. Find x in terms of n.

(A) $\dfrac{n}{6}$

(B) $\dfrac{n}{3}$

(C) $\dfrac{n}{2}$

(D) n

(E) $3n$

(B) The total number of people surveyed was $n + x$. Since 70 percent of the total preferred brand A, that means $.7(n + x)$ preferred brand A. However, 60 percent of the n people and all of the x people preferred brand A. So $.6n + x$ preferred brand A. Therefore, $.7(n + x)$ must equal $.6n + x$. So we have $.7n + .7x = .6n + x$. Solving for x gives $0.1n = 0.3x$ or $x = \dfrac{n}{3}$. (I-4)

★★☆ **4.** Is x greater than y?

(1) $3x = 2k$

(2) $k = y^2$

(E) Since STATEMENT (1) describes only x and STATEMENT (2) describes only y, both are needed to get an answer. Using STATEMENT (2), STATEMENT (1) becomes $3x = 2k = 2y^2$, so $x = \dfrac{2}{3}y^2$. However, this is not sufficient since if $y = -1$, then $x = \dfrac{2}{3}$ and x is greater than y, but if $y = 1$, then again $x = \dfrac{2}{3}$ but now x is less than y.

Therefore, STATEMENTS (1) and (2) together are not sufficient. (II-7)

★★☆ **5.** Is $ABCD$ a parallelogram?

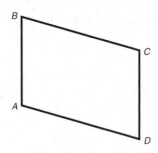

(1) $AB = CD$

(2) AB is parallel to CD

(C) $ABCD$ is a parallelogram if AB is parallel to CD and BC is parallel to AD. STATEMENT (2) tells you that AB is parallel to CD, but this is not sufficient since a trapezoid has only one pair of opposite sides parallel. Thus, STATEMENT (2) alone is not sufficient.

STATEMENT (1) alone is not sufficient since a trapezoid can have the two nonparallel sides equal.

However, using STATEMENTS (1) and (2) together we can deduce that BC is parallel to AD since the distance from BC to AD is equal along two different parallel lines. (III-5)

6. The hexagon *ABCDEF* is regular. That means all its sides are the same length and all its interior angles are the same size. Each side of the hexagon is 2 feet. What is the area of the rectangle *BCEF*?

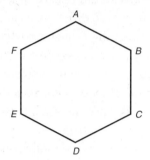

(A) 4 square feet

(B) $4\sqrt{3}$ square feet

(C) 8 square feet

(D) $4 + 4\sqrt{3}$ square feet

(E) 12 square feet

(B) A diagram always helps. You are given that *BC* and *EF* are each 2 feet. Since the area of a rectangle is length times width, you must find the length (*CE* or *BF*). Look at the triangle *ABF*. It has two equal sides (*AB* = *AF*), so the perpendicular from *A* to the line *BF* divides *ABF* into two congruent right triangles, *AHF* and *AHB*, each with hypotenuse 2.

★ ★ ★

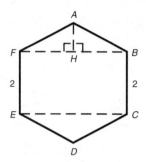

The angle *FAB* is 120° since the total of all the angles of the hexagon is 720°. So each of the two triangles is a 30° – 60° – 90° right triangle with hypotenuse 2. So *AH* = 1, and *FH* and *HB* must equal $\sqrt{3}$. Therefore, *BF* is $2\sqrt{3}$ and the area is $2 \times 2\sqrt{3} = 4\sqrt{3}$ square feet.

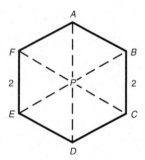

(You can find the sum of the angles of any convex polygon by connecting all vertices to a fixed interior point, *P*. In the case of the hexagon this will give 6 triangles. The total of all the triangles' angles is $6 \times 180° = 1,080°$. Since the angles at the fixed point, which are not part of the hexagon angles, will add up to 360°, the sum of the hexagon's angles is $1,080° - 360° = 720°$.) (III-3, III-4)

★★★ **7.** In Motor City 90 percent of the population own a car, 15 percent own a motorcycle, and everybody owns one or the other or both. What is the percentage of motorcycle owners who own cars?

(A) 5%

(B) 15%

(C) $33\frac{1}{3}$%

(D) 50%

(E) 90%

(C) You want the ratio of the percentage who own both a car and a motorcycle to the percentage who own a motorcycle. You know that 15 percent own a motorcycle, so you need to find the percentage who own both a car and a motorcycle. Let A stand for the percentage who own both a car and a motorcycle. Then (the percentage who own a car) plus (the percentage who own a motorcycle) minus A must equal the percentage who own one or the other or both. Since 100 percent own one or the other or both, we obtain $90\% + 15\% - A = 105\% - A = 100\%$. So $A = 5\%$. Since 15 percent own motorcycles, the percentage of motorcycle owners who own cars is $\frac{5\%}{15\%} = \frac{1}{3} = 33\frac{1}{3}\%$. (II-4)

★★★ **8.** Jim's weight is 140 percent of Marcia's weight. Bob's weight is 90 percent of Lee's weight. Lee weighs twice as much as Marcia. What percentage of Jim's weight is Bob's weight?

(A) $64\frac{2}{7}$

(B) $77\frac{7}{9}$

(C) 90

(D) $128\frac{4}{7}$

(E) $155\frac{5}{9}$

(D) To do computations, change percentages to decimals. Let J, M, B, and L stand for Jim's, Marcia's, Bob's, and Lee's respective weights. Then we know $J = 1.4M$, $B = .9L$, and $L = 2M$. We need to know B as a percentage of J. Since $B = .9L$ and $L = 2M$, we have $B = .9(2M) = 1.8M$. $J = 1.4M$ is equivalent to $M = \left(\frac{1}{1.4}\right)J$. So $B = 1.8M = 1.8\left(\frac{1}{1.4}\right)J = \left(\frac{9}{7}\right)J$. Converting to a percentage, we have $\frac{9}{7} = 1.28\left(\frac{4}{7}\right) = 128\frac{4}{7}\%$, so (D) is the correct answer. (Once you know $B = \frac{9}{7}J$, this means the correct answer must be greater than 100 percent so you should guess (D) or (E) if you can't finish the problem.) (I-4, II-2)

9. What is the two-digit number whose first digit is a and whose second digit is b? The number is greater than 9.

(1) $2a + 3b = 11a + 2b$

(2) The two-digit number is a multiple of 19.

(A) Two-digit numbers are the integers from 10 to 99. Since you are told that the number is greater than 9, the only possible choices are integers 10, 11, . . ., 99. ★★★

STATEMENT (1) alone is sufficient since (1) is equivalent to $9a = b$. In this case if a is greater than 1, then $9a$ is not a digit, and if a is 0, then the number is not greater than 9. Thus there is only one possible choice, $a = 1$, which yields the number 19, which satisfies (1).

STATEMENT (2) alone is not sufficient since 19, 38, 57, 76, and 95 satisfy (2) and are two-digit numbers greater than 9.

So (A) is the correct choice. (I-1)

---

10. A chair originally cost $50.00. The chair was offered for sale at 108 percent of its cost. After a week, the price was discounted 10 percent and the chair was sold. The chair was sold for

(A) $45.00

(B) $48.60

(C) $49.00

(D) $49.50

(E) $54.00

(B) Since 108 percent of $50 = (1.08)(50) = $54, the chair was offered for sale at $54.00. It was sold for 90 percent of $54 since there was a 10 percent discount. Therefore, the chair was sold for (.9)($54) or $48.60. (I-4) ★★☆

---

11. k is a positive integer. Is k a prime number?

(1) No integer between 2 and $\sqrt{k}$, inclusive, divides k evenly.

(2) No integer between 2 and $\dfrac{k}{2}$, inclusive, divides k evenly, and k is greater than 5.

(D) k is a prime if none of the integers 2, 3, 4, . . . up to $k - 1$ divide k evenly. STATEMENT (1) alone is sufficient since if k is not a prime, then $k = (m)(n)$, where m and n must be integers less than k. But this means either m or n must be less than or equal to $\sqrt{k}$ since if m and n are both larger than $\sqrt{k}$, $(m)(n)$ is larger than $\left(\sqrt{k}\right)\left(\sqrt{k}\right)$ or k. So STATEMENT (1) implies k is a prime. ★★☆

STATEMENT (2) alone is also sufficient since if $k = (m)(n)$ and m and n are both larger than $\dfrac{k}{2}$, then $(m)(n)$ is greater than $\dfrac{k^2}{4}$, but $\dfrac{k^2}{4}$ is greater than k when k is larger than 5. Therefore, if no integer between 2 and $\dfrac{k}{2}$, inclusive, divides k evenly, then k is a prime. (I-1)

★★☆ **12.** Towns *A* and *C* are connected by a straight highway that is 60 miles long. The straight-line distance between town *A* and town *B* is 50 miles, and the straight-line distance from town *B* to town *C* is 50 miles. How many miles is it from town *B* to the point on the highway connecting towns *A* and *C* that is closest to town *B*?

(A) 30

(B) 40

(C) $30\sqrt{2}$

(D) 50

(E) 60

(B) The towns can be thought of as the vertices of a triangle.

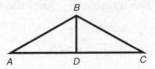

Since the distance from *A* to *B* is equal to the distance from *B* to *C*, the triangle is isosceles. The point *D* on *AC* that is closest to *B* is the point on *AC* such that *BD* is perpendicular to *AC*. (If *BD* were not perpendicular to *AC*, then there would be a point on *AC* closer to *B* than *D*; in the diagram, *E* is closer to *B* than *D* is.)

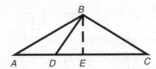

So the triangles *ABD* and *CBD* are right triangles with two corresponding sides equal. Therefore, *ABD* is congruent to *CBD*. Thus, *AD* = *DC*, and since *AC* is 60, *AD* must be 30. Since *ABD* is a right triangle with hypotenuse 50 and another side equal to 30, the remaining side (*BD*) must be 40. (III-4)

	Mon.	Tues.	Wed.	Thurs.	Fri.	Wages for week
Hours worked	8	8	8	8	8	$5x$
Excess worked over 8 hr	0	3	1	2	1	$(0+3+1+2+1)y = 7y$

★★☆ **13.** A worker is paid *x* dollars for the first 8 hours he works each day. He is paid *y* dollars per hour for each hour he works in excess of 8 hours. During one week he works 8 hours on Monday, 11 hours on Tuesday, 9 hours on Wednesday, 10 hours on Thursday, and 9 hours on Friday. What is his average daily wage in dollars for the 5-day week?

(A) $x + 1.4y$

(B) $2x + y$

(C) $\dfrac{(5x + 8y)}{5}$

(D) $8x + 1.4y$

(E) $5x + 7y$

(A) Here's a table of the hours worked:

The average daily wage equals $\dfrac{(5x+7y)}{5}$ or

$x + \dfrac{7}{5}y = x + 1.4y$. (I-7, II-3).

14. A club has 8 male and 8 female members. The club is choosing a committee of 6 members. The committee must have 3 male and 3 female members. How many different committees can be chosen?

(A) 112,896
(B) 3,136
(C) 720
(D) 112
(E) 9

(B) There are 8 choices for the first female, then 7 choices for the second female, and 6 choices for the third female on the committee. So there are $8 \times 7 \times 6$ different ways to pick the 3 females in order. However, if member A is chosen first, then member B, and then member C, the same 3 females are chosen as when C is followed by A and B is chosen last. In fact, the same 3 members can be chosen in $3 \times 2 \times 1$ different orders. So to find the number of different groups of 3 females, DIVIDE $(8 \times 7 \times 6)$ by $(3 \times 2 \times 1)$ to obtain 56.

In the same way, there are $8 \times 7 \times 6 = 336$ ways to choose the 3 males in order, but any group of 3 males can be put in order $3 \times 2 \times 1 = 6$ different ways. So there are $\frac{336}{6} = 56$ different groups of 3 males.

Therefore, there are $56 \times 56 = 3{,}136$ different committees. (II-4)

★★★

15. The towns A, B, and C lie on a straight line. C is between A and B. The distance from A to B is 100 miles. How far is it from A to C?

(1) The distance from A to B is 25 percent more than the distance from C to B.

(2) The distance from A to C is $\frac{1}{4}$ of the distance from C to B.

(D) Since we are given the fact that 100 miles is the distance from A to B, it is sufficient to find the distance from C to B. This is so because 100 minus the distance from C to B is the distance from A to C. STATEMENT (1) says that 125 percent of the distance from C to B is 100 miles. Thus, we can find the distance from C to B, which is sufficient. Since the distance from A to C plus the distance from C to B is the distance from A to B, we can use STATEMENT (2) to set up the equation 5 times the distance from A to C equals 100 miles.

Therefore, STATEMENTS (1) and (2) are each sufficient. (II-3)

★★☆

★★☆ **16.** A club has 10 male and 5 female members. Each member of the club writes his/her name on a ticket, and the tickets are deposited in a box. The club chooses 2 members to go to a national meeting by drawing 2 tickets from the box. What is the probability that both members picked for the trip are female?

(A) $\dfrac{2}{21}$

(B) $\dfrac{1}{10}$

(C) $\dfrac{2}{7}$

(D) $\dfrac{5}{15}$

(E) $\dfrac{2}{5}$

(A) Each member has a $\dfrac{1}{15}$ chance to be the first one picked. So the probability that the first person picked is female is $\dfrac{5}{15}$. If the first person picked is female, then there are 14 tickets left in the box with only 4 female members of the club left. So the probability that the second person picked is female if the first person picked was female is $\dfrac{4}{14}$. In order for both persons to be female, the first person must be female and then the second person must be female, so the probability that both persons are female is $\left(\dfrac{5}{15}\right)\left(\dfrac{4}{14}\right) = \dfrac{2}{21}$.

Another method of solving the problem follows. The number of ways the 2 tickets can be picked in order is 15 × 14, and the number of ways 2 females can be picked in order is 5 × 4. So the probability that both persons picked are female is

$\left(\dfrac{5 \times 4}{15 \times 14}\right) = \left(\dfrac{1}{3}\right)\left(\dfrac{2}{7}\right) = \dfrac{2}{21}$.

(I-7 or II-4)

★★☆ **17.** The distribution of scores on a math test had a mean of 82 percent with a standard deviation of 5 percent. The score that is exactly 2 standard deviations above the mean is

(A) 72%
(B) 82%
(C) 92%
(D) 95%
(E) cannot be determined

(C) Since the standard deviation is 5 percent, 2 standard deviations is 10 percent. The mean is 82 percent, so the score that is 2 standard deviations above the mean is 82% + 10% = 92 percent. Notice that this problem really has nothing to do with statistics because all you need to do is plug in the values. (II-3)

★★☆ **18.** What is the value of $x - y$?

(1) $x + 2y = 6$
(2) $x = y$

(B) STATEMENT (2) alone is sufficient since $x = y$ implies $x - y = 0$.

STATEMENT (1) alone is not sufficient. An infinite number of pairs satisfy STATEMENT (1), for example, $x = 2$, $y = 2$, for which $x - y = 0$, and $x = 4$, $y = 1$, for which $x - y = 3$. (II-2)

19. The number of eligible voters is 100,000. How many eligible voters voted?

    (1) 63 percent of the eligible men voted.

    (2) 67 percent of the eligible women voted.

(E) Since there is no information on how many of the eligible voters are men or how many are women, STATEMENTS (1) and (2) together are not sufficient. (II-4)

★★☆

---

20. A motorcycle costs $2,500 when it is brand new. At the end of each year it is worth 80 percent of what it was worth at the beginning of the year. What is the motorcycle worth when it is 3 years old?

    (A) $1,000
    (B) $1,200
    (C) $1,280
    (D) $1,340
    (E) $1,430

(C) Let x_n be what the motorcycle is worth after n years. Then we know $x_0 = \$2,500$ and $x_{n+1} = .8x_n$. So $x_1 = .8 \times 2,500$, which is $2,000. x_2 is $.8 \times 2,000$, which is 1,600, and finally x_3 is $.8 \times 1,600$, which is 1,280. Therefore, the motorcycle is worth $1,280 at the end of three years *or* $x_3 = .8x_2 = .8(.8x_1) = .8(.8)(.8\,x_0) = .512 \times 2,500 = 1,280$. (II-6)

★★☆

---

21. Which of the following inequalities is the solution to the inequality $7x - 5 < 12x + 18$?

    (A) $x < -\dfrac{13}{5}$

    (B) $x > -\dfrac{23}{5}$

    (C) $x < -\dfrac{23}{5}$

    (D) $x > \dfrac{23}{5}$

    (E) $x < \dfrac{23}{5}$

(B) Simply use the properties of inequalities to solve the given inequality. Subtract $12x$ from each side to get $-5x - 5 < 18$. Next add 5 to each side to obtain $-5x < 23$. Finally, divide each side by -5 to get $x > -23/5$. Remember that if you divide each side of an inequality by a negative number, the inequality is reversed. You can make a quick check of your answer by using $x = -5$, which is not greater than $-\dfrac{23}{5}$, and $x = -4$, which is greater than $-\dfrac{23}{5}$ in the original inequality. Since $x = -5$ does not satisfy the original inequality (-40 is not less than -42) and $x = -4$ does satisfy the inequality (-33 is less than -30), the answer is correct. You could use the method of checking values to find the correct answer, but it would take longer. (II-7)

★★☆

★★★ **22.** The hexagon *ABCDEF* is inscribed in the circle with center *O*. What is the length of *AB*?

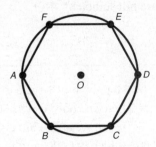

(1) The radius of the circle is 4 inches.
(2) The hexagon is a regular hexagon. That means all its sides are the same length and all its interior angles are the same size.

(C) Draw the radii from *O* to each of the vertices. These lines divide the hexagon into six triangles. STATEMENT (2) says that all the triangles are congruent since each of their pairs of corresponding sides is equal. Since there are 360° in a circle, the central angle of each triangle is 60°. And, since all radii are equal, each angle of the triangle equals 60°. Therefore, the triangles are equilateral, and *AB* is equal to the radius of the circle. Thus, if we assume STATEMENT (1), we know the length of *AB*. Without STATEMENT (1), we can't find the length of *AB*.

Also, STATEMENT (1) alone is not sufficient since *AB* need not equal the radius unless the hexagon is regular. (III-4)

★★☆ **23.** What was the percentage of defective items produced at a factory?

(1) The total number of defective items produced was 1,234.
(2) The ratio of defective items to nondefective items was 32 to 5,678.

(B) STATEMENT (2) alone is sufficient. If (2) holds, then $\frac{32}{(32+5,678)}$ represents the ratio of defective items to total items produced. Since any fraction can be changed into a percentage by multiplying by 100, STATEMENT (2) alone is sufficient.

STATEMENT (1) alone is not sufficient since the total number of items produced is also needed to find the percentage of defective items.

Therefore, (B) is the correct choice. (I-4, II-5)

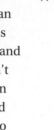
24. On a list of people's ages the tabulator made an error that resulted in 20 years being added to each person's age. Which of the following statements is true?

   I. The mean of the listed ages and the mean of the actual ages are the same.

   II. The standard deviation of the listed ages and the actual ages are the same.

   III. The range of the listed ages and the actual ages are the same.

(A) only II
(B) I and II
(C) I and III
(D) II and III
(E) I, II, and III

(D) Since 20 was added to each age, the mean of the listed ages will be 20 more than the mean of the actual ages. [Note that this means you can eliminate (B), (C), and (E) and that you should guess (A) or (D) if you can't solve the problem.] The standard deviation and the range of a list measure how spread out the data is; adding the same number to every measurement in the list will not change either of these, so the correct answer is (D). (I-7)

★★★

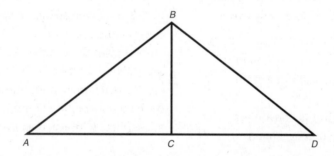

25. Is *ABC* a right triangle? *AB* = 5; *AC* = 4.

   (1) *BC* = 3
   (2) *AC* = *CD*

(A) STATEMENT (1) alone is sufficient. Since $3^2 + 4^2 = 5^2$, *ABC* is a right triangle by the Pythagorean Theorem.

   STATEMENT (2) alone is not sufficient since you can choose a point *D* so that *AC* = *CD* for *any* triangle *ABC*. (III-4)

★★☆

---

26. Did the price of energy rise last year?

   (1) If the price of energy rose last year, then the price of food would rise this year.

   (2) The price of food rose this year.

(E) (1) and (2) are not sufficient. The price of food could rise for other reasons besides the price of energy rising. (See analysis of #7 on page 52.)

★★☆

★★★ **27.** Mary, John, and Karen ate lunch together. Karen's meal cost 50 percent more than John's meal, and Mary's meal cost $\frac{5}{6}$ as much as Karen's meal. If Mary paid $2 more than John, how much was the total that the three of them paid?

(A) $28.33
(B) $30.00
(C) $35.00
(D) $37.50
(E) $40.00

(B) Let M, J, and K be the amounts paid by Mary, John, and Karen, respectively. Then $K = 1.5J$, $M = \left(\frac{5}{6}\right)K$, and $M = J + 2$.

So M, which is $\frac{5}{6}K$, must be $\left(\frac{5}{6}\right)(1.5)J = \left(\frac{5}{6}\right)\left(\frac{3}{2}\right)J = \frac{5}{4}J$. Therefore, we have $\left(\frac{5}{4}\right)J = J + 2$ or $\left(\frac{1}{4}\right)J = 2$, which means $J = 8$. So $K = 1.5J$, or 12, and $M = J + 2$, or 10. So the total is $8 + 12 + 10 = \$30$. (II-2)

★★★ **28.** A group of 49 consumers were offered a chance to subscribe to three magazines: A, B, and C. Thirty-eight of the consumers subscribed to at least one of the magazines. How many of the 49 consumers subscribed to exactly two of the magazines?

(1) Twelve of the 49 consumers subscribed to all three of the magazines.

(2) Twenty of the 49 consumers subscribed to magazine A.

(E) The number who subscribed to at least one magazine is the sum of the numbers who subscribed to exactly one, two, and three magazines. So $38 = N1 + N2 + N3$, where $N1$, $N2$, and $N3$ are the numbers who subscribed to 1, 2, and 3 magazines, respectively. We need to find $N2$. STATEMENT (1) is not sufficient since it gives the value of $N3$ but $N1$ and $N2$ are still both unknown. Even if we also use STATEMENT (1), we cannot find $N2$ since we have no information about the number of subscribers to magazines B and C. (II-4)

★★☆ **29.** If a and b are digits and the sum of the numbers $2a3$, $b31$, and 431 is 925 as shown

$$2a3$$
$$b31$$
$$+\ 431$$
$$\overline{925}$$

then the value of $a - b$ is

(A) −4
(B) 2
(C) 4
(D) 6
(E) 10

(C) The digit a is either 0, 1, 2, 3, 4, 5, 6, 7, 8, or 9. You know $6 \leq 3 + 3 + a \leq 12$. Since the tens place in the sum is 2, $3 + 3 + a$ must be 12. So $a = 6$. Since $3 + 3 + a = 12$, the hundreds place in the sum is $2 + b + 4 + 1$ must equal 9. So $7 + b = 9$ and $b = 2$. You can check that these values are correct by adding 263, 231, and 431. Since their sum is 925, $a = 6$ and $b = 2$ is correct. So $a - b = 4$. (I-1)

30. If the angles of a triangle are in the ratio 1 : 2 : 2, the triangle

   (A) is isosceles
   (B) is obtuse
   (C) is a right triangle
   (D) is equilateral
   (E) has one angle greater than 80°

(A) The angles are in the ratio 1 : 2 : 2, so two angles are equal to each other and both are twice as large as the third angle of the triangle. Since a triangle with two equal angles must have the sides opposite equal, the triangle is isosceles. (Using the fact that the sum of the angles of a triangle is 180°, you can see that the angles of the triangle are 72°, 72°, and 36°, so only (A) is true.) (III-4)

---

31. How much was a certain Rembrandt painting worth in January 1991?

   (1) In January 1997 the painting was worth $2 million.
   (2) Over the ten years 1988–1997 the painting increased in value by 10 percent each year.

(C) (1) alone is obviously insufficient. To use (2) you need to know what the painting was worth at some time between 1988 and 1997. So (2) alone is insufficient, but by using (1) and (2) together you can figure out the worth of the painting in January 1991. NOTE: You should not waste time actually figuring out the value. (II-6)

---

32. A sequence of numbers $a_1, a_2, a_3, \ldots$ is given by the rule $a_n^2 = a_{n+1}$. Does 3 appear in the sequence?

   (1) $a_1 = 2$
   (2) $a_3 = 16$

(D) (1) alone is sufficient since the rule enables you to compute all successive values once you know a_1. Also, the rule and (1) tell you that the numbers in the sequence will always increase. Thus, since $a_2 = 4$, 3 will never appear. In the same way, by using (2) and the rule for the sequence, you can determine that $a_2 = 4$ and a_1 is 2 or –2, so the reasoning used above shows that 3 will never appear. (II-6)

---

33. A wall with no windows is 11 feet high and 20 feet long. A large roll of wallpaper costs $25 and will cover 60 square feet of wall. A small roll of wallpaper costs $6 and will cover 10 square feet of wall. What is the least cost for enough wallpaper to cover the wall?

   (A) $75
   (B) $99
   (C) $100
   (D) $120
   (E) $132

(B) The area of the wall is 11 feet × 20 feet = 220 square feet. Since a large roll of wallpaper gives more square feet per dollar, you should try to use large rolls. Since $\frac{220}{60} = 3$ with a remainder of 40, if you buy 3 large rolls, which cost 3 × $25 = $75, you will have enough to cover the entire wall, except for 40 square feet. You can cover 40 square feet by either buying 1 large roll or 4 small rolls. A large roll costs $25 but 4 small rolls cost only $24. So the minimum cost is $75 + $24 = $99. (II-3)

★★☆ **34.** A jar is filled with 60 marbles. All the marbles in the jar are either red or green. What is the smallest number of marbles that must be drawn from the jar in order to be certain that a red marble is drawn?

(1) The ratio of red marbles to green marbles is 3 : 1.

(2) There are 15 green marbles in the jar.

(D) If there are x red marbles and y green marbles in the jar, then $(y + 1)$ marbles must contain at least one red marble. So it is sufficient to know the number of red marbles and the number of green marbles. Since you are given that $x + y = 60$, STATEMENT (2) is obviously sufficient. Also, STATEMENT (1) is sufficient since it implies that $x = 3y$, which enables you to find x and y. Therefore, the correct answer choice is (D). (I-7)

★★☆ **35.** Is $\frac{1}{x}$ greater than $\frac{1}{y}$?

(1) x is greater than 1.

(2) x is less than y.

(C) STATEMENT (2) alone is not sufficient. −1 is less than 2, and $\frac{1}{-1}$ is less than $\frac{1}{2}$, but 1 is less than 2 and $\frac{1}{1}$ is greater than $\frac{1}{2}$.

STATEMENT (1) alone is insufficient since there is no information about y.

STATEMENT (1) and (2) together imply that x and y are both greater than 1, and for two positive numbers x and y, if x is less than y, then $\frac{1}{x}$ is greater than $\frac{1}{y}$. (II-7)

★★☆ **36.** Plane X flies at r miles per hour from A to B. Plane Y flies at S miles per hour from B to A. Both planes take off at the same time. Which plane flies at a faster rate? Town C is between A and B.

(1) C is closer to A than it is to B.

(2) Plane X flies over C before plane Y.

(E) Since C is closer to A, if plane X is flying faster than plane Y, it will certainly fly over C before plane Y. However, if plane X flies slower than plane Y, and C is very close to A, plane X will still fly over C before plane Y does. Thus, STATEMENTS (1) and (2) together are not sufficient. (II-3)

37. Is $\dfrac{x}{12} > \dfrac{y}{40}$?

(1) $10x > 3y$

(2) $12x < 4y$

(A) To compare two fractions, the fractions ★★☆ must have the same denominator. The least common denominator for both fractions is 120. Using this fact, $\dfrac{x}{12} = \dfrac{10x}{120}$ and $\dfrac{y}{40} = \dfrac{3y}{120}$. So the relation between the fractions is the same as the relation between $10x$ and $3y$. Therefore, STATEMENT (1) alone is sufficient. STATEMENT (2) alone is not sufficient. Using $y = 13$ and $x = 4$, STATEMENT (2) is true and $\dfrac{x}{12}$ is greater than $\dfrac{y}{40}$. However, using $y = 10$ and $x = 2$, STATEMENT (2) is still true, but now $\dfrac{x}{12}$ is less than $\dfrac{y}{40}$. (I-2)

Verbal Section

The passage for questions 1–4 appears on page 595.

★★☆　**1.** According to the author, no complete inventory exists of positions in the three highest levels of government because

　(A) no one has bothered to count them
　(B) computers cannot handle all the data
　(C) no one is responsible for completing the project
　(D) the President has never requested such information
　(E) the Classification Act prohibits such a census

　(C) There is no "central point" (line 11) with jurisdiction over upper-level appointees.

★★☆　**2.** It may be inferred from the passage that top Presidential appointees have as their central responsibility

　(A) the prevention of politically motivated interference with the actions of their agencies
　(B) the monitoring of government actions on behalf of the President's own political party
　(C) developing courses of action following administration objectives
　(D) investigating charges of corruption within the government
　(E) maintaining adequate controls over the rate of government spending

　(C) See paragraph 3. "Top Presidential appointees . . . bear the brunt of translating the philosophy and aims of the current administration into practical programs."

★★☆　**3.** One exception to the general rule that top Presidential appointees must be in agreement with the President's political philosophy may be found in

　(A) most cabinet-level officers
　(B) members of the White House staff
　(C) bi-partisan boards and commission
　(D) those offices filled by patronage
　(E) offices requiring scientific or technical expertise

　(C) Bi-partisan boards and commissions are exempt from this requirement (lines 24–25).

★☆☆　**4.** The primary purpose of the passage is to

　(A) describe the qualifications for Presidential appointees
　(B) show how policy makers are selected
　(C) distinguish among different levels of federal service employees
　(D) describe who are the major influences among federal employees
　(E) show why the federal government is well managed

(C) The passage describes the various levels of government employees, from top appointees to lower-level employees. There is only one discussion of qualifications (line 22), so answer choice (A) is not relevant. The passage mainly discusses how top appointees are selected, without reference to other levels. Although the passage states that top-level employees carry out the administration's policy, there is no reference to "influence," choice (D). Why the federal government is well managed is not discussed, as in choice (E).

---

5. Richard is a terrible driver. He has had at least five traffic violations in the past year. ★★★

Which of the following can be said about the above claim?

(A) This is an example of an argument that is directed against the source of the claim rather than the claim itself.
(B) The statement is fallacious because it contains an illegitimate appeal to authority.
(C) The above argument obtains its strength from a similarity of two compared situations.
(D) The argument is built upon an assumption that is not stated but rather is concealed.
(E) In the above statement, there is a shifting in the meaning of terms, causing a fallacy of ambiguity.

(D) Analysis of the two sentences indicates the presence of an assumption that anyone who has had at least five traffic violations in a year is a terrible driver. This assumption is understood but is not stated. Rather, it is a hidden assumption, making (D) the appropriate answer. Alternative (A) is incorrect because there is no attack on the source of the claim. (B) is wrong because there is no appeal to authority—illegitimate or not. (C) is not the correct answer because there is no comparison of two similar situations in the statement. (E) is incorrect because there is no term with a confusing or double meaning.

---

6. The exchange rate is the ruling official rate of exchange of dollars for other currencies. It determines the value of American goods in relation to foreign goods. If the dollar is devalued in terms of other currencies, American exports (which are paid for in dollars) become cheaper to foreigners and American imports (paid for by purchasing foreign currency) become more expensive to holders of dollars. ★★☆

What conclusion can be drawn from the above?

(A) There are certain disadvantages for the United States economy attached to devaluation.
(B) The prospect of devaluation results in a speculative outflow of funds.
(C) By encouraging exports and discouraging imports, devaluation can improve the American balance of payments.
(D) The difference between imports and exports is called the Trade Gap.
(E) It is possible that inflation neutralizes the beneficial effects of devaluation.

(C) The best conclusion that can be drawn from the statement is one that sums up the facts that are given in one sentence; thus, (C) is the best answer. Although the given paragraph states that if there is devaluation of the dollar, American imports will become more expensive, this will not necessarily be a disadvantage for the U.S. economy. Hence, (A) is not appropriate. Alternative (B) is also inappropriate, because it highlights a disadvantage that may arise from the expectation of devaluation, but which is not dealt with in the paragraph. Alternatives (D) and (E) are both helpful pieces of information, but they cannot be concluded from the given text.

★★☆   **7.** Although I calculate that he will be here any minute, I cannot wait much longer for him to arrive.

(A) Although I calculate that he will be here

(B) Although I reckon that he will be here

(C) Because I calculate that he will be here

(D) Although I think that he will be here

(E) Because I am confident that he will be here

(D) Choices (A), (B), and (C) incorrectly use *calculate* or *reckon* to substitute for *think*. Choice (E) changes the meaning of the sentence.

★★★   **8.** The fourteen-hour day not only has been reduced to one of ten hours but also, in some lines of work, to one of eight or even six.

(A) The fourteen-hour day not only has been reduced

(B) Not only the fourteen-hour day has been reduced

(C) Not the fourteen-hour day only has been reduced

(D) The fourteen-hour day has not only been reduced

(E) The fourteen-hour day has been reduced not only

(E) This is correct because the words *not only . . . but also* are both idiomatically correct and parallel. The position of *not only* in choices (A), (B), (C), and (D) is unidiomatic and not parallel.

9. In the human body, platelets promote blood clotting by clumping together. Aspirin has been found to prevent clotting by making platelets less sticky. Research has now shown that heart attacks and strokes caused by blood clots could be avoided by taking one aspirin a day. Statistics show that the incidence of second heart attacks has been reduced by 21% and overall mortality rates by 15% as a result of taking aspirin. ★★★

Unfortunately, the drug has several unpleasant side effects, including nausea, gastric bleeding, and, in severe cases, shock. In children, it has been linked to Reye's Syndrome, a rare, but occasionally fatal, childhood illness.

On balance, however, for men aged 40 and over, an aspirin a day may present an excellent prophylactic measure for a disease that affects 1.5 million Americans yearly and claims the lives of about 540,000.

Which of the following conclusions can most properly be drawn from the information above?

(A) All people should take an aspirin a day to prevent heart attacks.
(B) Painkillers prevent heart attacks.
(C) Smokers can safely continue smoking, provided that they take at least one aspirin a day.
(D) The majority of people suffering second subsequent cardiac arrests could have been saved by taking an aspirin a day.
(E) Aspirin can be used to reduce mortality rates in patients who have already suffered heart attacks.

(E) According to the passage, all people cannot take aspirin without undesirable side effects, and in some cases, the danger caused by aspirin itself outweighs its benefits. The passage, by saying "On balance, however, for men aged 40 and over, an aspirin a day may present. . ." also implies that not all, but only some people (men over 40) should take an aspirin a day. Alternative answer (A) clearly cannot be concluded from the passage. Answer alternative (B) is also inappropriate. No painkiller other than aspirin is mentioned in the passage, and it cannot be inferred that all painkillers reduce the "stickiness" of platelets. (C) is incorrect. Smoking is not mentioned in the passage and since studies of the effects of smoking and aspirin have not been reported, no conclusions can be drawn. (D) is wrong because the statistics given in the passage say that 15% of second heart attack victims were saved from death by taking aspirin, and 15% does not constitute a majority. (E) is the correct choice since it simply states that mortality rates can be reduced in patients who have already suffered a heart attack (as stated in the passage), without giving any specific statistics.

★★★ **10.** In the past, to run for one's country in the Olympics was the ultimate achievement of any athlete. Nowadays, an athlete's motives are more and more influenced by financial gain, and consequently we do not see our best athletes in the Olympics, which is still only for amateurs.

Which of the following will most weaken the above conclusion?

(A) The publicity and fame that can be achieved by competing in the Olympics draws the best amateur athletes, who then become more "marketable" by agents and potential sponsors.

(B) The winning of a race is not as important as participating.

(C) There is a widely held belief that our best Olympic athletes already receive enough in terms of promotion and sponsorship.

(D) It has been suggested that professional athletes should be allowed to compete in the games.

(E) Athletics as an entertainment is like any other entertainment job and deserves a financial reward.

(A) Amateur athletes can attract sponsorship and make money through participation in the Olympics. This sponsorship can then provide financial gain. If an athlete's motives are more and more influenced by financial gain, as stated, the conclusion that "we do not see our best athletes in the Olympics" is weakened. Alternative (B) is an oft-used maxim. In this case, it is not relevant to the argument. Choice (C) may or may not be true but is not related to the conclusion that the best athletes do not compete in the Olympics. Choice (D) states that professionals should be allowed to compete in the Olympics. However, using professional athletes would change the nature of the Olympic games. Choice (E) equates the games to entertainment, assuming that the analogy is relevant. In fact, the analogy is flawed because qualifications for athletes are different from those for entertainers.

★★★ **11.** <u>We want the teacher to be him</u> who has the best rapport with the students.

(A) We want the teacher to be him

(B) We want the teacher to be he

(C) We want him to be the teacher

(D) We desire that the teacher be him

(E) We anticipate that the teacher will be him

(B) "He" is the subject of the sentence which takes *who* as the relative pronoun.

★★☆ **12.** <u>If she were to win the medal,</u> I for one would be disturbed.

(A) If she were to win the medal,

(B) If she was to win the medal,

(C) If she wins the medal,

(D) If she is the winner of the medal,

(E) In the event that she wins the medal,

(A) No error.

13. The function of a food technologist in a large marketing chain of food stores is to ensure that all foodstuffs that are offered for sale in the various retail outlets meet certain standard criteria for nonperishability, freshness, and fitness for human consumption.

    It is the technologist's job to visit the premises of suppliers and food producers (factory or farm), inspect the facilities, and report thereon. Her responsibility also includes receiving new products from local and foreign suppliers and performing exhaustive quality control testing on them. Finally, she should carry out surprise spot-checks on goods held in the marketing chain's own warehouses and stores.

What conclusion can best be drawn from the preceding paragraph?

(A) A university degree in food technology is a necessary and sufficient condition for becoming a food technologist.

(B) Imported products, as well as home-produced goods, must be rigorously tested.

(C) The food technologist stands between the unhygienic producer and the unsuspecting consumer.

(D) Home-produced foodstuffs are safer to eat than goods imported from abroad because they are subject to more regular and closer inspection procedures.

(E) Random checking of the quality of goods stored on the shelves in a foodstore is the best way of ensuring that foodstuffs of an inferior quality are not purchased by the general public.

(C) The paragraph demonstrates from beginning to end that the function of the food technologist is to prevent unfit foodstuffs from being marketed by the stores and passed on to the consumer, who relies on the store's control procedures. (C), therefore, is the most appropriate answer. Answer alternative (A) is inappropriate because it cannot be inferred from the text (even if it were true). Answer (B) and possibly answer (D) are factually correct, but these conclusions cannot be drawn from the text itself. (E) is not a correct interpretation of the facts; random checking is not the best way, since below-standard goods are caught in the net only by chance.

---

14. The scouts were told <u>to take an overnight hike, pitch camp, prepare dinner, and that they should be in bed by 9 P.M.</u>

(A) to take an overnight hike, pitch camp, prepare dinner, and that they should be in bed by 9 P.M.

(B) to take an overnight hike, to pitch camp, to prepare dinner, and that they should be in bed by 9 P.M.

(C) to take an overnight hike, pitch camp, prepare dinner, and be in bed by 9 P.M.

(D) to take an overnight hike, pitching camp, preparing dinner and going to bed by 9 P.M.

(E) to engage in an overnight hike, pitch camp, prepare dinner, and that they should be in bed by 9 P.M.

(C) Everything in the list in choice (C) is parallel. Choice (A) incorrectly uses *that they should be*. Choice (B) incorrectly uses *should be*. (D) incorrectly uses *pitching, preparing, and going*, which are not parallel to *were told*. Choice (E) changes the meaning and uses nonparallel construction.

The passage for questions 15–18 appears on page 600.

★★★ **15.** The academic debate mentioned in line 30 concerning the role of the so-called "multi-versity" did not consider which of the following?

(A) Student unrest
(B) Social problems
(C) Community college enrollments
(D) Open admissions
(E) Community service

(E) Community service. According to lines 12–14, "institutions of higher learning . . . commonly face the challenge of defining their programs in such a way as to contribute to the service of the community." In line 28, this statement is buttressed by "the thrust of these discussions obscures the larger meaning of the emergence of the service-university . . . ." Choices (A) through (D) are secondary to the "phenomenon" mentioned in line 31.

★★★ **16.** According to the passage, the purpose of American higher education in the past was *not* to

(A) advance learning
(B) solve societal problems
(C) impart knowledge
(D) provide useful knowledge
(E) prepare future managers

(B) See paragraph 1: "The successful institution of higher learning had never been . . . providing vocational skills or . . . resolving societal problems."

★★☆ **17.** According to the author, one of the recent, important changes in higher education is

(A) student representation on college boards
(B) faculty tenure requirements
(C) curriculum updates
(D) service-education concepts
(E) cost constraints

(D) The idea that a university must relate to the problems of society is discussed in paragraph 2. The passage states that this emphasis has become one of community service.

18. According to the passage, American secondary education ★★☆

(A) is geared to help solve social problems
(B) has become more useful in the long run
(C) has a relatively low attrition rate
(D) is known for its emphasis on vocational skills
(E) pioneered distance learning

(B) On lines 8–10, the author states that it was believed that secondary education was not of immediate use but "became beneficial in later life."

---

19. The <u>government's failing to keep it's pledges</u> will earn the distrust of all the other nations in the alliance. ★★☆

(A) government's failing to keep it's pledges
(B) government failing to keep it's pledges
(C) government's failing to keep its pledges
(D) government failing to keep it's pledges
(E) governments failing to keep their pledges

(C) Choice (C) is the only answer that correctly uses the possessive *its* rather than the conjunction *it's* (which means *it is*) and that correctly also uses the possessive *government's*.

---

20. Most students like to read <u>these kind of books</u> during their spare time. ★★☆

(A) these kind of books
(B) these kind of book
(C) this kind of book
(D) this kinds of books
(E) those kind of books

(C) Only choice (C) uses the singular pronoun *this* with the singular nouns *kind* and *book*. Choices (A), (B), (D), and (E) all incorrectly mix singular and plural.

---

21. In the normal course of events, <u>John will graduate high school and enter</u> college in two years. ★☆☆

(A) John will graduate high school and enter
(B) John will graduate from high school and enter
(C) John will be graduated from high school and enter
(D) John will be graduated from high school and enter into
(E) John will have graduated high school and enter

(B) The correct idiom is *graduate from*, therefore choice (A) is incorrect. Choices (C) and (D) use the wordy and awkward *will be graduated from*. Choice (D) also adds an unnecessary word, *into*. Choice (E) uses the incorrect verb tense.

★★☆   **22.** The daily journey from his home to his office takes John Bond on average an hour and 35 minutes by car. A friend has told him of a different route that is longer in mileage, but will only take an hour and a quarter on average, because it contains stretches of roads where it is possible to drive at higher speeds.

John Bond's only consideration apart from the time factor is the cost, and he calculates that his car will consume 10% less gasoline if he takes the suggested new route. John decides to take the new route for the next two weeks as an experiment.

If the above were the only other considerations, which one of the following may have an effect on the decision John has made?

(A) Major road work is begun on the shorter (in distance) route, which holds up traffic for an extra 10 minutes. The project will take six months, but after it, the improvements will allow the journey to be made in half an hour less than at present.
(B) There is to be a strike at local gas stations and the amount of gasoline drivers may purchase may be rationed.
(C) John finds a third route that is slightly longer than his old route, but shorter than the suggested route.
(D) The old route passes the door of a work colleague, who without a ride, would have to go to work by bus.
(E) None of the above.

(C) John's decision is to experiment with the new longer (in mileage) route for two weeks, and it is this decision that we have to consider. Choice (C), by offering a third alternative, gives John another possibility and, therefore, another outcome. It may affect his decision, and therefore, is the appropriate answer. Alternatives (A), (B), and (D) alter factors within the calculation affecting the decision, but taken individually and not making any other changes, will definitely not result in a different decision being made. These three are, therefore, not appropriate answers. The existence of a definite answer—in this case, (C)—means that alternative (E) is not appropriate.

★★★   **23.** This year the Consumer Price Index, a measure of inflation, was 6 percent, while last year it was only 4 percent. Analysts conclude from these figures that inflation is on an upward trend and we can expect that it will be even higher next year.

Which of the following statements, if true, could most weaken the analysts' prediction?

(A) Inflation in other countries with similar economies is not predicted to increase in the future.
(B) The price of natural gas, a major component of the consumer price index, rose by 8 percent year, owing to a temporary decrease in its supply.
(C) Increases in inflation can be predicted on the basis of two years' experience.
(D) The cost of production of most products has increased over the last five years.
(E) The ability of labor unions to force employers to increase wages has been a recurring phenomenon.

(B) If supply is expected to increase in the future, its price should decrease, thus mitigating its effect on the Consumer Price Index, since natural gas is a major component of the index. Since there is no evidence to show that inflation rates in similar economies follow the same trend, Choice (A) is incorrect. Choice (C) is wrong because inflation increases can be predicted on the basis of two years experience, this would support, not weaken, the conclusion. Choice (D) supports the conclusion because an increase in production costs over five years signals an inflationary trend. Choice (E) also supports the conclusion because the expectation of increased wages is a factor.

---

24. Although the Internet is a vital source of information, research has shown that head-quarters executives of global companies obtain as much as two-thirds of the information about competitors they need from personal sources. Headquarters executives generally acknowledge that company managers overseas are the people who know best what is going on in their areas. Therefore, they are the best source of information needed for strategic planning.

★★☆

Which of the following, if true, would weaken the above conclusion?

(A) In many global companies, both personal sources of information and the Internet are used.
(B) In many global companies, one-third of the information collected comes from personal sources.
(C) Strategic planning requires collecting information about all aspects of the market including consumer behavior.
(D) Overseas company managers only collect information relevant to their local operations.
(E) It is difficult to judge the accuracy of information available on the Internet.

(C) This statement shows that the information about competition collected by overseas managers is necessary but not sufficient for strategic planning. Therefore, it casts doubt about their being the best source. Choice (A) is incorrect because even if it were true, this statement does not weaken the conclusion. Overseas managers may still be the better source of information, regardless of whether the Internet is used as well. Choice (B) is inappropriate because it may refute the two-thirds claim but it does not refute the claim that overseas managers are the best source of information. Choice (D) is inappropriate because it is stated in the passage that overseas managers know best what is going on in their area. Therefore, it is expected that they collect information only in that area. Finally, Choice (E) supports the use of overseas managers as an information source, rather than the Internet.

The passage for questions 25–30 appears on page 603.

---

25. Changes in tradition-oriented universities' education are caused by

★★★

(A) increased enrollments
(B) globalization
(C) online education
(D) more qualified students
(E) lack of resources

(B) The reasons for the changes are given in lines 13–42. Choice (B) is found in line 31.

★★★ **26.** The best possible title for the passage is

(A) *Massification*
(B) *The Business of Education*
(C) *The Decline of Tradition-Loving Universities*
(D) *Downfall of Academic Dogma*
(E) *Globalization of Higher Education*

(B) The passage is about the business of education, or brains. Answer choices (A) and (E) are mentioned, but they do not touch on the central idea. There is no basis for choices (C) or (D). Oxford University and other tradition-oriented universities are not in decline. (D) is not mentioned at all.

★★☆ **27.** The passage suggests that mass higher education is forcing universities to become

(A) more democractic
(B) better managed
(C) more liberal
(D) more teaching oriented
(E) more competitive

(E) Traditional universities are being forced to compete for students (last paragraph). The other answer choices are not mentioned in the passage.

★★☆ **28.** According to the passage, younger universities try to

(A) compete with older ones
(B) create an image like that of more traditional universities
(C) diversify their student bodies
(D) rely less on outside financing
(E) diversify income sources

(B) The old universities attempt to maintain their image, whereas younger ones try to create "an aura of antiquity" (line 6). Younger universities do compete with older ones, but that is the second-best answer.

★★☆ **29.** The author states that universities react to the challenges facing them by

(A) making curriculum more relevant to societal needs
(B) entering alliances in order to survive
(C) creating distance learning programs
(D) encouraging donations from the public
(E) becoming more democratic

(B) The author gives a number of reasons why universities are being challenged and what their reactions are. Among these reactions are "partnerships with private companies" and "mergers and acquisitions" (lines 10–11). In other words, universities are forging alliances with others.

30. The passage states that in business terms, higher education has become ★★☆

    (A) more profitable

    (B) an export industry

    (C) better managed

    (D) bottom-line oriented

    (E) customer oriented

(B) The correct answer is given in paragraph 4. One of the major forces for change in higher education is globalization of the industry. None of the other alternatives is mentioned.

---

31. The owners of a local supermarket have decided to make use of three now-redundant checkout counters. They believe that they will attract those customers who lately have been put off by the long checkout lines during the mid-morning and evening rush hours. The owners have concluded that in order to be successful, the increased revenue from existing and added counters will have to be more than the increase in maintenance costs for the added counters. ★★★

The underlying goal of the owners can be summarized thus:

(A) To improve services to all customers.

(B) To attract people who have never been to the store.

(C) To make use of the redundant counters.

(D) To keep maintenance costs on the added counters as low as possible.

(E) To increase monthly profits.

(E) Services will be improved, it is hoped, for a certain segment of customers—those that shop during the rush hours—but not for all customers. This fact makes choice (A) inappropriate. To attract new customers is not stated in the passage as an objective, so (B) is inappropriate. The utilization of excess capacity, as in (C) is a useful byproduct of the new system, but it is not the main goal. If maintenance costs are kept low, it will probably make the achievement of the main goal that much easier, but this is not the major objective so choice (D) is not appropriate. The principal purpose of the owners is to make more money from the change, by increasing income more than the added costs. Therefore, (E) is the appropriate answer.

★★☆ **32.** The cost of housing in many parts of the United States has become so excessive that many young couples, with above-average salaries, can only afford small apartments. Mortgage commitments are so huge that they cannot consider the possibility of starting a family. A new baby would probably mean either the mother or father giving up a well-paid position. The lack of or great cost of child-care facilities precludes the return of both parents to work.

Which of the following adjustments could practically be made to the situation described above that would allow young couples to improve their housing prospects?

(A) Encourage couples to remain childless.

(B) Encourage couples to have one child only.

(C) Encourage couples to postpone starting their families until a later age than previously acceptable to society.

(D) Encourage young couples to move to cheaper areas of the United States.

(E) Encourage fathers to remain at home while mothers return to work.

(C) Choices (A) and (B) are not supported by information in the passage. If couples move to cheaper areas in the country, as suggested in (D), the chances are that work would be less available or possibly that the couple would have a less positive economic future, so the change may not necessarily be financially advantageous. If fathers stayed at home rather than mothers, there would be no improvement in financial status, so suggestion (E) is invalid. Suggestion (C) is the only sensible solution, since financial stability is likely to increase with the length of time in employment.

★★☆ **33.** With the exception of <u>Frank and I, everyone in the class finished</u> the assignment before the bell rang.

(A) Frank and I, everyone in the class finished

(B) Frank and me, everyone in the class finished

(C) Frank and me, everyone in the class had finished

(D) Frank and I, everyone in the class had finished

(E) Frank and me everyone in the class finished

(C) This corrects the two errors in this sentence. The first error is using *I* instead of *me*. The subject of the sentence is *everyone*. Therefore, *Frank* must be coupled with *me*, which is the object. The second error is tense. The verb must be *had finished* insead of *finished* because there are two events. First, everyone else finished. Then they finished. Therefore, *had finished* must be used for *everyone in the class*.

34. Many middle-class individuals find that they cannot obtain good medical attention, <u>despite they need it badly.</u>

    (A) despite they need it badly
    (B) despite they badly need it
    (C) in spite of they need it badly
    (D) however much they need it
    (E) therefore, they need it badly

    (D) *Despite*, as in choices (A) and (B), requires *the fact that* to form the idiom *despite the fact that*. Choice (C) is awkward and wordy. The word *therefore*, in choice (E), begins a new sentence and requires either a capital letter or a semicolon.

---

35. Unless new reserves are found soon, the world's supply of coal is being depleted in such a way that with demand continuing to grow at present rates, reserves will be exhausted by the year 2050.

    Which of the following, if true, will most weaken the above argument?

    (A) There has been a slowdown in the rate of increase in world demand for coal over the last 5 years from 10% to 5%.
    (B) It has been known for many years that there are vast stocks of coal under Antarctica that have yet to be economically exploited.
    (C) Oil is being used increasingly in place of coal for many industrial and domestic uses.
    (D) As coal resources are depleted, more and more marginal supplies, which are more costly to produce and less efficient in use, are being mined.
    (E) None of the above.

    (E) Even if the rate of increase in demand has slowed from 10% per annum to 5% per annum over the last five years, that means that demand is still increasing at 5% per annum. If, as the passage states, demand continues to grow at the present rate—that is, by 5% per annum—the world's resources will be used up by the year 2050. Therefore, the argument is not weakened by the statement in answer alternative (A). Choice (B) introduces the matter of supply, but apparently the reserves in Antarctica have been known for some time, and this, therefore, does not affect the argument that stocks will be depleted unless new reserves are found. Choice (C) informs us that there is an alternative to coal which is being used increasingly. However, the questions of the supply of and the rate of growth of demand for oil do not affect the argument in the paragraph. Choice (D) states an economic fact of life that will have to be faced if the statements in the paragraph are true. It may lead to a search for alternative fuels and consequent decrease in demand for coal, but this is uncertain and cannot be inferred. So, neither (A), (B), (C), nor (D) is appropriate. Choice (E) is, therefore, the correct answer.

36. In accordance with their powers, many state authorities are introducing fluoridation of drinking water. This follows the conclusion of 10 years of research that the process ensures that children and adults receive the required intake of fluoride that will strengthen teeth. The maximum level has been set at one part per million. However, there are many who object, claiming that fluoridation removes freedom of choice.

Which of the following will best weaken the claim of the proponents of fluoridation?

(A) Fluoridation over a certain prescribed level has been shown to lead to a general weakening of teeth.
(B) There is no record of the long-term effects of drinking fluoridated water.
(C) The people to be affected by fluoridation claim that they have not had sufficient opportunity to voice their views.
(D) Fluoridation is only one part of general dental health.
(E) Water already contains natural fluoride.

(B) Choice (A) contains an important point that would have been considered in setting the maximum treatment level. So it does not weaken the argument of the authorities and is inappropriate. Choice (C) is incorrect as the passage states that the authorities are carrying out this policy in accordance with their powers. Choice (D) is a fact that would be acknowledged by both sides and weakens neither's case, while choice (E) is also a well-known fact, which like the fact in (A), would have been taken into consideration by the researchers, so it is also not appropriate. The fact that the authorities have no record of the long-term good or damage of fluoridation is a significant weakness in their case, and therefore, (B) is the appropriate answer.

---

37. When one eats in this restaurant, you often find that the prices are high and that the food is poorly prepared.

(A) When one eats in this restaurant, you often find
(B) When you eat in this restaurant, one often finds
(C) As you eat in this restaurant, you often find
(D) If you eat in this restaurant, you often find
(E) When one ate in this restaurant, he often found

(C) Choices (A),(B), and (E) incorrectly shift between the pronoun *one* and *you*. Choice (D) incorrectly uses *if,* changing the meaning. Choice (E) contains an unnecessary shift of pronoun. Do not shift from *one* to *he.* Choice (D) changes the meaning unnecessarily.

38. Ever since the bombing, there has been much opposition <u>from they who maintain that it was an unauthorized war.</u>

   (A) from they who maintain that it was an unauthorized war
   (B) from they who maintain that it had been an unauthorized war
   (C) from those who maintain that it was an unauthorized war
   (D) from they maintaining that it was unauthorized
   (E) from they maintaining that it had been unauthorized

   (C) Choices (A), (B), (D), and (E) all use the incorrect pronoun *they* instead of *those*.

---

39. <u>I am not to eager to go to this play because it did not get good reviews.</u>

   (A) I am not to eager to go to this play because it did not get good reviews.
   (B) Because of its poor reviews, I am not to eager to go to this play.
   (C) Because of its poor revues, I am not to eager to go to this play.
   (D) I am not to eager to go to this play because the critics did not give it good reviews.
   (E) I am not too eager to go to this play because of its poor reviews.

   (E) Choices (A), (B), (C), and (D) all misspell *too*, which means "in addition."

---

40. In 1980, global service exports totaled about $370 billion, approximately 20 percent of world trade. Still, no coherent system of rules, principles, and procedures exists to govern trade in services.

Which of the following best summarizes the argument?

   (A) Regulatory systems lag behind reality.
   (B) A regulatory system ought to reflect the importance of service exports.
   (C) World trade totaled $1850 billion in 1980.
   (D) Service trade legislation is a veritable wasteland.
   (E) While trade legislation exists, it is uncoordinated.

   (B) Choice (A) is vague, while (D) equates service trade with legislation. Choice (C) is irrelevant to the argument. (E) comes close to summarizing the argument, but it is incomplete; *uncoordinated* is not an antonym for coherent.

41. We had decided that the emphasis would be placed on the results that might be attained.

   (A) We had decided that the emphasis would be placed on the results that might be attained.

   (B) We decided that the emphasis had been placed on the results that might be attained.

   (C) We decided to emphasize the results which we might attain.

   (D) We decided to emphasize the results that we attain.

   (E) We decided that the emphasis be placed on the results we might attain.

(E) Choices (A) and (B) incorrectly use the past perfect tense. Choice (C) is missing a comma after the non-defining clause, while Choice (D) uses the incorrect tense of *attain*.

EVALUATING YOUR SCORE

Tabulate your score for each section of the Sample Test according to the directions on pages 11–12 and record the results in the Self-Scoring Table below. Then find your rating for each score on the Self-Scoring Scale and record it in the appropriate blank.

SELF-SCORING TABLE

Section	Score	Rating
Quantitative		
Verbal		

SELF-SCORING SCALE—RATING

Section	Poor	Fair	Good	Excellent
Quantitative	0–15	15–25	26–30	31–37
Verbal	0–15	15–25	26–30	31–41

Study again the Review sections covering material in Sample Test 3 for which you had a rating of FAIR or POOR. Find your approximate GMAT score by using the scoring table on the next page.

*Important note: Up-to-date scoring guidelines for the Integrated Reasoning section can be found at *mba.com.*

SCORING TABLE

Add the number of correct answers on the Quantitative test and the number of correct answers on the Verbal test to find **T**, your total number of correct answers.

T should be a number less than or equal to 78. Find your equivalent scaled score in the table below.

Again, this table refers to Quantitative and Verbal scores only. For specifics on Integrated Reasoning scoring, go to *mba.com*.

T	Score	T	Score	T	Score	T	Score
78	800	59	660	40	510	21	370
77	790	58	650	39	500	20	360
76	790	57	640	38	490	19	350
75	780	56	630	37	490	18	340
74	770	55	620	36	480	17	340
73	760	54	620	35	470	16	330
72	760	53	610	34	460	15	320
71	750	52	600	33	460	14	310
70	740	51	590	32	450	13	300
69	730	50	580	31	440	12	290
68	720	49	580	30	430	11	280
67	720	48	570	29	430	10	270
66	710	47	560	28	420	9	260
65	700	46	550	27	410	8	250
64	690	45	550	26	400	7	240
63	690	44	540	25	400	6	230
62	680	43	530	24	390	5	220
61	670	42	520	23	380	4	210
60	660	41	520	22	370	<4	200

Acknowledgments

The authors gratefully acknowledge the kindness of all organizations concerned with granting us permission to reprint material. Every effort has been made to trace the copyright holders of items appearing in this book, and we apologize for any unintentional omissions. We would be pleased to insert the appropriate acknowledgment in any subsequent editions of this publication.

Sources and permissions for charts and graphs appear on the appropriate pages in the book through the courtesy of the following organizations: the New York Times Company; U.S. Department of Labor; Dow Jones & Company, Inc.; U.S. Department of Health, Education, and Welfare; United Nations Economics Bulletin for Europe; Social Security Bulletin, Statistical Abstract of the U.S., U.S. Department of Commerce, Bureau of Economic Analysis; Federal Reserve Bank of New York; European Economic Community; U.S. Department of Commerce, Bureau of the Census; New York State Department of Labor; Federal Power Commission; U.S. Treasury Department; U.S. Bureau of Labor Statistics; Institute of Life Insurance; and the Statistical Abstract of Latin America.

Other copyright holders and publishers of quoted material are listed below:

Page 26, Sample Passage: Reprinted with permission of the author, Virgil Thomson.

Pages 82–83, Passage: Excerpts, pp. 202–203, 207–208, and 211 from POLITICS AND CHANGE IN THE MIDDLE EAST, 5th by Roy R. Andersen, Robert F. Seibert, and Jon G. Wagner. Copyright © 1998 by Prentice-Hall, Inc. Reprinted by permission of Pearson Education, Inc.

Page 86, Passage: Bob Doyle, "Is There a 10th Planet," *Cumberland Times-News*, September 14, 2005. © 2006 *Cumberland Times-News*. Reprinted with the permission of the *Cumberland Times-News*.

Pages 88–89, Passage: Michael Useem, Professor of Sociology, Boston University, "Government Patronage of Science and Art in America," from *The Production of Culture*, Richard A. Peterson, ed., © 1976 SAGE Publications, Inc. Reprinted by permission of SAGE Publications.

Page 164, Essay Topic: Excerpt from "Beyond Those Health Care Numbers," by Gregory N. Mankiw. From *The New York Times*, November 24, 2007. © 2007 *The New York Times*. All rights reserved. Used by permission and protected by the Copyright Laws of the United States. The printing, copying, redistribution, or retransmission of this Content without express written permission is prohibited.

Page 187, Example: "Skye, Lonely Scottish Isle," *Newark Sunday News*, June 9, 1968, C 16, Sec. 2.

Page 189, Example: David Gunter, "Kibbutz Life Growing Easier," *Newark News*, May 6, 1968, p. 5.

Index

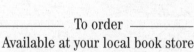

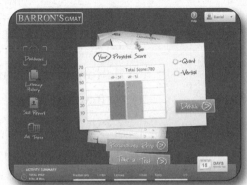
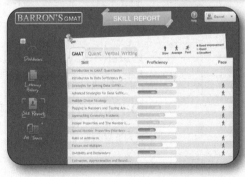

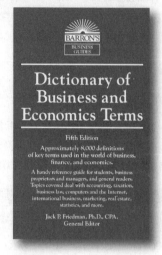
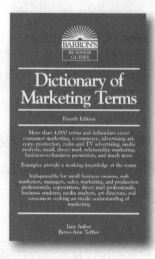